COUNTER THE COUNTERFEIT & BUILD A STRONG FOUNDATION FOR SUCCESS

Books are our best friends, is the adage we have grown up with. However, the pirates of piracy are continuously forging 'our best friends'. Our books and their supplementary online resources are copyrighted, and we don't lend any right-to-copy. Piracy is synonymous to stealing books.

Knowledge comes real, let's not encourage its counterfeit. Therefore, we appeal all our readers to discourage pirated books and **choose authentic ones**.

HOW TO IDENTIFY THE PIRATED BOOKS?

1 Cover and Spine

- Look and feel (new or used book)
- Blurred images on the cover
- Hologram pasted on front
- Defective spine (wrinkles) or air pocket at its bottom
- Unclear ISBN/bar codes
- Missing/non-operational access codes for supplemental online or e-learning materials

2 Text/Printing/Binding

- Uneven inking of pages
- Poor quality or blurred photographs/images/charts
- Substandard paper quality and opacity
- Misaligned pages
- Missing pages
- Inferior binding quality

You can further watch this video on How to identify a pirated book

For more information about identifying piracy, visit **https://www.mheducation.co.in/piracy**

To report a pirated book, send 'Hi' on WhatsApp code given on the back cover or write to us at **support.india@mheducation.com**.

Reported pirated books are examined to combat their piracy.

Let's fight the Pirates of Piracy and resolve to go for original!

About the Author

Vijay Kalyan Jha has been a veteran in the test preparation industry for the last two decades. He has cleared a gamut of tests – including the prestigious CAT and CLAT – multiple times. He also appeared for the CUET (UG) in 2022 and 2023 and scored 100%ile in many subjects: General Test, English Language Test, Political Science, etc. He is the topper of the General Test (COQP11) of CUET-PG 2023. Vijay has also claimed AIR 1 in the Maharashtra CET (5-year law) 2023. Having led teams in Academics, Marketing, Business etc. in the past, he has rich experience in many exams like Law (CLAT, AILET, etc.), CUET-UG, CUET-PG, CAT (and other MBA competitions), Civil Services, SSC, Banking, Defence, Teaching, NET & JRF, etc.

Crack CUET-UG General Test

with a 100%iler

Vijay Kalyan Jha

McGraw Hill Education (India) Private Limited

Published by McGraw Hill Education (India) Private Limited
Registered Office: Anjana Complex No: 5/90 A, Butt Road, St. Thomas Mount, Chennai – 600016

Crack CUET-UG General Test with a 100%iler

Print Edition
ISBN (13): 978-93-5532-919-6
ISBN (10): 93-5532-919-9

E-Book Edition
ISBN (13): 978-93-5532-804-5
ISBN (10): 93-5532-804-4

1 2 3 4 5 6 7 8 9 7101558 28 27 26 25 24

Printed and bound in India

Typeset at Transcend Content Solution, 163F Jaigirghat Road, Panchanantala, Kolkata – 700 063 and printed at Rajkamal Electric Press, Kundli, Haryana.

Cover Source: Adobe Stock
Cover Designer: Gyanendra Swamy

Visit us at: www.mheducation.co.in
Write to us at: info.india@mheducation.com

CIN: U80302TN2010PTC111532

Toll Free Number: 1800 103 5875

To

Maa (Nirmala Jha), who initiated me into Mathematics

and

Daddy (Prakash Kumar Jha), who took it to the next level ...

PREFACE

The CUET-UG is a mandatory test for admission into undergraduate (Bachelor's) programs offered by the central universities (University of Delhi, JNU, BHU, University of Allahabad, etc.). Many state universities (Dr. B.R. Ambedkar University Delhi, Jiwaji University Gwalior, etc.), Deemed Universities (TISS, NRTI Vadodara, etc.), as well as private universities have also accepted the CUET (UG) as the entrance for their undergraduate programs. Almost 15 lakh candidates had applied for CUET-UG 2023.

The General Test (GT) is the 2nd most popular test within the CUET-UG umbrella. More than six and a half lakh students took the General Test paper of CUET-UG 2023, and only 36 of them scored 100%ile in it.

The General Test (Section 3) of CUET (UG) is very important as it is mandatory for many popular courses, e.g. all undergraduate courses of the University of Allahabad, all undergraduate courses of the Tata Institute of Social Sciences (TISS), all undergraduate courses of the Jawaharlal Nehru University, etc. It is mandatory for some top-rated courses at some other universities too, e.g. Bachelor of Management Studies (BMS), Bachelor of Business Economics (BBE), B.Tech (Information Technology & Mathematical Innovation), etc. of the University of Delhi; B.A. LL.B. (Hons.) of Banaras Hindu University (BHU), etc.

The idea behind this book is to make you score heavily on this test. It is an easy test in which you must do 50 out of 60 questions in 60 minutes. The questions are broadly from 3 areas: Quantitative Aptitude, Reasoning and General Awareness.

Highlights of the book

- prepared by a 100%iler of the General Test of CUET-UG
- has 20 actual CUET-UG General Test papers along with the explanations
- has updates on the General Awareness questions
- has shortcuts and elimination techniques suggested for many questions
- has 100% accurate answer keys

Overall, the book has more than 1300 questions asked in different shifts of CUET-UG 2023 and 2022.

You may write to me at vijaykalyanjha@gmail.com if you have any queries.

All the best!

Acknowledgement

First, I am thankful to McGraw Hill India for giving me this opportunity, as that is how it started!

I am indebted to the people at McGraw Hill India, as they were very supportive of my ideas and accommodative of perennial delays on my part despite very demanding timelines.

This book 'would not have been possible', veritably, without the eye-time of Uroosa Shah, incidentally my wife!

Contents

Study Scheme for Getting a 100%ile Score on the General Test by a 100%iler!

Congratulations on having this book with you! It is a crucial step towards Mission 100!

What is the General Test of the CUET-UG?

General Test checks your preparedness in 3 parts: Analytical and Logical Reasoning (or Reasoning), Quantitative Aptitude and General Awareness. The tests in 2023 typically had 15–18 questions on Reasoning, 20–24 questions on Quantitative Aptitude and 20–22 questions on General Awareness. We have categorised calendars and clocks as Quantitative Aptitude.

These are the areas you are tested in:

Analytical & Logical Reasoning: syllogism, assertion & reason, statements & conclusions, Venn diagram, puzzles, inequalities, sitting arrangement, data sufficiency, analogy, odd one out, coding-decoding, order and ranking, series (on numbers as well as letters), direction-sense, cubes and cuboids, dice, figure-counting, mirror image, etc.

Quantitative Aptitude:

Geometry (lines & angles, triangle, rectangle, square, rhombus, parallelogram, kite)

Coordinate Geometry (straight lines)

Mensuration (triangle, quadrilateral, rectangle, square, parallelogram, rhombus, trapezium, circle, polygon, cube, cuboid, cylinder, cone, etc.)

Algebra (factoring and simplifying algebraic expressions, expressions and identities, linear equations in one variable, exponents and powers, quadratic equations, arithmetic progression, geometric progression, permutations and combinations, probability, etc.)

Arithmetic (percentage, ratio and proportion, profit-loss-discount, simple and compound interest, Time-speed-distance, Time & Work, etc.)

Number System (odd & even integers, prime numbers, rational numbers, LCM and HCF, number line, divisibility, etc.)

Simplification, square and cube roots, fractions & decimals, number series, calendars, clocks, etc.

General Awareness, including Current Affairs: You may revise the Social Science (History + Geography + Civics) books for grades 9 and 10. You may also get a few questions from General Science (Physics + Chemistry + Biology).

Current Affairs: Not many questions were asked from this section in most of the slots in 2022 and 2023.

The biggest relief for you is that **you can leave 10 questions** (out of the 60) in this test, and these questions can protect **your weak areas** to a great extent.

Almost all the questions in this test are from the areas you studied in grades 6–10 of your school. Please revise the concepts of only topics you are uncomfortable with. You may not need to do anything else for Reasoning if you solve all the Reasoning questions given in these 20 tests. There are 20 tests in this book, and we want you to use each as a mock with strict time limits. Please go through the solutions to even those questions you are already comfortable with, as you may discover a new way of solving them. Please get into the habit of using the 4 options given with each question to your advantage. We have demonstrated the option-elimination techniques for some of the questions in this book. It may be a good idea to solve the 2022 tests before you do the 2023 ones. Please solve all 1320 questions given in the book for optimal performance. Happy prepping!

CUET UG 2023 GENERAL TEST

June 11

INSTRUCTIONS:

1. You need to attempt any 50 out of the 60 questions in 60 minutes.
2. You get 5 marks for a correct response and –1 for an incorrect one. However, there is no reward or penalty for a question not attempted.

1. Which gland in the human body is called the master gland?
(1) Thyroid gland (2) Mucous gland
(3) Pituitary gland (4) Digestive gland

2. The difference between the cost price and the selling price of an article is ₹240. If the profit is 20%, then the selling price is:
(1) ₹1200 (2) ₹1240
(3) ₹1440 (4) ₹1600

3. Which of the following was not among the first 'Bharat Ratna' recipients in 1954?
(1) C. Rajagopalachari
(2) Dr. S. Radhakrishnan
(3) C.V. Raman
(4) Bhagwan Das

4. Which fraction among $\frac{2}{3}, \frac{4}{5}, \frac{7}{11}, \frac{1}{3}$ is the largest?
(1) $\frac{2}{3}$ (2) $\frac{7}{11}$
(3) $\frac{4}{5}$ (4) $\frac{1}{3}$

5. A point on the y-axis which is equidistant from the points A(6, 5) and B(−4, 3) is:
(1) (0, 9) (2) (0, −9)
(3) (9, 0) (4) (0, 6)

6.

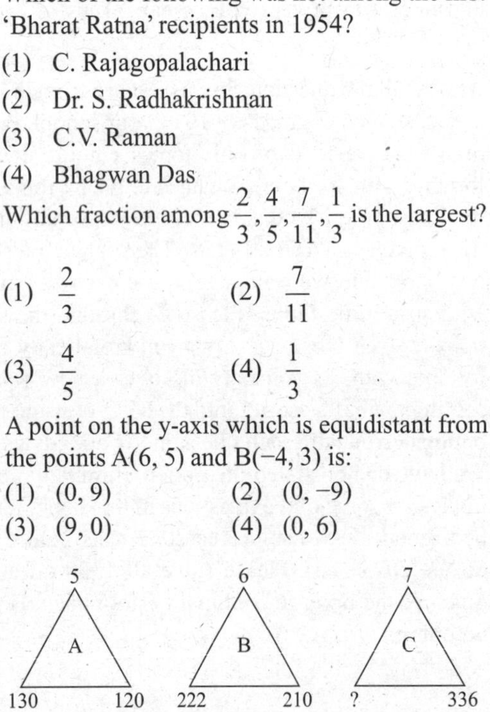

What would come in place of the question mark (?)?
(1) 343 (2) 329
(3) 350 (4) 366

7. Who among the following was not the Vice-President of India?
(1) V.V. Giri
(2) B.D. Jatti
(3) K.R. Narayanan
(4) Sarojini Naidu

8. Which number will appear on the face opposite to 1?

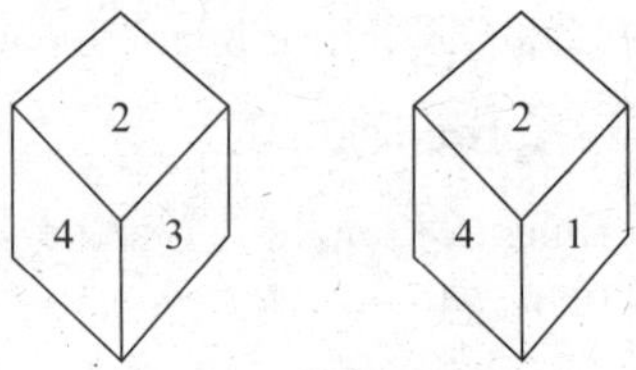

(1) 6 (2) 4
(3) 5 (4) 3

9. The distance between two parallel sides of a trapezium is 15 m, and its area is 480 m^2. If one of the parallel sides is 20 m long, then the length of the other side is:
(1) 42 m (2) 44 m
(3) 40 m (4) 46 m

10. In a certain language, 'AUSTRALIA' is written as @ $! # ^ @* ? @. Then "STRAIT" in that code language can be written as ________.
(1) ! # ^ @ ? # (2) ! # @ ^ ? #
(3) ! # ^ ? @ # (4) ! # ^ ? @ ?

11. Two numbers are in the ratio 3: 5. If 10 is added to each number, then the ratio becomes 5: 7. Find the numbers.

(1) 30, 50 (2) 45, 60
(3) 15, 25 (4) 36, 60

12. If English alphabets are written in the backward order, then which is the 7th letter to the right of K?

(1) A (2) B
(3) C (4) D

13. In the following question, figure (A) is embedded in any one of the four alternative figures (1), (2), (3) and (4). Find the alternative which contains (A) as its part.

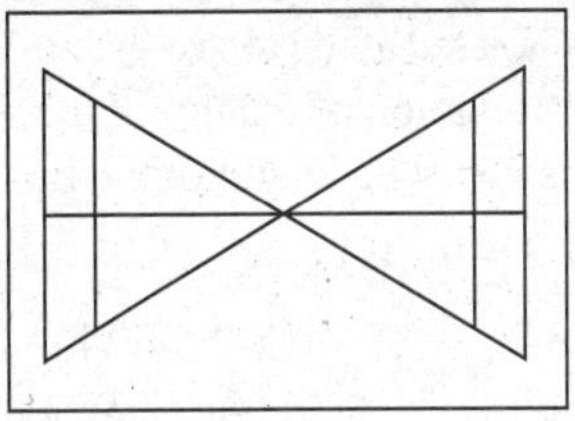

(A)

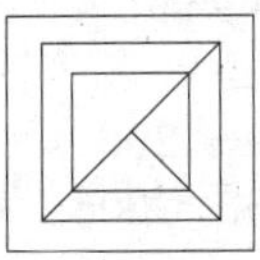 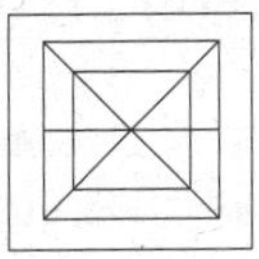 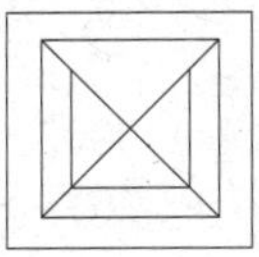 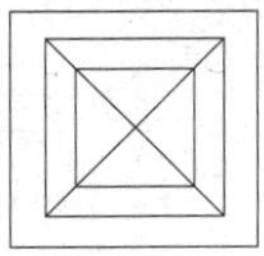

(1) (2) (3) (4)

14. Indian Air Force Day is celebrated on ________.

(1) 13 September (2) 3 December
(3) 13 August (4) 8 October

15. In a certain code language, 'it bit pit' means 'I am student' and 'it mit pit' means 'I am poet'. Which of the following means 'poet'?

(1) it (2) mit
(3) pit (4) bit

16. Match **List I** with **List II**.

List I (Shortcut Keys)	**List II (Description)**
(A) Ctrl + B	(I) open existing document
(B) F1	(II) left alignment
(C) Ctrl + L	(III) bold
(D) Ctrl + O	(IV) help

Choose the correct answer from the options given below:

(1) (A)-(III), (B)-(IV), (C)-(II), (D)-(I)
(2) (A)-(II), (B)-(I), (C)-(III), (D)-(IV)
(3) (A)-(I), (B)-(II), (C)-(IV), (D)-(III)
(4) (A)-(III), (B)-(IV), (C)-(I), (D)-(II)

17. Which of the following is India's highest gallantry award?

(1) Maha Vir Chakra
(2) Vir Chakra
(3) Param Vir Chakra
(4) Bharat Ratna

18. Match **List I** with **List II**.

List I Scientific Instruments	**List II Uses**
(A) Barometer	(I) helps examine the internal parts of body
(B) Calorimeter	(II) measures electrical power
(C) Dynamometer	(III) measures atmospheric pressure
(D) Endoscope	(IV) measures quantities of heat

Choose the correct answer from the options given below:

(1) (A)-(I), (B)-(II), (C)-(III), (D)-(IV)
(2) (A)-(II), (B)-(I), (C)-(III), (D)-(IV)
(3) (A)-(I), (B)-(II), (C)-(IV), (D)-(III)
(4) (A)-(III), (B)-(IV), (C)-(II), (D)-(I)

19. The fourth proportional to 5, 8, 15 is:

(1) 18
(2) 24
(3) 19
(4) 20

20. Which of the following options should replace the question mark in the following?

$$(4.25 + 2.75)^2 + ? = 5^3 - (9 \times 8)$$

(1) 3 (2) 4
(3) 5 (4) 6

21. Who won the French Open 2021 men's single title?

(1) Daniil Medvedev
(2) Novak Djokovic
(3) Stefanos Tsitsipas
(4) Rafael Nadal

22. A certain sum on $13\frac{1}{2}\%$ per annum simple interest amounts to ₹2502.50 in 4 years. Find the sum.

(1) ₹1500 (2) ₹1625
(3) ₹1650 (4) ₹1720

23. Ram starts walking in the north direction. Which of the following options will bring him going southwards?

(1) two consecutive right turns
(2) one right turn and then one left turn
(3) three consecutive left turns
(4) one left turn and then one right turn.

24. At what angle are the hour hand and minute hand of a clock inclined at 15 minutes past 5?

(1) $58\frac{1}{2}°$ (2) $64°$
(3) $67\frac{1}{2}°$ (4) $72\frac{1}{2}°$

25. Which number should replace the question mark?

53	87	61
62	89	54
32	?	12

(1) 54 (2) 53
(3) 44 (4) 20

26. A train running at a speed of 45 km/h crosses a 100 m long platform in 60 seconds. The time taken by the train to cross an electric pole is:

(1) 52 seconds (2) 8 seconds
(3) 1 minute (4) 1 minute 2 seconds

27. What is the value of $\left(1-\frac{1}{n}\right)+\left(1-\frac{2}{n}\right)+\left(1-\frac{3}{n}\right)+\cdots$ up to n terms?

(1) $\frac{1}{n}$ (2) $\frac{n}{2}$
(3) $\frac{n(n-1)}{2}$ (4) $\frac{n-1}{2}$

28. A, B, C, D, E, F, G and H are sitting around in an octagonal enclosed group facing the centre. B is sitting between D and G. H is to the immediate left of E, who sits beside D. F is sitting between A and H.
Who is sitting third to the left of E?

(1) A (2) B
(3) G (4) H

29. From a point P on the ground, the angle of elevation of the top of a 10 m high building is 30°. A flag is hoisted at the top of the building, and the angle of elevation of the top of the flagstaff from point P is 45°. The length of the flagstaff is:
(Take $\sqrt{3}=1.732$)

(1) 7 m (2) 7.24 m
(3) 7.56 m (4) 7.32 m

30. RTI (Right to Information) act came into force in ________?

(1) October, 2005 (2) December, 2004
(3) October, 2003 (4) December, 2006

31. Venus planet is also known as:

(A) Morning star (B) Winter star
(C) Evening star (D) Red planet

Choose the most appropriate answer from the options given below:

(1) (A), (B) and (D) only
(2) (A) and (C) only
(3) (A), (B), (C) and (D) only
(4) (B), (C) and (D) only

32. **Direction:** KLM ltd. bank is recruiting a senior manager for its 10 branches in Bangalore. There are some requirements for any willing candidate to fulfil; otherwise, he/she will be rejected.
The following conditions must be satisfied by the applicant:

i. The candidate must have passed class 12 with a minimum of 60% marks.
ii. The candidate must have scored at least 55% marks in graduation.

iii. The candidate must have scored at least 60% marks in the MBA.

iv. The candidate's age must be between 25 years and 35 years as of 1st March 2018.

Question: Which option is correct for Amit if Amit was born on the 11th of July 1987? He obtained 65% in graduation. He scored 66% marks in the MBA.

(1) if the data provided is inadequate to make a decision
(2) if Amit is to be selected
(3) if Amit is not to be selected
(4) if the case is referred to the HR Manager

33. In the pie chart shown here, what are the expenditures on food and house rent (in rupees) if the total monthly expenditure is ₹50,000?

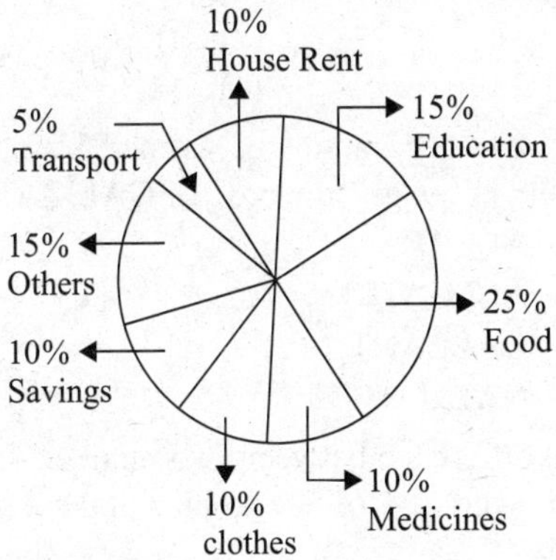

(1) 16,000 (2) 17,500
(3) 16,500 (4) 17,000

34. Dudhwa National Park is situated in ________?
(1) Mysuru, Karnataka
(2) Shivpuri, M.P.
(3) Lakhimpur Khiri, U.P.
(4) Garo Hills, Meghalaya

35. In the given figure DE||BC, the value of x is:

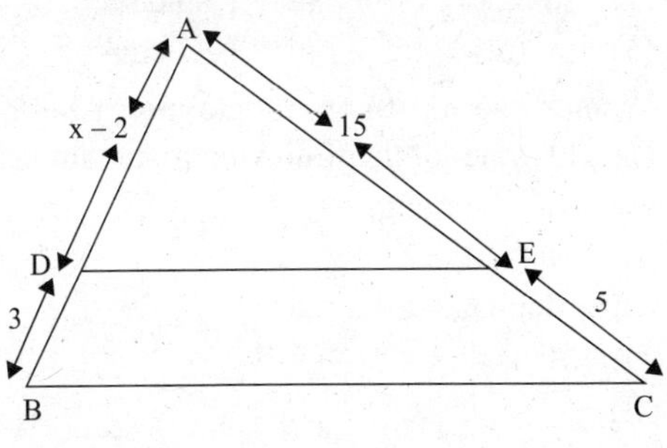

(1) 12 (2) 11
(3) 10 (4) 9

36. Mirror image of the word 'TRIUMPHS' is:
(1) ƧHꟼMUIЯT (2) SHPMUIRT
(3) SPMIURT (4) STRIUMPH

37. RTGS stands for __________.
(1) Revised Time Gross Settlement
(2) Revised Time Global Settlement
(3) Real Time Gross Settlement
(4) Real Time Global Survey

38. If 'GIVE' is written as 'VIEG' and 'OVER' as 'EVRO', how will 'DISK' be written in the same code?
(1) SIDK (2) KISD
(3) KDSI (4) SIKD

39. One Horse-Power (1 HP) is equal to ________ Watts.
(1) 726 watt (2) 706 watt
(3) 746 watt (4) 736 watt

40. Who discovered the 'Harappa Civilization' in 1921?
(1) B.D. Banerji (2) R.D. Banerji
(3) John Marshal (4) Dayaram Sahni

41.

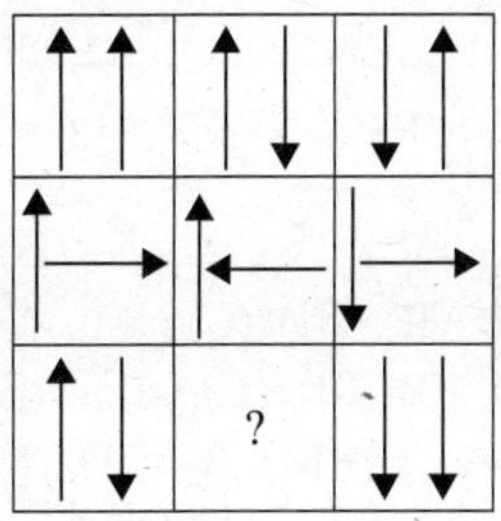

In the above figure, what will replace the '?' mark?

(1) 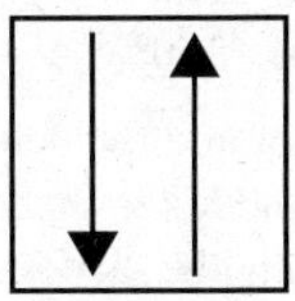
(2) 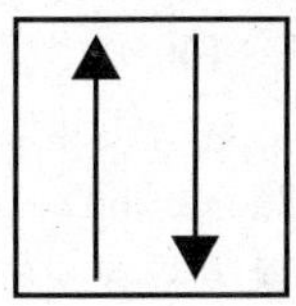
(3) 
(4) 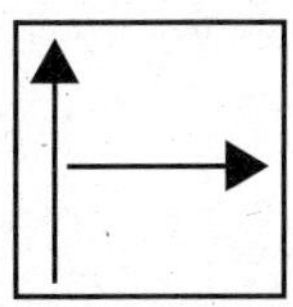

42. The smallest five-digit number which is exactly divisible by 12, 15 and 18 is:
(1) 10000 (2) 10020
(3) 10080 (4) 10260

43. 'An Area of Darkness' is written by ________.
(1) Louis Fischer
(2) James Harriot
(3) V.S. Naipaul
(4) Adam Smith

44. Ram ranks 7th from the top and 26th from the bottom in a class. How many students are there in the class?
(1) 31 (2) 32
(3) 33 (4) 34

45. Match **List I** with **List II**.

List I	List II
(A) Manometer	(I) measures very high temperature
(B) Micrometre	(II) measures small sub-division of scale
(C) Pyrometer	(III) measures the pressure of gases
(D) Vernier	(IV) measures distances/ angles

Choose the correct answer from the options given below:
(1) (A)-(III), (B)-(IV), (C)-(I), (D)-(II)
(2) (A)-(II), (B)-(III), (C)-(IV), (D)-(I)
(3) (A)-(I), (B)-(III), (C)-(II), (D)-(IV)
(4) (A)-(IV), (B)-(III), (C)-(II), (D)-(I)

46. A's weight is 25% of that of B and 40% of C. What percentage of C's weight is B's weight?
(1) 120% (2) 150%
(3) 160% (4) 200%

47. The sum of the numerator and the denominator of a fraction is 11. If 1 is added to the numerator and 2 is subtracted from the denominator, it becomes $\frac{2}{3}$. The fraction is:
(1) $\frac{5}{6}$ (2) $\frac{6}{5}$
(3) $\frac{3}{8}$ (4) $\frac{8}{3}$

48. The book ________ is written by Khushwant Singh.
(1) Kagaz te Canvas
(2) Sakharam Binder
(3) Burial at Sea
(4) Unhappy India

49. Which of the following is valid for the data 11, 15, 13, 12, 10, 8, 11, 7, 15, 11, 13, 7, 11?
(1) Mean = Median = Mode
(2) Mean > Median > Mode
(3) Mean > Mode = Median
(4) Mean < Median < Mode

50. A is twice as good a workman as B, and together, they finish a work in 14 days. The number of days that A alone will take to complete the work is:
(1) 11 (2) 21
(3) 28 (4) 42

51. Which word cannot be formed by using the letters of the given word? LEGALIZATION
(1) ALERT
(2) ALEGATION
(3) GALLANT
(4) NATAL

52. The difference between two numbers is 4, and their average is 6. The product of these numbers is:
(1) 24 (2) 12
(3) 32 (4) 48

53. From a solid cylinder whose height is 2.4 cm and diameter is 1.4 cm, a conical cavity of the same height and diameter is carved out. The total surface area of the remaining solid is: $\left(Use\ \pi = \frac{22}{7}\right)$
(1) 18 cm^2 (2) 17.6 cm^2
(3) 17 cm^2 (4) 16.7 cm^2

54. What is the most appropriate increasing order (height-wise) of the following mountain peaks?
(A) Kanchenjunga
(B) Makalu
(C) Dhaulagiri I
(D) Manaslu I
(E) Annapurna I

Choose the most appropriate answer from the options below:
(1) (A), (B), (D), (C), (E)
(2) (E), (D), (C), (B), (A)
(3) (A), (B), (C), (D), (E)
(4) (E), (D), (A), (B), (C)

55. Which option will represent the Venn diagram of dogs, pets and cats:

(1) 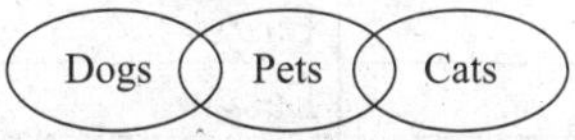

(2) 

(3) 

(4) 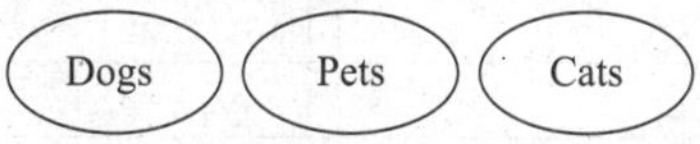

56. Which statement(s) is/are true about Article 19?
(A) Freedom of speech and expression
(B) Right to Education
(C) Right to Equality
(D) Right to Constitutional Remedy
Choose the most appropriate answer from the options given below:
(1) (A) and (B) only
(2) (B) and (C) only
(3) (C) and (D) only
(4) (A) only

57. A game consists of tossing a coin 3 times. Hanif wins if all the tosses give the same result. What is the probability that he loses the game?
(1) $\frac{1}{2}$ (2) $\frac{3}{4}$
(3) $\frac{1}{3}$ (4) $\frac{2}{3}$

58. What is the gain per cent if the cost price of 12 pens equals the selling price of 8 pens?
(1) $33\frac{1}{3}\%$ (2) 50%
(3) $66\frac{2}{3}\%$ (4) 70%

59. Find the distance covered by a man who walked for 15 minutes at a 3 km/h speed.
(1) 700 m (2) 750 m
(3) 600 m (4) 1200 m

60. Which among the following statements are not correct?
(A) Raman Research Institute _____ Bengaluru
(B) National Chemical Laboratory ____ Pune
(C) Solid State Physics Laboratory ____ Delhi
(D) National Physical Laboratory ____ Mumbai
(E) Regional Research Laboratories ____ Delhi
Choose the most appropriate answer from the options below:
(1) (A) and (B) only
(2) (B) and (C) only
(3) (C) and (D) only
(4) (D) and (E) only

Answer Key

1. **(3)**	2. **(3)**	3. **(4)**	4. **(3)**	5. **(1)**	6. **(3)**	7. **(4)**	8. **(4)**	9. **(2)**	10. **(1)**
11. **(3)**	12. **(4)**	13. **(2)**	14. **(4)**	15. **(2)**	16. **(1)**	17. **(3)**	18. **(4)**	19. **(2)**	20. **(2)**
21. **(2)**	22. **(2)**	23. **(1)**	24. **(3)**	25. **(2)**	26. **(1)**	27. **(4)**	28. **(1)**	29. **(4)**	30. **(1)**
31. **(2)**	32. **(1)**	33. **(2)**	34. **(3)**	35. **(2)**	36. **(1)**	37. **(3)**	38. **(4)**	39. **(3)**	40. **(4)**
41. **(3)**	42. **(3)**	43. **(3)**	44. **(2)**	45. **(1)**	46. **(3)**	47. **(3)**	48. **(3)**	49. **(3)**	50. **(2)**
51. **(1)**	52. **(3)**	53. **(2)**	54. **(2)**	55. **(1)**	56. **(4)**	57. **(2)**	58. **(2)**	59. **(2)**	60. **(4)**

Classification of Questions

Question No.	Subject	Topic	Level of Difficulty
1.	General Awareness	Science (Biology)	Medium
2.	Quantitative Aptitude	Profit, Loss & Discount	Easy
3.	General Awareness	Awards	Medium
4.	Quantitative Aptitude	Fractions	Easy
5.	Quantitative Aptitude	Coordinate Geometry	Easy
6.	Reasoning	Missing Number	Easy
7.	General Awareness	Polity	Easy
8.	Reasoning	Dice	Easy
9.	Quantitative Aptitude	Mensuration	Easy
10.	Reasoning	Coding	Easy
11.	Quantitative Aptitude	Ratios	Easy
12.	Reasoning	Rankings and Orders	Easy
13.	Reasoning	Non-verbal	Easy
14.	General Awareness	Miscellaneous	Easy
15.	Reasoning	Coding	Easy
16.	General Awareness	Computers	Easy
17.	General Awareness	Awards	Easy
18.	General Awareness	Science	Easy
19.	Quantitative Aptitude	Ratios and Proportions	Easy
20.	Quantitative Aptitude	Basic Arithmetic Operations	Easy
21.	General Awareness	Sports	Easy
22.	Quantitative Aptitude	Simple Interest	Easy
23.	Reasoning	Directions	Easy
24.	Quantitative Aptitude	Clocks	Easy
25.	Reasoning	Missing Number	Medium
26.	Quantitative Aptitude	Time, Speed & Distance	Medium
27.	Quantitative Aptitude	Basic Arithmetic Operations	Medium
28.	Reasoning	Circular arrangement	Easy
29.	Quantitative Aptitude	Trigonometry (Heights & Distances)	Medium
30.	General Awareness	Polity	Easy
31.	General Awareness	Geography	Medium
32.	Reasoning	Selection Criteria	Easy
33.	Data Interpretation	Pie-Chart	Easy
34.	General Awareness	Geography	Easy
35.	Quantitative Aptitude	Geometry	Easy

Question No.	Subject	Topic	Level of Difficulty
36.	Reasoning	Mirror Image	Easy
37.	General Awareness	Basic Banking Terms	Easy
38.	Reasoning	Coding	Easy
39.	General Awareness	Science (physics)	Easy
40.	General Awareness	History	Difficult
41.	Reasoning	Non-verbal	Easy
42.	Quantitative Aptitude	L.C.M.	Easy
43.	General Awareness	Books & Authors	Medium
44.	Reasoning	Rankings & Order	Easy
45.	General Awareness	Science (Physics)	Difficult
46.	Quantitative Aptitude	Percentages	Easy
47.	Quantitative Aptitude	Fractions	Easy
48.	General Awareness	Books & Authors	Medium
49.	Quantitative Aptitude	Statistics (Mean, Median, Mode)	Easy
50.	Quantitative Aptitude	Time & Work	Easy
51.	Reasoning	Miscellaneous	Easy
52.	Quantitative Aptitude	Algebra (Linear Equations)	Easy
53.	Quantitative Aptitude	Mensuration	Medium
54.	General Awareness	Geography	Difficult
55.	Reasoning	Venn Diagram	Easy
56.	General Awareness	Polity	Easy
57.	Quantitative Aptitude	Probability	Easy
58.	Quantitative Aptitude	Profit, Loss & Discount	Easy
59.	Quantitative Aptitude	Time, Speed and Distance	Easy
60.	General Awareness	Miscellaneous	Difficult

Explanation to Select Questions

2. The difference between the selling price and the cost price is ₹240, and the profit is 20%.
It means the profit is ₹240, which is 20% of the cost price.

$\Rightarrow$ the cost price $= \dfrac{240 \times 100}{20} = 1200.$

$\Rightarrow$ the selling price $= 1200 + 240 = 1440.$
Hence, Option 3.

3. Bharat Ratna – India's highest civilian award – was given for the first time in 1954. The first awardees were C.V. Raman, C. Rajagopalachari and Dr. S. Radhakrishnan. Bhagwan Das was awarded with it in 1955.
Hence, Option 4.

4. $\dfrac{2}{3} = \dfrac{110}{165}, \dfrac{4}{5} = \dfrac{132}{165}, \dfrac{7}{11} = \dfrac{105}{165}$ and $\dfrac{1}{3} = \dfrac{55}{165}$.

Of these four, $\dfrac{132}{165} = \dfrac{4}{5}$ is the largest.

Hence, Option 3.

5. Let the point on the y-axis equidistant from the points (6, 5) and (–4, 3) be (0, a).

The distance between (6, 5) and (0, a)

$= \sqrt{(6-0)^2 + (5-a)^2}$

$= \sqrt{36 + 25 - 10a + a^2}$

$= \sqrt{a^2 - 10a + 61}.$

The distance between (–4, 3) and (0, a)

$= \sqrt{(-4-0)^2 + (3-a)^2}$

$= \sqrt{16 + 9 - 6a + a^2} = \sqrt{a^2 - 6a + 25}$

But, $\sqrt{a^2 - 10a + 61} = \sqrt{a^2 - 6a + 25}$

or, $a^2 - 10a + 61 = a^2 - 6a + 25$

or, $4a = 36$ or, $a = 9$.

Therefore, the required point is (0, 9).

Hence, Option 1.

6. In triangle A,
$130 = 120 + 2 \times 5$
In triangle B,
$222 = 210 + 2 \times 6$
In triangle C,
$? = 336 + 2 \times 7 = 336 + 14 = 350.$
Hence, Option 3.

7. V.V. Giri was the 3rd vice president of India. B.D. Jatti was the 5th vice president of India. K.R. Narayanan was the 9th vice president of India.
Hence, Option 4.

8. The intended answer is option 4, but both positions given in the question cannot be on the same die! Therefore, the question is wrong.

9. 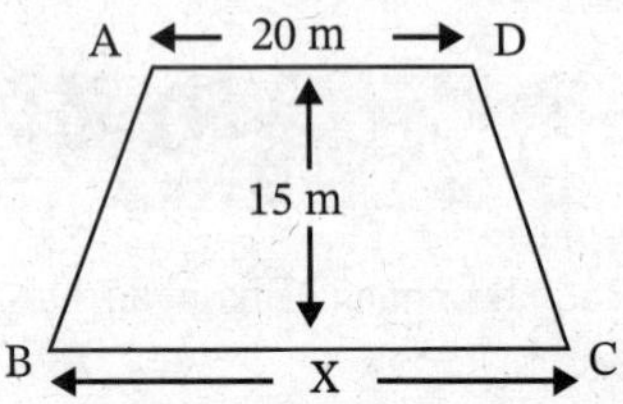

Let the length of the other parallel side be x.

The area of the trapezium $= \frac{1}{2} \times$ (the sum of the parallel sides) $\times$ (the distance between them)

or, $480 = \frac{1}{2}(x + 20) \times 15$

or, $(x + 20) = \frac{480 \times 2}{15} = 64.$

or, $x = 64 - 20 = 44$.

Hence, Option 2.

11. Let the numbers be $3x$ and $5x$.

We have, $\frac{3x + 10}{5x + 10} = \frac{5}{7}$

or, $21x + 70 = 25x + 50$, or, $4x = 20$, or, $x = 5$.

Therefore, the numbers are 15 and 20.

Hence, Option 3.

12. If the letters in the alphabet are written in backward order, then the letters originally left to K will become right to it.
K ranks 11 in the alphabet, and the 7th letter to the left of it is D (rank 4).
In the new arrangement, D will be the 7th letter to the right of K.
Hence, Option 4.

14. The Indian Air Force (IAF) was established on 8 October 1932, and to commemorate that, the Indian Air Force Day is celebrated on 8 October every year.
Hence, Option 4.

17. Param Vir Chakra (PVC) is India's highest war-time gallantry award. Maha Vir Chakra (MVC) is India's 2nd highest war-time gallantry award. Vir Chakra is India's 3rd highest war-time gallantry award.
Hence, Option 3.

19. Let the 4th proportional to 5, 8 and 15 be x.

Therefore, $\frac{5}{8} = \frac{15}{x}$ or, $x = \frac{15 \times 8}{5} = 24.$

Hence, Option 2.

20. $? = 5^3 - (9 \times 8) - (4.25 + 2.75)^2$

$= 125 - 72 - 7^2 = 125 - 72 - 49 = 125 - 121 = 4.$

Hence, Option 2.

22. Let the principal be p.

We have, $p + \frac{p \times 4 \times \frac{27}{2}}{100} = 2502.50$

or, $\frac{100p + 54p}{100} = 2502.50$

or, $154p = 2502.50 \times 100$

or, $p = \frac{250250}{154} = 1625.$

Hence, Option 2.

23. 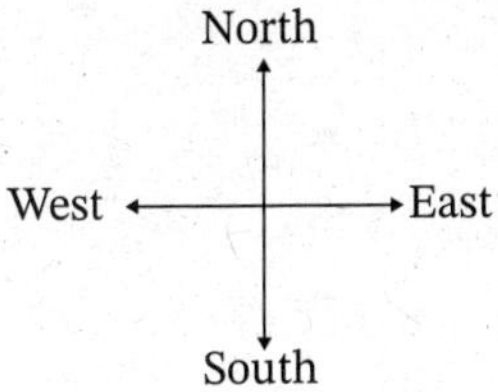

Option 1: 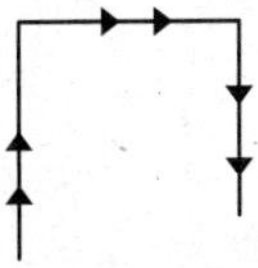

The final direction is south.

Option 2: 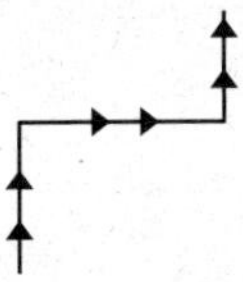

The final direction is north.

Option 3: 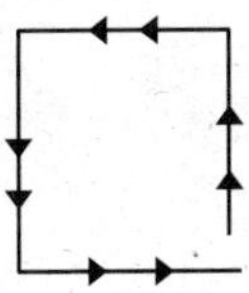

The final direction is east.

Option 4: 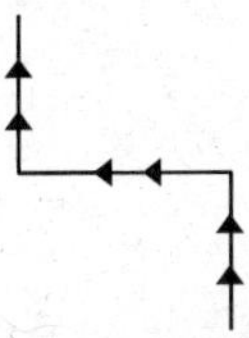

The final direction is north.

Hence, Option 1.

24. At 5 O' clock, the angular distance between the minute hand and the hour hand is $30° \times 5 = 150°$.

In 60 minutes, the minute hand covers $360° - 30° = 330°$ more than the hour hand.

In 15 minutes, the minute hand will cover $\frac{330°}{4} = 82.5°$ more than the hour hand.

Hence, the angle between the hands at 15 minutes past 5 is $150° - 82.5° = 67.5°$.

Hence, Option 3.

25. 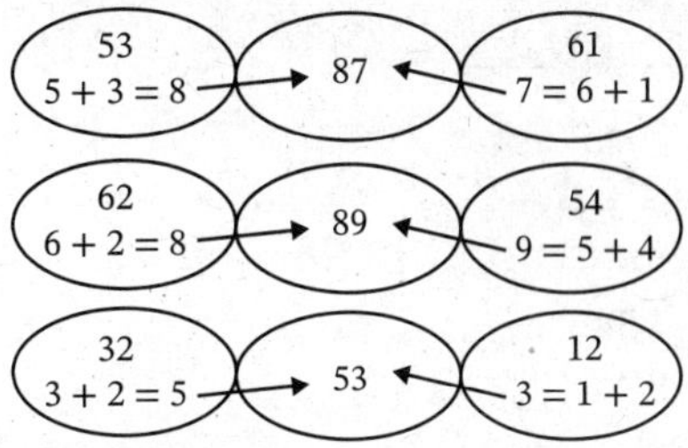

Hence, Option 2.

26. The speed of the train = 45 kmph = $\frac{45000}{3600}$ m/s

$= \frac{50}{4}$ m/s

Therefore, in 60 seconds it must have travelled $\frac{50}{4} \times 60 = 750$ m.

In crossing a platform, a train travels the sum of the lengths of the platform and itself.

Therefore, the length of the train = 750 – 100 = 650.

When a train passes an electric pole, it has to travel its own length.

The time taken by the train to pass the electric pole $= \frac{650}{\frac{50}{4}} = \frac{650 \times 4}{50} = 52$ seconds.

Hence, Option 1.

Alternative: the speed of the train $\frac{50}{4}$ m/sec.

Time taken in crossing a pole

$= 60 - \frac{100}{\frac{50}{4}} = 60 - 8 = 52$ seconds.

If a 100-meter-long platform collapses to become a pole, the train will save time to travel 100 meters.

27. $\left(1 - \frac{1}{n}\right) + \left(1 - \frac{2}{n}\right) + \left(1 - \frac{3}{n}\right) + \cdots$ up to n terms

$= \frac{n - 1 + n - 2 + n - 3 + n - 4 + \cdots \text{up to } n \text{ terms}}{n}$

$$= \frac{(n + n + n + n + \cdots n \text{ times}) - (1 + 2 + 3 + 4 + \cdots + n)}{n}$$

$$= \frac{n \times n - \frac{n(n+1)}{2}}{n} = n - \frac{(n+1)}{2}$$

$$= \frac{2n - n - 1}{2} = \frac{n-1}{2}.$$

Hence, Option 4.

Shortcut:

In $\left(1 - \frac{1}{n}\right) + \left(1 - \frac{2}{n}\right) + \left(1 - \frac{3}{n}\right) + \cdots$

If $n = 1$,

Then the value is $1 - \frac{1}{1} = 0$

Hence, the correct option should give us 0 for $n = 1$.

As Options 1 and 2 do not give 0 for $n = 1$, they can be eliminated.

Now, for $n = 2$, the value is $\left(1 - \frac{1}{2}\right) + \left(1 - \frac{2}{2}\right) = \frac{1}{2} + 0 = \frac{1}{2}$.

Of options 3 and 4, only Option 4 gives us $\frac{1}{2}$ by putting $n = 2$.

Hence, Option 4.

28.

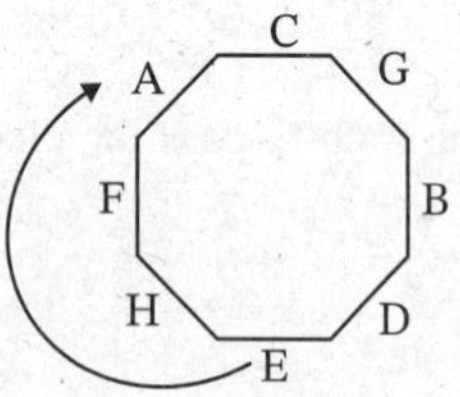

Hence, Option 1.

29.

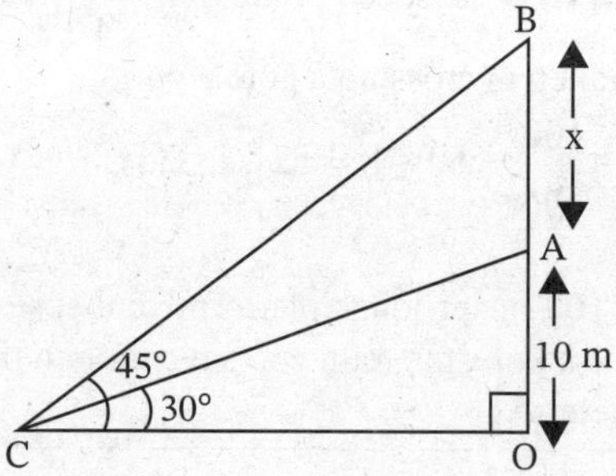

Let OA be the 10-m-high building and AB be the flagstaff. C is the point on the ground from where the angle of elevation for the top of the building is 30°.

Let the height of the flagstaff be x.

In ΔBOC,

$$\tan 45° = \frac{BO}{OC} = \frac{10 + x}{OC}$$

or, $1 = \frac{10 + x}{OC}$

or, OC = $10 + x$.

Now, in ΔAOC

$$\tan 30° = \frac{AO}{OC} = \frac{10}{x + 10}$$

or, $\frac{1}{\sqrt{3}} = \frac{10}{x + 10}$

or, $x + 10 = 10\sqrt{3} = 10 \times 1.732 = 17.32$

or, $x = 17.32 - 10 = 7.32$.

Hence, Option 4.

31. Even if you do not know about the other names of Venus but know that Mars is also known as the 'Red Planet', you can eliminate all the options with 'Red Planet' in them.

Only Option 2 does not have 'Red Planet' in it!

33. The expenditure on food and house rent is $25\% + 10\% = 35\%$

Total monthly expenditure = 50000

Therefore, the required value =

$$50000 \times \frac{35}{100} = 17500.$$

Hence, Option 2.

35.

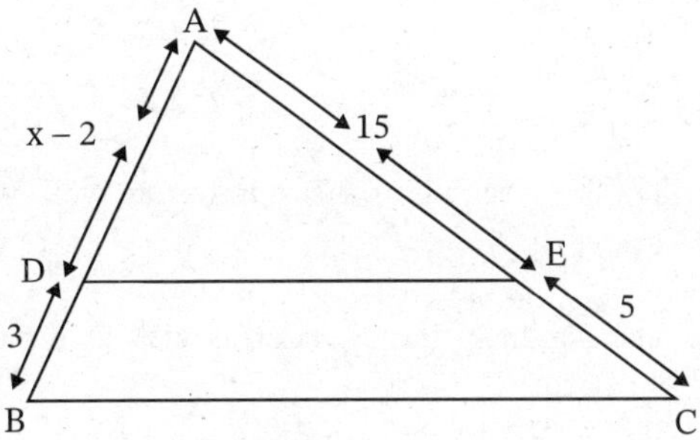

As DE || BC, $\frac{AD}{DB} = \frac{AE}{EC}$

or, $\frac{x-2}{3} = \frac{15}{5}$ or, $x - 2 = 3 \times 3 = 9$.

or, $x = 9 + 2 = 11$.

Hence, Option 2.

38.

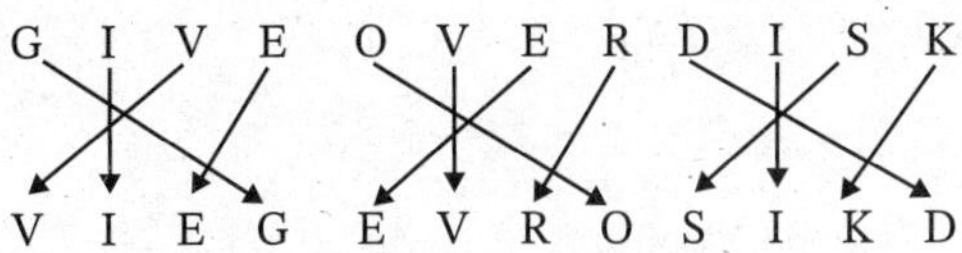

Hence, Option 4.

42. The LCM of 12, 15 and 18 is 180.

So, any number of the from 180k will be divisible by each of 12, 15 and 18, where k is a natural number.

The smallest 5-digit number is 10,000.

$10000 = 55 \times 180 + 100$

$\Rightarrow 55 \times 180 + 100 + 80$ will be of the form 180k.

$\Rightarrow$ 10080 is the smallest 5-digit number divisible by each of 12, 15 and 18.

Hence, Option 3.

Alternative: Try out the options.

Options 1 and 2 are not divisible by 18 and hence can be eliminated. Options 3 and 4 are divisible by each of 12, 15 and 18 and hence we have to go for the smaller of these two numbers.

Hence, Option 3.

44. Ram's rank from the top is 7th, so there are 6 students above him. Similarly, there are 25 students below him.

Therefore, the number of students other than Ram = 25 + 6 = 31.

So, the total number of students is 31 + 1 = 32.

Hence, Option 2.

Alternative:

The total number of students = an individual's rank from the top + that individual's rank from the bottom – 1.

= 7 + 26 – 1 = 32.

46. Let C's weight be 100.

$\Rightarrow$ A's weight must be 40% of 100 = 40.

Now, as A's weight is 25% of that of B and hence B's weight should be 4 times of A's weight that is $40 \times 4 = 160$.

Now, C's weight = 100 and B's weight = 160.

So, B's weight is 160% of C's weight.

Hence, Option 3.

47. Let the numerator and the denominator of the fraction be x and $11 - x$.

We have, $\frac{x+1}{11-x-2} = \frac{2}{3}$, or, $\frac{x+1}{9-x} = \frac{2}{3}$

or, $3x + 3 = 18 - 2x$

or, $5x = 15$ or, $x = 3$.

Therefore, the fraction is $\frac{3}{8}$.

Hence, Option 3.

Alternative: Check the Options.

The sum of the numerator and the denominator is 11 in each of them.

Option 1: $\frac{5+1}{6-2} = \frac{6}{4} = \frac{3}{2} \neq \frac{2}{3}$, hence it CANNOT be the answer.

Option 2: $\frac{6+1}{5-2} = \frac{7}{3} \neq \frac{2}{3}$, hence it CANNOT be the answer.

Option 3: $\frac{3+1}{8-2} = \frac{4}{6} = \frac{2}{3}$, hence, it is the answer.

48. Amrita Pritam wrote Kagaz te Canvas; Sakharam Binder is a play by Vijay Tendulkar; Khushwant Singh wrote Burial at Sea; and Lala Lajpat Rai wrote Unhappy India.

Hence, Option 3.

49. The given numbers in ascending order are: 7, 7, 8, 10, 11, 11, $\boxed{11}$, 11, 12, 13, 13, 15, 15.

As we can see, out of these 13 numbers, 11 is the middle one.

So, the median is 11.

Also, 11 is the most frequent number (it is 4 times).

So, the mode = 11.

$$\text{Mean} = \frac{7+7+8+10+11+11+11+11+12+13+13+15+15}{13}$$

$$= \frac{144}{13} = 11\frac{1}{13}.$$

Thus, Mean > Mode = Median.

Hence, Option 3.

50. Let the work be of $3x$ units.

A and B finish the work together in 14 days.

So, out of $3x$ units, A must have done $2x$ and B only x units (as A is twice as efficient as B).

Now, $2x$ can be done by A in 14 days.

1 can be done by him in $\frac{14}{2x}$ days.

$3x$ can be done by him in $\frac{14}{2x} \times 3x = 21$ days.

Hence, Option 2.

52. Let the numbers be x and y.

We have,

$\frac{x+y}{2} = 6 \Rightarrow x + y = 12$ (i)

and $x - y = 4$ (ii)

From (i) & (ii),

We get $x = 8$ and $y = 4$.

Therefore, the product of the numbers = $8 \times 4 = 32$.

Hence, Option 3.

53.

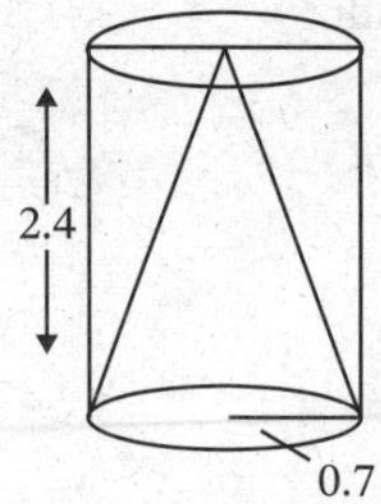

The base radius of the cylinder as well as the cone is $\frac{1.4}{2} = 0.7$

The height of the cylinder as well as the cone = 2.4 cm

The total surface area (TSA) of the remaining solid = the lateral surface area of the cone + the lateral surface area of the cylinder + the area of one of the bases of the cylinder.

So, the TSA

$= \pi(0.7)\sqrt{(2.4)^2 + (0.7)^2} + 2\pi(0.7)(2.4) + \pi(0.7)^2$

$= \pi(0.7)(2.5) + 2\pi(0.7)(2.4) + \pi(0.7)^2$

$= (0.7)\pi(2.5 + 4.8 + 0.7)$

$= 0.7 \times \frac{22}{7} \times 8 = 17.6 \text{ cm}^2$

Hence, Option 2.

Shortcut: As $\pi = \left(\frac{22}{7}\right)$ is a multiplier of each of the factors here, the answer must have an 11 in it.

Only Option 2 has an 11 in it as $17.6 = 1.6 \times 11$.

54.

Peak	Rank in the World (height)	Location	Height (in metre)
Annapurna 1	10th	Nepal	8091
Manaslu 1	8th	Nepal	8163
Dhaulagiri 1	7th	Nepal	8167
Makalu	5th	Nepal-China border	8463
Kanchenjunga	3rd	India-Nepal border	8586

Hence, Option 2.

Trick: Kanchenjunga is the tallest among these five. It is well known that only Everest and K2 are higher than Kanchenjunga. Only one option (Option 2) ends with Kanchenjunga.

Note: Manalsu is a river in Himachal Pradesh in India, and Manaslu is a mountain peak in Nepal. They should not be confused with each other.

56.

Fundamental Rights	Article in the Constitution of India
Freedom of Speech and Expression	Article 19
Right to Education	Article 21-A
Right to Equality	Articles 14–18
Right to Constitutional Remedy	Article 32

Hence, Option 4.

57. Hanif wins if all the results are heads or all of them are tails.

Probability of getting 3 heads in 3 tosses

$= \frac{1}{2} \times \frac{1}{2} \times \frac{1}{2} = \frac{1}{8}$.

Probability of getting 3 tails in 3 tosses

$= \frac{1}{2} \times \frac{1}{2} \times \frac{1}{2} = \frac{1}{8}$.

Therefore, the probability that Hanif wins

$= \frac{1}{8} + \frac{1}{8} = \frac{1}{4}$.

$\Rightarrow$ The probability that Hanif loses

$= 1 - \frac{1}{4} = \frac{3}{4}$.

Hence, Option 2.

Alternative: If you do not know probability, think about the possible scenarios:

The result of the 3 tosses can be one of these:

(T)	(T)	(T)	(i)
(T)	(T)	(H)	(ii)
(T)	(H)	(T)	(iii)
(H)	(T)	(T)	(iv)
(H)	(H)	(H)	(v)
(H)	(H)	(T)	(vi)
(H)	(T)	(H)	(vii)
(T)	(H)	(H)	(viii)

Hanif will win in only 2 cases: (i) and (v).

Therefore, he loses in 6 out of the 8 cases.

$\Rightarrow$ the required probability $= \frac{6}{8} = \frac{3}{4}$.

58. Let the cost price of each pen be x.

Now,

The cost price of 8 pens = 8 x.

The selling price of 8 pens = the cost price of 12 pens = 12x.

The profit percentage $= \frac{12x - 8x}{8x} \times 100 = 50$.

Hence, Option 2.

59. In 60 minutes, the man travels 3 km = 3000 m.

In 1 minutes, he travels $\frac{3000}{60}$ m.

In 15 minutes, he travels $\frac{3000}{60} \times 15 = 750$ m.

Hence, Option 2.

60. The National Physical Laboratory is in New Delhi (NOT Mumbai). The Regional Research Laboratories are in different states and union territories (NOT in Delhi).

Hence, Option 4.

SHIFT - I

CUET UG 2023
GENERAL TEST

June
8

INSTRUCTIONS:

1. You need to attempt any 50 out of the 60 questions in 60 minutes.
2. You get 5 marks for a correct response and –1 for an incorrect one. However, there is no reward or penalty for a question not attempted.

1. In the question below, find out which figure can be formed from the pieces given in the problem figure.

Problem figure

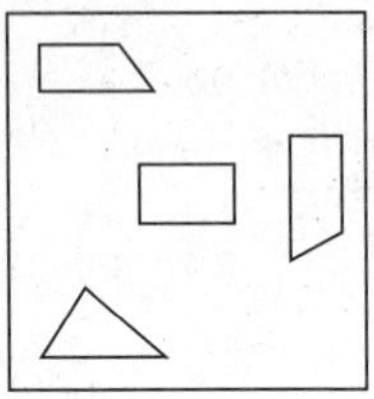

(1) 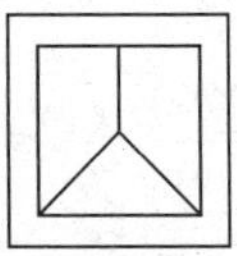 (2) 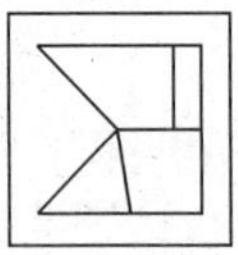

(3) 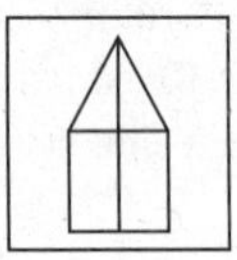 (4) 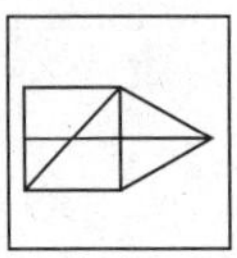

2. The average salary of employees of a factory is ₹15,000. The average salary of 250 employees is ₹16000, and that of the remaining employees is ₹13750. The total number of employees in the factory is:

(1) 420 (2) 450
(3) 456 (4) 475

3. The lengths of the three sides of a triangular field are 15 m, 19 m and 22 m. What is the area of the field? (correct to one decimal place)

(1) 138.5 m^2 (2) 150.8 m^2
(3) 140.2 m^2 (4) 150.5 m^2

4. Who is known as the "Grand Old Man of India"?

(1) Mahatma Gandhi
(2) Sardar Patel
(3) Bal Gangadhar Tilak
(4) Dada Bhai Naoroji

5. The Taj Mahal (Agra U.P.) was declared as one of the UNESCO's World Heritage sites in __________.

(1) 1975 (2) 1980
(3) 1983 (4) 1990

6. Which of the following supercomputers has not been developed in India?

(1) Flosolver (2) Pace
(3) Param-10000 (4) Deep Blue

7. Complete the figure.

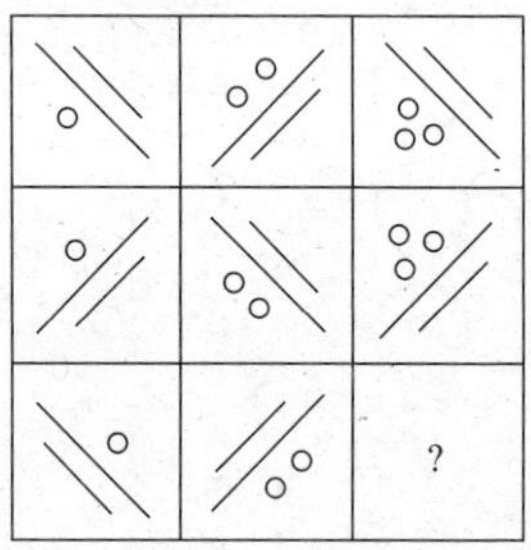

(1) 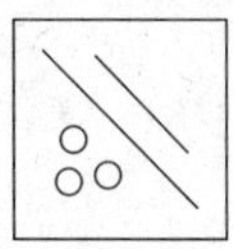 (2) 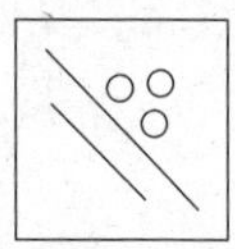

(3) 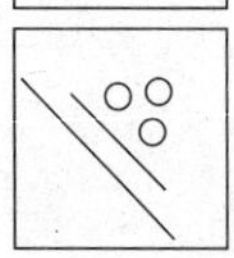 (4) 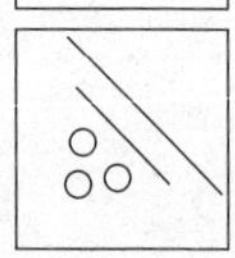

8. Find the missing term in the given series.
AZ, GT, MN, ?, YB
(1) JH (2) TS
(3) SK (4) SH

9. Manu started his journey at 10:45 am with a speed of 45 km/h. At what time will he reach his destination 150 km away?
(1) 1:45 pm (2) 1:55 pm
(3) 2:05 pm (4) 2:45 pm

10. Six persons, A, B, C, D, E and F, are sitting in two parallel rows of three persons in each row, and they are all facing north. C is sitting to the right of E. B is sitting to the right of D, who is sitting opposite to A. F is sitting diagonally opposite A, who is to the left of E.
Who is sitting opposite to B?
(1) F (2) C
(3) E (4) A

11. Find the value of $\frac{5x+1}{3}$ if $25^{4x-3} = 5^{6x+8}$.
(1) $\frac{11}{3}$ (2) 27
(3) 12 (4) $\frac{17}{6}$

12. Find the missing figure.
Problem figure

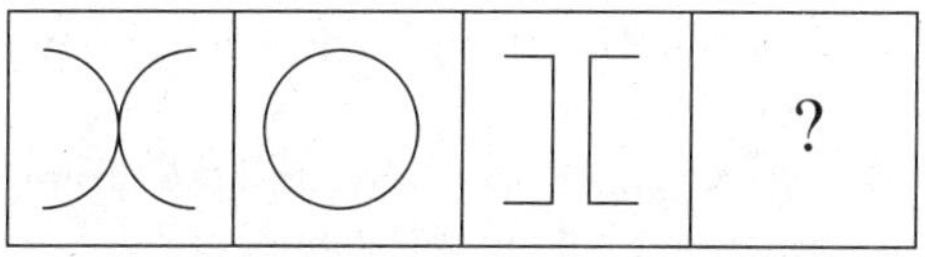

(1)  (2) 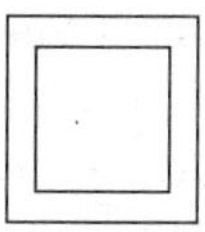
(3) 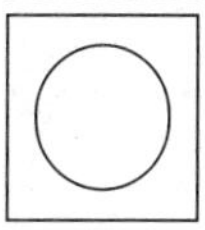 (4) 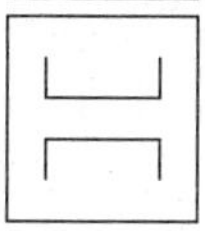

13. The value of $0.1^8 \div 0.01^5$ is:
(1) $\frac{1}{10}$ (2) $\frac{1}{1000}$
(3) 10 (4) 100

14. Given below are two statements:
Statement I: Arithmetic Progression is a sequence in which the sum of two consecutive terms is a constant.
Statement II: In a Geometric Progression, the ratio of any term to its preceding term is a constant.
In light of the above statements, choose the most appropriate answer from the options below.
(1) Both Statement I and Statement II are correct.
(2) Both Statement I and Statement II are incorrect.
(3) Statement I is correct, but Statement II is incorrect.
(4) Statement I is incorrect, but Statement II is correct.

15. Which term comes next in sequence:
AC, FH, KM, PR, ?
(1) TV (2) UX
(3) VW (4) UW

16. Match **List I** with **List II**.

List I (President of India)	List II (Tenure)
A. Dr. Zakir Hussain	I. 25 July 1997– 25 July 2002
B. Shri V.V. Giri	II. 25 July 1982– 25 July 1987
C. Shri K.R. Narayanan	III. 24 August 1969– 24 August 1974
D. Giani Zail Singh	IV. 13 May 1967– 03 May 1969

Choose the correct answer from the options given below:
(1) A-I, B-II, C-III, D-IV
(2) A-II, B-III, C-IV, D-I
(3) A-III, B-IV, C-II, D-I
(4) A-IV, B-III, C-I, D-II

17. Find two numbers such that their mean proportion is 6 and their third proportion is 20.25.
(1) 4 and 9 (2) 5 and 10.15
(3) 2 and 18 (4) 9 and 13.5

18. If $2\cos\theta = \sqrt{3}$, then what is the value of tan 2θ?
(1) $\frac{1}{\sqrt{3}}$ (2) $\sqrt{3}$
(3) $\frac{\sqrt{3}}{2}$ (4) $\frac{2}{\sqrt{3}}$

19. India's' 1st Gold ATM' that dispenses gold coins was launched in which city?
(1) Warangal (2) Hyderabad
(3) Gurugram (4) Delhi

20. If E and F are events such that P (E) = $\frac{5}{8}$, P(F) = $\frac{1}{2}$ and P (E and F) = $\frac{1}{4}$, then what is P (not E and not F)?
(1) $\frac{1}{8}$ (2) $\frac{3}{16}$
(3) $\frac{3}{4}$ (4) $\frac{7}{8}$

21. Ascorbic Acid is the correct chemical name of:
(1) Vitamin D (2) Vitamin C
(3) Vitamin E (4) Vitamin B12

22. Arrange the following in increasing order of lengths of boundaries that these countries share with India.
A. Nepal
B. Pakistan
C. China
D. Bhutan
E. Myanmar
Choose the correct answer from the options given below:
(1) A, B, C, D, E (2) D, E, A, C, B
(3) D, E, C, A, B (4) D, E, A, B, C

23. The position of how many digits in the number 726801 will remain unchanged after the digits within the number are rearranged in descending order (from left to right)?
(1) One (2) Two
(3) Three (4) Zero

24. The Elephanta Caves are located in:
(1) Gwalior (2) Mumbai
(3) Jodhpur (4) Bhubaneswar

25. In __________, the Indian National Congress passed a resolution of Poorna Swaraj (complete independence) as its ultimate goal.
(1) Madras Session (1927 AD)
(2) Lahore Session (1929 AD)
(3) Karachi Session (1931 AD)
(4) Calcutta Session (1928 AD)

26. Find the mean of the prime numbers between 1 and 30.
(1) 15 (2) 12.9
(3) 16 (4) 15.5

27. How many solid spherical balls, each with a diameter of 1.5 cm, can be made by melting a solid cylinder with a height of 36 cm and a base radius of 8 cm?
(1) 4,096 (2) 1,458
(3) 729 (4) 5,832

28. Who wrote the famous book - "The Story of My Experiments with Truth"?
(1) Lala Lajpat Rai
(2) M.K. Gandhi
(3) Sarojini Naidu
(4) V.S. Naipaul

29. A man, a woman and a boy can do a work in 6, 9 and 18 days, respectively. How many boys must assist one man and one woman to do the work in 1 day?
(1) 13 (2) 9
(3) 5 (4) 1

30. **Statement:** Money plays a vital role in politics.
Conclusion I: The poor can never become politicians.
Conclusion II: All the rich men take part in politics.
Which of them logically follows from the information given in the statement?
(1) Only I follows.
(2) Only II follows.
(3) Neither I nor II follows.
(4) Both I and II follow.

31. 'Exercise' is to 'Obesity' as 'Water' is to __________?
(1) Thirst (2) Alcohol
(3) Drink (4) Purity

32. Given below are two statements: one is labelled as Assertion A, and the other is labelled as Reason R.
Assertion A: The filament in an electric bulb does not burn up, although its temperature is about 2700° C when it glows.
Reason R: A bulb filament is made of tungsten.

In light of the above statements, choose the most appropriate answer from the options below.

(1) Both A and R are correct, and R is the correct explanation of A.
(2) Both A and R are correct, but R is NOT the correct explanation of A.
(3) A is correct, but R is not correct.
(4) A is not correct, but R is correct.

33. Choose the correct option for the missing term 27: 18: 102: ?

(1) 54 (2) 68
(3) 76 (4) 84

34. Find the next term in the alphanumeric series: C4X, F9U, I16R, ?

(1) K25P (2) L25P
(3) L25O (4) L27P

35. During a festival season, an item was available for ₹918 after a 15% discount. Smriti bargained with the shopkeeper and availed of a 20% discount; how much did Smriti pay for it?

(1) ₹864 (2) ₹872.10
(3) ₹888 (4) ₹902

36. The angles of a cyclic quadrilateral, taken in order, are $x°$, $(3x - 30)°$, $(y + 30)°$ and $(2x - y)°$. Find the measure of the smallest angle of the quadrilateral.

(1) 20° (2) 30°
(3) 40° (4) 50°

37. If the Republic Day of India was celebrated on Friday in 1996, on which day of 2000 was the Independence Day of India celebrated?

(1) Saturday (2) Sunday
(3) Monday (4) Tuesday

38. Find the missing term: 12: 36: : 15: ?

(1) 99 (2) 45
(3) 60 (4) 39

39. At what angle are a clock's hour and minute hands inclined at 15 min past 5?

(1) 64° (2) 58½°
(3) 72½° (4) 67½°

40. In which year was the 'Panchayati Raj Bill' passed by the Lok Sabha and the Rajya Sabha?

(1) 1992 (2) 1993
(3) 1994 (4) 1995

41. Heavy water is used as a coolant in Nuclear Reactors because heavy water is:

(1) Water rich in minerals
(2) Water containing minerals with heavy metal
(3) Ozonised water
(4) Water containing heavy isotopes of hydrogen

42. Find the compound interest on ₹64000 at 10% per annum for 9 months when interest is compounded quarterly.

(1) ₹2791 (2) ₹4912
(3) ₹4921 (4) ₹6615.70

43. The energy of a body due to its motion is called:

(1) Kinetic energy
(2) Potential energy
(3) Static energy
(4) Conservation of energy

44. Match **List I** with **List II**.

List I (Indian State/Union Territory)	List II (No. of Lok Sabha seats)
A. NCT of Delhi	I. 42
B. Uttar Pradesh	II. 25
C. West Bengal	III. 7
D. Rajasthan	IV. 80

Choose the correct answer from the options given below:

(1) A-IV, B-III, C-II, D-I
(2) A-I, B-II, C-III, D-IV
(3) A-I, B-IV, C-II, D-III
(4) A-III, B-IV, C-I, D-II

45. The relation between the velocity of light (c), Frequency (v) and Wavelength (λ) is:

(1) $c = v\lambda$ (2) $v = c\lambda$
(3) $\lambda = cv$ (4) $c = v\lambda^2$

46. Consider the following events and arrange them in ascending order.

A. Gandhi-Irwin Pact
B. First Round Table Conference
C. Simon Commission
D. Quit India Movement
E. Poona Pact

Choose the correct answer from the options given below:

(1) B, C, A, D, E (2) C, B, A, E, D
(3) A, B, C, D, E (4) B, D, A, C, E

47. India's first experimental remote sensing satellite carrying TV and microwave cameras was:

(1) Aryabhata (2) Bhaskar–1
(3) Rohini RS–1 (4) Rohini RS–2

48. Which of the following counties is NOT a G20 member?

(1) Indonesia (2) Turkey
(3) Mexico (4) Singapore

49. A triangle with vertices (3, 1), (–1, 0), (2, 5) is

(1) Isosceles and right-angled
(2) Right-angled but not isosceles
(3) Isosceles but not right-angled
(4) Neither isosceles nor right-angled

50. If the base radius of a cone is doubled and its height is halved, then the volume of the new cone will be:

(1) Same as of the original cone
(2) 1.5 times of the original cone
(3) 2 times of the original cone
(4) 4 times of the original cone

51. The Union Government launched the "Bharat Nirman Yojana" in:

(1) December 2005 (2) February 2006
(3) May 2015 (4) April 2016

52. A man moves to the east side, then turns left, then turns right and then further turns right again and then moves left. Now, which direction is the man in?

(1) East (2) West
(3) South (4) North

53. In this question, choose the correct water image of the given figure:

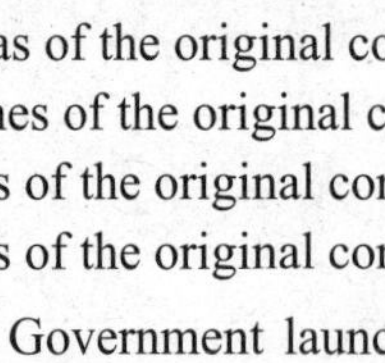

(1)
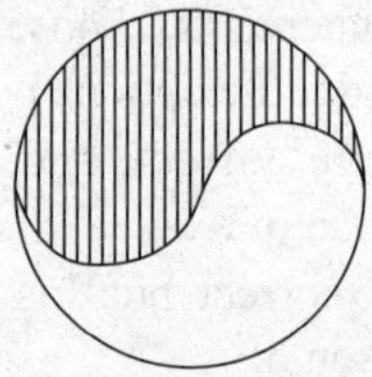
(2)
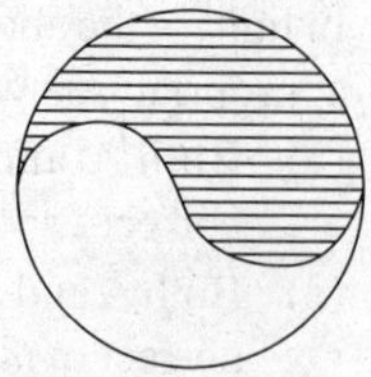

(3)
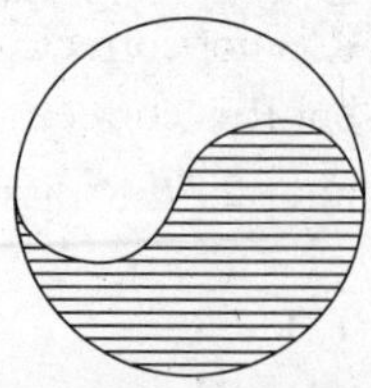
(4)
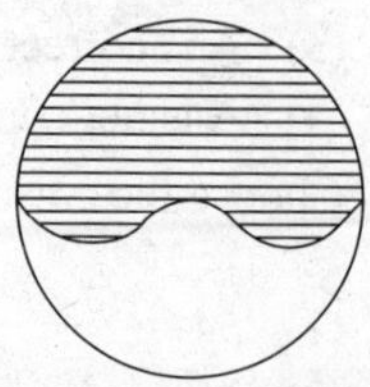

54. Match **List I** with **List II**.

List I (Player)	List II (Sports)
A. MC Mary Kom	I. Cricket
B. Dipika Pallikal	II. Archery
C. Deepika Kumari	III. Squash
D. Smriti Mandhana	IV. Boxing

Choose the correct answer from the options given below.

(1) A-IV, B-III, C-I, D-II
(2) A-IV, B-I, C-II, D-III
(3) A-IV, B-III, C-II, D-I
(4) A-IV, B-II, C-III, D-I

55. If $a = 12$, $b = -8$ and $c = -4$, then find the value of $a^3 + b^3 + c^3$.

(1) 384 (2) 1152
(3) –1448 (4) 2304

56. What would replace the question mark in the given series?

ADG, BEH, CFI, __? EHK

(1) DEH (2) DFH
(3) DGJ (4) DFI

57. What should be subtracted from 20% of 450 to get 25% of 240?

(1) 50 (2) 40
(3) 30 (4) 20

58. Shyam said Deepak's Mother is the mother of my father's wife. How is Deepak related to Shyam?

(1) Mother's brother (2) Grandfather
(3) Father's brother (4) Brother

59. Find the number of triangles in the given figure.

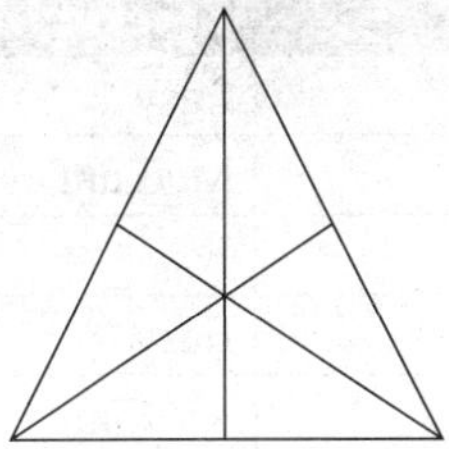

(1) 7 (2) 9
(3) 13 (4) 16

60. Simple interest on a certain sum at 8% per annum for 5 years is ₹2400. What will be the compound interest on the same sum at the same rate for 2 years?

(1) ₹990
(2) ₹998.40
(3) ₹960
(4) ₹1015.50

Answer Key

1. **(2)**	2. **(2)**	3. **(3)**	4. **(4)**	5. **(3)**	6. **(4)**	7. **(2)**	8. **(4)**	9. **(3)**	10. **(3)**
11. **(3)**	12. **(2)**	13. **(4)**	14. **(4)**	15. **(4)**	16. **(4)**	17. **(1)**	18. **(2)**	19. **(2)**	20. **(1)**
21. **(2)**	22. **(4)**	23. **(1)**	24. **(2)**	25. **(2)**	26. **(2)**	27. **(1)**	28. **(2)**	29. **(1)**	30. **(3)**
31. **(1)**	32. **(2)**	33. **(2)**	34. **(3)**	35. **(1)**	36. **(2)**	37. **(4)**	38. **(2)**	39. **(4)**	40. **(1)**
41. **(4)**	42. **(3)**	43. **(1)**	44. **(4)**	45. **(1)**	46. **(2)**	47. **(2)**	48. **(4)**	49. **(1)**	50. **(3)**
51. **(1)**	52. **(1)**	53. **(2)**	54. **(3)**	55. **(2)**	56. **(3)**	57. **(3)**	58. **(1)**	59. **(4)**	60. **(2)**

Classification of Questions

Question No.	Subject	Topic	Level of Difficulty
1.	Reasoning	Non-verbal	Easy
2.	Quantitative Aptitude	Averages	Easy
3.	Quantitative Aptitude	Geometry	Medium
4.	General Awareness	History	Easy
5.	General Awareness	Art & Culture	Difficult
6.	General Awareness	Science & Tech	Difficult
7.	Reasoning	Non-verbal	Easy
8.	Reasoning	Alphabetical Series	Easy
9.	Quantitative Aptitude	Time, Speed & Distance	Easy
10.	Reasoning	Linear Arrangement	Easy
11.	Quantitative Aptitude	Powers & Indices	Easy
12.	Reasoning	Non-verbal	Easy
13.	Quantitative Aptitude	Simplification	Easy
14.	Quantitative Aptitude	Algebra (Progression)	Easy

Question No.	Subject	Topic	Level of Difficulty
15.	Reasoning	Alphabetical Series	Easy
16.	General Awareness	Polity	Medium
17.	Quantitative Aptitude	Ratio & Proportions	Easy
18.	Quantitative Aptitude	Trigonometry	Easy
19.	General Awareness	Current Affairs	Medium
20.	Quantitative Aptitude	Probability	Medium
21.	General Awareness	Science (Biology)	Easy
22.	General Awareness	Geography	Tough
23.	Reasoning	Rankings & Orders	Easy
24.	General Awareness	Geography	Easy
25.	General Awareness	History	Easy
26.	Quantitative Aptitude	Averages	Easy
27.	Quantitative Aptitude	Mensuration	Medium
28.	General Awareness	Books & Authors	Easy
29.	Quantitative Aptitude	Time & Work	Easy
30.	Reasoning	Statements and Conclusions	Medium
31.	Reasoning	Analogy	Easy
32.	General Awareness	Science (Physics)	Difficult
33.	Reasoning	Missing Number	Easy
34.	Reasoning	Alphanumeric Series	Easy
35.	Quantitative Aptitude	Profit, Loss & Discount	Easy
36	Quantitative Aptitude	Geometry	Easy
37.	Quantitative Aptitude	Calendars	Easy
38.	Reasoning	Number-based Analogy	Easy
39.	Quantitative Aptitude	Clocks	Easy
40.	General Awareness	Polity	Difficult
41.	General Awareness	Science (Physics)	Medium
42.	Quantitative Aptitude	Compound Interest	Medium
43.	General Awareness	Science (Physics)	Easy
44.	General Awareness	Polity	Easy
45.	General Awareness	Science (Physics)	Easy
46.	General Awareness	History	Difficult
47.	General Awareness	Science & Technology	Difficult
48.	General Awareness	Polity	Easy
49.	Quantitative Aptitude	Coordinate Geometry	Medium
50.	Quantitative Aptitude	Mensuration	Easy

Question No.	Subject	Topic	Level of Difficulty
51.	General Awareness	Government Schemes	Difficult
52.	Reasoning	Directions	Easy
53.	Reasoning	Water Image	Easy
54.	General Awareness	Sports	Easy
55.	Quantitative Aptitude	Algebra (Basic Identities)	Easy
56.	Reasoning	Alphabetical Series	Easy
57.	Quantitative Aptitude	Percentages	Easy
58.	Reasoning	Blood Relations	Easy
59.	Quantitative Aptitude	Geometry	Medium
60.	Quantitative Aptitude	Simple Interest & Compound Interest	Medium

The no. of questions on Quantitative Aptitude: 23
The no. of questions on Reasoning: 16
The no. of questions on General Awareness: 21

Explanation to Select Questions

2. Let there be n employees in the factory.

$\therefore$ the total salary of these 'n' employees is $15000n$.

The total salary of the 250 employees with the average salary of $16000 = 250 \times 16000 = 4000000$.

The total salary of the remaining $(n - 250)$ employees with the average salary of $13750 = (n - 250)13750$.

$\therefore (n - 250)13750 + 4000000 = 15000n$

or, $13750n - 250 \times 13750 + 4000000 = 15000n$

or, $4000000 - 3437500 = 15000n - 13750n$

or, $1250n = 562500$

or, $n = \dfrac{562500}{1250} = 450.$

Hence, Option 2.

Shortcut: Use the method of alligation.

250 employees

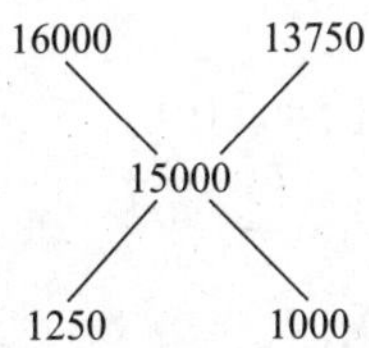

Therefore, the ratio of number of employees with the average salary of 16000 with the number of employees with the average salary of 13750 is $\dfrac{1250}{1000} = \dfrac{5}{4}$.

$\therefore$ the number of employees with the average salary of 13750 is $\dfrac{250 \times 4}{5} = 200.$

Thus, the total number of employees is $250 + 200 = 450$.

3. The lengths of the three sides of the triangle are 15, 19 and 22.

The semi-perimeter of the triangle

$= \dfrac{15 + 19 + 22}{2} = \dfrac{56}{2} = 28.$

The area of the triangle

$= \sqrt{28(28 - 15)(28 - 19)(28 - 22)}$

$= \sqrt{28 \times 13 \times 9 \times 6}$

$= \sqrt{4 \times 7 \times 13 \times 9 \times 6}$

$= \sqrt{4 \times 9 \times 6 \times 7 \times 13}$

$= 2 \times 3\sqrt{6 \times 7 \times 13}$

$= 6\sqrt{546}$
$= 6 \times 23.37$
$= 140.22$

Hence, Option 3.

6. Deep Blue was developed in the USA. It was programmed to play chess with the world chess champion Garry Kasparov. Kasparov defeated it first but lost to it subsequently.
Hence, Option 4.

8.

A	Z	G	T	M	N	?	Y	B
1	26	7	20	13	14		25	2

Comparing the 1st and the 2nd terms: 1 + 6 = 7 and 26 – 6 = 20.
Comparing the 2nd and the 3rd terms: 7 + 6 = 13 and 20 – 6 = 14.
Therefore, the 4th term should have 13 + 6 = 19 (S) and 14 – 6 = 8 (H).
The missing term is SH.
Hence, Option 4.

9. $\text{Time} = \frac{\text{Distance}}{\text{speed}} = \frac{150}{45} = \frac{10}{3}$ hours

$= 3\frac{1}{3}$ hours = 3 hours and 20 minutes.

He began at 10:45 am and took 3 hours and 20 minutes, so he reached at 2:05 pm.
Hence, Option 3.

10. This is how the arrangement is:

D B F
A E C

Please bear in mind that all 6 of them are facing North.
Hence, Option 3.

11. $25^{4x-3} = 5^{6x+8}$

or, $(5^2)^{4x-3} = 5^{6x+8}$

or, $5^{8x-6} = 5^{6x+8}$

or, $8x - 6 = 6x + 8$

or, $2x = 14$ or, $x = 7$.

Now, $\frac{5x+1}{3} = \frac{5 \times 7 + 1}{3} = \frac{36}{3} = 12.$

Hence, Option 3.

13. $(0.1)^8 \div (0.01)^5$

$= (10^{-1})^8 \div (10^{-2})^5$

$= \frac{10^{-8}}{10^{-10}} = 10^{10-8} = 10^2 = 100.$

Hence, Option 4.

14. Arithmetic progression is a sequence in which the difference (NOT the addition) of any two consecutive terms is a constant.
Hence, Statement I is incorrect.
Statement II is correct.
Hence, Option 4.

15.

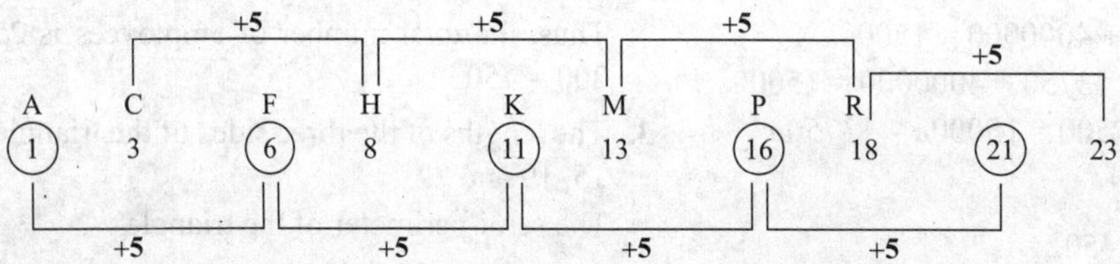

It is obvious that the next term will be UW. Hence, Option 4.

17. Let the numbers be a and b.
The mean proportional of a and b is $\sqrt{a \times b} = 6$.

or, $ab = 36$ (i)

As the third proportional of a and b is 20.25, we have,

$\frac{a}{b} = \frac{b}{20.25}$ or, $20.25 = \frac{b^2}{a}$

or, $\frac{b^2}{a} = \frac{81}{4}$ (ii)

Multiplying (i) and (ii),

$ab \times \frac{b^2}{a} = 36 \times \frac{81}{4}$

or, $b^3 = 9 \times 81$

or, $b^3 = 9 \times 9 \times 9$

or, $b = 9$

$\therefore\ a = \frac{36}{9} = 4.$

Therefore, the numbers are 4 and 9.

Hence, Option 1.

Shortcut: We are looking for two numbers whose product is 36. Hence, we can eliminate options 2 and 4.

The 3rd proportional in option 3 is $\frac{18 \times 18}{2} = 162.$

Hence, Option 3 can also be eliminated.

We are left with ONLY option I.

18. $2\cos\theta = \sqrt{3}$

or, $\cos\theta = \frac{\sqrt{3}}{2} = \cos 30°$

or, $\theta = 30°$

$\tan 2\theta = \tan 60° = \sqrt{3}.$

Hence, Option 2.

20. P (at least one of E and F) = P(E) + P(F) – P(E and F) $= \frac{5}{8} + \frac{1}{2} - \frac{1}{4} = \frac{5+4-2}{8} = \frac{7}{8}.$

Now, P(not E and not F) = 1 – P(at least one of E and F) $= 1 - \frac{7}{8} = \frac{1}{8}.$

Hence, Option 1.

Mathematically, P(at least one of E and F) = $P(E \cup F)$.

And P(E and F) = $P(E \cap F)$.

21.

Vitamin	Scientific/Chemical Name
Vitamin D	Calciferol
Vitamin C	Ascorbic acid
Vitamin E	Tocopherol
Vitamin B_{12}	Cobalamin

Hence, Option 2.

22. India shares its boundaries with 7 countries. These 7 countries arranged in ascending order of the length of their border with India are Afghanistan, Bhutan, Myanmar, Nepal, Pakistan, China and Bangladesh.

Hence, Option 4.

23. The original number: 7 2 6 8 0 1

Digits rearranged in descending order: 8 7 6 2 1 0

Thus, we see that the position of only 6 remains unchanged.

Hence, Option 1.

26. There are 10 prime numbers between 1 and 30: 2, 3, 5, 7, 11, 13, 17, 19, 23, and 29.

Their average

$= \frac{2+3+5+7+11+13+17+19+23+29}{10}$

$= \frac{129}{10} = 12.9.$

Hence, Option 2.

27. The volume of the cylinder $= \pi \times 8^2 \times 36$ $= \pi \times 64 \times 36.$

The volume of one such spherical ball

$= \frac{4}{3}\pi\left(\frac{1.5}{2}\right)^3.$

Therefore, the number of spherical balls

$= \frac{\pi \times 64 \times 36}{\frac{4}{3}\pi\frac{(1.5)^3}{8}}$

$= \frac{64 \times 36 \times 3 \times 8}{4 \times \frac{3^3}{2^3}} = \frac{64 \times 36 \times 3 \times 8 \times 8}{4 \times 27}$

$= 4096.$

Hence, Option 1.

29. Let the work be of 18 units.

A man can do $\frac{18}{6} = 3$ units in a day.

A woman can do $\frac{18}{9} = 2$ units in a day.

A boy can do $\frac{18}{18} = 1$ unit in a day.

One man and one woman can do 3 + 2 = 5 units in a day.

So, the remaining 18 – 5 = 13 units can be done by 13 boys in 1 day.

Hence, Option 1.

32. A and R are correct, but R is NOT the reason for A. The filament does not burn up as it is held in an environment of inert gases (mostly

Argon) to prevent its oxidation. Also, carbon and platinum can be used as filaments, but many factors, such as affordability, make tungsten the most suitable choice.
Hence, Option 2.

33. $18 = \frac{2}{3} \times 27$

Similarly $\frac{2}{3} \times 102 = 68.$

Hence, Option 2.

34.

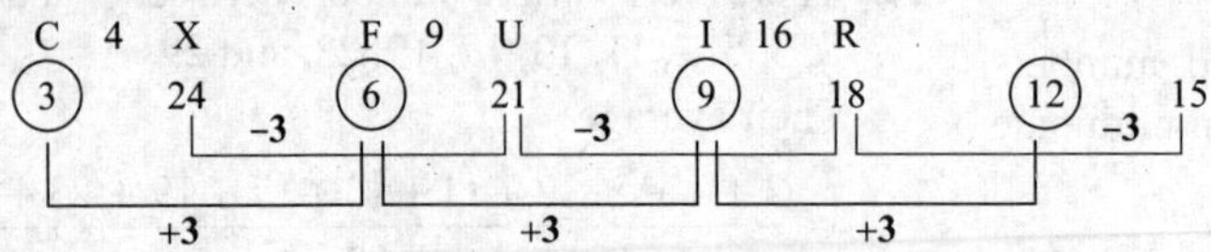

Therefore, the next term will have the letters L and O. Also, the number between the letters must be 25.
Hence, Option 3.

35. A 15% discount means 85% of the marked price.
A 20% discount means 80% of the marked price.

Therefore, Smriti paid $\frac{918 \times 80}{85} =$ ₹864.
Hence, Option 1.

36.

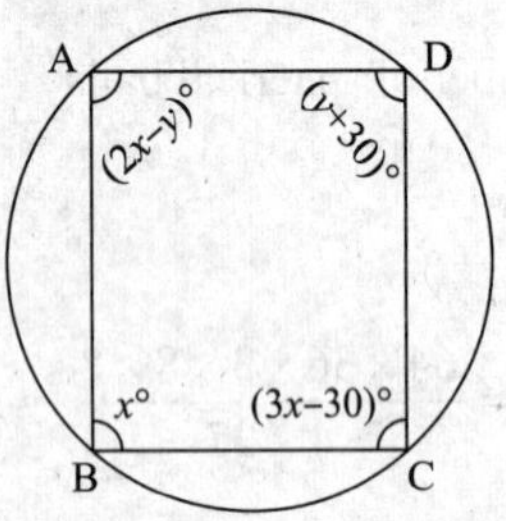

Let ABCD be a cyclic quadrilateral.
In any cyclic quadrilateral, the sum of the opposite angles is 180°.
Therefore, $\angle A + \angle C = 180°$.
or, $2x - y + 3x - 30 = 180$
or, $5x - y = 180 + 30$
or, $5x - y = 210$ (i)
Again, $\angle B + \angle D = 180°$, or, $x + y + 30° = 180°$
or, $x + y = 150°$ (ii)
Adding (i) and (ii), we get:
$6x = 360°$ or, $x = 60°$.
Therefore, $y = 150 - 60 = 90°$
So, the angles are 60°, 180 – 30° = 150°, 90 + 30 = 120° and 120 – 90 = 30°.
Therefore, the smallest angle is 30°.
Hence, Option 2.

37. The number of odd days between 26 January 1996 and 26 January 2000 = 5.

Therefore, 26 January 2000 was 5 days after a Friday, a Wednesday.
The number of odd-days between 26 January 2000 and 15 August 2000 is
5 (in January) + 1 (in February) + 3 (in March) + 2 (in April) + 3 (in May) + 2 (in June) + 3 (in July) + 1 (in August) = 20 = 7 × 2 + 6.
Therefore, 15 August 2000 was 6 days after a Wednesday, a Tuesday.
Hence, Option 4.

38. 36 = 12 × 3.
Hence, the missing term = 15 × 3 = 45.
Hence, Option 2.

39. Let the clock be divided into 12 parts.

A part is of $\frac{360°}{12} = 30°$.

At 15 minutes past 5, the minute hand is at mark 3 and the hour hand has travelled exactly $\frac{1}{4}$ of the distance between 5 and 6.

Therefore, the angle between them

$= \left(2\frac{1}{4}\right) \times 30° = 67.5°$.

Hence, Option 4.

40. The Constitution (Seventy-third Amendment) Act, 1992, came into force on 24th April 1993, but the Lok Sabha and the Rajya Sabha had passed the bill in 1992 itself.
Hence, Option 1.
Caution: Option 2 is a trap here.

41. Water containing heavy isotopes of Hydrogen is called Heavy Water or Deuterium Oxide (^2H_2O or D_2O). The answer is Option 4.

42. As the interest is compounded quarterly:
There would be 3 terms in 9 months, and the rate of interest per quarter will be $\frac{10}{4}$%.

The amount $= 64000\left(1+\frac{10}{400}\right)^3$

$= 64000\left(1+\frac{1}{40}\right)^3$

$= 64000\left(\frac{41}{40}\right)^3$

$= 64000 \times \frac{41}{40} \times \frac{41}{40} \times \frac{41}{40}$

$= 41^3 = 68921.$

Therefore, the interest = 68921 – 64000 = 4921.
Hence, Option 3.

44. Even if you do not know the exact numbers, you can guess that Uttar Pradesh should have the maximum, and the NCT of Delhi should have the minimum number of seats (among the options). There is only one option that supports it: Option 4.

46.

Event	Time
Simon Commission	1928
First Round Table Conference	12 November 1930 to 19 January 1931
Gandhi-Irwin Pact	5 March 1931
Poona Pact	24 September 1932
Quit India Movement	1942

Hence, Option 2.
Even if you do not remember the exact years, you must know that the Quit India Movement must be the last of these 5, and that is there only in Option 2.

47. Bhaskar-1 was manufactured by the ISRO (Indian Space Research Organisation) and launched in 1979.
Hence, Option 2.

49. Let the vertices of the Δ be A (3, 1), B (–1, 0) and C (2, 5).
Distance, between A and B

$= \sqrt{\{3-(-1)\}^2 + (1-0)^2}$

$= \sqrt{4^2+1^2} = \sqrt{17},$

Similarly, $BC = \sqrt{(-1-2)^2 + (0-5)^2}$

$= \sqrt{3^2+5^2} = \sqrt{34},$

$CA = \sqrt{(2-3)^2+(5-1)^2}$

$= \sqrt{1^2+4^2} = \sqrt{17}.$

Thus, we see that AB = AC.

Also, $\left(\sqrt{34}\right)^2 = \left(\sqrt{17}\right)^2 + \left(\sqrt{17}\right)^2.$

Thus, we see that the triangle is isosceles as well as right-angled.
Hence, Option 1.

50. Let the radius and height of the cone be r and h, respectively.

The volume of the cone $= \frac{1}{3}\pi r^2 h = v_1$ (say).

The volume of a new cone with the radius $2r$ and height $\frac{h}{2}$

$= \frac{1}{3}\pi(2r)^2 \times \frac{h}{2} = \frac{1}{3}\pi 4r^2 \times \frac{h}{2}$

$= 2 \times \frac{1}{3}\pi r^2 h = 2v_1.$

Hence, Option 3.

51. The Bharat Nirman Yojna was launched in December 2005 to improve India's rural infrastructure.
Hence, Option 1.

52.

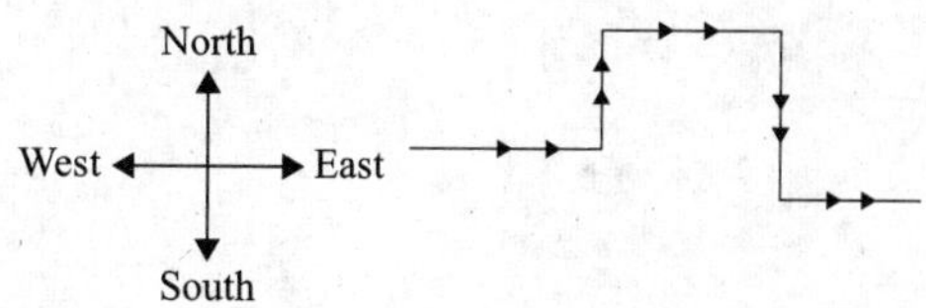

It is clear that the man is facing the East.
Hence, Option 1.

55. $a + b + c = 12 - 8 - 4 = 0.$
If $a + b + c = 0$, then $a^3 + b^3 + c^3 = 3abc.$
$\therefore a^3 + b^3 + c^3 = 3(12)(-8)(-4) = 36 \times 32 = 1152.$
Hence, Option 2.

56. A D G   B E H   C F I   **?**   E H K

1 4 7   2 5 8   3 6 9   5 8 11

Therefore, the ranks of the letters in the missing term in the alphabet should be 4, 7 and 10.

Hence, the term is DGJ.

Hence, Option 3.

57. 20% of 450 = $\frac{450}{5} = 90$.

25% of 240 = $\frac{240}{4} = 60$.

We must subtract 30 from 90 to get 60.

Hence, Option 3.

58.

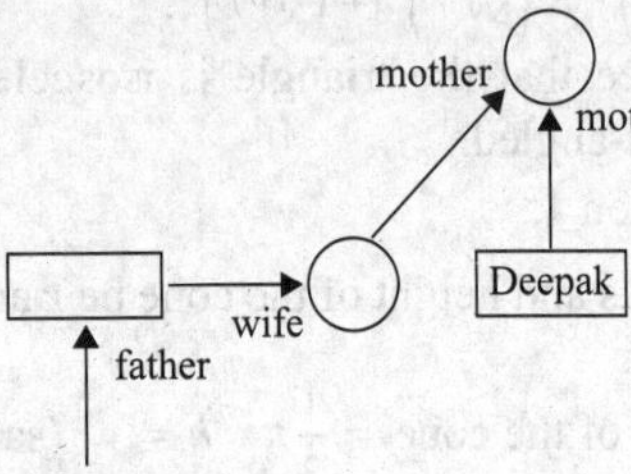

Thus, it is clear that Deepak is Shyam's maternal uncle.

Hence, Option 1.

59.

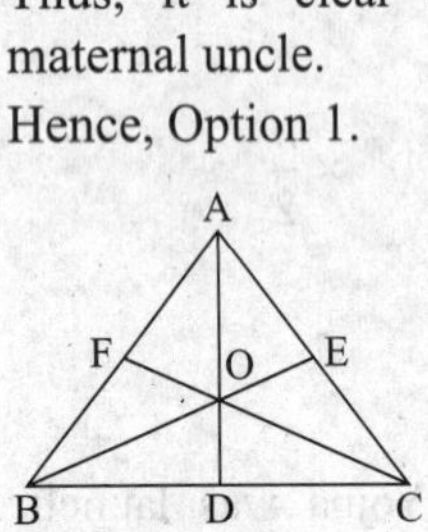

The triangles are ADB, ADC, BEC, BEA, CFA, CFB, AOF, FOB, BOD, DOC, COE, EOA, OAB, OBC, OCA and ABC.

Hence, Option 4.

60. The principal $= \frac{\text{S.I.} \times 100}{\text{rate} \times \text{time}}$

$= \frac{2400 \times 100}{8 \times 5}$

$= 6000.$

Now, at 8% compound interest for 2 years, ₹6000 will become

$$6000\left(1+\frac{8}{100}\right)^2 = 6000\left(1+\frac{2}{25}\right)^2$$

$$= 6000 \times \frac{27}{25} \times \frac{27}{25}$$

$$= 6998.40.$$

Therefore, the CI = 998.40

Hence, Option 2.

CUET UG 2023
GENERAL TEST

June
7

INSTRUCTIONS:
1. You need to attempt any 50 out of the 60 questions in 60 minutes.
2. You get 5 marks for a correct response and –1 for an incorrect one. However, there is no reward or penalty for a question not attempted.

1. Sunita rode her scooty northwards, turned left and then rode to her left again for 4 km. She found herself exactly 2 km West of her starting point. How far did she ride northwards initially?
(1) 5 km (2) 6 km
(3) 4 km (4) 2 km

2. Divide 243 kg weight into three parts such that half of the first part, one-third of the second part and one-fourth of the third part are equal.
(1) 63 kg, 84 kg, 96 kg
(2) 44 kg, 93 kg, 66 kg
(3) 48 kg, 63 kg, 132 kg
(4) 54 kg, 81 kg, 108 kg

3. Match **List I** with **List II**.

List I (Name of the Prime Minister)	List II (Tenure)
(A) Atal Bihari Vajpayee	(I) 10 November 1990 – 21 June 1991
(B) P.V. Narasimha Rao	(II) 28 July 1979 – 14 January 1980
(C) Chaudhari Charan Singh	(III) 16 May 1996 – 1 June 1996
(D) Chandra Shekhar	(IV) 21 June 1991 – 16 May 1996

Choose the most appropriate answer from the options given below:
(1) (A)-(I), (B)-(II), (C)-(III), (D)-(IV)
(2) (A)-(II), (B)-(I), (C)-(III), (D)-(IV)
(3) (A)-(III), (B)-(IV), (C)-(II), (D)-(I)
(4) (A)-(III), (B)-(IV), (C)-(I), (D)-(II)

4. ________ is the basic structural and functional unit of all known living organisms.
(1) Bacteria (2) Tissue
(3) Cell (4) Fungi

5. Match **List I** with **List II**.

List I (Jain Tirthankara)	List II (Symbolic Representation)
(A) Rishabha	(I) Lion
(B) Mahavira	(II) Elephant
(C) Parshvanath	(III) Bull
(D) Ajitnath	(IV) Serpent

Choose the most appropriate answer from the options given below:
(1) (A)-(III), (B)-(I), (C)-(IV), (D)-(II)
(2) (A)-(I), (B)-(IV), (C)-(II), (D)-(III)
(3) (A)-(II), (B)-(IV), (C)-(III), (D)-(I)
(4) (A)-(I), (B)-(IV), (C)-(III), (D)-(II)

6. A sum of money doubles itself in 10 years on compound interest. In how many years will it become four times?
(1) 18 (2) 20
(3) 21 (4) 19

7. How many times do the hour hand and minute hand of a clock coincide in a day?
(1) 24 (2) 20
(3) 21 (4) 22

8. Choose an alternative that most closely resembles the water image of the given figure.

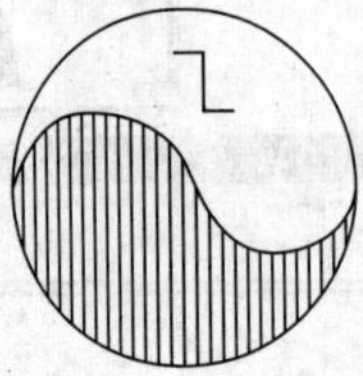

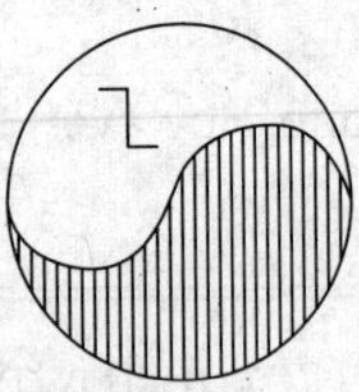

(A)

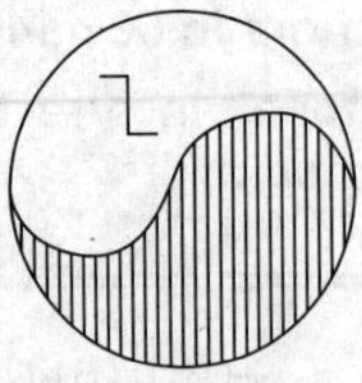

(B)

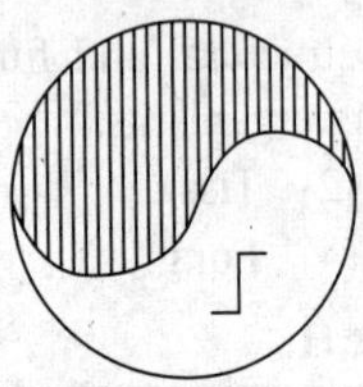

(C)

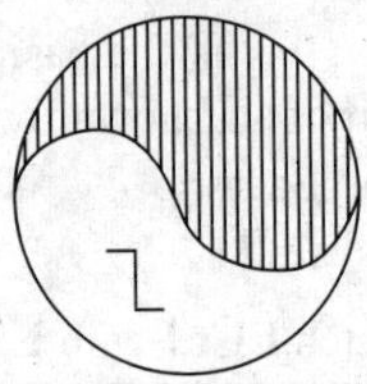

(D)

(1) (A) (2) (B)
(3) (C) (4) (D)

9. A coat is priced at ₹6000. In the sale, its price is reduced by 25%. After the sale, its price will be increased by 25% of the reduced price. What will be the price of the coat (in ₹) after the sale?

(1) 5265 (2) 5625
(3) 6125 (4) 6000

10. The 19th term of the A.P. 10, 7, 4, . . . is

(1) – 47 (2) – 44
(3) – 10 (4) – 35

11. Given below are one statement and one assumption:

Statement: Ashish wrote a second letter to his father after two months when he did not receive any reply to the first letter.

Assumption:

(I) Ashish's father did not receive the letter.

(II) His father promptly sends a reply to his letters.

Which Assumption is implicit based on the given statement?

(1) Only (I) is implicit.
(2) Only (II) is implicit.
(3) Both (I) and (II) are implicit.
(4) Either I or II is implicit.

12. A, B and C worked together for 5 days to build a wall, and then B left the work. A and C together finished the remaining work in 5 days. How many days can A and C work together to finish building the whole wall if B alone can do it in 25 days?

(1) $6\frac{1}{4}$ (2) 10
(3) 12 (4) $12\frac{1}{2}$

13. The speed of a boat in still water is 5 km/h. If it can travel 26 km downstream and 14 km upstream in the same time, then the speed of the stream is

(1) 1.5 km/h (2) 2 km/h
(3) 2.5 km/h (4) 3 km/h

14. ______ cell converts light energy directly into electric energy.

(1) Photovoltaic
(2) Photoelectric
(3) Photothermal
(4) Photocatalytic

15. How many types of muscles are there in the Human body?

(1) 2 (2) 3
(3) 4 (4) 5

16. If the mode and mean of a data are 18 and 21, respectively, then the median of the data is

(1) 60 (2) 19.5
(3) 20 (4) 30

17. If AMAZON is coded as ZNZALM, then FLIPKART will be coded as:

(1) UORKZIPG (2) UORKPZIG
(3) UROKPZIG (4) UROUPZIG

18. Involuntary actions like blood pressure, salivation and vomiting are controlled by the ______.

(1) Cerebrum (2) Cranium
(3) Spiral Cord (4) Medulla

19. Match **List I** with **List II**.

List I (Currency)	List II (Country)
(A) Euro	(I) Iceland
(B) Riel	(II) Turkey
(C) Krona	(III) Cambodia
(D) Lira	(IV) Belgium

Choose the correct answer from the options given below:

(1) (A)-(I), (B)-(II), (C)-(III), (D)-(IV)
(2) (A)-(II), (B)-(III), (C)-(IV), (D)-(I)
(3) (A)-(III), (B)-(IV), (C)-(II), (D)-(I)
(4) (A)-(IV), (B)-(III), (C)-(I), (D)-(II)

20. If February 1, 2004, was a Wednesday, Then which Day was March 3, 2004?

(1) Sunday (2) Monday
(3) Friday (4) Saturday

21. Which statements are true?

(A) Hecataeus is known as the father of Geography.
(B) Aristotle is known as the father of Geography.
(C) Historia Naturalia is a famous book of Pliny.
(D) Historia Naturalia is the famous book of Thalis.
(E) Hipparchus is known as the father of Geography.

Choose the **most appropriate** answer from the options given below:

(1) (E) and (A) only
(2) (A) and (C) only
(3) (B) and (C) only
(4) (D) and (E) only

22. Who was the founder of Arya Samaj?

(1) Raja Ram Mohan Roy
(2) Swami Vivekananda
(3) Swami Dayanand Saraswati
(4) Keshab Chandra Sen

23. X-rays were discovered by _______.

(1) Goldstein
(2) William Crooke
(3) Roentgen
(4) Chadwick

24. A man invested, on simple interest, $\frac{1}{4}$ of his capital at 7% p.a., another $\frac{1}{4}$ of the capital at 8% p.a. and the remaining capital at 10% p.a. He earned ₹700 as interest in one year. Find his total capital invested.

(1) ₹6000 (2) ₹7000
(3) ₹8000 (4) ₹9000

25. There is a certain relationship between two given numbers on one side of : : and one number is given on another side of : : while another number is to be found from the given alternatives, having the same relationship with this number as the numbers of the given pair. Choose the best alternative.

22:8::55: ?

(1) 18 (2) 19
(3) 20 (4) 21

26. Match **List I** with **List II**.

List I (Exponent)	List II (Musical Instrument)
(A) Pt. Ravi Shankar	(I) Sarod
(B) Zakir Hussain	(II) Sitar
(C) Ustad Ali Akbar Khan	(III) Shehnai
(D) Ustad Bismillah Khan	(IV) Tabla

Choose the most appropriate answer from the options given below:

(1) (A)-(II), (B)-(IV), (C)-(I), (D)-(III)
(2) (A)-(III), (B)-(IV), (C)-(I), (D)-(II)
(3) (A)-(II), (B)-(IV), (C)-(III), (D)-(I)
(4) (A)-(IV), (B)-(II), (C)-(III), (D)-(I)

27. The altitude of an equilateral triangle having a perimeter of 18 m is

(1) $3\sqrt{3}$ m (2) $4\sqrt{3}$ m
(3) $\frac{\sqrt{3}}{4}$ m (4) $5\sqrt{3}$ m

28. Indira Gandhi National Centre for Art was established in the year _______.

(1) 1985 (2) 1986
(3) 1987 (4) 1988

29. Swati throws a die twice. What is the probability that she throws at least one six?

(1) $\frac{1}{36}$ (2) $\frac{1}{4}$

(3) $\frac{11}{36}$ (4) $\frac{35}{36}$

30. Who was invited as the chief guest for India's Republic Day 2023?

(1) Mostafa Madbouly

(2) Abdel Fattah El-Sisi

(3) Joe Biden

(4) Rishi Sunak

31. The 17th Pravasi Bharatiya Divas in 2023 was held in ________.

(1) Mumbai (2) Delhi

(3) Ahmedabad (4) Indore

32. Three cubes, each with a volume of 343 cm^3, are placed side by side. What will be the surface area of the solid so formed (in cm^2)?

(1) 343 (2) 686

(3) 720 (4) 882

33. The sum of two numbers is 14, and their ratio is $\frac{5}{2}$. The numbers are:

(1) 7, 7 (2) 8, 6

(3) 9, 5 (4) 10, 4

34. Among the four answer figures, which one can be formed from the cut-outs given below?

(A)
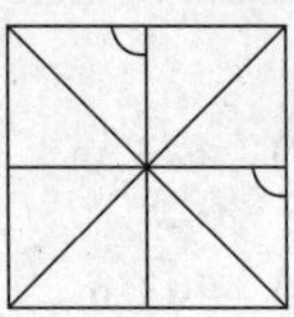
(B)
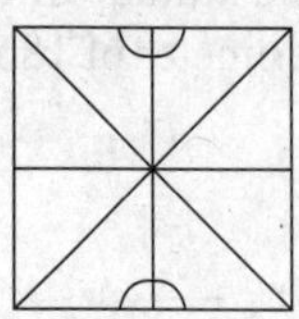

(C)
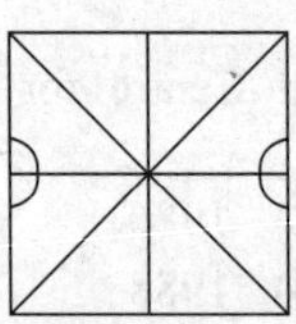
(D)
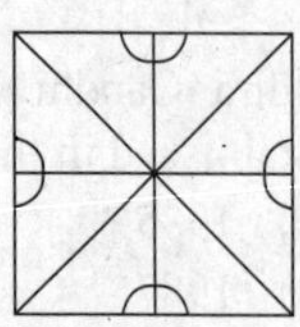

(1) (A) (2) (B)

(3) (C) (4) (D)

35. Which authority appoints the vice chancellor of a state university?

(1) President (2) Prime Minister

(3) Governor (4) Home Minister

36. If some words are coded from artificial language, like -

"Pono dakb" means LIVE RIGHTY.

"dakb Rnato" means LIVE PROFITABLY.

"Htbl dakb" means JUST LIVE.

Which code could mean "LIVE URGENTLY"?

(1) Wakbo Htbl (2) dakb Wakbo

(3) Htbl Pono (4) Pono Wakbo

37. The area (in square units) of the triangle formed by joining the points (3, 0), (0, 6) and (–5, 0) is

(1) 6 (2) 12

(3) 24 (4) 48

38. Figure out how the pattern would appear when the transparent sheet is folded at the dotted line from amongst the four alternatives.

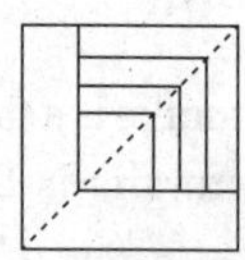

Transparent Sheet

(A)
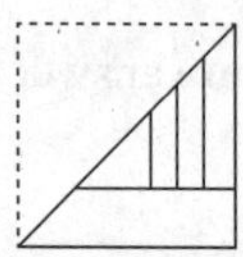
(B)
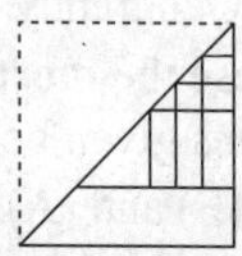

(C)
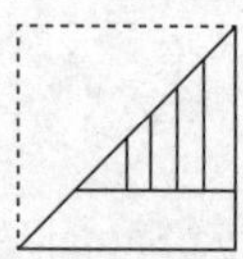
(D)
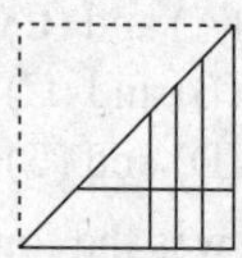

(1) (A) (2) (B)

(3) (C) (4) (D)

39. Find the next term in the given series.

2, 5, 10, 17, 26, ?

(1) 35 (2) 36

(3) 37 (4) 47

40. A Hockey Coach is trying to put together a team of 4 players for a forthcoming tournament. For this, 7 players are available. Males P, Q and R

and females S, T, U and Z. All players have equal capability, and at least 2 males will be there in the team. For a team of 4, all players must be able to play with each other. But Q cannot play with S, and R cannot play with Z and S.
If U is selected and Q is rejected, then which of the following groups will the team consist of?
(1) P, R, S and U (2) P, R, T and U
(3) P, R, U and Z (4) P, S, U and Z

41. Match **List I** with **List II**.

List I 1857 Revolt (Centre)	List II (Leader)
(A) Delhi	(I) Khan Bahadur Khan
(B) Kanpur	(II) Rani Lakshmi Bai
(C) Jhansi	(III) Nana Sahib
(D) Bareilly	(IV) Bahadur Shah and Gen. Bakht Khan

Choose the most appropriate answer from the options given below:
(1) (A)-(I), (B)-(II), (C)-(III), (D)-(IV)
(2) (A)-(II), (B)-(I), (C)-(IV), (D)-(III)
(3) (A)-(IV), (B)-(III), (C)-(II), (D)-(I)
(4) (A)-(III), (B)-(IV), (C)-(I), (D)-(II)

42. Which book was written by R.K. Narayan?
(1) The Z Factor (2) Zest For Life
(3) The Dark Room (4) Black Taj

43. In the figure, lines AB, CD and EF intersect at P. If $\angle CPE = 56°$, $\angle APD = 60°$ and PB = PF, then what is the measure of $\angle PBF$?

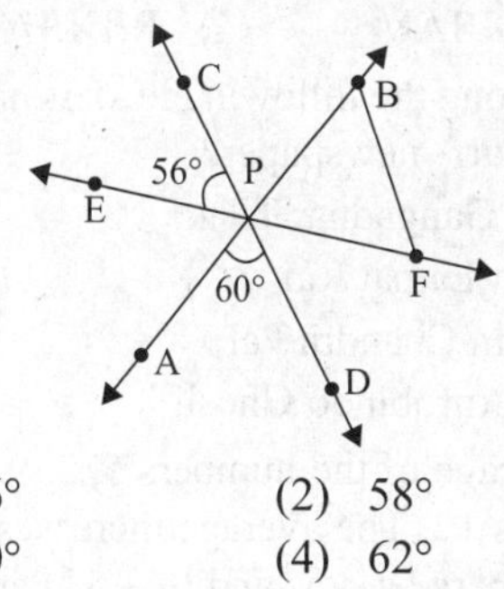

(1) 56° (2) 58°
(3) 60° (4) 62°

44. If $\cos(x - y) = \frac{\sqrt{3}}{2}$ and $\sin(x + y) = 1$ where $x > y$, then the value of y is:
(1) 0° (2) 30°
(3) 60° (4) 90°

45. Anuj notices that the reflection of the hands of the wall clock in a mirror shows the time to be 6 hours 15 minutes. What is the actual time shown by the clock?
(1) 5:45 (2) 5:15
(3) 6:45 (4) 6:15

46. Find which statements are sufficient to answer the given question.
What does 'Brown' represent in a code language?
(A) 'hiw ka tac' means 'Brown and Grey' in that code language.
(B) 'ma ta da' means 'you are Green' in that code language.
(C) 'ka da rac' means 'you can Brown' in that code language.
(1) Only (A) and (C)
(2) Only (A) and (B)
(3) Only (B) and (C)
(4) All (A), (B) and (C)

47. Sumit sold a television at ₹15,500 and suffered a loss of 20%. At what price did he buy the television?
(1) ₹21,350 (2) ₹18,730
(3) ₹19,375 (4) ₹12,916

48. Which state/UT of India is the 'Tower of Silence' situated in?
(1) Gujarat (2) Maharashtra
(3) Delhi (4) Rajasthan

49. Find the odd one out in the given series.
6, 24, 60, 120, 211, 336
(1) 120 (2) 211
(3) 336 (4) 60

50. Find the alternative which contains the problem figure as its part.
Problem Figure

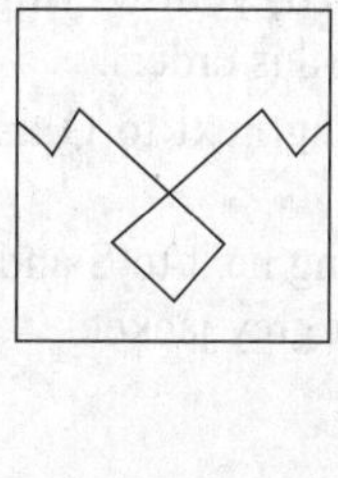

(A)  (B) 

(C) 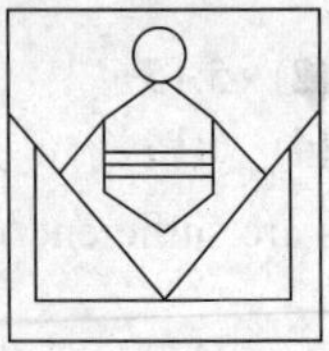 (D) 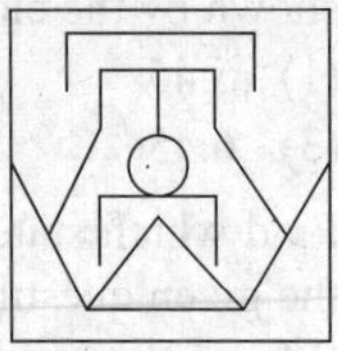

(1) (A) (2) (B)
(3) (C) (4) (D)

51. Find the alternative which contains the problem figure as its part.

Problem Figure

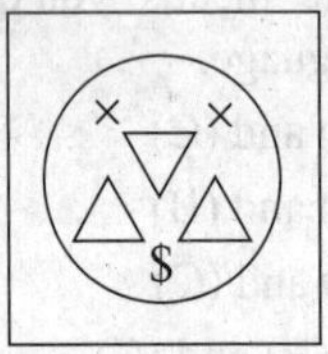

(A) 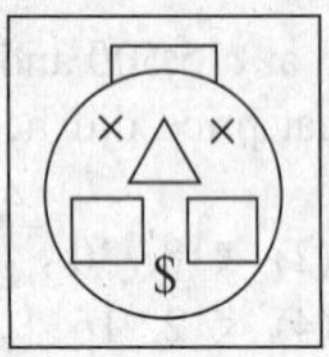 (B) 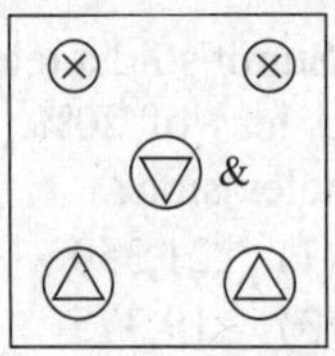

(C) 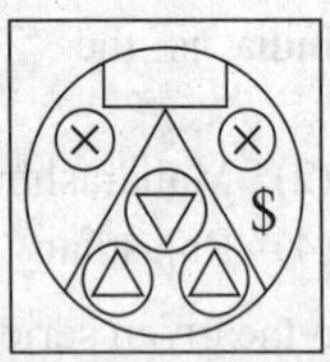 (D) 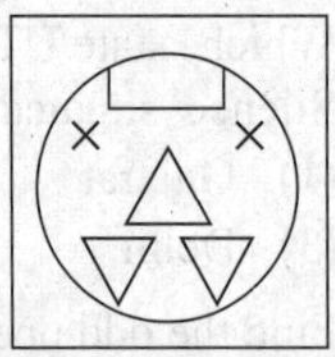

(1) (A) (2) (B)
(3) (C) (4) (D)

52. Read the following information carefully to answer the given question.

Five friends, P, Q, R, S and T, are sitting on a bench and wearing different colour jackets, i.e., brown, red, yellow, white and grey (not necessarily in this order).

(A) P is sitting next to Q and wearing a red jacket.
(B) R is sitting next to S and is not wearing a brown or grey jacket.
(C) S is not sitting with T, and T is wearing a brown jacket.
(D) T is on the left end of the bench.
(E) R is in the second position from the right.
(F) P is on the right of Q and T, and Q is wearing a grey jacket.
(G) P and R are sitting together.
(H) S is not wearing a white jacket.

What is the colour of R's jacket?

(1) Brown (2) Red
(3) White (4) Yellow

53. Select a figure from the given four alternatives, which, when placed in the blank space of the problem figure, would complete the pattern.

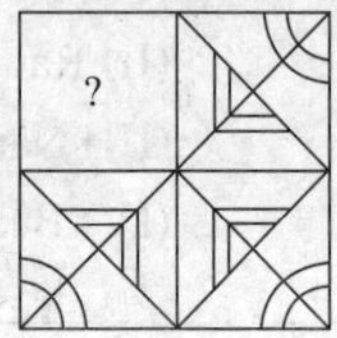

(A) 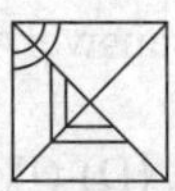 (B) 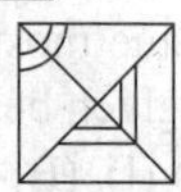

(C)  (D) 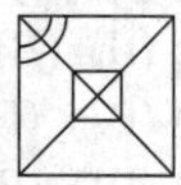

(1) (A) (2) (B)
(3) (C) (4) (D)

54. Choose the alternative that most closely resembles the mirror image of the given combination.

MARKER

(1) ЯƎKЯAM (2) ЯƎꓘЯAW
(3) ЯƎꓘЯAM (4) RƎꓘЯAW

55. Who among the following leaders had launched the "Kesari" newspaper?

(1) Bal Gangadhar Tilak
(2) Lala Lajpat Rai
(3) Bipin Chandra Pal
(4) Sri Aurobindo Ghosh

56. The average of the numbers 5, 3, 9, 11, 29 and $(p + 1)$ is 12. The average increases by 2 when the numbers $(q - 5)$ and $(q + 11)$ are included. Find the value of q.

(1) 12 (2) 14
(3) 17 (4) 18

57. Find the radius of a circle in which a sector with a central angle of 45° has an area of 154 cm². $\left(\text{Use } \pi = \frac{22}{7}\right)$

(1) $14\sqrt{2}$ cm (2) 14 cm

(3) $7\sqrt{2}$ cm (4) $\frac{21\sqrt{2}}{2}$ cm

58. A person crosses a 700 m long bridge in $3\frac{1}{2}$ minutes. The speed of the person in km/h is

(1) 6 (2) 8

(3) 10 (4) 12

59. Which was India's first state to establish the Panchayati Raj system?

(1) Rajasthan (2) Uttar Pradesh

(3) Maharashtra (4) Gujarat

60. Simplify $\frac{\sqrt{81}+\sqrt[3]{64}}{\sqrt{3^3+4^2+\sqrt[3]{216}}}$

(1) $\frac{17}{7}$ (2) $\frac{13}{7}$

(3) $\frac{12}{13}$ (4) $\frac{13}{17}$

Answer Key

1. (3) 2. (4) 3. (3) 4. (3) 5. (1) 6. (2) 7. (4) 8. (3) 9. (2) 10. (2)
11. (2) 12. (4) 13. (1) 14. (1) 15. (2) 16. (3) 17. (2) 18. (4) 19. (4) 20. (4)
21. (2) 22. (3) 23. (3) 24. (3) 25.* (2) and (3) 26. (1) 27. (1) 28. (1) 29. (3)
30. (2) 31. (4) 32. (2) 33. (4) 34. (1) 35. (3) 36. (2) 37. (3) 38. (1) 39. (3)
40. (2) 41. (3) 42. (3) 43. (2) 44. (2) 45. (1) 46. (1) 47. (3) 48. (2) 49. (2)
50.** It was dropped. 51. (3) 52. (3) 53. (2) 54. (3) 55. (1) 56. (3) 57. (1) 58. (4)
59. (1) 60. (2)

*In question 25, the official answer was Option 2, but we believe it can be Option 2 as well as Option 3.
**In question 50, Option 2 appears to be the answer, but all four options are incorrect; hence, the CUET dropped this question.

Classification of Questions

Question No.	Subject	Topic	Level of Difficulty
1.	Reasoning	Directions	Easy
2.	Quantitative Aptitude	Ratios	Easy
3.	General Awareness	Polity	Easy
4.	General Awareness	Science (Biology)	Easy
5.	General Awareness	History	Difficult
6.	Quantitative Aptitude	Compound Interest	Easy
7.	Quantitative Aptitude	Clocks	Easy

Question No.	Subject	Topic	Level of Difficulty
8.	Reasoning	Water Image	Easy
9.	Quantitative Aptitude	Profit, Loss and Discount	Easy
10.	Quantitative Aptitude	Algebra (A.P.)	Easy
11.	Reasoning	Statement and Assumption	Medium
12.	Quantitative Aptitude	Time and Work	Medium
13.	Quantitative Aptitude	Time, Speed and Distance	Easy
14.	General Awareness	Science	Medium
15.	General Awareness	Science (Biology)	Medium
16.	Quantitative Aptitude	Statistics (Mean, Median and Mode)	Medium
17.	Reasoning	Coding	Easy
18.	General Awareness	Science (Biology)	Medium
19.	General Awareness	Country & Currency	Difficult
20.	Quantitative Aptitude	Calendars	Easy
21.	General Awareness	Miscellaneous	Difficult
22.	General Awareness	History	Easy
23.	General Awareness	Science (Physics)	Easy
24.	Quantitative Aptitude	Simple Interest	Medium
25.	Reasoning	Analogy (Number-based)	Easy
26.	General Awareness	Art & Culture	Easy
27.	Quantitative Aptitude	Geometry	Easy
28.	General Awareness	Miscellaneous	Difficult
29.	Quantitative Aptitude	Probability	Easy
30.	General Awareness	Current Affairs	Easy
31.	General Awareness	Current Affairs	Medium
32.	Quantitative Aptitude	Mensuration	Medium
33.	Quantitative Aptitude	Algebra	Easy
34.	Reasoning	Non-verbal	Easy
35.	General Awareness	Polity	Easy
36.	Reasoning	Coding	Easy
37.	Quantitative Aptitude	Coordinate Geometry	Medium
38.	Reasoning	Non-verbal	Easy
39.	Reasoning	Number Series	Easy
40.	Reasoning	Team Selection	Easy
41.	General Awareness	History	Easy
42.	General Awareness	Books & Authors	Difficult
43.	Quantitative Aptitude	Geometry	Easy

Question No.	Subject	Topic	Level of Difficulty
44.	Quantitative Aptitude	Trigonometry	Easy
45.	Reasoning	Mirror Image	Easy
46.	Reasoning	Coding	Easy
47.	Quantitative Aptitude	Profit, Loss & Discount	Easy
48.	General Awareness	Miscellaneous	Difficult
49.	Reasoning	Number Series	Easy
50.	Reasoning	Non-verbal	Question was wrong
51.	Reasoning	Non-verbal	Easy
52.	Reasoning	Linear Arrangement	Easy
53.	Reasoning	Non-verbal	Easy
54.	Reasoning	Mirror Image	Easy
55.	General Awareness	History	Medium
56.	Quantitative Aptitude	Averages	Easy
57.	Quantitative Aptitude	Mensuration	Medium
58.	Quantitative Aptitude	Time, Speed and Distance	Easy
59.	General Awareness	Polity	Easy
60.	Quantitative Aptitude	Simplification	Easy

The no. of questions on Reasoning: 18
The no. of questions on Quantitative Aptitude: 22
The no. of questions on General Awareness: 20

Explanation to Select Questions

1.

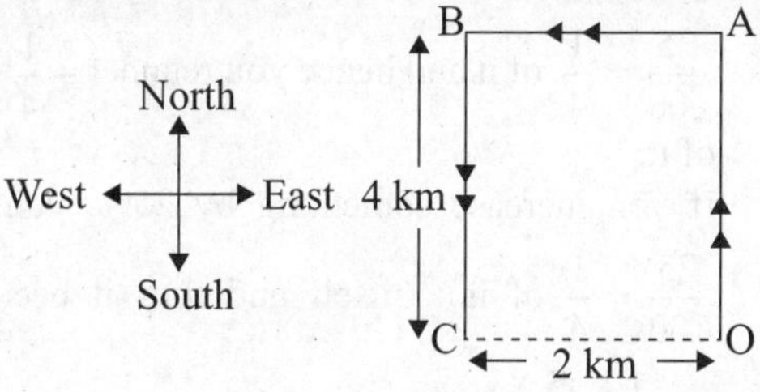

Sunita started from point O, took a left turn at point A, took another left turn at B and stopped at C.

We have OC = 2 km and BC = 4 km.

OABC is a rectangle, and OA = BC = 4.

So, Sunita rode 4 km towards the North.

Hence, Option 3.

2. Let the first part be $2x$, second $3x$ and third $4x$.

Of course, $\frac{2x}{2} = \frac{3x}{3} = \frac{4x}{4}$.

Now, $2x + 3x + 4x = 243$

or, $9x = 243$

or, $x = 27$

Therefore, the parts are 54, 81 and 108.

Hence, Option 4.

Shortcut: Try the options.

In none of options 1, 2 and 3, half of the first part is equal to one-third of the second part, and hence, we do not even need to check for the third part.

Hence, Option 4 is the answer.

Option 1: $\frac{63}{2} \neq \frac{84}{3}$, it cannot be the answer,

Option 2: $\frac{44}{2} \neq \frac{93}{3}$, it cannot be the answer,

Option 3: $\frac{48}{2} \neq \frac{63}{3}$, it cannot be the answer.

Hence, option 4.

6. Let the principal be P, and the rate of interest be r.

We have $2P = P\left(1+\frac{r}{100}\right)^{10}$

or, $\left(1+\frac{r}{100}\right)^{10} = 2$ (i)

Let the principal become 4 times itself in n years.

So, $4P = P\left(1+\frac{r}{100}\right)^{n}$

or, $\left(1+\frac{r}{100}\right)^{n} = 4 = 2^2$

or, $\left(1+\frac{r}{100}\right)^{n} = \left\{\left(1+\frac{r}{100}\right)^{10}\right\}^2$ (from (i))

or, $\left(1+\frac{r}{100}\right)^{n} = \left(1+\frac{r}{100}\right)^{20}$

$\Rightarrow n = 20$ years.

Hence, Option 2.

Shortcut: P becomes $2P$ in 10 years.
So, $2P$ will become $4P$ in 10 more years.
Hence, total time = 10 years + 10 years = 20 years.

7. Minute hand and hour hand of a watch meet once between 1 and 2, once between 2 and 3, once between 3 and 4, once between 4 and 5, once between 5 and 6, once between 6 and 7, once between 7 and 8, once between 8 and 9, once between 9 and 10, once between 10 and 11, but between 11 and 1, they meet just once (at 12). Hence, these hands meet 11 times in 12 hours. So, they meet 22 times in 24 hours.

Alternative I: The minute hand and hour hand are in circular motion, and the minute hand is faster than the hour hand. Every time the minute hand overtakes the hour hand, the hands meet. In 12 hours, the minute hand does 12 rounds of the watch, but the hour hand does just one round. Hence, the minute hand takes a lead of 11 rounds over the hour hand.

Therefore, they meet 11 times in 12 hours and 22 times in 24 hours.

Alternative II: The hour hand covers 30° in 60 minutes, but the minute hand covers 360° in 60 minutes.

So, the minute hand takes a lead of 360° – 30° = 330° over the hour hand in 60 minutes.

Once these hands are together, they will coincide again once the minute hand takes a lead of 360° over the hour hand.

Minute hand takes a lead of 330° over hour hand in 60 minutes,

$\therefore$ it will take a lead of 360° in $\frac{60}{330°} \times 360°$

$= \frac{720}{11}$ minutes $= 65\frac{5}{11}$ minutes.

Therefore, these hands meet every $\frac{720}{11}$ minutes.

There are 24 × 60 = 1440 minutes in a day.

$\Rightarrow$ they meet $\frac{1440}{\frac{720}{11}} = 22$ times in a day.

Caution: Do NOT think they meet 24 times in a day!

9. If you reduce 25% of something, you take out $\frac{25}{100} = \frac{1}{4}$ of it and hence you retain $1 - \frac{1}{4} = \frac{3}{4}$ of it.

If you increase something by 25%, you add $\frac{25}{100} = \frac{1}{4}$ of it to itself and thus it becomes $1 + \frac{1}{4} = \frac{5}{4}$ of its earlier value.

The price of the coat = ₹ 6000.

The price after a 25% discount = $6000 \times \frac{3}{4}$.

The price after an increase of 25% = $6000 \times \frac{3}{4} \times \frac{5}{4} = 5625$.

Hence, Option 2.

Alternative: If we increase something by $x\%$ and then reduce it by $x\%$ (in any order), it will reduce by $\frac{x^2}{100}\%$.

Here, $x = 25\%$, Hence, the reduction $= \frac{25^2}{100}\% = 6.25\%$.

6.25% of 6000 = 375.

Therefore, the final price of the coat = 6000 – 375 = 5625.

10. The first term a of the AP = 10

The common difference d of the AP = – 3

The 19th term = $a + (19 - 1)d$

$= 10 + 18(-3) = 10 - 54 = -44$.

Hence, Option 2.

12. B can do the work in 25 days.

Therefore, he must have done $\frac{5}{25} = \frac{1}{5}$ of the work in 5 days.

$\therefore$ A and C did $1 - \frac{1}{5} = \frac{4}{5}$ work in 10 days (5 days with B and another 5 days without B).

$\therefore$ A and C can do the complete work in $\frac{10 \times 5}{4} = 12\frac{1}{2}$ days.

Hence, Option 4.

Note: The answer has to be more than 10, and hence, Options 1 and 2 can be eliminated.

13. Let the speed of the stream be y km/h.

Time taken in travelling 26 km downstream $= \frac{26}{5 + y}$

Time taken in travelling 14 km upstream $= \frac{14}{5 - y}$

We have, $\frac{26}{5 + y} = \frac{14}{5 - y}$

or, $\frac{5 - y}{5 + y} = \frac{14}{26} = \frac{7}{13}$ or, $65 - 13y = 35 + 7y$

or, $20y = 30$

or, $y = 1.5$ km/hr.

Hence, Option 1.

Alternative: Try out the options.

$\frac{26}{5 + 1.5} = \frac{14}{5 - 1.5}$ and hence, option 1 is the answer.

15. The human body has three types of muscles: Skeletal, Smooth and Cardiac.

Hence, Option 2.

16. Mean – Mode = 3 (Mean – Median)

or, 21 – 18 = 3 (21 – Median)

or, 3 = 3 (21 – Median)

or, 21 – Median $= \frac{3}{3} = 1$

or, Median = 21 – 1 = 20.

Hence, Option 3.

17.

1	13	1	26	15	14
A	M	A	Z	O	N
Z	N	Z	A	L	M
26	14	26	1	12	13

6	12	9	16	11	1	18	20
F	L	I	P	K	A	R	T
U	O	R	K	P	Z	I	G
21	15	18	11	16	26	9	7

The sum of the rank of a letter and that of its code is always 27. E.g. the code for M(13) is N(27 – 13 = 14), etc.

Hence, Option 2.

20. The number of days between 1 February 2004 and 3 March 2004 = 28 + 3 = 31.

The number of odd days in 31 = 3 (as 31 = 7 × 4 + 3).

Therefore, 3 March would be 3 days after a Wednesday, that is, a Saturday.

Hence, Option 4.

Note: 2004 was a leap year, and it had 29 days in February.

21. Aristotle is known as the father of Political Science (NOT Geography).

Hipparchus is considered the founder of Trigonometry (NOT the father of Geography).

Two people are considered the fathers of Geography: Hecataeus and Eratosthenes.

Hence, Option 2.

22.

Organisation	Founder
Brahmo Samaj	Raja Ram Mohan Roy
Arya Samaj	Swami Dayanand Saraswati
Ramakrishna Mission	Swami Vivekananda
Brahmo Samaj of India	Keshab Chandra Sen

Hence, Option 3.

24. Let his total investment be $4x$.

Therefore, he invested $\frac{4x}{4} = x$ at 7% another $\frac{4x}{4} = x$ at 8% and the remaining $2x$ at 10%.

Total interest earned in one year

$= \frac{x \times 7}{100} + \frac{x \times 8}{100} + \frac{2x \times 10}{100}$

$= \frac{7x + 8x + 20x}{100} = \frac{35x}{100}$

Given that $= \frac{35x}{100} = 700$.

or, $x = \frac{700 \times 100}{35} = 2000$.

Therefore, the total investment $= 4x = 4 \times 2000$ = ₹8000.

Hence, Option 3.

Alternative: As one-half of the investment is at 10% and the remaining at less than 10%, the total returns in one year will be less than 10%. Try out the option now:

1. 700 > 10% of 6000: it cannot be the answer.
2. 700 = 10% of 7000: it cannot be the answer.
3. Break it into 3 parts:

7% of 2000 = 140

8% of 2000 = 160

10% of 4000 = 400

Total = 700.

Thus, it is the answer.

All this has to be done mentally.

25. $\frac{22 + 2}{3} = 8$ and $\frac{55 + 2}{3} = 19$

Hence, Option 2 (It was the official answer).

Again, $\frac{22}{8} = \frac{55}{20}$.

Hence, 20 should also have been accepted as the answer, especially when it is among the options.

27.

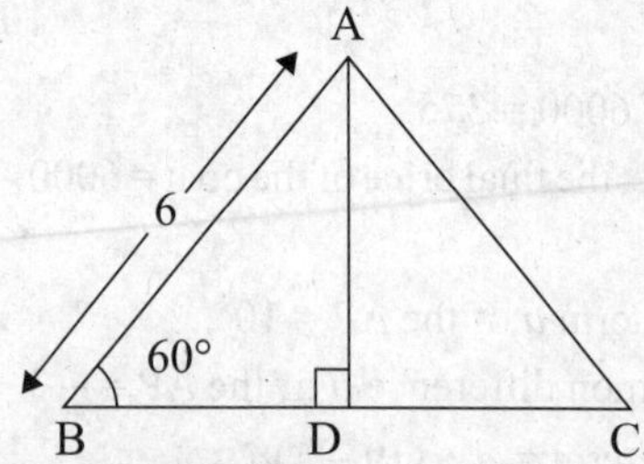

Let AD be the altitude drawn on side BC of the equilateral ΔABC.

As the perimeter of the triangle is 18,

AB = BC = CA = 6.

Also, ∠A = ∠B = ∠C = 60°

In Δ ADB,

$\text{Sin}\,60° = \frac{AD}{AB}$

or, $\frac{\sqrt{3}}{2} = \frac{AD}{6}$

or, $AD = \frac{6\sqrt{3}}{2} = 3\sqrt{3}$

Hence, Option 1.

Note: The **altitudes** of an equilateral triangle of side x are of length $\frac{\sqrt{3}x}{2}$.

28. The Indira Gandhi National Centre for Art (IGNCA) was established on 19 November 1985 on Indira Gandhi's birth anniversary.

Hence, Option 1.

29. The probability that Swati does NOT throw a single six $= \frac{5}{6} \times \frac{5}{6} = \frac{25}{36}$.

Therefore, the probability that she throws at least one six $= 1 - \frac{25}{36} = \frac{11}{36}$.

Hence, Option 3.

Note: Even if you do not know probability, you know that the total number of results on throwing a die twice is $6 \times 6 = 36$.

Out of the 36 results, in 11 of them, you can get at least one six: (6, 1), (6, 2), (6, 3), (6, 4), (6, 5), (6, 6), (1, 6), (2, 6), (3, 6), (4, 6), and (5, 6).

30. Abdel Fattah El-Sisi (the president of Egypt) was the chief guest for India's Republic Day in 2023. Emmanuel Macron, the president of France, was the chief guest for India's Republic Day in 2024.
Hence, Option 2.

31. Pravasi Bharatiya Diwas is celebrated on 9th January to commemorate the return of Mahatma Gandhi from South Africa to India. The year 2015 onwards, it is celebrated every two years. The 17th Pravasi Bharatiya Diwas was held in Indore in 2023. The 18th Pravasi Bharatiya Diwas will be held in 2025.
Hence, Option 4.

32.

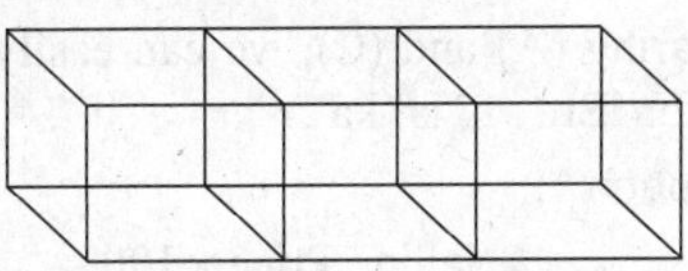

When we put 3 cubes of the same size side by side, we get a cuboid of the same width and height as those of the cubes but length 3 times the edge of the cubes.
The volume of a cube = 343 cm^3 = (7 cm)^3.
The edge of a cube = $\sqrt[3]{343}$ = 7 cm.
Now, the total surface area of the cuboid = 14 × the area of one face of a cube = 14 × (7 × 7) = 686 cm^2.
Note: When this cuboid is formed, 5 faces of each of the cubes on extremes are exposed, but only 4 faces of the middle cube are exposed.
Hence, Option 2.
Caution: 18 × 49 = 882 (Option 4) is a good trap.

33. Let the numbers be x and y.

We have $x + y = 14$ and $\frac{x}{y} = \frac{5}{2}$

or, $2x = 5y$ or, $x = \frac{5y}{2}$

So, $\frac{5y}{2} + y = 14$ or, $\frac{7y}{2} = 14$ or, $y = 4$

Therefore, $x = 14 - y = 14 - 4 = 10$.
So, the numbers are 10 and 4.
Hence, Option 4.

Alternative: Try out the options.

The sum of the numbers is 14 in all the options, but their ratio is $\frac{5}{2}$, only in Option 4.

36. Pono dakb: Live Rightly (i)
dakb Rnato: Live Profitably (ii)
Htbl dakb: Just live (iii)
On comparing (i), (ii) and (iii), it is clear that the code for 'Live' is 'dakb', the code for 'Rightly' is 'Pono', and the code for 'Just' is 'Htbl'.
The code for "Live Urgently' must have 'dakb' and must NOT have either 'Pono' or 'htbl'.
Hence, Option 2.

37.

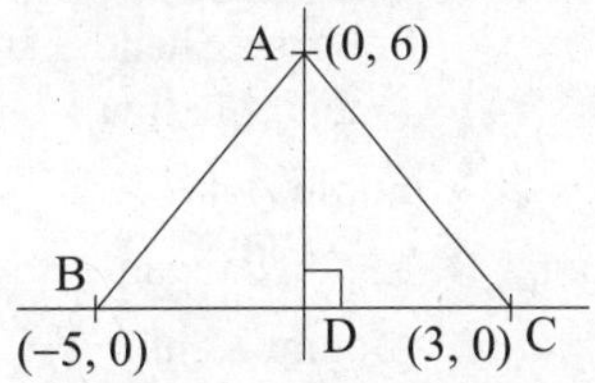

Let points (0, 6) be A, (–5, 0) be B, and (3, 0) be C. Points B and C are on the x-axis, and point A is on the y-axis.
BC = 3 – (– 5) = 8
AD = 6

$\therefore$ the area $= \frac{1}{2} \times 8 \times 6 = 24$ sq. units.

Alternative: the area of a triangle with vertices $(x_1, y_1), (x_2, y_2)$ and (x_3, y_3) is given by the value of the determinant $\frac{1}{2}\begin{vmatrix} x_1 & y_1 & 1 \\ x_2 & y_2 & 1 \\ x_3 & y_3 & 1 \end{vmatrix}$.

Here, the area $= \frac{1}{2}\begin{vmatrix} -5 & 0 & 1 \\ 3 & 0 & 1 \\ 0 & 6 & 1 \end{vmatrix}$

$= \frac{1}{2}\{-6(-5 \times 1 - 3 \times 1)\}$

$= \frac{1}{2}\{-6(-5 - 3)\} = \frac{1}{2}(6 \times 8) = 24$ sq. units.

39. Here, the nth term $T_n = n^2 + 1$.
$T_1 = 1^2 + 1 = 2, T_2 = 2^2 + 1 = 5, T_3 = 3^2 + 1 = 10$, etc.
$T_6 = 6^2 + 1 = 37$.
Hence, Option 3.

40. Male players: P, Q and R
Female Players: S, T, U and Z
As at least 2 males have to be selected and Q is rejected, P and R have to be there.
Also, as we have selected 2 males, we need to select 2 females as well because a team has to be made up of 4 players.
R is on the team, but he cannot play with either S or Z, and hence, the remaining 2 female players, T and U, have to be there.
Therefore, the team is P, R, T and U.
Hence, Option 2.

42.

Book	Writer/s
The Z Factor	Subhash Chandra and Pranjal Sharma
Zest For Life	Emile Zola
The Dark Room	R. K. Narayan
Black Taj	Mohini Kent

Hence, Option 3.

43.

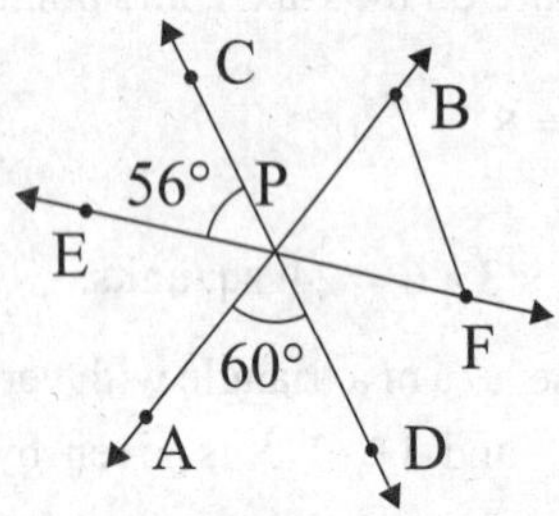

$\angle DPF = \angle CPE = 56°$ (opposite angles)
As APB is a straight line:
$\angle APD + \angle DPF + \angle BPF = 180°$
or, $60° + 56° + \angle BPF = 180°$
or, $\angle BPF = 180° - 60° - 56° = 64°$
In Δ PBF,
PB = PF.
$\Rightarrow \angle PBF = \angle PFB$.
Also, $\angle PBF + \angle PFB + \angle BPF = 180°$
or, $\angle PBF + \angle PBF + 64° = 180°$
or, $2\angle PBF = 180° - 64°$
or, $\angle PBF = \frac{116°}{2} = 58°$.
Hence, Option 2.

44. $\cos(x - y) = \frac{\sqrt{3}}{2} = \cos 30°$
or, $x - y = 30°$ (i)
$\sin(x + y) = 1 = \sin 90°$
or, $x + y = 90°$ (ii)
Adding (i) and (ii), we get
$2x = 120°$ or, $x = 60°$
$y = 90° - x = 90° - 60° = 30°$.
Hence, Option 2.

45. The actual time = 12:00 – the time shown in the image
= 12:00 – 6:15 = 05:45
Hence, Option 1.

46. (A) 'hiw ka tac': 'Brown and Grey"
(C) 'Ka da rac': 'You can Brown'
On comparing (A) and (C), we can easily see the code for 'Brown' is 'ka'.
Hence, Option 1.

47. The cost price $= \frac{\text{Selling Price} \times 100}{100 - \text{loss percentage}}$
$= \frac{15,500 \times 100}{100 - 20} = \frac{15,500 \times 100}{80}$
= ₹19375.
Hence, Option 3.

48. The 'Tower of Silence' is the burial place for Zoroastrians. In India, it is in Mumbai. This place is also known as Mumbai Dakhma.

49. Here, the nth term $T_n = (n + 1)^3 - (n + 1)$.
$T_1 = (1 + 1)^3 - (1 + 1) = 8 - 2 = 6$,
$T_2 = (2 + 1)^3 - (2 + 1) = 27 - 3 = 24$, etc.
Now, $T_5 = (5 + 1)^3 - (5 + 1) = 6^3 - 6 = 210$
Therefore, 211 is the odd one out.
Hence, Option 2.

50. Option 2 appears to be the correct answer, but if you look at the problem figure carefully, the quadrilateral does NOT touch the bottom of the figure. In option 2, that quadrilateral touches the bottom of the figure. Hence, none of the options is correct, and hence the CUET-UG dropped the question.

52. The seating arrangement is like:
T Q P R S

Person	Colour of Jacket
P	red
Q	grey
R	white
S	yellow
T	brown

Hence, Option 3.

55. Bal Gangadhar Tilak had launched two newspapers: Kesari (in Marathi) and Mahratta (in English).
Hence, Option 1.

56. The sum of 5, 3, 9, 11, 29 and $(p + 1) = 12 \times 6 = 72$
When we include $(q - 5)$ and $(q + 11)$, the average becomes $12 + 2 = 14$ and the number of numbers becomes $6 + 2 = 8$.
Therefore, the sum of these 8 numbers $= 14 \times 8 = 112$
But the sum of the original 6 numbers was 72.
So, the sum of the 2 new numbers $= 112 - 72 = 40$.
Now, $(q - 5) + (q + 11) = 40$, or, $2q + 6 = 40$, or, $2q = 40 - 6 = 34$.
or, $q = \frac{34}{2} = 17$.
Hence, Option 3.

57. Let the radius of the circle be r.
We have $\frac{45°}{360°} \times \pi r^2 = 154$
or, $\frac{1}{8} \times \frac{22}{7} r^2 = 154$
or, $r^2 = \frac{154 \times 8 \times 7}{22} = 7 \times 7 \times 8$
$= 7 \times 7 \times 2 \times 2 \times 2$
or, $r = \sqrt{7 \times 7 \times 2 \times 2 \times 2} = 7 \times 2\sqrt{2}$
$= 14\sqrt{2}$.
Hence, Option 1.

58. In $3\frac{1}{2} = \frac{7}{2}$ minutes, he travels 700 m,
$\therefore$ in 1 minute, he travels $\frac{700}{\frac{7}{2}}$ m,
$\therefore$ in 60 minutes, he travels
$= \frac{700 \times 60}{\frac{7}{2}}$ m
$= \frac{700 \times 60 \times 2}{7}$
$= 12000$ m.
$= \frac{12000}{1000} = 12$ km.
Hence, his speed is 12 km/hr.

60. $\frac{\sqrt{81} + \sqrt[3]{64}}{\sqrt{3^3 + 4^2 + \sqrt[3]{216}}} = \frac{9 + 4}{\sqrt{27 + 16 + 6}} = \frac{13}{\sqrt{49}}$
$= \frac{13}{7}$.
Hence, Option 2.

Shift - I

CUET UG 2023 General Test

June

5

Instructions:

1. You need to attempt any 50 out of the 60 questions in 60 minutes.
2. You get 5 marks for a correct response and –1 for an incorrect one. However, there is no reward or penalty for a question not attempted.

1. Which of the following are incorrect?

(A) sin 0° = 0

(B) tan 0° = 0

(C) cos 0° = 0

(D) cosec 0° = 0

(E) sec 0° = 0

Choose the correct answer from the options given below:

(1) (A) and (B) only

(2) (A), (C) and (D) only

(3) (D) and (E) only

(4) (C), (D) and (E) only

2. If point (x, y) is equidistant from the points (7, 1) and (3, 5), then which of the following options is correct?

(1) $x - y = 2$

(2) $x + y = 2$

(3) $x - y = 1$

(4) $x - y = -2$

3. The average of five consecutive natural numbers is 13. If the next two natural numbers are also included, find the new average.

(1) 13 (2) 13.5

(3) 14 (4) 13.75

4. Mirror image of D L 9 C G 4 7 2 8 is

(1) 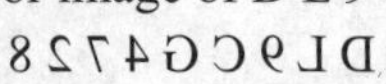

(2) 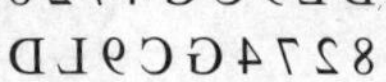

(3) 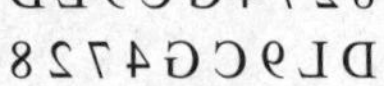

(4) 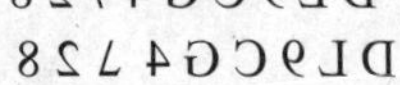

5. Complete the figure:

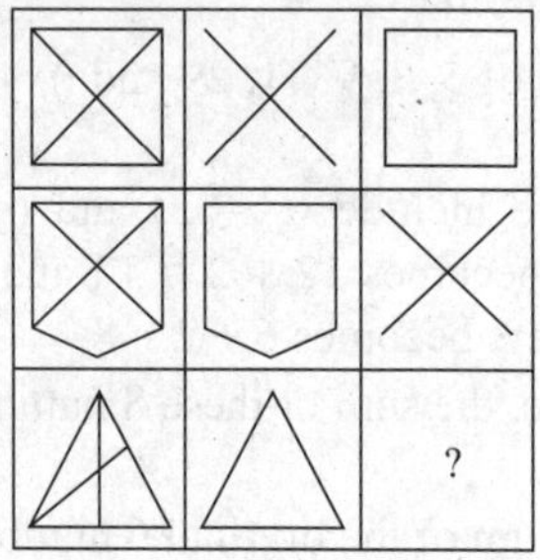

(1) 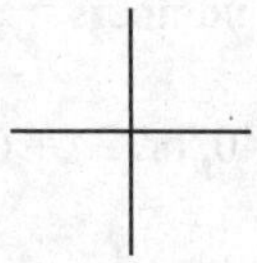

(2) 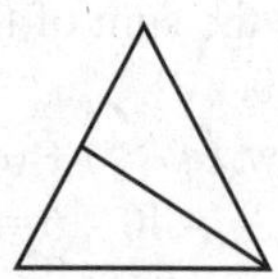

(3) 

(4) 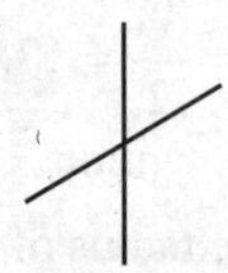

6. Who said, "Swaraj is my birthright, and I will have it"?

(1) Jawahar Lal Nehru

(2) Mahatma Gandhi

(3) Lala Lajpat Rai

(4) Bal Gangadhar Tilak

7. The cost of 5 kg apples and 3 kg oranges is ₹535. If the cost of 8 kg apples and 6 kg oranges is ₹910, then what is the cost of 2 kg apples and 8 kg oranges?

(1) ₹803 (2) ₹680

(3) ₹520 (4) ₹650

8. ISRO launched a digital platform on August 12, 2022. This platform is known as:
(1) SAMARTH (2) SARTHAK
(3) SPARK (4) INSAT

9. **Statements:**
(I) Some books are erasers.
(II) Some erasers are black.
(III) No black is green.
Conclusions:
(I) Some books are green.
(II) All erasers are green.
Which of the following **conclusions** can be drawn from the given **statements**?
(1) Only (I) follows.
(2) Neither (I) nor (II) follows.
(3) Only (II) follows.
(4) Either (I) or (II) follows.

10. Rome (Italy) is situated on the bank of ________ river.
(1) Tiber (2) Vistula
(3) Thames (4) Seine

11. You go north, then turn right, then right again and then go to the left. In which direction are you now?
(1) South (2) West
(3) East (4) North

12. A box contains $(12 + x)$ red balls and $(18 + x)$ green balls. A ball is drawn randomly and is found to be red. If the probability of this event is $\frac{5}{12}$, then find the value of x.
(1) 4 (2) 3
(3) 2 (4) 5

13. The author of the book "The Story of My Experiments with Truth" is __________.
(1) Mahatma Gandhi
(2) Rabindra Nath Tagore
(3) Chetan Bhagat
(4) Salman Rushdie

14. In a given number 1 2 3 4 5 6 7 8 9 1, we interchange the first and the second digits, the third and the fourth digits and so on. Then which digit will be sixth from the right?
(1) 2 (2) 4
(3) 7 (4) 6

15. The word 'Cell' was first coined by Robert Hook in __________.
(1) 1665 (2) 1838
(3) 1839 (4) 1668

16. China does not share its boundary with which Indian State/UT?
(1) Arunachal Pradesh
(2) Sikkim
(3) Bihar
(4) Jammu & Kashmir

17. An ice cream is in the form of a cone surmounted by a hemisphere.
If the base radius of the cone is 3.5 cm and the height of the ice cream is 10 cm, then find the volume of the ice cream (in cm³).
$\left(\pi = \frac{22}{7}\right)$
(1) 186.92 (2) 109.08
(3) 173.25 (4) 218.16

18. Match **List I** with **List II**.

List I (UNESCO World Heritage Site)	List II (State)
(A) Mahabalipuram Temple	(I) Karnataka
(B) Manas Wild Life Sanctuary	(II) Tamil Nadu
(C) Monuments at Hampi	(III) Sikkim
(D) Khangchendzonga National Park	(IV) Assam

Choose the correct answer from the options given below:
(1) (A)-(II), (B)-(IV), (C)-(III), (D)-(I)
(2) (A)-(II), (B)-(IV), (C)-(I), (D)-(III)
(3) (A)-(III), (B)-(II), (C)-(IV), (D)-(I)
(4) (A)-(IV), (B)-(II), (C)-(I), (D)-(III)

19. An exterior angle of a regular polygon is 24°. How many sides does the polygon have?
(1) 12 (2) 10
(3) 15 (4) 16

20. In which state did Prime Minister Narendra Modi inaugurate 'Jal Jan Abhiyan'?
(1) Rajasthan
(2) Jharkhand
(3) Himachal Pradesh
(4) Bihar

21. The value of $\frac{(4.2)^3}{(2.1)^2}$ is:
(1) 2 (2) 8
(3) 16.8 (4) 19.4

22. Who is the father of Indian Archaeology?
(1) James Burgess
(2) Sir John Marshall
(3) Sir Alexander Cunningham
(4) Carl Ortwin Sauer

23. P sold an item for ₹70 and earned 100% profit. What should be the selling price of the item to earn 150% profit?
(1) ₹105 (2) ₹52.50
(3) ₹87.50 (4) ₹150

24. Given below are two statements: one is labelled as Assertion (A), and the other is labelled as Reason (R).
Assertion (A): DDT has nowadays lost its use as an Insecticide.
Reason (R): DDT is harmful to man.
In the light of the above statements, choose the most appropriate answer from the options given below:
(1) Both (A) and (R) are correct, and (R) is the correct explanation of (A).
(2) Both (A) and (R) are correct, but (R) is not the correct explanation of (A).
(3) (A) is correct, but (R) is not correct.
(4) (A) is not correct, but (R) is correct.

25. The wrong number in the given series is:
7, 28, 63, 124, 215, 342, 511
(1) 215
(2) 124
(3) 28
(4) 7

26. At what time between 5 and 6 o'clock do the hands of a clock coincide?
(1) $27\frac{3}{11}$ min past 5
(2) $22\frac{8}{11}$ min past 4
(3) 30 min past 5
(4) 22 min past 4

27. Find the mean of the following frequency distribution:

Scores	5	6	7	8	9
Frequency	2	1	3	2	2

(1) 7 (2) 9
(3) 7.1 (4) 7.9

28. Match **List I** with **List II**.

List I (Name of Revolution)	List II (Field of the Revolution)
(A) Green Revolution	(I) Fruits production in horticulture
(B) Blue Revolution	(II) Agriculture
(C) Golden Revolution	(III) Egg production
(D) Silver Revolution	(IV) Fish production

Choose the correct answer from the options given below:
(1) (A)-(II), (B)-(IV), (C)-(III), (D)-(I)
(2) (A)-(II), (B)-(IV), (C)-(I), (D)-(III)
(3) (A)-(II), (B)-(I), (C)-(III), (D)-(IV)
(4) (A)-(III), (B)-(II), (C)-(IV), (D)-(I)

29.
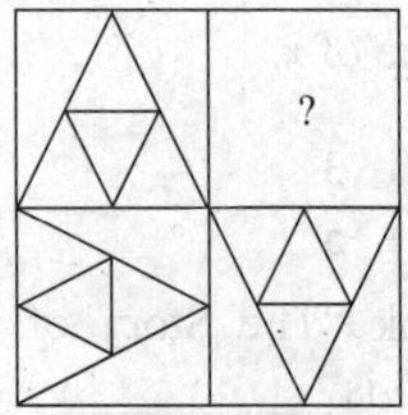

Choose the correct option to complete the figure.
(1)
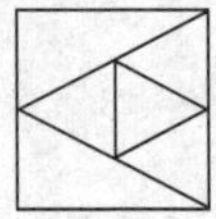
(2)
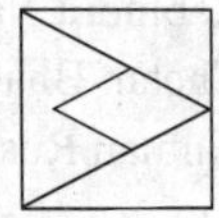
(3)
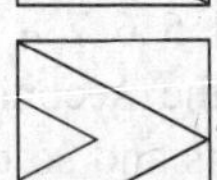
(4)
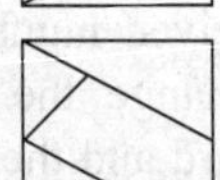

30. Fractions $\frac{3}{4}, \frac{2}{3}, \frac{5}{6}, \frac{11}{18}$ when written in descending order are:

(1) $\frac{11}{18}, \frac{2}{3}, \frac{5}{6}, \frac{3}{4}$ (2) $\frac{5}{6}, \frac{2}{3}, \frac{3}{4}, \frac{11}{18}$

(3) $\frac{2}{3}, \frac{5}{6}, \frac{3}{4}, \frac{11}{18}$ (4) $\frac{5}{6}, \frac{3}{4}, \frac{2}{3}, \frac{11}{18}$

31. Milk always contains:

(1) Water (2) Calcium
(3) Fats (4) Sugar

32. In a certain coding system, the word STATEMENT is written as TNEMETATS. What is the code for "POLITICAL" in the same system?

(1) LACITILOP (2) LCATILIOP
(3) OPILIT ACL (4) OPILATACL

33. Find the correct relationships:

(A) Jaundice - Bones
(B) Jaundice - Liver
(C) Dengue - Lungs
(D) Rickets - Bones
(E) Tuberculosis - Bones

Choose the correct answer from the options given below:

(1) (A), (B) and (D) only
(2) (B) and (D) only
(3) (B), (D) and (E) only
(4) (C), (B) and (D) only

34. E: 130: I: __?

Choose the correct option for the missing term.

(1) 729 (2) 734
(3) 738 (4) 758

35. The Republic Day of India in 1980 falls on a Saturday. Mohan was born on 3rd March 1980, and Sohan is 4 days older than Mohan. Sohan was born on a:

(1) Wednesday (2) Thursday
(3) Sunday (4) Saturday

36. Which scientist is known as the "Birdman of India"?

(1) Salim Ali (2) Ghulam Ali
(3) Noshad Ali (4) J.C. Bose

37. If a man starts at 7 a.m. at $\frac{5}{4}$ his usual speed, he reaches the office 30 minutes earlier than usual. So, with the new speed, at what time did he reach his office?

(1) 9:30 a.m. (2) 10 a.m.
(3) 9 a.m. (4) 8:25 a.m.

38. Match **List I** with **List II**.

List I (Player)	List II (Game)
(A) Dhanraj Pillay	(I) Shooting
(B) P.V. Sindhu	(II) Wrestling
(C) Gagan Narang	(III) Badminton
(D) Geeta Phogat	(IV) Hockey

Choose the correct answer from the options given below:

(1) (A)-(III), (B)-(I), (C)-(II), (D)-(IV)
(2) (A)-(IV), (B)-(III), (C)-(I), (D)-(II)
(3) (A)-(IV), (B)-(III), (C)-(II), (D)-(I)
(4) (A)-(III), (B)-(IV), (C)-(I), (D)-(II)

39. Match **List I** with **List II**.

List I (Committee)	List II (Report/Subject)
(A) Balwant Rai Mehta Committee	(I) Working of Panchayats
(B) Ashok Mehta Committee	(II) Panchayati Raj
(C) Hanumantha Rao Committee	(III) Constitutional status of Panchayats
(D) L.M. Singhvi Committee	(IV) District level Planning

Choose the correct answer from the options given below:

(1) (A)-(I), (B)-(II), (C)-(III), (D)-(IV)
(2) (A)-(II), (B)-(I), (C)-(IV), (D)-(III)
(3) (A)-(I), (B)-(IV), (C)-(III), (D)-(II)
(4) (A)-(III), (B)-(IV), (C)-(I), (D)-(II)

40. Find the area (in cm^2) of the figure ABCDEF; all its sides are perpendicular to their adjacent sides.

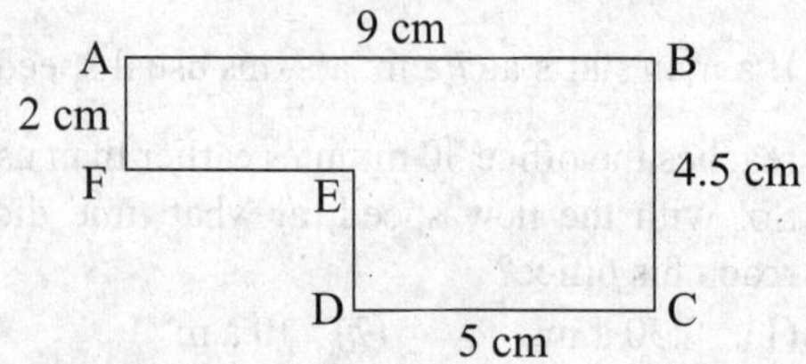

(1) 28.5 (2) 30
(3) 30.5 (4) 33

41. Five students are standing in a circle, and all are facing towards the centre of the circle. Apurva is on the left of Abhishek. Alok is on the left of Apurva. Abhinav is between Alok and Ankur. Who is sitting next to Abhinav on his immediate Right?

(1) Alok (2) Abhishek
(3) Apurva (4) Ankur

42. How many daughters does D have?

Statement (I): B and F are sisters of A.

Statement (II): C is a brother of A and F.

Statement (III): C and E are sons of D.

Choose the correct option to decide whether the data provided in the statements are sufficient to answer the question:

(1) I alone is sufficient.
(2) I & II together are sufficient.
(3) II & III together are sufficient.
(4) Even all the statements together are not sufficient.

43. Ministry of Social Justice and Empowerment decided to observe the "Constitution Day" on ________.

(1) 26th November (2) 26th December
(3) 16th November (4) 16th December

44. Given that:

(A) P is the brother of Q
(B) R is the father of P
(C) S is the brother of T
(D) T is the daughter of Q

Who is the uncle of S?

Choose the correct answer from the options given below:

(1) P (2) Q
(3) R (4) T

45. A sum of ₹5100 is divided amongst A, B and C, such that the ratio of shares of A and B is 1:2 and that of B and C is 3:4. Find the sum of the shares of A and B.

(1) ₹3400 (2) ₹3060
(3) ₹2880 (4) ₹2700

46. If x and y vary inversely to each other and x = 7 when y = 12, then find y when x = 21.

(1) 3 (2) 4
(3) 5 (4) 6

47. On compound interest, a certain sum amounts to ₹7350 in 2 years and to ₹8575 in 3 years. Find the rate of interest.

(1) $\frac{25}{3}\%$ (2) $\frac{50}{3}\%$
(3) 25% (4) 33%

48. Quit India resolution was passed by the Indian National Congress in its ________ session.

(1) Bombay (2) Lahore
(3) Calcutta (4) Lucknow

49. Who did the partition of Bengal in 1905?

(1) Lord Mountbatten
(2) Lord Curzon
(3) Lord Wavell
(4) Lord Simon

50. On dividing a number by 38, we get 90 as the quotient and 19 as the remainder. What is the number?

(1) 3439 (2) 3401
(3) 3382 (4) 3458

51. Which are the correct examples of Newton's 3rd law of motion?

(A) Recoil of a gun
(B) Running horse stops suddenly, the rider bends forward
(C) Motion of rocket
(D) It gives the definition of force
(E) Swimming

Choose the correct answer from the options given below:

(1) (A), (B) and (C) only
(2) (A), (C) and (E) only
(3) (B), (C) and (D) only
(4) (C), (D) and (E) only

52. Which Fundamental Right has been described as the heart and soul of the Constitution of India?
(1) Right to Equality
(2) Right against exploitation
(3) Right of Freedom
(4) Rights to Constitutional Remedies

53. Quantum theory was discovered by:
(1) Marconi (2) Albert Einstein
(3) Max Plank (4) James Chadwick

54. A can do a work in 12 days. B's efficiency in doing the work is 50% more than that of A. In how many days will B be able to do the work?"
(1) 8 (2) 10
(3) 5 (4) 11

55. In a Geometric Progression, if the product of the first three terms is $\frac{27}{8}$ then its second term is:
(1) $\frac{3}{2}$ (2) $\frac{9}{4}$
(3) $\frac{9}{2}$ (4) 1

56. Which one of the following will be the same as its mirror image?
(1) WYTOTYW
(2) WYOTTZW
(3) WYOTTWZ
(4) WYTOTWZ

57. How many such pairs of distinct letters are there in the word 'CHANNEL', which has as many letters between them in the word as in the English alphabet?
(1) 1 (2) 2
(3) 3 (4) 4

58. In a right triangle, the length of the hypotenuse is 17 cm. If the length of one of its other sides is 15 cm, then the area of the triangle is:
(1) 127.5 cm^2 (2) 122.5 cm^2
(3) 60 cm^2 (4) 66.5 cm^2

59. If 30 ml solution of 20% alcohol is mixed with 20 ml solution of 25% alcohol, then what is the strength of alcohol in the mixture?
(1) 23% (2) 21.5%
(3) 22% (4) 22.5%

60. Mahatma Buddha was born at ________.
(1) Vaishali (2) Kapilvastu
(3) Lumbini (4) Patliputra

Answer Key

1. **(4)** 2. **(1)** 3. **(3)** 4. **(1)** 5. **(4)** 6. **(4)** 7. **(3)** 8. **(3)** 9. **(2)** 10. **(1)**
11. **(3)** 12. **(2)** 13. **(1)** 14. **(4)** 15. **(1)** 16. **(3) and (4)** 17. **(3)** 18. **(2)** 19. **(3)**
20. **(1)** 21. **(3)** 22. **(3)** 23. **(3)** 24. **(2)** 25. **(3)** 26. **(1)** 27. **(3)** 28. **(2)** 29. **(1)**
30. **(4)** 31. **(2)** 32. **(1)** 33. **(2)** 34. **(3)** 35. **(2)** 36. **(1)** 37. **(3)** 38. **(2)** 39. **(2)**
40. **(3)** 41. **(1)** 42. **(4)** 43. **(1)** 44. **(1)** 45. **(4)** 46. **(2)** 47. **(2)** 48. **(1)** 49. **(2)**
50. **(1)** 51. **(2)** 52. **(4)** 53. **(3)** 54. **(1)** 55. **(1)** 56. **(1)** 57. **(2)** 58. **(3)** 59. **(3)**
60. **(3)**

Classification of Questions

Question No.	Subject	Topic	Level of Difficulty
1.	Quantitative Aptitude	Trigonometry	Easy
2.	Quantitative Aptitude	Coordinate Geometry	Easy
3.	Quantitative Aptitude	Averages	Easy
4.	Reasoning	Mirror Image	Easy
5.	Reasoning	Non-verbal	Easy
6.	General Awareness	History	Easy
7.	Quantitative Aptitude	Algebra (Linear Equations)	Medium
8.	General Awareness	Current Affairs	Difficult
9.	Reasoning	Syllogism	Easy
10.	General Awareness	Geography	Medium
11.	Reasoning	Directions	Easy
12.	Quantitative Aptitude	Probability	Medium
13.	General Awareness	Books and Authors	Easy
14.	Reasoning	Linear Arrangement	Easy
15.	General Awareness	Science (Biology)	Difficult
16.	General Awareness	Geography	Easy
17.	Quantitative Aptitude	Mensuration	Medium
18.	General Awareness	Geography	Medium
19.	Quantitative Aptitude	Geometry	Medium
20.	General Awareness	Current Affairs	Difficult
21.	Quantitative Aptitude	Arithmetic Operations	Easy
22.	General Awareness	History	Medium
23.	Quantitative Aptitude	Profit, Loss and Discount	Easy
24.	General Awareness	Science and Technology	Medium
25.	Reasoning	Number Series	Easy
26.	Quantitative Aptitude	Clocks	Easy
27.	Quantitative Aptitude	Statistics (Mean)	Easy
28.	General Awareness	Economics	Difficult
29.	Reasoning	Non-verbal	Easy
30.	Quantitative Aptitude	Arithmetic Operations	Easy
31.	General Awareness	Science	Medium
32.	Reasoning	Coding	Easy
33.	General Awareness	Science (Biology)	Medium
34.	Reasoning	Alpha-numeric Series	Medium

Question No.	Subject	Topic	Level of Difficulty
35.	Quantitative Aptitude	Calendars	Easy
36.	General Awareness	Miscellaneous	Easy
37.	Quantitative Aptitude	Time, Speed and Distance	Medium
38.	General Awareness	Sports	Easy
39.	General Awareness	Polity	Difficult
40.	Quantitative Aptitude	Mensuration	Easy
41.	Reasoning	Circular Arrangement	Easy
42.	Reasoning	Blood Relations	Easy
43.	General Awareness	Polity	Easy
44.	Reasoning	Blood Relations	Easy
45.	Quantitative Aptitude	Ratios	Easy
46.	Quantitative Aptitude	Ratio and Proportions	Easy
47.	Quantitative Aptitude	Compound Interest	Easy
48.	General Awareness	History	Easy
49.	General Awareness	History	Easy
50.	Quantitative Aptitude	Arithmetic Operations	Easy
51.	General Awareness	Science (Physics)	Difficult
52.	General Awareness	Polity	Easy
53.	General Awareness	Science (Physics)	Easy
54.	Quantitative Aptitude	Time and work	Easy
55.	Quantitative Aptitude	Algebra (G.P.)	Easy
56.	Reasoning	Mirror Image	Easy
57.	Reasoning	Letter Arrangement	Easy
58.	Quantitative Aptitude	Mensuration	Easy
59.	Quantitative Aptitude	Mixtures and Solutions	Easy
60.	General Awareness	History	Easy

Explanation to Select Questions

1. (C), (D) and (E) are incorrect.
$\cos 0° = 1$ (NOT 0)
cosec 0° is undefined
Sec 0° = 1 (NOT 0)
Hence, Option 4.

2. The locus of the points equidistant from the points (7, 1) and (3, 5) is a straight line that is the perpendicular bisector of the line segment joining these points.
Therefore, this line will pass through the mid-point of (7, 1) and (3, 5) and the product of its slope with the slope of the line joining (7, 1) and (3, 5) will be –1.
The mid-point of (7, 1) and (3, 5) =

$$\left(\frac{7+3}{2}, \frac{1+5}{2}\right) = (5, 3).$$

The slope of the line joining (7, 1) and (3, 5) is

$$\frac{5-1}{3-7} = \frac{4}{-4} = -1.$$

Therefore, the slope of the locus $= \frac{-1}{-1} = 1$.

$\therefore$ the required line is $(y - 3) = 1\,(x - 5)$

or, $y - 3 = x - 5$

or, $x - y = 2$

Hence, Option 1.

Shortcut: The correct answer must satisfy the mid-point of (7, 1) and (3, 5), that is (5, 3). Only Option 1 does!

3. As the average of five consecutive natural numbers is 13, 13 must be the median of these 5 natural numbers. Hence, the numbers are 11, 12, 13, 14, and 15. If we include the next two natural numbers, the numbers are 11, 12, 13, 14, 15, 16, 17.

The median value is 14 now. Hence, 14 is the new average.

Hence, Option 3.

Note: For a set of consecutive natural numbers, the mean and median are the same.

7. Let the prices per kg of apples and oranges be x and y.

We have

$5x + 3y = 535$ (i)

and

$8x + 6y = 910$ (ii).

Subtracting (i) from (ii), we get

$3x + 3y = 375$

or, $x + y = 125$.

Now, $5x + 3y = 535$

or, $2x + 3(x + y) = 535$

or, $2x + 3 \times 125 = 535$

or, $2x = 535 - 375 = 160$

or, $x = 80$.

$y = 125 - 80 = 45$.

We have to get the value of $2x + 8y$.

It is $2 \times 80 + 8 \times 45 = 160 + 360 = 520$.

Hence, Option 3.

9.

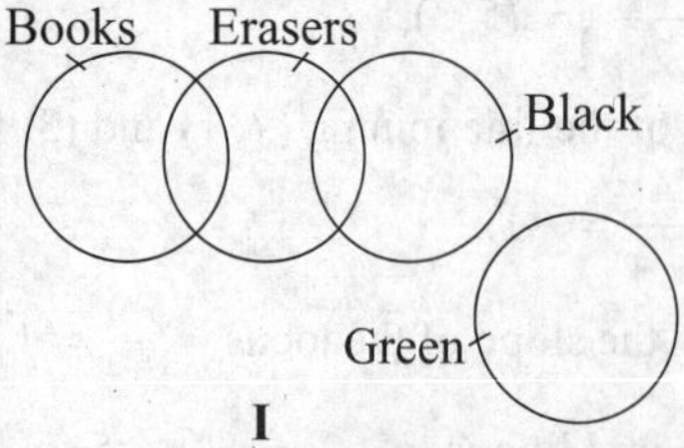

I

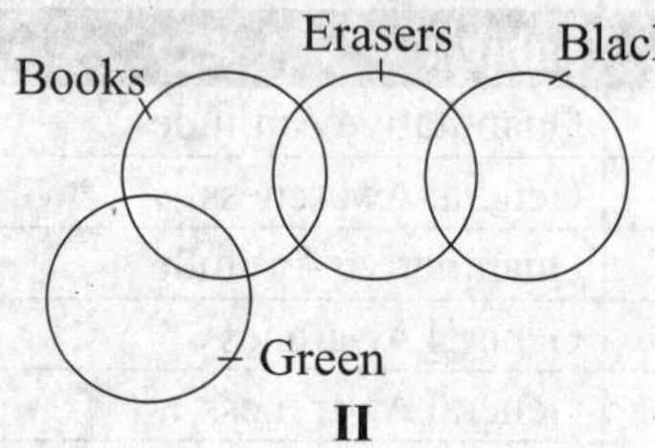

II

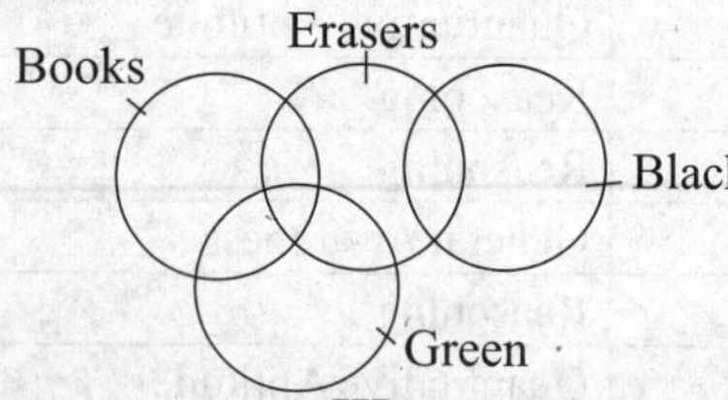

III

'Some books are green' is just a possibility. It may be there (II) and may NOT be there (I). It CANNOT be concluded.

Some Erasers may be Green (III), and it is just a possibility. Some Erasers are Black, and no Black is Green.

Therefore, at least those Erasers that are Black cannot be Green. Hence, 'all erasers are Green' is impossible.

Hence, Option 2.

11.

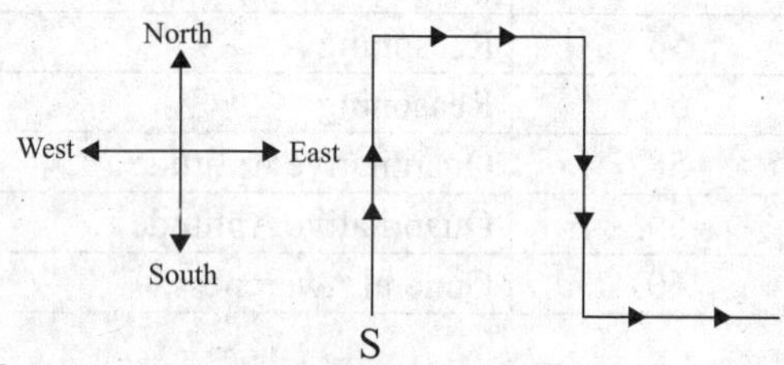

Let S be your starting point.

It is clear that after taking the final turn, you would be facing the East.

Hence, Option 3.

12. The total number of red balls: $12 + x$.

The total number of green balls: $18 + x$.

The total number of balls $= (12 + x) + (18 + x)$ $= 30 + 2x$

If a ball is drawn randomly, the probability of it being red $= \dfrac{12 + x}{30 + 2x}$.

As per the question, $\dfrac{12 + x}{30 + 2x} = \dfrac{5}{12}$

or, $144 + 12x = 150 + 10x$

or, $2x = 6$ or, $x = 3$.

Hence, Option 2.

14. After effecting all 5 interchanges, the new number is

2 1 4 3 6 5 8 7 1 9.

The 6th digit from the right is 6.

Hence, Option 4.

16. China shares its boundary with Ladakh (UT), Himachal Pradesh, Uttarakhand, Sikkim and Arunachal Pradesh. Thus, there are two correct answers to this question: Options 3 and 4.

As stated above, China used to share a boundary with the erstwhile state of Jammu and Kashmir, but it does not share its boundary with the union territory of Jammu and Kashmir.

17.

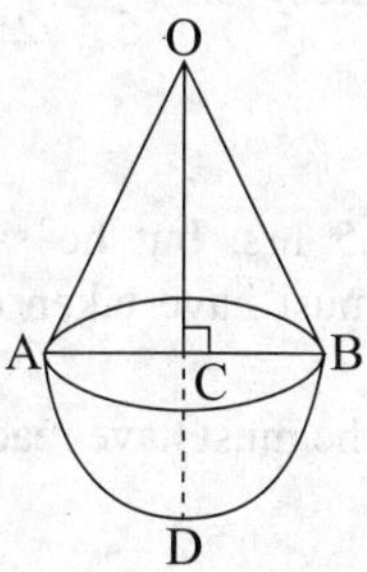

As per the question,

AC = CB = CD = 3.5 cm.

OD = 10 cm.

$\Rightarrow$ OC = OD – CD = 10 – 3.5 = 6.5 cm.

Therefore, the height of the cone is 6.5 cm.

The volume of the ice cream = volume of the hemisphere + volume of the cone

$$= \frac{2}{3}\pi (3.5)^3 + \frac{1}{3}\pi (3.5)^2 \times 6.5$$

$$= 2\frac{\pi}{3} \times \frac{7^3}{2^3} + \frac{\pi}{3} \times \frac{7^2}{2^2} \times \frac{13}{2}$$

$$= \frac{\pi}{24} \times 49\,(2 \times 7 + 13)$$

$$= \frac{22}{7} \times \frac{1}{24} \times 49 \times 27 = 173.25 \text{ cm}^3$$

Hence, Option 3.

Shortcut:

The volume of the ice cream $= \frac{2}{3}\pi r^3 + \frac{1}{3}\pi r^2 h$

$$= \pi\left(\frac{2r^3}{3} + \frac{r^2 h}{3}\right)$$

(Where r is the base radius of the cone and h is the height of the cone.)

As this expression is a multiple of $\pi\left(=\frac{22}{7}\right)$, the answer should have an 11 in it.

Only Option 3 has an 11 in it.

173.25 = 15.75 × 11.

Ignoring the decimal, you can easily check the number with an 11 in it using the divisibility rule by 11.

Of course, you are lucky here as only one Option has an 11 in it.

19. The number of sides of a regular polygon $= \frac{360°}{\text{The exterior angle}}$.

$\therefore$ the number of sides $= \frac{360°}{24°} = 15$.

Hence, Option 3.

21. $\frac{(4.2)^3}{(2.1)^2} = \frac{(2 \times 2.1)^3}{(2.1)^2} = \frac{2^3 \times (2.1)^3}{(2.1)^2}$

$= 8 \times 2.1 = 16.8$.

Hence, Option 3.

23. The selling price on 100% profit = 200% of the cost price.

The selling price on 150% profit = 250% of the cost price.

Now, 200% of the cost price = ₹70

$\therefore$ 250% of the cost price $= \frac{70}{200} \times 250 =$ ₹87.5

Hence, Option 3.

24. DDT is classified as a Persistent Organic Pollutant, and that is the reason why it lost its use as an insecticide.

Hence, Option 2.

25.

$7 = 2^3 - 1$

$28 = 3^3 + 1$

$63 = 4^3 - 1$

$124 = 5^3 - 1$

$215 = 6^3 - 1$

$342 = 7^3 - 1$

$511 = 8^3 - 1$

It is obvious that 28 is the wrong number in the sequence.

Hence, Option 3.

26. At 5, the hour hand is $30° \times 5 = 150°$ ahead of minute hand. So, in order to coincide with it, the minute hand needs to take a lead of 150° over the hour hand.

Minute hand takes a lead of 330° over hour hand in 60 minutes

$\therefore$ the minute hand takes a lead of 150° over hour hand in $\frac{60}{330°} \times 150°$

$= \frac{300}{11}$ minute $= 27\frac{3}{11}$ minutes.

Therefore, the hands will coincide at $27\frac{3}{11}$ minutes past 5.

Hence, Option 1.

Shortcut:

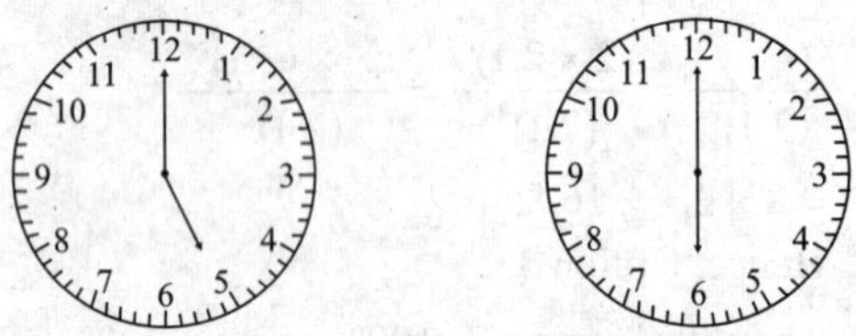

5 O' clock 6 O' clock

If you look at the images above, it is clear that the hands must have coincided between 5:25 and 5:30 as the hour hand moves only between 5 and 6. There is only one option between 5:25 and 5:30, Option 1.

27. The mean $= \frac{5 \times 2 + 6 \times 1 + 7 \times 3 + 8 \times 2 + 9 \times 2}{2 + 1 + 3 + 2 + 2}$

$= \frac{10 + 6 + 21 + 16 + 18}{10} = \frac{71}{10} = 7.1$

Hence, Option 3.

30. $\frac{3}{4} = \frac{27}{36}, \frac{2}{3} = \frac{24}{36}, \frac{5}{6} = \frac{30}{36}, \frac{11}{18} = \frac{22}{36}$

Therefore, the fractions in descending order:

$\frac{30}{36}, \frac{27}{36}, \frac{24}{36}, \frac{22}{36}$

or, $\frac{5}{6}, \frac{3}{4}, \frac{2}{3}, \frac{11}{18}$

Hence, Option 4.

34. E:130

E is the 5th letter in the alphabet.

$130 = 5^3 + 5$.

I is the 9th letter in the alphabet.

Therefore, $9^3 + 9 = 729 + 9 = 738$.

Hence, Option 3.

37. Let the time taken in reaching the office at his usual speed be t.

At $\frac{5}{4}$ of the usual speed, time taken is $\frac{4}{5}$ of the usual time or $\frac{4t}{5}$.

$t - \frac{4t}{5} = \frac{1}{2}$ hrs (30 minutes) or, $\frac{t}{5} = \frac{1}{2}$ or,

$t = \frac{5}{2}$ hrs.

So, his usual time is 2.5 hrs, but he saved 30 minutes and, hence, must have taken only 2 hours.

He had begun at 7 am, so he must have reached the office at 9 am.

Hence, Option 3.

40.

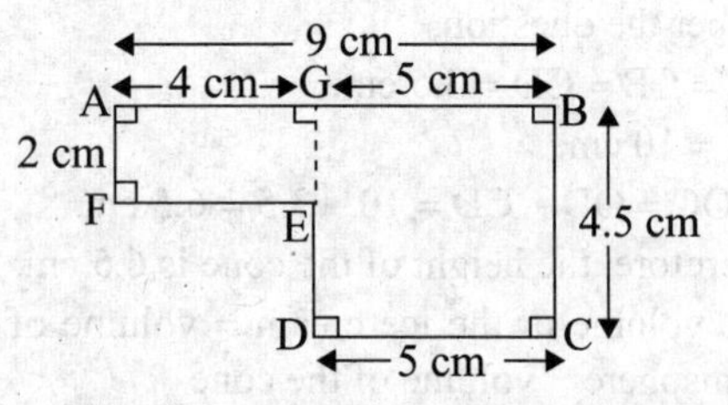

We have dropped perpendicular EG on the side AB.

Now, the figure is divided into 2 rectangles: BCDG and GEFA.

GB = DC = 5

AG = AB – GB = 9 – 5 = 4.

Area of the rectangle BCDG = 4.5 × 5 = 22.5 cm^2.

Area of the rectangle GEFA = 4 × 2 = 8 cm^2

Therefore, the area of the hexagon ABCDEF

= 22.5 + 8 = 30.5 cm^2

Hence, Option 3.

41. I: Apurva is on the left of Abhisek.
II: Alok is on the left of Apurva.
From I and II, we can draw:

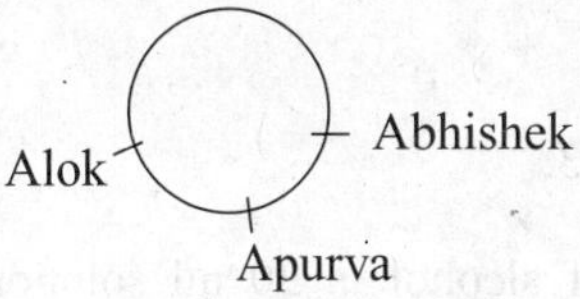

III: Abhinav is between Alok and Ankur.
We can now complete the arrangement:

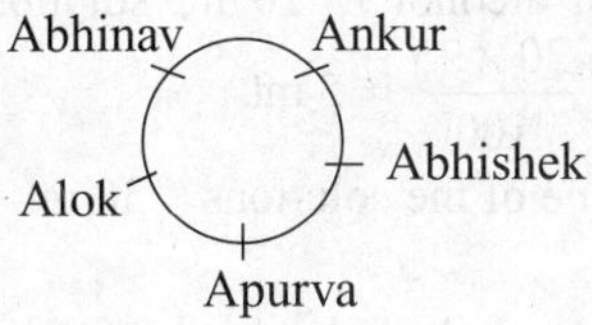

Therefore, Alok is sitting to the immediate right of Abhinav.
Hence, Option 1.

42.

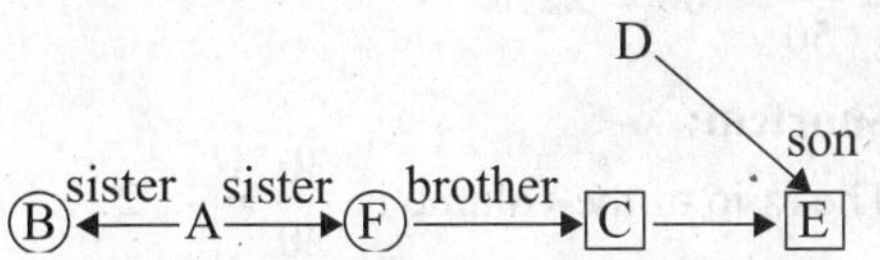

Even if we take all 3 statements together, we can only conclude that:
1. D has at least 5 children: A, B, C, E and F
2. D has at least 2 sons: C and E
3. D has at least 2 daughters: B and F
Therefore, we can not ascertain the number of daughters D has.
Note: We do not know about the genders of D and A.
Hence, Option 4.

43. The Indian Constitution was adopted on 26 November 1949, and this is why we celebrate 26 November as Constitution Day.
Hence, Option 1.

44.

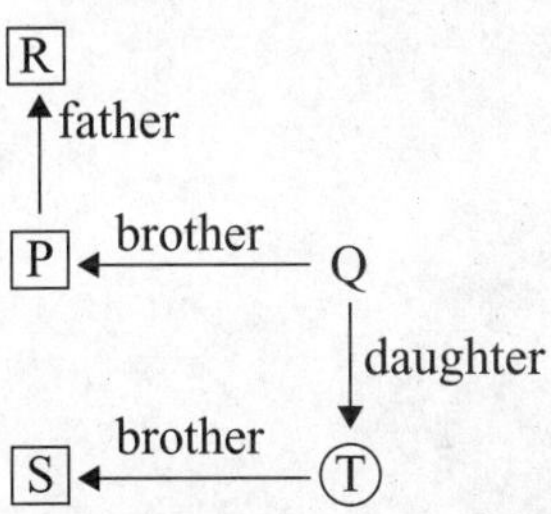

Q is one of the parents of S, and P is the brother of S. Therefore, P is an uncle of S (maternal or paternal, we do not know).
Hence, Option 1.

45. The ratio of shares of A and B = 1:2 = 3:6
The ratio of shares of B and C = 3:4 = 6:8
The ratio of the shares of A, B and C is = 3:6:8.
Let A, B and C get $3x$, $6x$ and $8x$ respectively.
So, $3x + 6x + 8x = 5100$
or, $17x = 5100$
or, $x = 300$.
Therefore, the shares of A, B and C are 900, 1800 and 2400.
Therefore, the sum of the shares of A and B is $900 + 1800 = 2700$.
Hence, Option 4.

46. $x \propto \frac{1}{y}$ or, $x = \frac{k}{y}$
(where κ is a proportionality constant)
We have, $7 = \frac{k}{12}$ or, $k = 84$
Thus $x = \frac{84}{y}$ or, $y = \frac{84}{x}$.
When $x = 21$, $y = \frac{84}{21} = 4$.
Hence, Option 2.

47. On compound interest, the amount at the end of the 2nd year is the principal for the 3rd year.
For the 3rd year:
Principal = 7350
Amount = 8575
∴ Interest = 8575 – 7350 = 1225.
The rate of interest $= \frac{1225}{7350} \times 100 = \frac{50}{3}\%$
Hence, Option 2.

50. The number = Divisor × Quotient + Remainder $= 38 \times 90 + 19 = 3439$.
Hence, Option 1.

51. (B) is an example of Newton's First Law of Motion. (D) is the example of Newton's Second Law of Motion.
Hence, Option 2.

54. Let the work be of 12 units.
As A completes the work in 12 days,

He does 1 unit in 1 day.
As B is 50% more efficient, he does 1.5 units in a day.
Hence, B can complete the work in $\frac{12}{1.5} = 8$ days.
Hence, Option 1.

Shortcut: As B is 50% more efficient, he is $\frac{3}{2}$ of A and hence will take $\frac{2}{3}$ of time taken by A, i.e. $\frac{2}{3} \times 12 = 8$ days.

55. Let the first three terms of the GP be $\frac{a}{r}$, a and ar.
The product of these terms $= \frac{a}{r} \cdot a \cdot ar$
$= a^3 = \frac{27}{8} = \frac{3^3}{2^3} = \left(\frac{3}{2}\right)^3$

Or, $a = \frac{3}{2}$.
Hence, Option 1.

57. C H A N N E L

3 8 1 14 14 5 12

Thus, we see that there are only two such pairs: C and A and the 2nd N and L.
Hence, Option 2.

58.

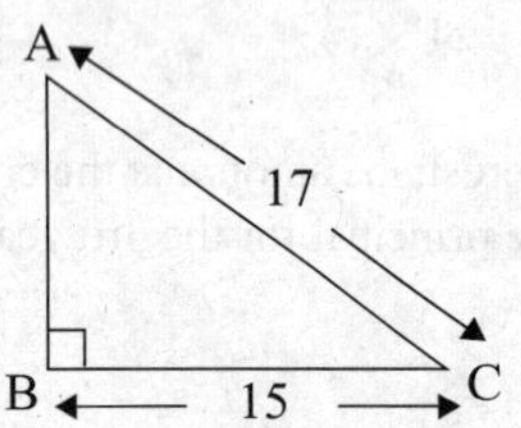

Here, the 3rd side $AB = \sqrt{17^2 - 15^2}$
$= \sqrt{289 - 225} = \sqrt{64} = 8.$

The area of the triangle $= \frac{1}{2} \times AB \times BC$
$= \frac{1}{2} \times 8 \times 15$
$= 60\ cm^2$
Hence, Option 3.

59. The volume of alcohol in 30 ml solution of 20% alcohol $= \frac{30 \times 20}{100} = 6$ ml.
The volume of alcohol in 20 ml solution of 25% alcohol $= \frac{20 \times 25}{100} = 5$ ml.
The total volume of the solutions = 30 ml + 20 ml = 50 ml.
The total volume of alcohol = 6 ml + 5 ml = 11 ml.
The strength of the alcohol in the mixture $= \frac{11}{50} \times 100 = 22\%$.

Shortcut:
The ratio of the volume is $\frac{30}{20} = 3 : 2$.
Therefore, the strength of alcohol =
$\frac{3 \times 20 + 2 \times 25}{3 + 2} = \frac{110}{5} = 22\%$.
Hence, Option 3.

60. Buddha was born at Lumbini (in present-day Nepal) and died at Kushinagar (in present-day Uttar Pradesh of India).
Hence, Option 3.

CUET UG 2023 GENERAL TEST

June **2**

INSTRUCTIONS:

1. You need to attempt any 50 out of the 60 questions in 60 minutes.
2. You get 5 marks for a correct response and –1 for an incorrect one. However, there is no reward or penalty for a question not attempted.

1. Choose the correct Venn diagram for the given elements:

Boys, Students, Athletes

(1)  (2) 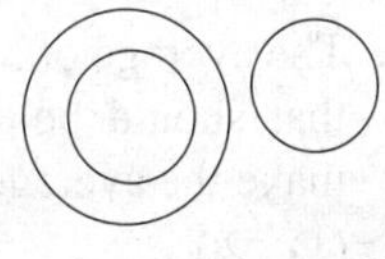

(3) 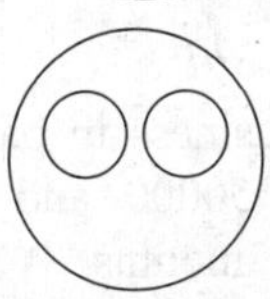 (4) 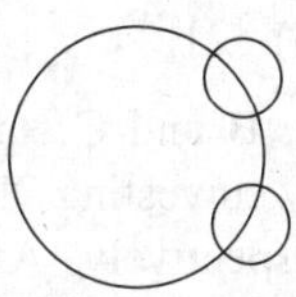

2. If the base radius of a cylinder is doubled, then how many times will its volume become with respect to its original volume?

(1) 2 (2) 4
(3) 6 (4) 8

3. In how many years will a sum of ₹90 become ₹108 at $6\frac{1}{4}$ % simple interest?

(1) $3\frac{1}{5}$ years (2) $4\frac{1}{5}$ years
(3) $2\frac{1}{5}$ years (4) $6\frac{1}{5}$ years

4. There are five different houses, H1, H2, H3, H4 and H5 in a row. H1 is to the right of H2, and H5 is to the left of H3 and right of H1. H2 is to the right of H4. Which of the houses is in the middle?

(1) H1 (2) H2
(3) H4 (4) H5

5. Here are some phrases translated from an artificial language:

'id nim nop' means 'they are innocent'.
'gob ots al' means 'we like roses'.
'nop ed al' means 'they like flowers'.

Which code represents 'flowers' in this language?

(1) nop (2) al
(3) ed (4) ots

6. Choose the odd one:

9105, 9837, 7125, 4314, 3927, 2958

(1) 9105 (2) 9837
(3) 7125 (4) 4314

7. A girl is facing North. She turns 90° in the anti-clockwise direction and then 45° in the clockwise direction. Which direction is she facing now?

(1) West (2) North-East
(3) North-West (4) South-West

8. The string of a kite is 100 meters long, and it makes an angle of 30° with the horizontal. Find the height of the kite from the ground.

(1) 100 m (2) 50 m
(3) 60 m (4) 48 m

9. Who wrote the book "Poverty and Un-British Rule in India"?

(1) Pt. Jawaharlal Nehru
(2) Mahatma Gandhi
(3) Dadabhai Naoroji
(4) Sardar Vallabhbhai Patel

10. Which among the following figures will be formed after folding the given figure along the dotted line?

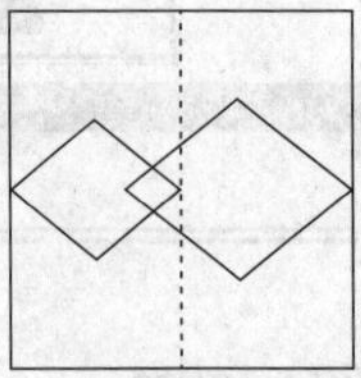

(1) 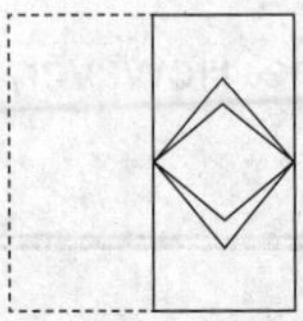 (2) 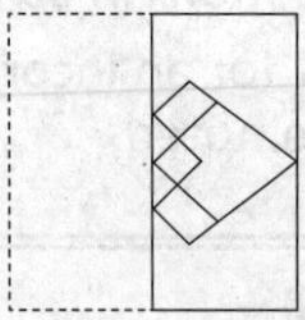

(3) 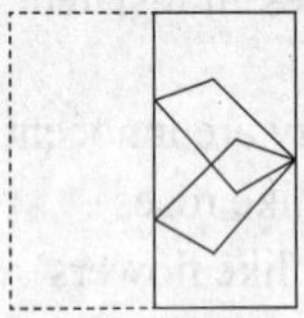 (4) 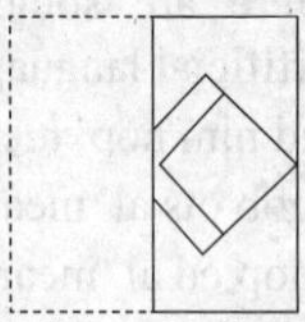

11. A. Andrology is the study of the male reproductive organs.

B. Agrology is the study of grass.

C. Angiology is the study of the blood vascular system, including arteries and veins.

D. Agronomy is the science of soil management and the production of crops.

Choose the Most appropriate answer from the options given below:

(1) A and B only (2) A and D only
(3) B and D only (4) A, C and D only

12. If March 24, 2011 was Thursday, what was the day on June 24, 2012?

(1) Saturday (2) Sunday
(3) Thursday (4) Friday

13. The Central Government has renamed Rajpath as:

(1) Azad Path (2) Atal Path
(3) Kartavya Path (4) Bharat Path

14. Which of India's neighbouring countries is the Himalayan peak Makalu situated in?

(1) Bhutan (2) China
(3) Nepal (4) Pakistan

15. When an article is sold for ₹115, the profit is twice as much as when it is sold for ₹95. The cost price of the article is

(1) ₹65 (2) ₹75
(3) ₹85 (4) ₹90

16. A mother, daughter and son can do a work in 3, 4 and 5 days, respectively. How many days will they take to complete the work if they work together?

(1) $\frac{47}{60}$ days (2) $2\frac{13}{47}$ days
(3) $1\frac{13}{47}$ days (4) $\frac{13}{47}$ days

17. The book "The Last Queen" is written by:

(1) Chitra Banerjee
(2) Rumaan Alam
(3) Roman Pina Chan
(4) Richard Wright

18. The average of 5 numbers is 15. Find a number that should be included in these numbers to make the average 16.

(1) 20 (2) 19
(3) 21 (4) 17

19. A, B and C started a business in partnership by investing ₹40000, ₹50000 and ₹70000, respectively. After four months, A invested ₹20000 more. After two more months, D also joined the business by investing ₹60000. After two more months, C withdrew ₹10000. Find the sum of the shares of C and D in the profit of ₹92100 earned at the end of the year.

(1) ₹42800 (2) ₹43500
(3) ₹44265 (4) ₹44515

20. 23rd January is celebrated as "Parakram Diwas" every year to honour the services and indomitable spirit of ________.

(1) Jawaharlal Nehru
(2) Narendra Modi
(3) Sardar Bhagat Singh
(4) Netaji Subhas Chandra Bose

21. Statement: 'Buy pure & natural Honey of company X'- an advertisement.

Assumptions

I: Artificial honey can be prepared.

II: No other company supplies pure honey.

Choose the correct option.
(1) Only I is implicit.
(2) Only II is implicit.
(3) Neither I nor II is implicit.
(4) Both I & II are implicit.

22. Find the sum of the smallest and the greatest 3-digit numbers formed by using the digits 0, 1, 2, 3 and 4 without any repetition of digits.
(1) 1099 (2) 544
(3) 534 (4) 555

23. Which of the following is/are true about the Union Budget 2021?
A. Atmanirbhar health care system was announced
B. big boost for roads and infrastructure
C. vehicle scrappage policy
D. fuel and liquor cess imposed
Choose the most appropriate answer from the options given below:
(1) A and B only (2) A, B and C only
(3) A, B, C and D (4) A only

24. Simplify $\left(\frac{x^m}{x^n}\right)^{m+n} \cdot \left(\frac{x^n}{x^p}\right)^{n+p} \cdot (x^p \times x^m)^{p-m}$
(1) mnp (2) 0
(3) 1 (4) $m^2 - p^2 + n^2$

25. If the sum of the first 14 terms of an AP is 1050 and its first term is 10, then its 20th term is:
(1) 200 (2) 100
(3) 300 (4) 400

26. What will be the angle between the hour hand & the minute hand of a clock when the time is 5:36 am?
(1) 47° (2) 48°
(3) 49° (4) 50°

27. Which article of the Indian constitution has provisions for the Uniform Civil Code?
(1) Article 42 (2) Article 43
(3) Article 51-A (4) Article 44

28. A rectangle has a length of 24 cm and diagonals of length 25 cm each. The area of the rectangle (in cm²):
(1) 576 (2) 312.5
(3) 288 (4) 168

29. Complete the figure:

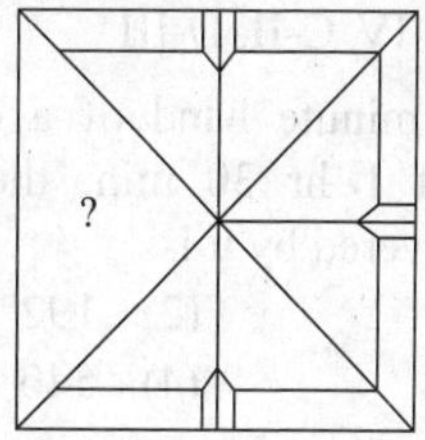

(1)
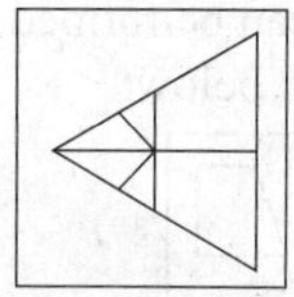
(2)
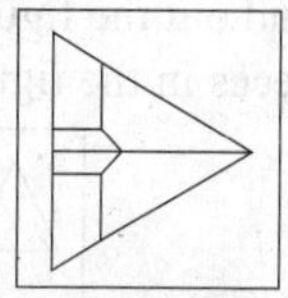
(3)
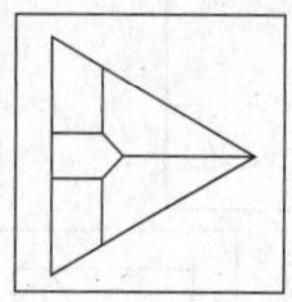
(4)
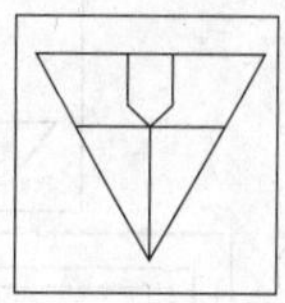

30. P is directly proportional to Q, and Q = 7 when P = 15. Find P when Q = 14.
(1) 10 (2) 20
(3) 30 (4) 22

31. If in ΔABC, AB = 5 cm, BC = 12 cm and AC = 13 cm, then the length of the median BE is:
(1) 5.5 cm (2) 7.5 cm
(3) 6.5 cm (4) 4.5 cm

32. Disease due to deficiency of Vitamin D is:
(1) Night Blindness (2) Covid-19
(3) Scurvy (4) Osteomalacia

33. Match **List I** with **List II**.

List I (Year of Launch)	List II (Programme/Measure)
A. 2015	I. National Rural Livelihood Mission
B. 2000	II. Pradhan Mantri Gram Sadak Yojana
C. 2011	III. National Skill Development Mission
D. 2018	IV. Ayushman Bharat

Choose the most appropriate answer from the options given below:
(1) A-III, B-I, C-IV, D-II
(2) A-III, B-II, C-I, D-IV

(3) A-IV, B-I, C-II, D-III
(4) A-I, B-IV, C-II, D-III

34. When the minute hand of a clock covers a distance of 1 hr 30 min, then the angular distance covered by it is:
(1) 480° (2) 192°
(3) 420° (4) 540°

35. Find out the figure that can be formed from the pieces in the figure given below:

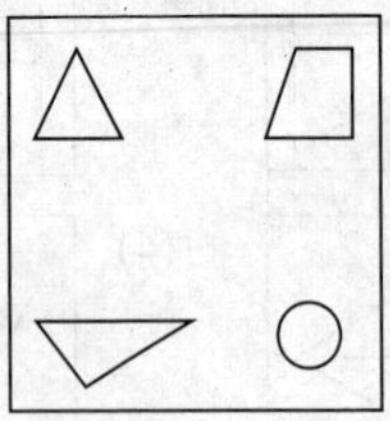

(1) 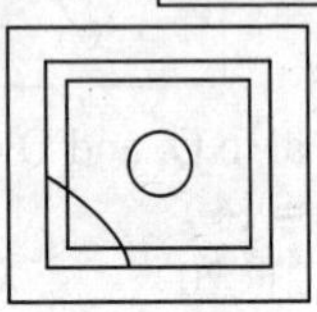 (2) 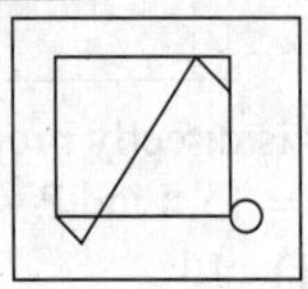

(3) 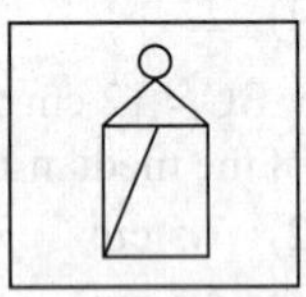 (4) 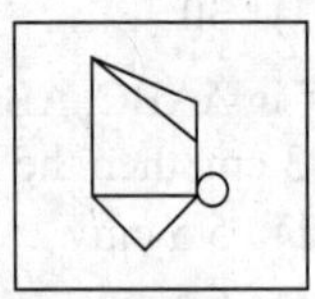

36. The pair of linear equations $2x + ky = 5$ and $4x + 6y = p$ is inconsistent. Which of the following cannot be the value of $(k + p)$?
(1) 11 (2) 12
(3) 13 (4) 15

37. Given below are two statements: one is labelled as Assertion A, and the other is labelled as Reason R.
Assertion A: Copper is used to make electrical wires.
Reason R: Copper has very low electrical resistance.
In light of the above statements, choose the correct answer from the options below.
(1) Both A and R are true, and R is the correct explanation of A.
(2) Both A and R are true, but R is NOT the correct explanation of A.
(3) A is true, but R is false.
(4) A is false, but R is true.

38. On July 22, 2019, Chandrayaan-2 was launched by ISRO through its rocket:
(1) GSLV-MKIII-M1
(2) PSLV
(3) SLV
(4) Ariane Rocket

39. Match **List I** with **List II**.

List I (Dance)	List II (State)
A. Bharatanatyam	I. Andhra Pradesh
B. Bihu	II. Assam
C. Kathakali	III. Kerala
D. Kuchipudi	IV. Tamil Nadu

Choose the most appropriate answer from the options given below:
(1) A-II, B-I, C-IV, D-III
(2) A-II, B-I, C-III, D-IV
(3) A-I, B-II, C-III, D-IV
(4) A-IV, B-II, C-III, D-I

40. Pointing to a woman in a picture, Raju said, "Her mother-in-law has only one grandchild whose mother is my wife". How is the woman in the picture related to Raju?
(1) cousin (2) wife
(3) sister (4) aunt

41. Find the missing term.
R9I, T6G, V11E, ?, Z13A
(1) X4C (2) X9C
(3) W4C (4) Y9D

42. Which state/UT of India does the territory known as Yanam (Puducherry) share boundaries with?
(1) Ladakh
(2) Kerala
(3) Goa
(4) Andhra Pradesh

43. Rohit ranks seventeenth from the top in a class of 40 students. What is his rank from the bottom?
(1) 23 (2) 24
(3) 25 (4) 26

44. Insert the missing term:

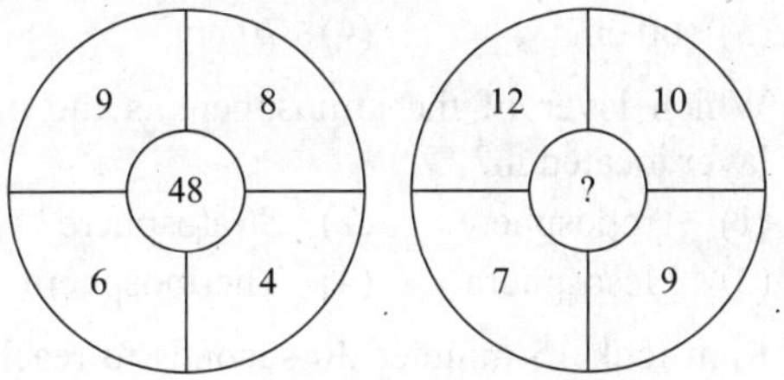

(1) 69 (2) 57
(3) 53 (4) 60

45. The ratio between two numbers is 2:3. If each number is increased by 2, then the ratio becomes 3:4. Find the sum of the original numbers.

(1) 10 (2) 6
(3) 8 (4) 5

46. Ethanol is obtained commercially by:

(1) dehydration (2) distillation
(3) fermentation (4) evaporation

47. One evening before sunset, two friends, Shahrukh and Rakesh, were talking to each other face-to-face. If Rakesh's shadow is precisely to his right side, which direction was Shahrukh facing?

(1) North (2) South
(3) West (4) East

48. In which quadrants do the points (–2, 3) and (3, –2) lie?

(1) both in the Second quadrant
(2) First and Fourth quadrants
(3) Second and Third quadrants
(4) Second and Fourth quadrants

49. The Saffron (Kesari) colour in the Indian national flag is a symbol of:

(1) renunciation of material gains
(2) path of truth
(3) relation of soil and plant life
(4) dharma

50. The atomic energy program in India was launched by:

(1) C.V. Raman
(2) Dr. APJ Abdul Kalam
(3) Satish Dhawan
(4) Homi J. Bhabha

51. Choose the missing term in the series from the options given below:

J2AZ, M4BY, L6CX, O8DW, ?, Q12FU

(1) N9EV (2) P10GH
(3) N10EV (4) P10EV

52. If the mean of the numbers 2, (p + 1), 8, 19, 16, 3 and p is 9, then find the mode of the numbers.

(1) 2 (2) 8
(3) 16 (4) 19

53. Who has the authority to decide all doubts and disputes connected with the election of the President of India?

(1) Vice President
(2) Speaker of the Lok Sabha
(3) Parliament
(4) Supreme Court

54. Match **List I** with **List II**.

List I	List II
A. Probability of getting a prime number in a single throw of a die is	I. $\frac{1}{6}$.
B. Probability of getting neither a prime nor a composite number in a single throw of a die is	II. $\frac{1}{3}$.
C. Probability of getting a multiple of 3 in a single throw of a die is	III. $\frac{1}{2}$.
D. Probability of getting a number greater than 2 in a single throw of a die is	IV. $\frac{2}{3}$.

Choose the correct answer from the options given below:

(1) A-III, B-I, C-IV, D-II
(2) A-II, B-I, C-III, D-IV
(3) A-III, B-I, C-II, D-IV
(4) A-I, B-II, C-III, D-IV

55. The founder of the "Servants of India Society" is

(1) Mahatma Gandhi
(2) Bal Gangadhar Tilak
(3) Gopal Krishna Gokhale
(4) Lala Lajpat Rai

56. Pankaj is younger than Sonali, and Rupali is older than Tinu. Who among them is the oldest?

Statements:

A. Rupali is older than Pankaj.

B. Sonali is older than Rupali.

C. Tinu is the youngest among all.

What all statements are needed to answer the question?

(1) B only

(2) C only

(3) A and B only

(4) A, B and C together required

57. The volume of a wall, which is 5 times as high as it is broad and 8 times as long as it is high, is 12.8 m^3. The breadth of the wall is

(1) 40 cm (2) 50 cm

(3) 60 cm (4) 70 cm

58. Which layer of the atmosphere is the ozone layer located in?

(1) Troposphere (2) Stratosphere

(3) Mesosphere (4) Thermosphere

59. Ram took 15 minutes 30 seconds to reach his friend's house, which is 900 meters away. The speed of Ram (in km/h) is (correct to two decimal places):

(1) 3.48 (2) 4.48

(3) 34.80 (4) 13.48

60. Jamshedpur is situated on the bank of river:

(1) Ganga (2) Mahanadi

(3) Subarnarekha (4) Godavari

Answer Key

1. (1)	2. (2)	3. (1)	4. (1)	5. (3)	6. (2)	7. (3)	8. (2)	9. (3)	10. (2)
11. (4)	12. (2)	13. (3)	14. (3)	15. (2)	16. (3)	17. (1)	18. (3)	19. (4)	20. (4)
21. (1)	22. (3)	23. (3)	24. (3)	25. (1)	26. (2)	27. (4)	28. (4)	29. (2)	30. (3)
31. (3)	32. (4)	33. (2)	34. (4)	35. (3)	36. (3)	37. (1)	38. (1)	39. (4)	40. (2)
41. (1)	42. (4)	43. (2)	44. (2)	45. (1)	46. (3)	47. (2)	48. (4)	49. (1)	50. (4)
51. (3)	52. (2)	53. (4)	54. (3)	55. (3)	56. (1)	57. (1)	58. (2)	59. (1)	60. (3)

Classification of Questions

Question No.	Subject	Topic	Level of Difficulty
1.	Reasoning	Venn Diagram	Easy
2.	Quantitative Aptitude	Mensuration	Easy
3.	Quantitative Aptitude	Simple Interest	Easy
4.	Reasoning	Linear arrangement	Easy
5.	Reasoning	Coding	Easy
6.	Reasoning	Odd-one-out (numbers)	Difficult
7.	Reasoning	Directions	Easy
8.	Quantitative Aptitude	Trigonometry (Heights & Distances)	Easy
9.	General Awareness.	Books & Authors	Medium
10.	Reasoning	Non-verbal	Medium

Question No.	Subject	Topic	Level of Difficulty
11.	General Awareness	Science (Biology)	Difficult
12.	Quantitative Aptitude	Calendars	Easy
13.	General Awareness	Current Affairs	Easy
14.	General Awareness	Geography	Medium
15.	Quantitative Aptitude	Profit, Loss & Discount	Easy
16.	Quantitative Aptitude	Time & Work	Easy
17.	General Awareness	Books & Authors	Difficult
18.	Quantitative Aptitude	Averages	Easy
19.	Quantitative Aptitude	Partnership	Easy
20.	General Awareness	Current Affairs	Easy
21.	Reasoning	Statement-Assumption	Easy
22.	Quantitative Aptitude	Number System	Medium
23.	General Awareness	Current Affairs	Medium
24.	Quantitative Aptitude	Simplification	Easy
25.	Quantitative Aptitude	Algebra (AP)	Easy
26.	Quantitative Aptitude	Clocks	Medium
27.	General Awareness	Polity	Easy
28.	Quantitative Aptitude	Mensuration	Easy
29.	Reasoning	Non-verbal	Easy
30.	Quantitative Aptitude	Ratio & Proportions	Easy
31.	Quantitative Aptitude	Geometry	Easy
32.	General Awareness	Science (Biology)	Easy
33.	General Awareness	Government Schemes	Difficult
34.	Quantitative Aptitude	Clocks	Easy
35.	Reasoning	Non-verbal	Easy
36.	Quantitative Aptitude	Algebra (Linear Equations)	Easy
37.	General Awareness	Science (Physics)	Medium
38.	General Awareness	Science & technology	Difficult
39.	General Awareness	Art & Culture	Easy
40.	Reasoning	Blood Relations	Easy
41.	Reasoning	Alphanumeric Series	Medium
42.	General Awareness	Geography	Difficult
43.	Reasoning	Rankings & Orders	Easy
44.	Reasoning	Missing Term	Easy
45.	Quantitative Aptitude	Ratios	Easy
46.	General Awareness	Science (Chemistry)	Easy
47.	Reasoning	Directions	Easy
48.	Quantitative Aptitude	Coordinate Geometry	Easy

Question No.	Subject	Topic	Level of Difficulty
49.	General Awareness	Polity	Easy
50.	General Awareness	Science & Technology	Easy
51.	Reasoning	Alphanumeric Series	Easy
52.	Quantitative Aptitude	Statistics (Mean, Median & Mode)	Easy
53.	General Awareness	Polity	Difficult
54.	Quantitative Aptitude	Probability	Medium
55.	General Awareness	History	Easy
56.	Reasoning	Rankings and Orders	Easy
57.	Quantitative Aptitude	Mensuration	Easy
58.	General Awareness	Geography	Medium
59.	Quantitative Aptitude	Time, Speed & Distance	Easy
60.	General Awareness	Geography	Medium

No. of questions on General Awareness: 21
No. of questions on Reasoning: 16
No. of questions on Quantitative Aptitude: 23

Explanation to Select Questions

1. Some boys are athletes, and some boys are not. Some boys are students, and some boys are not. Some students are athletes, and some students are not.
Hence, Option 1.

2. Let the original base radius of the cylinder be r and the height be h.
Volume of the cylinder $= \pi r^2 h$.
The volume of the cylinder once the base radius is doubled: $\pi(2r)^2 h = 4\pi r^2 h$.
$= 4 \times$ (*the original volume*)
Hence, Option 2.

3. Here, $P = 90$, $A = 108$ and $r = 6\frac{1}{4}\% = \frac{25}{4}\%$
Interest $= A - P = 108 - 90 = 18$.

$$\text{Time} = \frac{S.I. \times 100}{P \times r} = \frac{18 \times 100}{90 \times \frac{25}{4}} = \frac{18 \times 100 \times 4}{90 \times 25}$$

$= 3\frac{1}{5}$ years
Hence, Option 1.

Shortcut: Here the interest is 20% of the principal and 6.25% of the principal gets generated in 1 year.
Therefore, 20% of the principal will get generated in $\frac{20}{6.25}$ years.
As, $3 < \frac{20}{6.25} < 4$, only Option 1 gives us something between 3 and 4 years.

4. H_1 is to the right of H_2: H_2, H_1 (i)
H_5 is to the left of H_3 and right of H_1:
H_1, H_5, H_3 (ii)
H_2 is to the right of H_4: H_4, H_2 (iii)
Assimilating all (i), (ii) and (iii), we get:
H_4, H_2, H_1, H_5, H_3
Therefore, H_1 is in the middle.
Hence, Option 1.

5. id nim nop: they are innocent (i)
gob ots al: we like roses (ii)
nop ed al: they like flowers (iii)

Comparing (ii) and (iii), we deduce that 'al' is the code for 'like' as 'al' is common to both on the left and 'like' is common to both on the right. Similarly, comparing (i) and (iii), we deduce that 'nop' is the code for 'they'.
Therefore, 'ed' is the code for 'flowers'.
Hence, Option 3.

6. In 9105, the rightmost digit 5 is half of the sum of the other digits 9, 1 and 0

$$5 = \frac{9+1+0}{2}$$

Similarly, in 7125,

$$5 = \frac{7+1+2}{2},$$

in 4314,

$$4 = \frac{4+3+1}{2},$$

in 3927,

$$7 = \frac{3+9+2}{2}$$

in 2958,

$$8 = \frac{2+9+5}{2},$$

but in 9837, $7 \neq \frac{9+8+3}{2}$.

Hence, Option 2.

7.

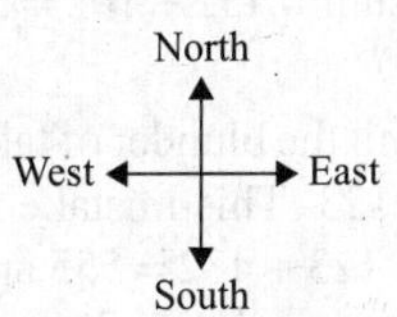

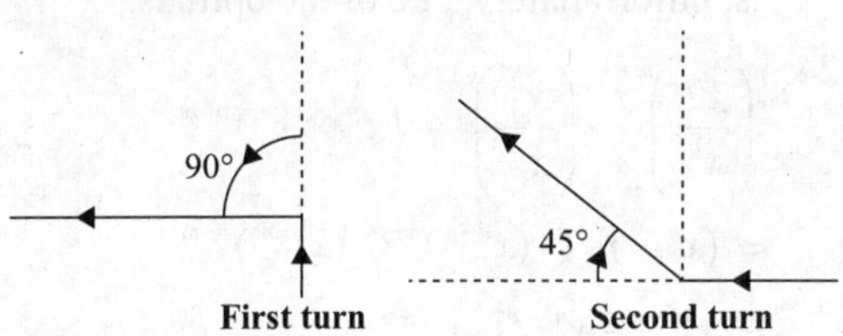

The girl is clearly facing the North-West direction after the second turn.
Hence, Option 3.

8.

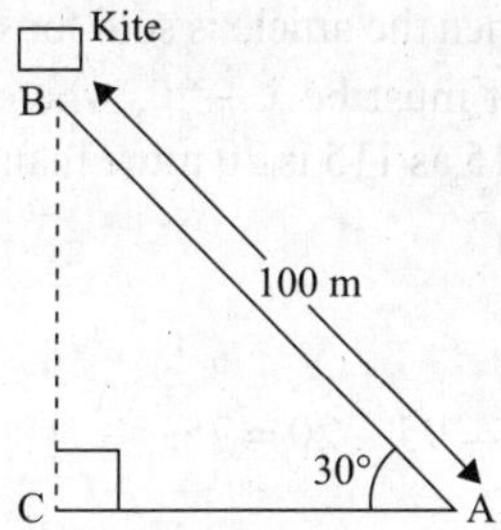

Let, AB be the string of the kite.
The height of the kite is BC.

In ΔABC, $\sin 30° = \frac{BC}{BA}$

or, $\frac{1}{2} = \frac{BC}{100}$

or, $BC = \frac{100}{2} = 50$ m.

Hence, Option 2.

10. The dotted line in the question figure is a base to two triangles and is touched by one of the vertices of a quadrilateral. This must not change even after the sheet is folded.
Hence, Option 2.

11. Only statement B is incorrect. Agrology is a branch of soil sciences that deals with the production of crops. Agrostology is the study of grass.
Hence, Option 4.

12. The number of days from 24 March 2011 to 24 March 2012 = 366
(Please take into account 29 February 2012)
There are 2 odd days in 366 days ($52 \times 7 + 2$).
Therefore, 24 March 2012 must have been 2 days after a Thursday, that is Saturday.
The number of days from 24 March 2012 to 24 June 2012 is 7 (in March) + 30 (in April) + 31 (in May) + 24 (in June) = 92.
The number of odd days in 92 days is 1 as $92 = 13 \times 7 + 1$.
Therefore, 24 June 2012 must be a day after a Saturday, that is a Sunday.
Hence, Option 2.

14. Makalu is the 5th highest peak in the world, situated on the border of Nepal and Tibet (China).
Hence, Option 3.

15. Let the profit be x when the article is sold for ₹95. Therefore, the profit must be $x + 20$, when the article is sold for ₹115 as 115 is 20 more than 95.
As per the question,
$x + 20 = 2x$
or, $x = 20$
Thus, the cost price = 95 – 20 = 75.
Hence, Option 2.
Alternative: Just work with the options.
Option 1: CP = 65
Profit, when the article is sold for 95, is 30.
Profit when the article is sold 115, is 50.
And $50 \neq 2(30)$.
When we check it for Option 2, we get the answer.

16. As the mother, daughter and son can do the work in 3, 4 and 5 days,
they can do 1/3 ,1/4 and 1/5 of the work in 1 day, respectively.
So, together they can do $\frac{1}{3}+\frac{1}{4}+\frac{1}{5} = \frac{20+15+12}{60} = \frac{47}{60}$ of the work in 1 day.
Hence, they can finish the work in $\frac{60}{47}$ days = $1\frac{13}{47}$ days.
Hence, Option 3.
Caution: Do NOT mark Option 1 $\left(\frac{47}{60}\text{ days}\right)$.
Alternative: Let the work be of 60 units.
I have taken 60 as it is the LCM of 3, 4, and 5.
As the mother, daughter and son can do the work in 3, 4 and 5 days respectively, they do 20, 15 and 12 units in a day, respectively.
So, together, they do 47 units in a day.
Therefore, they can complete 60 units in $\frac{60}{47} = 1\frac{13}{47}$ days.
I want you to work using this method as it is faster once you get habituated.

17. 'The Last Queen' is a book written by Chitra Banerjee. It is based on the life of Maharani Jind Kaur, the last queen of Punjab.
Hence, Option 1.

18. The sum of the 5 numbers with an average of $15 = 5 \times 15 = 75$.
The sum of the 6 numbers with an average of $16 = 6 \times 16 = 96$.
Therefore, the new number = 96 – 75 = 21.
Hence, Option 3.
Alternative: If the new number is 15, the average of the 6 numbers will remain 15. So, if we want the average to go up by 1 (from 15 to 16), we must add 6 to 15 to make it 21.

19. Suppose one rupee invested for a month is 1 month-rupee.
A's investment = $40000 \times 4 + 60000 \times 8$ = 640000 month-rupee.
B's investment = 50000×12 = 600000 month-rupee.
C's investment = $70000 \times 8 + 60000 \times 4$ = 80000 month-rupee.
D's investment = 60000×6 = 360000 month-rupee.
The combined investment of C and D = 800000 + 360000 = 1160000 month-rupee.
Total investment = 640000 + 600000 + 1160000 = 2400000 month-rupee.
Sum of the shares of C & D = $92100 \times \frac{1160000}{2400000}$ = 44515.
Hence, Option 4.

22. The smallest 3-digits number as per the conditions = 102.
The greatest 3-digit number as per the conditions = 432
Therefore, the required sum = 432 + 102 = 534.
Hence, Option 3.
Caution: Do NOT commit the blunder of taking the smallest number as 123. This mistake will give the required sum as 123 + 432 = 555 and it is, unfortunately, one of the options.

24. $\left(\frac{x^m}{x^n}\right)^{m+n} \cdot \left(\frac{x^n}{x^p}\right)^{n+p} \cdot (x^p \times x^m)^{p-m}$

$= (x^{m-n})^{m+n} \cdot (x^{n-p})^{n+p} \cdot (x^{p+m})^{p-m}$

$= x^{m^2-n^2} \cdot x^{n^2-p^2} \cdot x^{p^2-m^2}$

$= x^{m^2-n^2+n^2-p^2+p^2-m^2}$

$= x^0 = 1$.

Hence, Option 3.

25. Let the first term of the AP be a, common difference be d, the nth term be T_n and the sum of the first n terms be S_n.

Given that $a = 10$ and

$$S_{14} = \frac{2a + (n-1)d}{2} \times n$$

$$= \frac{20 + 13d}{2} \times 14 = 1050.$$

or, $20 + 13d = \frac{1050 \times 2}{14}$

or, $20 + 13d = 150$

or, $d = \frac{150 - 20}{13} = 10.$

$T_{20} = a + 19d = 10 + 19 \times 10 = 200.$

Hence, option 1.

26. At 5:36, the minute hand is at the distance of $36 \times 6° = 216°$ from 12.

And the hour hand is at $150° + 30° \times \frac{36}{60} = 168°$ from 12.

Therefore, the angle between these two hands is $216° - 168° = 48°$.

Alternative: At 5:00, the minute hand is at 12 and the hour hand is making an angle of $30° \times 5 = 150°$ with it.

Now,

In 60 minutes, the minute hand takes a lead of 330° over hour hand.

Therefore, in 36 minutes, it will take a lead of $330° \times \frac{36}{60} = 198°$.

Thus, the angle between them $= 198° - 150° = 48°$.

27. Article 44 of the Indian constitution is on the Uniform Civil Code. It is one of the Directive Principles of State Policy.

Hence, Option 4.

Mnemonic: The number 44 is also uniform as its digits are the same.

28.

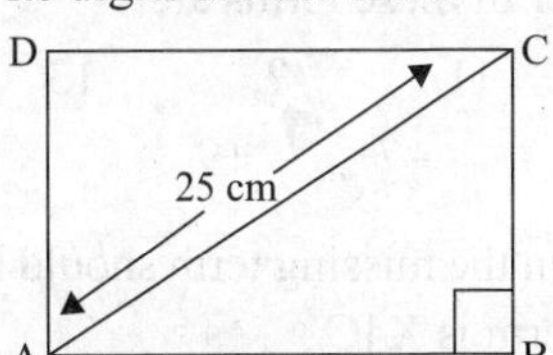

The width of the rectangle

$= \sqrt{25^2 - 24^2} = \sqrt{49} = 7.$

Therefore, the area $= 24 \times 7 = 168$.

Hence, Option 4.

30. Given that:

$P \propto Q$ or, $P = KQ$

Where k is a proportionality constant.

Also, when $Q = 7$, $P = 15$.

or, $15 = k \times 7$

or, $k = \frac{15}{7}$

So, $P = \frac{15}{7}Q$

Putting $Q = 14$ in it,

$P = \frac{15}{7} \times 14 = 30.$

Hence, Option 3.

31.

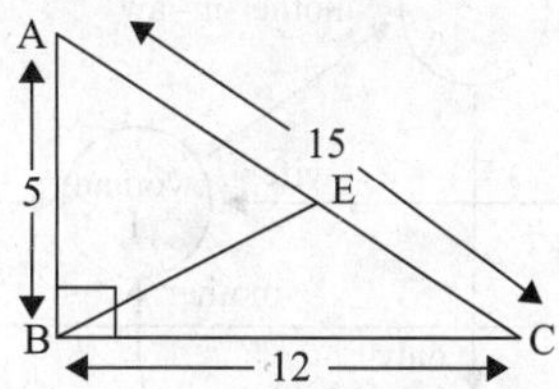

As 5, 12 and 13 are Pythagorean triplets, ΔABC is right angled.

In any right-angled triangle, the length of the median drawn on the hypotenuse is half the length of the hypotenuse.

Therefore, $BE = \frac{13}{2} = 6.5$ cm.

Hence, Option 3.

32. Osteomalacia is also known as 'soft bone disease' and is caused by Vitamin D deficiency.

Hence, Option 4.

'Osteo' is a Greek word root that means bone.

34. In 60 minutes, the minute hand of a clock covers 360°.

$\therefore$ in 1 minute, it covers $\frac{360°}{60} = 6°$.

$\therefore$ in 90 minutes (1 hour and 30 minutes), it covers $90 \times 6° = 540°$.

Hence, Option 4.

36. The equations

$2x + ky = 5$

And $4x + 6y = p$ are inconsistent.

For the equations to be NOT inconsistent, we should have

$$\frac{2}{4} = \frac{k}{6} = \frac{5}{p}$$

$$\left(\text{They are inconsistent if } \frac{2}{4} = \frac{k}{6} \neq \frac{5}{p}.\right)$$

$\Rightarrow k = 3$ and $p = 10$.

Thus, if $(k + p) = 13$, the equations are not inconsistent.

Hence, Option 3.

40.

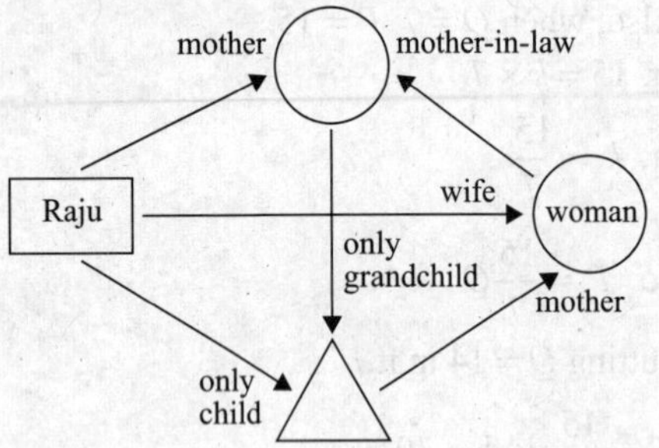

Case I

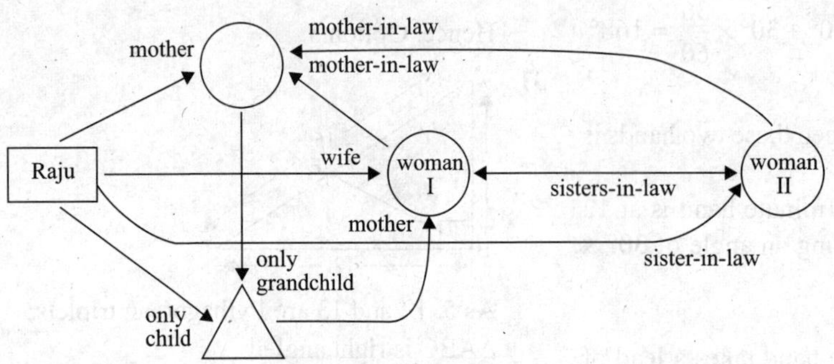

Case II

The question has assumed only one possibility (case I) and in that the woman in picture is Raju's wife.

There can be another case also (case II) in which the woman in picture could be Raju's sister-in-law (the wife of his brother).

As sister-in-law is not among the choices, wife is the best answer.

Hence, Option 2.

41.

R	9	I	T	6	G	V	11	E	◯	Z	13	A
18		9	20		7	22		5		26		1

The first letters of the terms have ranks 18, 20, 22 and hence the first letter of the next term should have a rank 24.

So, the first letter of the missing term is *x*.

Also, the sum of the ranks of the two letters in each of the terms is 27.

So, the 2nd letter of the missing term is C.

Now, the number of these terms are

9,	6,	11,	?,	13
−3	+5	−7	+9	

So, the number in the missing term should be 4.

Therefore, the term is X4C.

Hence, Option 1.

42. The union territory of Puducherry comprises the erstwhile French colonies of Yanam, Mahe, Karaikal and Puducherry. Puducherry and Karaikal are surrounded by Tamil Nadu; Mahe is surrounded by Kerala, and Yanam is surrounded by Andhra Pradesh.
Hence, Option 4.

43. As Rohit's rank is 17 from the top, there must be 16 people above him.
As there are 39 students other than Rohit and 16 are above him, there must be 39 – 16 = 23 students below him.
Thus, Rohit's rank from the bottom is 24.
Shortcut: If there are n people in a row, for any individual in the row, the rank from the top + the rank from the bottom = $n + 1$
Here, $n = 40$, and Rohit's rank from the top = 17
Therefore, Rohit's rank from the bottom = $(40 + 1) - 17 = 24$.
Hence, Option 2.

44.

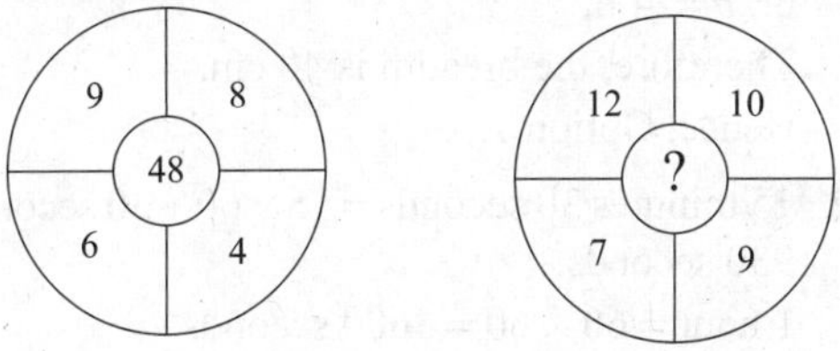

$48 = 9 \times 8 - 6 \times 4$

$? = 12 \times 10 - 7 \times 9 = 120 - 63 = 57$

Hence, Option 2.

45. Let the numbers be $2x$ and $3x$.
We have,

$$\frac{2x+2}{3x+2} = \frac{3}{4}, \text{ or, } 8x + 8 = 9x + 6$$

or, $x = 2$
Therefore, the numbers are 4 and 6. The sum of 4 and 6 is 10.

Alternative: As the ratio of the numbers is 2:3, their sum should be a multiple of 5. When we add 2 to each of these numbers, the ratio becomes 3:4.
Therefore, if we add 4 to the sum of these numbers, that should be divisible by 7.
We have only one such number among the options: 10.
We have, of course, assumed the numbers to be integers in this method.

46. Ethanol (CH_3CH_2OH or alcohol or drinking alcohol) is obtained by fermentation. Distillation is used for its purification (to remove the by-products).
Hence, Option 3.
Caution: Option 2 is a good trap.

47.

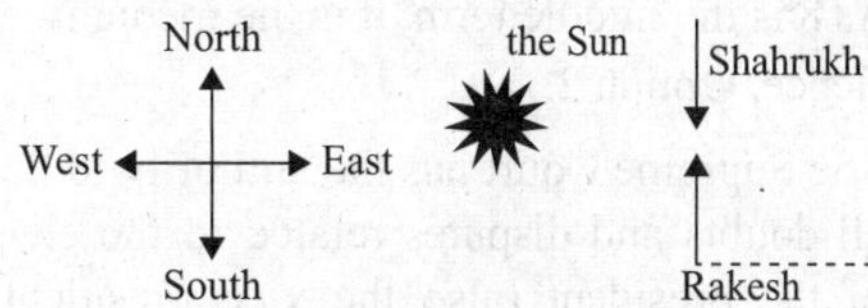

As it is evening, the sun is in the west. Rakesh's shadow is falling to his right, it means, Rakesh is facing north and Shahrukh is facing south.
Hence, Option 2.

48.

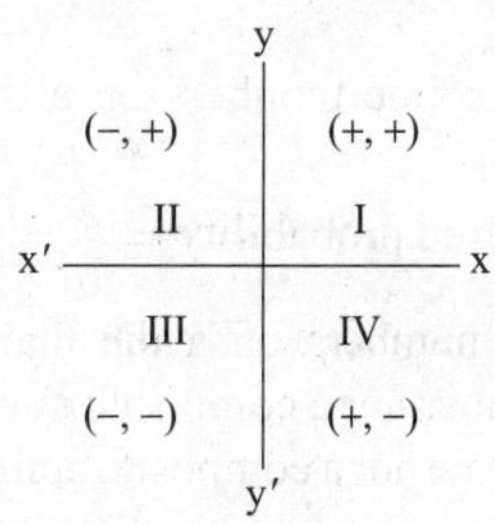

Thus, (– 2, 3) is in the Second and (3, – 2) is in the Fourth quadrant.

51.

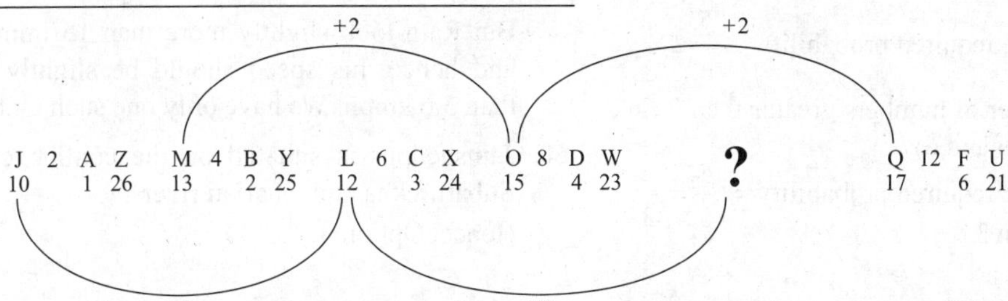

The first letter of missing term has rank 12 + 2 = 14 in the alphabet.
So, it is N.
N should, of course, be followed by 10 E and V.
Hence, Option 3.

52. The mean of the 7 numbers is 9.
Therefore,

$$\frac{2+(p+1)+8+19+16+3+p}{7}=9$$

or, $49 + 2p = 63$
or, $2p = 14$ or, $p = 7$.
$\therefore$ the numbers are 2, 8, 8, 19, 16, 3 and 7.
Arranging the numbers in ascending order, we get:
2, 3, 7, $\boxed{8}$, 8, 16, 19.
As 8 is the middle term, it is the median.
Hence, Option 2.

53. The Supreme Court has the authority to decide all doubts and disputes related to the election of the president (also the vice president) of India. This provision is in Article 71 of the Constitution of India.
Hence, Option 4.

54. The number of numbers on a die = 6 (1, 2, 3, 4, 5 and 6)
A. The number of prime numbers on a die = 3 (2, 3 and 5)
Therefore, the required probability $= \frac{3}{6} = \frac{1}{2}$.
B. The number of numbers on a die that are neither a prime number nor a composite number = 1 (1 is neither a prime nor a composite number)
Therefore, the required probability $\frac{1}{6}$.
C. The number of multiples of 3 on a die = 2 (3 and 6).
Therefore, the required probability $= \frac{2}{6} = \frac{1}{3}$.
D. The number of numbers greater than 2 on a die = 4 (3, 4, 5 and 6)
Therefore, the required probability $= \frac{4}{6} = \frac{2}{3}$.
Hence, Option 3.

56. Pankaj is younger than Sonali and Tinu is younger than Rupali.
So, of these four people, neither Pankaj nor Tinu can be the oldest as each of them is younger to at least one person.
Therefore, one of Sonali and Rupali is the oldest.
Statement B answers this and with it we can conclude that Sonali is the oldest.
Hence, Option 1.

57. Let the breadth of the wall be b.
The height of the wall = $5b$
The length of the wall = $8 \times 5b = 40b$.
The volume of the wall = $b \times 5b \times 40b$
$= 200b^3 = 12.8 \text{ m}^3$
or, $b^3 = \frac{12.8}{200} \text{ m}^3 = 0.064 \text{ m}^3$
or, $b = \sqrt[3]{0.064}$ m
or, $b = .4$ m
Therefore, the breadth is 40 cm.
Hence, Option 1.

59. 15 minutes 30 seconds = 15 × 60 + 30 seconds = 930 seconds
1 hour = 60 × 60 = 3600 seconds
Speed of Ram $= \frac{900}{930}$ metres/second
$= \frac{900}{930} \times \frac{3600}{1000}$ km/hr
= 3.48 km/hr. (approx.)
Shortcut: Had Ram taken 15 minutes to travel 900 metres, his speed would have been 900 × 4 = 3600 metre per hour
or, 3.6 kmph (as 15 minutes in $\frac{1}{4}$ of an hour).
But Ram took slightly more than 15 minutes, and hence, his speed should be slightly less than 3.6 kmph. We have only one such Option.

60. Jamshedpur is situated on the confluence of Subarnrekha and Kharkai rivers.
Hence, Option 3.

CUET UG 2023 GENERAL TEST

June 1

INSTRUCTIONS:

1. You need to attempt any 50 out of the 60 questions in 60 minutes.
2. You get 5 marks for a correct response and –1 for an incorrect one. However, there is no reward or penalty for a question not attempted.

1. If in ΔABC $\angle A + \angle B = 90°$ and $\sin B = \frac{4}{5}$, then find the value of cos A.

(1) 1 (2) $\frac{3}{5}$

(3) $\frac{4}{5}$ (4) 0

2. If 18th February 1997 fell on Tuesday, then what was the day on 18th February 1999?

(1) Friday (2) Monday

(3) Tuesday (4) Thursday

3. Tickets numbered 1 to 20 are mixed, and a ticket is drawn randomly.
What is the probability that the ticket drawn bears a number which is a multiple of 3?

(1) $\frac{3}{10}$ (2) $\frac{3}{20}$

(3) $\frac{2}{5}$ (4) $\frac{1}{2}$

4. Find the missing term in the given series.
20:17: : 104:?

(1) 52 (2) 55

(3) 59 (4) 61

5. The circumference of a circular field is 396 m, and that of the other circular field is 132 m. Find the area (in m^2) of the third circular field whose radius is the sum of the radii of the first two fields. $\left(\text{Take } \pi = \frac{22}{7}\right)$

(1) 13860 (2) 19536

(3) 22176 (4) 23984

6. Who wrote the famous novel "The Guide"?

(1) R.K. Narayan (2) Sarojini Naidu

(3) B.M. Kaul (4) Vijay Tendulkar

7. Five students are standing in a circle, and all are facing the centre of the circle. Abhinav is between Alok and Ankur. Apurva is on the left of Abhishek. Alok is on the left of Apurva. Who is sitting next to Abhinav on his right?

(1) Apurva (2) Ankur

(3) Abhishek (4) Alok

8. Which of the following represents the Boyle's Law?

(1) $V \propto T$ (at constant P)

(2) $V \propto \frac{1}{P}$ (at constant T)

(3) $P \propto T$ (at constant V)

(4) $V \propto n$ (at constant T&P)

9. Find the missing figure and complete it:

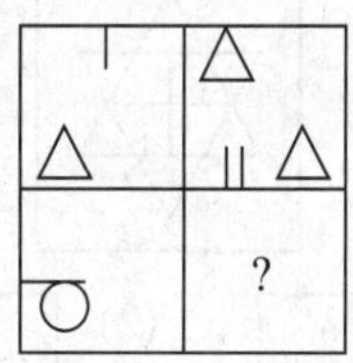

(1) 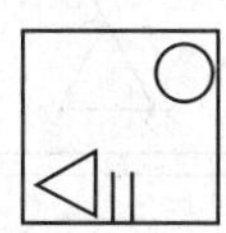 (2) 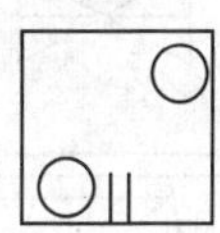

(3) 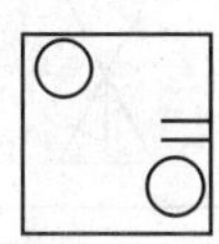 (4) 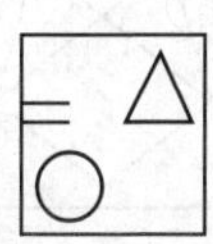

10. A sum of ₹1250 is divided among A, B and C such that A gets $\frac{2}{9}$ of B's share and C gets $\frac{3}{4}$ of A's share. Find the shares of A, B and C (in ₹).
(1) 200, 900, 150
(2) 200, 800, 250
(3) 150, 800, 300
(4) 190, 850, 210

11. Match **List I** with **List II**.

List I (Prime Minister of India)	List II (Period)
(A) Lal Bahadur Shastri	(I) 1984 to 1989
(B) Rajiv Gandhi	(II) 1991 to 1996
(C) Atal Bihari Vajpayee	(III) 1964 to 1966
(D) P.V. Narasimha Rao	(IV) 1998 to 2004

Choose the most appropriate answer from the options given below:
(1) (A)-(II), (B)-(III), (C)-(IV), (D)-(I)
(2) (A)-(III), (B)-(I), (C)-(IV), (D)-(II)
(3) (A)-(I), (B)-(III), (C)-(II), (D)-(IV)
(4) (A)-(III), (B)-(II), (C)-(IV), (D)-(I)

12. ________ is a famous folk dance in Maharashtra.
(1) Kathi (2) Lavani
(3) Jatra (4) Garba

13. Choose the alternative figure which is embedded in the problem figure:
Problem figure

(1)
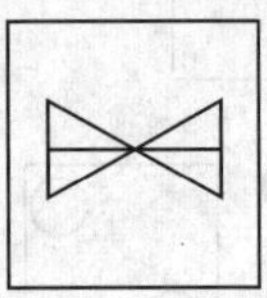
(2)
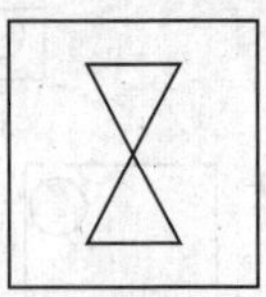
(3)
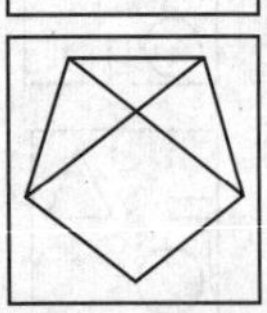
(4)
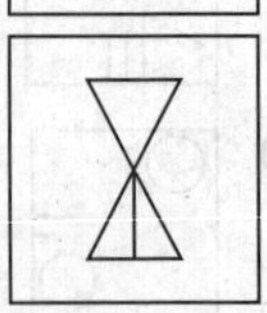

14. If CAT is 12, then LION is:
(1) 24 (2) 25
(3) 48 (4) 50

15. A man walking at a speed of 5 km/h passes a bridge in 15 minutes.
What is the length of the bridge (in meters)?
(1) 1000 (2) 1200
(3) 1250 (4) 1500

16. A toy is made in the shape of a hemisphere with a diameter of 7 cm surmounted by a cone. If this 15.5 cm high toy is polished at 20 paise per cm^2, then find the cost of polishing. $\left(\text{Take } \pi = \frac{22}{7}\right)$
(1) ₹39 (2) ₹40.50
(3) ₹42.90 (4) ₹45

17. Arrange the following in the correct chronological order:
(A) Dandi March
(B) Chauri Chaura incident
(C) Quit India Movement
(D) Formation of the Indian National Congress
(E) Swadeshi Movement
Choose the most appropriate answer from the options given below:
(1) (D), (E), (B), (A), (C)
(2) (A), (C), (B), (D), (E)
(3) (E), (B), (C), (A), (D)
(4) (C), (A), (B), (E), (D)

18. A quadrilateral has vertices in the order (0, −1), (−2, 3), (6, 7) and (8, 3). The quadrilateral is a:
(1) Trapezium (2) Square
(3) Rhombus (4) Rectangle

19. In which language were most of the Ashokan inscriptions written?
(1) Sanskrit & Pali (2) Prakrit & Brahmi
(3) Hindi & Pali (4) Urdu & Sanskrit

20. Given below are two statements: one is labelled as Assertion (A), and the other is labelled as Reason (R).
Assertion (A): Earth is the only planet known to have life.
Reason (R): Earth has an atmosphere that is a mixture of oxygen, nitrogen, and carbon dioxide.

In the light of the above statements, choose the most appropriate answer from the options given below:

(1) Both (A) and (R) are correct, and (R) is the correct explanation of (A)
(2) Both (A) and (R) are correct, but (R) is not the correct explanation of (A)
(3) (A) is correct, but (R) is not correct
(4) (A) is not correct, but (R) is correct

21. Linear equations $3x + 5y = 19$ and $10x - 3y = 24$ have a solution $x = \frac{\alpha}{3}$ and $y = \frac{\beta}{2}$, then the value of $\alpha + \beta$ is:

(1) 5 (2) 13
(3) 10 (4) 7

22. Find the A.P. whose 3rd term is 18 and 12th term is 72.

(1) 6, 12, 18 … (2) 0, 9, 18 …
(3) 12, 15, 18 … (4) 4.5, 9, 18 …

23. Which of the following countries shares the shortest border with India?

(1) Bhutan (2) Myanmar
(3) Nepal (4) Pakistan

24. Eight persons with an average weight of 49 kg were in a lift. Two more persons, Anita and Kamal, boarded the lift, and the average weight of the persons in the lift increased by 2.8 kg. What is the average weight of Anita and Kamal?

(1) 51.8 kg (2) 54.6 kg
(3) 59 kg (4) 63 kg

25. According to the months they are celebrated in, arrange the following festivals in ascending order in the calendar:

(A) Bihu
(B) Pongal
(C) Holi
(D) Christmas
(E) Onam

Choose the most appropriate answer from the options given below:

(1) (B), (A), (C), (D), (E)
(2) (B), (C), (A), (E), (D)
(3) (A), (B), (C), (D), (E)
(4) (E), (C), (A), (B), (D)

26. If the mean of the numbers 2, $(2p + 2)$, 7, 13, 17, 4 and $(p - 1)$ is 8, then find their median.

(1) 4 (2) 6
(3) 7 (4) 13

27. 'Venus' is to 'Earth' as 'Mercury' is to ________.

(1) Sun (2) Pluto
(3) Mars (4) Moon

28. A boy runs 4 km to the East side, then turns to the right side and runs 6 km, then turns left and runs 8 km, then turns left to run 3 km, again turns left and runs 4 km, then turns right and runs 1 km. Now the boy is in which direction?

(1) West (2) South
(3) North (4) East

29. The provision for the anti-defection law is given under which schedule of the constitution:

(1) 10th Schedule (2) 9th Schedule
(3) 8th Schedule (4) 12th Schedule

30. The greatest football player 'Pele' belonged to ________.

(1) Belgium (2) Argentina
(3) Brazil (4) Germany

31. If the first three letters of the word "SOCIOLOGIST" are reversed, then the last three letters are added, and then the remaining letters are reversed and added, then which letter will be exactly in the Middle?

(1) G (2) T
(3) I (4) C

32. Choose a set of numbers similar to the given set from the four alternative sets.

(8, 12, 18)

(1) (6, 12, 18) (2) (7, 11, 15)
(3) (7, 11, 17) (4) (9, 13, 20)

33. Who was the first Chief Justice of India?

(1) S.R. Das
(2) N.V. Ramana
(3) Harilal J. Kania
(4) Patanjali Shastri

34. If $\sin\theta + \text{cosec}\theta = 2$, then what is the value of $\sin^2\theta + \text{cosec}^2\theta$?

(1) 4 (2) 8
(3) 2 (4) 16

35. ________ is known as the father of Indian Nuclear Physics.
(1) Vikram Sarabhai
(2) J.C. Bose
(3) Dr. Homi J. Bhabha
(4) A.P.J. Abdul Kalam

36. Joseph gifted ₹20000 to his wife and some money to his three children aged 12, 14 and 16 years in the ratio of their ages. If he gave ₹3000 to his youngest child, then how much money did he gift to his family?
(1) ₹30000 (2) ₹30150
(3) ₹30225 (4) ₹30500

37. Match **List II** with **List II**.

List I	List II
(A) Indian Rare Earths Limited	(I) Bangalore
(B) Indian Space Research Organisation	(II) Thiruvananthapuram
(C) Vikram Sarabhai Space Centre	(III) Jadugoda
(D) Uranium Corporation of India	(IV) Aluva (Kerala)

Choose the most appropriate answer from the options given below:
(1) (A)-(I), (B)-(III), (C)-(II), (D)-(IV)
(2) (A)-(IV), (B)-(III), (C)-(II), (D)-(I)
(3) (A)-(IV), (B)-(I), (C)-(II), (D)-(III)
(4) (A)-(I), (B)-(IV), (C)-(II), (D)-(III)

38. Palk Strait Separates which of the following countries from India?
(A) Pakistan
(B) Bangladesh
(C) Sri Lanka
(D) Myanmar
Choose the most appropriate answer from the options given below:
(1) (A) only (2) (B) only
(3) (C) only (4) (B) and (C) only

39. A certain sum becomes $\frac{36}{25}$ of itself after 2 years on compound interest. Find the rate of interest per annum.
(1) 15% (2) 20%
(3) 25% (4) 10%

40. The angular distance covered by the minute hand in 1 hour and 20 minutes is:
(1) 420° (2) 480°
(3) 192° (4) 310°

41. ________, an Indian patriot from Punjab, shot down General Reginald Dyer in London.
(1) Sardar Bhagat Singh
(2) Shah Nawaz
(3) Sardar Udham Singh
(4) Sohan Singh

42. 1 kilo Watt-hour (kWh) is equal to ________
(1) 3.6×10^4 joule (2) 3.6×10^7 joule
(3) 3.6×10^5 joule (4) 3.6×10^6 joule

43. Choose the alternative in which the problem figure is embedded:

Problem Figure

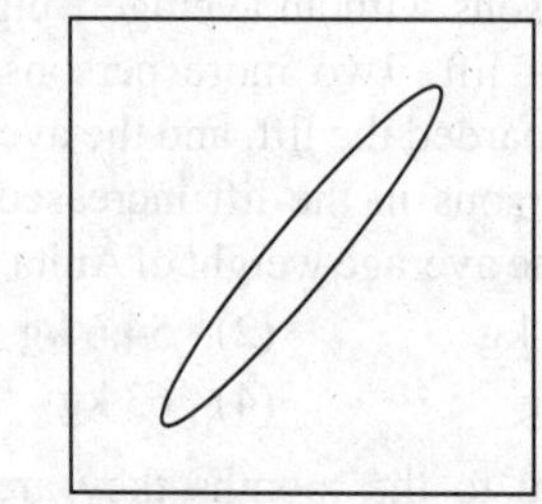

(1)
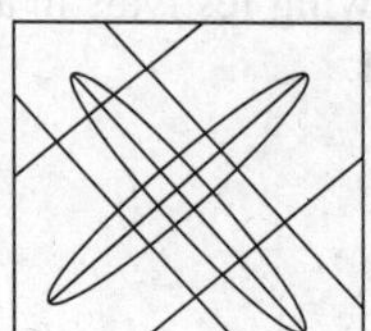
(2)
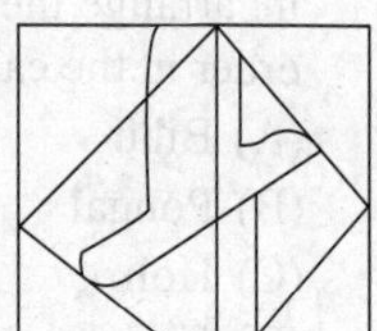
(3)
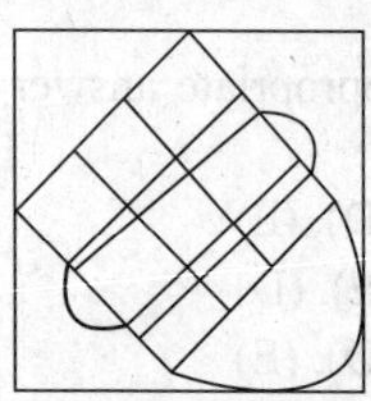
(4)
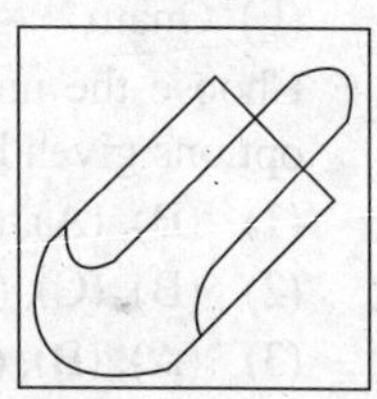

44. Match **List I** with **List II**.

List I (Quantity)	List II (Unit)
(A) Acceleration	(I) newton-meter^{-2}
(B) Pressure	(II) meter^{-1}
(C) Power of Lens	(III) second^{-1}
(D) Frequency	(IV) meter-second^{-2}

Choose the most appropriate answer from the options given below:

(1) (A)-(I), (B)-(II), (C)-(III), (D)-(IV)
(2) (A)-(IV), (B)-(I), (C)-(II), (D)-(III)
(3) (A)-(I), (B)-(IV), (C)-(III), (D)-(II)
(4) (A)-(II), (B)-(IV), (C)-(I), (D)-(III)

45. Find the missing term in the given series: DF, GJ, KM, NQ, RT, ?

(1) UW (2) UX
(3) YZ (4) XZ

46. Rajan does $\frac{7}{11}$ of a work in 21 days. How many more days will he take to complete the work?

(1) $9\frac{1}{4}$ (2) 12
(3) 15 (4) $13\frac{1}{2}$

47. **Statement** (I): All children are students.
(II): All students are players.
Conclusions (I): All students are children.
(II): All children are players.
Which of the conclusions follow/s from the given statements?

(1) Only I follows.
(2) Only II follows.
(3) Both I & II follow.
(4) Neither I nor II follows.

48. The volumes of 3 solid cubes made of metal are 125 cm^3, 64 cm^3 and 27 cm^3, respectively. After melting all three cubes, a solid cube is made. Find the edge of the new cube.

(1) 2.5 cm (2) 4 cm
(3) 6 cm (4) 5 cm

49. Fill up the gap with a proper group of letters. IKM, JLN, KMO, __?_

(1) PNL (2) QNS
(3) LNP (4) SNQ

50. "Namami Gange" was launched in the year _______ to comprehensively clean and protect the river Ganga.

(1) 2014 (2) 2015
(3) 2016 (4) 2017

51. Which of the following is/are the possible commercial industrial applications of bacteria?

(A) fermentation of sugar
(B) cleaning of oil spills
(C) tanning and making ink
(D) production of vaccine
(E) to make varnish, polish, paint, etc.

Choose the most appropriate answer from the options given below:

(1) (A), (B) and (C) only
(2) (A), (B) and (D) only
(3) (B), (C) and (D) only
(4) (C) and (E) only

52. Which of the following is correct for divisibility?

(A) A number is divisible by 6 if it is divisible by 3 or 2.
(B) A number is divisible by 5 if its unit digit is 0 or 5.
(C) A number is divisible by 3 if its unit digit is divisible by 3.
(D) A number is divisible by 4 if the number formed by its last two digits is divisible by 4.

Choose the correct answer from the options given below:

(1) (A), (B) and (D) only
(2) (B) and (D) only
(3) (A), (C) and (D) only
(4) (B) and (C) only

53. Find the answer figure that can be formed from the pieces in the question figure.

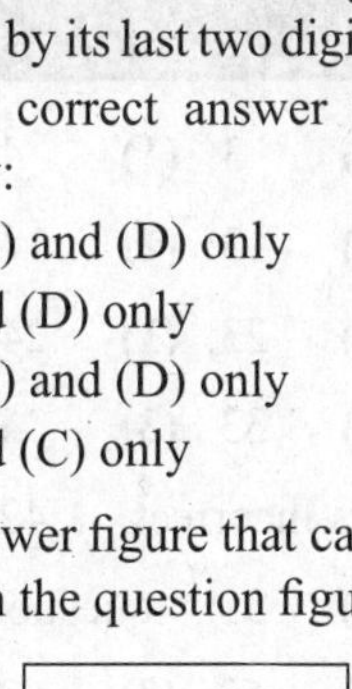

(1) 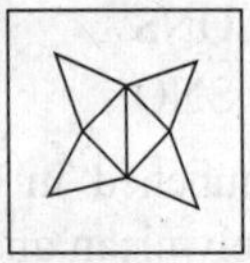 (2) 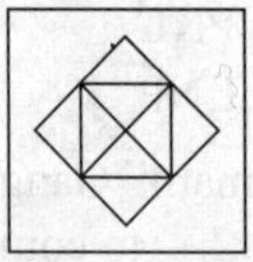

(3) 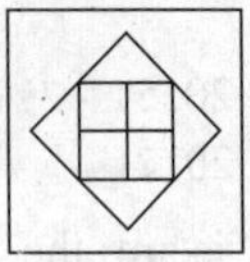 (4) 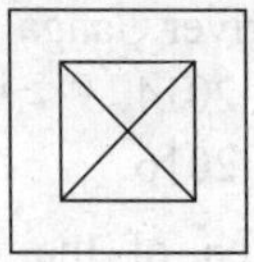

54. 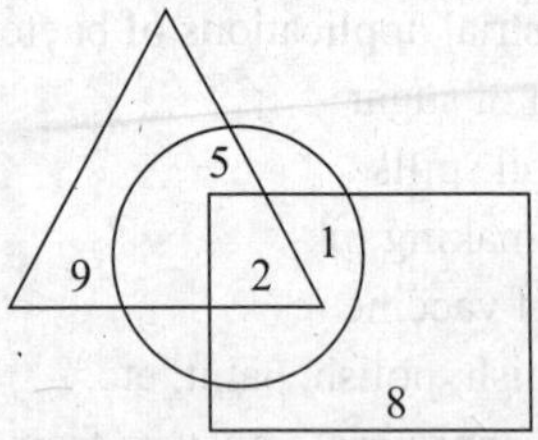

Which number lies inside all the figures?

(1) 2 (2) 5
(3) 9 (4) 1

55. In a certain code, GONE is written as 4%1* and MEDAL as 2*7$@. How will 'GOLD' be written in that code?

(1) 4@%7 (2) 4#@7
(3) 4%@7 (4) 4%#7

56. A wholesaler sells 20 pens at the marked price of 16 to a retailer. The retailer sells them at the marked price. Determine the gain per cent of the retailer.

(1) 30% (2) 23%
(3) 25% (4) 28%

57. Who was the first female Chief Minister in India?

(1) Shakuntala Devi
(2) Sarojini Naidu
(3) Anita B. George
(4) Sucheta Kripalani

58. An angle is $\frac{3}{7}$ times its supplementary angle. Find the angle.

(1) 54° (2) 63°
(3) 27° (4) 126°

59. If $243^{3x} = 27^{(4x-1)}$, then the value of 4^x is:

(1) 4 (2) −4
(3) $\frac{1}{4}$ (4) $\frac{1}{16}$

60. Pointing to a man, a lady said, "His mother is the only daughter of my mother." How is the lady related to the man?

(1) Aunt (2) Sister
(3) Daughter (4) Mother

Answer Key

1. (3) 2. (4) 3. (1) 4. (3) 5. (3) 6. (1) 7. (4) 8. (2) 9. (3) 10. (1)
11. (2) 12. (2) 13. (2) 14. (2) 15. (3) 16. (3) 17. (1) 18. (4) 19. (2) 20. (2)
21. (2) 22. (1) 23. (1) 24. (4) 25. (2) 26. (3) 27. (1) 28. (3) 29. (1) 30. (3)
31. (2) 32. (3) 33. (3) 34. (3) 35. (3) 36. (4) 37. (3) 38. (3) 39. (2) 40. (2)
41.* question was incorrect 42. (4) 43. (1) 44. (2) 45. (2) 46. (2) 47. (2) 48. (3)
49. (3) 50. (1) 51.* question was incorrect 52. (2) 53. (2) 54. (1) 55. (3) 56. (3)
57. (4) 58. (1) 59. (3) 60. (4)

Classification of Questions

Question No.	Subject	Topic	Level of Difficulty
1.	Quantitative Aptitude	Trigonometry	Easy
2.	Quantitative Aptitude	Calendars	Easy
3.	Quantitative Aptitude	Probability	Easy
4.	Reasoning	Number Series	Medium
5.	Quantitative Aptitude	Mensuration	Medium
6.	General Awareness	Books and Authors	Easy
7.	Reasoning	Circular Arrangement	Easy
8.	General Awareness	Science	Easy
9.	Reasoning	Non-verbal	Easy
10.	Quantitative Aptitude	Ratios	Easy
11.	General Awareness	Polity	Easy
12.	General Awareness	Art and Culture	Medium
13.	Reasoning	Non-verbal	Medium
14.	Reasoning	Coding	Easy
15.	Quantitative Aptitude	Time, Speed and Distance	Easy
16.	Quantitative Aptitude	Mensuration	Medium
17.	General Awareness	History	Medium
18.	Quantitative Aptitude	Coordinate Geometry	Medium
19.	General Awareness	History	Easy
20.	General Awareness	Science	Difficult
21.	Quantitative Aptitude	Algebra	Easy
22.	Quantitative Aptitude	Algebra	Easy
23.	General Awareness	Geography	Medium
24.	Quantitative Aptitude	Averages	Medium
25.	General Awareness	Art and Culture	Medium
26.	Quantitative Aptitude	Statistics (Median)	Medium
27.	Reasoning	Analogy (Geography based)	Easy
28.	Reasoning	Directions	Easy
29.	General Awareness	Polity	Easy

Question No.	Subject	Topic	Level of Difficulty
30.	General Awareness	Sports	Easy
31.	Reasoning	Letter Arrangement	Easy
32.	Reasoning	Miscellaneous	Easy
33.	General Awareness	Polity	Easy
34.	Quantitative Aptitude	Trigonometry	Medium
35.	General Awareness	Science and Tech	Easy
36.	Quantitative Aptitude	Ratios	Easy
37.	General Awareness	Geography	Medium
38.	General Awareness	Geography	Easy
39.	Quantitative Aptitude	Compound Interest	Easy
40.	Quantitative Aptitude	Clocks	Easy
41.	General Awareness	History	Question was wrong
42.	General Awareness	Science	Medium
43.	Reasoning	Non-verbal	Easy
44.	General Awareness	Science	Easy
45.	Reasoning	Series	Easy
46.	Quantitative Aptitude	Time and Work	Easy
47.	Reasoning	Syllogism	Easy
48.	Quantitative Aptitude	Mensuration	Easy
49.	Reasoning	Series	Easy
50.	General Awareness	Government Schemes	Difficult
51.	General Awareness	Science	Question was wrong
52.	Quantitative Aptitude	Divisibility	Medium
53.	Reasoning	Non-verbal	Medium
54.	Reasoning	Venn Diagram	Easy
55.	Reasoning	Coding	Easy
56.	Quantitative Aptitude	Profit, Loss and Discount	Easy
57.	General Awareness	Polity	Easy
58.	Quantitative Aptitude	Geometry	Easy
59.	Quantitative Aptitude	Powers and Indices	Easy
60.	Reasoning	Blood Relations	Easy

The no. of questions on Quantitative Aptitude: 22
The no. of questions on General Awareness: 21
The no. of questions on Reasoning: 17

Explanation to Select Questions

1. 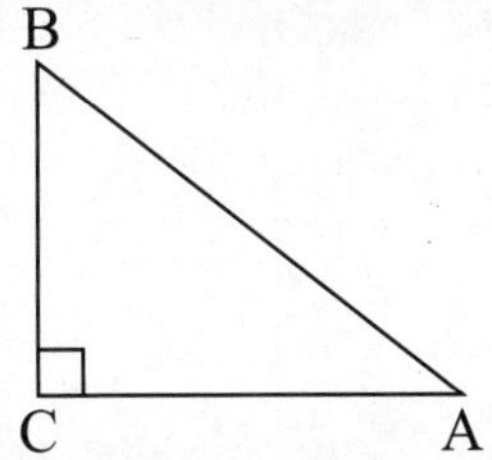

In ΔABC,

As $<A + <B = 90°$, $<C = 90°$.

Now, $\text{CosA} = \frac{AC}{AB} = \text{SinB} = \frac{4}{5}$.

Hence, Option 3.

2. There are exactly 2 non-leap years in between 18th February 1997 and 18th February 1999.
Two non-leap years have 2 odd days.
Therefore, if 18th February 1997 was a Tuesday, 18th February 1999 would be 2 days after a Tuesday, that is a Thursday.
Hence, Option 4.

3. Total number of possibilities: 20.
Total Number of favourable cases: 6 (3, 6, 9, 12, 15, 18).

$\therefore$ the required probability $= \frac{6}{20} = \frac{3}{10}$.

Hence, Option 1.

4. $17 = \frac{20}{2} + 7$.

Similarly $59 = \frac{104}{2} + 7$.

Hence, Option 3.

5. Let the radii of these circular fields be r_1 and r_2.
We have,

$2\pi r_1 = 396$

or, $2 \times \frac{22}{7} \times r_1 = 396$

or, $r_1 = 63$

Again,

$2\pi r_2 = 132$

or, $2 \times \frac{22}{7} \times r_2 = 132$

or, $r_2 = 21$

$\therefore$ the radius of the 3rd circular field $= r_1 + r_2 = 63 + 21 = 84$.

$\therefore$ the area of the 3rd circular field $= \pi(84)^2$

$= \frac{22}{7} \times 84 \times 84$

$= 22176$

Hence, Option 3.

6. 'The Guide' was written by R. K. Narayan.
Hence, Option 1.
The famous Hindi film Guide is based on it.

7. As Apurva is on the left of Abhishek and Alok is on the left of Apurva, only this is possible:

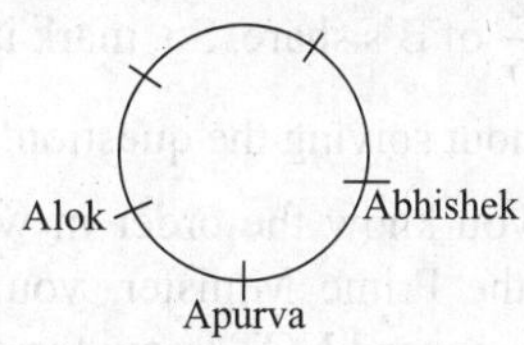

Also, Abhinav is between Alok and Ankur and hence, the only possible arrangement is:

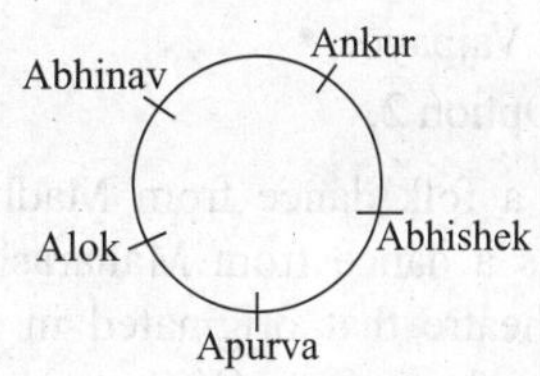

It is Alok, who is on the right of Abhinav.
Hence, Option 4.

8. Option 1 - Volume and Temperature of a gas are directly proportional when Pressure is constant- is Charles's Law.
Option 2 - The Volume of a gas is inversely proportional to its Pressure when Temperature is constant - is Boyle's Law.
Hence, Option 2.

10. Let B's share be x.

$\therefore$ A's share $= \frac{2x}{9}$

and C's share $= \frac{2x}{9} \times \frac{3}{4} = \frac{x}{6}$

We have

$$\frac{2x}{9} + x + \frac{x}{6} = 1250$$

or, $\frac{4x + 18x + 3x}{18} = 1250$

or, $x = 900$.

Therefore, A's share $= \frac{2x}{9} = \frac{2 \times 900}{9} = 200$,

B's share $= x = 900$ and

C's share $= \frac{x}{6} = \frac{900}{6} = 150$.

Hence, Option 1.

Alternative: It is ONLY in Option 1 that A's share is $\frac{2}{9}$ of B's share. So, mark it confidently, even without solving the question!

11. Even if you know the order in which these 4 became the Prime Minister, you can get the answer. You need NOT know the exact periods of their reign. The order was:

L.B. Shastri, Rajiv Gandhi, P.V. Narasimha Rao and A.B. Vajpayee.

Hence, Option 2.

12. Kathi is a folk dance from Madhya Pradesh. Lavani is a dance from Maharashtra. Jatra is a folk theatre that originated in Bengal, and Garba is a dance from Gujarat.

Hence, Option 2.

13.

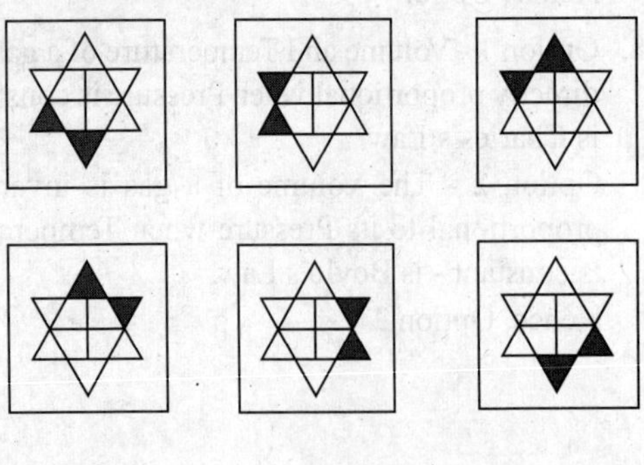

There are 6 such figures embedded in the problem figure! Please notice the shaded regions in the figures above.

Hence, Option 2.

14. **C A T**

3 1 20

$12 = \frac{3 + 1 + 20}{2}$.

L I O N

12 9 15 14

$\therefore$ the code for LION $= \frac{12 + 9 + 15 + 14}{2} = 25$.

Hence, Option 2.

15. $\because$ In 60 minutes, the man walks 5 km

$\therefore$ In 15 minutes, he walks $\frac{5}{4}$ km = 1.25 km = 1250 m

$\therefore$ the length of the bridge is 1250 m.

Hence, Option 3.

16.

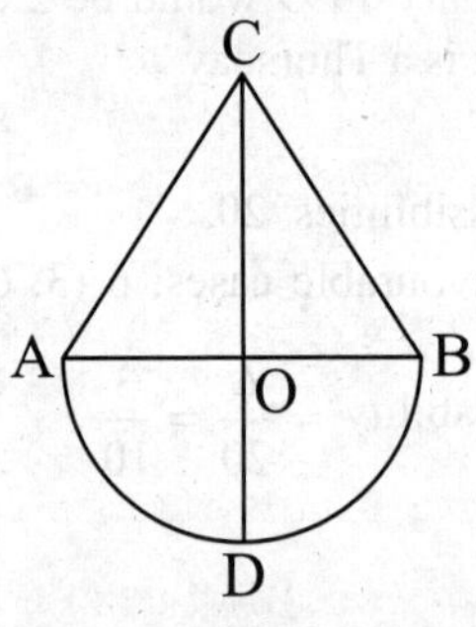

Let AB be a diameter of the hemisphere, O its centre and D the point where the toy touches the ground.

Let C be the vertex of the cone.

We have, AB = 7.

$\therefore$ OA = OB = OD $= \frac{7}{2} = 3.5$ cm.

Also, the height DC of the toy is 15.5 cm.

CO = CD – OD = 15.5 – 3.5 = 12 cm.

So, the height CO of the cone is 12 cm.

The slant height BC of the cone

$= \sqrt{12^2 + (3.5)^2} = \sqrt{144 + 12.25}$

$= \sqrt{156.25} = 12.5$.

The surface area of the toy = the lateral surface area of the hemisphere + the lateral surface area of the cone

$= 2\pi\left(\frac{7}{2}\right)^2 + \pi \times \frac{7}{2} \times 12.5$

$= 2 \times \frac{22}{7} \times \frac{49}{4} + \frac{22}{7} \times \frac{7}{2} \times \frac{25}{2}$

$= 77 + 137.5 = 214.5$.

The cost of polishing $= 214.5 \times \frac{1}{5}$

$= 42.90$.

Alternative: We know the answer has to be a multiple of π, and $\pi = \frac{22}{7}$.

Therefore, the answer should be a multiple of 11 (maybe a fraction multiplied by 11).

Only option 3 has an 11 in it as $42.9 = 11 \times 3.9$.

Hence, Option 3.

17.

Event	Period
Formation of the Indian National Congress	1885
Swadeshi Movement	1905
Chauri Chaura incident	1922
Dandi March	1930
Quit India Movement	1942

Hence, Option 1.

18. Let the quadrilateral be ABCD with points A, B, C and D at (0, –1), (–2, 3), (6, 7) and (8, 3), respectively.

The length of AB $= \sqrt{2^2 + (-4)^2} = \sqrt{20} = 2\sqrt{5}$

The length of BC $= \sqrt{(-8)^2 + (-4)^2} = \sqrt{80} = 4\sqrt{5}$

The length of CD $= \sqrt{(-2)^2 + 4^2} = \sqrt{20} = 2\sqrt{5}$

The length of DA $= \sqrt{8^2 + 4^2} = \sqrt{80} = 4\sqrt{5}$

The slope of AB $= \frac{3-(-1)}{-2-0} = \frac{4}{-2} = -2$

The slope of BC $= \frac{7-3}{6-(-2)} = \frac{4}{8} = \frac{1}{2}$

The slope of CD $= \frac{3-7}{8-6} = \frac{-4}{2} = -2$

The slope of DA $= \frac{-1-3}{0-8} = \frac{-4}{-8} = \frac{1}{2}$

As the product of the slopes of any two adjacent sides is (–1), the adjacent sides are perpendicular to each other.

Also, the opposite sides are equal in length and parallel (they have equal slopes).

Therefore, ABCD is a rectangle.

Hence, Option 4.

19. Most of the Ashokan inscriptions were written in the Prakrit language (in Brahmi script).

20. Just having an atmosphere with oxygen, nitrogen and carbon dioxide is insufficient to support life on a planet. Liquid water, energy, nutrients and heat are also essential to sustain life.

Hence, Option 2.

21. $3x + 5y = 19$ (i)

and

$10x - 3y = 24$ (ii)

Multiplying (i) with 3 and (ii) with 5 and then adding them, we get

$59x = 177$ or, $x = 3$.

Now, $3 \times 3 + 5y = 19$

or, $y = 2$.

Given,

$x = \frac{\alpha}{3}$ or, $\alpha = 3x$.

$y = \frac{\beta}{2}$ or, $\beta = 2y$.

Therefore, $\alpha + \beta = 3x + 2y = 3 \times 3 + 2 \times 2 = 13$.

Hence, Option 2.

22. Let the first term of the AP be a and the common difference be d. Let the nth term be Tn.

We have, $T_3 = a + 2d = 18$ and

$T_{12} = a + 11d = 72$.

Solving these two equations for a and d, we get: a = 6 and d = 6.

Hence, the AP is 6, 12, 18, 24, ---

Hence, option 1.

Alternative: As $T_3 = 3 \times 6 = 18$ and $T_{12} = 12 \times 6 = 72$, this AP is actually the table of 6 in which $T_n = 6n$.
Hence, Option 1.

23. India shares a land border with seven countries. These countries - in descending order of the length of their borders with India - are Bangladesh, China, Pakistan, Nepal, Myanmar, Bhutan and Afghanistan.
Hence, Option 1.
Do NOT get surprised at seeing Afghanistan here! Yes, India shares a small border with Afghanistan that is now in Pakistan-occupied Kashmir (PoK).

24. The total weight of 8 people with an average weight of 49 kg = 8 × 49 = 392 kgs.
When Anita and Kamal board,
the average weight = 49 + 2.8 = 51.8
Number of people = 8 + 2 = 10
Total weight = 51.8 × 10 = 518.
Therefore, the combined weight of the Anita and Kamal = 518 – 392 = 126.

So, their average weight $= \frac{126}{2} = 63$ kg.

Hence, Option 4.
Alternative: The initial average = 49
When 2 new people come in, the average increases by 2.8 kg for 10 people. So, they have brought 2.8 × 10 = 28 kgs above the average weight.

So, each newcomer has carried $\frac{28}{2} = 14$ kg above the average weight of the 8 people.

Hence, the average weight of these two = 49 + 14 = 63 kg.

25.

Festival	Month of Celebration
Pongal (Tamil Nadu)	January
Holi	March (mostly)
Bihu (Bohag Bihu, Assam)	April
Onam (Kerala)	August-September
Christmas	25 December

Hence, Option 2.

26. The mean of the 7 given numbers = 8,
∴ their sum = 7 × 8 = 56.
So, 2 + (2p + 2) + 7 + 13 + 17 + 4 + (p – 1) = 56
or, 3 p + 44 = 56 or, 3p = 12 or, $p = \frac{12}{3} = 4$.
Hence, the numbers are:
2, (2 × 4 + 2), 7, 13, 17, 4 and (4 – 1).
i.e., 2, 10, 7, 13, 17, 4 and 3
Arranging these numbers in ascending order, we get:
2, 3, 4, 7, 10, 13, 17.
As 7 is the middle number, it is the median.
Hence, Option 3.

27. Venus is the Earth's neighbour, and Mercury is the Sun's.
Hence, Option 1.

28. The graph of the movement of the boy is like:

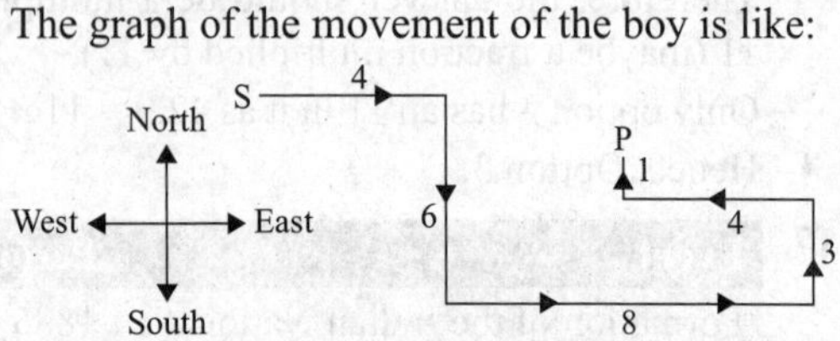

Let's say that he starts from point S and stops at point P.
He clearly faces the North at P.
Hence, Option 3.

29. The 10th schedule of the Indian Constitution contains the provision for the anti-defection law. The 9th schedule includes the list of central and state laws that cannot be challenged in court. The 8th schedule has the official languages, and the 12th schedule includes municipalities' powers, authorities and responsibilities.

31. The restructured arrangement is COSISTGOLOI. The letter T is in the middle of it.
Hence, Option 2.

32. The set (8, 12, 18) has three numbers: the second number is 4 more than the first, and the third number is 6 more than the second. This pattern is only in Option 3.

34. It is given that $\sin\theta + \operatorname{cosec}\theta = 2$.
Let's assume $\sin\theta$ to be x.

$\therefore \operatorname{cosec}\theta = \frac{1}{\sin\theta} = \frac{1}{x}$.

We have $x+\frac{1}{x}=2$ or, $\frac{x^2+1}{x}=2$

or, $x^2+1=2x$ or, $x^2-2x+1=0$ or, $(x^2-1)=0$

or, $x=1$.

$\Rightarrow \text{Sin}\,\theta=1$ and $\text{cosec}\,\theta=\frac{1}{\sin\theta}=\frac{1}{1}=1.$

Now $\sin^2\theta+\text{cosec}^2\theta=1^2+1^2=1+1=2.$

Interestingly, the value of $\sin^n\theta+\text{cosec}^n\theta$ will always be 2 regardless of the value of n if $\text{Sin}\,\theta=1$ (n is a real number).

Hence, Option 3.

36. Let Joseph gifted $12x$, $14x$ and $16x$ rupees to his children aged 12, 14 and 16 respectively.

Also, it is given that

$12x=3000$

or, $x=250$.

His total gift to his 3 children $=12x+14x+16x=42x=42\times250=10500.$

His gift to his wife = 20,000.

Therefore, his total gift to his family = 20000 + 10500 = 30500.

Hence, Option 4.

37. The Indian Rare Earths Limited (IREL) is headquartered in Mumbai. It had its first production facility at Aluva. The Uranium Corporation of India has its headquarters at Jadugoda in the East Singhbhum district of Jharkhand.

Hence, Option 3.

39. Let the sum be P and the rate of interest per annum be r%.

$\therefore$ the amount after 2 years $=P\left(1+\frac{r}{100}\right)^2$

Given that, $P\left(1+\frac{r}{100}\right)^2=P\times\frac{36}{25}$

or, $\left(1+\frac{r}{100}\right)^2=\left(\frac{6}{5}\right)^2$

or, $1+\frac{r}{100}=1.20$

or, $\frac{r}{100}=0.20$

or, $r=20$.

Hence, Option 2.

Alternative: If a sum on compound interest becomes $\frac{36}{25}$ in 2 years, it becomes $\sqrt{\frac{36}{25}}=\frac{6}{5}$ times itself every year. So, the rate of interest is 20%.

40. The minute hand of a clock completes 1 round = 360° in 60 minutes.

$\therefore$ it moves $\frac{360°}{60}=6°$ per minute.

$\therefore$ it will cover $80\times6°=480°$ in 80 minutes (1 hour and 20 minutes).

Hence, Option 2.

41. The question is incorrect, and it was dropped by the CUET-UG. No one shot at General Reginald Dyer. It was Michael O'Dwyer who was shot dead by Sardar Udham Singh in London.

42. 1 Watt-Second = 1 Joule,

1 Kilo Watt-hour (kWh) = 1000 Watt × 3600 Seconds = 3.6×10^6 Joule.

Hence, Option 4.

45.

DF	GJ	KM	NQ	RT	☐
4 6	7 10	11 13	14 17	18 20	
6 – 4 = 2	10 – 7 = 3	13 – 11 = 2	17 – 14 = 3	20 – 18 = 2	

Thus, we see that the difference between the ranks of the letters in the same term are alternately 2 and 3. As the difference between the ranks of R and T is 2, the difference between the ranks of the letters of the next term will be 3, and it is there in only Option 2.

Also, from the 2nd term onwards, the first letter of every term is the next letter of the second letter of the preceding term, and hence, the first letter of the term after RT has to be U.

46. As Rajan has already done $\frac{7}{11}$ of the work, $1-\frac{7}{11}=\frac{4}{11}$ of it is left.

Now, if $\frac{7}{11}$ of the work can be done in 21 days, $\frac{4}{11}$ of it can be done in $\frac{21}{7}\times 4 = 12$ days.

Alternative: If $\frac{7}{11}$ can be done in 21 days, 1 can be done in $\frac{21\times 11}{7} = 33$ days.

So, he needs 33 – 21 = 12 more days. Hence, Option 2.

47.

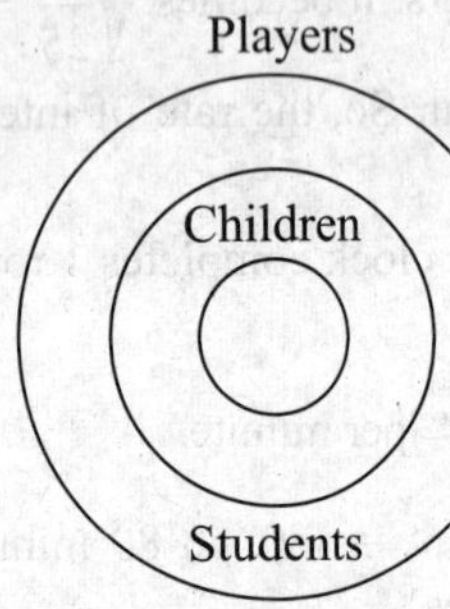

We cannot conclude that all students are children; it is just a possibility.
It is obvious that all children are players.
Hence, option 2.

48. The volume of the new cube = 125 + 64 + 27 = 216 cm^3
$\therefore$ the edge of the new cube $= (216)^{\frac{1}{3}} = 6$ cm.
Hence, Option 3.

49. IKM JLN KMO
We can see that every term has a group of 3 letters that are alternate in the alphabet.
Also, as the first 3 terms start with the letters I, J and K, the 4th term will start with L, and this term will be LNP.
Hence, Option 3.

51. This question was incorrect and was dropped by the CUET-UG.

52. Statements A and C are incorrect.
A number is divisible by 6 if it is divisible by 3 and 2 (NOT 3 or 2).
Also, a number is divisible by 3 if the sum of its digits is divisible by 3.
Hence, Option 2.

53. The question figure has 4 sets of quadrilaterals, each divided into 2 triangles. Thus, it has 8 triangles. Answer figure (1) has only 6 triangles, and (3) and (4) have 4 triangles each. Answer figure (2) has 8 triangles (a combination of 4 quadrilaterals).
Hence, Option 2.

55.

G	O	N	E	and	M	E	D	A	L
4	%	1	*		2	*	7	$	@

On observing the above two codes, it becomes obvious that:
the code for G is 4,
the code for O is %,
the code for L is @ and
the code for D is 7.
Therefore, GOLD will be written as 4%@7.
Hence, Option 3.

56. Let the marked price of a pen be x.
For the retailer,
the cost price of the 20 pens = the marked price of 16 pens = 16x.
the selling price of these 20 pens = 20x (at the marked price).
Therefore, the gain percent

$$= \frac{20x - 16x}{16x}\times 100 = 25$$

Hence, Option 3.

57. Sucheta Kripalani was the first woman chief minister in India. She was the chief minister of Uttar Pradesh from 2 October 1963 to 13 March 1967.
Hence, Option 4.

58. Two angles are supplementary if their sum is 180°.
Let the angle be x.
The supplementary angle of $x = 180° - x$.

As per the question, $x = \frac{3}{7}(180° - x)$

or, $7x = 540° - 3x$

or, $10x = 540°$

or, $x = 54°$.

Hence, Option 1.

Note: we must NOT get confused between the supplementary angles and the complementary angles. Two angles are complementary if their sum is 90°.

Mnemonic: 90° comes before 180° and C (Complementary) comes before S (Supplementary).

59. Given, $243^{3x} = 27^{(4x-1)}$

or, $(3^5)^{3x} = (3^3)^{(4x-1)}$

or, $3^{15x} = 3^{(12x-3)}$

or, $15x = 12x - 3$

or, $3x = -3$

or, $x = -1$.

Now, $4^x = 4^{-1} = \frac{1}{4}$.

Hence, Option 3.

60. If a woman refers to someone as the 'only daughter of my mother', she is certainly referring to herself.

Therefore, she is the mother of the man she is pointing to.

Hence, Option 4.

CUET UG 2023
GENERAL TEST

June
1

INSTRUCTIONS:
1. You need to attempt any 50 out of the 60 questions in 60 minutes.
2. You get 5 marks for a correct response and –1 for an incorrect one. However, there is no reward or penalty for a question not attempted.

1. How many Indian state/s or UT/s share their borders with Afghanistan?
(1) One (2) Two
(3) Three (4) Four

2. Find the point on the X-axis which is equidistant from (2, –5) and (–2, 9).
(1) (–7, 0) (2) (7, 0)
(3) (–5, 0) (4) (5, 0)

3. Which planet is the Titan the largest natural satellite of?
(1) Venus (2) Saturn
(3) Pluto (4) Neptune

4. Moon is also known as the ___________.
(1) Fossil Planet (2) Blue Planet
(3) Red Planet (4) Evening Planet

5. Which option will give the same relationship on both sides:

SNAKE: REPTILE: :
(1) Fish: Water (2) Man: Mammal
(3) Owl: Fly (4) Cow: Grass

6. In ΔABC, right angled at B, if AB = 4 cm and ∠C = 60°, then the length of AC is:
(1) $\frac{8\sqrt{3}}{3}$ cm (2) $\frac{2}{\sqrt{3}}$ cm
(3) $\sqrt{3}$ cm (4) $\frac{1}{\sqrt{3}}$ cm

7. Given below are two statements: one is labelled as Assertion (A), and the other is labelled as Reason (R).

Assertion (A): Mercury is the second farthest planet from the Sun.

Reason (R): Mercury is the smallest planet in the entire solar system.

In the light of the above statements, choose the most appropriate answer from the options given below:
(1) Both (A) and (R) are correct, and (R) is the correct explanation of (A).
(2) Both (A) and (R) are correct, but (R) is not the correct explanation of (A).
(3) (A) is correct, but (R) is not correct.
(4) (A) is not correct, but (R) is correct.

8. In the following question, choose one option that is similar to the numbers in the given set:
(273, 365, 367)
(1) (246, 257, 358)
(2) (145, 235, 325)
(3) (143, 253, 246)
(4) (233, 343, 345)

9. In a class of 39 students, there are 26 girls with an average weight of 42 kg. If the average weight of the whole class is 48 kg, then what is the average weight of the boys?
(1) 54 kg (2) 66 kg
(3) 60 kg (4) 62 kg

10. Where is the Chilika Lake situated?
(1) Jammu & Kashmir
(2) Rajasthan
(3) Odisha
(4) Himachal Pradesh

11. The two numbers whose arithmetic mean is 34 and geometric mean 16 are:

(1) 60, 8 (2) 34, 34
(3) 64, 4 (4) 40, 28

12. Choose the correct alternative that will continue the same pattern.

1, 1, 4, 7, 22, 43, ?

(1) 101 (2) 111
(3) 121 (4) 130

13. The simplified value of $\dfrac{\frac{1}{3}\div 2+10}{\frac{1}{3}\times 2+10}$ is:

(1) $\dfrac{61}{64}$ (2) $\dfrac{61}{24}$
(3) $\dfrac{1}{384}$ (4) $\dfrac{31}{24}$

14. In which year did the Indian Space Research Organization (ISRO) successfully launch "Chandrayaan- I"?

(1) 22nd October 2009
(2) 22nd October 2010
(3) 22nd October 2008
(4) 22nd July 2019

15. Select the pair in which the numbers are similarly related as in the given pair.

8:448:: _______?

(1) 9:729 (2) 7:1029
(3) 6:216 (4) 11:1210

16. Match **List I** with **List II**.

List I (Nickname)	List II (Eminent Person)
(A) Deenbandhu	(I) Khan Abdul Ghaffar Khan
(B) Andhra Kesari	(II) C.R. Das
(C) Deshbandhu	(III) T. Prakasam
(D) Frontier Gandhi	(IV) C.F. Andrews

Choose the most appropriate answer from the options given below:

(1) (A)-(IV), (B)-(III), (C)-(II), (D)-(I)
(2) (A)-(I), (B)-(III), (C)-(II), (D)-(IV)
(3) (A)-(I), (B)-(III), (C)-(IV), (D)-(II)
(4) (A)-(II), (B)-(I), (C)-(IV), (D)-(III)

17. In a fort, there was a food provision for 120 men for 200 days. After 5 days, 30 men moved to another place. How long will the remaining food last?

(1) 140 days (2) 260 days
(3) 300 days (4) 290 days

18. Ram, Mohan and Sohan started a business with a total capital of ₹50000. Mohan invested ₹10000 less than Ram and ₹8000 more than Sohan. What is Mohan's share of profit in a total profit of ₹20000?

(1) ₹6400 (2) ₹3200
(3) ₹2800 (4) ₹7200

19. A man makes his onward journey at 16 km/hr and return journey at 28 km/hr. What is his average speed during the entire journey (correct to 2 decimal places)?

(1) 22 km/hr (2) 20.36 km/hr
(3) 32.15 km/hr (4) 30.56 km/hr

20. A student has to obtain 33% of the total marks to pass an examination. She got 148 marks and failed by 50 marks. The maximum marks for the examination is

(1) 400 (2) 450
(3) 500 (4) 600

21. On which date is India's National Youth Festival celebrated on the Birthday of Swami Vivekananda?

(1) 5 January (2) 12 January
(3) 15 January (4) 2 February

22. Which Blood Group in humans is a Universal donor?

(1) A Group (2) AB Group
(3) O Group (4) B Group

23. A sum becomes its double in 5 years on simple interest. What is the rate of interest?

(1) 5% (2) 10%
(3) 15% (4) 20%

24. In the following question, select the related option from the given alternatives:

DXH:4X8::MXQ: ?

(1) MX18 (2) 12X16
(3) 13X17 (4) 12X17

25.

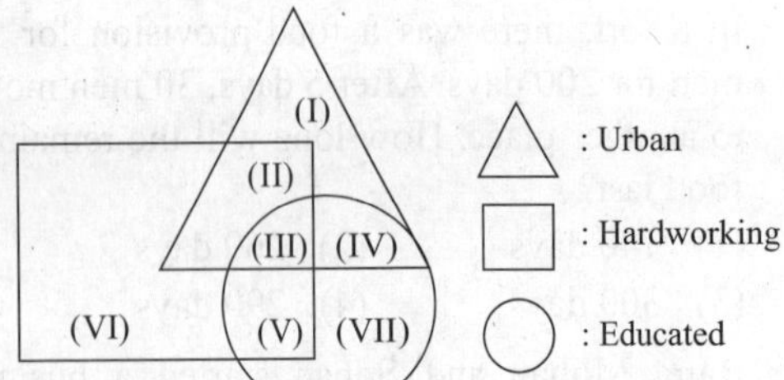

Which part shows the urban educated who are not hardworking?
(1) II (2) I
(3) IV (4) V

26. In which year was the "One Nation, One FASTag Scheme" implemented?
(1) 1 December 2020
(2) 1 December 2019
(3) 1 December 2021
(4) 1 December 2022

27. During the revolt of 1857, who was the loyal commander of Nana Sahib from Kanpur?
(1) Liaqat Ali
(2) Amar Singh
(3) Bakht Khan
(4) Tantiya Tope

28. What is the pH value of human blood, which is basic in nature?
(1) 9.5 (2) 10.4
(3) 7.4 (4) 8.7

29. The speed of sound will be the fastest in ________.
(1) iron bar (2) water
(3) hilltop (4) vacuum

30. When is the World Statistics Day celebrated?
(1) 13 December (2) 22 October
(3) 20 October (4) 9 December

31. Five Boys, P, Q, R, S and T, are sitting around a pentagonal table, and their faces are towards each other. P is between Q and R. S is to the left of T. Q is to the left of S. Who is to the right of P?
(1) T (2) Q
(3) R (4) S

32. Cathode Rays consist of ________.
(1) Neutrons (2) Alpha Particles
(3) Electrons (4) Protons

33. Read the following information carefully and answer the question given below:
Anil and Kamal are good at Hockey and Volleyball. Suresh and Anil are good at Hockey and Baseball. Gopal and Kamal are good at Cricket and Volleyball. Suresh, Gopal and Mahesh are good at Football and Baseball.
Who is good at Hockey, Cricket and Volleyball?
(1) Gopal (2) Mahesh
(3) Anil (4) Kamal

34. Choose the correct mirror image of fig. (X) from amongst the four alternatives (A), (B), (C) and (D) given along with it.

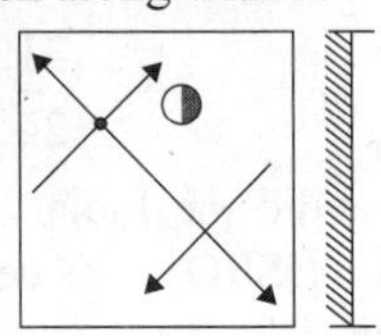

(X)

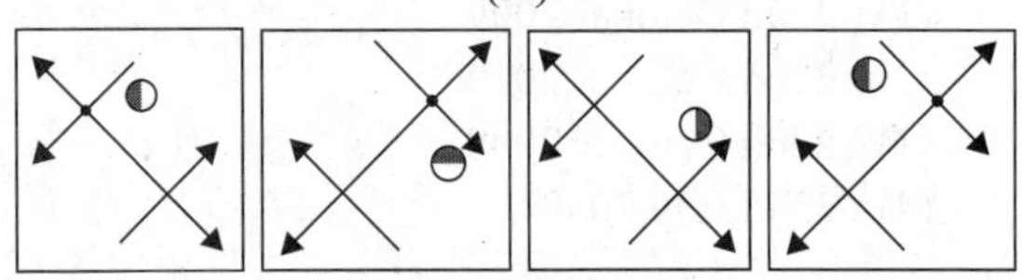

(A) (B) (C) (D)

(1) (A) (2) (B)
(3) (C) (4) (D)

35. Find the curved surface area of a cone having a base diameter of 42 cm and a height of 20 cm. $\left(\pi = \frac{22}{7}\right)$
(1) 1642 cm^2 (2) 1876 cm^2
(3) 1914 cm^2 (4) 2016 cm^2

36. Match **List I** with **List II**.

List I (Books)	List II (Authors)
(A) Train to Pakistan	(I) Salman Rushdie
(B) Languages of Truth	(II) APJ Abdul Kalam
(C) The Righteous Life	(III) Khushwant Singh
(D) It Is Always Possible	(IV) Kiran Bedi

Choose the most appropriate answer from the options given below:
(1) (A)-(I), (B)-(III), (C)-(IV), (D)-(II)
(2) (A)-(II), (B)-(IV), (C)-(III), (D)-(I)
(3) (A)-(III), (B)-(I), (C)-(II), (D)-(IV)
(4) (A)-(III), (B)-(II), (C)-(IV), (D)-(I)

37. Which among the following is not a type of direct tax?
(1) Sales Tax (2) Property Tax
(3) Stamp Duties (4) Land Revenue

38. From the given figure, find the relation between x, y and z if AB, EF and DC are perpendicular to BC.

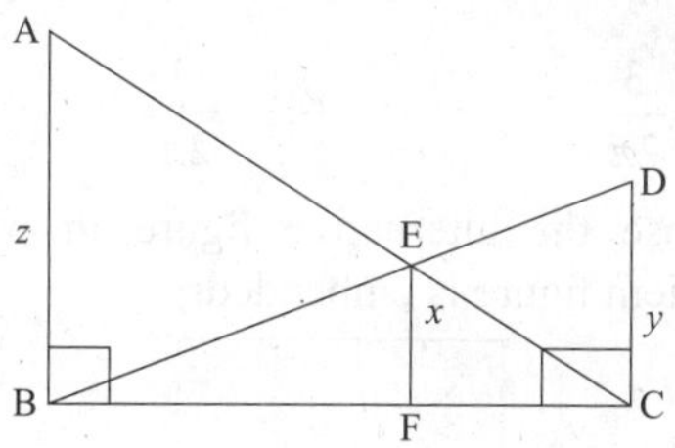

(1) $xyz = x + y + z$ (2) $zx = y(x+z)$
(3) $xy = z(x+y)$ (4) $yz = x(y+z)$

39. Figure out how the pattern would appear when the transparent sheet is folded at the dotted line from amongst the four alternatives.

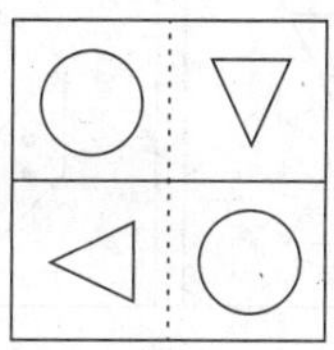
(X)

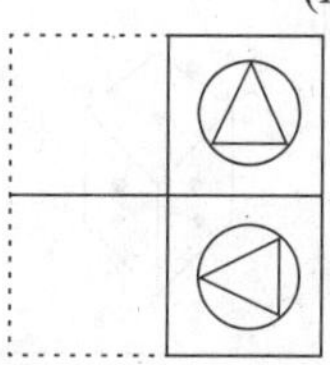
(A)

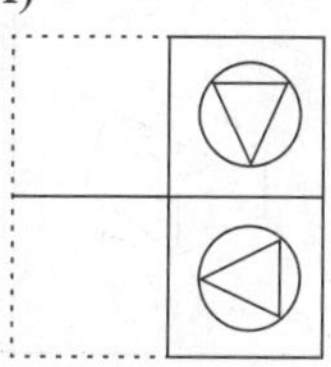
(B)

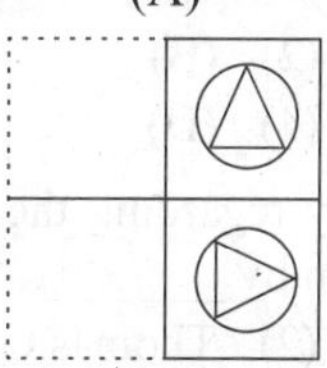
(C)

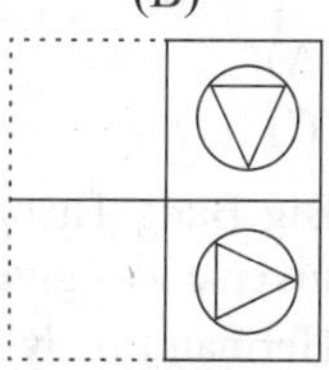
(D)

(1) (A) (2) (B)
(3) (C) (4) (D)

40. Match **List I** with **List II**.

List I (International Line)	List II (Between Two Countries)
(A) Maginot Line	(I) North Korea and South Korea
(B) Durand Line	(II) France and Germany
(C) 38th Parallel	(III) USA and Canada
(D) 49th Parallel	(IV) Pakistan and Afghanistan

Choose the most appropriate answer from the options given below:
(1) (A)-(II), (B)-(IV), (C)-(I), (D)-(III)
(2) (A)-(II), (B)-(III), (C)-(IV), (D)-(I)
(3) (A)-(I), (B)-(IV), (C)-(III), (D)-(II)
(4) (A)-(I), (B)-(II), (C)-(IV), (D)-(III)

41. Which of the following is the maximum speed?
(1) 35 m/sec. (2) 2500 m/min.
(3) 90 km/hr. (4) 98000 m/hr.

42. If it were a Friday on January 1, 1998, then January 1, 2000, would have been:
(1) Monday (2) Wednesday
(3) Friday (4) Sunday

43. An artificial language has been given for some sentences:
'zongo talb' means 'Leave Application'.
'txlo zongo' means 'Sunday Leave'.
'pokto zongo' means 'Festival Leave'.
Which of the following could be the artificial language for 'Indian Festival'?
(1) bueot talb (2) pokto bueot
(3) beolk talb (4) zongo txlo

44. Half-life of C^{14} is around ________ years.
(1) 4700 (2) 5700
(3) 5000 (4) 4500

45. Statements:
Some Bottles are Papers.
Some Papers are Pens.
No Pen is a Pencil.

Conclusions:

(I) Some Bottles are Pencils.

(II) No Bottle is a Pencil.

(III) Some Bottles are Pens.

(1) Only (I) follows.

(2) Only (II) follows.

(3) Only (III) follows.

(4) Either (I) or (II) follows.

46. Facing a man in the eye, Aman said, "Your son is my son's uncle". How is the man related to Aman?

(1) grandfather (2) brother

(3) father (4) uncle

47. A father's age is thrice the age of his daughter. Ten years ago, his age was five times his daughter's age. Find the present age of the father.

(1) 50 years (2) 60 years

(3) 45 years (4) 40 years

48. The following pie chart shows a student's study time in different subjects in a day.

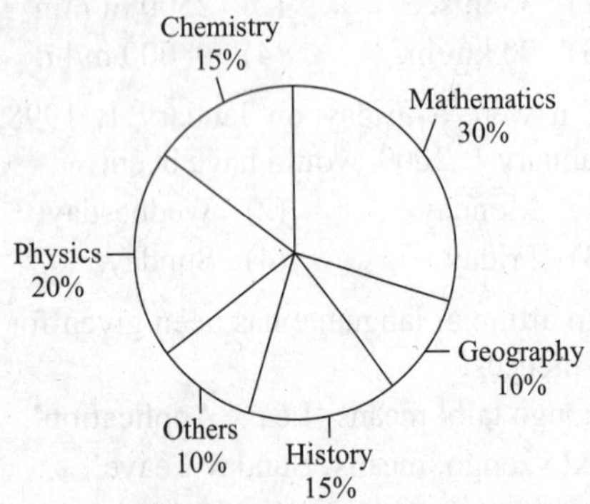

If the total time spent to study History and Chemistry is 4 hours and 30 minutes, then the student studied Physics for:

(1) 1.5 hours (2) 2.9 hours

(3) 2 hours (4) 3 hours

49. When the minute hand covers a distance of 1 hour and 10 minutes, then what is the angular distance covered by it?

(1) 400° (2) 410°

(3) 420° (4) 430°

50. The sides of a triangle are in the ratio 8:9:10, and its perimeter is 270 cm. What is its area?

(1) $175\sqrt{17}$ cm^2 (2) $45\sqrt{231}$ cm^2

(3) $225\sqrt{231}$ cm^2 (4) $375\sqrt{15}$ cm^2

51. By looking in a mirror, it appears that it is 6:30 on the clock. What is the actual time?

(1) 5:30 (2) 6:00

(3) 4:30 (4) 6:30

52. If a rectangular sheet of paper of length 6 cm and width 3 cm is rolled to form a cylinder with a height equal to the width of the paper, then what is the base radius of the cylinder (in cm)?

(1) $\frac{6}{\pi}$ (2) $\frac{3}{\pi}$

(3) $\frac{3}{2\pi}$ (4) $\frac{9}{2\pi}$

53. Choose the alternative figure in which the problem figure is embedded:

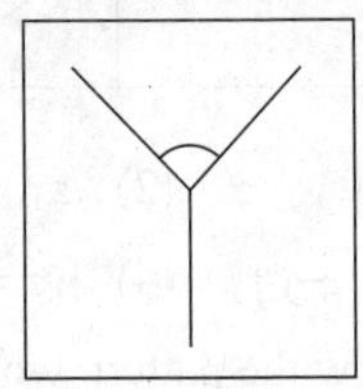

(X)

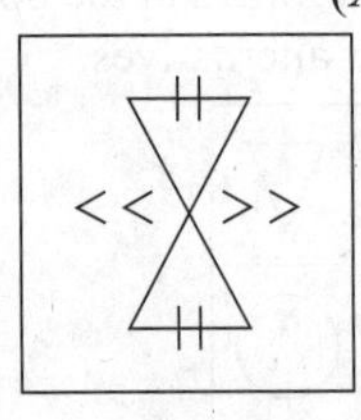

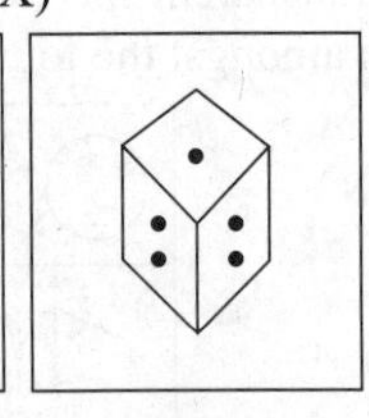

(A) (B)

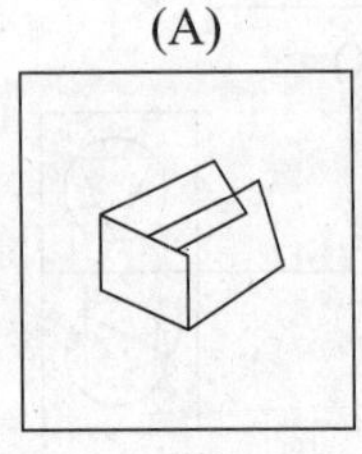

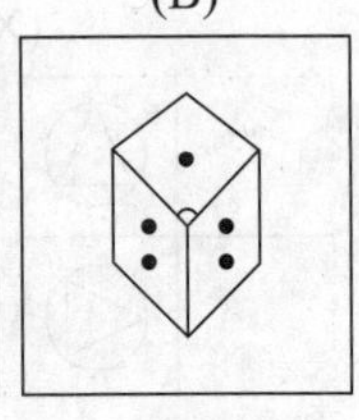

(C) (D)

(1) (A) (2) (B)

(3) (C) (4) (D)

54. The Big Bang Theory regarding the origin of the universe was given by _______.

(1) Herman Bondy (2) Thomas Gold

(3) Georges Lemaitre (4) Dr. Allen Sundes

55. In which one of the following, pq = 3?

(1) 2p:3 = 1:q
(2) 2:p = 3q:1
(3) 3:p = q:2
(4) 3:p = q:1

56. The salaries of Ravi, Anil and Kavita are in the ratio 1: 3: 6. If their salaries are increased by 5%, 10% and 15%, respectively, then what is the new ratio of their salaries?

(1) 1:2:3 (2) 7:22:46
(3) 7:11:23 (4) 7:22:15

57. Shivani moved a distance of 45 meters towards the north. She then turned to the left and walked for about 15 meters, turned left again and walked 50 meters. Finally, she turned to the right at an angle of 45°. In which direction was she moving finally?

(1) North-West (2) South-West
(3) North-East (4) South

58. The probability that a man will live for more than 10 years is $\frac{1}{4}$, and the probability that his wife will live for more than 10 years is $\frac{1}{3}$. The probability that none of them will live for more than 10 years is

(1) $\frac{5}{12}$ (2) $\frac{7}{12}$
(3) $\frac{1}{2}$ (4) $\frac{11}{12}$

59. What is 'Blue Moon'?

(1) Moon during total lunar eclipse
(2) a sequence of four total lunar eclipse
(3) second full moon of the two full moons in a month
(4) full moon closest to the earth

60. Identify the diagram that best represents the relationship among the classes given below:
Animal, Land Animal, Sea Animal

(1) 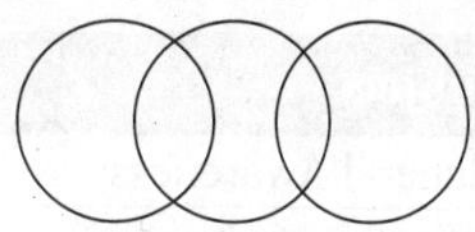

(2) 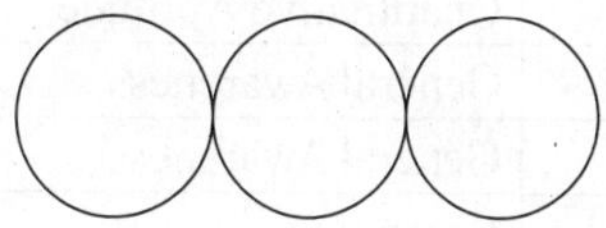

(3) 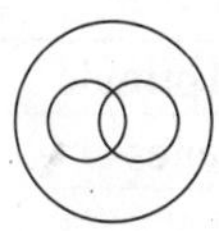

(4) 

Answer Key

1. (1) 2. (1) 3. (2) 4. (1) 5. (2) 6. (1) 7. (4) 8. (1) 9. (3) 10. (3)
11. (3) 12. (4) 13. (1) 14. (3) 15. (4) 16. (1) 17. (2) 18. (1) 19. (2) 20. (4)
21. (2) 22. (3) 23. (4) 24. (3) 25. (3) 26. (2) 27. (4) 28. (3) 29. (1) 30. (3)
31. (2) 32. (3) 33. (4) 34.* all options were incorrect 35. (3) 36. (3)
37.** 1 as well as 3 38. (4) 39. (4) 40. (1) 41. (2) 42. (4) 43. (2) 44. (2) 45. (4)
46.*** 3 as well as 4 47. (2) 48. (4) 49. (3) 50. (3) 51. (1) 52. (2) 53. (4) 54. (3)
55. (4) 56. (2) 57. (2) 58. (3) 59. (3) 60. (3)

*34. All options were incorrect, and hence, this question was dropped. The following figure is the correct answer:

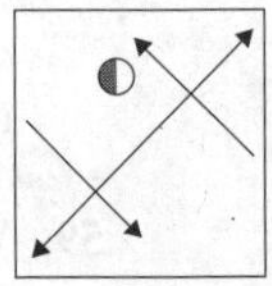

(D)

**37. Sales tax and stamp duties are both indirect taxes, and hence, both these options were accepted as the correct answer.

***46. The answer can be father as well as uncle, and hence, both options 3 and 4 were accepted as the correct answers. In fact, the answer can be father-in-law, too, but that is not among the options.

Classification of Questions

Question No.	Subject	Topic	Level of Difficulty
1.	General Awareness	Geography	Easy
2.	Quantitative Aptitude	Coordinate Geometry	Easy
3.	General Awareness	Geography	Medium
4.	General Awareness	Geography	Difficult
5.	Reasoning	Analogy (science-based)	Easy
6.	Quantitative Aptitude	Trigonometry	Easy
7.	General Awareness	Geography	Medium
8.	Reasoning	Number Pattern	Medium
9.	Quantitative Aptitude	Averages	Easy
10.	General Awareness	Geography	Easy
11.	Quantitative Aptitude	Algebra (AP and GP)	Easy
12.	Reasoning	Number Series	Easy
13.	Quantitative Aptitude	Simplification	Easy
14.	General Awareness	Science & Tech	Medium
15.	Reasoning	Analogy (Number-based)	Medium
16.	General Awareness	History	Easy
17.	Quantitative Aptitude	Time, Speed & Distance	Easy
18.	Quantitative Aptitude	Partnership	Easy
19.	Quantitative Aptitude	Time, Speed & Distance	Easy
20.	Quantitative Aptitude	Percentages	Easy
21.	General Awareness	Art & Culture	Easy
22.	General Awareness	Science (Biology)	Easy
23.	Quantitative Aptitude	Simple Interest	Easy
24.	Reasoning	Analogy (Alphanumeric)	Easy
25.	Reasoning	Venn Diagram	Easy

Question No.	Subject	Topic	Level of Difficulty
26.	General Awareness	Current Affairs	Medium
27.	General Awareness	History	Easy
28.	General Awareness	Science (Chemistry)	Easy
29.	General Awareness	Science (Physics)	Medium
30.	General Awareness	Miscellaneous	Difficult
31.	Reasoning	Circular Arrangement	Easy
32.	General Awareness	Science (Physics)	Medium
33.	Reasoning	Miscellaneous	Easy
34.	Reasoning	Non-verbal	Easy
35.	Quantitative Aptitude	Mensuration	Medium
36.	General Awareness	Books & Authors	Medium
37.	General Awareness	Economics	Easy
38.	Quantitative Aptitude	Geometry	Medium
39.	Reasoning	Non-verbal	Easy
40.	General Awareness	Geography	Easy
41.	Quantitative Aptitude	Time, Speed & Distance	Easy
42.	Quantitative Aptitude	Calendars	Easy
43.	Reasoning	Coding	Easy
44.	General Awareness	Science (Chemistry)	Difficult
45.	Reasoning	Syllogism	Easy
46.	Reasoning	Blood Relations	Easy
47.	Quantitative Aptitude	Algebra (Linear Equations)	Easy
48.	Data Interpretation	Pie Chart	Easy
49.	Quantitative Aptitude	Clocks	Easy
50.	Quantitative Aptitude	Mensuration	Medium
51.	Reasoning	Mirror Image	Easy
52.	Quantitative Aptitude	Mensuration	Medium
53.	Reasoning	Non-verbal	Easy
54.	General Awareness	Science (Physics)	Difficult
55.	Quantitative Aptitude	Ratios	Easy
56.	Quantitative Aptitude	Ratios	Easy
57.	Reasoning	Directions	Medium
58.	Quantitative Aptitude	Probability	Easy
59.	General Awareness	Geography	Difficult
60.	Reasoning	Venn Diagram	Medium

The no. of questions in General Awareness: 21
The no. of questions in Quantitative Aptitude: 21
The no. of questions in Data Interpretation: 1
The no. of questions in Reasoning: 17

Explanation to Select Questions

1. The only state/UT of India that shares its borders with Afghanistan is Jammu and Kashmir. The part of Jammu and Kashmir that shares its borders with Afghanistan is in Pakistan-Occupied Kashmir (POK).
Hence, Option 1.

2. A point on the x-axis has its y-coordinate zero. Let this point, equidistant from (2, –5) and (–2, 9), be $(a, 0)$.
The distance between (2, –5) and $(a, 0)$
$= \sqrt{(2-a)^2 + (-5-0)^2} = \sqrt{(2-a)^2 + 25}$
The distance between (–2, 9) and (a, 0)
$= \sqrt{(-2-a)^2 + (9-0)^2} = \sqrt{(2+a)^2 + 81}$
But, $\sqrt{(2-a)^2 + 25} = \sqrt{(2+a)^2 + 81}$
or, $(2-a)^2 + 25 = (2+a)^2 + 81$
or, $(2+a)^2 - (2-a)^2 = 25 - 81$
or, $8a = -56$ or, $a = -7$.
Thus, the required point is (–7, 0).
Hence, Option 1.

6. 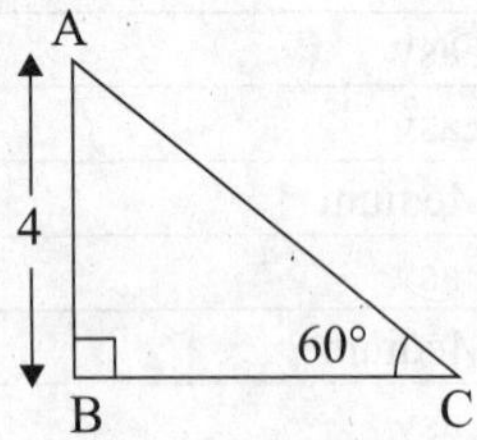

In ΔABC,
$\text{Sin } 60° = \frac{4}{AC}$
or, $\frac{\sqrt{3}}{2} = \frac{4}{AC}$
or, $AC = \frac{4 \times 2}{\sqrt{3}} = \frac{8}{\sqrt{3}} = \frac{8\sqrt{3}}{3}$.
Hence, Option 1.

7. The Assertion is incorrect, as Mercury is the nearest planet to the Sun.
Hence, Option 4.

8. The sum of the digits of 273 is 12; the sum of the digits of 365 is 14, and the sum of the digits of 358 is 16. This pattern is only in the numbers in the set in Option 1.
The sum of the digits of 246 is 12; the sum of the digits of 257 is 14, and the sum of the digits of 358 is 16.
Hence, Option 1.

9. The number of students in the class = 39
The number of girls in the class = 26
∴ the number of boys = 39 – 26 = 13
The average weight of the 26 girls = 42 kg
The total weight of the 26 girls = 42 × 26 kg
The average weight of the 39 students = 48 kg
The total weight of the 39 students = 39 × 48 kg
Total weight of the boys = Total weight of all 39 students – total weight of the 26 girls = $39 \times 48 - 26 \times 42 = 13(3 \times 48 - 2 \times 42)$
Therefore, the average weight of the 13 boys
$= \frac{13(3 \times 48 - 2 \times 42)}{13} = 3 \times 48 - 2 \times 42$
$= 144 - 84 = 60$.
Hence, Option 3.
Shortcut: There are 39 students in the class, of which 26 are girls and 13 are boys. For the purpose of calculating the average weight of the boys, we can just take the ratio of the numbers 39, 26, and 13 for ease of calculation.
So, we can say there are 3 students: 2 girls and a boy.
The average weight of the boy
$= \frac{3 \times 48 - 2 \times 42}{1} = 144 - 84 = 60.$

11. Let the numbers be a and b.
We have, $\frac{a+b}{2} = 34$ and $\sqrt{ab} = 16$.
$\Rightarrow a + b = 68$ and $ab = 256$
$\Rightarrow a + \frac{256}{a} = 68$
or, $a^2 + 256 = 68a$

or, $a^2 - 68a + 256 = 0$

or, $a^2 - 4a - 64a + 256 = 0$

or, $a(a-4) - 64(a-4) = 0$

or, $(a-64)(a-4) = 0$

or, $a = 4, 64$

When $a = 4$, $b = \frac{256}{4} = 64$.

When $a = 64$, $b = \frac{256}{64} = 4$.

Thus, the numbers are 4 and 64.

Alternative: We are actually looking for two numbers such that their sum is 68 and the product is 256. Try out the options. In all the options, the sum of the numbers is 68, but the product is 256 only in Option 3.

12. This is how the pattern is:
$(1 \times 2) - 1 = 1$,
$(1 \times 3) + 1 = 4$,
$(4 \times 2) - 1 = 7$,
$(7 \times 3) + 1 = 22$,
$(22 \times 2) - 1 = 43$ and
$(43 \times 3) + 1 = 130$.
Hence, Option 4.

15. $448 = 8^3 - 8^2$ and $1210 = 11^3 - 11^2$.
Hence, Option 4.

16. T. Prakasam was the first CM of the Andhra State in 1953. Andhra State should NOT be confused with Andhra Pradesh, which came into existence on 1 November 1956.
The answer is Option 1.

17. The total food = 120×200 man-day.
The food exhausted by 120 men in 5 days = $120 \times 5 = 600$ man-days.
Food left = $120 \times 200 - 600 = 23400$ man-days.
The number of men left after 5 days = $120 - 30 = 90$.
The number of days the remaining food will last $= \frac{23400}{90} = 260$.
Hence, Option 2.
Note: 1 man-day is the amount of food eaten by 1 man in 1 day.

18. Let's assume that Ram invested Rs. x.
Therefore, Mohan invested $x - 10000$ and Sohan invested $x - 10000 - 8000 = x - 18000$.
Now, $x + x - 10000 + x - 18000 = 50000$.
or, $3x - 28000 = 50000$
or, $3x = 50000 + 28000 = 78000$
or, $x = \frac{78000}{3} = 26000$.
Mohan invested $= x - 10000 = 26000 - 10000 = 16000$.
Therefore, Mohan's proportion in the investment $= \frac{16000}{50000} = \frac{8}{25}$.
Hence, Mohan's profit $= \frac{8}{25} \times 20000 =$ ₹6400.
Hence, Option 1.

19. Let the one-side distance be d km.
The time taken in the onward journey $= \frac{d}{16}$ hours
The time taken in the backward journey $= \frac{d}{28}$ hours
The total distance travelled $= d + d = 2d$.
The total time taken
$$= \frac{d}{16} + \frac{d}{28} = \frac{7d + 4d}{112} = \frac{11d}{112}.$$
The average speed
$$= \frac{2d}{\frac{11d}{112}} = \frac{2d \times 112}{11d} = \frac{224}{11} = 20.36 \text{ km/hr.}$$
Hence, Option 2.

Shortcut: If you go to a place at a speed of x and come back at a speed of y, your average speed for the overall journey $= \frac{2xy}{x+y}$.
Applying the formula here:
The average speed
$$= \frac{2 \times 16 \times 28}{16 + 28} = \frac{32 \times 28}{44}$$
$$= \frac{32 \times 7}{11} = \frac{224}{11} = 20.36 \text{ km/hr.}$$

20. The student scored 148 but failed by 50 marks. Therefore, the pass marks = 148 + 50 = 198 marks.

Also, as per the question,
the pass marks is 33% of the total marks.
So, 198 is 33% of the total marks.

$\Rightarrow$ Total marks $= 198 \times \frac{100}{33} = 600$.

Hence, Option 4.

22. The 'O' Group is the universal donor, and the 'AB' Group is the universal acceptor of blood.
Hence, Option 3.

23. Let the sum be ₹100.
The amount after 5 years = 100 × 2 = 200.

$\therefore$ the interest = 200 – 100 = 100

$$\text{Rate} = \frac{\text{S.I.} \times 100}{\text{Principal} \times \text{Time}} = \frac{100 \times 100}{100 \times 5} = 20\%.$$

Hence, Option 4.

Shortcut: If the sum doubles itself in 5 years, 100% of the sum is created in 5 years. Therefore, $\frac{100\%}{5} = 20\%$ is created in 1 year.

$\Rightarrow$ rate of interest = 20%.

24. D is the 4th and H is the 8th letter in the alphabet. Similarly, M is the 13th, and Q is the 17th letter in the alphabet.
Hence, Option 3.

29. Sound CANNOT travel in a vacuum. Sound travels the fastest in solid, then in liquid, and then in gas.
Hence, Option 1.

30. The World Statistics Day is celebrated on October 20, every five years. It will next be celebrated on 20 October 2025.
Hence, Option 3.

31. As S is to the left of T and Q is to the left of S, they will be sitting in the following order:

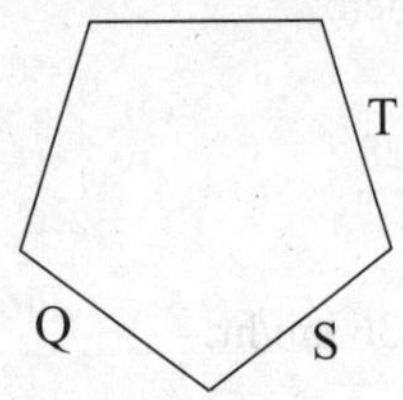

We also know that P is between Q and R.
Hence, the arrangement can be completed in only one way:

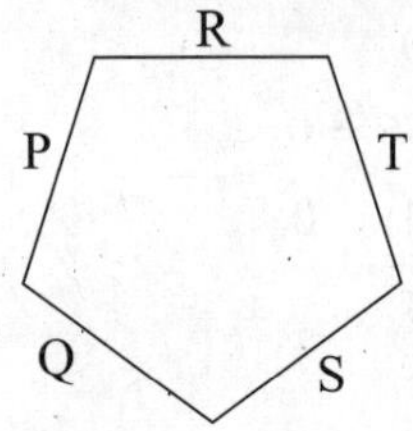

It is Q who is to the right of P.
Hence, Option 2.

34. All options for this question are incorrect. It was dropped by the CUET-UG.

35.

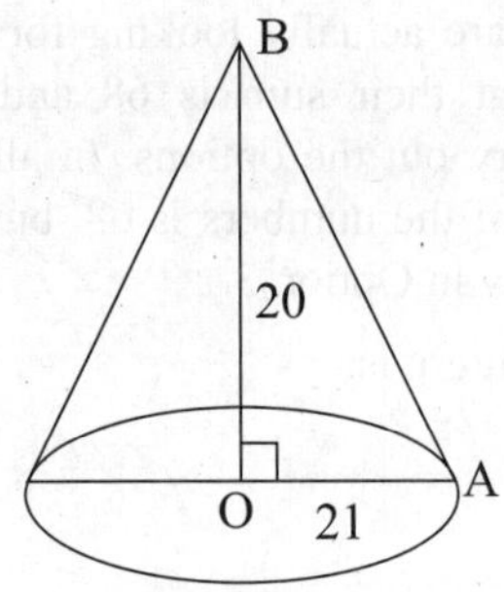

The base diameter of the cone = 42 cm

The base radius r of the cone $= \frac{42}{2} = 21$ cm

The height of the cone = 20 cm

The slant height l of the cone $= \sqrt{20^2 + 21^2} = 29$.

The lateral surface area of the cone

$= \pi r l = \frac{22}{7} \times 21 \times 29 = 1914 \text{ cm}^2$.

Hence, Option 3.

Shortcut: we know the lateral surface area of a cone $= \pi r l$, where r is the base radius and l slant height.

As $\pi r l$ is a multiple of π, it should be a multiple of 11 as $\pi = \frac{11 \times 2}{7}$.

Among the options, only Option 3 (1914) is a multiple of 11.

38.

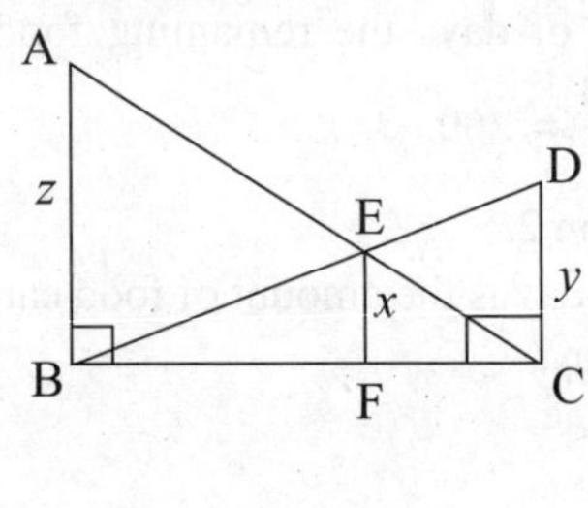

As ΔCFE is similar to ΔCBA,

$$\frac{EF}{AB} = \frac{CF}{CB}$$

$$\text{or, } \frac{x}{z} = \frac{CF}{CB}$$

$$\text{or, } CF = CB\left(\frac{x}{z}\right) \qquad \text{(i)}$$

Now, as ΔBFE is similar to ΔBCD,

$$\frac{FE}{CD} = \frac{BF}{BC} \text{ or, } \frac{x}{y} = \frac{BF}{BC}$$

$$\text{or, } BF = BC\left(\frac{x}{y}\right) \qquad \text{(ii)}$$

Adding (i) and (ii), we get:

$$CF + BF = BC\left(\frac{x}{z} + \frac{x}{y}\right)$$

$$\text{or, } BC = BC\left(\frac{x}{z} + \frac{x}{y}\right)$$

$$\text{or, } \frac{x}{z} + \frac{x}{y} = 1$$

$$\text{or, } x\left(\frac{1}{y} + \frac{1}{z}\right) = 1$$

$$\text{or, } x\left(\frac{y+z}{yz}\right) = 1$$

$$\text{or, } x = \frac{yz}{y+z}$$

$$\text{or, } yz = x(y+z).$$

Hence, Option 4.

41. Option 1: 35 m/sec = 35 × 60 m/min
= 2100 m/min

Option 2: 2500 m/min

Option 3: 90 km/hr = $\frac{90000}{60}$ m/min
= 1500 m/min

Option 4: 98000 m/hr = $\frac{98000}{60}$ m/min
= $1633\frac{1}{3}$ m/min

Hence, Option 2 is the maximum.

42. There are 2 non-leap years between January 1, 1998 and January 1, 2000.
Two non-leap years have 2 odd days.
As January 1, 1998, is a Friday, January 1, 2000, will be 2 days after a Friday, that is a Sunday.
Hence, Option 4.
Important: Though the year 2000 was a leap year, its extra day (29 February) does NOT come between 1 January 1998 and 1 January 2000.
Hence, the number of odd days will not be impacted by this.
Do NOT commit the blunder of going for Option 1 (Monday).
Option 1 is a good trap!

43. Zongo talb: Leave Application (i)
Txlo Zongo: Sunday Leave (ii)
Pokto Zongo: Festival Leave (iii)
On comparing (i) and (ii), it is obvious that 'Zongo' is the code for 'Leave'. So, in (iii) 'Pokto' must be the code for 'Festival'. Therefore, the code for 'Indian Festival' must contain 'Pokto', and it is there only in Option 2.

45.

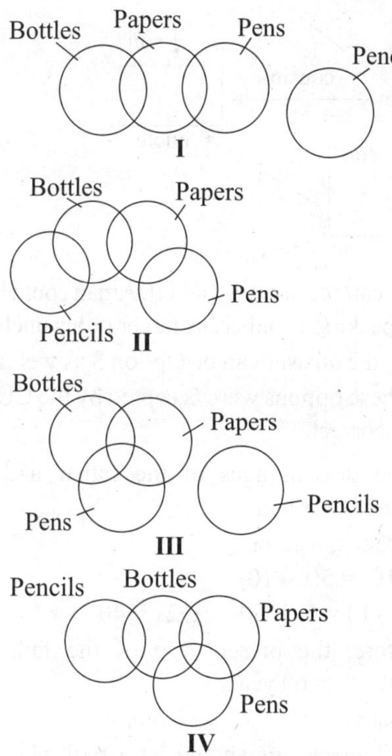

'Some Bottles are Pencils' is just a possibility, as you can see in Figures II and IV; it cannot be concluded.
'No Bottle is Pencil' is just a possibility, as you can see in Figures I and III. Even this cannot be concluded.

'Some Bottles are Pens' is also just a possibility. It may be there (III and IV) and may NOT be there (I and II). It cannot be concluded.

As statements I and II are exhaustive, one of them will certainly follow.

Hence, Option 4.

46.

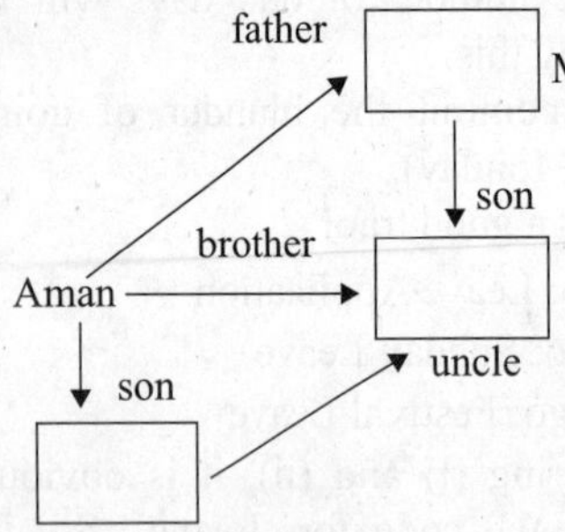

Case I

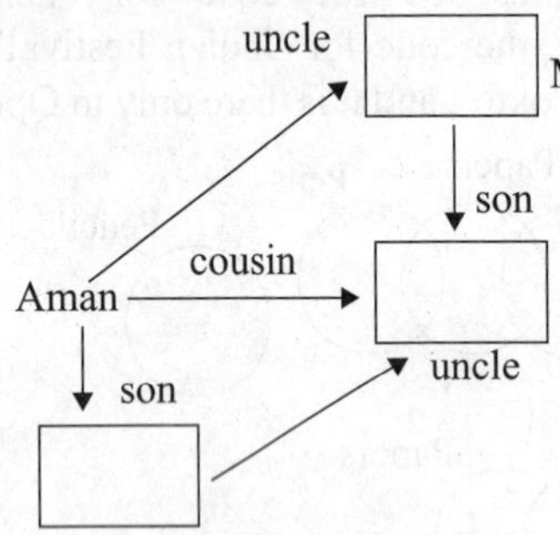

Case II

As you can see in cases I and II, Aman could have been speaking to either his father or his uncle. Hence, the answer can be Option 3 as well as 4. Both these options were accepted by the CUET-UG as correct.

47. Let the present ages of the father and his daughter be $3x$ and x.

As per the question:

$(3x - 10) = 5(x - 10)$

or, $3x - 10 = 5x - 50$ or, $2x = 40$ or, $x = 20$.

Therefore, the present age of the father is $3x = 3 \times 20 = 60$ years.

Alternative:

I. The father's age should be a multiple of 3; hence, we can rule out options 1 and 4.

II. If the present age of the father is 45 years (as in option 3), his daughter is $\frac{45}{3} = 15$ years of age.

Ten years ago, the ages of the father and daughter would have been $45 - 10 = 35$ and $15 - 10 = 5$ years.

But, $35 \neq 5(5)$.

So, option 3 can also be eliminated.

Hence, Option 2.

48. History + Chemistry = 15% + 15% = 30% = 4 hrs 30 minutes

Physics $= 20\% = \frac{2}{3}(30\%) = \frac{2}{3}$ (4 hrs 30 minutes) = 3 hours.

Hence, Option 4.

49. The minute hand of a watch completes 1 round (360°) of the watch in 60 minutes.

$\therefore$ In 1 minute, it covers $\frac{360°}{60} = 6°$

$\therefore$ In 70 minutes (1 hour and 10 minutes), it covers $70 \times 6° = 420°$.

Hence, Option 3.

50. Let the sides of the triangle be $8x$, $9x$ and $10x$.

$\Rightarrow$ its perimeter $= 8x + 9x + 10x = 27x$.

Now, $27x = 270$ cm

or, $x = 10$ cm

Thus, the sides are 80, 90 and 100 cm.

The semi-perimeter $s = \frac{270}{2} = 135$.

The area of the triangle

$= \sqrt{135(135-80)(135-90)(135-100)}$

$= \sqrt{135 \times 55 \times 45 \times 35}$

$= \sqrt{45 \times 3 \times 11 \times 5 \times 45 \times 5 \times 7}$

$= \sqrt{45^2 \times 5^2 \times 3 \times 11 \times 7}$

$= 45 \times 5\sqrt{231} = 225\sqrt{231}$ cm^2.

Hence, Option 3.

51. The actual time = 12:00 – the time in the image = 12 – 6:30 = 5:30.

Hence, Option 1.

52. As the height of the cylinder is along the width of the paper, the length of the paper will become the circumference of the base of the cylinder.

Let the base radius be r.

The circumference of the base $= 2\pi r = 6$ cm

or, $r = \frac{6}{2\pi} = \frac{3}{\pi}$.

Hence, Option 2.

54. Georges Lemaitre, a Belgian cosmologist, had given the Big Bang Theory regarding the origin of the universe.

Hence, Option 3.

55. Option 1:

$2p:3 = 1:q$ or, $\frac{2p}{3} = \frac{1}{q}$ or, $pq = \frac{3}{2} \neq 3$.

Option 2:

$2:p = 3q:1$ or, $\frac{2}{p} = \frac{3q}{1}$ or, $pq = \frac{2}{3} \neq 3$.

Option 3:

$3:p = q:2$ or, $\frac{3}{p} = \frac{q}{2}$ or, $pq = 6 \neq 3$.

Option 4:

$3:p = q:1$ or, $\frac{3}{p} = \frac{q}{1}$ or, $pq = 3$.

Hence, Option 4.

56. Let the salaries of Ravi, Anil and Kavita be x, $3x$ and $6x$, respectively.

Ravi's new salary after a 5% increase

$= 1.05x = \frac{21x}{20}$

Anil's new salary after a 10% increase

$= 3x \times 1.1 = \frac{33x}{10}$

Kavita's new salary after a 15% increase

$= 6x \times 1.15 = \frac{69x}{10}$

Therefore, the ratio of the new salaries of Ravi and Anil $= \frac{21x}{20} \times \frac{10}{33x} = 7:22$.

And the ratio of the new salaries of Anil and Kavita $= \frac{33x}{10} \times \frac{10}{69x} = \frac{22}{46}$.

Thus, the ratio of the new salaries of Ravi, Anil and Kavita is 7:22:46.

Hence, Option 2.

Shortcut: The ratio of the salaries of Ravi and Anil is 1:3 initially, and then they get hikes of 5% and 10%, respectively.

Therefore, the new salary of Anil will be more than 3 times Ravi's new salary. This is there only in Options 2 and 4.

So, we can eliminate Options 1 and 3.

Now, the ratio of the original salaries of Anil and Kavita is 1:2. As Kavita gets a percentage hike more than Anil, her new salary will be more than 2 times that of Anil.

Thus, we can eliminate Option 4 as well.

We are left with only Option 2.

57.

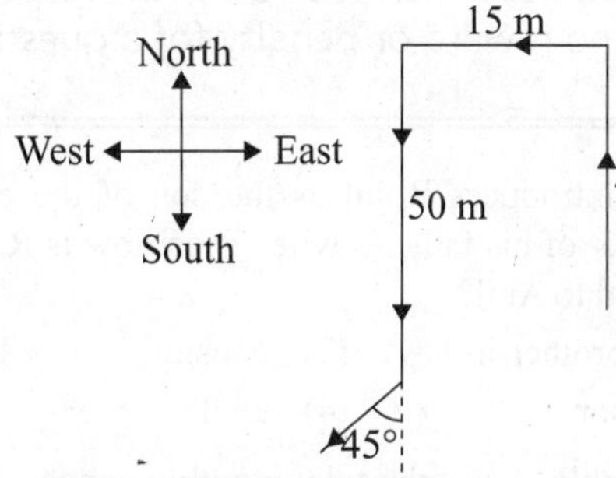

It is obvious that after taking a right turn at an angle of 45°, Shivani was moving in the South-West direction.

Hence, Option 2.

58. The probability that the man will live for 10 more years is $\frac{1}{4}$.

$\therefore$ the probability that he will NOT live for 10 more years is $1 - \frac{1}{4} = \frac{3}{4}$.

The probability that his wife will live for 10 more years is $\frac{1}{3}$.

$\therefore$ the probability that she will NOT live for 10 more years $= 1 - \frac{1}{3} = \frac{2}{3}$.

So, the probability that none of them will live for 10 more years $= \frac{3}{4} \times \frac{2}{3} = \frac{1}{2}$.

Hence, Option 3.

60. Both land animals and sea animals are proper subsets of animals. Also, there are some animals that are land animals as well as sea animals.

Hence, option 3.

SHIFT - I

CUET UG 2023 GENERAL TEST

May 30

INSTRUCTIONS:

1. You need to attempt any 50 out of the 60 questions in 60 minutes.
2. You get 5 marks for a correct response and –1 for an incorrect one. However, there is no reward or penalty for a question not attempted.

1. Anil introduces Rohit as the son of the only brother of his father's wife. Then how is Rohit related to Anil?

(1) brother-in-law (2) cousin
(3) son (4) uncle

2. The table shows the total monthly expenditure of a family on various items.

Commodity	Expenses (in ₹)
food items	4,000
weight	2,000
fare	1,500
education	1,500
miscellaneous	1,000

What is the difference between the angles of sectors of food and fare when the data given in the table is shown in a pie chart?

(1) 75° (2) 90°
(3) 105° (4) 54°

3. The circumference of a car's wheel is $4\frac{2}{7}$ m, and it makes 14 revolutions in 2 seconds. What is the speed of the car (m/s)?

(1) 25 (2) 27
(3) 30 (4) 32

4. In which state is Gir National Park situated?

(1) Madhya Pradesh
(2) Gujarat
(3) Assam
(4) Karnataka

5. Select the number which is similar to the numbers in the following set:
(471, 489, 759)

(1) 581 (2) 479
(3) 382 (4) 633

6. Which number should be substituted in place of the question mark?

4	2	3	4
2	1	6	4
5	1	2	5
2	8	3	?

(1) 0 (2) 1
(3) 2 (4) 3

7. Who developed India's first supercomputer, "PARAM 8000", which was the second fastest computer in the world?

(1) Professor Arun Bhattar
(2) Professor Vijay Bhatkar
(3) Professor Bina Agarwal
(4) Professor Anil Bhatkar

8. Who is India's Minister of External Affairs as of April 2023?

(1) Prahlad Joshi
(2) Sarbananda Sonowal
(3) Dr. Subrahmanyam Jaishankar
(4) Giriraj Singh

9. What is the common name of 'Canis familiaris'?

(1) dog (2) cat
(3) deer frog (4) frog

10. In the given figure, *ABCD* is a square. The area of the shaded part is:

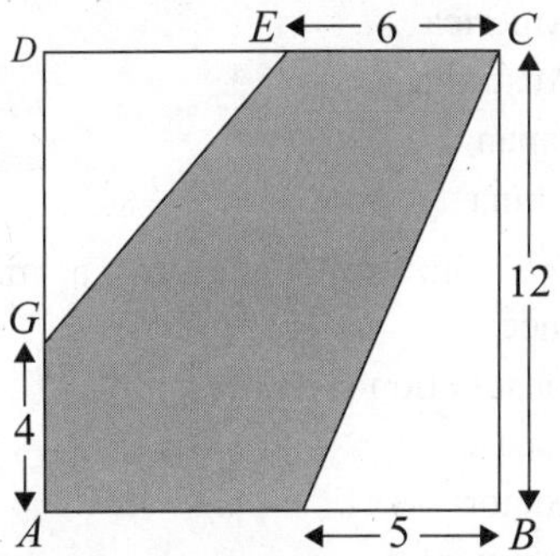

(1) 90 square units (2) 100 square units
(3) 84 square units (4) 72 square units

11. If a + b + c = 6 and ab + bc + ca = 10 then what will be the value of $a^3 + b^3 + c^3 - 3abc$?

(1) 36 (2) 48
(3) 42 (4) 40

12. Three dice are thrown simultaneously. Find the probability of getting a total of at least 6 as the sum of the numbers on the top faces of these dice.

(1) $\frac{5}{108}$ (2) $\frac{5}{18}$
(3) $\frac{101}{108}$ (4) $\frac{103}{108}$

13. National Research Centre for Grapes is located in________.

(1) Pune (2) Mumbai
(3) Delhi (4) Hyderabad

14. Three partners, A, B and C, started a business. Twice, the capital of A is equal to thrice the capital of B, which is four times that of C. If the profit at the end of the year is ₹16,500, then B's share in the profit is

(1) ₹4,500 (2) ₹5,300
(3) ₹6,000 (4) ₹6,250

15. What is the mean proportional of 48 and 12?

(1) 12 (2) 24
(3) 36 (4) 48

16. Given below are two statements: one is written as Assertion (A), and the other is written as Reason (R).

Assertion (A): The leaves of plants are green.

Reason (R): Plants contain chromoplasts, which have green pigment.

In the context of the above statements, select the most appropriate answer from the options given below:

(1) Both (A) and (R) are true, and (R) is the correct explanation of (A).
(2) Both (A) and (R) are true, but (R) is not the correct explanation of (A).
(3) (A) is true, but (R) is false.
(4) (A) is false, but (R) is true.

17. What is the correct time if a clock shows 8:30 when seen in a mirror?

(1) 8:30 (2) 5:30
(3) 2:30 (4) 3:30

18. What stands for the "ZSI"?

(1) Zoological Serving of India
(2) Zoological Survey of India
(3) Zoo Survey of India
(4) Zoological Setup of India

19. Select the cube formed by folding the sheet shown in Figure (X) from the given options:

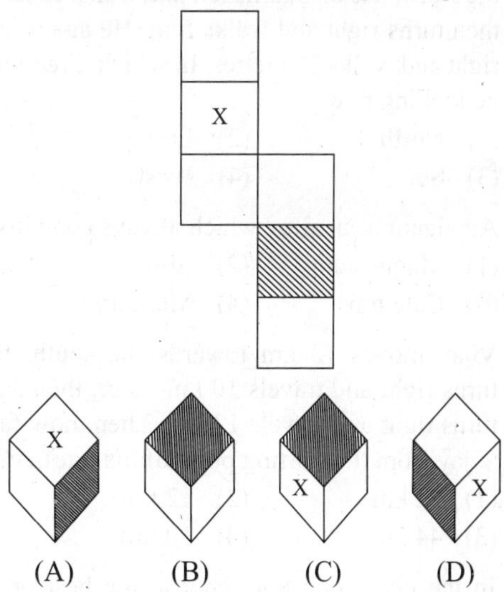

(1) Only (B)
(2) Only (A), (B) and (D)
(3) Only (A), (B) and (C)
(4) Only (B) and (D)

20. "National Master Plan for Multi-Modal Connectivity" is related to which scheme?
(1) PM Gati Shakti Yojana
(2) Bharatmala Project
(3) Char Dham Highway Development Project
(4) Green National Highways Corridor Project

21. Find the compound interest on ₹1,25,000 at 8% per annum for 9 months, when the interest is compounded quarterly:
(1) ₹5,672 (2) ₹7,651
(3) ₹5,625 (4) ₹3,750

22. A number is first increased by 10% and then decreased by 10%. By what per cent does the original number increase or decrease?
(1) decreased by 1%
(2) increased by 1%
(3) neither increased nor decreased
(4) increased by 10%

23. Currency of Iran is ______.
(1) Taka (2) Baht
(3) Toman (4) Somoni

24. A man leaves his home and walks 10 m towards the North. He then turns left and walks 25 m. He then turns right and walks 5 m. He again turns right and walks 25 metres. In which direction is he looking now?
(1) North (2) East
(3) South (4) West

25. Amalgam is an alloy which always contains:
(1) Magnesium (2) Iron
(3) Calcium (4) Mercury

26. Vijay moves 12 km towards the south, then turns right and travels 10 km more, then again turns right and travels 12 km. Then, how far is Vijay from the starting point of his journey?
(1) 22 km (2) 12 km
(3) 44 km (4) 10 km

27. In the given question, choose the best option for '?'.
Assam:Bihu : : Andhra Pradesh:?
(1) Kathakali (2) Kathak
(3) Kuchipudi (4) Bharatanatyam

28. Which country won the maximum number of medals in the 2020 Tokyo Olympics?
(1) America
(2) Australia
(3) Japan
(4) China

29. Arrange the following in a meaningful sequence:
(A) consultation
(B) disease
(C) Doctor
(D) treatment
Select the correct answer from the options given below:
(1) (A), (B), (C), (D)
(2) (D), (C), (B), (A)
(3) (B), (C), (A), (D)
(4) (C), (B), (D), (A)

30. Which number should be substituted in place of the question mark?

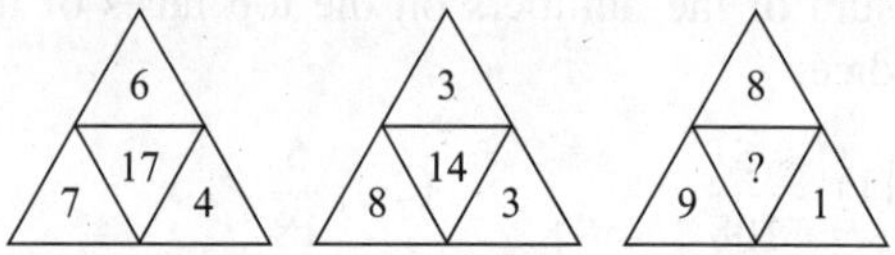

(1) 15 (2) 16
(3) 18 (4) 19

31. In a class of forty students, Suresh is five ranks below the top-ranked Sameer. Then what is Suresh's rank from the bottom in the class?
(1) 34th (2) 36th
(3) 35th (4) 33rd

32. Kailash remembers that his brother Deepak's birthday falls after 20th of May but before 28th of May. Meanwhile, Geeta remembers that Deepak's birthday falls before the 22nd of May but after the 12th of May. When is Deepak's birthday?
(1) 22 May (2) 21 May
(3) 20 May (4) 25 May

33. BEGK is related to ADFJ in the same way as PSVY is related to ______.
(1) ORUX (2) OTUZ
(3) ROUX (4) LOQT

34. The unit of luminous intensity is __________.
(1) Candela (cd) (2) Kelvin (K)
(3) Steradian (Sr) (4) Radian (rad)

35. Where is the headquarters of the West Central Railway?
(1) Bilaspur (2) Jabalpur
(3) Jaipur (4) Mumbai

36. Statement: 70 percent of government employees went on strike. Shri Ram is a government employee.
Conclusion:
(I) Shri Ram went on strike.
(II) Shri Ram did not participate in the strike.
(1) Only conclusion-I follows.
(2) Only conclusion-II follows.
(3) Both conclusion-I and conclusion-II follow.
(4) Either conclusion-I or conclusion-II follows.

37. Who among the following was the first Vice-President of India?
(1) Dr. Zakir Hussain
(2) Dr. Sarvepalli Radhakrishnan
(3) Gopal Swaroop Pathak
(4) B.D. Jatti

38. The sum of how many terms of the A.P. 6, 12, 18, 24, ... is 1800?
(1) 18 (2) 20
(3) 24 (4) 26

39. Match **List I** with **List II**.

List I (Famous Place)	List II (Location)
(A) Ajanta Caves	(I) Udaipur (Rajasthan)
(B) Brindavan Gardens	(II) Bijapur (Karnataka)
(C) Gol Gumbaz	(III) Mysore (Karnataka)
(D) Lake Pichola	(IV) Maharashtra

Select the correct answer from the options given below:
(1) (A)-(I), (B)-(II), (C)-(III), (D)-(IV)
(2) (A)-(IV), (B)-(III), (C)-(II), (D)-(I)
(3) (A)-(I), (B)-(II), (C)-(IV), (D)-(III)
(4) (A)-(III), (B)-(IV), (C)-(I), (D)-(II)

40. A man standing at the top of a tower finds that a boat coming towards the tower takes 10 minutes for the angle of depression to change from 30° to 60°. How much more time will the boat take to reach the tower?
(1) 3 minutes (2) 15 minutes
(3) 10 minutes (4) 5 minutes

41. An article whose cost price is ₹80 is sold for ₹68. The percentage loss from this is:
(1) 12% (2) 15%
(3) $17\frac{11}{17}\%$ (4) 20%

42. Match **List I** with **List II**.

List I (Invention)	List II (Inventor)
(A) Ballpoint pen	(I) Willis H. Carrier
(B) Radio	(II) E.G. Otis
(C) Air Conditioner	(III) G. Marconi
(D) Lift	(IV) L.J. Biro

Select the correct answer from the options given below:
(1) (A)-(I), (B)-(II), (C)-(III), (D)-(IV)
(2) (A)-(IV), (B)-(III), (C)-(I), (D)-(II)
(3) (A)-(I), (B)-(II), (C)-(IV), (D)-(III)
(4) (A)-(III), (B)-(IV), (C)-(I), (D)-(II)

43. The curved surface area of a cylindrical pillar is 264 m^2, and its volume is 924 m^3. What is the ratio of its diameter to its height $\left(\pi = \frac{22}{7}\right)$?
(1) 5:7 (2) 7:3
(3) 4:1 (4) 3:5

44. What is the slogan of the "Pradhan Mantri Jan Dhan Yojana (PMJDY)?
(1) Mera Khata-Mera Vidhata
(2) Mera Khata-Bhagya Vidhata
(3) Mera Paisa-Mera Khata
(4) Mera Khata-Mera Sathi

45. In what ratio does the line $x + y - 6 = 0$ divide the line segment formed by joining the points A (3, 5) and B (2, –7)?
(1) 3:5 (2) 4:7
(3) 2:11 (4) 5:9

46. What is the scientific name of peacock?
(1) Felis catus
(2) Pavo cristatus
(3) Anura Ranidae
(4) Pablo Cris

47. The average of nine numbers is 7. If the average of 6 of these numbers is 8, then what is the average of the remaining numbers?
(1) 4 (2) 5
(3) 6 (4) 7

48. A and B can do a piece of work in 15 days and 20 days, respectively. If they work together for 4 days, what portion of the work will be left?
(1) 1/4 (2) 1/10
(3) 7/15 (4) 8/15

49. How many glass spheres of radius 3 cm each can be formed by melting a solid cuboid of dimensions 9 cm × 22 cm × 12 cm $\left(\pi = \frac{22}{7}\right)$?
(1) 50 (2) 63
(3) 42 (4) 21

50. Six years ago, A's age was 18 times B's present age. B is 2 years younger than C. If the present age of C is 5 years, then what is the present age of A?
(1) 84 years (2) 48 years
(3) 60 years (4) 72 years

51. In the given question, choose the best option for '?'.
Lemur:Monkey : : Rook:?
(1) Owl (2) Vulture
(3) Crow (4) Cat

52. If Paper is called Wood, Wood is called Straw, Straw is called Grass, Grass is called Rubber and Rubber is called Cloth, then what is furniture made of?
(1) Paper (2) Grass
(3) Wood (4) Straw

53. If $<$ means subtraction, $>$ means addition, $=$ means multiplication and \$ means division, then what is the value of the following?
$27 > 81 \ \$ \ 9 < 6$
(1) 36 (2) 30
(3) 54 (4) 40

54.

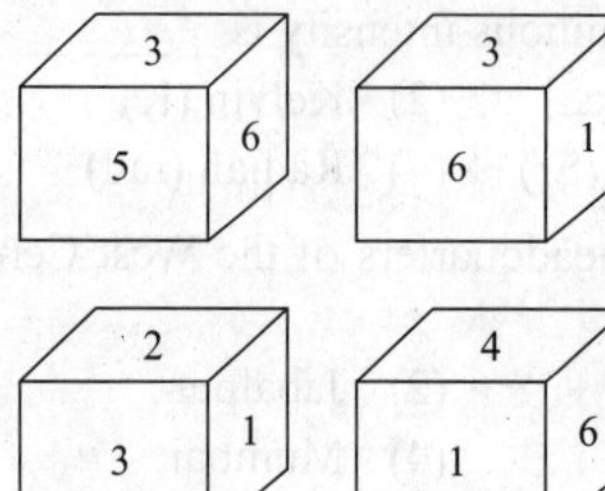

Which number is on the opposite side of the number 3?
(1) 4 (2) 6
(3) 5 (4) 1

55. Which conclusion/s will follow from the given statements:
Statements: Some trees are birds. Some birds are rice. No rice is wheat.
Conclusions:
(I) Some trees are wheat.
(II) Some trees being wheat is a possibility.
(III) Some birds are not wheat.
(1) Only conclusion (I) follows.
(2) Only conclusion (I) and conclusion (II) follow.
(3) Either conclusion (I) or (III) follows.
(4) Only conclusions (II) and (III) follow.

56. A train leaves Delhi at 4:10 pm and reaches Aligarh at 7:25 pm. The average speed of this train is 40 km/h. What is the distance from Delhi to Aligarh?
(1) 120 km (2) 130 km
(3) 135 km (4) 140 km

57. Match **List I** with **List II**.

List I (Vitamin)	List II (Deficiency Disease)
(A) Vitamin – K	(I) Beriberi
(B) Vitamin – A	(II) cracks in skin
(C) Vitamin – B2	(III) non-clotting of blood
(D) Vitamin – B1	(IV) Colour Blindness

Select the correct answer from the options given below:
(1) (A)-(II), (B)-(III), (C)-(IV), (D)-(I)
(2) (A)-(III), (B)-(IV), (C)-(II), (D)-(I)

(3) (A)-(I), (B)-(III), (C)-(II), (D)-(IV)
(4) (A)-(III), (B)-(II), (C)-(I), (D)-(IV)

58. In a code language, RUSTICATE is written as QTTUIDBSD. How will STATISTIC be written in that code?
(1) RSBUJTUHB
(2) RSBUITUHB
(3) RSBUIRSJD
(4) TUBUITUMB

59. What is the point of intersection of the medians of a triangle called?
(1) Orthocentre
(2) Incentre
(3) Circumcentre
(4) Centroid

60. Match **List I** with **List II**.

List I (Units)	List II (Prefixes)
(A) Giga	(I) 10^{-2} m.
(B) Nano	(II) 10^{2} m.
(C) Hecto	(III) 10^{-9} m.
(D) Centi	(IV) 10^{9} m.

Select the correct answer from the options given below:
(1) (A)-(IV), (B)-(III), (C)-(II), (D)-(I)
(2) (A)-(I), (B)-(II), (C)-(III), (D)-(IV)
(3) (A)-(II), (B)-(III), (C)-(IV), (D)-(I)
(4) (A)-(IV), (B)-(I), (C)-(II), (D)-(III)

Answer Key

1. **(2)**	2. **(2)**	3. **(3)**	4. **(2)**	5. **(4)**	6. **(1)**	7. **(2)**	8. **(3)**	9. **(1)**	10. **(1)**
11. **(1)**	12. **(4)**	13. **(1)**	14. **(3)**	15. **(2)**	16. **(3)**	17. **(4)**	18. **(2)**	19. **(1)**	20. **(1)**
21. **(2)**	22. **(1)**	23. **(3)**	24. **(2)**	25. **(4)**	26. **(4)**	27. **(3)**	28. **(1)**	29. **(3)**	30. **(3)**
31. **(3)**	32. **(2)**	33. **(1)**	34. **(1)**	35. **(2)**	36. **(4)**	37. **(2)**	38. **(3)**	39. **(2)**	40. **(4)**
41. **(2)**	42. **(2)**	43. **(2)**	44. **(2)**	45. **(3)**	46. **(2)**	47. **(2)**	48. **(4)**	49. **(4)**	50. **(3)**
51. **(3)**	52. **(4)**	53. **(2)**	54. **(1)**	55. **(4)**	56. **(2)**	57. **(2)**	58. **(2)**	59. **(4)**	60. **(1)**

Classification of Questions

Question No.	Subject	Topic	Level of Difficulty
1.	Reasoning	Blood Relations	Easy
2.	Data Interpretation	Pie Chart	Easy
3.	Quantitative Aptitude	Time, Speed & Distance	Easy
4.	General Awareness	Geography	Easy
5.	Reasoning	Similar Numbers	Easy
6.	Reasoning	Missing Number	Easy
7.	General Awareness	Science & Technology	Difficult
8.	General Awareness	Polity	Easy
9.	General Awareness	Science (Biology)	Easy
10.	Quantitative Aptitude	Mensuration	Easy

Question No.	Subject	Topic	Level of Difficulty
11.	Quantitative Aptitude	Algebra (Identities)	Medium
12.	Quantitative Aptitude	Probability	Medium
13.	General Awareness	Geography	Medium
14.	Quantitative Aptitude	Partnership	Easy
15.	Quantitative Aptitude	Ratios & Proportions	Easy
16.	General Awareness	Science (Biology)	Medium
17.	Reasoning	Mirror Image	Easy
18.	General Awareness	Miscellaneous	Easy
19.	Reasoning	Cubes	Medium
20.	General Awareness	Government Projects	Difficult
21.	Quantitative Aptitude	Compound Interest	Medium
22.	Quantitative Aptitude	Percentages	Easy
23.	General Awareness	Geography (Currency)	Medium
24.	Reasoning	Directions	Easy
25.	General Awareness	Science (Chemistry)	Easy
26.	Reasoning	Directions	Easy
27.	General Awareness	Art & Culture	Easy
28.	General Awareness	Sports	Medium
29.	Reasoning	Sequencing	Easy
30.	Reasoning	Missing Number	Easy
31.	Reasoning	Rankings & Orders	Easy
32.	Reasoning	Miscellaneous	Easy
33.	Reasoning	Coding	Easy
34.	General Awareness	Science (Physics)	Easy
35.	General Awareness	Geography	Medium
36.	Reasoning	Statements & Conclusions	Easy
37.	General Awareness	Polity	Easy
38.	Quantitative Aptitude	Algebra (AP)	Easy
39.	General Awareness	Geography	Medium
40.	Quantitative Aptitude	Trigonometry (Heights & Distances)	Medium
41.	Quantitative Aptitude	Profit, Loss & Discount	Easy
42.	General Awareness	Miscellaneous (Inventors & Inventions)	Easy
43.	Quantitative Aptitude	Mensuration	Easy
44.	General Awareness	Government Projects	Difficult
45.	Quantitative Aptitude	Coordinate Geometry	Medium
46.	General Awareness	Science (Biology)	Easy

Question No.	Subject	Topic	Level of Difficulty
47.	Quantitative Aptitude	Averages	Easy
48.	Quantitative Aptitude	Time & Work	Easy
49.	Quantitative Aptitude	Mensuration	Easy
50.	Quantitative Aptitude	Age-based Problems	Easy
51.	General Awareness	Analogy (Science-based)	Medium
52.	Reasoning	Coding	Easy
53.	Reasoning	Coding	Easy
54.	Reasoning	Cubes	Easy
55.	Reasoning	Syllogism	Medium
56.	Quantitative Aptitude	Time, Speed & Distance	Easy
57.	General Awareness	Science (Biology)	Easy
58.	Reasoning	Coding	Easy
59.	Quantitative Aptitude	Geometry	Easy
60.	Quantitative Aptitude	Prefixes of Units of Length	Medium

Number of questions on General Awareness: 21
Number of questions on Reasoning: 18
Number of questions on Quantitative Aptitude: 20
Number of questions on Data Interpretation: 1

Explanation to Select Questions

1. 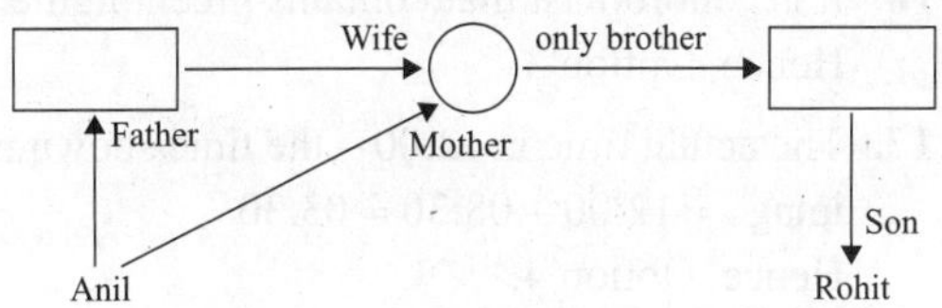

Therefore, Rohit is the son of Anil's maternal uncle, and Anil and Rohit are cousins.
Hence, Option 2.

2. The total monthly expenses = 4000 + 2000 + 1500 + 1500 + 1000 = ₹10,000.
The difference between the expenses on food and fare = 4000 – 1500 = 2500.
This difference, 2500, is 25% of the total.

$\therefore$ it will make an angle of $360 \times \frac{25}{100} = 90°$.

Hence, Option 2.

3. The circumference of the wheel $= 4\frac{2}{7} = \frac{30}{7}$ m
The wheel makes 14 revolutions in 2 seconds.
$\Rightarrow$ It makes 7 revolutions in 1 second.

$\Rightarrow$ It travels $\frac{30}{7} \times 7 = 30$ metres in 1 second.

Hence, Option 3.

4. The Gir National Park, also known as the Sasan Gir, is the only place in Asia where Asiatic lions are found in their natural habitat. It is in the Junagadh district of Gujarat.
Hence, Option 2.

5. All the numbers in the set (471, 489, 759) are multiples of 3. There is only one multiple of 3 among the options: 633.
Hence, Option 4.

6. The sum of the four numbers in each of the first three rows is 13. To get a sum of 13 in the 4th row, we need to put 0 in place of ?.
Hence, Option 1.

10.

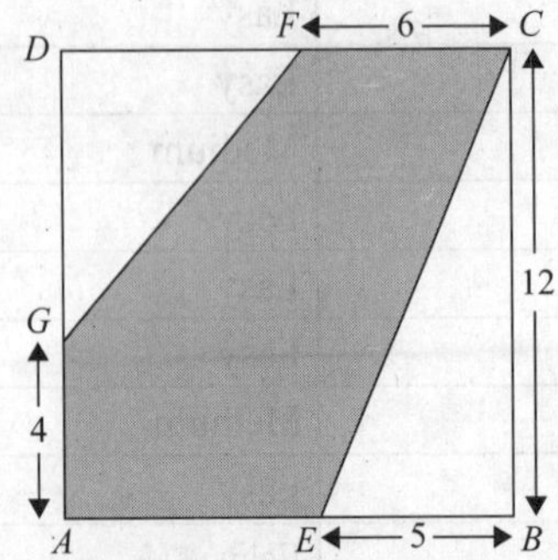

$DG = DA - GA = 12 - 4 = 8.$
$DF = CD - CF = 12 - 6 = 6.$
The area of the square $ABCD = 12 \times 12 = 144.$
The area of the shaded region
= the area of the square – (the area of the ΔEBC + the area of the ΔDGF)

$$= 144 - \left(\frac{1}{2} \times 12 \times 5 + \frac{1}{2} \times 6 \times 8\right)$$

$= 144 - (30 + 24) = 144 - 54 = 90.$

Hence, Option 1.

11. $a^3 + b^3 + c^3 = (a + b + c)$
$(a^2 + b^2 + c^2 - ab - bc - ca)$
$= (a + b + c)\{(a + b + c)^2 - 3(ab + bc + ca)\}$
$= 6\ \{6^2 - 3 \times 10\} = 6(36 - 30) = 6 \times 6$
$= 36.$
Hence, Option 1.

12. The total number of outcomes when 3 dice are rolled $= 6 \times 6 \times 6 = 216.$
For 3 dice, the minimum total can be 3 (1, 1, 1), and the maximum can be 18 (6, 6, 6).
We can get a total of 3 in 1 way: (1, 1, 1).
We can get a total of 4 in 3 ways: (1, 1, 2), (1, 2, 1) and (2, 1, 1).
We can get a total of 5 in 6 ways:
(3, 1, 1), (1, 3, 1), (1, 1, 3), (2, 2, 1), (2, 1, 2), & (1, 2, 2).

$\therefore$ Out of 216 ways, in $1 + 3 + 6 = 10$ ways, the total will be less than 6.
$\Rightarrow$ In $216 - 10 = 206$ ways, the total will be at least 6.
Therefore, the probability of getting a total of at least $6 = \frac{206}{216} = \frac{103}{108}.$
Hence, Option 4.

14. Let the capital of C be x.
$\Rightarrow$ the capital of $B = 4x.$
$\Rightarrow$ the capital of $A = \frac{4x \times 3}{2} = 6x.$
$\Rightarrow$ the total investment $= x + 4x + 6x = 11x.$
The proportion of the investment of B in the total investment $= \frac{4x}{11x} = \frac{4}{11}.$
$\therefore$ B's profit $= \frac{4}{11} \times 16{,}500 = 6{,}000.$
Hence, Option 3.

15. The mean proportional of 48 and 12 is $\sqrt{48 \times 12}$
$= \sqrt{12 \times 4 \times 12}$
$= \sqrt{12^2 \times 2^2} = 12 \times 2 = 24.$
Hence, Option 2.

16. It is Chloroplast that contains green pigment.
Hence, Option 3.

17. The actual time is 12:00 – the time shown in its image = 12:00 – 08:30 = 03:30.
Hence, Option 4.

18. The Zoological Survey of India was established on 1st July 1916. Its headquarters is in Kolkata.
The answer is Option 2.

19. The shaded face and the face marked X should be opposite, but they are adjacent in figures A, C and D.
Hence, Option 1.

21. As the interest is compounded quarterly, the effective rate $= \frac{8}{4} = 2\%$ per 3 months.
There are 3 time periods of 3 months in 9 months.

The total amount at the end of 9 months

$= 1,25,000\left(1+\frac{2}{100}\right)^3 = 1,25,000\times(1.02)^3$

$= 1,32,651.$

The interest = 1,32,651 – 1,25,000 = 7,651.

22. Let the number be 100.

After a 10% increase, 100 become 110.

110, after a reduction of 10% $= 110 - 110 \times \frac{10}{100} = 99.$

So, after a 10% increase and a 10% decrease, 100 becomes 99.

It is a 1% decrease.

Remember: If a number is increased by a% and then decreased by a% (irrespective of the order), overall, there will be a decrease of $\frac{a^2}{100}\%$.

Here, $a = 10$.

Hence, the decrease is $\frac{10^2}{100}\% = 1\%$.

23. The currency of Iran is Rial, and 10 Rials = 1 Toman. Thus, Toman is a super unit of the currency of Iran.

Hence, Option 3.

24.

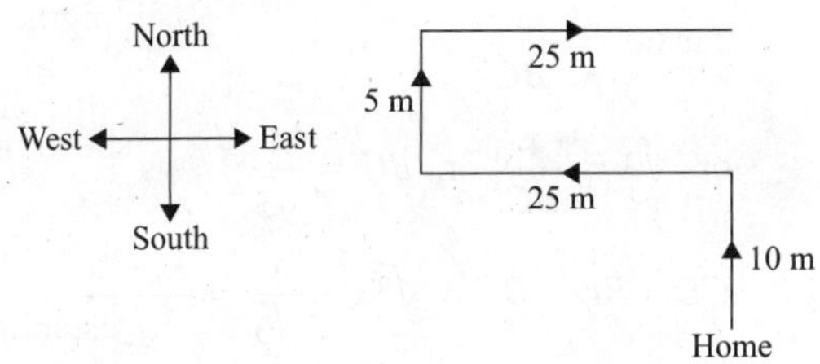

Hence, Option 2.

26.

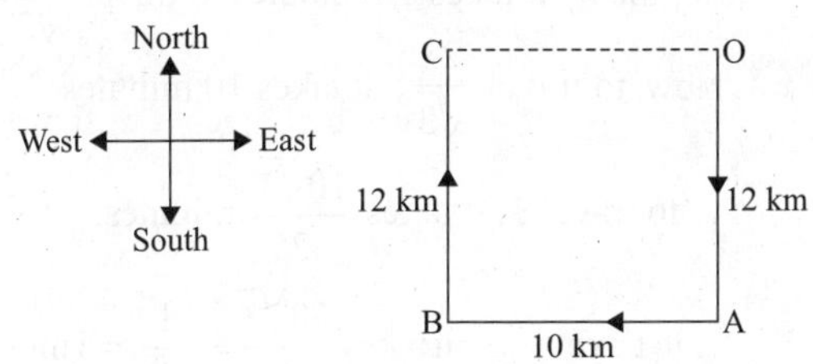

Let O be Vijay's initial position. His final position is C. The distance $OC = AB = 10$ km.

Hence, Option 4.

27. Bihu is a dance from Assam, and Kuchipudi is a dance from Andhra Pradesh. Hence, Option 3. Please bear in mind that Bihu is a festival, too, again from Assam.

28. The 2020 Tokyo Summer Olympics were held in 2021 because of the COVID. The USA won the maximum number of medals - 112 - and got the 1st position with 39 Golds. China won the 2nd highest number of medals - 89 - and got the 2nd position with 38 Golds. A country with the highest number of medals only gets the 1st position if it has the maximum number of Golds. Hence, Option 1.

29. After contracting a disease, one finds a doctor, avails consultation and then the treatment starts. Hence, Option 3.

30. The number in the central triangle is the sum of the numbers in the outer triangles in each of the first two figures:

$6 + 4 + 7 = 17,$

$3 + 3 + 8 = 14.$

Therefore, the number in the central triangle of the 3rd figure should be $8 + 1 + 9 = 18$.

Hence, Option 3.

31. The total no. of students = 40, so the no. of students other than Suresh is 39.

The no. of students ranked above Suresh = 5, so the number of students below Suresh = 39 – 5 = 34.

Therefore, Suresh's rank from the bottom is 35th.

Hence, Option 3.

32. The dates after 20th May, but before 28th May: 21, 22, 23, 24, 25, 26, 27

The dates after 12th May, but before 22nd May: 13, 14, 15, 16, 17, 18, 19, 20, 21

As 21 is the only common number in these two sequences, Deepak's birthday must be the 21st of May.

Hence, Option 2.

33. B E G K → A D F J

2 5 7 11   1 4 6 10

Here, $2-1=1, 5-1=4, 7-1=6$ and $11-1=10$

P S V Y

16 19 22 25

Here, 16 – 1 = 15, 19 – 1 = 18, 22 – 1 = 21 and 25 – 1 = 24.

Therefore, the answer is O R U X

15 18 21 24

Hence, Option 1.

34.

Physical Quantity	Unit
Candela	Luminous Intensity
Kelvin	Temperature
Steradian	Solid Angle
Radian	Plane Angle

Hence, Option 1.

36. 70% of the government employees went on strike, which also means that 30% of them did not. Shri Ram is a government employee, but he can be among the 70% who went on strike and also among those 30% who did not. Hence, we cannot conclude either (I) or (II), but one of (I) or (II) has to be correct as (I) and (II) are exhaustive events.

Hence, Option 4.

37. Dr. Sarvepalli Radhakrishnan was India's first vice president and second president. We celebrate Teachers' Day on 5th September as it was his birthday.

Hence, Option 2.

38. Here, the first term of the AP, $a = 6$.

the common difference, $d = 6$

Let there be n terms.

$S_n = 1800$ (given)

$$S_n = \left\{\frac{2a + (n-1)d}{2}\right\}n$$

$$\text{or, } 1800 = \left\{\frac{12 + (n-1)6}{2}\right\}n$$

$$\text{or, } \left(\frac{12 + 6n - 6}{2}\right)n = 1800$$

$$\text{or, } \frac{6n+6}{2} \cdot n = 1800$$

$$\text{or, } n(3n+3) = 1800$$

$$\text{or, } 3n^2 + 3n - 1800 = 0$$

$$\text{or, } 3n^2 - 72n + 75n - 1800 = 0$$

$$\text{or, } 3n(n-24) + 75(n-24) = 0$$

$$\text{or, } (3n+75)(n-24) = 0$$

$n = 24$ (n cannot be a negative number)

Hence, Option 3.

40.

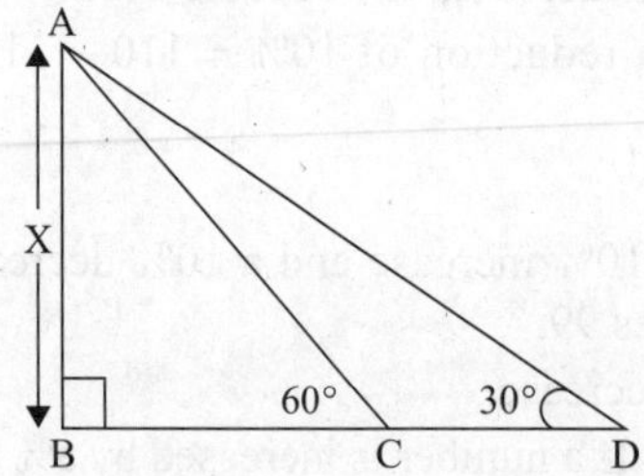

Let AB be the tower and let the boat be at point D initially and at point C after 10 minutes.

Let the height of the tower be x.

In ΔABD,

$$\tan 30° = \frac{x}{BD}$$

$$\text{or, } \frac{1}{\sqrt{3}} = \frac{x}{BD}$$

$$\text{or, } BD = \sqrt{3}x$$

In ΔABC,

$$\tan 60° = \frac{x}{BC}$$

$$\text{or, } \sqrt{3} = \frac{x}{BC} \text{ or, } BC = \frac{x}{\sqrt{3}}$$

$$CD = BD - BC = \sqrt{3}x - \frac{x}{\sqrt{3}} = \frac{3x - x}{\sqrt{3}} = \frac{2x}{\sqrt{3}}$$

So, the boat takes 10 minutes to travel $\frac{2x}{\sqrt{3}}$.

Now, to travel $\frac{2x}{\sqrt{3}}$, it takes 10 minutes.

$\therefore$ to travel 1, it takes $\frac{10\sqrt{3}}{2}$ minutes.

$\therefore$ to travel $\frac{x}{\sqrt{3}}$, it takes $\frac{10\sqrt{3}}{2} \times \frac{1}{\sqrt{3}} = 5$ minutes.

Hence, Option 4.

41. The cost price = 80

The selling price = 68

$\therefore$ the loss = 80 – 68 = 12

$\therefore$ the loss percentage = $\frac{12}{80} \times 100 = 15$.

Hence, Option 2.

43. Let the radius of the cylinder be r and the height h.

The curved surface area of the cylinder = $2\pi rh$

$= 2 \times \frac{22}{7} \times r \times h = 264$

or, $rh = \frac{264 \times 7}{22 \times 2} = 42$

The volume of the cylinder = $\pi r^2 h = \frac{22}{7} \times r^2 \times h = 924$

or, $r^2 h = \frac{924 \times 7}{22} = 294$

or, $r \times rh = 294$

or, $r \times 42 = 294$

or, $r = 7$

As $rh = 42, h = \frac{42}{7} = 6$

The diameter of the cylinder = 2 × 7 = 14.

The ratio of the diameter and height = $\frac{14}{6} = \frac{7}{3}$.

Hence, Option 2.

Alternative: $2\pi rh = 264$ (i)

and

$\pi r^2 h = 924$ (ii)

Dividing (ii) by (i), we get:

$\frac{r}{2} = \frac{924}{264}$, or, $r = 7$.

Putting the value of r in (i),

$2 \times \frac{22}{7} \times 7 \times h = 264$

or, $h = 6$.

The required ratio = $\frac{2 \times 7}{6} = \frac{7}{3}$.

45. Let the ratio in which the line $x + y - 6 = 0$ divides the line segment formed by joining the points $A(3, 5)$ and $B(2, -7)$ be m:n.

Therefore, the coordinates of this point are $\frac{2m + 3n}{m + n}$ and $\frac{-7m + 5n}{m + n}$.

As this point is on the line $x + y - 6 = 0$, it must satisfy the equation of the line.

Therefore, $\frac{2m + 3n}{m + n} + \frac{-7m + 5n}{m + n} - 6 = 0$

or, $\frac{2m + 3n - 7m + 5n}{m + n} = 6$

or, $-5m + 8n = 6m + 6n$

or, $2n = 11m$

or, $\frac{m}{n} = \frac{2}{11}$.

Hence, Option 3.

46. Pavo Cristatus is the scientific name of peacock. The peacock is India's National Bird.

Hence, Option 2.

Felis Catus is the scientific name of domestic cat or house cat. Anura Ranidae is the scientific name of frogs.

47. The sum of the 9 numbers with an average 7 = 9 × 7 = 63.

The sum of 6 of these numbers with an average 8 = 6 × 8 = 48.

The sum of the remaining 3 numbers = 63 – 48 = 15.

$\therefore$ The average of these 3 numbers = $\frac{15}{3} = 5$.

Hence, Option 2.

48. $\therefore$ A can do the work in 15 days,

$\therefore$ In 1 day, he does $\frac{1}{15}$.

Similarly, in 1 day, B does $\frac{1}{20}$.

The work done in 4 days = $4\left(\frac{1}{15} + \frac{1}{20}\right)$

$= 4\left(\frac{4+3}{60}\right) = \frac{7}{15}$.

Thus, $1 - \frac{7}{15} = \frac{8}{15}$ of the work will be left.

Hence, Option 4.

49. The volume of the solid cube = 9 × 22 × 12 cm^3.

Let's assume that we can form n spheres with a radius of 3 cm each.

The volume of these n spheres = $n \times \frac{4}{3}\pi \times 3^3$

$= n \times \frac{4}{3} \times \frac{22}{7} \times 27$.

So, $n \times \frac{4}{3} \times \frac{22}{7} \times 27 = 9 \times 12 \times 22$

or, $n = 21$.

Hence, Option 4.

50. The present age of $C = 5$ years

$\therefore$ The present age of $B = 5 - 2 = 3$ years.

$\therefore$ A's age, six years ago, was $18 \times 3 = 54$ years

$\therefore$ A's present age $= 54 + 6 = 60$ years.

Hence, Option 3.

51. Lemurs and monkeys are of the same family. Similarly, rooks and crows are of the same family.
Hence, Option 3.

52. Furniture is made of wood, and wood is called straw.
Hence, Option 4.

53. $27 > 81 \$ 9 < 6$

$= 27 + 81 \div 9 - 6$

$= 27 + 9 - 6 = 30.$

Hence, Option 2.

54. It is clear from the given figures that 5, 6, 1 and 2 are on the adjacent faces of 3. Therefore, only 4 can be opposite to 3.
Hence, Option 1.

55.

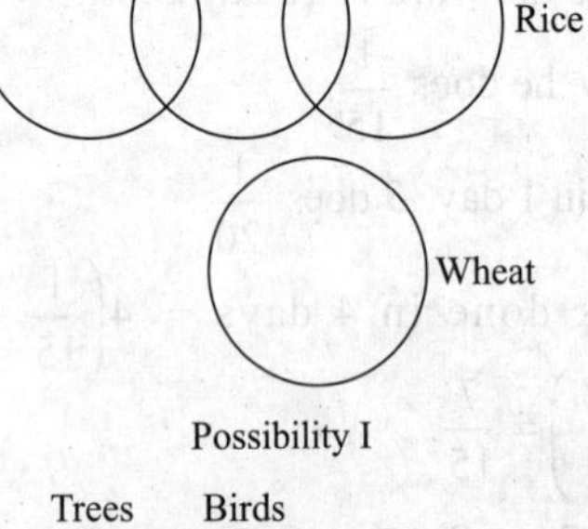

Possibility I

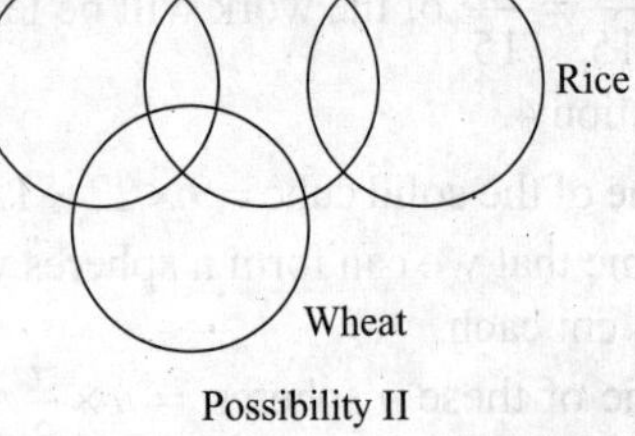

Possibility II

'Some Trees are Wheat' is just a possibility, as seen in II. It cannot be concluded.

No Rice is Wheat, and some Birds are Rice.
So, those Birds that are Rice are certainly not Wheat.
Therefore, we can conclude that some Birds are not Wheat.
Hence, Option 4.

56. The train travelled for 7:25 – 4:10 = 3:15 hours, i.e., $3\frac{1}{4}$ hours.

The distance travelled by the train

$= 40 \times \left(3\frac{1}{4}\right) = 40 \times \frac{13}{4} = 130$ km.

Hence, Option 2.

58. RUSTICATE is coded as QTTUIDBSD. For the first two letters, the code has the letters that immediately precede R and U. For the next two letters, the code has letters that immediately succeed S and T. The middle letter does not change. Then, for C and A, the code again has the letters that immediately succeed these two. The last two letters, T and E, are coded by the letters immediately preceding them.
Hence, Option 2.

59. The Orthocentre is the point of intersection of the altitudes of a triangle.
The Incentre is the point of intersection of the angle-bisectors of a triangle.
The Circumcentre is the point of intersection of the perpendicular bisectors of the sides of a triangle.
The Centroid (also called the Centre of Mass) is the point of intersection of the medians of a triangle.
Hence, Option 4.

CUET UG 2023 GENERAL TEST

May 30

INSTRUCTIONS:

1. You need to attempt any 50 out of the 60 questions in 60 minutes.
2. You get 5 marks for a correct response and –1 for an incorrect one. However, there is no reward or penalty for a question not attempted.

1. If E = 5, PEN = 35, then PAGE = ?

(1) 27 (2) 29
(3) 28 (4) 36

2. The curved surface area of a right circular cylinder with a height of 14 cm is 88 cm^2. The diameter of the base of the cylinder is $\left(\text{use } \pi = \dfrac{22}{7}\right)$:

(1) 2 cm (2) 4 cm
(3) 5 cm (4) 0.5 cm

3. Today is Monday. After 60 days, it will be?

(1) Thursday (2) Tuesday
(3) Friday (4) Wednesday

4. Nine boys can complete a work in 360 days, 18 men can complete the same work in 72 days and 12 women can complete it in 162 days. In how many days can 4 men, 12 women and 10 boys together finish the work?

(1) 79 (2) 81
(3) 83 (4) 85

5. A certain weight (in kg) is divided into two parts such that 5 times the first part added to 11 times the second part makes 7 times the whole weight. The ratio of the first part to the second part is

(1) 1:2 (2) 5:11
(3) 2:1 (4) 2:3

6. Which country has launched the world's first commercial moon lander?

(1) Japan (2) Russia
(3) India (4) U.S.A.

7. Match **List I** with **List II**.

List I (Animal)	List II (Natural Habitat)
(A) elephant	(I) Sundarbans National park
(B) camel	(II) Gir Forest National park
(C) Indian lion	(III) Thar Desert
(D) tiger	(IV) the hot wet forests of Assam and Kerala

Choose the most appropriate answer from the options given below:

(1) (A)-(IV), (B)-(III), (C)-(II), (D)-(I)
(2) (A)-(III), (B)-(IV), (C)-(II), (D)-(I)
(3) (A)-(IV), (B)-(III), (C)-(I), (D)-(II)
(4) (A)-(II), (B)-(III), (C)-(IV), (D)-(I)

8. A wholesaler sells a jacket to a retailer at a profit of 5%, and the retailer sells it to a customer at a profit of 10%. If the customer pays ₹4,158 for the jacket, then what was the cost price of the jacket for the wholesaler?

(1) ₹3,500 (2) ₹3,400
(3) ₹3,300 (4) ₹3,600

9. The average weight of A, B and C is 60 kg. If the average weight of B and C is 50 kg, and that of A and B is 52 kg, then what is the weight of B?

(1) 26 kg (2) 24 kg
(3) 30 kg (4) 32 kg

10. Two men, P and Q, start together from place A at 3 km/h and 3.75 km/h, respectively, for place B. Q reaches half an hour before P. What is the distance that each one has covered?

(1) 7 km (2) 7.2 km
(3) 7.5 km (4) 7.8 km

11. Find the missing term in the given series.

$4, 6, 9, 13\frac{1}{2}$, ______?

(1) $22\frac{3}{4}$ (2) $20\frac{1}{4}$
(3) 19 (4) $17\frac{1}{2}$

12. Study the following arrangement carefully and answer the question given below:

R D A K 7 B I 3 M J E N 6 7 U Z V 1 W 3 H 4 F Y 8 P 6

How many such numbers are there in the above sequence, each immediately preceded by a consonant and immediately followed by a vowel?

(1) Zero (2) One
(3) Two (4) Three

13. On compound interest, ₹2,000 amounts to ₹2,226.05 in 2 years.

What is the rate of interest per annum?

(1) 5% (2) 5.5%
(3) 6% (4) 6.5%

14. Atmospheric Pressure is measured by ______.

(1) Pedometer (2) Thermometer
(3) Odometer (4) Barometer

15. Who said, "INC (Indian National Congress) should distinguish between begging and claiming the Rights"?

(1) Aurobindo Ghosh
(2) Bal Gangadhar Tilak
(3) Bipin Chandra Pal
(4) Lala Lajpat Rai

16. A clock is set right at 5 a.m. The clock loses 16 minutes in 24 hours. What time will be the right time when the clock indicates 10 p.m. on the 4th day?

(1) 12:30 a.m. (2) 12:00 midnight
(3) 11:00 p.m. (4) 11:15 p.m.

17. Match **List I** with **List II**.

List I (Scheme)	List II (Year of Commencement)
(A) Vande Mataram Yojana	(I) 2000
(B) Swajal Dhara Yojana	(II) 2005
(C) Bharat Nirman Yojana	(III) 2002
(D) Janashree Bima Yojana	(IV) 2004

Choose the most appropriate answer from the options given below:

(1) (A)-(II), (B)-(III), (C)-(IV), (D)-(I)
(2) (A)-(I), (B)-(II), (C)-(III), (D)-(IV)
(3) (A)-(I), (B)-(III), (C)-(IV), (D)-(II)
(4) (A)-(IV), (B)-(III), (C)-(II), (D)-(I)

18. Complete the figure matrix:

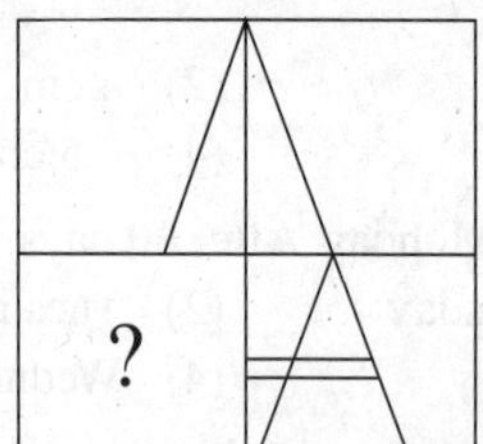

(1)
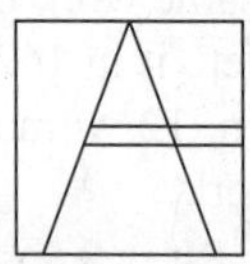

(2)
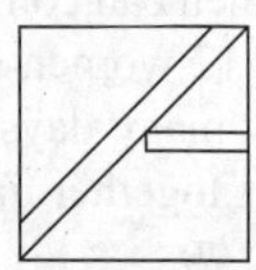

(3)
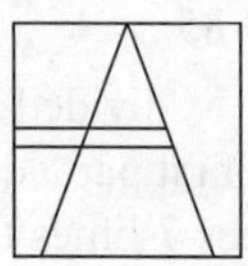

(4)
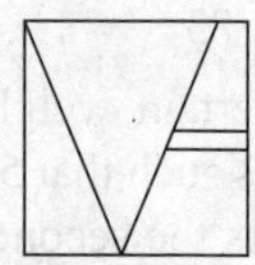

19. Who won the T20 Cricket World Cup-2022 held in Australia?

(1) Australia (2) England
(3) India (4) Pakistan

20. Keoladeo Bird Sanctuary is located in ______.

(1) Rajasthan (2) Delhi
(3) Haryana (4) Punjab

21. Which Indian scientist invented the crescograph for measuring plant growth?
(1) Jagdish Chander Bose
(2) C.V. Raman
(3) Homi J. Bhabha
(4) Vikram Sarabhai

22. Which of the following articles of the Constitution of India is related to the Finance Commission?
(1) Article 21A (2) Article 280
(3) Article 324 (4) Article 124

23. Which of the following will continue the same series established by the given figure?

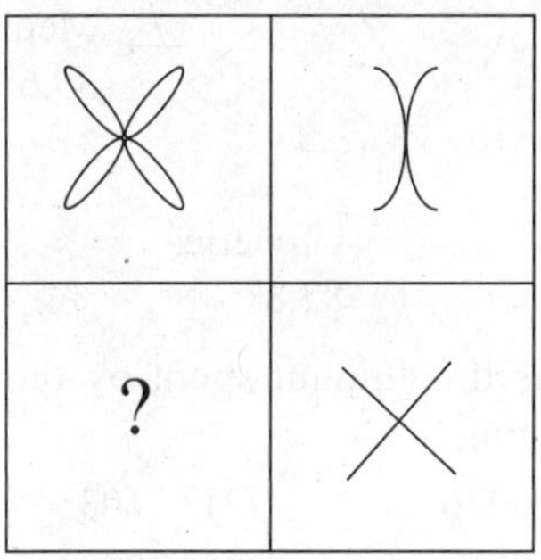

(1) 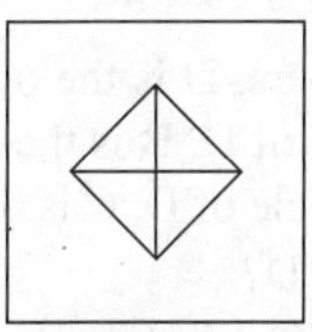 (2) 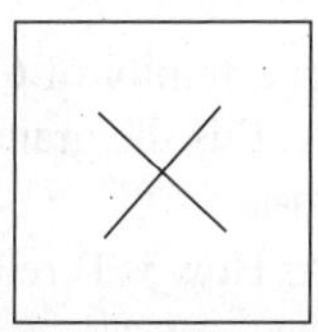

(3) 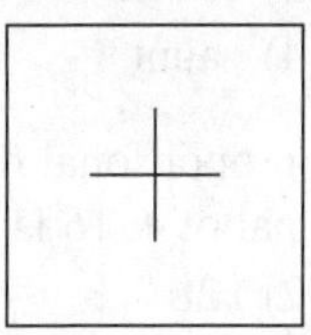 (4) 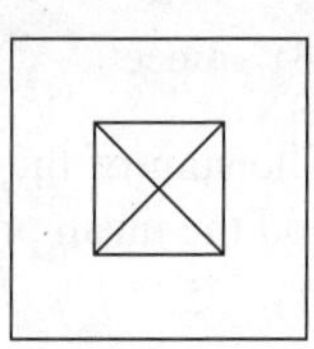

24. From the figure, find x.

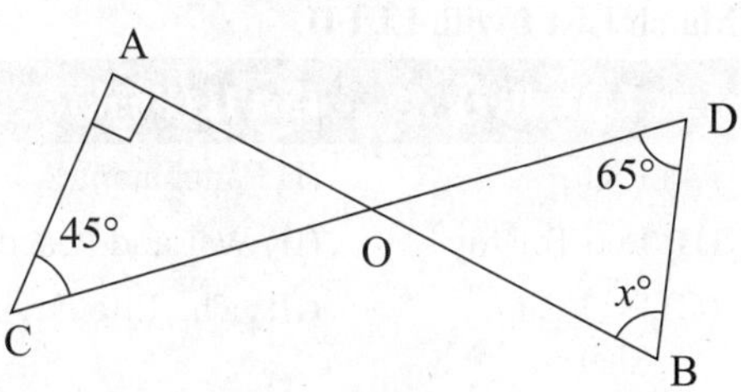

(1) 65 (2) 70
(3) 75 (4) 45

25. Given below are two statements: one is labelled as Assertion (A), and the other is labelled as Reason (R).
Assertion (A): Milk production in India is low compared to many other countries.
Reason (R): The animal rearers in India are poor.
In the light of the above statements, choose the most appropriate answer from the options given below:
(1) Both (A) and (R) are correct and (R) is the correct explanation of (A).
(2) Both (A) and (R) are correct but (R) is not the correct explanation of (A).
(3) (A) is correct, but (R) is not correct.
(4) (A) is not correct, but (R) is correct.

26. Study the following arrangement carefully and answer the question given below.
M D E K 7 B I 4 M J N E 7 6 Z U V W 1 3 H 4 F
How many such numbers are there in the above sequence, each immediately preceded by a consonant and immediately followed by a vowel?
(1) zero (2) one
(3) two (4) three

27. Find the value of $\sqrt{6+\sqrt{6+\sqrt{6+\sqrt{6 \ldots \ldots \ldots}}}}$.
(1) 3 (2) 2
(3) 6 (4) $\sqrt{8}$

28. Mohan is 14th in a row of 40 boys from the left end. What is his position from the right end?
(1) 21st (2) 24th
(3) 27th (4) 25th

29. As shown in the figure, a sector is assembled to form a cone. What is the base radius (in cm) of the cone so formed? $\left(\pi = \frac{22}{7}\right)$

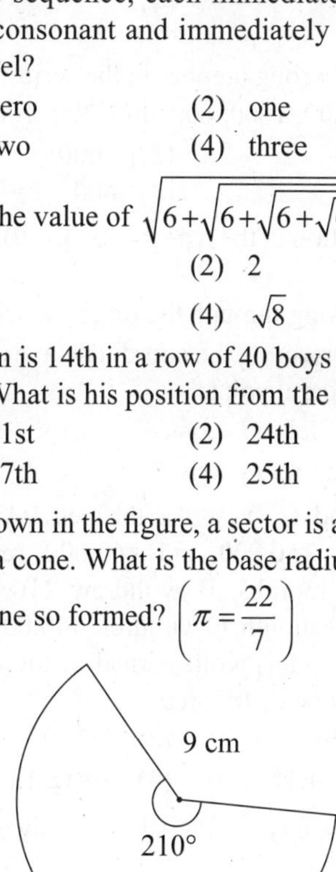

(1) 9 (2) 5.25
(3) 6.75 (4) 4.5

30. Which number is in the square, ellipse and triangle?

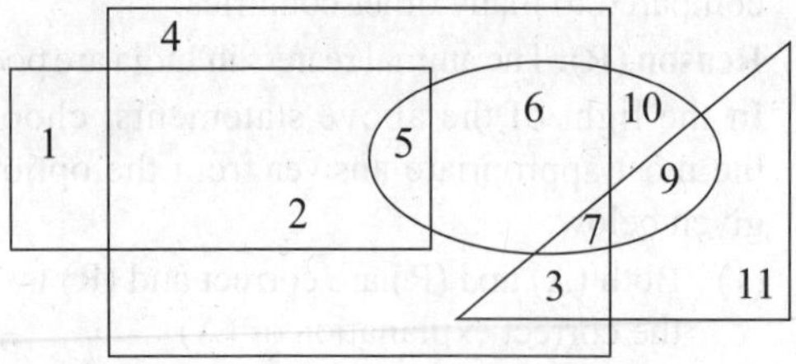

(1) 7 (2) 6
(3) 5 (4) 1

31. A dice is thrown twice. Find the probability of getting an odd number in the second throw and a multiple of 3 in the first throw.

(1) $\frac{1}{2}$ (2) $\frac{1}{3}$

(3) $\frac{1}{6}$ (4) $\frac{1}{9}$

32. Find the wrong number in the series.
6400, 3200, 1600, 600, 400, 200, 100, 50
(1) 200 (2) 1600
(3) 100 (4) 600

33. An equation of the type y = kx (k ≠ 0) represents a line:
(1) passing through the origin
(2) intersecting the coordinate axes at two different points
(3) parallel to x-axis
(4) parallel to y-axis

34. A, B and C started a business by investing ₹40,000, ₹50,000 and ₹60,000 respectively. After 8 months, B withdrew ₹10,000. After one more month, C withdrew ₹40,000. Find the ratio in which profit earned at the end of the year will be distributed.
(1) 4:5:6 (2) 2:2:1
(3) 12:14:15 (4) 10:12:13

35. In which city of Punjab are railway coaches manufactured?
(1) Ludhiana (2) Patiala
(3) Kapurthala (4) Bhatinda

36. If $\frac{2a^2 - 3b^2}{a^2 + b^2} = \frac{2}{41}$, then $a:b$ =
(1) 5:4 (2) 25:16
(3) 16:25 (4) 4:5

37. The pie chart shows the degree-wise breakdown of a family's monthly expenditure. The total amount spent in a month is ₹45800.

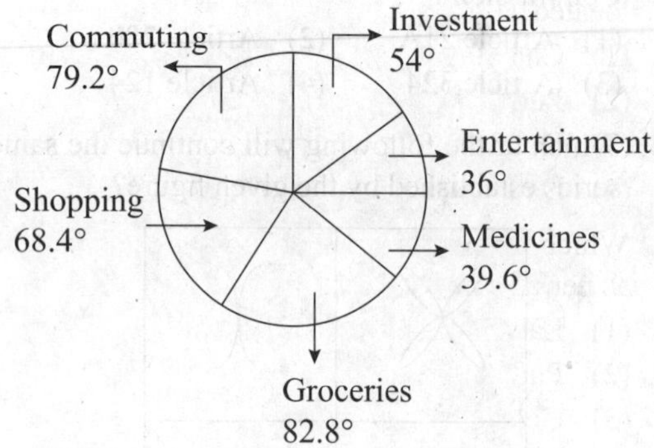

What is the amount spent by the family on commuting?
(1) ₹10076 (2) ₹10354
(3) ₹6870 (4) ₹8702

38. In a family of 6 members, D is the only son of A, E is the grandfather of D. B is the daughter-in-law of C. F is the uncle of D. C is the wife of A. How is B related to D?
(1) wife (2) sister
(3) niece (4) aunt

39. The sum of the fourth proportional of 4, 5, 16 and the mean proportional of 4, 16 is
(1) 25 (2) 28
(3) 30 (4) 32

40. Match **List I** with **List II**.

List I (Writer)	List II (Book)
(A) Plato	(I) Panchatantra
(B) Leo Tolstoy	(II) War and Peace
(C) Pt. Vishnu Sharma	(III) The Life Divine
(D) Sri Aurobindo Ghosh	(IV) The Republic

Choose the most appropriate answer from the options given below:

(1) (A)-(IV), (B)-(II), (C)-(I), (D)-(III)
(2) (A)-(II), (B)-(IV), (C)-(I), (D)-(III)
(3) (A)-(IV), (B)-(I), (C)-(II), (D)-(III)
(4) (A)-(II), (B)-(I), (C)-(III), (D)-(IV)

41. In which Union Territory of India is the "National Meat and Poultry Processing Board" located?

(1) Chandigarh
(2) Puducherry
(3) Delhi
(4) Dadra and Nagar Haveli

42. Which Union Territory of India is the smallest as per its area?

(1) Lakshadweep
(2) Puducherry
(3) Chandigarh
(4) Delhi

43. Find the odd pair out.

(1) 11:125 (2) 33:1093
(3) 35:1229 (4) 17:295

44. Which of the following is known as the "Island of Pearls"?

(1) Australia (2) Zanzibar
(3) Bahrain (4) Panama

45. If $\sin 2\theta = \cos 40°$, then the smallest positive value of θ is:

(1) 25° (2) 20°
(3) 40° (4) 30°

46. ______ is called the father of Indian Archaeology.

(1) James Prinsep
(2) John Marshall
(3) Alexander Cunningham
(4) Mortimer Wheeler

47. Find the missing term in 1, 4, 10, 22, 46, __?

(1) 100 (2) 98
(3) 96 (4) 94

48. The 10th term of the A.P. 1, 5, 9, 13, . . ., is:

(1) 36 (2) 33
(3) 37 (4) 41

49. Find the missing figure from the given options.

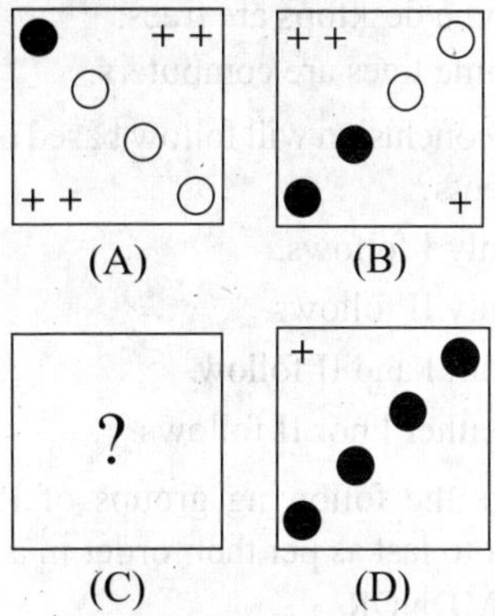

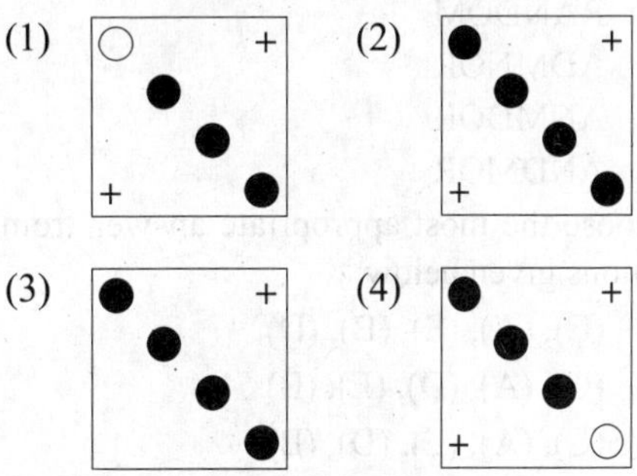

50. The ascending order of the numbers 0.8, 0.88, 0.808, 0.08 is

(1) 0.88, 0.808, 0.8, 0.08
(2) 0.808, 0.8, 0.08, 0.88
(3) 0.08, 0.8, 0.88, 0.808
(4) 0.08, 0.8, 0.808, 0.88

51. "CNG" stands for ______

(1) Common Natural Gas
(2) Compressed Natural Gas
(3) Common Effective Natural Gas
(4) Compressed Neutral Gas

52. A rectangular room can be partitioned into two equal square rooms by a 7-meter-long partition. What is the floor area of the rectangular room in m^2?

(1) 49 (2) 98
(3) 147 (4) 196

53. Statements:

(I) No tree is a desktop.
(II) All desktops are computers.

Conclusions:

(I) Some desktops are trees.

(II) Some trees are computers.

Which conclusion will follow based on the given statements?

(1) Only I follows.

(2) Only II follows.

(3) Both I and II follow.

(4) Neither I nor II follows.

54. Arrange the following groups of letters from the first to last as per their order in a dictionary.

(A) AMDNOR

(B) RANDOM

(C) ADMNOR

(D) ANMDOR

(E) ANDMOR

Choose the most appropriate answer from the options given below:

(1) (C), (A), (E), (B), (D)

(2) (C), (A), (D), (E), (B)

(3) (C), (A), (E), (D), (B)

(4) (C), (B), (A), (E), (D)

55. The life span of 'RBC' is ______.

(1) 48 Hours

(2) 24 Hours

(3) 12 Hours

(4) 120 days

56. How many times has Mithali Raj played in the ICC Women's Cricket World Cup?

(1) 4 (2) 3

(3) 5 (4) 6

57. Starting from point P, Sunil walked 30 m towards the South. He turned to his left and walked 40 m. Then, he again turned to his left and walked 30 m. Turning to his left, he walks 15 m and stops at point N. How far is Sunil from the starting point P?

(1) 30 m

(2) 15 m

(3) 25 m

(4) 10 m.

58. Match **List I** with **List II**.

List I (States)	List II (Bordering Countries)
(A) Punjab, Rajasthan, Gujarat	(I) Bhutan
(B) Himachal Pradesh, Uttarakhand, Sikkim, Arunachal Pradesh	(II) Pakistan
(C) West Bengal, Mizoram, Meghalaya, Tripura, Assam	(III) China
(D) West Bengal, Sikkim, Arunachal Pradesh, Assam	(IV) Bangladesh

Choose the most appropriate answer from the options given below:

(1) (A)-(III), (B)-(IV), (C)-(I), (D)-(II)

(2) (A)-(II), (B)-(III), (C)-(I), (D)-(IV)

(3) (A)-(III), (B)-(II), (C)-(IV), (D)-(I)

(4) (A)-(II), (B)-(III), (C)-(IV), (D)-(I)

59. Which Indian meteorological satellite was renamed Kalpana-I in 2003?

(1) INSAT-3A

(2) METSAT

(3) INSAT-3C

(4) GSAT-2

60. Statement: European economy is dependent mainly on forests.

Conclusions:

(I) Europe wants only the maintenance of forests to improve economic conditions.

(II) Trees should be preserved to improve the European economy.

Which conclusion will follow based on the given statement?

(1) Only Conclusion I follows.

(2) Only Conclusion II follows.

(3) Both Conclusions I and II follow.

(4) Either Conclusion I or II follows.

Answer Key

1. **(2)**	2. **(1)**	3. **(3)**	4. **(2)**	5. **(3)**	6. **(1)**	7. **(1)**	8. **(4)**	9. **(2)**	10. **(3)**
11. **(2)**	12. **(1)**	13. **(2)**	14. **(4)**	15. **(2)**	16. **(3)**	17. **(4)**	18. **(3)**	19. **(2)**	20. **(1)**
21. **(1)**	22. **(2)**	23. **(4)**	24. **(2)**	25. **(4)***	26. **(1)**	27. **(1)**	28. **(3)**	29. **(2)**	30. **(1)**
31. **(3)**	32. **(4)**	33. **(1)**	34. **(3)**	35. **(3)**	36. **(1)**	37. **(1)**	38. **(1)**	39. **(2)**	40. **(1)**
41. **(3)**	42. **(1)**	43. **(4)**	44. **(3)**	45. **(1)**	46. **(3)**	47. **(4)**	48. **(3)**	49. **(4)**	50. **(4)**
51. **(2)**	52. **(2)**	53. **(4)**	54. **(3)**	55. **(4)**	56. **(4)**	57. **(3)**	58. **(4)**	59. **(2)**	60. **(2)**

Classification of Questions

Question No.	Subject	Topic	Level of Difficulty
1.	Reasoning	Coding	Easy
2.	Quantitative Aptitude	Mensuration	Easy
3.	Quantitative Aptitude	Calendars	Easy
4.	Quantitative Aptitude	Time and Work	Medium
5.	Quantitative Aptitude	Ratios	Easy
6.	General Awareness	Current Affairs	Difficult
7.	General Awareness	Geography	Medium
8.	Quantitative Aptitude	Profit, Loss and Discount	Easy
9.	Quantitative Aptitude	Averages	Easy
10.	Quantitative Aptitude	Time, Speed and Distance	Medium
11.	Reasoning	Series	Easy
12.	Reasoning	Miscellaneous	Easy
13.	Quantitative Aptitude	Compound Interest	Easy
14.	General Awareness	Science	Easy
15.	General Awareness	History	Difficult
16.	Quantitative Aptitude	Clocks	Difficult
17.	General Awareness	Government Schemes	Difficult
18.	Reasoning	Non-verbal	Easy
19.	General Awareness	Sports	Easy
20.	General Awareness	Geography	Easy
21.	General Awareness	Science	Easy

Question No.	Subject	Topic	Level of Difficulty
22.	General Awareness	Polity	Medium
23.	Reasoning	Non-Verbal	Easy
24.	Quantitative Aptitude	Geometry	Easy
25.	General Awareness	Geography	Easy
26.	Reasoning	Miscellaneous	Easy
27.	Quantitative Aptitude	Algebra	Medium
28.	Reasoning	Ranking	Easy
29.	Quantitative Aptitude	Mensuration	Difficult
30.	Reasoning	Venn Diagram	Easy
31.	Quantitative Aptitude	Probability	Easy
32.	Reasoning	Series	Easy
33.	Quantitative Aptitude	Coordinate Geometry	Easy
34.	Quantitative Aptitude	Ratios	Easy
35.	General Awareness	Geography	Medium
36.	Quantitative Aptitude	Ratios	Easy
37.	Data Interpretation	Pie-Chart	Easy
38.	Reasoning	Blood Relation	Easy
39.	Quantitative Aptitude	Ratios and Proportions	Easy
40.	General Awareness	Books and Authors	Medium
41.	General Awareness	Geography	Difficult
42.	General Awareness	Geography	Easy
43.	Reasoning	Odd Pair	Easy
44.	General Awareness	Geography	Difficult
45.	Quantitative Aptitude	Trigonometry	Easy
46.	General Awareness	History	Medium
47.	Reasoning	Number Series	Easy
48.	Quantitative Aptitude	Algebra (A.P.)	Easy
49.	Reasoning	Non-verbal	Easy
50.	Quantitative Aptitude	Ascending Order of Numbers	Easy
51.	General Awareness	Science	Easy
52.	Quantitative Aptitude	Mensuration	Medium
53.	Reasoning	Syllogism	Easy
54.	Reasoning	Ranking	Easy
55.	General Awareness	Science	Medium
56.	General Awareness	Sports	Difficult

Question No.	Subject	Topic	Level of Difficulty
57.	Reasoning	Directions	Easy
58.	General Awareness	Geography	Difficult
59.	General Awareness	Science and Technology	Easy
60.	Reasoning	Statement-Conclusion	Easy

The no. of questions on Quantitative Aptitude: 21
The no. of questions on General Awareness: 21
The no. of questions on Data Interpretation: 1
The no. of questions on Reasoning: 17

Explanation to Select Questions

1. **E** — **5**

P E N — **16 5 14**; code = 16 + 5 + 14 = 35

P A G E — **16 1 7 5**; code = 16 + 1 + 7 + 5 = 29

Hence, Option 2.

2. Let the radius of the cylinder be r and height h.
It's height = 14 (given).
The curved surface area = $2\pi rh$

$= 2\times\frac{22}{7}\times r\times 14 = 88$

$\Rightarrow r = 1$

The diameter = $2r$ = 2.
Hence, Option 1.

3. $60 = 7\times 8 + 4$
Hence, there are 4 odd days in 60 days.
So, the answer is 4 days after a Monday, and that is a Friday.
Hence, Option 3.

4. $\because$ 9 boys can complete the work in 360 days,
$\therefore$ 1 boy can complete it in 360×9 days
$\therefore$ 10 boys can complete the work in

$\frac{360\times 9}{10}$ days = 324 days.

Similarly, 4 men can complete the work in $\frac{72\times 18}{4} = 324$ days.

The work done by 4 men, 12 women and 10 boys in a day $= \frac{1}{324}+\frac{1}{162}+\frac{1}{324} = \frac{4}{324} = \frac{1}{81}$.

Therefore, the work will be completed in 81 days.
Hence, Option 2.

5. Let the weight of the first part be x and that of the second part be y.
As per the question:

$5x + 11y = 7(x + y)$

or, $11y - 7y = 7x - 5x$ or, $4y = 2x$

or, $x = 2y$ or, $\frac{x}{y} = \frac{2}{1}$.

Hence, Option 3.

6. A Japanese space startup, iSpace, has launched its private lander to the Moon over a SpaceX rocket.
Hence, Option 1.

8. Let the cost price of the jacket for the wholesaler be x.
As per the question,
The cost price for the retailer $= x\times\frac{105}{100}$.

The cost price for the customer $= x\times\frac{105}{100}\times\frac{110}{100}$.

Also, $x\times\frac{105}{100}\times\frac{110}{100} = 4158$

or, $x = 3600$.
Hence, Option 4.

9. The average weight of A, B and C is 60 kg.

$\therefore$ The total weight of A, B and C is 60 × 3 = 180 kg.

The average weight of B and C is 50 kg.

$\therefore$ The total weight of B and C is 50 × 2 = 100 kg.

The average weight of A and B is 52 kg.

$\therefore$ the total weight of A and B is 52 × 2 = 104 kg.

So, $A + B + C = 180$ (i)

$A + B = 104$ (ii)

$B + C = 100$ (iii)

Adding (ii) and (iii), we get

$A + 2B + C = 204$ (iv)

Subtracting (i) from (iv), we get, B = 24.

Hence, Option 2.

10. Let the distance be d.

P's speed = 3 km/h, time taken by P to travel distance $d = \frac{d}{3}$.

Q's speed = 3.75 km/h = $\frac{15}{4}$ km/h, time taken by Q to travel distance $d = \frac{d}{\frac{15}{4}} = \frac{4d}{15}$.

As per the question:

$$\frac{d}{3} - \frac{4d}{15} = \frac{1}{2}$$

$$\text{or, } \frac{5d - 4d}{15} = \frac{1}{2}$$

$$\text{or, } \frac{d}{15} = \frac{1}{2} \quad \text{or, } d = \frac{15}{2} = 7.5 \text{ km.}$$

Hence, Option 3.

Alternative: Look for an option that is easily divisible by 3 as well as 3.75. You just need to check if the difference between the quotients is $\frac{1}{2}$.

11. The terms here form a GP with a common ratio of 1.5. So, starting with the 2nd term, every term is 1.5 times the preceding term.

$$6 = 4 \times 1.5, \quad 9 = 6 \times 1.5, \quad 13\frac{1}{2} = 9 \times 1.5.$$

The next term is

$$13\frac{1}{2} \times 1.5 = \frac{27}{2} \times \frac{3}{2} = \frac{81}{4} = 20\frac{1}{4}.$$

Hence, Option 2.

13. Let the rate of interest be r.

We have,

$$2226.05 = 2000\left(1 + \frac{r}{100}\right)^2$$

$$\text{or, } \frac{2226.05}{2000} = \left(1 + \frac{r}{100}\right)^2$$

$$\text{or, } \left(1 + \frac{r}{100}\right)^2 = \frac{2226.05}{2000} = (1.055)^2$$

$$\text{or, } \left(1 + \frac{r}{100}\right)^2 = \left(1 + \frac{5.5}{100}\right)^2$$

$\Rightarrow r = 5.5.$

Hence, Option 2.

Alternative:

Here, the interest is 226.05 < 240.

Hence, we can easily say that the rate of interest is less than 6%.

Even the simple interest on 2000 at 6% per annum for 2 years is 240, and the compound interest will be even more than 240.

Thus, we can rule out options 3 and 4 as they are 6% and 6.5%.

The compound interest on 2000 at 5% per annum for 2 years is 205.

As 226.05 > 205, we can rule out option 1 as well, and hence the answer is Option 2.

14. A Barometer measures atmospheric pressure.

Hence, Option 4.

An odometer is an instrument for measuring the distance a wheeled vehicle travels.

A pedometer is a device that counts the number of steps a person takes.

16. As the clock loses 16 minutes in 24 hours (1440 minutes), when it shows 1424 minutes, the actual time is 1440 minutes.

From 5 am on the 1st day to 10 pm on the 4th day is 89 hours as per this faulty clock.

89 hours = 89 × 60 minutes.

Now,

When the clock shows 1424 minutes, the actual time = 1440

When the clock shows 1 minute, the actual time is $= \frac{1440}{1424}$

When the clock shows 89 × 60 minutes, the actual time $= \frac{1440}{1424} \times 89 \times 60$

$= 90 \times 60$ minutes

$= 90$ hours.

Hence, the clock has lost 1 hour.

⇒ The actual time is 11 pm.

Hence, Option 3.

Alternative: The clock loses only 16 minutes in a day.

Hence, when it shows 89 hours, the actual time is certainly less than 4 days.

∵ In 1 day, the clock loses 16 minutes,

∴ in 4 days, the clock loses 64 minutes.

And, in less than 4 days, the clock loses less than 64 minutes. There is only one option in which the clock loses less than 60 minutes.

Hence, Option 3.

24.

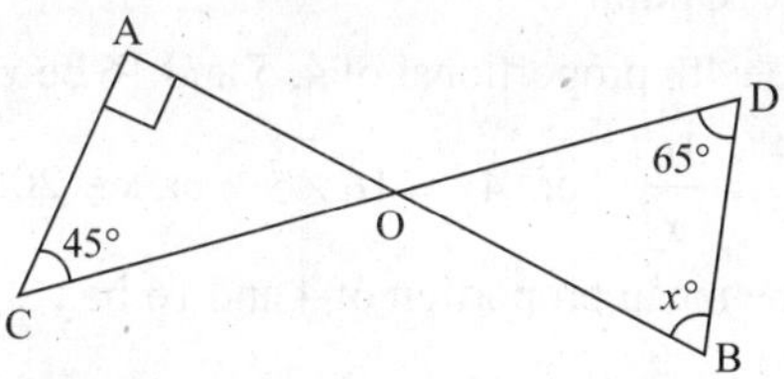

$\angle AOC = 180° - 90° - 45° = 45°$

$\angle BOD = \angle AOC = 45°$

$\angle OBD = 180° - 65° - 45° = 70° = x°$.

Therefore, $x = 70$.

Hence, Option 2.

25. It was a very poorly framed question; the official answer was Option 3. We strongly object to this answer. India is the largest milk producer in the world; hence, we CANNOT say that milk production in India is low compared to many other countries. What they probably meant by 'milk production' is 'milk yield'. Milk yield is defined as the amount of milk produced per day per animal. Milk yield in India is only about 2/3 of the world average. The statement given in the Reason (R) is also very vague.

27. Let $\sqrt{6+\sqrt{6+\sqrt{6+\sqrt{6+\ldots}}}}$ be x.

$x^2 = 6 + x$

or, $x^2 - x - 6 = 0$

or, $(x - 3)(x + 2) = 0$

or, $x = 3$ (x cannot be a negative number)

Hence, Option 1.

29.

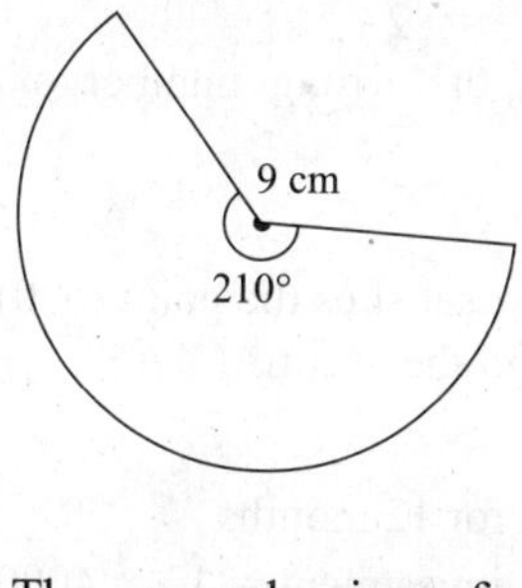

The curved circumference of the figure $= 2 \times \frac{22}{7} \times 9 \times \frac{210}{360} = 33$.

This curved circumference will become the circumference of the base of the cone.

Let the radius of the base of the cone be r.

$2\pi r = 33$

or, $2 \times \frac{22}{7} \times r = 33$

or, $r = \frac{33 \times 7}{22 \times 2} = 5.25$.

Hence, Option 2.

31. The first throw:

Favourable cases: 3 and 6

Total cases: 1, 2, 3, 4, 5 and 6

∴ the probability of getting a multiple of 3 in the first throw $= \frac{2}{6} = \frac{1}{3}$.

The second throw:

Favourable cases: 1, 3 and 5

Total cases: 1, 2, 3, 4, 5, and 6

∴ the probability of getting an odd number $= \frac{3}{6} = \frac{1}{2}$.

The overall probability $= \frac{1}{3} \times \frac{1}{2} = \frac{1}{6}$.

Hence, Option 3.

32. The given series is a GP with a common ratio of $\frac{1}{2}$.

The 2nd term $= 6400 \times \frac{1}{2} = 3200$

The 3rd term $= 3200 \times \frac{1}{2} = 1600$

The 4th term $= 1600 \times \frac{1}{2} = 800$ (NOT 600).

Therefore, 600 is the wrong number of the series.

Hence, Option 4.

33. The equation $y = kx$ satisfies the point (0, 0), so it must pass through the origin.

Hence, Option 1.

34. A invested 40,000 for 12 months.

Hence, A's month-investment $= 12 \times 40000 = 480000$.

B invested 50000 for 8 months and 40000 for 4 months.

Hence, B's month-investment $= 50000 \times 8 + 40000 \times 4 = 560000$.

C invested 60000 for 9 months and 20000 for 3 months.

Hence, C's month-investment $= 60000 \times 9 + 20000 \times 3 = 600000$.

Therefore, the ratio of the investments of A, B and C is 480000:560000:600000 = 12:14:15.

So, the profit will also be distributed in the ratio 12:14:15 among A, B and C, respectively.

Hence, Option 3.

Shortcut: Even if we get the ratio for only A and B, we will get the answer as there is only one option in which the ratio of the profits of A and B is 6:7.

35. The Rail Coach Factory (RCF) is situated at Kapurthala.

Hence, Option 3.

36. $\frac{2a^2 - 3b^2}{a^2 + b^2} = \frac{2}{41}$

or, $41(2a^2 - 3b^2) = 2(a^2 + b^2)$

or, $82a^2 - 123b^2 = 2a^2 + 2b^2$

or, $80a^2 = 125b^2$

or, $\frac{a^2}{b^2} = \frac{125}{80} = \frac{25}{16}$ or, $\frac{a}{b} = \frac{5}{4}$.

Hence, Option 1.

37. The amount spent by the family on commuting

$= \frac{79.2}{360} \times 45800 = 10076$.

Hence, Option 1.

38. We need to concentrate on just 3 facts:

1. D is the only son of A.
2. C is the wife of A and
3. B is the daughter-in-law of C

From these 3, we get:

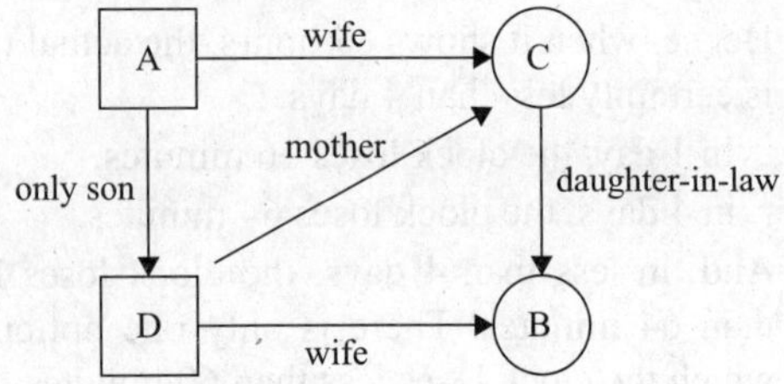

Therefore, B is D's wife.

Hence, Option 1.

39. Let the 4th proportional of 4, 5 and 16 be x.

So, $\frac{4}{5} = \frac{16}{x}$ or, $4x = 16 \times 5$ or, $x = 20$.

Let the mean proportion of 4 and 16 be y.

We have, $\frac{4}{x} = \frac{x}{16}$ or, $x^2 = 64$ or, $x = 8$.

The required sum = 20 + 8 = 28.

Hence, Option 2.

42.

Union Territory	Area
Delhi	1483 sq km
Puducherry	492 sq km
Chandigarh	114 sq km
Lakshadweep	32 sq km

Hence, Option 1.

43. $125 = 11^2 + 4$, $1093 = 33^2 + 4$, $1229 = 35^2 + 4$.

but $295 = 17^2 + 6$.

Hence, Option 4.

45. $\text{Sin } 2\theta = \text{Cos } 40° = \text{Sin } 50°$

or, $\text{Sin } 2\theta = \text{Sin } 50°$

$\Rightarrow 2\theta = 50°$

or, $\theta = \frac{50°}{2} = 25°$

Hence, Option 1.

46. Alexander Cunningham is considered the father of the Indian Archaeology. He was the first Director-General of the Archaeological Survey of India (ASI).

Hence, Option 3.

47. Here, $4 = 1 \times 2 + 2$, $10 = 4 \times 2 + 2$, $22 = 10 \times 2 + 2$, $46 = 22 \times 2 + 2$.

Therefore, the next term $= 46 \times 2 + 2 = 94$.

Hence, Option 4.

48. Here, the first term of the AP, a = 1

The common difference, d = 4

The nth term, $T_n = a + (n - 1)d$

The 10th term, $T_{10} = 1 + (10 - 1)4$

$= 1 + 36 = 37$.

Hence, Option 3.

51. Compressed Natural Gas (CNG) mainly comprises Methane (CH_4).

Hence, Option 2.

52.

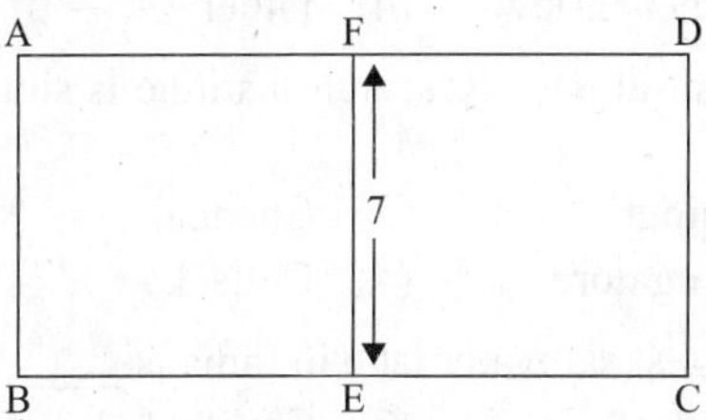

Let ABCD be the rectangular room and EF the 7-metre-long partition.

As ABEF and FECD are squares,

AB = BE = EF = FA = 7 and EC = CD = DF = FE = 7.

Hence, the length AD of the rectangle = AF + FD = 7 + 7 = 14.

the breadth AB of the rectangle = 7.

Therefore, the area of the rectangle $= 14 \times 7 = 98\ m^2$.

Hence, Option 2.

Shortcut: As the rectangular room can be partitioned into two squares, the area of the rectangle should be 2 times a perfect square, which is only in option 2.

53.

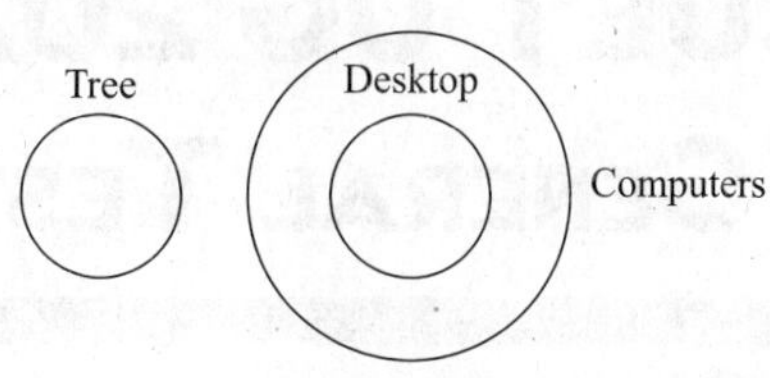

Possibility-I

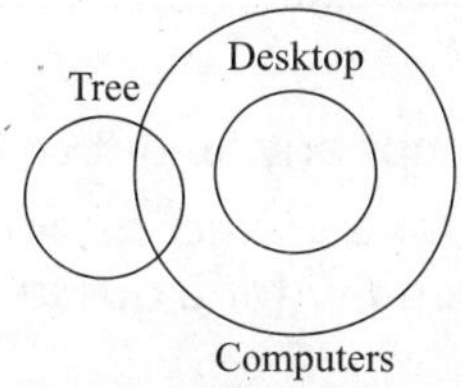

Possibility-II

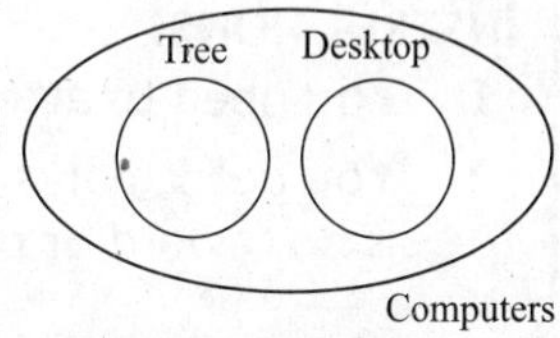

Possibility-III

There can be many possibilities here as the statements are silent on the relation between Trees and Computers.

Conclusion I is impossible.

Conclusion II is a possibility, as seen in II, but it cannot be concluded.

Hence, Option 4.

55. The life span of Red Blood Cells (RBC) is around 120 days.

Hence, Option 4.

The life span of White Blood Cells (WBC) is normally from 12 to 20 days.

57.

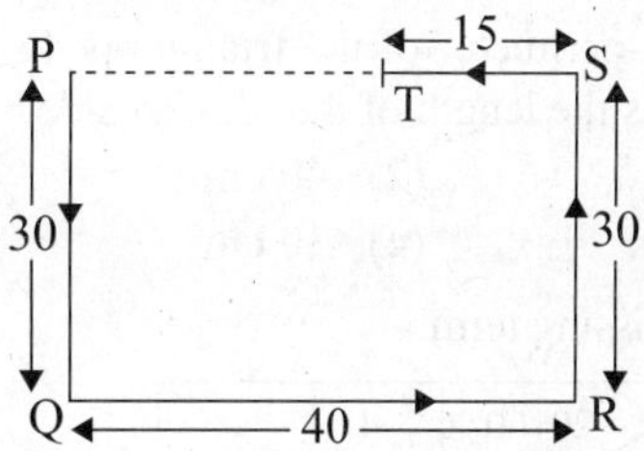

Let Sunil's final position be T.

As we can see from the figure, PQRS is a rectangle, and SP = QR = 40.

PT = SP – ST = 40 – 15 = 25.

Hence, Option 3.

59. The question is about a 'meteorological' satellite, and Option 2 is METSAT. The 'MET' of METSAT is for meteorological. It was an easy picking!

SHIFT - 3

CUET UG 2023
GENERAL TEST

May
24

INSTRUCTIONS:

1. You need to attempt any 50 out of the 60 questions in 60 minutes.
2. You get 5 marks for a correct response and –1 for an incorrect one. However, there is no reward or penalty for a question not attempted.

1. One of the Harappan sites known as Kalibangan is located in which state of India?
(1) Rajasthan
(2) Gujarat
(3) Madhya Pradesh
(4) Punjab

2. Sixty-four solid iron spheres of radius r are melted to form a sphere of radius R. Find R:r.
(1) 2:1 (2) 3:1
(3) 8:1 (4) 4:1

3. The sides of a triangle are in the ratio $\frac{1}{3}:\frac{1}{4}:\frac{1}{5}$.
If the semi-perimeter of the triangle is 47 cm, then what is the length of the longest side?
(1) 20 cm (2) 40 cm
(3) 44 cm (4) 30 cm

4. Find the missing term.

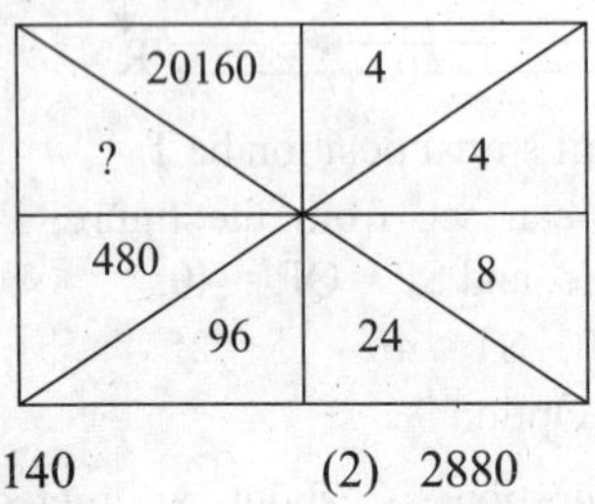

(1) 1140 (2) 2880
(3) 3240 (4) 860

5. If the arithmetic mean and geometric mean of roots of a quadratic equation are 8 and 5, respectively, then the quadratic equation is:
(1) $x^2 + 8x + 5 = 0$
(2) $x^2 - 8x + 25 = 0$
(3) $x^2 - 16x + 25 = 0$
(4) $2x^2 - 8x + 25 = 0$

6. Rahul told Anand, "Yesterday, I defeated the only brother of the daughter of my grandmother". Whom did Rahul defeat?
(1) son (2) brother
(3) father-in-law (4) father

7. The Central Rice Research Institute is situated in ______.
(1) Raipur (2) Chennai
(3) Bangalore (4) Cuttack

8. The largest saltwater lake in India is ______.
(1) Wular Lake (2) Chilika Lake
(3) Loktak Lake (4) Dal Lake

9. Here are some phrases translated from an artificial language:
'hirpa nig' means 'bat ball'.
'kirpa nig' means 'foot ball'.
'kirpa nad' means 'foot mark'.
Which word would mean "mark sheet" in that language?
(1) hirpa kirpa (2) nad tyan
(3) hirpa nad (4) kirpa nad

10. A pair of dice is thrown. What is the probability of getting the sum of the numbers on the two faces as an odd-prime number?
(1) $\frac{7}{18}$ (2) $\frac{1}{6}$
(3) $\frac{1}{2}$ (4) $\frac{5}{12}$

11. In the following question, if a mirror is placed on the line AB, then which of the answer figures is the right image of the given figure?

Problem Figure

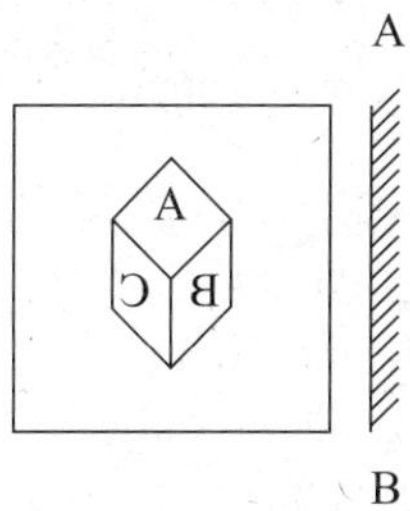

a b c d

(1) a (2) b

(3) c (4) d

12. A cuboidal slab of copper with dimensions 22 cm × 10 cm × 5 cm is melted and recast in the form of a wire of 1 mm diameter. The wire is rubber coated at ₹1.50 per meter. Find the cost of rubber coating (in ₹). Use $\left(\pi = \frac{22}{7}\right)$.

(1) 525 (2) 650

(3) 2100 (4) 2600

13. The value of $\sqrt[4]{(625)^3}$ is:

(1) 110 (2) 25

(3) 125 (4) 115

14. Pratap starts from school and walks 7 km towards the East. He takes a left and walks 4 km, then takes a right and walks 2 km. He, again, takes a right and walks 3 km. Which direction is he facing now?

(1) West (2) East

(3) North (4) South

15. Lift was invented by _______.

(1) Richard Gatling (2) E.G. Otis

(3) K.G. Johnson (4) J.C. Perier

16. If the average weight of 10 students is 25 kg and that of the other 10 students is 35 kg, then the average weight of these 20 students is:

(1) 30 kg (2) 35 kg

(3) 25 kg (4) 20 kg

17. Given below are two statements: one is labelled as Assertion (A), and the other is labelled as Reason (R).

Assertion (A): Leakages in household gas cylinders can be detected.

Reason (R): LPG has a strong smell.

In the light of the above statements, choose the most appropriate answer from the options given below:

(1) Both (A) and (R) are correct, and (R) is the correct explanation of (A).

(2) Both (A) and (R) are correct, but (R) is not the correct explanation of (A).

(3) (A) is correct, but (R) is not correct.

(4) (A) is not correct, but (R) is correct.

18. Match **List I** with **List II**.

List I (Sobriquets)	List II (Names)
(A) Sorrow of Bengal	(I) Udaipur
(B) Venice of the East	(II) river Kosi
(C) Sorrow of Bihar	(III) Ahmedabad
(D) Bostan of India	(IV) river Damodar

Choose the most appropriate answer from the options given below:

(1) (A)-(III), (B)-(II), (C)-(I), (D)-(IV)

(2) (A)-(IV), (B)-(I), (C)-(III), (D)-(II)

(3) (A)-(IV), (B)-(I), (C)-(II), (D)-(III)

(4) (A)-(I), (B)-(IV), (C)-(II), (D)-(III)

19. A 110 m long train takes 3 seconds to pass a pole. How long is the platform if the train passes it in 15 seconds?

(1) 440 m (2) 400 m

(3) 550 m (4) 450 m

20. Find the missing term:

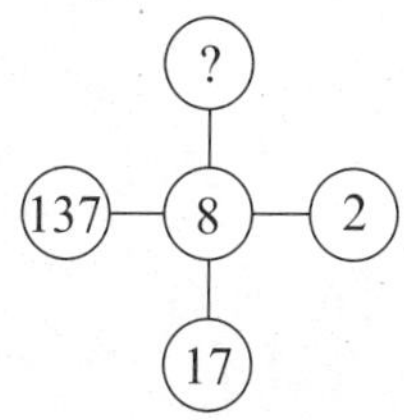

(1) 9107 (2) 907
(3) 1097 (3) 97

21. The age of a tree can be calculated by _______.
(1) measuring its height
(2) measuring the thickness of the trunk
(3) measuring the width of the tree
(4) measuring the number of annual rings

22. Match **List I** with **List II**.

List I	List II
(A) Bharatnatyam	(I) Sonal Mansingh
(B) Kathak	(II) Lakshmi Narayan Shastri
(C) Odissi	(III) Krishna Iyer
(D) Kuchipudi	(IV) Sitara Devi

Choose the most appropriate answer from the options given below:
(1) (A)-(II), (B)-(III), (C)-(I), (D)-(IV)
(2) (A)-(IV), (B)-(III), (C)-(II), (D)-(I)
(3) (A)-(I), (B)-(II), (C)-(IV), (D)-(III)
(4) (A)-(III), (B)-(IV), (C)-(I), (D)-(II)

23. Which of the following fundamental rights has been removed from our constitution?
(1) Right against exploitation
(2) Right to constitutional remedies
(3) Right to property
(4) Right to freedom of religion

24. Forty-four per cent of a number is 2288. What will be 87% of the number?
(1) 3614 (2) 4524
(3) 4815 (4) 3928

25. In ΔABC with $AB = 5$ cm, $BC = 12$ cm, $AC = 13$ cm and $\angle B = 90°$, which of the following are not correct?

(A) $\tan C = \frac{12}{13}$

(B) $\text{cosec } A = \frac{13}{12}$

(C) $\sin B = \frac{5}{13}$

(D) $\tan A = \frac{12}{15}$

(E) $\cos C = \frac{12}{13}$

Choose the correct answer from the options given below:
(1) (A), (B) and (C) only
(2) (A) and (B) only
(3) (A), (C) and (D) only
(4) (B), (C) and (D) only

26. Match **List I** with **List II**.

List I (Vitamin)	List II (Deficiency Disease)
(A) Vitamin – A	(I) Scurvy
(B) Vitamin – C	(II) Rickets
(C) Vitamin – D	(III) non-clotting of blood
(D) Vitamin – K	(IV) colour blindness

Choose the most appropriate answer from the options given below:
(1) (A)-(I), (B)-(IV), (C)-(II), (D)-(III)
(2) (A)-(IV), (B)-(I), (C)-(II), (D)-(III)
(3) (A)-(IV), (B)-(I), (C)-(III), (D)-(II)
(4) (A)-(I), (B)-(IV), (C)-(III), (D)-(II)

27. Choose the alternative figure in which the problem figure is embedded.

Problem Figure

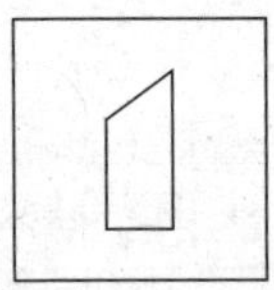

(1) 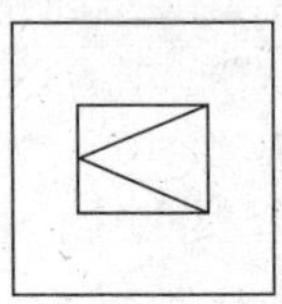 (2) 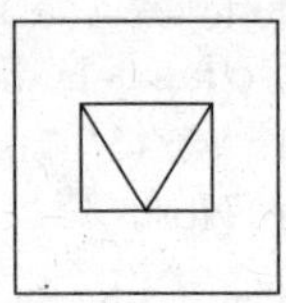

(3) 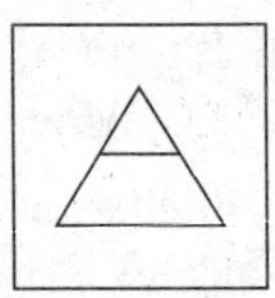 (4) 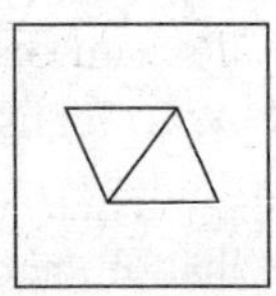

28. Find the wrong number in the given series:
89, 78, 86, 80, 85, 82, 83
(1) 78 (2) 86
(3) 82 (4) 83

29. Who was awarded the Booker Prize in 2022?
(1) Annie Ernaux (2) Mallika Sarabhai
(3) Arundhati Roy (4) Shehan Karunatilaka

30. Find the missing term in the given series:
1, 9, 25, 49, 81, ?, 169
(1) 91 (2) 144
(3) 121 (4) 64

31. Correct the following equation by interchanging the two signs:
$4 \times 2 + 6 \div 2 - 12 = 2$
(1) ÷ and × (2) + and –
(3) × and + (4) ÷ and –

32. The difference between two numbers, P and Q (P > Q), is 40% of their sum. The ratio of P:Q is:
(1) 6:4 (2) 7:3
(3) 8:5 (4) 5:4

33. Match **List I** with **List II**.

List I (Name of Sanctuaries)	List II (Locations)
(A) Achanakmar	(I) Jammu and Kashmir
(B) Dachigam	(II) Karnataka
(C) Chandraprabha	(III) Uttar Pradesh
(D) Bhadra	(IV) Chhattisgarh

Choose the most appropriate answer from the options given below:
(1) (A)-(IV), (B)-(I), (C)-(III), (D)-(II)
(2) (A)-(IV), (B)-(I), (C)-(II), (D)-(III)
(3) (A)-(I), (B)-(IV), (C)-(II), (D)-(III)
(4) (A)-(I), (B)-(IV), (C)-(III), (D)-(II)

34. Consider the following pairs:
(A) International Women's Day - 08 March
(B) World Earth Day - 22 March
(C) International Labour Day - 01 May
(D) International Yoga Day - 21 May
(E) World Health Day - 07 April

Choose the most appropriate answer from the options given below:
(1) (A), (B) and (D) only
(2) (A), (C) and (E) only
(3) (B) and (D) only
(4) (A), (B), (D) and (E) only

35. In the following question, select the related number from the given alternatives:
15:256::18:?
(1) 360 (2) 361
(3) 261 (4) 461

36. A and B working together can do a work in 10 days. If A can do the work in 15 days, how many days will B take to do the same work?
(1) 40 (2) 30
(3) 20 (4) 25

37. If 1st January 2001 was Monday, then which day of the week was it on 31 December 2001?
(1) Monday (2) Wednesday
(3) Friday (4) Saturday

38. For a certain period, simple interest on ₹1000 at 10% per annum is ₹100 more than that on ₹800. Find the period (in years).
(1) 4 (2) 10
(3) 5 (4) 2

39. Who amongst the following was shocked by the Chauri-Chaura incident, which took place near Gorakhpur, and withdrew the Non-Cooperation Movement on 5th February 1922?
(1) Mohandas Karamchand Gandhi
(2) Sardar Vallabhbhai Patel
(3) Motilal Nehru
(4) Lala Lajpat Rai

40. By knowing the pH value of a liquid, we can find the:
(1) density of the liquid
(2) viscosity of the liquid
(3) acidity of the liquid
(4) pressure of the liquid

41. The area of four walls of a rectangular hall, which has a length of 18 m and a height of 8 m, is 448 m^2. What is the breadth of the hall (in m)?
(1) 10 (2) 9
(3) 8 (4) 7

42. Choose the most appropriate mirror image of the figure.

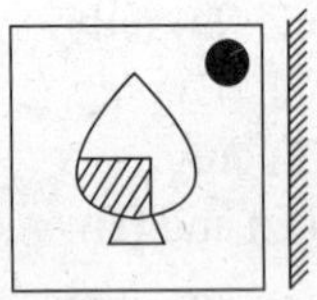

(1)  (2) 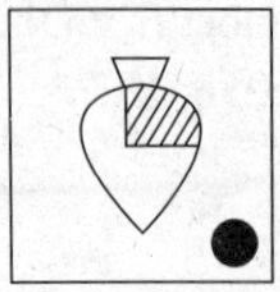

(3) 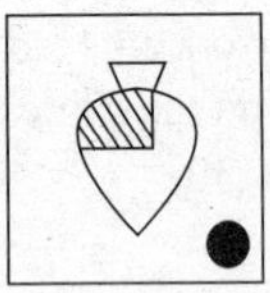 (4) 

43. Find the coordinates of the centroid of ΔABC if the midpoint of BC is $D(2, 4)$ and vertex $A(2, -3)$.

(1) (1, 0) (2) $\left(0, -\frac{2}{5}\right)$

(3) (2, 5) (4) $\left(2, \frac{5}{3}\right)$

44. Who is known as the Father of the Indian space program?

(1) Dr. C.V. Raman
(2) Vikram Sarabhai
(3) Subramanyan Chandrasekhar
(4) Dr. A.P.J. Abdul Kalam

45. Given below are two statements:

Statement (I): All natural numbers are rational numbers.

Statement (II): 1 is the smallest prime number.

In the light of the above statements, choose the most appropriate answer from the options given below:

(1) Both Statement I and Statement II are correct.
(2) Both Statement I and Statement II are incorrect.
(3) Statement I is correct, but Statement II is incorrect.
(4) Statement I is incorrect, but Statement II is correct.

46. Match **List I** with **List II**.

List I (Alloy)	**List II (Composition)**
(A) Amalgam	(I) Cu + Zn
(B) Brass	(II) Pb + Sn
(C) Bronze	(III) Cu + Sn
(D) Solder	(IV) Metal + Hg

Choose the most appropriate answer from the options given below:

(1) (A)-(IV), (B)-(I), (C)-(III), (D)-(II)
(2) (A)-(III), (B)-(II), (C)-(I), (D)-(IV)
(3) (A)-(III), (B)-(I), (C)-(II), (D)-(IV)
(4) (A)-(IV), (B)-(III), (C)-(II), (D)-(I)

47. P, Q, R, S and T are sitting around a circular table, facing the centre of the table. R is to the right of P and second to the left of S. T is not between P and S. Who is second to the left of R?

(1) P (2) Q
(3) S (4) T

48. The digits and numbers from 1 to 12, representing the dial of a clock, are replaced by the consecutive letters of the English alphabet. The replacement is started with the letter C. Find the letter which is represented by 9 O'clock. Consider hour hand only.

(1) N (2) H
(3) J (4) k

49. Match **List I** with **List II**.

List I (Boundary Lines)	**List II (Countries Sharing Borders)**
(A) 38th Parallel Line	(I) between the U.S.A and Canada
(B) Durand Line	(II) between India and China
(C) McMahon Line	(III) between North and South Korea
(D) 49th Parallel Line	(IV) between India and Afghanistan

Choose the most appropriate answer from the options given below:

(1) (A)-(II), (B)-(III), (C)-(IV), (D)-(I)
(2) (A)-(III), (B)-(IV), (C)-(II), (D)-(I)
(3) (A)-(IV), (B)-(III), (C)-(II), (D)-(I)
(4) (A)-(III), (B)-(IV), (C)-(I), (D)-(II)

50. 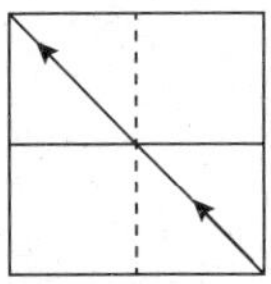

After folding the above figure along the dotted line, which figure will be obtained?

(1) 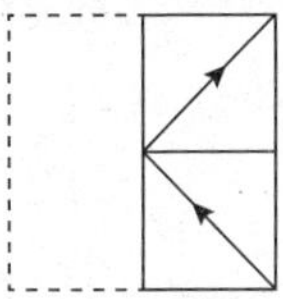
(2) 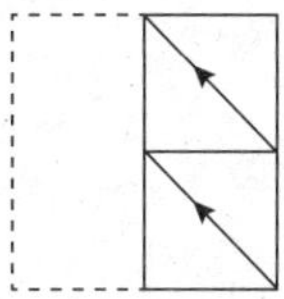
(3) 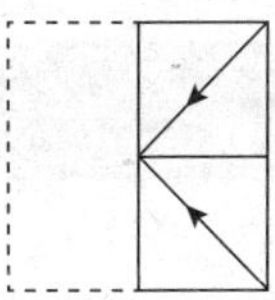
(4) 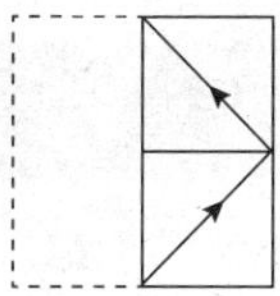

51. How many triangles are there in the given figure?

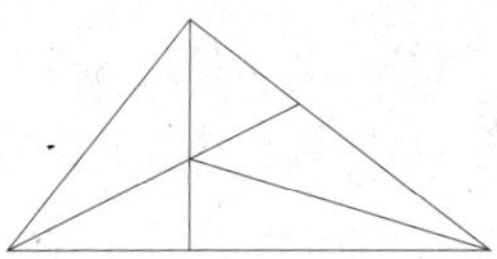

(1) 12 (2) 11
(3) 16 (4) 10

52. The mean of scores obtained by 50 students was 79.5. Later on, it was found that the score of one student was read as 94 in place of 49, and the score of another student was read as 69 in place of 89. Find the correct mean.

(1) 85.52 (2) 79.35
(3) 79 (4) 78

53. Match **List I** with **List II**.

List I (Quantities)	List II (Units)
(A) Force	(I) Coulomb
(B) Charge	(II) Hertz
(C) Heat	(III) Newton
(D) Frequency	(IV) Joule

Choose the most appropriate answer from the options given below:

(1) (A)-(IV), (B)-(II), (C)-(I), (D)-(III)
(2) (A)-(II), (B)-(IV), (C)-(III), (D)-(I)
(3) (A)-(III), (B)-(I), (C)-(IV), (D)-(II)
(4) (A)-(III), (B)-(IV), (C)-(I), (D)-(II)

54. According to Indian literature, who is known as the Father of plastic surgery?

(1) Charaka (2) Sushruta
(3) Panini (4) Patanjali

55. Among A, B, C, D and E, having different amounts of money, C has more money than only E, B and A. Who among them has the highest amount of money?

(1) C (2) D
(3) E (4) A

56. How many languages are presently scheduled in the Indian Constitution?

(1) 14 (2) 21
(3) 22 (4) 18

57. A shop and a car were sold for ₹2,70,000 each. Due to the improved scope of business, the shop was sold at a profit of 20%, but due to depreciation, the car could be sold at a loss of 10%. How much profit or loss resulted in the entire transaction?

(1) loss of ₹5,000
(2) loss of ₹10,000
(3) profit of ₹15,000
(4) profit of ₹15,480

58. **Statements:**

(I) All forces are energies.
(II) All energies are powers.
(III) No power is heat.

Conclusions:

(I) Some forces are definitely not powers.
(II) No heat is force.

Which of the following conclusions can be drawn from the statements in the question?

(1) If only (I) follows.
(2) If only (II) follows.
(3) If both (I) and (II) follow.
(4) If neither (I) nor (II) follows.

59. An interior angle of a regular polygon is 135°. The polygon is a/an:

(1) hexagon (2) square
(3) pentagon (4) octagon

60. Match **List I** with **List II**.

List I	List II
(A) $14 - \frac{x-1}{10} = \frac{x+5}{6} - 3$	(I) 4
(B) $(x-5)^2 - (x+3)^2 = 48$	(II) $-\frac{23}{2}$
(C) $6(x-4) = 4(x-3) - (3x-8)$	(III) 61
(D) $(2x-1)(2x+3) = (2x-7)(2x+7)$	(IV) -2

Choose the correct answer from the options given below:

(1) (A)-(I), (B)-(II), (C)-(III), (D)-(IV)
(2) (A)-(II), (B)-(I), (C)-(III), (D)-(IV)
(3) (A)-(III), (B)-(IV), (C)-(I), (D)-(II)
(4) (A)-(III), (B)-(IV), (C)-(II), (D)-(I)

Answer Key

1. **(1)**	2. **(4)**	3. **(2)**	4. **(2)**	5. **(3)**	6. **(4)**	7. **(4)**	8. **(2)**	9. **(2)**	10. **(1)**
11. **(1)**	12. **(3)**	13. **(3)**	14. **(4)**	15. **(2)**	16. **(1)**	17. **(3)**	18. **(3)**	19. **(1)**	20. **(3)**
21. **(4)**	22. **(4)**	23. **(3)**	24. **(2)**	25. **(3)**	26. **(2)**	27. **(2)**	28. **(2)**	29. **(4)**	30. **(3)**
31. **(1)**	32. **(2)**	33. **(1)**	34. **(2)**	35. **(2)**	36. **(2)**	37. **(1)**	38. **(3)**	39. **(1)**	40. **(3)**
41. **(1)**	42. **(1)**	43. **(4)**	44. **(2)**	45. **(3)**	46. **(1)**	47. **(2)**	48. **(4)**	49. **(2)**	50. **(1)**
51. **(1)**	52. **(3)**	53. **(3)**	54. **(2)**	55. **(2)**	56. **(3)**	57. **(3)**	58. **(2)**	59. **(4)**	60. **(3)**

Classification of Questions

Question No.	Subject	Topic	Level of Difficulty
1.	General Awareness	History	Easy
2.	Quantitative Aptitude	Mensuration	Easy
3.	Quantitative Aptitude	Geometry	Easy
4.	Reasoning	Missing Term Series	Easy
5.	Quantitative Aptitude	Algebra (Quadratic Equations)	Easy
6.	Reasoning	Blood Relations	Easy
7.	General Awareness	Geography	Difficult
8.	General Awareness	Geography	Easy
9.	Reasoning	Coding	Easy

Question No.	Subject	Topic	Level of Difficulty
10.	Quantitative Aptitude	Probability	Medium
11.	Reasoning	Mirror Image	Easy
12.	Quantitative Aptitude	Mensuration	Medium
13.	Quantitative Aptitude	Simplification	Easy
14.	Reasoning	Directions	Easy
15.	General Awareness	Discoveries & Inventions	Medium
16.	Quantitative Aptitude	Averages	Easy
17.	General Awareness	Science (Chemistry)	Difficult
18.	General Awareness	Geography	Medium
19.	Quantitative Aptitude	Time, Speed & Distance	Easy
20.	Reasoning	Missing Term	Medium
21.	General Awareness	Science	Medium
22.	General Awareness	Art & Culture	Difficult
23.	General Awareness	Polity	Easy
24.	Quantitative Aptitude	Percentages	Easy
25.	Quantitative Aptitude	Trigonometry	Easy
26.	General Awareness	Science (Biology)	Easy
27.	Reasoning	Non-verbal	Easy
28.	Reasoning	Number Series	Easy
29.	General Awareness	Current Affairs	Easy
30.	Reasoning	Number Series	Easy
31.	Quantitative Aptitude	Miscellaneous	Easy
32.	Quantitative Aptitude	Ratios	Easy
33.	General Awareness	Geography	Medium
34.	General Awareness	Miscellaneous	Medium
35.	Reasoning	Analogy (Number-based)	Easy
36.	Quantitative Aptitude	Time & Work	Easy
37.	Quantitative Aptitude	Calendars	Easy
38.	Quantitative Aptitude	Simple Interest	Easy
39.	General Awareness	History	Easy
40.	General Awareness	Science (Chemistry)	Easy
41.	Quantitative Aptitude	Mensuration	Easy
42.	Reasoning	Mirror Image	Easy
43.	Quantitative Aptitude	Coordinate Geometry	Medium
44.	General Awareness	Science & Technology	Easy
45.	Quantitative Aptitude	Number System	Easy
46.	General Awareness	Science (Chemistry)	Medium

Question No.	Subject	Topic	Level of Difficulty
47.	Reasoning	Circular Arrangement	Easy
48.	Reasoning	Coding	Easy
49.	General Awareness	Geography	Medium
50.	Reasoning	Non-verbal	Easy
51.	Reasoning	Figure Counting	Medium
52.	Quantitative Aptitude	Averages	Easy
53.	General Awareness	Science (Physics)	Easy
54.	General Awareness	History	Medium
55.	Reasoning	Orders & Rankings	Easy
56.	General Awareness	Polity	Easy
57.	Quantitative Aptitude	Profit, Loss & Discount	Easy
58.	Reasoning	Syllogism	Easy
59.	Quantitative Aptitude	Geometry	Easy
60.	Quantitative Aptitude	Algebra (Equations)	Easy

The no. of questions on Quantitative Aptitude: 22
The no. of questions on General Awareness: 21
The no. of questions on Reasoning: 17

Explanation to Select Questions

2. The volume of the sphere with radius $r = \frac{4}{3}\pi r^3$.

The volume of the sphere with radius $R = \frac{4}{3}\pi R^3$.

So, $\frac{4}{3}\pi R^3 = 64 \times \frac{4}{3}\pi r^3$.

or, $\frac{R^3}{r^3} = 64$ or, $\frac{R}{r} = \frac{4}{1}$

Hence, Option 4.

3. The ratio of the sides of the triangle $= \frac{1}{3}:\frac{1}{4}:\frac{1}{5}$ $= 20:15:12$.

Let the sides of the triangle be $20x$, $15x$ and $12x$.

So, the semi-perimeter of the triangle $= \frac{1}{2}(20x + 15x + 12x) = \frac{47x}{2}$.

As per the question, $\frac{47x}{2} = 47$

or, $x = 2$

Therefore, the length of the largest side $20x$ is $20 \times 2 = 40$.

Hence, Option 2.

4. The pattern is like this (in the clockwise direction):

$4 \times 1 = 4$

$4 \times 2 = 8$

$8 \times 3 = 24$

$24 \times 4 = 96$

$96 \times 5 = 480$

$\mathbf{480 \times 6 = 2880}$

$2880 \times 7 = 20160$

Hence, Option 2.

5. Let the roots of the quadratic equation be α and β.

As per the question,

The Arithmetic Mean of α and $\beta = \dfrac{\alpha+\beta}{2} = 8$
or, $\alpha + \beta = 16$.
The Geometric Mean of α and $\beta = \sqrt{\alpha\beta} = 5$
or, $\alpha\beta = 25$.
The quadratic equation with the roots α and β is

$x^2 - (\alpha+\beta)x + \alpha\beta = 0$

or, $x^2 - 16x + 25 = 0$
Hence, Option 3.

6. The only brother of daughter of someone's grandmother is that person's father.
Hence, Option 4.

7. The Central Rice Research Institute (CRRI) is in Cuttack (Odisha). The administrative control of the CRRI is with the Indian Council of Agricultural Research (ICAR).
Hence, Option 4.

8. The Wular Lake in Jammu and Kashmir is the largest freshwater lake in India. The Chilika Lake is the largest saltwater lake in India.
Hence, Option 2.

9. hirpa nig:bat ball (i)
kirpa nig:foot ball (ii)
kirpa nad:foot mark (iii)
On comparing (ii) and (iii), we find that 'kirpa' means foot. It also implies that 'nad' means mark.
On comparing (i) and (ii), we find that 'nig' means ball and 'hirpa' means bat.
Therefore, the phrase for 'mark sheet' must have 'nad' and must NOT have 'hirpa' or 'kirpa'. We have only one such option: 'nad tyan'.
Hence, Option 2.

10. When we roll two dice, we can get an odd prime no. as the sum of the numbers on the top faces of the dice in 4 cases:
Case I: 3 $\rightarrow$ possible in 2 ways: (1, 2) and (2, 1)
Case II: 5 $\rightarrow$ possible in 4 ways: (1, 4), (2, 3), (3, 2) and (4, 1)
Case III: 7 $\rightarrow$ possible in 6 ways: (1, 6), (2, 5), (3, 4), (4, 3) (5, 2) and (6, 1)
Case IV: 11 $\rightarrow$ possible in 2 ways: (6, 5) and (5, 6)

Thus, we can get an odd prime number in 14 ways (2 + 4 + 6 + 2).
The total number of outcomes = $6 \times 6 = 36$.
The required probability $= \dfrac{14}{36} = \dfrac{7}{18}$.
Hence, Option 1.

12. The volume of the cuboidal slab = $22 \times 10 \times 5$ cm^3 = 1100×1000 mm^3
(as 1 cm^3 = 1000 mm^3)
Let the length of the wire be l mm.
As a wire is always a cylinder, the volume of this wire $= \pi \times \left(\dfrac{1}{2}\right)^2 \times l = \dfrac{22}{7} \times \dfrac{1}{4} l$.

Now, $\dfrac{22}{7} \times \dfrac{1}{4} l = 1100 \times 1000$

or, $l = 1400000$ mm
= 1400 metre
(1 metre = 1000 mm)
The rate of coating is ₹1.5 per metre.
Therefore, the total cost = 1400×1.5 = ₹2100.
Hence, Option 3.

13. $\sqrt[4]{(625)^3} = (625)^{\frac{3}{4}} = \left((625)^{\frac{1}{4}}\right)^3 = 5^3 = 125$.

Hence, Option 3.

14.

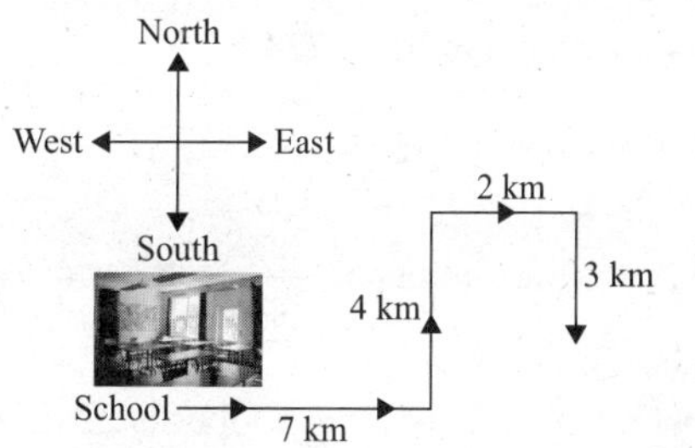

Hence, Option 4.

16. The total weight of the 10 students, with an average weight of 25 kg, is $25 \times 10 = 250$ kg.
The total weight of the 10 students with an average weight of 35 kg = 350 kg.
The total weight of all these 20 students = 250 + 350 = 600 kg.
The average weight of the 20 students $= \dfrac{600}{20} = 30$ kg.

Shortcut I: As both the groups have the same number of students (10), their combined average is the average of their averages $= \frac{25+35}{2} = 30$ kg .

Shortcut II: As the two groups of students have averages of 25 kg and 35 kg, their combined average must lie between 25 and 35 (excluding 25 and 35), and only Option 1 is strictly between 25 and 35.

17. The LPG has NO smell of its own. Ethyl mercaptan (Ethanethiol, CH_3CH_2SH) is added as a smelling agent to the LPG.
Hence, Option 3.

20. The pattern (in the clockwise direction) goes like this:
$2 \times 8 + 1 = 17$
$17 \times 8 + 1 = 137$
$137 \times 8 + 1 = 1097$
Hence, Option 3.

22. Sonal Mansingh specialises in Bharatanatyam as well as Odissi. Even if one knows the Sitara Devi - Kathak combination, one could get the answer as it is only in Option 4.
Hence, Option 4.

24. $\therefore$ 44% of the number = 2288

$\therefore$ 1% of the number $= \frac{2288}{44}$

$\therefore$ 87% of the number $= \frac{2288}{44} \times 87 = 4524$.

Hence, Option 2.

Shortcut: As 44% of the number is 2288, 87% of it will be slightly less than twice of 44% or 2288. There is only one option that is slightly less than $2288 \times 2 = 4576$.

25.

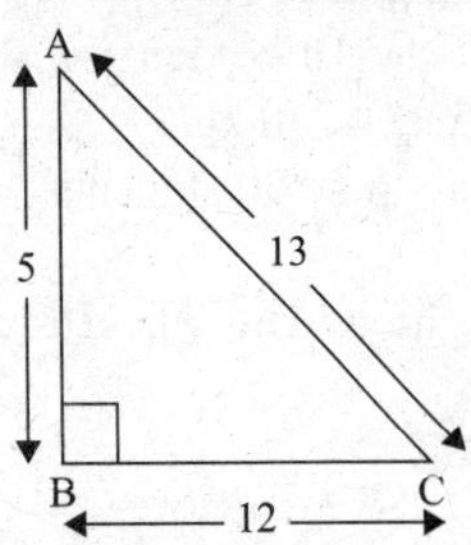

Hence, $\tan C = \frac{5}{12}$,

$\sin B = \sin 90° = 1$

$\tan A = \frac{12}{5}$.

29. UPDATE: The Booker Prize 2023 winner is Paul Lynch, who got it for his novel 'Prophet Song'. The winner in 2022 was Shehan Karunatilaka. Also, the Booker Prize is different from the International Booker Prize. The International Booker Prize 2023 winners are Georgi Gospodinov and Angela Rodel for the novel Time Shelter.

30. This sequence is of squares of the odd integers. We need to put the square of 11 in between the squares of 9 and 13.
Hence, Option 3.

32. As per the question
$P - Q = 40\% \text{ of } P + Q$

or, $P - Q = \frac{40}{100} \times (P + Q)$

or, $P - Q = \frac{2}{5} \times (P + Q)$

or, $5P - 5Q = 2P + 2Q$

or, $3P = 7Q$ or, $\frac{P}{Q} = \frac{7}{3}$

Hence, Option 2.

34. The World Earth Day is celebrated on 22 April (NOT 22 March). The International Yoga Day is celebrated on 21 June (NOT 21 May).
Hence, Option 2.

35. On the left-hand side, we have 15:256 as $256 = (15 + 1)^2$.
The last part on the right-hand side will be $(18 + 1)^2 = 361$.
Hence, Option 2.

36. Let's assume that the work is of 30 units.
As per the question:

A and B can do $\frac{30}{10} = 3$ units in a day.

A can do $\frac{30}{15} = 2$ units in a day.

$\Rightarrow$ B can do $3 - 2 = 1$ unit in a day.

$\Rightarrow$ B can do the work in $\frac{30}{1} = 30$ days.

Alternative: B can do the work in $\frac{1}{\frac{1}{10} - \frac{1}{15}} =$ 30 days.

37. The number of days between 1st January 2001 and 31st December 2001 = 364.

As 364 is 52×7, the number of odd days in it is zero.

Therefore, 31st December 2001 will also be a Monday.

Fact to remember: The first and the last day of any non-leap year always fall on the same day.

38. Let the period be n years.

As per the question,

$$\frac{1000 \times 10 \times n}{100} = \frac{800 \times 10 \times n}{100} + 100$$

or, $100n - 80n = 100$

or, $n = 5$

Hence, Option 3.

41. The area of the 4 walls of a room = 2 × height (length + breadth) = 448

or, $2 \times 8\ (18 + \text{breadth}) = 448$

or, $18 + \text{breadth} = \frac{448}{16} = 28$

or, breadth = 28 – 18 = 10.

Hence, Option 1.

42. The dark circle is on the top right corner of the object. Hence, the dark circle should be on the top left corner of the image of the object, and it is only in Option 1.

43.

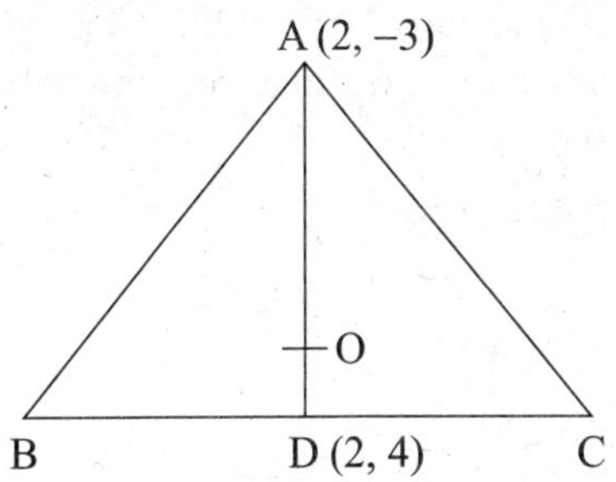

Let O be the centroid of the triangle.

The centroid O divides the median AD in the ratio 2:1.

$\frac{AO}{OD} = \frac{2}{1}$.

x-coordinate of point $O = \frac{2 \times 2 + 1 \times 2}{1 + 2} = 2$

y-coordinate of point $O = \frac{2 \times 4 + 1(-3)}{1 + 2} = \frac{5}{3}$.

Hence, Option 4.

45. 1 is neither prime nor composite.

Hence, Option 3.

46.

Element	Chemical Symbol
Lead	Pb
Tin	Sn
Copper	Cu
Mercury	Hg
Zinc	Zn

The answer is Option 1.

47. As R is to the right of P and second to the left of S, these three people would be placed in the following manner:

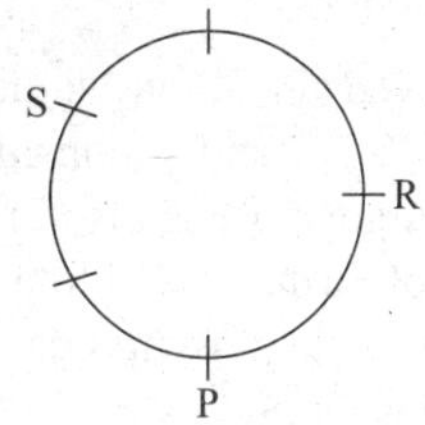

As T cannot be put between P and S, it must be placed between S and R. Also, the 5th person Q must be in between S and P.

The final arrangement would be like:

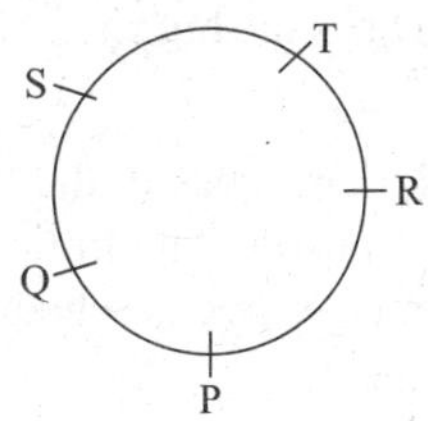

Of course, Q is 2nd to the left of R.

Hence, Option 2.

48. As 1 is represented by C, 9 will be represented by (9 + 2)th letter that is K.

Hence, Option 4.

51.

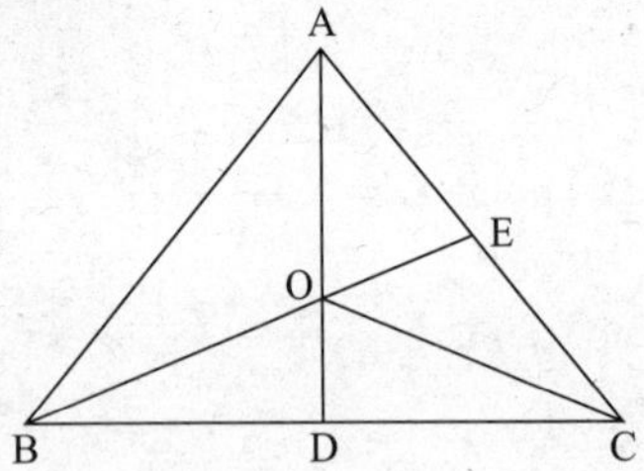

The triangles are:
1. ABC, 2. AOB, 3. OBD, 4. ODC, 5. OEC, 6. OAE, 7. ABD, 8. ADC, 9. ABE, 10. BEC, 11. BOC and 12. AOC.

52. The apparent total score of 50 students = $79.5 \times 50 = 3975$.
But, one of the scores was read as 94 in place of 49, so it caused a surplus of 45.
Similarly, one of the scores was read as 69 in place of 89, so it caused a deficit of 20.
Therefore, the actual total score of the 50 students = $3975 - 45 + 20 = 3950$.
The correct mean = $\frac{3950}{50} = 79$.
Hence, Option 3.

54. Sushruta lived in India sometime between 1000 and 800 BC and is considered the father of plastic surgery. He is also credited with the authorship of Sushruta Samhita. It is one of the foundational texts of Ayurveda.
The answer is Option 2.

55. As these five people have different amounts of money and C has more money than only E, B and A, it is evident that D has more money than even C; thus, 4 people have less than D. Therefore, D has the highest amount.
Hence, Option 2.

56. There are 22 languages in the 8th Schedule of the Indian Constitution. Initially, there were only 14 languages in this schedule.
Hence, Option 3.

57. The cost price of the car that was sold for 270000 at 20% profit = $\frac{270000}{1.2} = 225000$
The profit in this case = $270000 - 225000 = 45000$.
The cost price of the car sold for 270000 at a 10% loss = $\frac{270000}{0.9} = 300000$.
The loss in this case = $300000 - 270000 = 30000$.
Therefore, the overall profit = $45000 - 30000 = 15000$.
Hence, Option 3.

58.

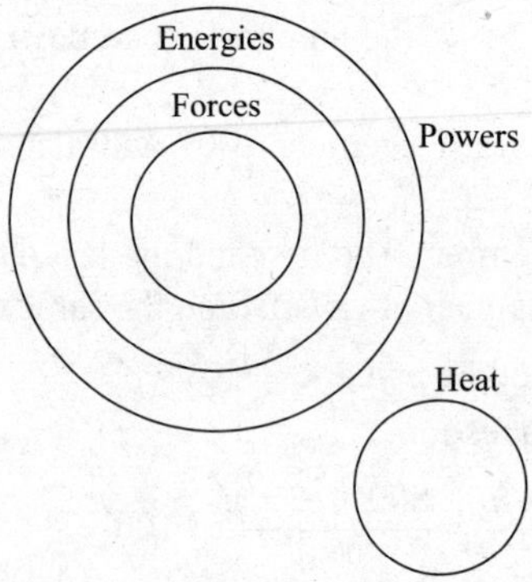

It is obvious that all forces are powers. As the superset of Forces, Powers is disjoint with heat. So, no heat can be Forces.
Hence, Option 2.

59. Let the polygon be of n sides.
The interior angle of a regular polygon of n sides
$= \frac{(2n-4)90^\circ}{n} = 135^\circ$.
or, $(2n-4)90^\circ = 135^\circ n$.
or, $2(2n-4) = 3n$
or, $4n - 8 = 3n$
or, $n = 8$.
Hence, Option 4.
Shortcut: Interior angle of the polygon = 135°
The exterior angle = $180^\circ - 135^\circ = 45^\circ$
The number of sides of a regular polygon
$= \frac{360^\circ}{\text{Exterior angle}}$
$= \frac{360^\circ}{45^\circ} = 8$.

60. A. $14 - \frac{x-1}{10} = \frac{x+5}{6} - 3$
or, $\frac{x+5}{6} + \frac{x-1}{10} = 14 + 3$

or, $\frac{5(x+5)+3(x-1)}{30} = 17$

or, $8x + 22 = 510$

or, $8x = 488$

or, $x = \frac{488}{8} = 61$.

B. $(x-5)^2 - (x+3)^2 = 48$

or, $x^2 - 10x + 25 - (x^2 + 6x + 9) = 48$

or, $-16x + 16 = 48$

or, $-16x = 48 - 16$

or, $x = -2$.

C. $6(x-4) = 4(x-3) - (3x-8)$

or, $6x - 24 = 4x - 12 - 3x + 8$

or, $6x - 24 = x - 4$

or, $6x - x = 24 - 4$

or, $5x = 20$

or, $x = 4$

D. $(2x-1)(2x+3) = (2x-7)(2x+7)$

or, $4x^2 + 6x - 2x - 3 = 4x^2 - 49$

or, $4x = 3 - 49$

or, $x = \frac{-46}{4} = -\frac{23}{2}$.

Shift - I

CUET UG 2023
General Test

May
21

Instructions:

1. You need to attempt any 50 out of the 60 questions in 60 minutes.
2. You get 5 marks for a correct response and –1 for an incorrect one. However, there is no reward or penalty for a question not attempted.

1. Match **List I** with **List II**.

List I (Deficiency)	List II (Disease)
A. Insulin	I. Kwashiorkor
B. Protein	II. Scurvy
C. Thyroxin	III. Diabetes
D. Vitamin C	IV. Goitre

Choose the correct answer from the options given below:

(1) A-III, B-I, C-IV, D-II
(2) A-I, B-III, C-IV, D-II
(3) A-II, B-I, C-IV, D-III
(4) A-IV, B-III, C-II, D-I

2. Match **List I** with **List II**.

List I (Physical Quantity)	List II (Unit)
A. electric charge	I. Newton
B. force	II. Coulomb
C. power	III. Joule
D. energy	IV. Watt

Choose the most appropriate answer from the options given below:

(1) A-I, B-II, C-IV, D-III
(2) A-II, B-I, C-IV, D-III
(3) A-II, B-IV, C-I, D-III
(4) A-III, B-II, C-IV, D-I

3. Find out which of the figures out of the given options can be formed from the pieces given in Figure (X).

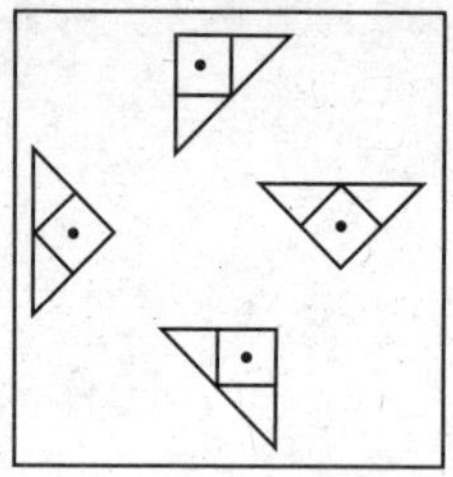

Figure X

(1) 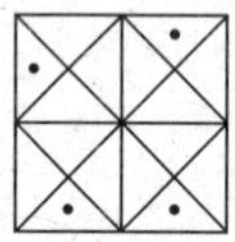
(2) 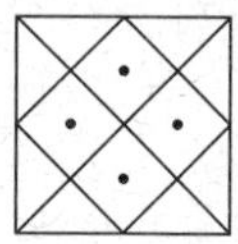
(3) 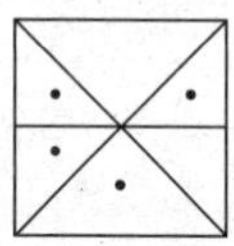

4. Find out which of the answer figures (1), (2), (3) and (4) completes the figure matrix?

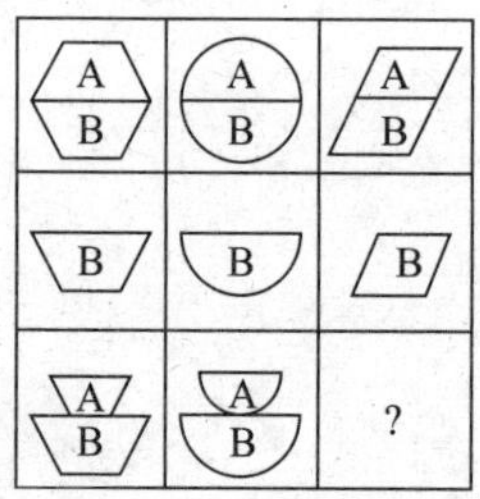

(1) 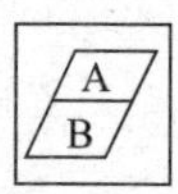

(2) 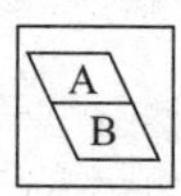

(3) 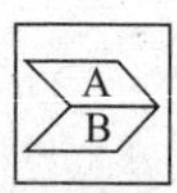

(4) 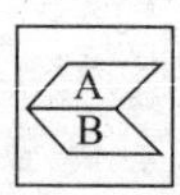

5. Match **List I** with **List II**.

List I (River)	List II (City)
A. Mahanadi	I. Ludhiana
B. Godavari	II. Cuttack
C. Sutlej	III. Lucknow
D. Gomti	IV. Nashik

Choose the most appropriate answer from the options given below:
(1) A-II, B-IV, C-III, D-I
(2) A-II, B-IV, C-I, D-III
(3) A-IV, B-II, C-I, D-III
(4) A-III, B-I, C-II, D-IV

6. **Statements**
I. Some cars are black.
II. Some lions are cars.
Conclusion
I. Some blacks are lions.
II. No black is a lion.
(1) Only I follows.
(2) Only II follows.
(3) Either I or II follows.
(4) None follows.

7. Arrange the following in meaningful sequence:
A. Key
B. Door
C. Lock
D. Room
Choose the most appropriate answer from the options given below:
(1) A, C, B, D
(2) D, C, A, B
(3) B, A, D, C
(4) C, B, D, A

8. Match **List I** with **List II**.

List I (Diet Deficiency)	List II (Disease)
A. Deficiency of Vitamin B	I. Anaemia
B. Deficiency of Vitamin A	II. Beri-Beri
C. Deficiency of Iron	III. Goitre
D. Deficiency of Iodine	IV. Night Blindness

Choose the most appropriate answer from the options given below:
(1) A-IV, B-II, C-III, D-I
(2) A-II, B-IV, C-I, D-III
(3) A-I, B-III, C-IV, D-II
(4) A-III, B-I, C-II, D-IV

9. If today is Saturday, then what will be the day on the 363rd day?
(1) Sunday (2) Monday
(3) Thursday (4) Friday

10. What is the probability that any non-leap year will have 53 Sundays?
(1) $\frac{1}{53}$ (2) $\frac{2}{53}$
(3) $\frac{1}{7}$ (4) $\frac{2}{7}$

11. A man walks 2 km towards the East, and then he turns to the South and walks 6 km. Again, he turns to the East and walks 4 km; after this, he turns to the North and walks 14 km. How far is he from his starting point?
(1) 10 km (2) 15 km
(3) 20 km (4) 25 km

12. Find the perimeter of a rhombus, one of whose diagonals is 16 cm long and the area is 240 cm^2.
(1) 68 cm (2) 30 cm
(3) 24 cm (4) 36 cm

13. The area of a circle is numerically equal to its circumference. Find the diameter of the circle.
(1) 2 units (2) 4 units
(3) 1 unit (4) 5 units

14. Which of the following is not a state of India?
(1) Nagaland (2) Manipur
(3) Ladakh (4) Meghalaya

15. Here are some phrases translated from an artificial language:
'Holo polo' means 'base ball'.
'Moto prot' means 'my India'.
'Prot shot' means 'India won'.
Which phrase could mean "All India Radio"?
(1) Holo polo prot (2) Kud prot nid
(3) Prot polo nid (4) Polo nid prot

16. The average of 12 numbers is 15, and the average of the first two numbers is 14. What is the average of the remaining numbers?

(1) 15 (2) 15.2
(3) 14 (4) 14.2

17. Match **List I** with **List II**.

List I (Scientist)	List II (Discovery)
A. Har Gobind Khorana	I. discovery of Zero
B. C.V. Raman	II. genetic composition of cell
C. Jagdish Chandra Bose	III. scattering of light
D. Aryabhata	IV. measurement of plant growth

Choose the most appropriate answer from the options given below:

(1) A-II, B-III, C-I, D-IV
(2) A-III, B-II, C-IV, D-I
(3) A-II, B-III, C-IV, D-I
(4) A-I, B-III, C-II, D-IV

18. What is the smallest perfect square number divisible by 4, 6 and 32?

(1) 100 (2) 196
(3) 96 (4) 576

19. Major is related to Lieutenant in the same way as 'Squadron Leader' is related to ________?

(1) Pilot Officer (2) Flying Attendant
(3) Group Captain (4) Flying Officer

20. How many terms are there in the A.P. 3, 7, 11, ……. 407?

(1) 100 (2) 101
(3) 99 (4) 102

21. The ratio of the ages of 2 boys is 3:7. After 2 years, the ratio of their ages will become 5:9. The ratio of their ages after 10 years will be

(1) 15:16 (2) 5:17
(3) 17:18 (4) 13:17

22. If the median of $\frac{x}{5}, x, \frac{x}{4}, \frac{x}{2}$ and $\frac{x}{3}$ (where $x > 0$) is 8, then the value of x is

(1) 24 (2) 32
(3) 8 (4) 16

23. Which quadrant does the point (−2, 3) lie in?

(1) I (2) II
(3) III (4) IV

24. Find the angle of elevation of the Sun when the length of the shadow of a tree is $\frac{1}{\sqrt{3}}$ times the height of the tree.

(1) 30° (2) 45°
(3) 60° (4) 90°

25. Match **List I** with **List II**.

List I (Movement)	List II (Purpose)
A. Quit India Movement	I. to achieve self-government in India and demand for large political representation
B. Civil Disobedience Movement	II. to compel the British to leave India
C. Non-cooperation Movement	III. to refuse to obey certain laws and orders or commands of the government
D. Home Rule Movement	IV. Indians resigning their titles, boycotting foreign goods and government institutions refusing to pay taxes

Choose the most appropriate answer from the options given below:

(1) A-I, B-III, C-II, D-IV
(2) A-II, B-III, C-I, D-IV
(3) A-III, B-II, C-IV, D-I
(4) A-II, B-III, C-IV, D-I

26. A railway half-ticket costs half the full ticket. However, the reservation charge for all the tickets is a constant. One full reserved ticket for a journey is ₹525. If the cost of one full reserved ticket and one half reserved ticket for the same journey is ₹850, then what is the reservation charge per ticket?

(1) ₹120 (2) ₹150
(3) ₹125 (4) ₹115

27. Which of the following is not a satellite launched by India?

(1) Explorer (2) APPLE
(3) Bhaskar (4) INSAT

28. The minimum number of colours required to paint all sides of a cube so that no two adjacent faces may have the same colour is

(1) 5 (2) 4
(3) 3 (4) 6

29. If the selling price of 80 articles equals the cost price of 100 articles, then find the gain percentage.

(1) 30% (2) 25%
(3) 40% (4) 50%

30. From the figure, what is the value of x?

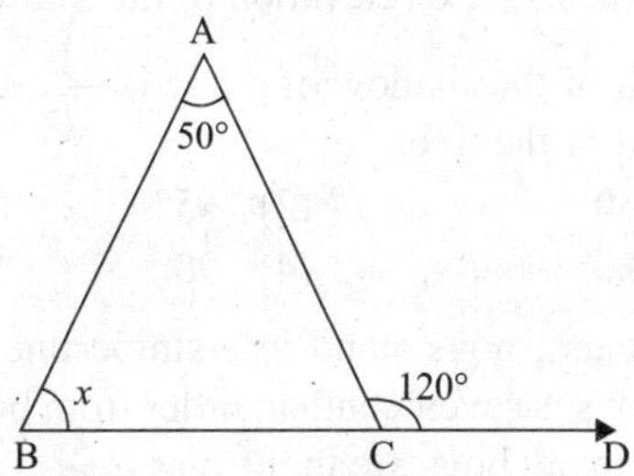

(1) 50° (2) 120°
(3) 60° (4) 70°

31. The only Indian who has received a Nobel Prize in literature is:

(1) Bankim Chandra Chatterjee
(2) Toru Dutt
(3) R.K. Narayan
(4) Rabindra Nath Tagore

32. Find a single equivalent increase if a number is successively increased by 20%, 25% and 30%.

(1) 75% (2) 85%
(3) 95% (4) 35%

33. Which of the following is a metal?

(1) Carbon (2) Mercury
(3) Sulphur (4) Iodine

34. The Bhoodan-Gram Dan Movement was initiated by:

(1) Mahatma Gandhi
(2) Vinoba Bhave
(3) Shri Ram Chandra Reddy
(4) Sardar Patel

35. Which of the following players didn't receive a medal in the Tokyo Olympics 2020?

(1) P.V. Sindhu
(2) Neeraj Chopra
(3) Abhinav Bindra
(4) Ravi Kumar Dahiya

36. Match **List I** with **List II**.

List I	List II
A. Blue Revolution	I. increase in crop yield and agricultural products
B. White Revolution	II. increase in oil-seeds production
C. Yellow Revolution	III. increase in fish production
D. Green Revolution	IV. increase in milk production

Choose the most appropriate answer from the options given below:

(1) A-IV, B-III, C-II, D-I
(2) A-III, B-IV, C-II, D-I
(3) A-I, B-III, C-II, D-IV
(4) A-III, B-I, C-II, D-IV

37. Consider the diagram: Five hundred candidates appeared in an examination comprising English, Hindi and Math tests. The diagram gives the number of students who failed in different tests. What is the percentage of students who failed in at least two subjects?

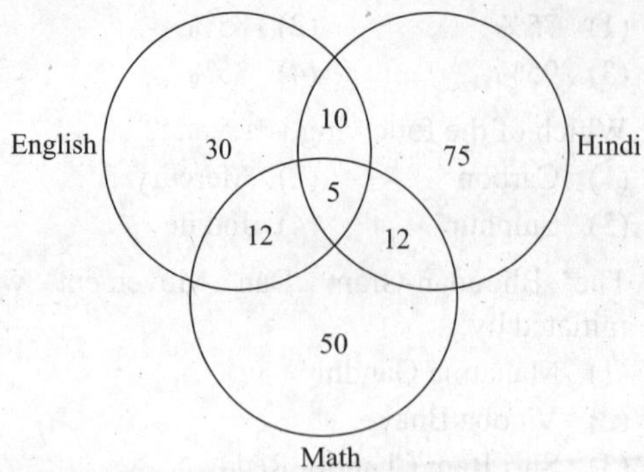

(1) 6.8% (2) 7.8%
(3) 1.0% (4) 0.078%

38. A is 3 years younger than C but one year older than D. D is one year older than B but 4 years younger than C. C is 15 years old. What is B's age in years?
(1) 13 (2) 12
(3) 11 (4) 10

39. In a row of 40 children, A is 13th from the left end, and B is ninth from the right end. How many children are there between A and C if C is fourth to the left of B?
(1) 13 (2) 14
(3) 15 (4) 16

40. Choose the one that is different from the other three.
(1) 431 (2) 162
(3) 831 (4) 232

41. A significant constituent of the natural gas is:
(1) Propane
(2) Butane
(3) Methane
(4) Carbon

42. Match **List I** with **List II**.

List I (City)	List II (Nickname)
A. Nagpur	I. Diamond City
B. Surat	II. Pink City
C. Jaisalmer	III. Orange City
D. Jaipur	IV. Golden City

Choose the most appropriate answer from the options given below:
(1) A-III, B-I, C-IV, D-II
(2) A-I, B-III, C-IV, D-II
(3) A-III, B-I, C-II, D-IV
(4) A-II, B-I, C-III, D-IV

43. X got 98 marks on his exam, which is 56% of the total marks. What is the maximum marks in the exam?
(1) 150 (2) 175
(3) 200 (4) 225

44. The relationship between the values of a country's imports and exports is called:
(1) Balance of Trade
(2) Balance of Payment
(3) Balance of currency
(4) Bill of exchange

45. Who won a Nobel Prize in the field of "physiology or medicine"?
(1) C.V. Raman
(2) Jagdish Chandra Bose
(3) Homi Jehangir Bhabha
(4) Har Gobind Khorana

46. Find the angle of elevation of the Sun when the length of the shadow of a tree is $\frac{1}{\sqrt{3}}$ times the height of the tree.
(1) 30° (2) 45°
(3) 60° (4) 90°

47. In a class, boys stand in a single line. One of the boys is seventeenth in order from both ends. How many boys are in the class?
(1) 34 (2) 33
(3) 32 (4) 27

48. A bag contains 5 black balls, 3 white balls and 2 red balls. Three balls are drawn in succession. What is the probability that the first ball is red, the second black and the third white?
(1) $\frac{1}{24}$ (2) $\frac{3}{10}$
(3) $\frac{1}{10}$ (4) $\frac{1}{2}$

49. If the word 'LEADER' is coded as 20-13-9-12-13-26. How would you write "LIGHT" in that code?
(1) 20-16-15-17-22 (2) 20-17-15-16-28
(3) 20-15-16-18-23 (4) 20-16-17-15-27

50. Find the angle traced by the hour hand of a correct clock between 7 pm and 2 am.
(1) 200° (2) 210°
(3) 310° (4) 290°

51. A and B can do a work in 9 days and 12 days, respectively. If they work on alternate days starting with A, then in how many days will the work be completed?
(1) 36 days (2) 10 days
(3) $10\frac{1}{4}$ days (4) 13 days

52. What money will amount to ₹520 in 5 years and to ₹568 in 7 years on simple interest?
(1) ₹400 (2) ₹120
(3) ₹510 (4) ₹220

53. **Statement I:** The Constitution is the framework for the governance of a country, which delegates power and authority to the executive, legislative and judiciary.
Statement II: It helps a country maintain good relationships with neighbouring countries.
In light of the above statements, choose the most appropriate answer from the options below.
(1) Both Statement I and Statement II are correct.
(2) Both Statement I and Statement II are incorrect.
(3) Statement I is correct, but Statement II is incorrect.
(4) Statement I is incorrect, but Statement II is correct.

54. Find the next term in the alphanumeric series D4T, F9R, H20P, J43N.
(1) L 90 M (2) N 90 N
(3) L 90 L (4) J 90 L

55. When seen through a mirror, a clock shows 3:30. What is the correct time?
(1) 2:30 (2) 8:30
(3) 5:30 (4) 4:30

56. If the 2nd half of the letters of the word INTERMEDIATE are reversed and placed before the 1st half of the letters, which letter will be 2nd to the right of the 10th letter from the right?
(1) A (2) D
(3) E (4) I

57. In the given figure, find out which number indicates doctors who are not married.

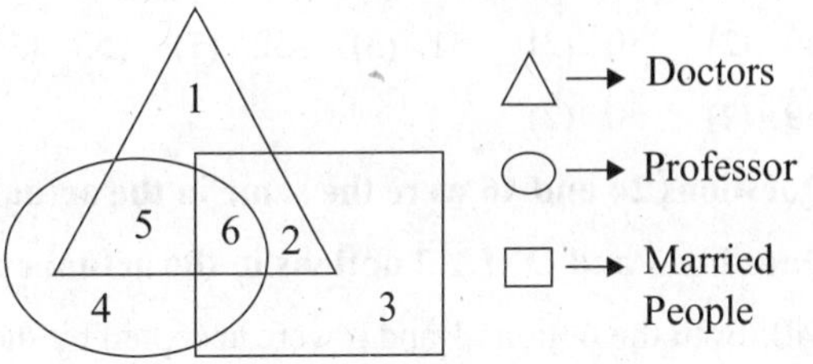

(1) 2 (2) 4
(3) 1 (4) 6

58. Which book was written by Dr. S. Radhakrishnan?
(1) The World's Largest Democracy
(2) India Divided
(3) Indian Philosophy
(4) India's Priceless Heritage

59. Which of the following speeds is the least?
(1) 50 meter/second (2) 50 meter/minute
(3) 70 km/hour (4) 5 km/minute

60. Match **List I** with **List II**.

List I (Book)	List II (Author)
A. India Wins Freedom	I. R.K. Narayan
B. The Guide	II. Mahatma Gandhi
C. India from Midnight to Millennium	III. Abdul Kalam Azad
D. Conquest of Self	IV. Shashi Tharoor

Choose the most appropriate answer from the options given below:
(1) A-I, B-III, C-IV, D-II
(2) A-III, B-I, C-IV, D-II
(3) A-III, B-I, C-II, D-IV
(4) A-I, B-IV, C-II, D-III

Answer Key

1. (1) 2. (2) 3. (2) 4. (3) 5. (2) 6. (3) 7. (1) 8. (2) 9. (3) 10. (3)
11. (1) 12. (1) 13. (2) 14. (3) 15. (2) 16. (2) 17. (3) 18. (4) 19. (4) 20. (4)
21. (4) 22. (1) 23. (2) 24. (3) 25. (4) 26. (3) 27. (1) 28. (3) 29. (2) 30. (4)
31. (4) 32. (3) 33. (2) 34. (2) 35. (3) 36. (2) 37. (2) 38. (4) 39. (2)
40*. (1) as well as (3) 41. (3) 42. (1) 43. (2) 44. (1) 45. (4) 46. (3) 47. (2) 48. (1)
49. (2) 50. (2) 51. (3) 52. (1) 53. (3) 54. (3) 55. (2) 56. (2) 57. (3) 58. (3)
59. (2) 60. (2)

Questions 24 and 46 were the same in the actual examination also.

Question 3 had ONLY 3 options in the actual examination also.

*40. Both the options 1 and 3 were accepted by the CUET-UG as the answers.

Classification of Questions

Question No.	Subject	Topic	Level of Difficulty
1.	General Awareness	Science (Biology)	Easy
2.	General Awareness	Science (Physics)	Easy
3.	Reasoning	Non-verbal	Easy
4.	Reasoning	Non-verbal	Easy
5.	General Awareness	Geography	Medium
6.	Reasoning	Syllogism	Easy
7.	Reasoning	Sequencing	Easy
8.	General Awareness	Science (Biology)	Easy
9.	Quantitative Aptitude	Calendars	Medium
10.	Quantitative Aptitude	Probability	Medium
11.	Reasoning	Directions	Easy
12.	Quantitative Aptitude	Mensuration	Medium
13.	Quantitative Aptitude	Geometry	Easy
14.	General Awareness	Polity	Easy
15.	Reasoning	Coding	Easy
16.	Quantitative Aptitude	Averages	Easy
17.	General Awareness	Discoveries & Inventions	Easy
18.	Quantitative Aptitude	Number System (LCM)	Easy
19.	General Awareness	Miscellaneous	Difficult
20.	Quantitative Aptitude	Algebra (AP)	Easy

Question No.	Subject	Topic	Level of Difficulty
21.	Quantitative Aptitude	Ratios	Easy
22.	Quantitative Aptitude	Statistics (Median)	Easy
23.	Quantitative Aptitude	Coordinate Geometry	Easy
24.	Quantitative Aptitude	Trigonometry	Easy
25.	General Awareness	History	Easy
26.	Quantitative Aptitude	Algebra (Linear Equations)	Easy
27.	General Awareness	Science & Technology	Medium
28.	Reasoning	Miscellaneous	Easy
29.	Quantitative Aptitude	Profit, Loss & Discount	Easy
30.	Quantitative Aptitude	Geometry	Easy
31.	General Awareness	Awards	Easy
32.	Quantitative Aptitude	Percentages	Easy
33.	General Awareness	Science (Chemistry)	Easy
34.	General Awareness	Social Work	Easy
35.	General Awareness	Sports	Easy
36.	General Awareness	Economics	Easy
37.	Quantitative Aptitude	Set Theory	Easy
38.	Quantitative Aptitude	Algebra (Linear Equations)	Easy
39.	Reasoning	Rankings & Orders	Easy
40.	Reasoning	Odd-one-out (Numbers)	Easy
41.	General Awareness	Science (Chemistry)	Easy
42.	General Awareness	Geography	Easy
43.	Quantitative Aptitude	Percentages	Easy
44.	General Awareness	Economics	Easy
45.	General Awareness	Awards	Easy
46.	Quantitative Aptitude	Trigonometry (Heights & Distances)	Easy
47.	Reasoning	Rankings & Orders	Easy
48.	Quantitative Aptitude	Probability	Easy
49.	Reasoning	Coding	Easy
50.	Quantitative Aptitude	Clocks	Easy
51.	Quantitative Aptitude	Time & Work	Medium
52.	Quantitative Aptitude	Simple Interest	Easy
53.	General Awareness	Polity	Medium
54.	Reasoning	Alphanumeric Series	Easy
55.	Reasoning	Mirror Image	Easy
56.	Reasoning	Rankings & Orders	Easy

Question No.	Subject	Topic	Level of Difficulty
57.	Reasoning	Venn Diagram	Easy
58.	General Awareness	Books & Authors	Medium
59.	Quantitative Aptitude	Time, Speed & Distance	Easy
60.	General Awareness	Books & Authors	Easy

No. of questions on General Awareness: 21
No. of questions on Quantitative Aptitude: 24
No. of questions on Reasoning: 15

Explanation to Select Questions

3. The 4 pieces in Figure X are all congruent. Moreover, these pieces have a dot inside a square. In Option 1, the dots are inside the triangles (NOT squares). In Option 3, the pieces are not congruent.
Hence, Option 2.

4. The 3rd row is made by retaining the lower halves of the figures in the first row but placing the upper halves upside down.
Hence, Option 3.

6.

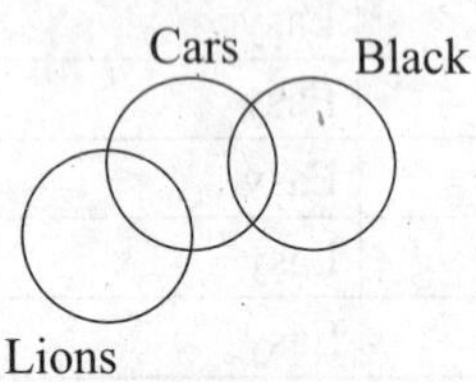

Figure I

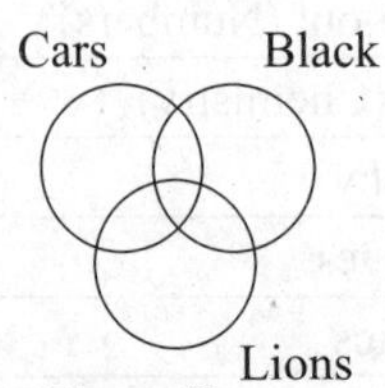

Figure II

Figures I and II depict 2 possibilities.
Conclusion I is just a possibility, and so is conclusion II, but one of these two will certainly be the case.
Hence, Option 3.

7. A key is put in a lock on the door, part of a room. Hence, Key, Lock, Door and Room is the most logical sequence among the options.
Hence, Option 1.

9. We need to be very careful here. This question does NOT ask the day of the week after 363 days; the answer would have been Option 4 (Friday) in that case. It asks the day of the week on the 363rd day.

The 363rd day Will come after only 362 days. For example, after 2 days, it is the 3rd day.

Today: 1st day

Tomorrow: 2nd day (or after 1 day)

The day after tomorrow: 3rd day (or after 2 days)

Now, $362 = 51 \times 7 + 5$.

So, there are 5 odd days in it.

Hence, on the 363rd day (or after 362 days), it would be 5 days after a Saturday, which is a Thursday.

Hence, Option 3.

Option 4 (Friday) is a perfect trap for those who cannot distinguish between "on 363rd day" and "after 363 days".

10. A non-leap year has 365 days.

Now, $365 = 52 \times 7 + 1$.

So, a non-leap year has one day in excess of 52 weeks.

52 weeks would always have 52 Sundays.

The extra day (above 364 days) can be any of the 7 days. Hence, the required, probability is $\frac{1}{7}$.

$\frac{1}{7}$ is the best option that you get in most of the examinations.

However, the reality is slightly different. In the Gregorian calendar, everything gets repeated after 400 years.

The first day of the calendar – 01.01.0001 – was a Monday, and 01.01.0401 was again a Monday.
From year 1 to year 400, there were 97 leap years and 303 non-leap years. Out of 303 non-leap years, 43 years started and ended with a Sunday, i.e., they had 53 Sundays. Therefore, the actual answer to the question is 43/303 (very close to $\frac{1}{7}$, but NOT exactly $\frac{1}{7}$)

The distribution of Sundays on the last day of a calendar year is NOT even.

11. Let's assume the person started from point O and finally reached Point A.

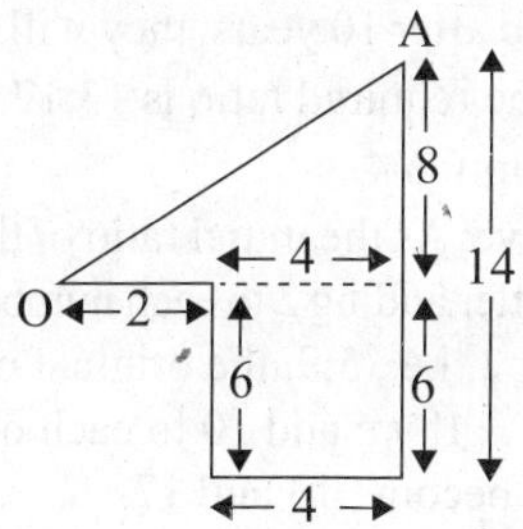

$OA = \sqrt{6^2 + 8^2} = 10$.

Hence, Option 1.

12.

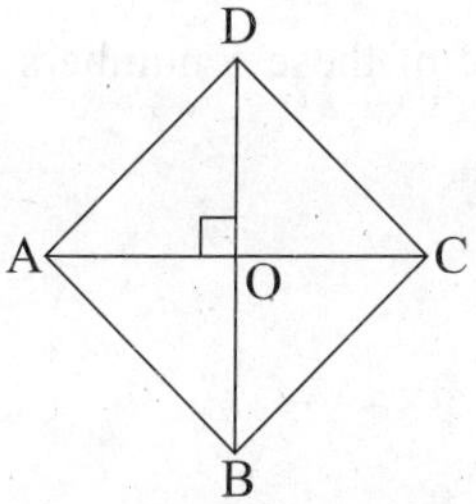

Area of a rhombus

$= \frac{1}{2} \times d_1 \times d_2$

(Where d_1 and d_2 are the lengths of the diagonals)

Here, $\frac{1}{2} \times 16 \times d_2 = 240$

or, $d_2 = 30$.

In the figure above, let AC be 30, and BD be 16

$OA = \frac{AC}{2} = \frac{30}{2} = 15$ and $OD = \frac{BD}{2} = \frac{16}{2} = 8$.

(Diagonals of a rhombus bisect each other at 90°).

$AD = \sqrt{15^2 + 8^2} = 17$.

The perimeter $= 4 \times 17 = 68$.

Hence, option 1.

13. Let the radius of the circles be r.
Area of the circle $= \pi r^2$

Circumference of the circle $= 2\pi r$

It is given that, $2\pi r = \pi r^2$

or, $r = 2$.

The diameter of the circle $= 2r = 2 \times 2 = 4$.
Hence, option 2.
Caution: Many people tend to mark 2 (Option 1) as the answer the moment they get $r = 2$. Two is the radius, but you are supposed to find the diameter.

14. Ladakh is a union territory. It was a part of the erstwhile state of Jammu and Kashmir but became a union territory in August 2019.
Hence, Option 3.

15. Holo polo: Base Ball (i)
Moto prot: my India (ii)
Prot shot: India won (iii)
On comparing (ii) and (iii), it is clear that the code for India is prot. Also, the code for "All India Radio" should not have any of Holo or polo as they are the codes for base and ball (not necessarily in the order).
Hence, Option 2.

16. The average of the 12 numbers = 15.
The sum of these 12 numbers $= 15 \times 12 = 180$.
The average of the first 2 numbers = 14
The sum of these 2 numbers $= 2 \times 14 = 28$.
Hence, the sum of the remaining 10 numbers $= 180 - 28 = 152$.

The average of these 10 numbers $= \frac{152}{10} = 15.2$.

Hence, option 2.

Shortcut 1: The overall average is 15, but the average of the first 2 numbers is 14, which is less than 15.

Hence, the average of the remaining numbers will be more than 15 and ONLY option 2 is more than 15.

Shortcut 2: The first two numbers have an average of 14 (1 less than 15); thus, these 2 numbers have left a sum of 2 to be distributed among the remaining 10 numbers.

Hence, the average of the remaining 10 numbers

$= 15 + \frac{2}{10} = 15.2$.

18. LCM of 4, 6 and 32 is 96.

Now, $96 = 2^5 \times 3^1$.

So, 96 is divisible by 4, 6 and 32, but it is not a perfect square. As the powers of 2 and 3 are odd in 96, we must multiply it by 2 and 3 to get a perfect square.

Hence, the required number is $= 2^5 \times 3^1 \times 2 \times 3$

$= 2^6 \times 3^2$

$= 576$

The answer is Option 4.

Alternative: Work with the options.

Option 1: 100 is not divisible by 6; it cannot be the answer.

Option 2: 196 is not divisible by 6; it cannot be the answer.

Option 3: 96 is NOT a perfect square; it cannot be the answer.

As we have already eliminated the first 3 options, the answer has to be option 4.

19. In the Indian Army, a major is two ranks above a lieutenant. Similarly, in the Indian Air Force, a squadron leader is two ranks above a flying officer.

Hence, Option 4.

20. Here, the first term, $a = 3$.

The common difference is $d = 4$, and the last term $T_n = 407$.

$T_n = a + (n-1)d$

or, $407 = 3 + (n-1)4$

or, $407 - 3 = (n-1)4$

or, $(n-1) = \frac{404}{4} = 101$

or, $n = 102$

Hence, Option 4.

Alternative: If we increase each of the terms by 1, the series will become:

4, 8, 12, __ __ __, 408.

It is a table of 4 and the total no. of terms is $\frac{408}{4} = 102$.

21. Let the ages of the boys be $3x$ and $7x$.

As per the question:

$\frac{3x+2}{7x+2} = \frac{5}{9}$ or, $27x + 18 = 35x + 10$

or, $8x = 8$

or, $x = 1$

Therefore, the actual ages of the boys are 3 and 7, and after 10 years, they will be 13 and 17.

Hence, the required ratio is 13:17.

Hence, Option 4.

Alternative: As the initial ratio of the numbers is 3:7 and after adding 2 to each number, it becomes 3 + 2:7 + 2, i.e., 5:9, the original numbers must be 3 and 7. If we add 10 to each of 3 and 7, the numbers become 13 and 17.

22. The numbers in ascending order are:

$\frac{x}{5}, \frac{x}{4}, \frac{x}{3}, \frac{x}{2}$ and x.

$\frac{x}{3}$ is in the middle of these 5 numbers and, hence, is the median.

$\frac{x}{3} = 8$ (given)

$x = 24$

Hence, Option 1.

23. For point (–2, 3), the x-coordinate is negative and the y-coordinate is positive.

Hence, the point is in the 2nd quadrant.

24.

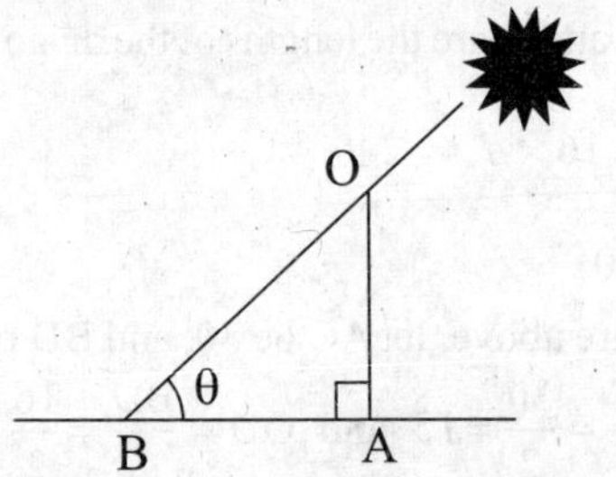

Let OA be the tree, AB be its shadow, and $\angle OBA$ be θ.

As per the question,

$$\frac{BA}{OA} = \frac{1}{\sqrt{3}}$$

or $\frac{OA}{BA} = \sqrt{3}$.

Now, $\tan\theta = \frac{OA}{BA} = \sqrt{3} = \tan 60°$

$\theta = 60°$

Hence, Option 3.

26. Let the cost of a full ticket be x, and the reservation be y.

Given that:

$$x + y = 525 \quad \text{(i)}$$

$$\text{and } \frac{3x}{2} + 2y = 850 \quad \text{(ii)}$$

From (i) and (ii), we get:

$x = 400$

$y = 125$.

Hence, Option 3.

27. Explorer was the first satellite launched by the USA in 1958.
Hence, Option 1.

28. We can put the same colour on the opposite surfaces of a cube but not on the adjacent surfaces. As a cube has 3 pairs of opposite surfaces, we require a minimum of 3 colours.
Hence, Option 3.

29. Let the cost price of each article be x.
Given that:
the selling price of 80 articles
= the cost price of 100 articles = $100x$
but the cost price of 80 articles = $80x$

Hence, profit $= 100x - 80x = 20x$.

The profit percentage = $\frac{20x}{80x} \times 100 = 25\%$

Hence, Option 2.

30.

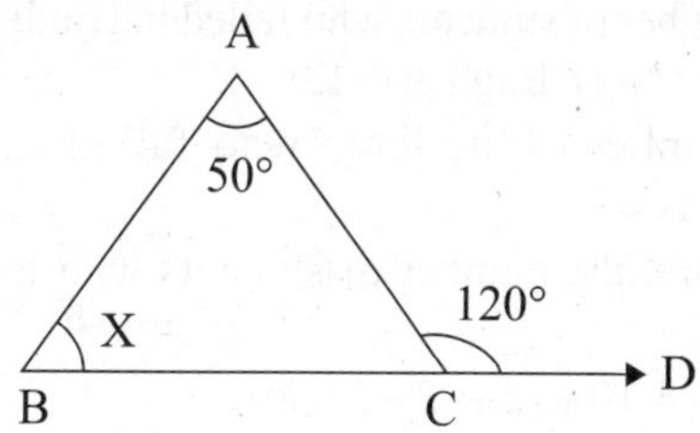

In the figure, $\angle ACD = \angle CAB + \angle ABC$
or, $120° = 50° + x$
or, $x = 70°$
Hence, Option 4.

31. Among the people in the 4 options here, only Rabindra Nath Tagore was a Nobel laureate.
Hence, Option 4.

32. Let the initial no. be 100.
Once we increase 100 by 20%, 25% and 30%, it becomes:

$$100 \times \frac{120}{100} \times \frac{125}{100} \times \frac{130}{100} = 195.$$

So, the increase is 95%.
Hence, Option 3.

33. Mercury, also called quicksilver, is the only metallic element in a liquid state at standard temperature and pressure.
Hence, Option 2.

35. Abhinav Bindra was the first Indian to get an individual gold medal in the Summer Olympics. He had achieved this feat in 2008.
Hence, Option 3.

37.

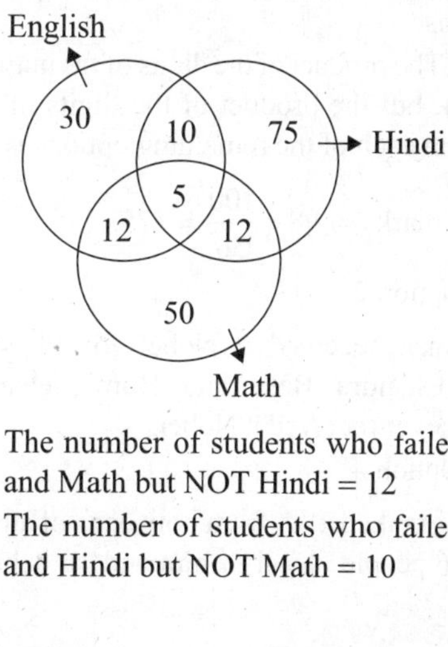

The number of students who failed in English and Math but NOT Hindi = 12
The number of students who failed in English and Hindi but NOT Math = 10

The number of students who failed in Hindi and Math but NOT English = 12

The number of students who failed in all 3 subjects = 5

Therefore, the number of students who failed in at least 2 subjects = $10+12+12+5=39$.

The total number of students = 500.

The required percentage $= \frac{39}{500} \times 100$

$= 7.8$.

Hence, Option 2.

38. The age of C is 15.

The age of A is $15 - 3 = 12$.

So, the age of $D = 12 - 1 = 11$.

The age of $B = 11 - 1 = 10$.

Hence, Option 4.

39. 12 children A _ _ _ _ C _ _ _ _ B 8 children

There are 40 children in the row. There are 12 children to the left of A and 8 to the right of B. There are 3 children in between C and B.

The no. of children to the right of $C = 12$

So, there should be 27 children to the left of C. There are 13 children, including A and the children to A's left.

Hence, the number of children between A and C is $27 - 13 = 14$.

40. There are two answers to this question, and both were accepted by the CUET-UG.

Option 1: 431 is the only prime number among the options.

Option 3: The product of the digits of the number 831 is 24, but the product of the digits of the numbers in each of the remaining options is 12.

43. The total marks $= 98 \times \frac{100}{56} = 175$.

Hence, Option 2.

45. C.V. Raman received a Nobel for Physics; Jagdish Chandra Bose and Homi Jehangir Bhabha never received a Nobel.

Hence, Option 4.

47. If a boy is ranked 17th from both ends of a line, he has 16 people ahead of him and 16 behind.

Therefore, the total no. of people in the line is $16 + 1 + 16 = 33$.

Hence, Option 2.

48. The number of red balls = 2

The number of black balls = 5

The number of white balls = 3

The total number of balls = 2 + 5 + 3 = 10

The probability of getting a red ball $= \frac{2}{10} = \frac{1}{5}$.

Now, only 9 balls are left in the bag.

The probability of getting a black ball $= \frac{5}{9}$.

Now, only 8 balls are left in the bag.

The probability of getting a white ball $= \frac{3}{8}$.

The required probability $\frac{1}{5} \times \frac{5}{9} \times \frac{3}{8} = \frac{1}{24}$.

Hence, Option 1.

49. Here, the code for a letter is 8 more than its rank in the alphabet. For example, the rank of L in the alphabet is 12, and its code in this question is $12 + 8 = 20$.

Hence, Option 2.

50. There are 7 hours between 7 pm and 2 am.

The hour hand travels 30° in an hour.

Hence, it will travel $30° \times 7 = 210°$.

Hence, Option 2.

51. Let the work be of 36 units.

As A can complete the work in 9 days, it does $\frac{36}{9} = 4$ units in a day.

Similarly, B does $\frac{36}{12} = 3$ units in a day.

If A and B start working on alternate days, starting with A,

A will do 4 units on day 1,

B will do 3 units on day 2, etc.

Thus, they will do 4 +3 = 7 units in the first 2 days.

Therefore, they will do $7 \times 5 = 35$ units in $2 \times 5 = 10$ days.

On the 11th day, it is A's turn, and he has to do $36 - 35 = 1$ unit.

A can do 4 units in a day, so he will take $\frac{1}{4}$ days to do 1 unit.

Hence, the total time taken $= 10 + \frac{1}{4} = 10\frac{1}{4}$ days.

Hence, Option 3.

52. The amount in 5 years = 520,
the amount in 7 years = 568.

So, the interest in 2 years is $568 - 520 = 48$.

$\Rightarrow$ the interest in 1 year $= \frac{48}{2} = 24$.

$\Rightarrow$ the interest in 5 years $= 24 \times 5 = 120$.

Therefore, the principal $= 520 - 120 = 400$.

Hence, Option 1.

54. The first letters of the terms of the series are the alternate letters of the alphabet in increasing order, starting with D: D, F, H, J. The next letter will be L. The last letters of the terms of the series are alternate letters of the alphabet in decreasing order, starting with T: T, R, P, N. The next letter will be L.

The numbers in the series follow this pattern:

$4 \times 2 + 1 = 9$,

$9 \times 2 + 2 = 20$,

$20 \times 2 + 3 = 43$.

The next term will be:

$43 \times 2 + 4 = 90$.

Therefore, the next term is L90L.

Hence, Option 3.

55. There is a simple trick for the time in mirror questions:

Just subtract 03:30 from 12:00 to get the answer.

Therefore, it is 08:30.

Hence, Option 2.

56. The 2nd half of the word INTERMEDIATE is EDIATE. If we put the letters of EDIATE in reverse order, it becomes ETAIDE. So, the final output is ETAIDEINTERM.

The 10th letter from the right in ETAIDEINTERM is A, and the 2nd letter to the right of A is D.

Hence, Option 2.

57. Two numbers indicate doctors who are not married: 1 and 5. Of these two numbers, only 1 is among the options.

Hence, Option 3.

59. Option 2:

$$50 \text{ metre/minute} = \frac{50}{60} \text{ meter/second}$$

$$= \frac{5}{6} \text{ meter/second}$$

Option 3:

$$70 \text{ km/hour} = \frac{70 \times 1000}{3600} \text{ meter/second}$$

$$= \frac{175}{9} \text{ meter/second}$$

Option 4:

$$5 \text{ km/minute} = \frac{5 \times 1000}{60} \text{ meter/second}$$

$$= \frac{250}{3} \text{ meter/second.}$$

Now, $\frac{250}{3} > 50 > \frac{175}{9} > \frac{5}{6}$.

Hence, Option 2.

CUET UG 2023 GENERAL TEST

May 21

INSTRUCTIONS:

1. You need to attempt any 50 out of the 60 questions in 60 minutes.
2. You get 5 marks for a correct response and –1 for an incorrect one. However, there is no reward or penalty for a question not attempted.

1. Five students are standing in a circle, and they are facing the centre of the circle. Ajay is between Amar and Aman. Alok is on the left of Amit. Amar is on the immediate left of Alok. Who is sitting on the immediate right of Ajay?

(1) Amar (2) Aman
(3) Alok (4) Amit

2. Which of the following is not a member of the 'SAARC'?

(1) Nepal (2) Sri Lanka
(3) China (4) Bangladesh

3. In which year was the organisation named 'Lalit Kala Akademi' established?

(1) 1951 (2) 1952
(3) 1953 (4) 1954

4. Which city is known as the Lake City of India?

(1) Jaipur (2) Udaipur
(3) Bikaner (4) Bhiwadi

5. Necklace is related to jewellery in the same way as shirt is related to __________?

(1) cloth (2) apparel
(3) cotton (4) thread

6. Match **List I** with **List II**.

List I (Event)	List II (Year)
A. Partition of Bengal	I. 1885
B. Foundation of the Indian National Congress	II. 1917
C. Champaran Satyagraha	III. 1930
D. Civil Disobedience Movement	IV. 1905

Choose the correct answer from the options given below:

(1) A-I, B-III, C-IV, D-II
(2) A-III, B-II, C-I, D-IV
(3) A-IV, B-I, C-II, D-II
(4) A-IV, B-I, C-III, D-II

7. The incomes of A and B are in the ratio 5:3. The expenditures of A, B and C are in the ratio 8:5:2. If C spends ₹2000 and B saves ₹700, then what amount does A save?

(1) ₹1500 (2) ₹1000
(3) ₹2000 (4) ₹500

8. Indian Grain Storage Management and Research Institute (IGMRI) is situated at:

(1) Hapur (2) Bagpat
(3) Amroha (4) Varanasi

9. If the vertices of a ΔABC are $A(1, 3)$, $B(3, 5)$ and $C(x, y)$ and the centroid is $\left(\frac{11}{3}, \frac{16}{3}\right)$, then (x, y) is:

(1) (8, 7) (2) (7, 8)
(3) (4, 8) (4) (7, 7)

10. A capsule of medicine is in the shape of a sphere with a diameter of 2.8 mm. How much medicine is needed to fill this capsule (correct to one place of decimal)? $\left(\pi = \frac{22}{7}\right)$

(1) 11.5 mm^3
(2) 12.2 mm^3
(3) 22.4 mm^3
(4) 15.4 mm^3

11. If the mean of p, q and r is M and pq + qr + rp = 0, then the mean of p^2, q^2 and r^2 is

(1) M^2 (2) $3\ M^2$
(3) $6\ M^2$ (4) $9\ M^2$

12. What is the shape of our Milky Way galaxy?

(1) Circular (2) Spiral
(3) Elliptical (4) Diamond shape

13. If in a code language, 'WORD' is written as '1234', 'GOD' as '524' and 'PUT' as '678', then 'GOOD' can be written as ________.

(1) 7224 (2) 6224
(3) 5224 (4) 4223

14. Read the following arrangement carefully and answer the question given below.

A B 3 D 4 C 9 O & Q Y X * N M K 8 Q R G

Which of the following is exactly in the middle of 9 and 8?

(1) X, * (2) X
(3) Y (4) *

15. Complete the following series.

9, 12, 18, 30, 54, ?

(1) 78 (2) 84
(3) 72 (4) 102

16. Abhijit Vinayak Banerjee won the Nobel Prize in economic sciences in 2019 for his experimental approach to ________.

(1) alleviating global poverty
(2) struggle against the suppression of children
(3) making a transition from Physics to Biology
(4) breakthrough in the field of medicine

17. Match **List I** with **List II**.

List I (Liquid)	List II (pH Value)
A. milk	I. 3
B. pure water	II. 6.5
C. blood	III. 7
D. apple juice	IV. 7.4

Choose the correct answer from the options given below:

(1) A-II, B-IV, C-III, D-I
(2) A-II, B-III, C-IV, D-I
(3) A-III, B-IV, C-I, D-II
(4) A-III, B-II, C-IV, D-I

18. Arrange the given events in the ascending order of their probabilities:

A = target is hit 2 times in 20 shots
B = target is hit 175 times in 200 shots
C = target is hit 92 times in 100 shots
D = target is hit 2 times in 5 shots
E = target is hit 5 times in 13 shots

Choose the correct answer from the options given below:

(1) E, A, D, B, C
(2) E, B, A, D, C
(3) A, E, D, B, C
(4) E, A, B, C, D

19. Which one of the following is not an A.P.?

(1) 11, 7, 3, −1, −5
(2) 0, −3, −6, −9
(3) 3, 9, 19, 33, 51
(4) 9, 13, 17, 21, 25

20. A and B can do a work in 45 days and 40 days, respectively. They started working together, but A left after some days and B alone completed the remaining work in 23 days. After how many days did A leave?

(1) 8 (2) 6
(3) 11 (4) 9

21. A tower stands vertically on the ground. From a point on the ground, which is 18 m away from the foot of the tower, the angle of elevation of the top of the tower is found to be 30°. Find the height of the tower.

(1) $15\sqrt{3}$ m (2) $6\sqrt{3}$ m
(3) $5\sqrt{3}$ m (4) $10\sqrt{3}$ m

22. If a 10-digit number M30348462N is divisible by both 8 and 11, then what is the value of $M^2 + N^2 - 18$?

(1) 5 (2) 6
(3) 7 (4) 8

23. The 'Kanha National Park' is situated in ________.

(1) Rajasthan
(2) Uttar Pradesh
(3) Madhya Pradesh
(4) Gujarat

24. Which number can be filled in place of the question mark?

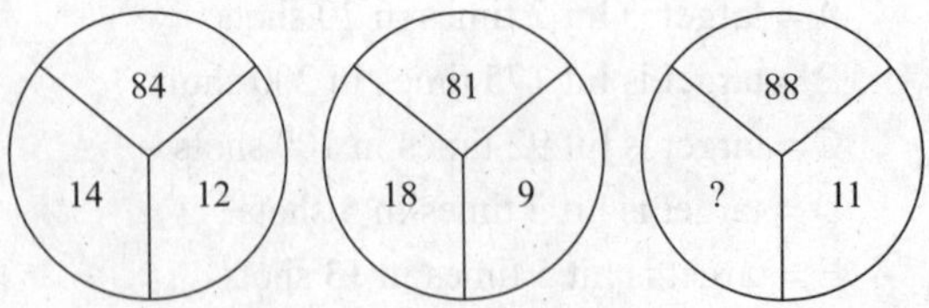

(1) 16 (2) 14
(3) 12 (4) 10

25. A sum was invested on simple interest at a certain rate for 3 years. Had it been invested at a rate 2% higher, it would have fetched ₹360 more as interest. The value of the invested sum is:

(1) ₹6500 (2) ₹5000
(3) ₹6000 (4) ₹4020

26. Asha is twice as old as Anita. Three years ago, she was three times as old as Anita. How old is Asha now?

(1) 12 years (2) 8 years
(3) 7 years (4) 6 years

27. Statement: XYZ company has marked its product, "Go ahead and purchase it, if price and quality are your considerations.

Conclusions:

I. The product must be good in quality.
II. The price of the product must be reasonable.

(1) If only conclusion I follows.
(2) If only conclusion II follows.
(3) If either conclusion I or II follows.
(4) If both conclusions I and II follow.

28. Which of the following texts deals with the philosophical matters of Buddha?

(1) Vinaya Pitaka
(2) Sutta Pitaka
(3) Abhidhamma Pitaka
(4) Dipavamsa

29. Find the next term in the following series.

ZAY, XBW, VCU, TDS, ______.

(1) REQ (2) QER
(3) RES (4) OEP

30. The chemical name of washing soda is ______.

(1) Sodium Carbonate Decahydrate
(2) Sodium Carbonate Octahydrate
(3) Sodium Carbonate Pentahydrate
(4) Sodium Carbonate Tetrahydrate

31. Sundarbans National Park is situated in ______.

(1) Odisha (2) Assam
(3) West Bengal (4) Bihar

32. If the circumference of a circle is increased by 20%, then the area of the circle will increase by:

(1) 40% (2) 44%
(3) 48% (4) 46%

33. Match **List I** with **List II**.

List I (Constellations)	List II (Indian Names)
A. Taurus	I. Mithun
B. Sagittarius	II. Kumbh
C. Aquarius	III. Dhanu
D. Gemini	IV. Vrish

Choose the correct answer from the options given below:

(1) A-IV, B-I, C-III, D-II
(2) A-IV, B-III, C-II, D-I
(3) A-IV, B-I, C-II, D-III
(4) A-II, B-IV, C-III, D-I

34. Out of the given options, which name will come in the last in a telephone directory?

(1) Mahender (2) Mohendra
(3) Mohinder (4) Mahinder

35. Alka is older than Mala, Gopal is older than Mala but younger than Alka. Kapil is younger than Ram and Mala. Mala is older than Ram. Who is the youngest?

(1) Kapil (2) Alka
(3) Ram (4) Mala

36. Given below are two statements:

Statement I: Only one rhombus ABCD can be drawn with AB = 4 cm and diagonal BD = 5 cm.

Statement II: Only one parallelogram ABCD can be drawn with AB = 6 cm and diagonal BD = 8 cm.

In light of the above statements, choose the correct answer from the options below.

(1) Both statement I and statement II are true.
(2) Both statement I and statement II are false.
(3) Statement I is true, but statement II is false.
(4) Statement I is false, but statement II is true.

37. If $\frac{2}{3}$ of A = 75% of B = 0.6 of C, then A:C:B is:

(1) 9:8:10 (2) 9:10:8
(3) 8:9:10 (4) 10:9:8

38. Match **List I** with **List II**.

List I (Players)	List II (Nicknames)
A. Flying Fish	I. Harbhajan Singh
B. Black Pearl	II. K.D. Jadhav
C. The Turbanator	III. Pele
D. Pocket Dynamo	IV. Michael Phelps

Choose the correct answer from the options given below:

(1) A-IV, B-II, C-I, D-III
(2) A-I, B-II, C-IV, D-III
(3) A-IV, B-III, C-I, D-II
(4) A-II, B-III, C-I, D-IV

39. Who was the founder of the 'ISRO'?

(1) Vikram Sarabhai
(2) APJ Abdul Kalam
(3) Srinivasa Ramanujan
(4) Homi Jehangir Bhabha

40. According to the Big Bang theory of the origin of the universe, which basic unit is termed the 'God Particle'?

(1) Proton (2) Higgs Boson
(3) Nebula (4) Electron

41. If 'when' means 'multiplication', 'you' means 'division', 'come' means 'subtraction' and 'will' means 'addition', then what will be the value of "8 when 12 will 16 you 2 come 10"?

(1) 112 (2) 96
(3) 94 (4) 45

42. Five years ago, Nuri was thrice as old as Sonu. Ten years from now, Nuri will be twice as old as Sonu. The present ages of Nuri and Sonu, respectively, are

(1) 40 years, 20 years
(2) 30 years, 20 years
(3) 20 years, 50 years
(4) 50 years, 20 years

43. A, B, C and D are playing cards. A and B are partners. D faces the North. If A faces the West, then who faces the South?

(1) A (2) B
(3) C (4) D

44. The ratio of the base radii of a cylinder and a cone is 3:4, and their heights are in the ratio 2:3. Then the ratio of their volumes is

(1) 8:9 (2) 9:8
(3) 7:13 (4) 12:15

45. Find the answer figure in which the problem figure is embedded:

Problem Figure

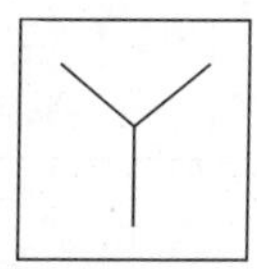

(1)

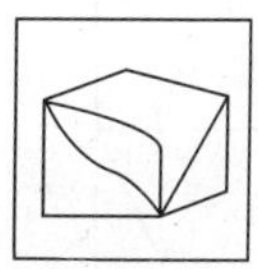

(2)

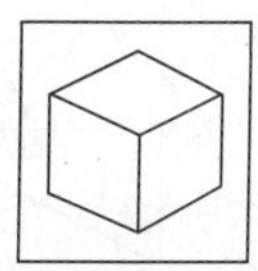

(3)

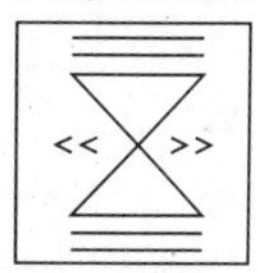

(4)

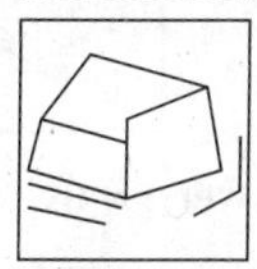

46. A and B are two stations 455 km apart. A train starts from station A at 9 am and runs towards station B at a speed of 55 kmph. Another train starts from station B at 10 am and runs towards station A at a speed of 45 kmph. At what time do the trains meet?

(1) 2 pm (2) 2:15 pm
(3) 2:30 pm (4) 2:45 pm

47. Who wrote the book 'Panchatantra'?

(1) Kalidas (2) Pt. Vishnu Sharma
(3) Mahadevi Verma (4) Ashwa Ghosh

48. In a Physics test, the average mark of girls in a class is 40. If the average mark of the first 20 girls is 50, and that of the remaining girls is 20, then the total number of girls in the class is:

(1) 30 (2) 40
(3) 25 (4) 45

49. A bus for Delhi leaves every 30 minutes from a bus stand. An enquiry clerk, Ramesh, told Anil, a passenger, that a bus had already left 10 minutes ago, and the next bus would leave at 9:35 am. At what time did the enquiry clerk give this information to Anil?

(1) 9:10 am (2) 9:20 am
(3) 9:15 am (4) 9:05 am

50. If January 1 is a Friday in a leap year, then what is the last day of March in that year?

(1) Monday (2) Tuesday
(3) Wednesday (4) Thursday

51. In the following question, find out which of the answer figures (1), (2), (3) and (4) completes the figure matrix.

Problem Figure

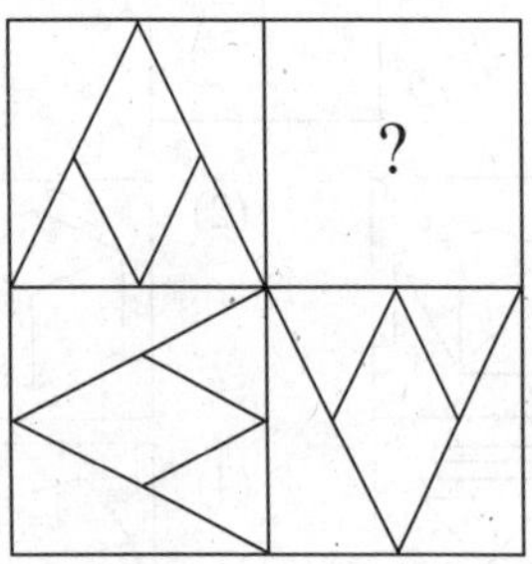

Answer Figures

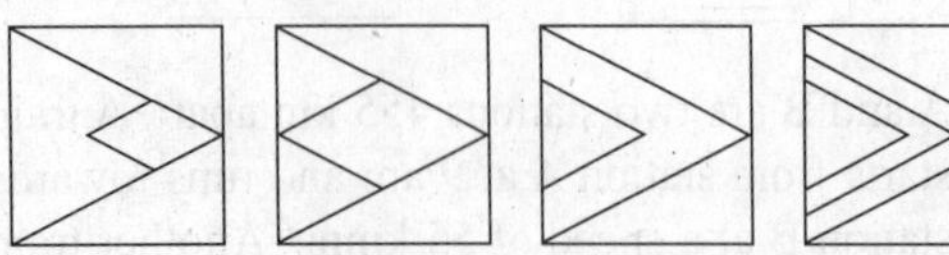

(1) (2) (3) (4)

52. The given reaction is called a ________.

$$CaO + H_2O \rightarrow Ca(OH)_2$$

(1) Dissociation Reaction
(2) Substitution Reaction
(3) Combination Reaction
(4) Addition Reaction

53. Rakesh, Amit and Suresh started a business. Rakesh invested $\frac{1}{2}$ part, Amit $\frac{1}{3}$ part and the rest of the capital was invested by Suresh. The ratio of their profits will be:

(1) 2:3:1 (2) 3:2:1
(3) 2:3:6 (4) 6:3:2

54. A cube painted green on all faces is cut into 27 small cubes of equal size. How many small cubes are painted on one face only?

(1) 12 (2) 8
(3) 6 (4) 1

55. Who amongst the following is associated with the Law of Inheritance?

(1) Gregor Johann Mendel
(2) Charles Robert Darwin
(3) Leeuwenhoek
(4) Isaac Newton

56. Five students, A, B, C, D and E, are good at various subjects. B and E are good at Dramatics and Computer Science, and A and B are good at Computer Science and Physics. A, D and C are good at Physics and History. C and A are good at Physics and Mathematics, D and E are good at History and Dramatics. Who is good at Computer Science, History and Dramatics?

(1) A (2) C
(3) B (4) E

57. Savvy invested $\frac{1}{3}$ of her capital at a 10% gain, $\frac{1}{4}$ at a 20% gain and the remaining at a 30% gain. If her income from the investment is ₹50,000, then the value of the capital is:

(1) ₹72,20,000 (2) ₹2,40,000
(3) ₹2,60,000 (4) ₹2,80,000

58. How many parallelograms are there in the following figure?

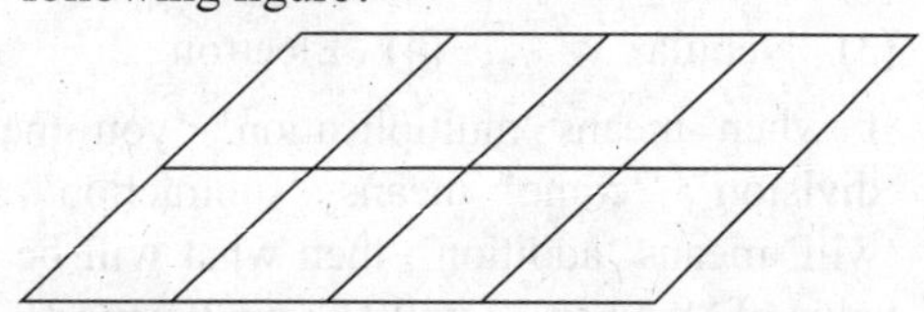

(1) 22 (2) 30
(3) 28 (4) 24

59. Match **List I** with **List II**.

List I	List II
A. LCM of $2^2 \times 3^3 \times 5^4 \times 7$ and $2^3 \times 3 \times 5 \times 7^4$	I. $2^6 \times 7^4$
B. HCF of $2^3 \times 3^2 \times 5$ and $3^2 \times 2^4 \times 5^3$	II. $2^{12} \times 3^5 \times 5^7 \times 7^{14}$
C. LCM of $5^7 \times 7^5 \times 2^{12}$ and $3^5 \times 7^{14} \times 2^6$	III. $2^3 \times 3^3 \times 5^4 \times 7^4$
D. HCF of $5^7 \times 7^5 \times 2^{12}$ and $3^5 \times 7^4 \times 2^6 \times 11$	IV. $2^3 \times 3^2 \times 5$

Choose the correct answer from the options given below:

(1) A-III, B-II, C-IV, D-I

(2) A-IV, B-III, C-I, D-II

(3) A-III, B-IV, C-II, D-I

(4) A-III, B-IV, C-I, D-II

60. Which of the following were the causes of the revolt of 1857?

A. Indian soldiers were paid low salaries

B. Jhansi was annexed owing to the Doctrine of Lapse

C. partition of Bengal

D. Jallianwala Bagh massacre

E. heavy taxation

Choose the correct answer from the options given below:

(1) B and E only

(2) A, B and E only

(3) A and B only

(4) C, D and E only

Answer Key

1. **(1)**	2. **(3)**	3. **(4)**	4. **(2)**	5. **(2)**	6. **(3)**	7. **(1)**	8. **(1)**	9. **(2)**	10. **(1)**
11. **(2)**	12. **(2)**	13. **(3)**	14. **(2)**	15. **(4)**	16. **(1)**	17. **(2)**	18. **(3)**	19. **(3)**	20. **(4)**
21. **(2)**	22. **(3)**	23. **(3)**	24. **(1)**	25. **(3)**	26. **(1)**	27. **(4)**	28. **(3)**	29. **(1)**	30. **(1)**
31. **(3)**	32. **(2)**	33. **(2)**	34. **(3)**	35. **(1)**	36. **(3)**	37. **(2)**	38. **(3)**	39. **(1)**	40. **(2)**
41. **(3)**	42. **(4)**	43. **(3)**	44. **(2)**	45. **(2)**	46. **(1)**	47. **(2)**	48. **(1)**	49. **(3)**	50. **(4)**
51. **(2)**	52. **(3)**	53. **(2)**	54. **(3)**	55. **(1)**	56. **(4)**	57. **(2)**	58. **(2)**	59. **(3)**	60. **(2)**

Classification of Questions

Question No.	Subject	Topic	Difficulty Level
1.	Reasoning	Circular Arrangement	Easy
2.	General Awareness	Polity	Easy
3.	General Awareness	Art and Culture	Difficult
4.	General Awareness	Miscellaneous	Easy
5.	Reasoning	Analogy	Easy
6.	General Awareness	History	Medium
7.	Quantitative Aptitude	Ratio	Medium
8.	General Awareness	Miscellaneous	Difficult

Question No.	Subject	Topic	Difficulty Level
9.	Quantitative Aptitude	Coordinate Geometry	Medium
10.	Quantitative Aptitude	Mensuration	Easy
11.	Quantitative Aptitude	Algebra	Medium
12.	General Awareness	Geography	Easy
13.	Reasoning	Coding	Easy
14.	Reasoning	Miscellaneous	Easy
15.	Reasoning	Number Series	Easy
16.	General Awareness	Recognition and Awards	Easy
17.	General Awareness	Chemistry	Medium
18.	Quantitative Aptitude	Probability	Medium
19.	Quantitative Aptitude	Algebra (Arithmetic Progression)	Easy
20.	Quantitative Aptitude	Time and Work	Medium
21.	Quantitative Aptitude	Trigonometry (Heights and Distances)	Medium
22.	Quantitative Aptitude	Divisibility	Easy
23.	General Awareness	Geography	Easy
24.	Reasoning	Missing Number	Medium
25.	Quantitative Aptitude	Simple Interest	Medium
26.	Quantitative Aptitude	Age-based Problems	Easy
27.	Reasoning	Statements and Conclusions	Medium
28.	General Awareness	History	Difficult
29.	Reasoning	Alphabetical Series	Easy
30.	General Awareness	Chemistry	Medium
31.	General Awareness	Geography	Easy
32.	Quantitative Aptitude	Mensuration	Medium
33.	General Awareness	Miscellaneous	Difficult
34.	Reasoning	Rank and Order	Easy
35.	Reasoning	Rank and Order	Easy
36.	Quantitative Aptitude	Geometry	Difficult
37.	Quantitative Aptitude	Ratios	Easy
38.	General Awareness	Sports	Difficult
39.	General Awareness	Science and Technology	Easy
40.	General Awareness	Physics	Medium
41.	Reasoning	Basic Arithmetic Operations	Easy
42.	Quantitative Aptitude	Age-based Problems	Easy
43.	Reasoning	Directions	Easy
44.	Quantitative Aptitude	Mensuration	Medium
45.	Reasoning	Non-verbal	Easy
46.	Quantitative Aptitude	Time, Speed and Distance	Easy

Question No.	Subject	Topic	Difficulty Level
47.	General Awareness	Books and Authors	Easy
48.	Quantitative Aptitude	Averages	Medium
49.	Reasoning	Miscellaneous	Easy
50.	Quantitative Aptitude	Calendars	Easy
51.	Reasoning	Non-verbal	Easy
52.	General Awareness	Chemistry	Medium
53.	Quantitative Aptitude	Ratios	Easy
54.	Reasoning	3-Dimensional Arrangements	Medium
55.	General Awareness	Biology	Easy
56.	Reasoning	Miscellaneous	Easy
57.	Quantitative Aptitude	Profit, Loss and Discount	Medium
58.	Quantitative Aptitude	Permutation and Combination	Medium
59.	Quantitative Aptitude	LCM & HCF	Easy
60.	General Awareness	History	Medium

Explanation to Select Questions

1. It is given that:

a. Ajay is between Amar and Aman,

b. Alok is on the left of Amit and

c. Amar is on the immediate left of Alok.

From b and c, we can conclude that Alok has Amit on his right and Amar on his left.

This gives only one possible arrangement:

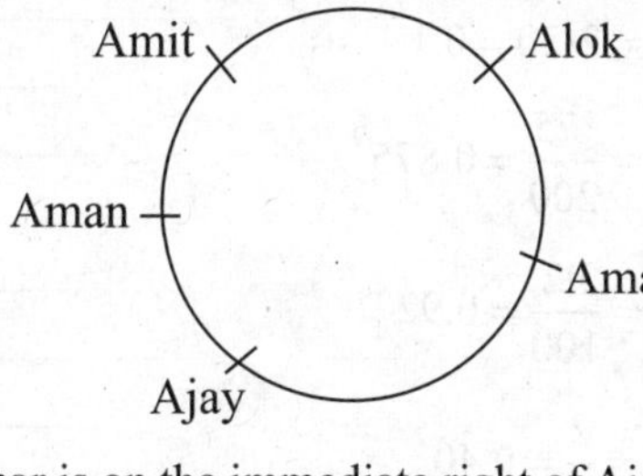

Amar is on the immediate right of Ajay.

Hence, option 1.

2. SAARC stands for South Asian Association for Regional Cooperation, and it has 8 members: Afghanistan, Bangladesh, Bhutan, India, Maldives, Nepal, Pakistan and Sri Lanka.

Hence, Option 3.

3. The Lalit Kala Akademi (National Academy of Art) is in New Delhi, and it was established in 1954. Its parent organisation is the Ministry of Culture, Government of India.

Hence, Option 4.

4. Jaipur is also known as the "Pink City". Bikaner is also known as the "Camel Country". Udaipur is also known as the "Lake City of India".

Hence, Option 3.

5. A necklace is a type of jewellery, and a shirt is a type of apparel. An apparel is designed to be worn to cover the body.

So, the correct answer is Option 2.

Apparel is made of cloth; jewellery is primarily made of metal.

We need to be careful with Option 1 (cloth).

7. Let the incomes of A and B be $5x$ and $3x$, respectively.

Let the expenditures of A, B and C be $8y$, $5y$ and $2y$, respectively.

We, of course, cannot assume that $x = y$.

It is given that $2y = 2000$,

$\Rightarrow y = 1000$.

So, the expenditures of A and B are 8000 and 5000 respectively.

B's saving = $3x - 5000 = 700$ (given in the question)

or, $3x = 5700$

or, $x = 1900$.

A's income is $5x = 9500$.

He spends 8000.

Thus, he saves $9500 - 8000 = 1500$.

Hence, Option 1.

8. The Indian Grain Storage Management and Research Institute (IGMRI) is situated at Hapur in Uttar Pradesh. Its parent organisation is Department of Food & Public Distribution, Ministry of Consumer Affairs, Food and Public Distribution.

Hence, Option 1.

9. The centroid of a triangle with vertices (x_1, y_1), (x_2, y_2) and (x_3, y_3) is $\frac{x_1 + x_2 + x_3}{3}, \frac{y_1 + y_2 + y_3}{3}$.

Here, $\frac{11}{3} = \frac{1+3+x}{3}$

$\Rightarrow x = 7$

and $\frac{16}{3} = \frac{3+5+y}{3}$

$\Rightarrow y = 8$.

Hence, Option 2.

10. The radius of the sphere $r = \frac{2.8}{2} = 1.4\,\text{mm}$.

The volume $= \frac{4}{3}\pi r^3 = \frac{4}{3} \times \frac{22}{7} \times 1.4 \times 1.4 \times 1.4$

$= 11.486....$

$\simeq 11.50$

Hence, Option 1.

11. It is given that $M = \frac{p+q+r}{3}$

or, $p+q+r = 3M$.

$p^2 + q^2 + r^2 = (p+q+r)^2 - 2(pq+qr+rp)$

$(3M)^2 - 2 \times 0$

(given that $pq+qr+rp = 0$)

or, $p^2 + q^2 + r^2 = 9M^2$.

The mean of p^2, q^2 and r^2 is $\frac{p^2 + q^2 + r^2}{3}$

$= \frac{9M^2}{3} = 3M^2$.

Hence, Option 2.

Option 4 $(9M^2)$ is a trap option.

13. WORD is written as 1234 and GOD as 524. It is evident that the W is coded as 1, O as 2, R as 3, D as 4 and G as 5.

The code for GOOD is 5224.

Hence, Option 3.

14. There are 9 characters between the 8 and the 9. Hence, the character exactly in between is the 5th character to the right of 9 or the left of 8.

The obvious answer is X.

Hence, Option 2.

15. 9, 12, 18, 30, 54, ?

Here, the differences between any two consecutive terms of the series are in a Geometric Progression.

The differences are 3, 6, 12 and 24. Hence, the next difference will be $24 \times 2 = 48$.

Now, the next term is $54 + 48 = 102$.

Hence, Option 4.

17. The pH stands for "Potential of Hydrogen". It indicates the acidity or basicity of an aqueous solution. The range of its values is 0-14, with 7 being neutral. A pH value of more than 7 indicates basicity and a value of less than 7 indicates acidity.

Here, the answer is Option 2.

18. $P(A) = 2/20 = 0.1$

$P(B) = \frac{175}{200} = 0.875$

$P(C) = \frac{92}{100} = 0.92$

$P(D) = \frac{2}{5} = 0.40$

$P(E) = \frac{5}{13} = 0.3846$ (approximately)

Hence, A<E<D<B<C.

Hence, Option 3.

19. In an Arithmetic Progression (A.P.), the difference between any two consecutive terms is a constant.

In Option 3, the difference between the second and first terms is 9 – 3 = 6, but the difference between the third and second terms = 19 – 9 = 10. As $6 \neq 10$, this sequence is NOT an A.P.
Hence, Option 3.

20. Let the work be of 360 units.
(We can take any number of our choice, but I have taken 360 as it is a multiple of both 45 and 40.)
As A can finish 360 units in 45 days,
he does 8 units in a day.
Similarly, B does $\frac{360}{40} = 9$ units in a day.
B must have done $23 \times 9 = 207$ units in the last 23 days.
It means A and B together did 360 – 207 = 153 units.
A and B do 8 + 9 = 17 units in a day.
They worked together for $\frac{153}{17} = 9$ days.
Hence, Option 4.

21.

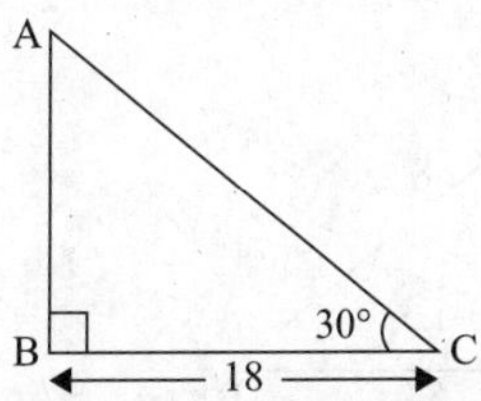

Let AB be the tower, with point B being its foot.
In ΔABC,

$$\tan 30° = \frac{AB}{BC} = \frac{AB}{18}$$

or, $\frac{1}{\sqrt{3}} = \frac{AB}{18}$

or, $AB = \frac{18}{\sqrt{3}} = 6\sqrt{3}$.

Hence, Option 2.

22. As M30348462N is divisible by 8, its last three digits - 62N - should be divisible by 8, and that is possible only if N = 4.
Again, as M30348462N is divisible by 11, N + 6 + 8 + 3 + 3 - (M + 0 + 4 + 4 + 2) should either be zero or a multiple of 11.
$\Rightarrow$ N + 20 – (M + 10) = 0 or 11K (k is a natural number)
$\Rightarrow$ 24 – M – 10 = 0 or 11k (as N = 4)
$\Rightarrow$ 14 – M = 0 or 11k
Hence, M can only be 3.
Now, $M^2 + N^2 - 18 = 3^2 + 4^2 - 18 = 25 - 18 = 7$.
Hence, Option 3.

23. The Kanha National Park is situated in the Balaghat and Mandla districts of Madhya Pradesh.
Hence, Option 3.

24. The number at the top of each of the first two figures is half of the product of the remaining two numbers.

E.g., $84 = \frac{12 \times 14}{2}, 81 = \frac{9 \times 18}{2}$

Let the number in place of ? be x.

So, $88 = \frac{11x}{2}$ or, $x = \frac{88 \times 2}{11} = 16$.

Hence, Option 1.

25. At a 2% higher rate of interest for 3 years, the investment would have fetched 6% more of the principal.
So, 6% of the investment is 360.

$\Rightarrow$ The investment $= 360 \times \frac{100}{6} = 6000$.

Hence, Option 3.

26. Let the ages of Asha and Anita be $2x$ and x, respectively.
As per the question,
$(2x - 3) = 3(x - 3) \Rightarrow 2x - 3 = 3x - 9$
or, $x = 6$.
Asha's age is $2x$; hence, the answer is 12 years.
Hence, Option 1.

28. Vinaya Pitaka literally means 'Basket of Discipline'. It is the collection of monastic laws. Sutta Pitaka literally means 'Basket of Discourses'.
It contains discourses delivered by Buddha and his close disciples.
Abhidhamma Pitaka mainly deals with the psychology and philosophy of the Theravada school of Buddhism.

Hence, Option 3.

Dipavamsa is the oldest available historical record of Sri Lanka and it mentions Buddha's three visits to the island.

29. $\underset{26\ 1\ 25}{ZAY}$ $\underset{24\ 2\ 23}{XBW}$ $\underset{22\ 3\ 21}{VCU}$ $\underset{20\ 4\ 19}{TDS}$ ____

It is clear from the figure above that the next term is $\underset{18\ 5\ 17}{REQ}$

Hence, Option 1.

30. The chemical name of Washing Soda is Sodium Carbonate Decahydrate ($Na_2CO_3 \cdot 10H_2O$).

Hence, Option 1.

The chemical name of Baking Soda is Sodium Bicarbonate or Sodium Hydrogencarbonate ($NaHCO_3$).

31. The Sundarbans National Park is situated in West Bengal.

Hence, Option 3.

It contains the world's largest area of mangrove forests. It is one of the 42 UNESCO World Heritage Sites in India.

32. Let the initial radius of the circle be r, hence its circumference will be $2\pi r$.

When the circumference increases by 20%, the radius must have increased by 20% as 2 and π are constants.

So, the new radius must be 1.2r.

The initial area of the circle $= \pi r^2$

The subsequent area of the circle $= \pi(1.2r)^2 = 1.44\pi r^2$.

So, the area goes up by 44%.

Hence, Option 2.

34. The order of the words in a telephone directory will be as per their order in a dictionary.

Words starting with Ma (Mahender and Mahinder) will come before the words starting with Mo (Mohendra and Mohinder). Of Mohendra and Mohinder, Mohendra will come first. Thus, the last entry will be Mohinder.

Hence, Option 3.

35. It is given that: Alka>Mala, Alka>Gopal>Mala, Kapil<Mala, Kapil<Ram and Mala>Ram.

Combining these all, we get:

Alka>Gopal>Mala>Ram>Kapil.

Thus, Kapil is the youngest.

Hence, Option 1.

36. Statement I

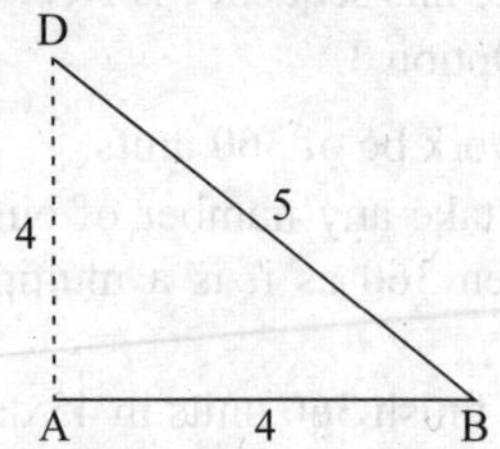

As *ABCD* is a rhombus, each of its sides is 4cm in length.

In ΔABC, all three sides are known: $AB = 4$, $BD = 5$ and $DA = 4$; hence, *ABD* is a unique triangle.

Now, point *C* can also be uniquely determined as line *AC* is a perpendicular bisector of the line *BD*, and $DC = CB = 4$.

Thus, only one rhombus *ABCD* can be drawn.

Statement II

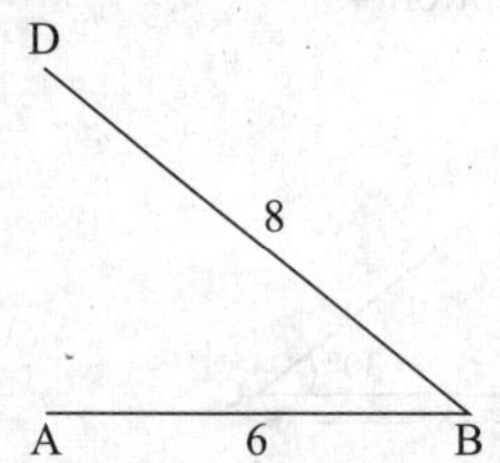

Here, *D* is a variable point as the length of *AD* is NOT fixed. Thus, there can be infinitely many parallelograms *ABCD* with the given information.

So, statement I is correct, but statement II is incorrect.

Hence, Option 3.

37. $\frac{2}{3}$ of A = 75% of B = 0.6 of C

$$\text{or, } \frac{2A}{3} = \frac{3B}{4} = \frac{6C}{10}$$

$$\text{or, } \frac{2A}{3} = \frac{6C}{10} = \frac{3B}{4}$$

$$\text{or, } \frac{2A}{2} = \frac{3C}{5} = \frac{3B}{4} = K \text{ (say)}$$

$A = \frac{3K}{2}, C = \frac{5K}{3}$ *and* $B = \frac{4K}{3}$

$A:C:B = 9:10:8.$

Hence, Option 2.

We must be careful as we are being asked about $A:C:B$ and NOT $A:B:C$.

39. The Indian National Committee for Space Research (INCOSPAR) was set up in 1962. It was subsumed by the ISRO when it came into existence on 15 August 1969. Vikram Sarabhai - the father of Indian space research - founded the ISRO.

Hence, Option 1.

41.

when	×
you	÷
come	–
will	+

Now, 8 when 12 will 16 you 2 come 10

$= 8 \times 12 + 16 \div 2 - 10$

$= 8 \times 12 + 8 - 10 = 104 - 10 = 94.$

We need to follow the BODMAS rule and must do the division before doing anything else.

Hence, Option 3.

42. Let the present ages of Nuri and Sonu be $3x + 5$ and $x + 5$. It is clear that 5 years ago, Nuri was thrice as old as Sonu.

After 10 years,

Nuri's age $= 3x + 5 + 10 = 3x + 15$ and Sonu's age $= x + 5 + 10 = x + 15$.

$3x + 15 = 2(x + 15)$

or, $3x - 2x = 30 - 15$

or $x = 15$.

Hence, the present age of Nuri is $3x + 5 = 3(15) + 5 = 50$ years.

Hence, option 4.

Alternative: 10 years from now, Nuri will be twice as old as Sonu, and it is possible only in Option 4.

43. There are 4 players: A, B, C and D. As A and B are partners, C and D must also be partners, and partners sit facing each other while playing cards. As D faces North, its partner C must be facing South.

Hence, Option 3.

44. Let the base radii of the cylinder and the cone be $3x$ and $4x$, respectively and their heights be $2y$ and $3y$, respectively.

The volume of the cylinder $= \pi(3x)^2 2y = 18\pi x^2 y$.

The volume of the cone $= \frac{1}{3}\pi(4x)^2 3y = 16\pi x^2 y$.

The required ratio is $\frac{18\pi x^2 y}{16\pi x^2 y} = 9:8$.

Hence, Option 2.

46. By the time the train from station B starts at 10 am, the train from station A has already travelled 55 km in 1 hour. At 10 am, the distance between the two trains is $455 - 55 = 400$ km.

The relative speed of these trains $= 55 + 45 = 100$ kmph (as they move towards each other).

The time they will take to meet $= \frac{400}{100} = 4$ hrs.

Hence, the trains will meet at 2 pm.

Hence, Option 1.

48. Let there be n girls in the class. Total marks scored by these girls $= 40n$.

The total marks scored by the first 20 girls is $20 \times 50 = 1000$.

The total marks scored by the remaining $(n - 20)$ girls is $20(n - 20)$.

So, $1000 + 20(n - 20) = 40n$

or, $1000 + 20n - 400 = 40n$

or, $600 = 20n$

or, $n = 30$.

Hence, Option 1.

49. As a bus leaves every 30 minutes and the next bus is at 9:35, the last bus must have left at 9:05. At the time of Anil's enquiry, it had been 10 minutes since the bus had left. Hence, the time, then, must have been 9:15 am.

Hence, Option 3.

50. The number of days between 1st January and 31st March in a leap year is $30 + 29 + 31 = 90$.

The number of odd days is the remainder when 90 is divided by 7.

Thus, the number of odd days = 6.

Hence, 31st March would be 6 days after Friday, that is Thursday.

Hence, Option 4.

51. Here, the figures that are diagonally opposite are mirror images of each other.
Also, all three figures in the Problem figure are the same but face different directions. There is only one such figure among the options.
Hence, Option 2.

53. Let the total investment be x.

Rakesh's investment = $\frac{x}{2}$

Amit's investment = $\frac{x}{3}$

Suresh's investment = $x - \frac{x}{2} - \frac{x}{3} = \frac{x}{6}$.

Hence, the ratio of their investments is $\frac{x}{2}:\frac{x}{3}:\frac{x}{6} = 3:2:1$.

So, the ratio of their profits will also be 3:2:1.
Hence, Option 2.

54. There will be exactly one cube on each of the 6 faces of the bigger cube with exactly one painted face.

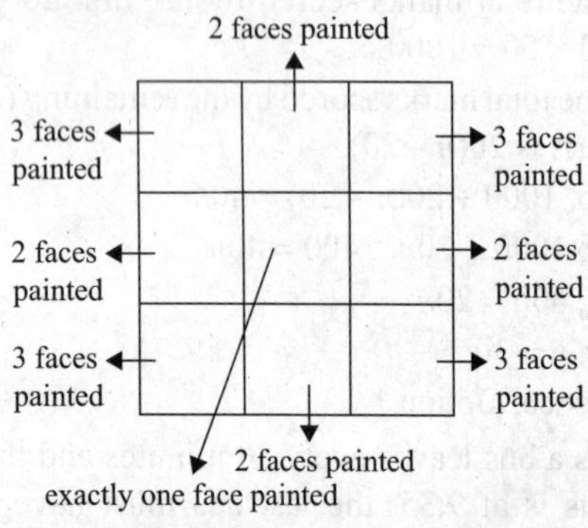

Hence, Option 3.

55. Gregor Mendel - a biologist - is known for discovering fundamental laws of inheritance.
Hence, Option 1.

Darwin - a biologist - is known for his Theory of Evolution.
Leeuwenhoek is considered the father of microbiology.
Isaac Newton was a polymath but primarily a physicist and mathematician.

56.

Dramatics	→	B, E, D
Computer Science	→	B, E, A
Physics	→	A, B, D, C
History	→	A, D, C, E
Mathematics	→	C, A

Only E is good at computer Science, History and Dramatics.
Hence, Option 4.

57. Let the total capital of Savvy be $12x$.

She invests $\frac{12x}{3} = 4x$ at 10% gain, $\frac{12x}{4} = 3x$ at 20% gain and the remaining $5x$ at 30% gain.

Her total gain is 10% of $4x$ + 20% of $3x$ + 30% of $5x = \frac{4x}{10} + \frac{3x}{5} + \frac{5x \times 3}{10} = \frac{25x}{10}$.

Given, $\frac{25x}{10} = 50{,}000$.

Or, $x = 20{,}000$.

Her total capital is $12x = 12 \times 20{,}000 = 2{,}40{,}000$.
Hence, Option 2.

58. The given figure has 3 horizontal and 5 slant lines. We can get a parallelogram by selecting any 2 of the 3 horizontal lines and any 2 of the 5 slant lines.
Hence, the number of parallelograms is ${}^3C_2 \times {}^5C_2 = 3 \times 10 = 30$.
Hence, Option 2.

CUET UG 2022
GENERAL TEST

August 30

INSTRUCTIONS:

1. You need to attempt any 60 out of the 75 questions in 60 minutes.
2. You get 5 marks for a correct response and –1 for an incorrect one. However, there is no reward or penalty for a question not attempted.

1. Which team won the ICC Women's World Cup 2022?

A. West Indies B. India
C. Australia D. England

2. Read the following statements and find the value of m.

(a) 'm' and 'n' both are even numbers
(b) $m > n$
(c) $0 < m \leq 8$
(d) $2n = 12$

Choose the correct answer from the options given below:

A. $m = 7$ B. $m = 8$
C. $m = 6$ D. $m = 4$

3. The value of $\dfrac{1}{1+\dfrac{1}{1+\dfrac{1}{5}}}$ is

A. $\dfrac{5}{11}$ B. $\dfrac{1}{7}$
C. $\dfrac{11}{6}$ D. $\dfrac{6}{11}$

4. Pointing to a photograph, a woman said, "This man is the son of the father-in-law of my husband."
How is the woman related to the man in the photograph?

A. mother B. wife
C. daughter D. sister

5. Which is the correct diagram showing the relation among students, teachers and schools?

A.
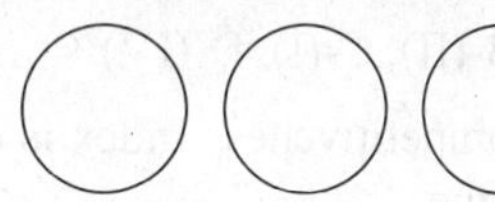

B.
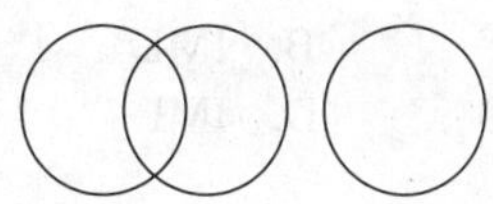

C.

D.
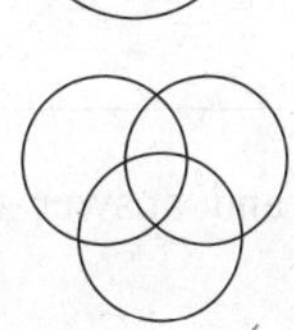

6. The value of $\dfrac{275\times275-175\times175}{275+175}$ is

A. 100 B. 450
C. $\dfrac{200}{9}$ D. 1

7. Which is the third word among the following if arranged in dictionary order?

A. SPACE
B. SPIRAL
C. SPRINT
D. SPORT

8. Match **List I** with **List II**.

List I	List II
(A) $x^2 - 4x + 4 = 0$	(I) $x = \frac{7}{2}$
(B) $2x - 7 = 0$	(II) quadratic equation
(C) $\frac{1}{x^2} - 1 = 0$	(III) $x = 2$
(D) $4x^2 + 4x + 1 = 0$	(IV) $x = \pm 1$

Choose the **correct** answer from the options given below:

A. A-(I), B-(II), C-(III), D-(IV)
B. A-(III), B-(I), C-(IV), D-(II)
C. A-(III), B-(I), C-(II), D-(IV)
D. A-(III), B-(II), C-(I), D-(IV)

9. The World Competitiveness Index is compiled and issued by the

A. UNDP B. IMD
C. UNESCO D. IMF

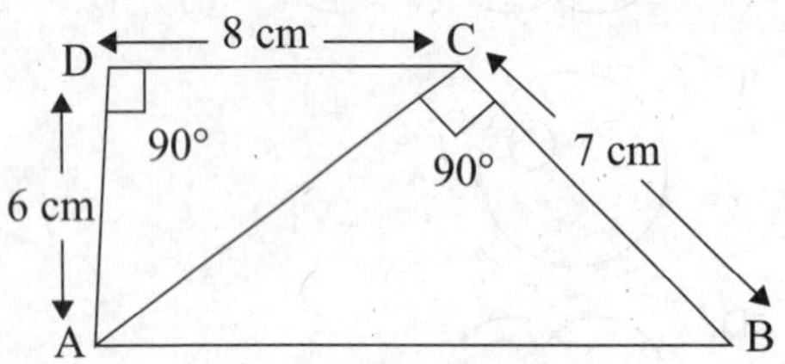

Observe the figure above and answer questions 10–12.

10. The length of AC is

A. 14cm B. 10 cm
C. 12 cm D. 13 cm

11. The area of ABCD is

A. 118 cm² B. 62 cm²
C. 59 cm² D. 90 cm²

12. The length of AB is

A. 149 cm B. 12 cm
C. 13 cm D. $\sqrt{149}$ cm

13. Which Indian writer won the 'International Booker Prize 2022?

A. Chetan Bhagat B. Arundhati Roy
C. Geetanjali Shree D. Shashi Tharoor

14. If '+' means '–', '–' means '÷' and '÷' means 'x' and 'x' means '+', then the value of 30 + 15 – 3 × 2 ÷ 4

A. 33 B. 43.5
C. 28 D. 26

15.

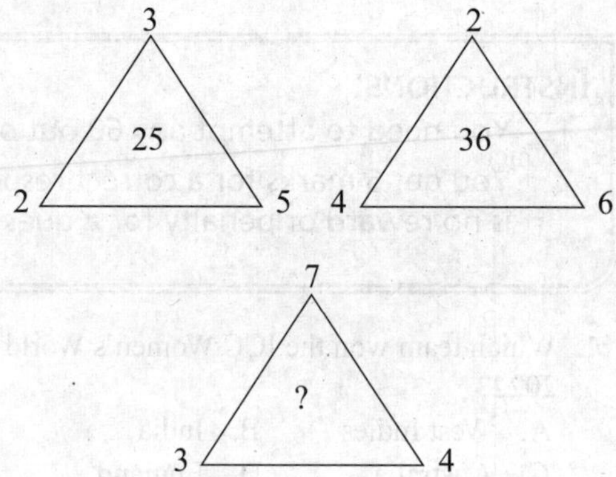

The missing number is

A. 100 B. 49
C. 40 D. 14

16. Observe the sequence:

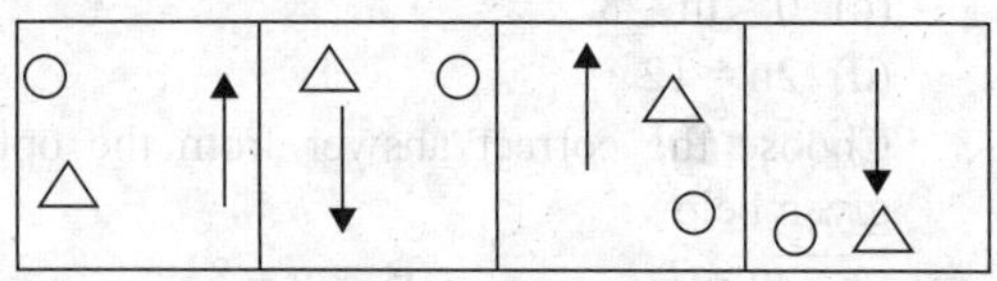

Which of the following should be the next figure?

A. 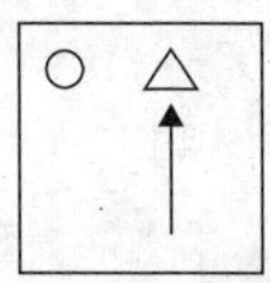 B. 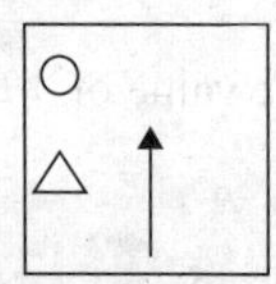

C. 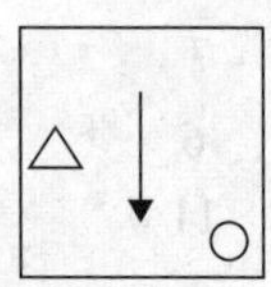 D. 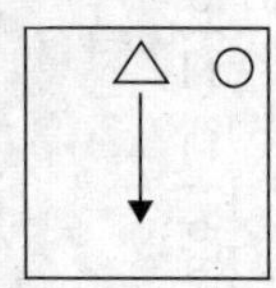

17. Which five-year plan was based on the Mahalanobis model?

A. First B. Second
C. Third D. Fourth

18. Pramod walks 10 m towards the east, then turns right and goes 8 m; he again turns right and walks 4 m. The distance of Pramod from the initial point is

A. 22 m B. 14 m
C. 10 m D. 24 m

19. 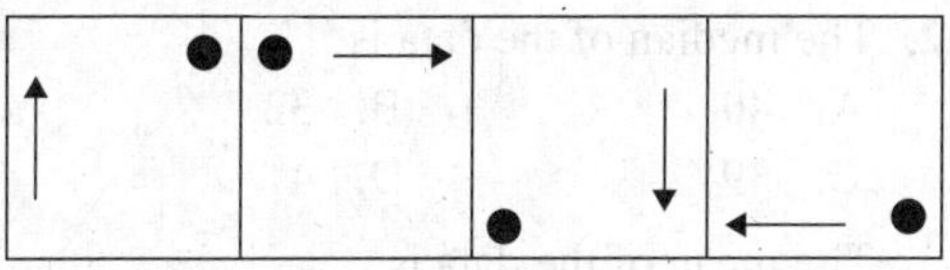

Which of the following should be the next figure?

A.  B. 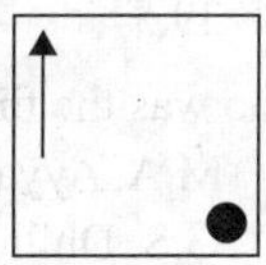

C. 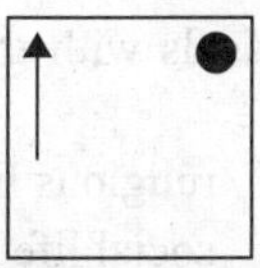 D. 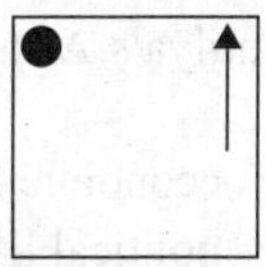

20. Match **List I** with **List II**.

List I	List II
(A) Ship	(I) Space
(B) Car	(II) Water
(C) Aeroplanes	(III) Road
(D) Train	(IV) Track

Choose the **correct** answer from the options given below:

A. A-(I), B-(II), C-(III), D-(IV)
B. A-(II), B-(III), C-(I), D-(IV)
C. A-(III), B-(II), C-(I), D-(IV)
D. A-(II), B-(III), C-(IV), D-(I)

21. 'Varuna' is the bilateral naval exercise between India and which country?

A. Japan
B. France
C. Russia
D. USA

22. A shopkeeper is giving two successive discounts of 30% and 20%. The selling price of an article after the discounts, whose MRP is 1200, is

A. 600 B. 572
C. 840 D. 672

23. If a:b = 3:4 and b:c = 3:5, then a:c is

A. 3:5 B. 7:8
C. 3:4 D. 9:20

24. The number of squares in the figure is

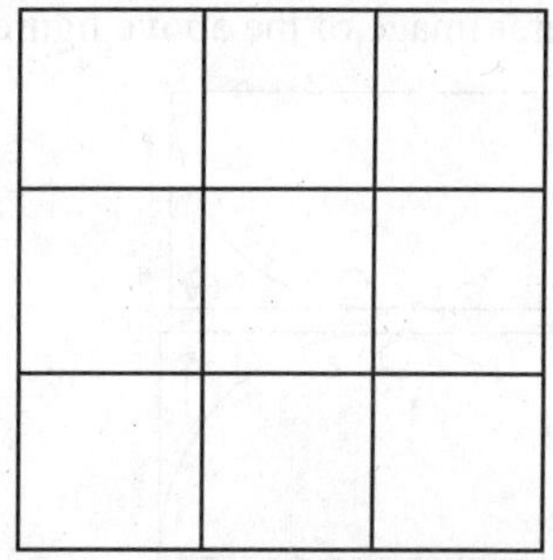

A. 10 B. 13
C. 14 D. 9

25. Match **List I** with **List II**.

List I (Indian National Congress Session)	List II (Headed by)
(A) Banaras Session, 1905	(I) M.K. Gandhi
(B) Calcutta Session, 1917	(II) Gopal Krishan Gokhale
(C) Belgaum Session, 1924	(III) Subhash Chandra Bose
(D) Haripura Session, 1938	(IV) Annie Besant

Choose the **correct** answer from the options given below:

A. A-(II), B-(I), C-(III), D-(IV)
B. A-(IV), B-(II), C-(III), D-(I)
C. A-(II), B-(IV), C-(I), D-(III)
D. A-(I), B-(III), C (II), D-(IV)

26. Which city was awarded the Cleanest City Award under 'The Swachh Survekshan Awards 2021'?

A. Varanasi
B. Delhi
C. Surat
D. Indore

27. 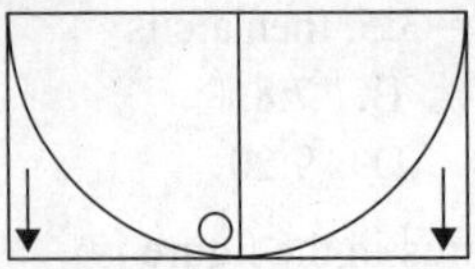

The water image of the above figure is

A. 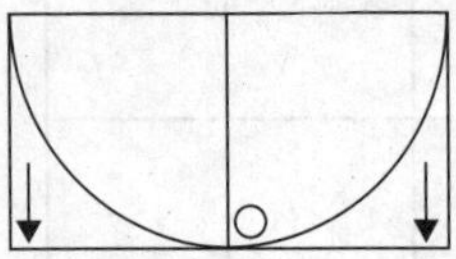

B. 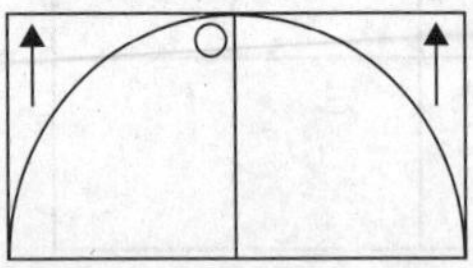

C. 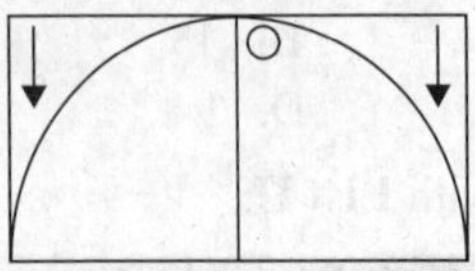

D. 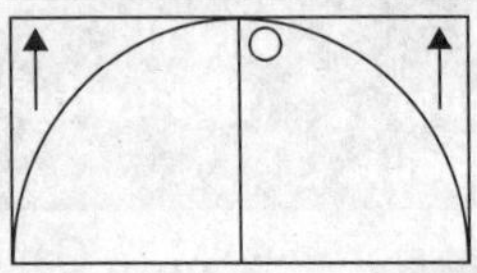

28. According to the Bloomberg Billionaires Index 2022, who is the world's richest person?

A. Elon Musk B. Gautam Adani
C. Jeff Bezos D. Bill Gates

29. When three-fourths of a number is added to the same number, it gives 28. One-fourth of the number is

A. 16 B. 4
C. 28 D. 7

30. 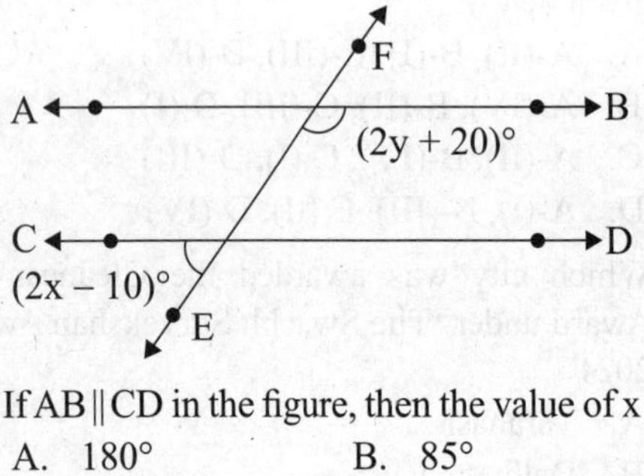

If AB || CD in the figure, then the value of x + y is

A. 180° B. 85°
C. 170° D. 90°

The marks of 12 students in mathematics are as follows:

47, 43, 39, 46, 37, 35, 29, 43, 41, 49, 35 and 30

Study the data above and answer questions 31–33.

31. The range of the data is

A. 17 B. 19
C. 20 D. 18

32. The median of the data is

A. 40 B. 32
C. 39 D. 41

33. The mean of the data is

A. 40 B. 39
C. 39.5 D. 40.5

34. Who was the first Lok Sabha speaker of India?

A. M.A. Ayyangar B. G.V. Mavalankar
C. G.S. Dhillon D. M.G. Joshi

35. Kautilya's Arthashastra deals with the aspects of

A. economic life B. religious life
C. political life D. social life

36. Which of the following countries is not a permanent member of the U.N. Security Council?

A. China B. Germany
C. France D. United Kingdom

37. Match **List I** with **List II**.

List I (Padma Vibhushan Winner)	List II (Field)
(A) Ms. Prabha Atre	(I) Civil Service
(B) Sh. Radheshyam Khemka	(II) Public Affair
(C) General Bipin Rawat	(III) Art
(D) Sh. Kalyan Singh	(IV) Literature and Education

Choose the **correct** answer from the options given below:

A. A-(III), B-(IV), C-(I), D-(II)
B. A-(IV), B-(III), C-(I), D-(II)
C. A-(IV), B-(III), C-(II), D-(I)
D. A-(III), B-(IV), C-(II), D-(I)

38. Recently, which of the following received the best film award at the Dadasaheb Phalke International Film Festival 2022?

A. Shershaah B. Pushpa: The Rise
C. KGF D. Major

39. Which of the following is the new National Education Policy (NEP) structure that will replace the 10 + 2 structure of school education?

A. 5 + 3 + 2 + 2 B. 5 + 4 + 2 + 1
C. 5 + 4 + 3 + 3 D. 5 + 3 + 3 + 4

40. Which body regulates the securities and commodities market in India?

A. Reserve Bank of India
B. Securities and Exchange Commission
C. Finance Ministry
D. Securities and Exchange Board of India

41.

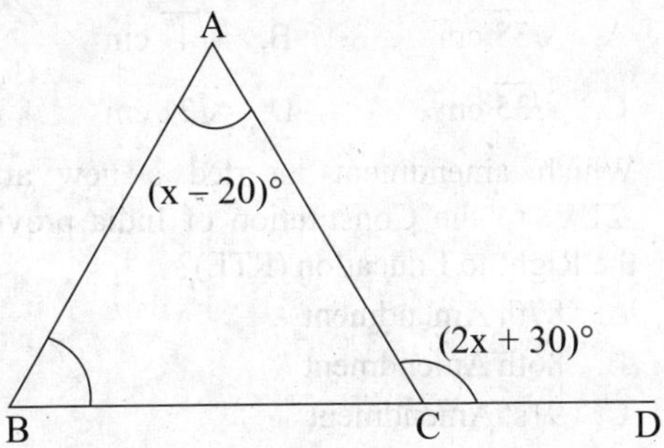

The value of ∠ACB is

A. 25° B. 75°
C. 100° D. 80°

42. Which of the following figures is the odd one?

A. 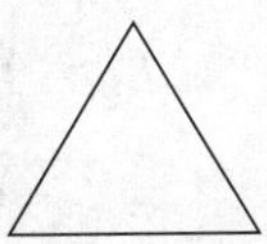 B. 

C. 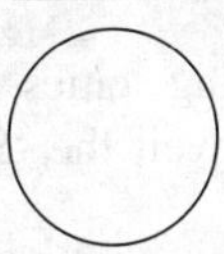 D. 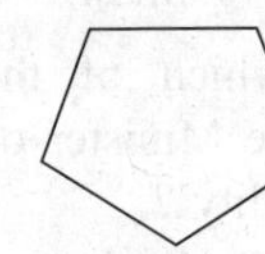

43. The National Education Day is celebrated on:

A. 11 September B. 24 January
C. 11 November D. 5 September

44. 15 kg is _____% of 50 kg.

A. 30 B. $\frac{10}{3}$
C. $\frac{3}{10}$ D. 20

45. Which among the following is the second most populated state in India, according to the 2011 census?

A. Bihar B. Maharashtra
C. Rajasthan D. Uttar Pradesh

46. Which of the following is the highest civilian award in India?

A. Padma Shri B. Padma Bhushan
C. Bharat Ratna D. Param Vir Chakra

47. If STUDENTS is written as TSDUNEST in a certain language, then FLOWER will be written as

A. ERWOLF B. EROWLF
C. LFOWRE D. LFWORE

48. 'A' is taller than 'B' but shorter than 'C'. 'D' is not the shortest among all. Who is the shortest among all?

A. D B. A
C. C D. B

49. Find the missing term: 2, 5, 10, 17, ?, 37

A. 25 B. 26
C. 24 D. 23

50. Acid rain is caused by the emission of which of the following into the atmosphere?

A. oxides of nitrogen and sulphur dioxide
B. carbon dioxide and carbon monoxide
C. ozone and carbon dioxide
D. carbon monoxide and nitrogen

51. The ozone layer in the upper part of the atmosphere protects us from

A. Cosmic Rays B. Ultrasonic Waves
C. Infra-red Rays D. Ultraviolet Rays

52. Which of the following high courts has jurisdiction over more than one State/Union Territory?

A. Kerala B. Madhya Pradesh
C. Jharkhand D. Delhi

53. Which country tested Inter Continental Ballistic Missile (ICBM) RS-28 Sarmat?

A. China B. Pakistan
C. Russia D. India

54. The mirror image of the figure given below is

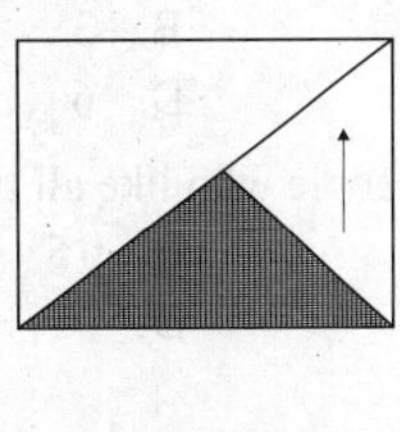

A. 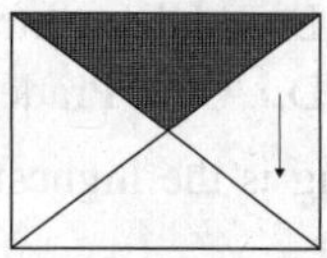 B. 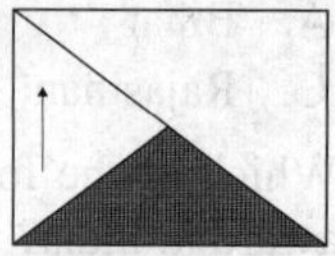

C. 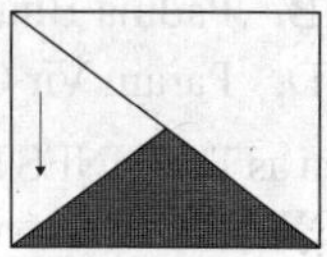 D. 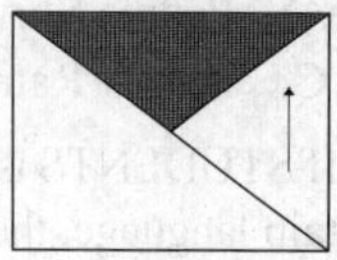

55. The Ministry of Human Resource and Development (MHRD) has been renamed as

A. Ministry of Health
B. Ministry of Education
C. Ministry of Women and Child Welfare
D. Ministry of Tribal Affairs

56. The average age of 4 family members is 15 years. The average age of that family before the birth of their 3-year-old twin kids was

A. 27 years B. 24 years
C. 20 years D. 30 years

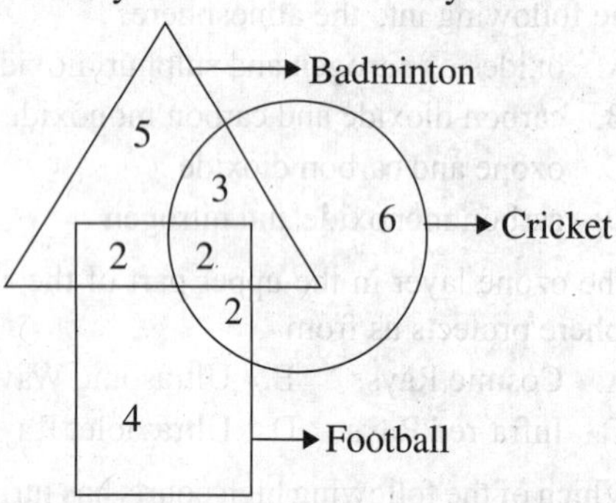

The diagram above shows the no. of people who like different sports. Observe it and answer questions 57–59.

57. The no. of people who like only cricket is

A. 9 B. 13
C. 8 D. 6

58. The no. of people who like Badminton and Cricket but not Football is

A. 2 B. 3
C. 5 D. 6

59. The no. of people who like all three sports is

A. 24 B. 15
C. 2 D. 9

60. The rate at which the RBI borrows money from commercial banks within the country is called

A. Repo Rate
B. Bank Rate
C. Reverse Repo Rate
D. Cash Reserve Ratio

61. The International Yoga Day is celebrated on

A. 21 July B. 22 June
C. 21 June D. 22 July

62. The area of a rectangle is 20 cm^2. Its length is 5 cm. Find the diagonal of the rectangle.

A. $\sqrt{38}$ cm B. $\sqrt{41}$ cm
C. $\sqrt{35}$ cm D. $\sqrt{21}$ cm

63. Which amendment inserted a new article, '21A', to the Constitution of India providing the Right to Education (RTE)?

A. 87th Amendment
B. 86th Amendment
C. 91st Amendment
D. 85th Amendment

64. The ratio between the speeds of two trains is 3:4, respectively. If the second train covers 2 km in 50 seconds, the speed of the first train is

A. 30 m/sec
B. 30 km/hr
C. 40 m/sec
D. 40 km/hr

65. In which of the following cities did the Prime Minister of India unveil the 'Statue of Equality'?

A. Hyderabad B. Surat
C. Vadodara D. Bangalore

66. Carbon dating is used to determine the age of

A. Plants B. Fossils
C. Humans D. Rocks

67. In which Indian state/UT is the 'Kaziranga National Park' located?

A. Bihar
B. Assam
C. Jharkhand
D. Jammu and Kashmir

68. 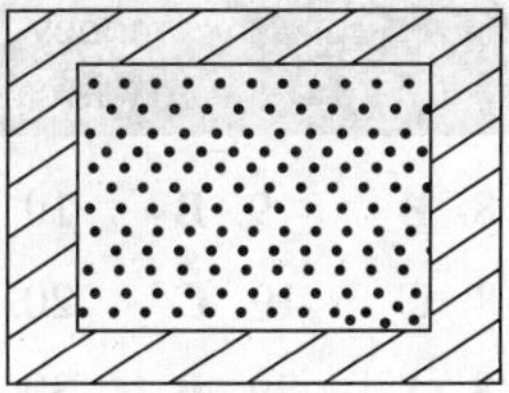

A carpet of size 3 m × 7 m has a red border. The width of the border is 25 cm. The inner part of the carpet is blue. The area of blue colour is

A. 21 m^2 B. 14.75 m^2
C. 18.5625 m^2 D. 16.25 m^2

69. In which state was the ancient Nalanda University located in India?

A. West Bengal B. Bihar
C. Odisha D. Uttar Pradesh

70. 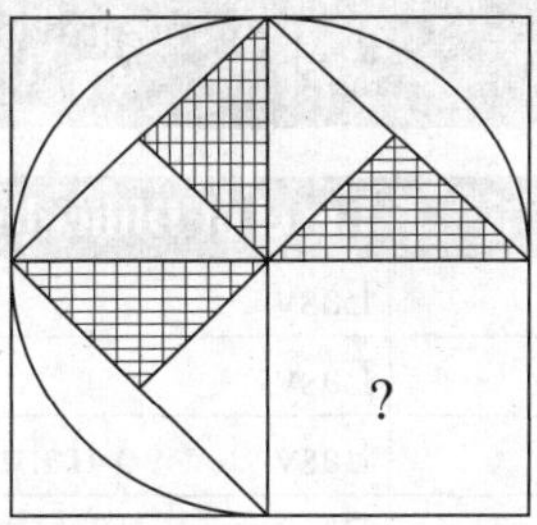

The figure which completes the adjoining figure is

A. 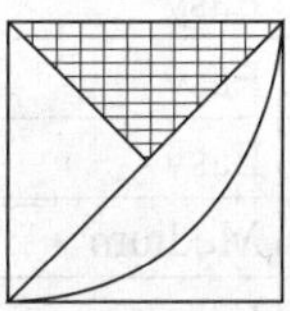 B. 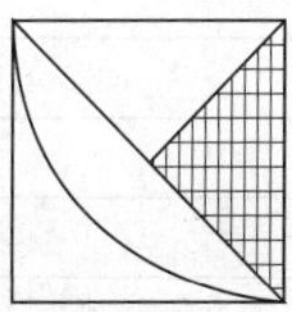

C. 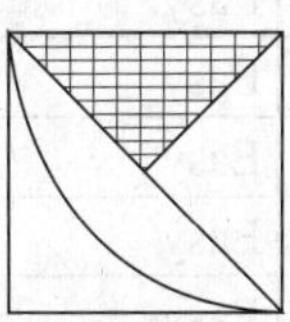 D. 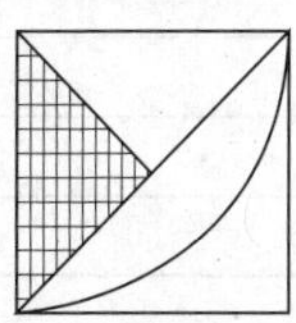

71. Match **List I** with **List II**.

List I (Agriculture Revolutions)	List II (Related to/Products)
(A) White Revolution	(I) fish
(B) Grey Revolution	(II) fertilisers
(C) Blue Revolution	(III) milk
(D) Silver Revolution	(IV) egg

Choose the **correct** answer from the options given below:

A. A-(III), B-(II), C-(I), D-(IV)
B. A-(III), B-(IV), C-(I), D-(II)
C. A-(III), B-(IV), C-(II), D-(I)
D. A-(IV), B-(III), C-(II), D-(I)

72. If x% of 24 = 10% of 72 then the value of x is

A. 30 B. 3
C. 300 D. 7.2

73. Match **List I** with **List II**.

List I	List II
(A) 2x + 5 = 15	(I) x = –10
(B) x + 3 = –7	(II) x = 6
(C) 2x – 10 = 8	(III) x = 5
(D) x + 3 = 2x – 3	(IV) x = 9

Choose the **correct** answer from the options given below:

A. A-(III), B-(IV), C-(I), D-(II)
B. A-(I), B-(III), C-(IV), D-(II)
C. A-(III), B-(I), C-(IV), D-(II)
D. A-(IV), B-(II), C-(I), D-(III)

74. The mean of three consecutive odd integers is 27. The largest among the integers is

A. 27 B. 29
C. 25 D. 31

75. A train crosses a 250 m long platform in 15 seconds and crosses a pole in 2.5 seconds. What is the length of the train?

A. 50 m B. 100 m
C. 150 m D. 250 m

Answer Key

1. **C**	2. **B**	3. **D**	4. **D**	5. **C**	6. **A**	7. **D**	8. **B**	9. **B**	10. **B**
11. **C**	12. **D**	13. **C**	14. **A**	15. **C**	16. **B**	17. **B**	18. **C**	19. **C**	20. **B**
21. **B**	22. **D**	23. **D**	24. **C**	25. **C**	26. **D**	27. **D**	28. **A**	29. **B**	30. **B**
31. **C**	32. **A**	33. **C**	34. **B**	35. **C**	36. **B**	37. **A**	38. **B**	39. **D**	40. **D**
41. Data Insufficient*			42. **C**	43. **C**	44. **A**	45. **B**	46. **C**	47. **D**	48. **D**
49. **B**	50. **A**	51. **D**	52. **A**	53. **C**	54. **B**	55. **B**	56. **B**	57. **D**	58. **B**
59. **C**	60. **C**	61. **C**	62. **B**	63. **B**	64. **A**	65. **A**	66. **B**	67. **B**	68. **D**
69. **B**	70. **D**	71. **A**	72. **A**	73. **C**	74. **B**	75. **A**			

*41. This question was incomplete.

Classification of Questions

Question No.	Subject	Topic	Level of Difficulty
1.	General Awareness	Sports	Easy
2.	Quantitative Aptitude	Numbers	Easy
3.	Quantitative Aptitude	Simplification	Easy
4.	Reasoning	Blood Relations	Easy
5.	Reasoning	Venn-diagram	Easy
6.	Quantitative Aptitude	Simplification	Easy
7.	Reasoning	Dictionary Order	Easy
8.	Quantitative Aptitude	Algebra (Equations)	Easy
9.	General Awareness	Economics	Medium
10.	Quantitative Aptitude	Geometry	Easy
11.	Quantitative Aptitude	Geometry	Easy
12.	Quantitative Aptitude	Geometry	Easy
13.	General Awareness	Current Affairs	Easy
14.	Reasoning	Miscellaneous	Easy
15.	Reasoning	Missing Number	Easy
16.	Reasoning	Non-verbal	Easy
17.	General Awareness	Economics	Easy
18.	Reasoning	Directions	Easy
19.	Reasoning	Non-verbal	Easy
20.	Reasoning	Miscellaneous	Easy
21.	General Awareness	Miscellaneous	Medium

Question No.	Subject	Topic	Level of Difficulty
22.	Quantitative Aptitude	Profit, Loss & Discount	Easy
23.	Quantitative Aptitude	Ratios	Easy
24.	Quantitative Aptitude	Permutations & Combinations	Easy
25.	General Awareness	History	Difficult
26.	General Awareness	Current Affairs	Easy
27.	Reasoning	Non-verbal (Water Image)	Easy
28.	General Awareness	Current Affairs	Medium
29.	Quantitative Aptitude	Basic Arithmetic Operations	Easy
30.	Quantitative Aptitude	Geometry	Easy
31.	Quantitative Aptitude	Statistics (Mean, Median, Mode & Range)	Easy
32.	Quantitative Aptitude	Statistics (Mean, Median, Mode & Range)	Easy
33.	Quantitative Aptitude	Statistics (Mean, Median, Mode & Range)	Easy
34.	General Awareness	Polity	Easy
35.	General Awareness	History	Easy
36.	General Awareness	Polity	Easy
37.	General Awareness	Current Affairs	Medium
38.	General Awareness	Current Affairs	Medium
39.	General Awareness	Current Affairs	Medium
40.	General Awareness	Economics	Easy
41*.	Quantitative Aptitude	Geometry	Incomplete Question
42.	Reasoning	Odd-one-out	Easy
43.	General Awareness	Miscellaneous	Easy
44.	Quantitative Aptitude	Percentages	Easy
45.	General Awareness	Geography	Easy
46.	General Awareness	Awards	Easy
47.	Reasoning	Coding	Easy
48.	Reasoning	Orders & Rankings	Easy
49.	Reasoning	Number Series	Easy
50.	General Awareness	Science (Chemistry)	Medium
51.	General Awareness	Science (Physics)	Easy
52.	General Awareness	Polity	Easy
53.	General Awareness	Science & Technology	Medium
54.	Reasoning	Non-verbal (Mirror Image)	Easy
55.	General Awareness	Current Affairs	Easy
56.	Quantitative Aptitude	Averages	Medium
57.	Reasoning	Venn-diagram	Easy

Question No.	Subject	Topic	Level of Difficulty
58.	Reasoning	Venn-diagram	Easy
59.	Reasoning	Venn-diagram	Easy
60.	General Awareness	Economics	Easy
61.	General Awareness	Miscellaneous	Easy
62.	Quantitative Aptitude	Geometry	Easy
63.	General Awareness	Polity	Medium
64.	Quantitative Aptitude	Time, Speed & Distance	Easy
65.	General Awareness	Current Affairs	Easy
66.	General Awareness	Science	Medium
67.	General Awareness	Geography	Easy
68.	Quantitative Aptitude	Mensuration	Medium
69.	General Awareness	History	Easy
70.	Reasoning	Non-verbal	Easy
71.	General Awareness	Economics	Medium
72.	Quantitative Aptitude	Percentages	Easy
73.	Quantitative Aptitude	Algebra (Linear Equations)	Easy
74.	Quantitative Aptitude	Averages	Easy
75.	Quantitative Aptitude	Time, Speed & Distance	Easy

The no. of questions on Reasoning: 19
The no. of questions on Quantitative Aptitude: 25
The no. of questions on General Awareness: 31

Explanation to Select Questions

1. Australia won the ICC Women's Cricket World Cup for the 7th time in 2022. Twelve editions of this tournament have taken place thus far, and the 13th edition will be played in India in 2025. India will be hosting this tournament for the 4th time.
Hence, Option C.

2. From (d) we get,
$2n = 12$ or, $n = 6$
From (a) and (b), we can conclude,
$m \geq 8$ (as m is an even number greater than n)
(c) says that $m \leq 8$.
So, $8 \leq m \leq 8$.
Therefore, $m = 8$.
Hence, Option B.

3. $$\frac{1}{1+\frac{1}{1+\frac{1}{5}}} = \frac{1}{1+\frac{1}{\frac{5+1}{5}}} = \frac{1}{1+\frac{5}{6}} = \frac{1}{\frac{6+5}{6}} = \frac{6}{11}.$$

Hence, Option D.

4.

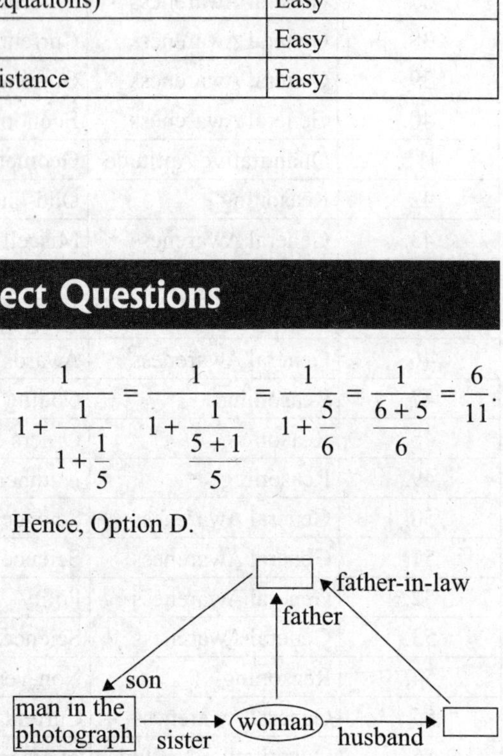

The father-in-law of a woman's husband is her father.

The woman is the sister of the man in the photograph.

Hence, Option D.

6. $\dfrac{275\times275-175\times175}{275+175}=\dfrac{275^2-175^2}{275+175}$

$=\dfrac{(275+175)(275-175)}{(275+175)}=275-175=100.$

Hence, Option A.

8. (A) $x^2-4x+4=0$

or, $x^2-2\times2\times x+2^2=0$

or, $(x-2)^2=0$ or, $x=2$.

(B) $2x-7=0$ or, $2x=7$ or, $x=\dfrac{7}{2}$.

(C) $\dfrac{1}{x^2}-1=0$ or, $\dfrac{1}{x^2}=1$ or, $x^2=1$

or, $x=\pm1$.

(D) $4x^2+4x+1=0$ (it is a quadratic equation)

or, $(2x)^2+2\times2x\times1+1^2=0$

or, $(2x+1)^2=0$ or, $(2x+1)=0$

or, $x=-\dfrac{1}{2}$.

Hence, Option B.

9. The International Institute of Management Development (IMD, not IIMD!) compiles and issues the World Competitiveness Index.

Hence, Option B.

Please refer to the following figure for explanations of questions 10–12:

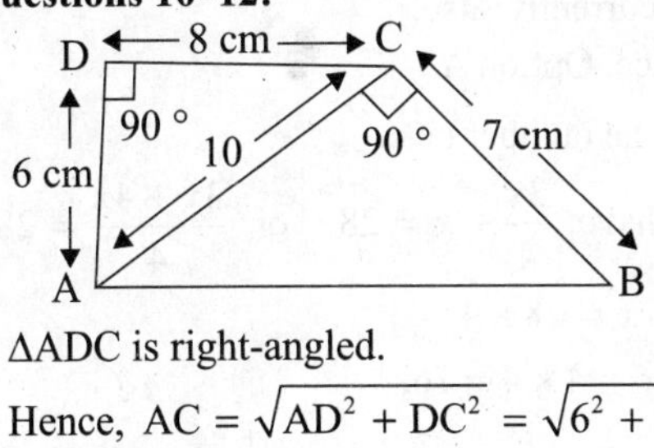

ΔADC is right-angled.

Hence, $AC=\sqrt{AD^2+DC^2}=\sqrt{6^2+8^2}$

$=\sqrt{100}$

or, AC = 10.

Now, ΔACB is also right-angled.

Hence, $AB=\sqrt{AC^2+BC^2}=\sqrt{10^2+7^2}$

or, $AB=\sqrt{149}$.

10. Option B.

11. The area of ABCD = area of ΔADC + area of ΔACB

$=\dfrac{1}{2}\times AD\times DC+\dfrac{1}{2}\times AC\times BC$

$=\dfrac{1}{2}\times6\times8+\dfrac{1}{2}\times10\times7=24+35=59\text{ cm}^2.$

Hence, Option C.

12. Option D.

13. Geetanjali Shree and Daisy Rockwell won the International Booker Prize in 2022. Geetanjali Shree got it for her novel Ret Samadhi (originally written in Hindi), which was translated into English by Daisy Rockwell. The English translation is 'Tomb of Sand'. It is the first book originally written in an Indian language to get this prize.

Hence, Option C.

The International Booker Prize is different from the Booker Prize.

Update: Georgi Gospodinov and Angela Rodel got the International Booker Prize in 2023 for their novel Time Shelter, the first novel originally published in Bulgarian to get this prize. Paul Lynch got the Booker Prize in 2023 for his novel Prophet Song.

14. $30+15-3\times2\div4$

$=30-15\div3+2\times4$ (BODMAS)

$=30-5+8=33.$

Hence, Option A.

15.

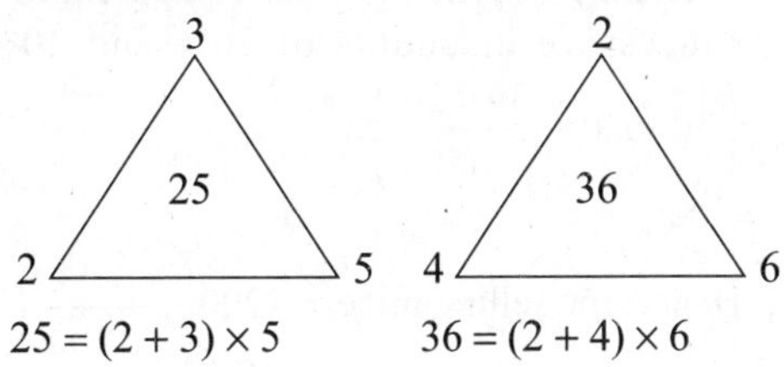

$25=(2+3)\times5$ $36=(2+4)\times6$

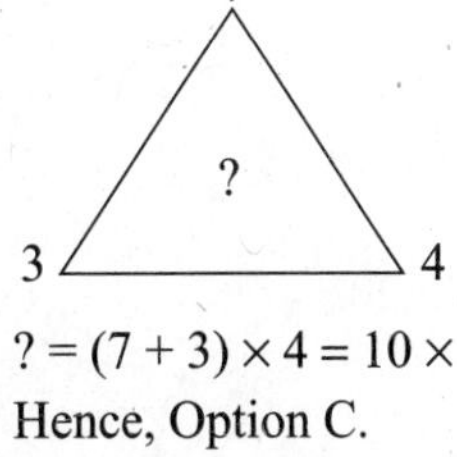

$?=(7+3)\times4=10\times4=40$

Hence, Option C.

18. 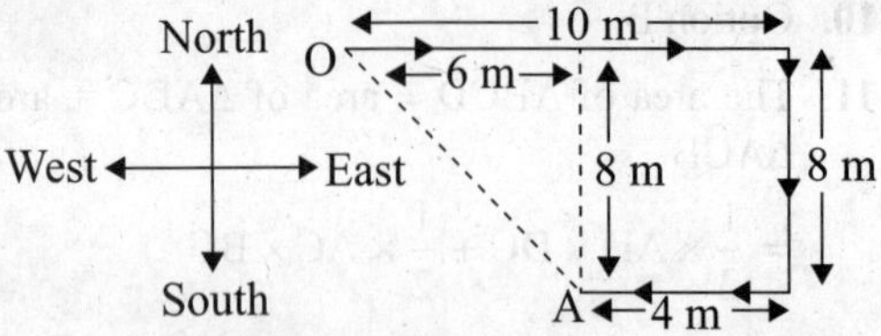

Let the starting point of Pramod be O, and the final point be A.

The required distance

$OA = \sqrt{6^2 + 8^2} = \sqrt{100} = 10$ m.

Hence, Option C.

21. Varuna is the bilateral naval exercise between India and France. Varun is the god of oceans and water in the Hindu mythology.

Hence, Option B.

India's naval exercise with Japan is JIMEX (Japan India Maritime Exercise).

India's naval exercise with Russia is INDRA (navy).

India's naval exercise with the USA, Japan and Australia is MALABAR.

22. The selling price $= 1200\left(1 - \frac{30}{100}\right)\left(1 - \frac{20}{100}\right)$

$= 1200 \times \frac{70}{100} \times \frac{80}{100}$

$= 840 \times \frac{4}{5} = 672.$

Hence, Option D.

Alternative: One discount equivalent to two successive discounts of 30% and 20% is

$\left(30 + 20 - \frac{30 \times 20}{100}\right)\%$

$= 44\%.$

Hence, the selling price $= 1200\left(1 - \frac{44}{100}\right)$

$= 1200 \times \frac{56}{100} = 672.$

23. a:b = 3:4 = 9:12.

b:c = 3:5 = 12:20

Therefore, a:b:c = 9:12:20.

Hence, a:c = 9:20.

Hence, Option D.

24. 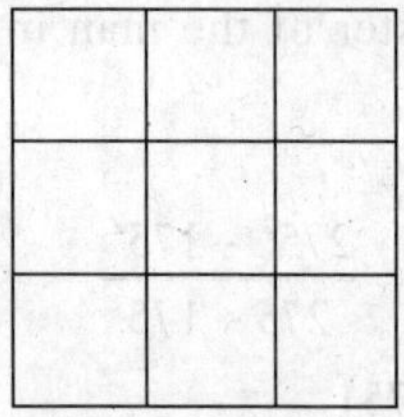

The total number of squares $= 3^2 + 2^2 + 1^2 = 14$.

Hence, Option C.

25. The Belgaum Session of the Congress in 1924 was the only Congress Session headed by M.K. Gandhi. Belgaum is a place in Karnataka. Belgaum is officially known as Belagavi now.

Netaji S.C. Bose headed a Congress Session only twice, Haripura in 1938 and Tripuri in 1939. Haripura is a village in the Surat district of Gujarat, and Tripuri is near Jabalpur in Madhya Pradesh.

Hence, Option C.

26. Indore was awarded the 'Cleanest City Award' under the Swachh Survekshan Award 2021.

Hence, Option D.

Update: Surat and Indore were jointly awarded this for 2023. This award is given by the Ministry of Housing and Urban Affairs under their Swachh Bharat Urban Mission. Indore got this award for the 7th time.

28. The Bloomberg Billionaires Index is a daily ranking of the world's 500 wealthiest people. Elon Musk was at the top in 2022 and is at the top currently, also.

Hence, Option A.

29. Let the number be x.

We have, $\frac{3x}{4} + x = 28$ or, $\frac{3x + 4x}{4} = 28$

or, $7x = 28 \times 4$

or, $x = 4 \times 4 = 16$.

Hence, one-fourth of 16 $= \frac{1}{4} \times 16 = 4$.

Hence, Option B.

Note: Option A is a trap. You are supposed to get $\frac{1}{4}$ of the number and not the number itself.

30. 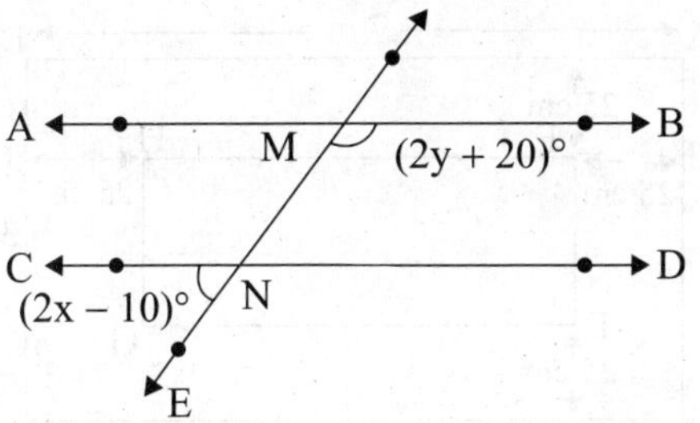

$\angle MND = \angle CNE = (2x - 10)°$ (opposite angles)

Now, $\angle BMN + \angle MND = 180°$ (as $AB \parallel CD$)

or, $(2y + 20)° + (2x - 10)° = 180°$

or, $(2x + 2y + 10)° = 180°$

or, $2x + 2y = 180 - 10 = 170.$

or, $x + y = \dfrac{170}{2} = 85.$

Hence, Option B.

Refer to the following data for explanations of questions 31–33:

The marks of the 12 students put in ascending order are:

29, 30, 35, 35, 37, [39, 41,] 43, 43, 46, 47, 49

31. The range of the data = the highest value – the lowest value = 49 – 29 = 20.

Hence, Option C.

32. As the number of numbers is an even number (12)

here, there are two middle terms: the 6th and the 7th.

The median = the average of the middle-terms

$= \dfrac{39 + 41}{2} = 40.$

Hence, Option A.

33. The mean of the data $= \dfrac{\text{the sum of these numbers}}{12}$

$= \dfrac{474}{12} = 39.5.$

Hence, Option C.

34. The first Speaker of the Lok Sabha was Ganesh Vasudev Mavalankar.

Hence, Option B.

38. The winner in 2022 was 'Pushpa: The Rise'.

Hence, Option B.

Update: The winner of the best film award at the Dadasaheb International Film Festival 2023 is 'The Kashmir Files'.

41. This question was incomplete.

44. The required percentage $= \dfrac{15}{50} \times 100 = 30.$

Hence, Option A.

45. As per the latest census conducted in India in 2011, Uttar Pradesh is the most populous state in the country, with 16.51% of India's population. Maharashtra is the 2nd most populous state, with 9.28% of India's population.

Hence, Option B.

47. 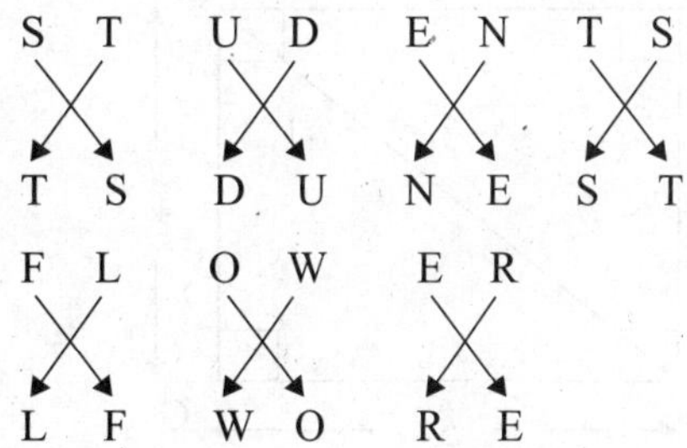

Hence, Option D.

48. A is taller than B and hence cannot be the shortest person in this group.

C is taller than at least 2 people: A and B.

Hence, C also cannot be the shortest.

Also, it is given that D is not the shortest.

Therefore, B is the shortest person in this group.

Hence, Option D.

49. 2, 5, 10, 17, (26), 37

+3 +5 +7 +9 +11

Hence, Option B.

Alternative:

$1^2 + 1 = 2$

$2^2 + 1 = 5$

$3^2 + 1 = 10$

$4^2 + 1 = 17$

$\boxed{5^2 + 1 = 26}$

$6^2 + 1 = 37.$

52. The High Court of Kerala, situated in Ernakulam, has jurisdiction over the state of Kerala and the Union Territory of Lakshadweep.
Hence, Option A.
The High Court of Madhya Pradesh is in Jabalpur and it has its benches in Gwalior and Indore.

56. The sum of the ages of all 4 family members = $4 \times 15 = 60$ years.
The sum of the ages of the family 3 years ago = $60 - 3 \times 4 = 48$ years.
But 3 years ago, there were only 2 family members as the twins were about to be born.
$\Rightarrow$ the average age then = $\frac{48}{2} = 24$ years.
Hence, Option B.

62.

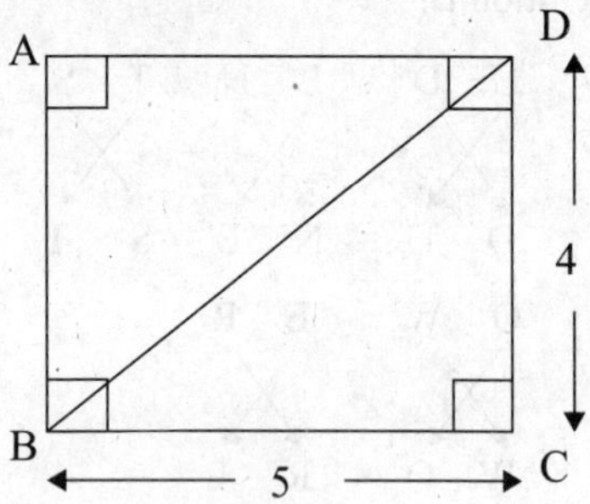

Breadth of the rectangle = $\frac{\text{Area}}{\text{length}} = \frac{20}{5} = 4$ cm.
Therefore, the length of the diagonal
$= \sqrt{4^2 + 5^2} = \sqrt{16 + 25} = \sqrt{41}$ cm.
Hence, Option B.

64. The speed of the second train = $\frac{2 \times 1000}{50}$
= 40 m/s.
Therefore, the speed of the first train =
$40 \times \frac{3}{4}$ m/s = 30 m/s.
Hence, Option A.

65. The Statue of Equality is in the Ranga Reddy district of Telangana near the city of Hyderabad.
Hence, Option A.
The statue is of the 11th-century reformer Ramanuja.
The Statue of Equality should not be confused with the Statue of Unity in Kevadia (Gujarat).

68.

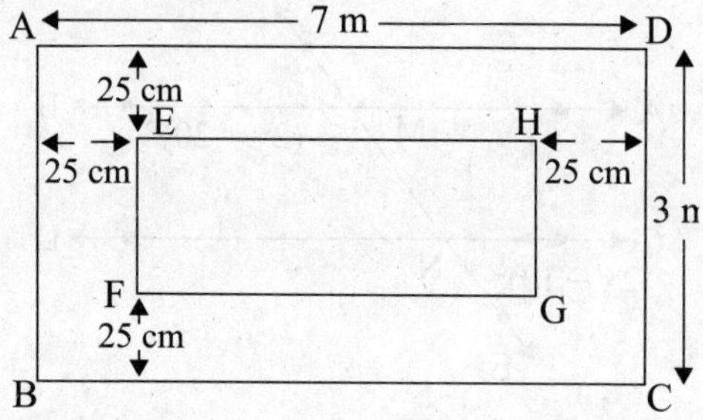

$25 \text{ cm} = \frac{25}{100} = \frac{1}{4}$ m.
We have to get the area of the rectangle EFGH.
$EF = 3 - 2 \times \frac{1}{4} = 2.5$ m.
$EH = 7 - 2 \times \frac{1}{4} = 6.5$ m.
Therefore, the area of the rectangle EFGH
$= EF \times EH$
$= 2.5 \times 6.5$
$= 16.25 \text{ m}^2$.
Hence, Option D.

72. $x\%$ of 24 = 10% of 72
or, $24 \times \frac{x}{100} = 72 \times \frac{10}{100}$
or, $x = \frac{72 \times 10 \times 100}{24 \times 100} = 30$.
Hence, Option A.

73. (A) $2x + 5 = 15$ or, $2x = 15 - 5$
or, $x = \frac{10}{2} = 5$.
(B) $x + 3 = -7$, or, $x = -7 - 3 = -10$.
(C) $2x - 10 = 8$ or, $2x = 8 + 10$
or, $x = \frac{18}{2} = 9$.
(D) $x + 3 = 2x - 3$ or, $2x - x = 3 + 3$
or, $x = 6$.
Hence, Option C.

74. Let the numbers be x, $x + 2$, and $x + 4$.
The mean of these numbers
$= \frac{x + x + 2 + x + 4}{3} = 27$.

or, $\frac{3x + 6}{3} = 27$ or, $3x + 6 = 81$

or, $3x = 75$ or, $x = 25$.

Therefore, the numbers are 25, 27 and 29.

Hence, Option B.

Alternative: These numbers are in an (Arithmetic Progression), and hence, their mean is their median.

Therefore, 27 is the median of these numbers.

As 27 is the middle of the 3 consecutive odd numbers, the other two are definitely 25 and 29.

75. In order to pass a platform, a train has to pass the length of the platform as well as its own length.

In order to pass a pole, the train has to pass its own length.

So, the train takes 2.5 seconds to pass its own length

$\Rightarrow$ The train takes $15 - 2.5 = 12.5$ seconds to pass the length of the platform.

Now, in 12.5 seconds, it travels 250 m,

Therefore, in 2.5 seconds, it travels $\frac{250}{12.5} \times 2.5$ = 50 metres.

Hence, the length of the train is 50 m.

Hence, Option A.

CUET UG 2022
General Test

August 23

Instructions:

1. You need to attempt any 60 out of the 75 questions in 60 minutes.
2. You get 5 marks for a correct response and –1 for an incorrect one. However, there is no reward or penalty for a question not attempted.

1. Choose the **correct** answer:

In which city is Major Dhyan Chand Sports University established?

A. New Delhi B. Amritsar
C. Meerut D. Ahmedabad

2. Match **List I** with **List II**.

List I (Nobel Prize winner)	List II (Area)
a. Abhijeet Banerjee	i. Peace
b. Kailash Satyarthi	ii. Literature
c. C.V. Raman	iii. Economics
d. Rabindranath Tagore	iv. Physics

Choose the **correct** answer from the options given below:

A. a-ii, b-iii, c-iv, d-i
B. a-iv, b-i, c-iii, d-ii
C. a-iii, b-i, c-iv, d-ii
D. a-i, b-ii, c-iv, d-iii

3. The rate at which banks part short-term excess liquidity with the RBI is called

A. Repo Rate B. Reverse Repo Rate
C. Bank Rate D. Cash Reserve Ratio

4. Who designed India's national flag?

A. Sarojini Naidu
B. Subhas Chandra Bose
C. Pingali Venkayya
D. C. Rajagopalachari

5. Which among the following are considered Vedangas?

(a) Kalp
(b) Ayurveda
(c) Vyakaran
(d) Manu Smriti
(e) Jyotish

Choose the **correct** answer from the option given below:

A. (a), (b) and (d) only
B. (b), (d) and (e) only
C. (a), (c) and (e) only
D. (a), (c) and (d) only

6. Match **List I** with **List II**.

List I (Author)	List II (Book)
a. Smriti Zubin Irani	i. India vs UK: The story of an Unprecedented Diplomatic Win
b. Dr. Shankar Acharya	ii. An Economist at Home and Abroad: A Personal Journey
c. Syed Akbaruddin	iii. Lal Salaam: A Novel
d. Brijinder Nath Goswamy	iv. Conversations: India's Leading Art Historian Engages with 101 Themes and More

Choose the **correct** answer from the options given below:

A. a-iv, b-ii, c-iii, d-i
B. a-iii, b-ii, c-i, d-iv
C. a-i, b-ii, c-iv, d-iii
D. a-iii, b-iv, c-i, d-ii

7. Match **List I** with **List II**.

List I (Agency)	List II (Headquarters)
a. United Nations World Tourism Organization	i. Paris, France
b. UNESCO	ii. Madrid, Spain
c. World Trade Organization	iii. Washington D.C., U.S.
d. IMF	iv. Geneva, Switzerland

Choose the **correct** answer from the options given below:

A. a-ii, b-i, c-iv, d-iii
B. a-iv, b-i, c-iii, d-ii
C. a-iii, b-i, c-iv, d-ii
D. a-i, b-iv, c-ii, d-iii

8. Match **List I** with **List II**.

List I	List II
a. World Lion Day	i. 26 August
b. World Elephant Day	ii. 10 August
c. World Mosquito Day	iii. 12 August
d. International Dog Day	iv. 20 August

Choose the **correct** answer from the options given below:

A. a-iii, b-i, c-ii, d-iv
B. a-iv, b-ii, c-iii, d-i
C. a-ii, b-iii, c-iv, d-i
D. a-iii, b-ii, c-i, d-iv

9. 2021 Yidan Prize for Education Development for Improving Learning Outcomes in Schools at Scale has been given to

(a) Eric A. Hanushek
(b) Angeline Murimirwa
(c) Lucky Lake
(d) Dr. Rukmini Banerji

Choose the **correct** answer from the options given below.

A. a and b only B. b and d only
C. a and d only D. c and d only

10. Which actor (Drama) won the Best Actor award at "Golden Globe Awards 2022"?

A. Will Smith
B. Andrew Garfield
C. Kodi Smit
D. Jane Campion

11. ______ of the total surface area of the earth is covered with water.

A. 72.5% B. 66.7%
C. 70.8% D. 71.6%

12. PROM stands for

A. Programmable Read-Only Memory
B. Programmed Random Only Memory
C. Programmable Random Objective Memory
D. Programmed Random Objective Memory

13. ______ is the structural and functional unit of the kidneys.

A. Nucleon B. Ribosome
C. Nephron D. Urochrome

14. The speed of light is:

A. 3×10^8 m/s B. 3×10^3 m/s
C. 8×10^3 m/s D. 8×10^8 m/s

15. Who was the first man to climb Mount Everest without Oxygen?

A. Sherpa Tenzing Norgay
B. Sir Edmund Hillary
C. Sir Everest
D. Messner and Habeler

16. A father told his child, "I was as old as you are at the time of your birth". If the father's age is 48 years now, the child's age six years back was:

A. 15 years B. 16 years
C. 17 years D. 18 years

17. A town had a population of 20,000 in 1980. In one year, i.e. by 1981, it increased by 25%. The following year, i.e. in 1982, it decreased by 20%. The next year, in 1983, there was an increase of 30%. What is the population at the end of 1983?

A. 28000 B. 24000
C. 26000 D. 25000

18. A man can row at 6 kmph in still water. If the speed of the current is 2 kmph, and it takes him 3 hours to row to a place and come back, how far is the place?

A. 8 km B. 5 km
C. 7 km D. 4 km

19. A car is sold for ₹85000 at a loss of 20%. What is the cost price (CP) of the car?

A. ₹107250 B. ₹105250
C. ₹104250 D. ₹106250

20. If I sell a cycle at ₹3600, I make a profit of 20%. At what price need I sell to make a profit of 10%?

A. ₹3500 B. ₹3000
C. ₹3300 D. ₹3600

21. A, B and C are in a cycle race of 1500 m. A cycles twice as fast as B and C cycles $\frac{1}{2}$ as fast as B. C completes the race in 40 minutes. Then, where was B from the finishing line when A finished the race?

A. 550 m from the finish line
B. 450 m from the finish line
C. 650 m from the finish line
D. 750 m from the finish line

22. Mohan asked 36 men to build his house in 30 days. Half of the work was completed in just 10 days. So, Mohan removed some workers. Now, how many persons does he need to complete the remaining work in the predecided time?

A. 20 B. 18
C. 16 D. 14

23. P alone can do a piece of work in 5 days, and Q alone can do it in 4 days. P and Q undertook to do it for ₹3000. With R's help, they completed the work in 2 days. How much is to be paid to R?

A. ₹300 B. ₹400
C. ₹500 D. ₹600

24. A tyre has two punctures. The first puncture alone would have made the tyre flat in 6 minutes, and the second alone would have done it in 9 minutes. If air leaks out at a constant rate, how long does it take both the punctures together to make it flat?

A. $3\frac{3}{5}$ minutes B. $4\frac{3}{5}$ minutes
C. $5\frac{3}{5}$ minutes D. $2\frac{3}{5}$ minutes

25. The length of the diagonals of a square is $7\sqrt{2}$ m. The area of the square is

A. 46 m^2 B. 49 m^2
C. 39 m^2 D. 48 m^2

26. If A:B is 2:5. Then, the value of 2A + 3B: A + B is

A. 14:5 B. 19:7
C. 3:11 D. 17:15

27. Find the greatest number that will divide 38, 88 and 163 to leave the same remainder in each case.

A. 18 B. 28
C. 25 D. 15

28. If Principal = P, Rate = R% per annum, T = Time (in years), SI = Simple Interest, then

(a) $T = \frac{100 \times SI}{P \times R}$

(b) $SI = \frac{P \times R \times T}{100}$

(c) $R = \frac{P \times SI \times T}{100}$

(d) $T = \frac{P \times SI \times T}{100}$

(e) $R = \frac{100 \times SI}{P \times T}$

A. a and c only
B. b, c and d only
C. a, b and e only
D. c, d and e only

29. Two numbers are in the ratio 4:3. If 2 is added to each of the numbers, the new ratio becomes 5:4. Find the numbers.
A. 20, 15 B. 16, 12
C. 8, 6 D. 12, 9

30. The average of the first 99 positive integers is:
A. 45 B. 50
C. 55 D. 60

31. 27:729 : : 31:?
A. 961 B. 916
C. 841 D. 814

32. Abundant : Scarce : : Artificial : ?
A. Manmade B. Sparse
C. Meager D. Genuine

33. GFE:KJI : : ONM:?
A. SRT B. SRQ
C. TSR D. RQP

34. Contaminated:Sinful : : Immense:?
A. Tiny B. Gigantic
C. Brave D. Beautiful

35. Ganga:Kanpur : : Narmada:?
A. Bhopal B. Amarkantak
C. Ahmedabad D. Jodhpur

36. Arrange the following words in the sequence in which they appear in a dictionary:
(a) Mechanics
(b) Mathematics
(c) Monuments
(d) Measurement
(e) Magnitude
Choose the **correct** answer from the options given below:
A. b, c, a, e, d B. a, c, d, e, b
C. d, a, c, e, b D. e, b, d, a, c

37. If 'BHARAT' stands for 'B – 8 – A – 18 – A – 20' and 'ENGLAND' stands for 'E – 14 – G – 12 – A – 14 – D', then how will you code SRILANKA?
A. S-18-I-12-A-14-11-A
B. S-15-I-9-A-11-10-A
C. S-17-I-11-A-13-K-1
D. S-18-I-12-A-14-K-1

38. Arpit travelled 3 km east from his home, then 2 km north, followed by 3 km east. He then took a 90° right turn and walked 5 km straight, then he again took a right turn and walked 6 km more. How far is he now from his home?
A. 5 km B. 3 km
C. 6 km D. 2 km

39. Complete the series:
29, 31, 37, 41, 43, ________
A. 45 B. 47
C. 49 D. 51

40. Today is Friday. After 91 days, it will be:
A. Wednesday B. Thursday
C. Friday D. Saturday

41. Complete the series:
15, 24, 35, 48, 63, ________
A. 80 B. 89
C. 94 D. 99

42. Complete the series:
76, 62, ... ?..., 34, 20, 6
A. 56 B. 48
C. 43 D. 36

43. In this question, four words have been given, of which three are alike in some way, and one is different. Find the odd one out.
A. Motorcycle B. Metro
C. Bus D. Car

44. How many triangles are there in the given figure?

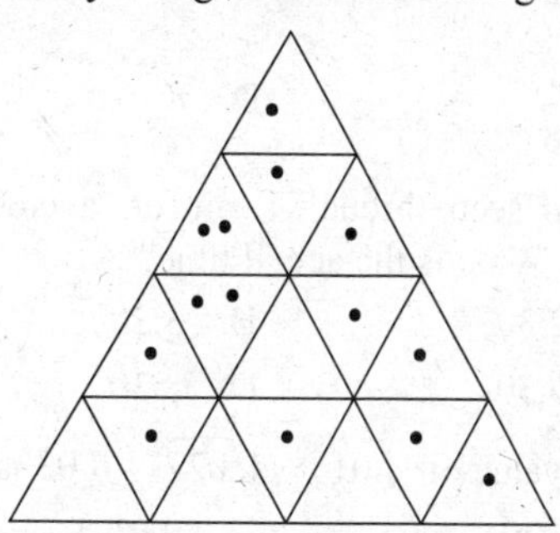

A. 21 B. 23
C. 27 D. 29

45. Anita, Baby and Charu are sisters. D is the brother of E, and E is the daughter of Baby. How is Anita related to D?

A. Niece B. Sister
C. Cousin D. Aunt

46. Find the value of $\frac{5^{\frac{2}{3}} \times \sqrt[3]{5^7}}{\sqrt[3]{5^6}}$.

A. 5 B. 1
C. $\sqrt{5}$ D. $3\sqrt{5}$

47. The angle of elevation for the top of a pole from a point situated at a distance 100 m from the base of a pole is 30°. Find the height of the pole.

A. $100(\sqrt{3}+1)$ m B. $\frac{100}{3}$ m
C. $\frac{100}{3}\sqrt{3}$ m C. $100\sqrt{3}$ m

48. The value of $13.7 \times 12.7 \times 0.8$ is ______.

A. 13.9193 B. 13.9192
C. 139.192 D. 139.191

49. The sum of the greatest five-digit and the smallest four-digit numbers is

A. 91999 B. 19999
C. 10999 D. 100999

50. If $\sqrt[3]{X} = 2y$, then the value of $\frac{Y^3}{X}$ is ______.

A. $\frac{1}{2}$ B. $\frac{2}{3}$
C. $\frac{1}{8}$ D. 8

51. When seen through a mirror, a clock shows 8:30. What is the actual time?

A. 2:30 B. 3:30
C. 5:30 D. 8:30

52. The value of $\sqrt{.01} \times \sqrt[3]{.027} - 0.03$ is

A. –0.1 B. 0.01
C. 0 D. 0.1

53. Two women and 3 men can do a piece of work in 10 days, while 3 women and 2 men can do the same work in 8 days. In how many days can 2 women and 1 man do the work?

A. $12\frac{1}{4}$ days B. 15 days
C. 25 days D. $12\frac{1}{2}$ days

54. It was a Monday on 7th March, 2005. What was the day of the week on 7th March 2004?

A. Monday B. Saturday
C. Sunday D. Friday

55. The value of $\frac{(793+232)^2-(793-232)^2}{(793\times 232)}$ is

A. 7930 B. 4
C. 2 D. 2320

56. The simple interest on a sum of money is $\frac{4}{5}$ of the principal. Find the rate of interest if both the rate of interest and time are numerically equal.

A. $4\sqrt{6}$ % P.A. B. $4\sqrt{2}$ % P.A.
C. $4\sqrt{3}$ % P.A. D. $4\sqrt{5}$ % P.A.

57. Find the odd-one-out in the series: 63, 48, 34, 24, 15, 8, 3

A. 24 B. 34
C. 15 D. 8

58. The average of the four consecutive odd numbers is 16. What is the third number in descending order?

A. 13 B. 15
C. 17 D. 19

59. A train running at a speed of 54 km/hr crosses a platform that is double the length of the train in 18 seconds. What are the lengths of the platform and the train, respectively?

A. 180 m and 90 m
B. 90 m and 180 m
C. 70 m and 140 m
D. 140 m and 70 m

60. Find the largest size of bamboo that can be placed in a square of area 338 m².

A. 13 m B. $13\sqrt{2}$ m
C. 26 m D. $26\sqrt{2}$ m

61. Arrange the following in a logical order:
(a) Frog
(b) Eagle
(c) Grasshopper
(d) Snake
(e) Grass

Choose the **correct** answer from the options given below:

A. a, c, e, b, d B. c, d, b, e, a
C. e, c, a, d, b D. e, c, d, b, a

62. Which of the following collections of letters looks the same in a mirror?

A. HIMOSTA B. HIMOVTA
C. AOSVMTA D. HVHRTAM

63. If 'book' is called 'watch', 'watch' is called 'bag', 'bag' is called 'dictionary' and 'dictionary' is called 'door', then what is used to carry books?

A. watch B. bag
C. dictionary D. door

64. Find out the figure which can be exactly made from the sum collection of the following symbols:

A. 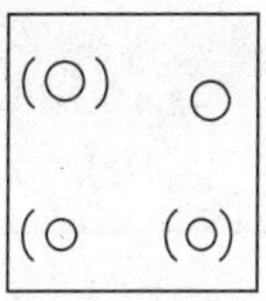
B. 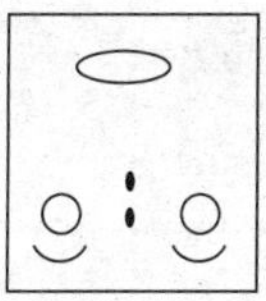
C. 
D. 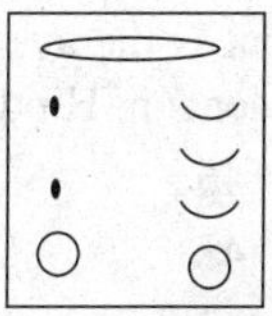

65. Match **List I** with **List II**.

List I	List II
A. book	I. editor
B. film	II. dramatist
C. play	III. author
D. newspaper	IV. producer

Choose the **correct** answer from the options given below:

A. A-III, B-II, C-IV, D-I
B. A-I, B-IV, C-III, D-II
C. A-I, B-II, C-III, D-IV
D. A-III, B-IV, C-II, D-I

66. Three different positions, P, Q and R, of a die are shown in the figures given below.

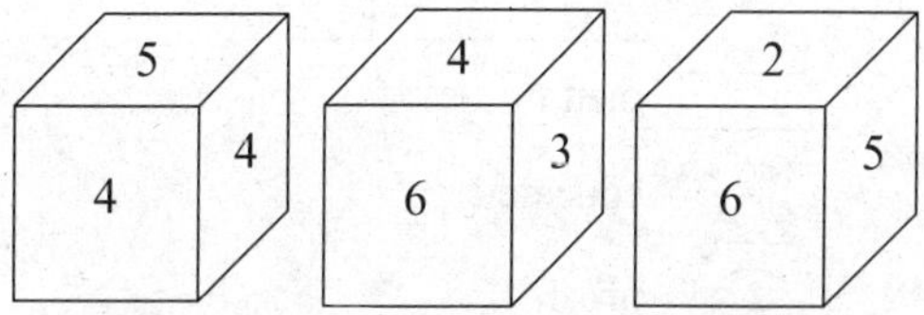

P Q R

Which number lies at the bottom face in position P?

A. 2 B. 3
C. 4 D. 5

67. Farming always comprises ______.
Choose the essential word from the options given below.

A. Tractor B. Plough
C. Land D. Spade

68. Which of the following diagrams correctly represents European countries, Arab countries and the countries that took part in the Gulf War?

A. 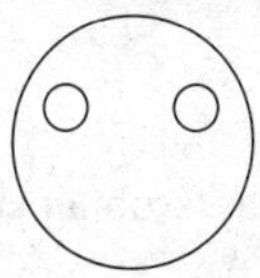
B. 
C. 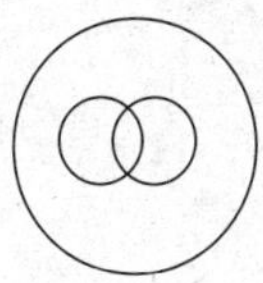
D. 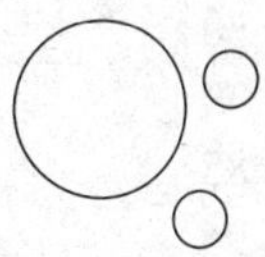

In the following diagram, the rectangle represents men, the triangle represents educated, the circle represents urban, and the square represents government employees.

Answer questions 69–71 based on the above information.

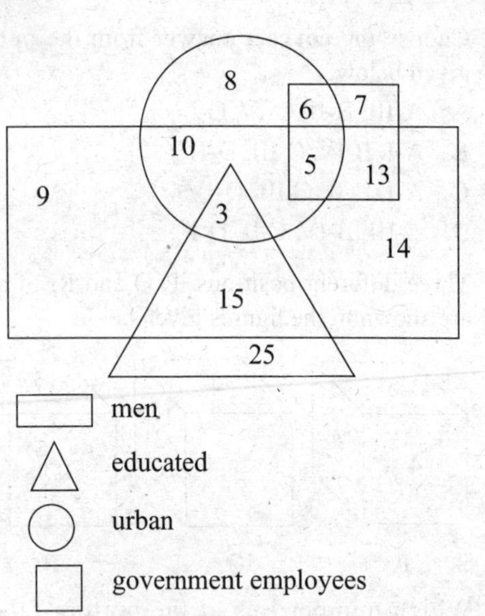

69. Which of the following numbers represents educated men who are not urban?
A. 14
B. 3
C. 15
D. 25

70. Which of the following numbers represents urban educated men?
A. 3
B. 15
C. 5
D. 25

71. Which of the following numbers represents urban men who are government employees?
A. 10
B. 3
C. 5
D. 13

Study the following table carefully to answer the questions that follow.

Marks obtained by the students in different subjects in the board examination:

Subject (Marks)/ Student	Math (75)	Science (75)	English (80)	Hindi (60)	Computer (110)
PK	60	62	70	50	90
QS	48	56	70	55	90
RP	70	68	72	40	80
SG	62	69	75	45	95
GP	66	60	62	30	85
FA	54	70	50	56	100

72. What is the average of marks obtained by all the students in Computer?
A. 80
B. 90
C. 85
D. 95

73. What is the overall percentage of marks obtained by GP in all subjects?
A. 72.88%
B. 76.75%
C. 74.50%
D. 75.75%

74. What is the average marks obtained by all the students in Hindi?
A. 46
B. 48
C. 47.8
D. 45.8

75. What is the ratio between total marks obtained by RP and FA in all subjects?
A. 84:89
B. 50:51
C. 1:1
D. 10:11

Answer key

1. **C** 2. **C** 3. **B** 4. **C** 5. **C** 6. **B** 7. **A** 8. **C** 9. **C** 10. **A**
11. **C** 12. **A** 13. **C** 14. **A** 15. **D** 16. **D** 17. **C** 18. **A** 19. **D** 20. **C**
21. **D** 22. **B** 23. **A** 24. **A** 25. **B** 26. **B** 27. **C** 28. **C** 29. **C** 30. **B**
31. **A** 32. **D** 33. **B** 34. **B** 35. **B** 36. **D** 37. **D** 38. **B** 39. **B** 40. **C**
41. **A** 42. **B** 43. **B** 44. **C** 45. **D** 46. **A** 47. **C** 48. **C** 49. **D** 50. **C**
51. **B** 52. **C** 53. **D** 54. **C** 55. **B** 56. **D** 57. **B** 58. **B** 59. **A** 60. **C**
61. **C** 62. **B** 63. **C** 64. **C** 65. **D** 66. **B** 67. **C** 68. * 69. **C** 70. **A**
71. **C** 72. **B** 73. **D** 74. **A** 75. **C**

*68. None of the options is correct.
The correct answer is

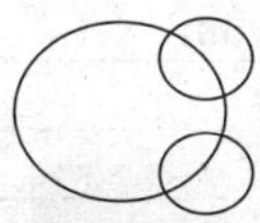

Classification of Questions

Question No.	Subject	Topic	Level of Difficulty
1.	General Awareness	Current Affairs	Medium
2.	General Awareness	Awards	Easy
3.	General Awareness	Economics	Easy
4.	General Awareness	Polity	Easy
5.	General Awareness	History	Difficult
6.	General Awareness	Books & Authors	Difficult
7.	General Awareness	Polity	Medium
8.	General Awareness	Miscellaneous	Difficult
9.	General Awareness	Current Affairs	Difficult
10.	General Awareness	Awards	Medium
11.	General Awareness	Science	Easy
12.	General Awareness	Computers	Easy
13.	General Awareness	Science (Biology)	Easy
14.	General Awareness	Science (Physics)	Easy
15.	General Awareness	Miscellaneous	Medium
16.	Quantitative Aptitude	Age-based problem	Easy
17.	Quantitative Aptitude	Percentages	Easy
18.	Quantitative Aptitude	Time, Speed & Distance	Easy
19.	Quantitative Aptitude	Profit, Loss & Discount	Easy
20.	Quantitative Aptitude	Profit, Loss & Discount	Easy

Question No.	Subject	Topic	Level of Difficulty
21.	Quantitative Aptitude	Time, Speed & Distance	Medium
22.	Quantitative Aptitude	Time & Work	Medium
23.	Quantitative Aptitude	Time & Work	Medium
24.	Quantitative Aptitude	Time & Work	Easy
25.	Quantitative Aptitude	Mensuration	Easy
26.	Quantitative Aptitude	Ratios	Easy
27.	Quantitative Aptitude	Numbers (LCM)	Easy
28.	Quantitative Aptitude	Simple Interest	Easy
29.	Quantitative Aptitude	Ratios	Easy
30.	Quantitative Aptitude	Averages	Easy
31.	Reasoning	Analogy (Number-based)	Easy
32.	Reasoning	Analogy (Word-based)	Easy
33.	Reasoning	Analogy (Letter-based)	Easy
34.	Reasoning	Analogy (Word-based)	Easy
35.	Reasoning	Analogy (Geography-based)	Medium
36.	Reasoning	Dictionary Order	Easy
37.	Reasoning	Coding	Easy
38.	Reasoning	Directions	Easy
39.	Reasoning	Number Series	Easy
40.	Quantitative Aptitude	Calendars	Easy
41.	Reasoning	Number Series	Easy
42.	Reasoning	Number Series	Easy
43.	Reasoning	Odd-one-out	Medium
44.	Reasoning	Figure counting	Difficult
45.	Reasoning	Blood Relations	Easy
46.	Quantitative Aptitude	Surds & Indices	Easy
47.	Quantitative Aptitude	Trigonometry (Heights & Distances)	Easy
48.	Quantitative Aptitude	Basic Arithmetic Operations	Easy
49.	Quantitative Aptitude	Numbers	Easy
50.	Quantitative Aptitude	Equations	Easy
51.	Reasoning	Mirror Image	Easy
52.	Quantitative Aptitude	Simplification	Easy
53.	Quantitative Aptitude	Time & Work	Medium
54.	Quantitative Aptitude	Calendars	Easy
55.	Quantitative Aptitude	Simplification	Easy
56.	Quantitative Aptitude	Simple Interest	Easy
57.	Reasoning	Number Series	Easy
58.	Quantitative Aptitude	Averages	Easy
59.	Quantitative Aptitude	Time, Speed & Distance	Medium
60.	Quantitative Aptitude	Mensuration	Easy
61.	Reasoning	Words in a Logical Sequence	Easy
62.	Reasoning	Mirror Image	Easy

Question No.	Subject	Topic	Level of Difficulty
63.	Reasoning	Miscellaneous	Easy
64.	Reasoning	Non-verbal	Easy
65.	Reasoning	Miscellaneous	Easy
66.	Reasoning	Die-based problem	Medium
67.	Reasoning	Miscellaneous	Easy
68.	Reasoning	Venn-diagram	All options incorrect
69.	Reasoning	Venn-diagram	Easy
70.	Reasoning	Venn-diagram	Easy
71.	Reasoning	Venn-diagram	Easy
72.	Data Interpretation	Table-based	Easy
73.	Data Interpretation	Table-based	Easy
74.	Data Interpretation	Table-based	Easy
75.	Data Interpretation	Table-based	Easy

The no. of questions on Reasoning: 27

The no. of questions on General Awareness: 15

The no. of questions on Quantitative Aptitude: 29

The no. of questions on Data Interpretation: 4

Explanation to Select Questions

5. There are 6 Vedangas: Shiksha, Chandas, Vyakaran, Nirukta, Kalp and Jyotish.
Hence, Option C.

9. Dr. Rukmini Banerji is the CEO of Pratham Education Foundation.
Hence, Option C.

10. In 2022, it went to Will Smith for his acting in King Richard.
Hence, Option A.

Update: In 2024, it went to Cillian Murphy for his acting in Oppenheimer.

16. Let's suppose that the father's age at the time of his son's birth was x years.

So, he must be $x + x = 2x$ years of age now as the son's present age is x years.

As $2x = 48$, the son's age in $\frac{48}{2} = 24$ years now.

Therefore, the son's age 6 years ago was 24 – 6 = 18 years.

Hence, Option D.

17. The population at the end of 1983

$$= 20000 \times \frac{100+25}{100} \times \frac{100-20}{100} \times \frac{100+30}{100}$$

$$= 20000 \times \frac{125}{100} \times \frac{80}{100} \times \frac{130}{100} = 26000.$$

Hence, Option C.

Shortcut: An increase of 25% followed by a decrease of 20% brings no change to the original number. So, at the end of 1982, the population was again 20000. You just need to increase it by 30% to get the answer.

18. The upstream speed = 6 – 2 = 4 kmph.
The downstream speed = 6 + 2 = 8 kmph.
Let the one-side distance be d.

We have, $\frac{d}{4} + \frac{d}{8} = 3$ or, $\frac{2d + d}{8} = 3$

or, $\frac{3d}{8} = 3.$ or, $d = 8$ km.

Hence, Option A.

19. The cost price = the selling price

$\times \dfrac{100}{100 - \text{loss percentage}} = 85000 \times \dfrac{100}{100-20}$

$= 85000 \times \dfrac{100}{80} = 106250.$

Hence, Option D.

20. A 20% profit means the selling price is 120% of the cost price and a 10% profit means the selling price is 110% of the cost price (CP).

Here, 120% of the CP = 3600.

So, 110% of the CP $= \dfrac{3600}{120} \times 110 = 3300.$

Hence, Option C.

21. This question has a lot more information than what you need to solve it.

Only two things are important:

1. the race is of 1500 m
2. A cycles twice as fast as B

As A is twice as fast as B, when he completes 1500 m, B must have done $\dfrac{1500}{2} = 750$ m.

Thus, when A finished the race, B was at a distance of 1500 – 750 = 750 m from the finish line.

Hence, Option D.

22. Thirty-six people did half the work in 10 days.

So, 36 people can do the remaining half also in 10 days.

To do the remaining work in 10 days, 36 people are needed.

So, to do the remaining work in 30 – 10 = 20 days, $\dfrac{36 \times 10}{20} = 18$ people are needed.

Hence, Option B.

23. Let the work be of 20 units.

As *P* can do the work in 5 days, in 1 day he does $\dfrac{20}{5} = 4$ units.

Similarly, *Q* can do $\dfrac{20}{4} = 5$ units in a day.

Therefore, in 2 days,

P did 2 × 4 = 8 units and *Q* did 2 × 5 = 10 units.

So, *R* must have done 20 – (10 + 8) = 2 units.

As *R* does $\dfrac{2}{20} = \dfrac{1}{10}$ of the work, he must be paid $\dfrac{1}{10} \times 3000 =$ ₹300.

Hence, Option A.

24. The time taken by both the punctures to make the tyre flat $= \dfrac{1}{\frac{1}{6}+\frac{1}{9}} = \dfrac{1}{\frac{3+2}{18}} = \dfrac{18}{5} = 3\dfrac{3}{5}$ minutes.

Hence, Option A.

25. The side of a square

$= \dfrac{\text{length of its diagonal}}{\sqrt{2}} = \dfrac{7\sqrt{2}}{\sqrt{2}} = 7.$

Therefore, the area of the square = 7 × 7 = 49 m^2.

Hence, Option B.

Alternative: A square is also a rhombus.

The area of a rhombus $= \dfrac{1}{2} \times$ product of the lengths of its diagonals

$= \dfrac{1}{2} \times 7\sqrt{2} \times 7\sqrt{2}$

$= \dfrac{1}{2} \times 49 \times 2 = 49 \text{ m}^2.$

26. We have $\dfrac{A}{B} = \dfrac{2}{5}$

$\dfrac{2A+3B}{A+B} = \dfrac{\frac{2A+3B}{B}}{\frac{A+B}{B}} = \dfrac{2\frac{A}{B}+3}{\frac{A}{B}+1}$

$= \dfrac{2 \times \frac{2}{5} + 3}{\frac{2}{5}+1} = \dfrac{\frac{4}{5}+3}{\frac{2+5}{5}} = \dfrac{4+15}{5} \times \dfrac{5}{7} = \dfrac{19}{7}$

Hence, Option B.

27. Let the greatest number be *N* and the quotients when it divides 38, 88 and 163 be q_1, q_2 and q_3, respectively.

Let the remainder be *r* in each case.

So, $38 = Nq_1 + r$,

$88 = Nq_2 + r$ and

$163 = Nq_3 + r$.

Now, $163 - 88 = Nq_3 + r - (Nq_2 + r) = N(q_3 - q_2)$

or, $75 = N(q_3 - q_2)$

Similarly, $88 - 38 = 50 = N(q_2 - q_1)$ and

$163 - 38 = 125 = N(q_3 - q_1)$.

So, we are necessarily looking for the largest N that divides 50, 75 and 125.

The answer is the HCF of 50, 75 and 125, which is 25.

Hence, Option C.

Alternative: Try with the options.

Option A: When 38 and 88 are divided by 18, the remainders are 2 and 16, respectively. As $2 \neq 16$, Option A is not the answer.

Option B: When 38 and 88 are divided by 28, the remainders are 10 and 4, respectively. As $10 \neq 4$, Option B cannot be the answer.

Option C: When 38, 88 and 163 are divided by 25, the remainder is 13 in each case. As this is the only option that satisfies the condition. It is the answer.

This can be done without putting pen on paper.

29. Let the numbers be $4x$ and $3x$.

We have $\dfrac{4x+2}{3x+2} = \dfrac{5}{4}$.

or, $16x + 8 = 15x + 10$.

or, $x = 2$

Therefore, the numbers are $4 \times 2 = 8$ and $3 \times 2 = 6$.

Hence, Option C.

Note: Working with the options should give the answer in 10–20 seconds!

The numbers in all 4 options are in the ratio 4:3, but it is only in Option C that when you add 2 to both the numbers, the new ratio is 5:4.

30. The sum of the first n natural numbers is $\dfrac{n(n+1)}{2}$ and the average of the first n natural numbers is $\dfrac{n+1}{2}$.

Therefore, the average of the first 99 naturals numbers $= \dfrac{99+1}{2} = 50$.

Hence, Option B.

Note: Positive integers are natural numbers.

31. $729 = 27^2$ and $961 = 31^2$.

Hence, Option A.

32. 'Abundant' and 'scarce' are opposites, and so are 'artificial' and 'genuine'.

Hence, Option D.

33. G F E : K J I

7 6 5   11 10 9

(−1, −1   −1, −1; +4)

O N M : [S R Q]

15 14 13   19 18 17

(−1, −1   −1, −1; +4)

Hence, Option B.

35. Kanpur is on the bank of the river Ganga, and Amarkantak (Madhya Pradesh) is on the bank of the river Narmada.

Hence, Option B.

38.

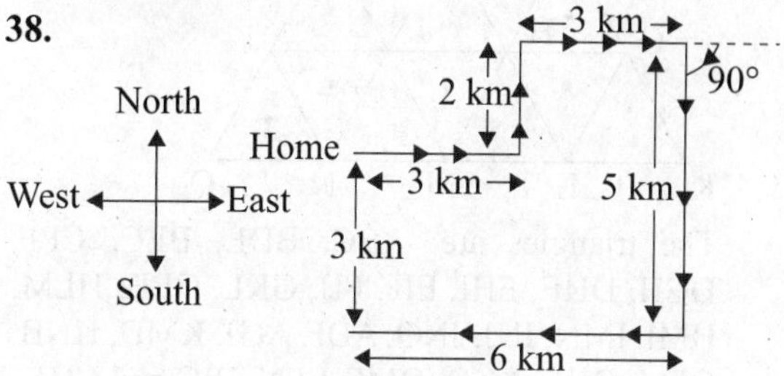

Hence, Option B.

39. The series has only prime numbers, starting with 29. The next prime after 43 is 47.

Hence, Option B.

40. As 91 (= 13 × 7) is a multiple of 7. There are zero odd days in it.

So, if it is a Friday today, after 91 days also, it would be a Friday.

Hence, Option C.

41. 15, 24, 35, 48, 63, (80)

+9 +11 +13 +15 +17

Hence, Option A.

Another way of looking at it:

$3 \times 5 = 15$

$4 \times 6 = 24$

$5 \times 7 = 35$

$6 \times 8 = 48$

$7 \times 9 = 63$

$8 \times 10 = \boxed{80}$

42. It is an AP with a common difference of –14.

$62 = 76 - 14$,

$\boxed{48} = 62 - 14$,

$34 = 48 - 14$,
$20 = 34 - 14$,
$6 = 20 - 14$.
Hence, Option B.

43. Motorcycles, buses and cars run on the roads, but the metro runs on tracks.
Hence, Option B.

44.

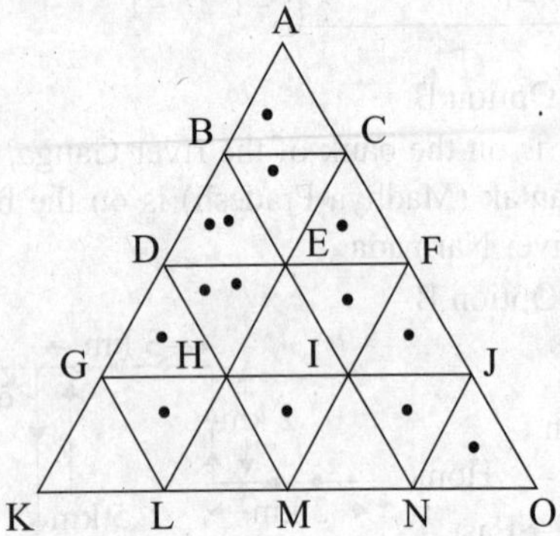

The triangles are: ABC, BDE, BEC, CEF, DGH, DHE, EHI, EIF, FIJ, GKL, GLH, HLM, HMI, IMN, INJ, JNO, ADF, AGJ, KMD, KNB, OFM, OCL, AKO, DMF, ELN, BIG and CHJ.
Hence, Option C.

45.

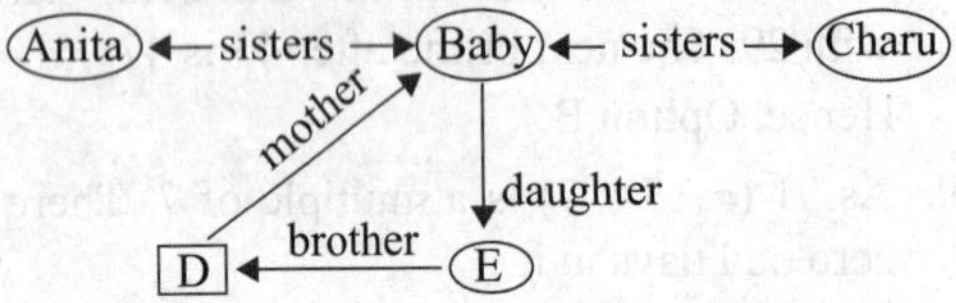

Anita is a sister of D's mother. So, Anita is D's aunt.
Hence, option D.

46. $$\frac{5^{\frac{2}{3}} \times \sqrt[3]{5^7}}{\sqrt[3]{5^6}} = \frac{5^{\frac{2}{3}} \times 5^{\frac{7}{3}}}{5^{\frac{6}{3}}} = \frac{5^{\frac{2}{3}+\frac{7}{3}}}{5^2} = \frac{5^3}{5^2} = 5.$$

Hence, Option A.

47.

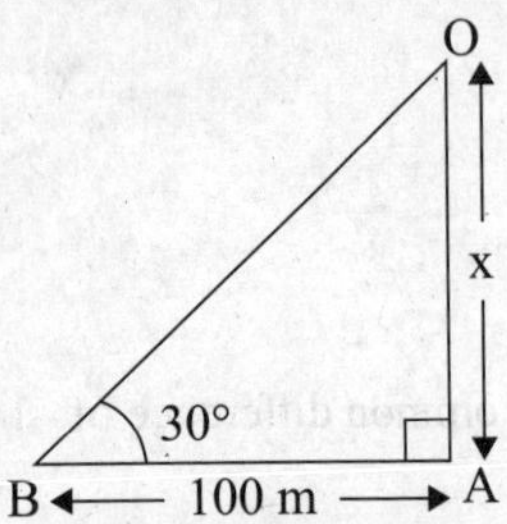

Let OA be the pole and x be its height.
Let B be the point from where the angle of elevation for the top of the pole is 30°.
In ΔOAB,

$$\tan 30^\circ = \frac{OA}{AB}$$

or, $\frac{1}{\sqrt{3}} = \frac{x}{100}$

or, $x = \frac{100}{\sqrt{3}} = \frac{100\sqrt{3}}{3}$.

Hence, Option C.

48. The product should have 3 digits on the right side of the decimal, and its last digit should be 2. There is only one such option.
Hence, Option C.

49. The largest five-digit number: 99999
The smallest four-digit number: 1000
Therefore, the required sum = 99999 + 1000 = 100999.
Hence, Option D.

50. $\sqrt[3]{X} = 2Y$

or, $(X)^{\frac{1}{3}} = 2Y$

or, $X = (2Y)^3$

or, $X = 8Y^3$

or, $\frac{Y^3}{X} = \frac{1}{8}$.

Hence, Option C.

51. The actual time = 12:00 – the mirror image of the time = 12:00 – 8:30 = 3:30.
Hence, Option B.

52. $\sqrt{0.01} \times \sqrt[3]{.027} - 0.03$

$= \sqrt{(0.1)(0.1)} \times \sqrt[3]{(0.3) \times (0.3) \times (0.3)} - 0.03$

$= \sqrt{(0.1)^2} \times \sqrt[3]{(0.3)^3} - 0.03$

$= (0.1) \times (0.3) - 0.03$

$= 0.03 - 0.03 = 0.$

Hence, Option C.

53. Let's assume that in 1 day, a man does m and a woman does w units of work.
As per the question,
The work is of $10(2\,w + 3\,m)$ units and also of $8(3\,w + 2\,m)$ units.

Therefore, $20w + 30m = 24w + 16m$
or, $14m = 4w$
or, $2w = 7m$.
Now, the work is of $(20w + 30m)$ units = $(70m + 30m)$ units (as $2w = 7m$, or, $20w = 70m$) = $100m$ units.
Two women and 1 man do $2w + m$ units in a day.
$2w + m = 7m + m = 8m$ (as $2w = 7m$).
Therefore, the required number of days
$= \frac{100m}{8m} = 12\frac{1}{2}$.
Hence, Option D.

54. The number of days between 7 March 2004 and 7 March 2005 is $365 = 52 \times 7 + 1$.
So, there is 1 odd day between these 2 dates.
Therefore, as 7 March 2005 was a Monday, 7 March 2004 would be a day before Monday, a Sunday.
Hence, Option C.
Note: Do NOT commit the blunder of taking 366 days (or 2 odd days) between these 2 dates. Though 2004 was a leap year, 29 February 2004 did not fall between the dates we are concerned with.
Option B (Saturday) is a trap for those people who mistakenly go for 2 odd days.

55. $\frac{(793+232)^2 - (793-232)^2}{793 \times 232}$

$$= \frac{(793)^2 + (232)^2 + 2 \times 793 \times 232 - \{(793)^2 + (232)^2 - (2 \times 793 \times 232)\}}{793 \times 232}$$

$$= \frac{4 \times 793 \times 232}{793 \times 232} = 4.$$

Hence, Option B.
Note: $(a + b)^2 - (a - b)^2 = 4ab$ is an identity that you need to keep in mind.

56. Let the principal be P, rate of interest r and time t.
We have simple interest (S.I.) $= \frac{4P}{5}$.
Also, S.I. $= \frac{Prt}{100}$
$= \frac{P.r.r}{100}$ (as $r = t$)
$= \frac{Pr^2}{100}$.
So, $\frac{4P}{5} = \frac{Pr^2}{100}$
or, $r^2 = \frac{100 \times 4}{5} = 80 = 4^2 \times 5$.
Therefore, $r = \sqrt{4^2 \times 5} = 4\sqrt{5}$.
Hence, Option D.

57. $63 = 9 \times 7$
$48 = 8 \times 6$
$\boxed{35 = 7 \times 5}$
$24 = 6 \times 4$
$15 = 5 \times 3$
$8 = 4 \times 2$
$3 = 3 \times 1$.
Hence, 34 is the odd-one in the series. It should have been 35.
Hence, Option B.

58. Let the numbers be $x, x + 2, x + 4$ and $x + 6$.
We have, $\frac{x + x + 2 + x + 4 + x + 6}{4} = 16$
or, $4x + 12 = 16 \times 4 = 64$
or, $4x = 52$
or, $x = \frac{52}{4} = 13$.
So, the numbers are 13, 15, 17 and 19.
Hence, the 3rd number in the descending order is 15.
Hence, Option B.
Note: These 4 numbers are in an AP, and for the numbers in an AP, the mean (average) and the median are equal.
For 4 numbers, the median is the average of the 2nd and the 3rd numbers and so is the mean.
As 16 is the average here, it should promptly come to our mind that 16 is between 15 and 17 and hence the 4 numbers are 13, 15, 17 and 19.
We need NOT put pen on paper to get the answer.

59. The speed of the train = 54 km/hr.
or, $= \frac{54 \times 1000}{3600}$ m/s
or, 15 m/s.
The total distance travelled by train in 18 seconds $= 18 \times 15 = 270$ m.

But 270 m must be the sum of the lengths of the platform and the train.
Also, the length of the platform is 2 times the length of the train.
So, the length of the platform

$= 270 \times \frac{2}{2+1} = 180$ m.

And, the length of the train = 270 – 180 = 90 m.

Hence, Option A.

60.

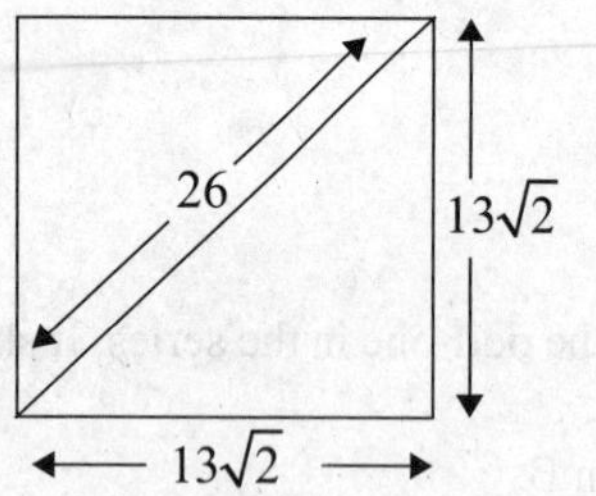

The area of the square = 338 m^2.
Therefore, the side of the square $= \sqrt{338}$
$= \sqrt{13 \times 13 \times 2} = 13\sqrt{2}$.

Now, the largest bamboo that can be placed in a square has to be put along its diagonal.
The diagonal of the square $= \sqrt{2} \times$ side
$= \sqrt{2} \times 13\sqrt{2} = 26$.
Hence, Option C.

66. This die is unusual!
If you look at the positions P, Q and R, it is clear that the numbers on it are
2, 3, 4, 4, 5 and 6.

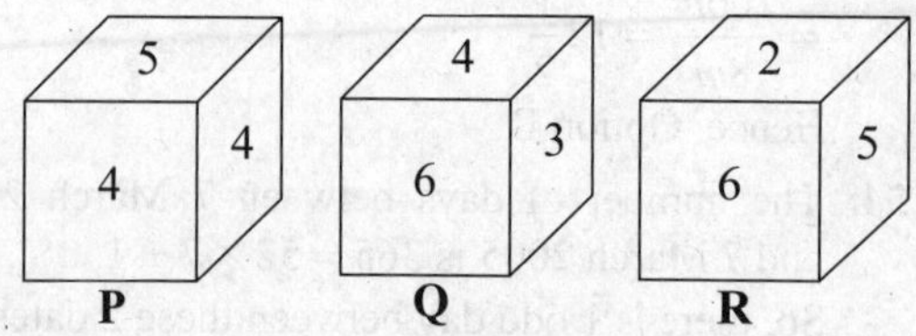

Also, from positions P and R, it is clear that 2, 4, 4 and 6 are on the adjacent faces of 5.
Therefore, 3 is on a face opposite to 5.
As 5 is the top face in position P, 3 must be at the bottom face.
Hence, Option B.

Please refer to the following table for explanations of questions 72–75.

Subject Marks/Student	Math (75)	Science (75)	English (80)	Hindi (60)	Computer (110)
PK	60	62	70	50	90
QS	48	56	70	55	90
RP	70	68	72	40	80
SG	62	69	75	45	95
GP	66	60	62	30	85
FA	54	70	50	56	100

72. The required average

$= \frac{90+90+80+95+85+100}{6} = \frac{540}{6} = 90.$

Hence, Option B.

73. GP's aggregate score in all 5 persons = 66 + 60 + 62 + 30 + 85 = 303.
The maximum marks in these papers = 75 + 75 + 80 + 60 + 110 = 400.

The required percentage $= \frac{303}{400} \times 100 = 75.75$.

Hence, Option D.

74. The required average

$= \frac{50+55+40+45+30+56}{6} = \frac{276}{6} = 46.$

Hence, Option A.

75. The total marks obtained by RP = 70 + 68 + 72 + 40 + 80 = 330.
The total marks obtained by FA = 54 + 70 + 50 + 56 + 100 = 330.

Therefore, the required ratio $= \frac{330}{330} = 1:1$.

Hence, Option C.

CUET UG 2022 General Test

August 21

Instructions:

1. You need to attempt any 60 out of the 75 questions in 60 minutes.
2. You get 5 marks for a correct response and –1 for an incorrect one. However, there is no reward or penalty for a question not attempted.

1. Which state is commonly known as the "Spice Garden of India"?

A. Sikkim B. Tripura
C. Kerala D. Goa

2. The Atal Innovation Mission (AIM) of NITI Aayog has launched a Digi-book named:

A. Science and Technology
B. Innovations for You
C. Innovations in Health Care
D. Innovations in Education

3. According to FICCI, India's GDP is expected to grow at ______ in 2021–22:

A. 8.5% B. 9.1%
C. 7.9% D. 9.6%

4. Arrange the following days in the order of the date of their observance in India:

A. National Sports Day
B. Children's Day
C. National Education Day
D. National Voter's Day
E. International Yoga Day

Choose the correct answer from the options given below:

A. A, C, E, B, D
B. C, E, B, D, A
C. D, E, A, C, B
D. B, D, E, C, A

5. Arrange the following Nobel prize-winning Indians in chronological order of the year of getting the Nobel:

A. CV Raman
B. Kailash Satyarthi
C. Rabindranath Tagore
D. Amartya Sen
E. Har Gobind Khorana

Choose the correct answer from the options given below:

A. A, C, E, B, D B. D, A, B, C, E
C. E, D, A, B, C D. C, A, E, D, B

6. At high altitudes, more time is required to cook food because the boiling point of water is:

A. less than 100°C
B. more than 100°C
C. less than 98°F
D. more than 200°C

7. ______ plays an important role in hypersensitivity.

A. Basophils B. Eosinophils
C. Neutrophils D. Monocytes

8. Which of the following is the largest island in the world?

A. Sumatra B. Maldives
C. Madagascar D. Greenland

9. Which among the following countries have the Euro as their currency?

A. Belgium
B. Chile
C. Ireland
D. Italy
E. UK

Choose the correct answer from the options given below:
A. A, C and D only
B. B, C and E only
C. A, B and D only
D. C, D and E only

10. Who was the first Indian to get Bharat Ratna?
A. Dr. Rajendra Prasad
B. Maharshi Karve
C. Dr. S. Radhakrishnan
D. Jawaharlal Nehru

11. Who among the following was appointed as the first Chief of the Defence staff of India?
A. General KM Cariappa
B. General SHFJ Manekshaw
C. General VP Malik
D. General Bipin Rawat

12. Match **List I** with **List II**.

List I	List II
A. Karnam Malleswari	I. Wrestling
B. Sakshi Malik	II. Weightlifting
C. Leander Paes	III. Shooting
D. Rajyavardhan Singh Rathore	IV. Tennis

Choose the correct answer from the options given below:
A. A-II, B-I, C-IV, D-III
B. A-III, B-IV, C-I, D-II
B. A-IV, B-II, C-III, D-I
D. A-I, B-III, C-II, D-IV

13. Which among the following nations is not among the five permanent members of the UN Security Council?
A. France
B. Russia
C. Germany
D. United Kingdom

14. Which among the following is not an operating system?
A. MS Office B. Windows
C. Linux D. Android

15. Match the **List I** with **List II**.

List I	List II
A. Jaishankar Prasad	I. Untouchable
B. Khushwant Singh	II. Ajatshatru
C. Mulk Raj Anand	III. Train to Pakistan
D. Mark Tully	IV. The Heart of India

A. A-IV, B-III, C-II, D-I
B. A-III, B-IV, C-I, D-II
C. A-II, B-III, C-I, D-IV
D. A-I, B-II, C-IV, D-III

16. A and B can complete a piece of work together in 6 days. If A alone can complete the work in 12 days, in how many days can B alone complete it?
A. 10 days B. 12 days
C. 6 days D. 18 days

17. Find the ratio of the swimming speed of Vikas in still water to the speed of the river if the ratio of time taken to go 5 km upstream to the time taken to go 5 km downstream is 10:5.
A. 5:10 B. 5:1
C. 3:1 D. 4:1

18. What is the value of 1800 km/hr in m/sec?
A. 600 B. 500
C. 400 D. 300

19. A gold bracelet is sold for ₹16500 at a loss of 25%. What is the cost price of it?
A. ₹21000 B. ₹22000
C. ₹23000 D. ₹20000

20. If 25% of an electricity bill is deducted, then ₹375 is still to be paid. How much was the original bill?
A. ₹400 B. ₹500
C. ₹600 D. ₹700

21. The average age of Radha and Mohan is 75 years. The average age of Radha, Mohan and Jay is 55 years. What is the age of Jay?
A. 14 years B. 15 years
C. 16 years D. 18 years

22. If X : Y = 7 : 3, then the value of $\frac{x^2+y^2}{x^2-y^2}$ is

A. 11/40 B. 19/30
C. 39/40 D. 29/20

23. If x, y, z are three sums of money such that y is the simple interest on x, z is the simple interest on y for the same time and at the same rate of interest, then which of the following holds?

A. $y^2 = zx$ B. $z^2 = xy$
C. $x^2 = zy$ D. $x = yz$

24. If the sum of two numbers is 60 and the HCF and the LCM of these numbers are 6 and 150, then the sum of their reciprocals is

A. $\frac{1}{15}$ B. $\frac{1}{12}$
C. $\frac{1}{18}$ D. $\frac{1}{16}$

25. A cube whose edge is 10 cm long has circles painted red on each of its faces. What is the total area of the unpainted surfaces of the cube if the circles are of the largest possible areas? (Take $\pi = 3.14$.)

A. 109 cm^2 B. 119 cm^2
C. 129 cm^2 D. 99 cm^2

26. The present ages of Sam and Amar are the ratio of 5:4, respectively. Three years later, the ratio of their ages will become 8:7, respectively. What is Amar's present age in years?

A. 5 years B. 4 years
C. 6 years D. 7 years

27. Match **List I** with **List II**.

List I	List II
A. $\frac{1}{20}$	I. 2%
B. $\frac{1}{5}$	II. 10%
C. $\frac{1}{10}$	III. 5%
D. $\frac{1}{50}$	IV. 20%

Choose the correct answer from the options given below:

A. A-I, B-II, C-III, D-IV
B. A-III, B-IV, C-II, D-I
C. A-II, B-III, C-IV, D-I
D. A-IV, B-I, C-II, D-III

28. A man buys an article for ₹25.50 and sells it for ₹ 28.60. Find his gain in per cent.

A. 12.15% B. 15.15%
C. 12.65% D. 15.65%

29. Ramesh covers one-fourth of the total distance at 30 km/hr, one-fourth at 20 km/hr and the rest of his journey at 60 km/hr. Find Ramesh's average speed for the whole distance?

A. 37.84 km/hr
B. 45.84 km/hr
C. 34.28 km/hr
D. 67.28 km/hr

30. A boat can go 360 m in still water in 2 min. If the speed of the stream is 2 m/sec. How much time shall it take to cover the same distance downstream?

A. 60 sec B. 48 sec
C. 56 sec D. 72 sec

31. What will come in the place of the question mark?

DE:10 : : HI:?

A. 18 B. 30
C. 36 D. 72

32. How many rectangles are there in the figure?

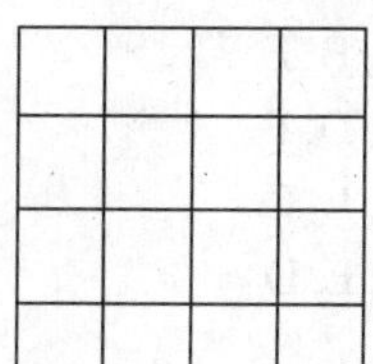

A. 16 B. 30
C. 72 D. 100

33. If the reflected time in a mirror is 3:43, then what is the actual time on the clock?

A. 3:17 B. 7:17
C. 8:17 D. 8:43

34. Which figure represents Cells, Tissues and Organs?

A. 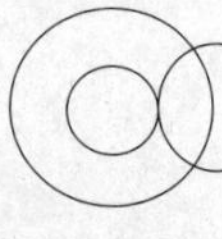

B. 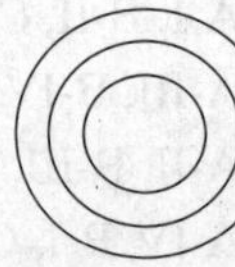

C. 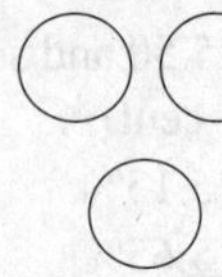

D. 

35. Find out the missing number in the following question.

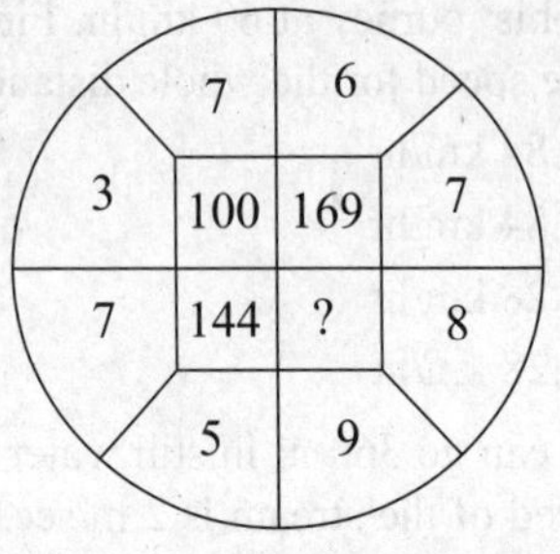

A. 72 B. 289
C. 81 D. 34

36. In BODMAS law, the sequence is
A. Brackets, Of
B. Addition
C. Multiplication
D. Divide
E. Subtraction
Choose the correct answer from the options given below:
A. A, D, C, B, E
B. A, B, C, D, E
C. B, D, A, E, C
D. B, A, C, E, D

37. Group the following figures into three classes based on identical properties.

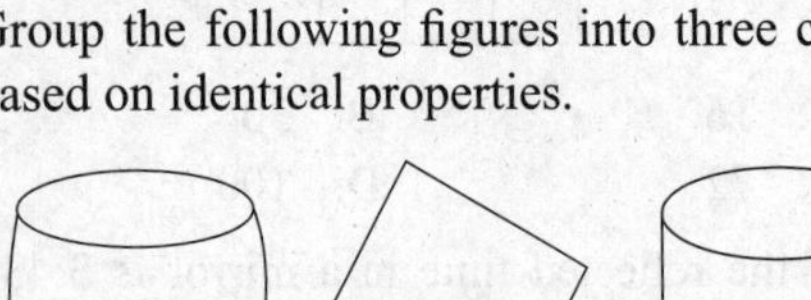

(1) (2) (3)

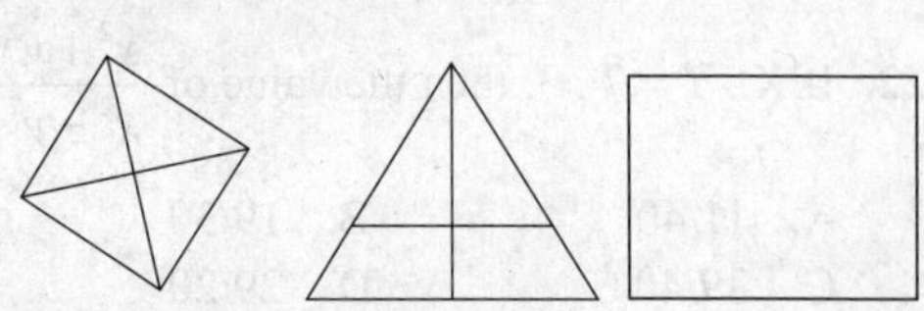

(4) (5) (6)

(7) (8) (9)

A. 1, 3, 8; 2, 6, 9; 4, 5, 7
B. 2, 3, 4; 1, 5, 6; 7, 8, 9
C. 1, 4, 8; 2, 6, 7; 3, 5, 9
D. 1, 3, 9; 2, 4, 5; 6, 7, 8

38. Two positions of a die are shown below. If the face with 1 is at the bottom, which number is on the top?

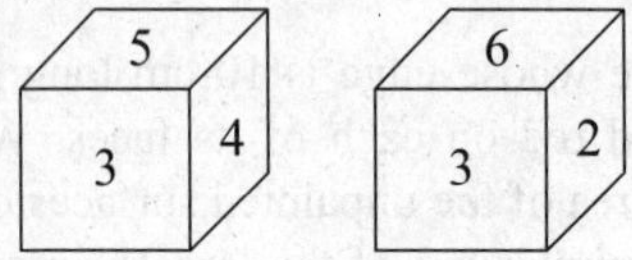

(i) (ii)

A. 2 B. 3
C. 4 D. 5

39. What is the mirror image of the term TRAIN6871?
A. ТЯAIИ68ΓI
B. ТЯAIN987I
C. ТЯAIИ98ΓI
D. TRAIN98ΓI

40. Find the missing number.

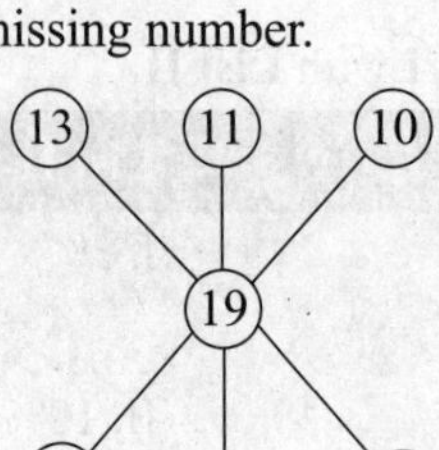

A. 10 B. 11
C. 9 D. 8

41. Choose the correct image after folding the transparent sheet.

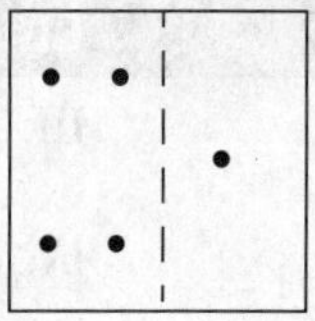

A. 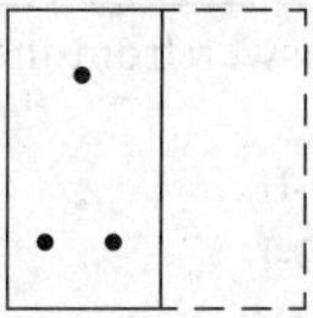 B. 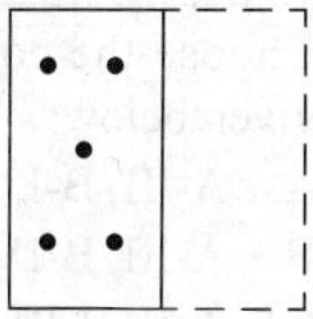

C. 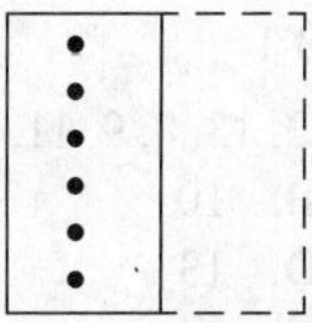 D. 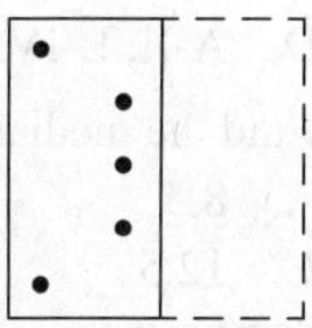

Read the following information carefully and answer questions 42–45.

1. A, B, C, D, E and F are six students procuring their Master's degree in six different subjects-Economics, Accountancy, Philosophy, Psychology, Zoology and Botany.
2. Two stay in hostels, two stay as paying guest (PG) and the remaining two stay at their home.
3. C does not stay as PG and studies Philosophy.
4. The students studying Zoology and Accountancy do not stay in PG.
5. E studies Botany and D studies Psychology. F and D stay in Hostels. E stays in PG, and B stays at home.

42. Who studies Economics?

A. C B. D
C. E D. A

43. Which of the following combinations of subject and place of stay is not correct?

A. Economics-Hostel
B. Botany-PG
C. Philosophy-Home
D. Psychology-Hostel

44. In which of the following pairs of students one has accommodation at a hostel and another one at home?

A. BC B. DC
C. FD D. AE

45. Which subject does B study?

A. Accountancy
B. Zoology
C. Accountancy or Zoology
D. Botany

46. 4:256 : : 9:?

A. 729 B. 6561
C. 1296 D. 2916

47. UY:PT : : KO:?

A. PN B. CD
C. FJ D. LK

48. Destitute:Poor : : ?:Excitable

A. Gigantic B. Devoted
C. Lively D. Credible

49. Physician:Stethoscope : : Radiologist:?

A. Surgical Gloves
B. X-ray
C. Spatula
D. Scissor

50. Arrange the following words in the sequence in which they appear in a dictionary:

A. Understood
B. Understanding
C. Undertrial
D. Undisputed
E. Unpleasant

Choose the correct answer from the options given below:

A. B, A, C, D, E B. B, A, D, E, C
C. A, C, D, E, B D. A, D, C, E, B

51. If in a certain language, G is coded as 4, M is coded as 5, S is coded as 2, D is coded as 3, A is coded as 8, C is coded as 9 and R is coded as 0, then how is MADAGASCAR coded in that language?

A. 5838482980 B. 5838824980
C. 5883849280 D. 5892488380

52. A dog is facing north. The dog turns 90° in the clockwise direction and then turns 60° in anti-clockwise direction. Which direction is the dog facing now?

A. South-east B. South-west
C. North-east D. North-west

53. Complete the series 69, 73, 75, 81, 85 ______.

A. 87 B. 89
C. 91 D. 93

54. If the 31st day of a month is Friday, what was the day on the 3rd day of that month?

A. Thursday B. Friday
C. Saturday D. Sunday

55. Complete the series 12, 20, 30, 42, 56 ______.

A. 72 B. 70
C. 80 D. 96

56. Complete the series 59049, 6561, …?..., 81, 9, 1.

A. 729 B. 324
C. 243 D. 162

57. How many squares are there in the given shape?

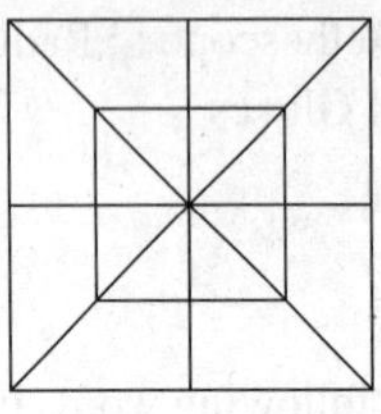

A. 08 B. 10
C. 12 D. 16

58. In this question, four words have been given, of which three are alike in some way, and one is different. Find the odd one out.

A. Brahmaputra B. Kaveri
C. Narmada D. Ganga

59. A man introduces a woman as the daughter of his mother's brother. How is the woman related to the man?

A. sister B. mother
C. grandmother D. sister-in-law

60. Interesting : Repulsive : : Intricate :

A. Proud B. Brave
C. Humble D. Unrefined

61. Match the **List I** with **List II**.

List I	List II
A. $5x+2=0$	I. $\frac{5}{4}$
B. $-2x+\frac{5}{2}=0$	II. $\frac{1}{4}$
C. $x+7=6$	III. $-\frac{2}{5}$
D. $-2x+\frac{3}{2}=1$	IV. -1

Choose the correct answer from the options given below:

A. A-III, B-I, C-IV, D-II
B. A-III, B-IV, C-II, D-I
C. A-II, B-III, C-I, D-IV
D. A-II, B-IV, C-III, D-I

62. Find the median of 18, 3, 13, 8, 9, 11, 14 and 9.

A. 8.5 B. 10
C. 12.5 D. 13

63. If PQRS is a parallelogram, then the value of 'x' is

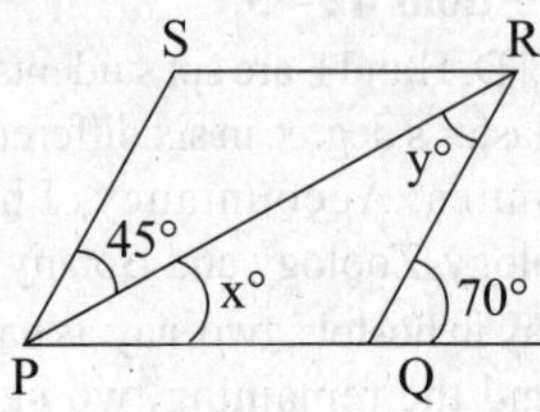

A. 70 B. 35
C. 55 D. 25

64. The value of 'x' in $8x+\frac{5}{7}=12x-\frac{3}{5}$ is

A. $\frac{23}{70}$ B. $\frac{23}{35}$
C. $-\frac{23}{35}$ D. $\frac{23}{70}$

65. A factorised form of $2x^2+3x+1$ is

A. $(2x-1)(x-1)$
B. $(x+1)(2x+1)$
C. $(x+1)(2x-1)$
D. $(2x+1)(x-1)$

66. The area of a rectangle whose sides are $(2x-7)$ and $(2x+7)$ is

A. $2x^2-49$ square units
B. $2x^2-7$ square units
C. $4x^2+49$ square units
D. $4x^2-49$ square units

67. A 150 m long train crossed a person standing on a platform in 9 seconds. The speed of the train in km/hr is

A. $\frac{50}{3}$ B. 60

C. $\frac{50}{9}$ D. $\frac{250}{54}$

68. The value of (2x + y) is

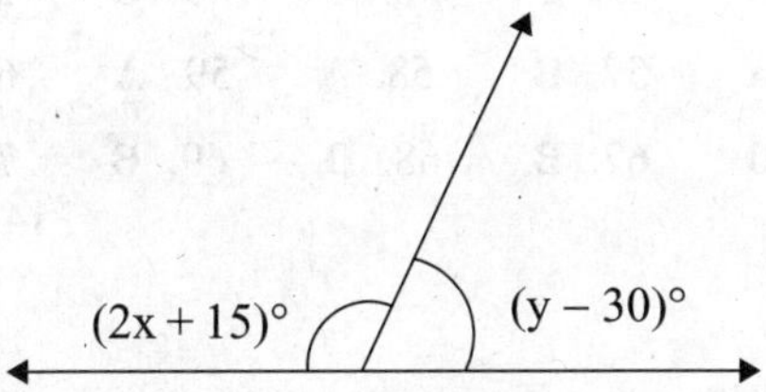

A. 180 B. 165
C. 210 D. 195

69. The value of 'x' is

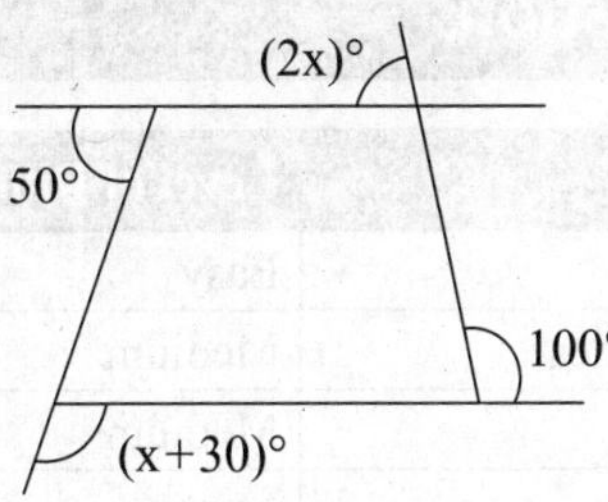

A. 50 B. 60
C. 30 D. 40

The adjoining histogram shows the frequency distribution of the ages of 20 teachers in a school. Based on the histogram, choose the correct option for questions 70–72.

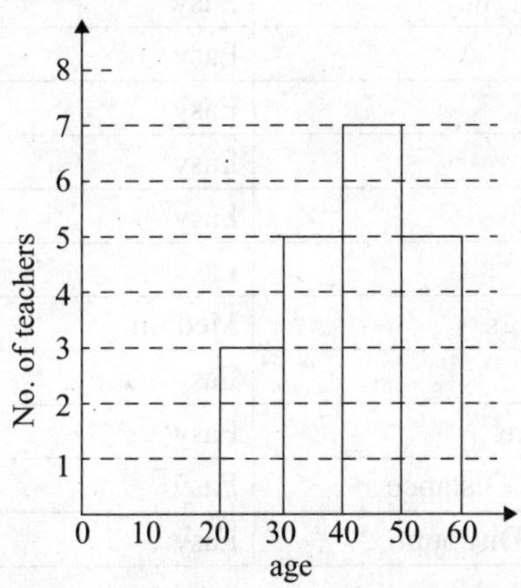

70. The number of teachers in the age group 20 to 40 is:

A. 20 B. 5
C. 8 D. 15

71. The size of the class is

A. 10–20 B. 10
C. 7 D. 20–60

72. The number of teachers in the age group 40–50 is more than the number of teachers in the age group 20–30 by

A. 10 B. 3
C. 4 D. 7

The adjoining figure shows '3' stairs of L = 85 cm, B = 45 cm and H = 30 cm.
Based on this information, choose the correct option for questions 73 to 75.

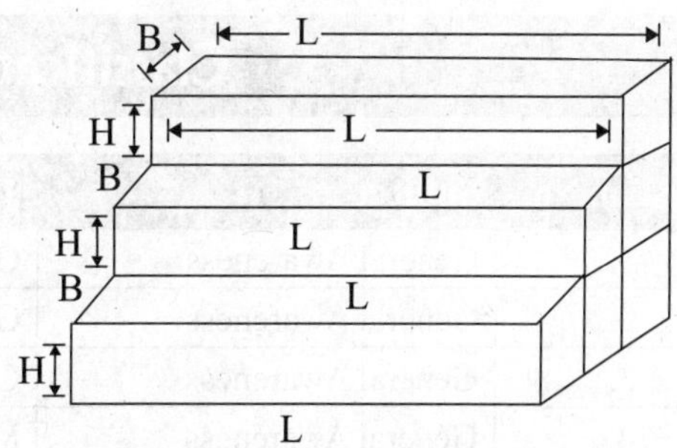

73. The perimeter of the side view is

A. 450 cm
B. 750 cm
C. 675 cm
D. 300 cm

74. Which of the following shows the area of the side view?

A. 15450 cm^2
B. 4050 cm^2
C. 8100 cm^2
D. 8500 cm^2

75. The perimeter of the bottom is

A. 340 cm
B. 330 cm
C. 320 cm
D. 440 cm

Answer Key

1. **C**	2. **B**	3. **B**	4. **C**	5. **D**	6. **A**	7. **C**	8. **D**	9. **A**	10. **C**
11. **D**	12. **A**	13. **C**	14. **A**	15. **C**	16. **B**	17. **C**	18. **B**	19. **B**	20. **B**
21. **B**	22. **D**	23. **A**	24. **A****	25. **C**	26. **B**	27. **B**	28. **A**	29. **C**	30. **D**
31. **C**	32. **D**	33. **C**	34. **B**	35. **B**	36. **A**	37. **A**	38. **B**	39. **C***	40. **C**
41. **B**	42. **D**	43. **A**	44. **B**	45. **C**	46. **B**	47. **C**	48. **C**	49. **B**	50. **A**
51. **A**	52. **C**	53. **C**	54. **B**	55. **A**	56. **A**	57. **B**	58. **A**	59. **A**#	60. **D**
61. **A**	62. **B**	63. **D**	64. **D**	65. **B**	66. **D**	67. **B**	68. **D**	69. **B**	70. **C**
71. **D**	72. **C**	73. **A**	74. **C**	75. **D**					

** The answer appears to be A, but the question is incorrect.

* C will be the answer if we read from right to left.

The woman is his cousin.

Classification of Questions

Question No.	Subject	Topic	Level of Difficulty
1.	General Awareness	Geography	Easy
2.	General Awareness	Government Schemes	Medium
3.	General Awareness	Current Affairs	Medium
4.	General Awareness	Miscellaneous	Medium
5.	General Awareness	Awards	Easy
6.	General Awareness	Science (Chemistry)	Easy
7.	General Awareness	Science (Biology)	Difficult
8.	General Awareness	Geography	Medium
9.	General Awareness	Country & Currency	Easy
10.	General Awareness	Awards	Easy
11.	General Awareness	Miscellaneous	Easy
12.	General Awareness	Sports	Easy
13.	General Awareness	Polity	Easy
14.	General Awareness	Computers	Easy
15.	General Awareness	Books & Authors	Medium
16.	Quantitative Aptitude	Time & Work	Easy
17.	Quantitative Aptitude	Boats & Streams	Easy
18.	Quantitative Aptitude	Time, Speed & Distance	Easy
19.	Quantitative Aptitude	Profit, Loss & Discount	Easy

Question No.	Subject	Topic	Level of Difficulty
20.	Quantitative Aptitude	Profit, Loss & Discount	Easy
21.	Quantitative Aptitude	Averages	Easy
22.	Quantitative Aptitude	Ratios	Easy
23.	Quantitative Aptitude	Simple Interest	Medium
24.	Quantitative Aptitude	Numbers (LCM & HCF)	Incorrect Question
25.	Quantitative Aptitude	Mensuration	Medium
26.	Quantitative Aptitude	Age-based problem	Easy
27.	Quantitative Aptitude	Percentages	Easy
28.	Quantitative Aptitude	Profit, Loss & Discount	Easy
29.	Quantitative Aptitude	Time, Speed & Distance	Easy
30.	Quantitative Aptitude	Boats & Streams	Medium
31.	Reasoning	Coding	Easy
32.	Quantitative Aptitude	Permutation & Combination	Medium
33.	Reasoning	Mirror Image	Easy
34.	Reasoning	Venn-diagram	Easy
35.	Reasoning	Missing Number	Easy
36.	Quantitative Aptitude	Miscellaneous	Easy
37.	Reasoning	Non-verbal	Easy
38.	Reasoning	Dice	Easy
39.	Reasoning	Mirror Image	Easy
40.	Reasoning	Missing Number	Easy
41.	Reasoning	Non-verbal	Easy
42.	Reasoning	Puzzle	Easy
43.	Reasoning	Puzzle	Easy
44.	Reasoning	Puzzle	Easy
45.	Reasoning	Puzzle	Easy
46.	Reasoning	Missing Number	Easy
47.	Reasoning	Analogy (letter-based)	Easy
48.	Reasoning	Analogy	Easy
49.	Reasoning	Analogy	Easy
50.	Reasoning	Dictionary Order	Easy
51.	Reasoning	Coding	Easy
52.	Reasoning	Directions	Easy
53.	Reasoning	Number Series	Easy
54.	Quantitative Aptitude	Calendars	Easy
55.	Reasoning	Number Series	Easy

Question No.	Subject	Topic	Level of Difficulty
56.	Reasoning	Number Series	Easy
57.	Reasoning	Figure Counting	Easy
58.	General Awareness	Geography	Easy
59.	Reasoning	Blood Relations	Easy
60.	Reasoning	Analogy	Easy
61.	Quantitative Aptitude	Algebra (Linear Equations)	Easy
62.	Quantitative Aptitude	Statistics (Median)	Easy
63.	Quantitative Aptitude	Geometry (Parallelograms)	Easy
64.	Quantitative Aptitude	Algebra (Linear Equations)	Easy
65.	Quantitative Aptitude	Algebra (Factorisation)	Easy
66.	Quantitative Aptitude	Mensuration	Easy
67.	Quantitative Aptitude	Time, Speed and Distance	Easy
68.	Quantitative Aptitude	Geometry (Supplementary Angles)	Easy
69.	Quantitative Aptitude	Geometry (Quadrilaterals)	Easy
70.	Data Interpretation	Histogram	Easy
71.	Data Interpretation	Histogram	Easy
72.	Data Interpretation	Histogram	Easy
73.	Quantitative Aptitude	Mensuration	Easy
74.	Quantitative Aptitude	Mensuration	Easy
75.	Quantitative Aptitude	Mensuration	Easy

No. of questions on Quantitative Aptitude: 30
No. of questions on General Awareness: 16
No. of questions on Reasoning: 26
No. of questions on Data Interpretation: 3

Explanation to Select Questions

3. The FICCI, in their Economic Outlook Survey, had expected India's GDP to grow at 9.1% in 2021–22.

Hence, Option B.

Update: FICCI's Economic Outlook Survey predicts that India's GDP will grow at 6.3% in 2023–24.

4.

Important Event	
National Voters' Day (25 January)	The Election Commission of India came into existence on this day in 1950.

Important Event	
International Yoga Day (21 June)	
National Sports Day (29 August)	This is the birth anniversary of Major Dhyan Chand.
National Education Day (11 November)	This is the birth anniversary of India's first education minister, Maulana Abul Kalam Azad.
Children's Day (14 November)	This is the birth anniversary of India's first prime minister, Jawaharlal Nehru.

Hence, Option C.

Note: Please do NOT confuse Teachers' Day (5 September) and National Education Day (11 November).

5.

Nobel Laureate	Year of the Award	Field
Rabindranath Tagore	1913	Literature
C.V. Raman	1930	Physics
Har Gobind Khorana*	1968	Physiology or Medicine
Amartya Sen	1998	Economics
Kailash Satyarthi	2014	Peace

Hence, Option D.

*Har Gobind Khorana was a US citizen at the time of this award.

8. These are the 6 largest islands of the world:
   1. Greenland
   2. New Guinea
   3. Borneo (the largest island in Asia)
   4. Madagascar
   5. Baffin Island (Canada)
   6. Sumatra

   Hence, Option D.

   Java (Indonesia) is the most populous island in the world.

   Note: Australia is NOT considered an island.

9. Chile's currency is the Chilean peso. The currency of the UK is Pound sterling. Chile is a country in South America and hence cannot be in the European Union or have Euro as its currency. The UK came out of the EU in 2020 itself. The answer is Option A.

10.

Person	The Year of Getting the Bharat Ratna
Dr. S. Radhakrishnan	1954
Jawaharlal Nehru	1955
Maharshi Karve	1958
Dr. Rajendra Prasad	1962

Hence, Option C.

Note: Bharat Ratna was awarded for the first time in 1954, and there were three recipients that year: C.V. Raman, Dr. S. Radhakrishnan and C. Rajagopalachari.

11. General K.M. Cariappa became the first Indian Commander-in-Chief of the Indian Army in 1949. General Manekshaw became the first Field Marshal of the Indian Army in 1973. General Bipin Rawat became India's first Chief of Defence Staff in 2020.

    Hence, Option D.

    Update: General Anil Chauhan is the 2nd and current Chief of Defence Staff.

16. B alone can complete the work in $\frac{1}{\frac{1}{6}-\frac{1}{12}} = \frac{12}{2-1} = 12$ days.

    Hence, Option B.

    Shortcut: As A and B can do $\frac{1}{6}$ of the work in 1 day and A alone can do $\frac{1}{12}$ of the work in 1 day, A does exactly half of the work done by both of them. It means A and B are equally efficient and take the same time.

You should be able to do this question without putting pen on paper.

17. Let the swimming speed of Vikas in still water be x km/hr and the speed of the river be y km/hr. We have,

$$\frac{\frac{5}{x-y}}{\frac{5}{x+y}} = \frac{10}{5}$$

or, $\frac{5}{x-y} \times \frac{x+y}{5} = \frac{2}{1}$

or, $\frac{x+y}{x-y} = 2:1 = \frac{2}{1}$

or, $x + y = 2x - 2y$

or, $x = 3y$

or, $\frac{x}{y} = \frac{3}{1} = 3:1.$

Hence, Option C.

Shortcut: As Vikas travels the same distance (5 km) upstream as well as downstream, the ratio of the upstream and downstream speeds is the reciprocal of 10:5, which is 1:2. Only Option C gives us this ratio, as $\frac{3-1}{3+1} = \frac{1}{2}$.

18. 1 km = 1000 m and 1hr = 60 × 60 = 3600 sec.

1800 km/hr = $\frac{1800 \times 1000}{3600}$ = 500 m/sec.

Hence, Option B.

Note: To convert km/hr to m/sec, just multiply the former with $\frac{5}{18}\left(=\frac{1000}{3600}\right)$.

19. The cost price = the selling price × $\frac{100}{100 - \text{loss percentage}}$

$= 16500 \times \frac{100}{100-25}$

$= 16500 \times \frac{100}{75}$

$= 22000.$

Hence, Option B.

20. The original bill = 375 × $\frac{100}{100 - \text{percentage Discount}}$

$= 375 \times \frac{100}{100-25} = 375 \times \frac{100}{75}$

$= 375 \times \frac{4}{3} = 500.$

Hence, Option B.

21. The sum of the ages of Radha and Mohan = 2 × 75 = 150 years.

The sum of the ages of Radha, Mohan and Jay = 3 × 55 = 165 years.

Therefore, the age of Jay = 165 – 150 = 15 years.

Hence, Option B.

22. $x:y = 7:3$

or, $\frac{x}{y} = \frac{7}{3}$

or, $\frac{x^2}{y^2} = \left(\frac{7}{3}\right)^2 = \frac{49}{9}.$

Now, $\frac{x^2+y^2}{x^2-y^2}$

$$= \frac{\frac{x^2+y^2}{y^2}}{\frac{x^2-y^2}{y^2}} = \frac{\frac{x^2}{y^2}+1}{\frac{x^2}{y^2}-1} = \frac{\frac{49}{9}+1}{\frac{49}{9}-1}$$

$$= \frac{\frac{49+9}{9}}{\frac{49-9}{9}} = \frac{58}{9} \times \frac{9}{40} = \frac{29}{20}.$$

Hence, Option D.

23. Let the time be t and rate r in both cases.

$$y = \frac{x \times r \times t}{100} \quad \text{(i)}$$

and

$$z = \frac{y \times r \times t}{100} \quad \text{(ii)}$$

On dividing (i) by (ii), we get,

$$\frac{y}{z} = \frac{\frac{x \times r \times t}{100}}{\frac{y \times r \times t}{100}}$$

or, $\frac{y}{z} = \frac{x \times r \times t}{100} \times \frac{100}{y \times r \times t}$

or, $\frac{y}{z} = \frac{x}{y}$ or, $y^2 = xz$.

Hence, Option A.

24. This question is **INCORRECT**.

Let the numbers be $6a$ and $6b$ (as their HCF is 6).

Of course, a and b have to be coprime.

Now, $6a + 6b = 60$,

or, $6(a + b) = 60$,

or, $(a + b) = \frac{60}{6} = 10$.

So, a and b have to be coprime to each other, and their sum should be 10.

There are 2 such pairs of Natural numbers: (1, 9) and (3, 7).

So, there can be 2 pairs of numbers such that their sum is 60 and the HCF is 6:

1. (6, 54), but the LCM of these numbers is 54 (not 150).
2. (18, 42), but the LCM of these numbers is 126 (NOT 150).

Thus, we see that if the HCF of 2 numbers is 6 and their sum is 60, their LCM CANNOT be 150.

25.

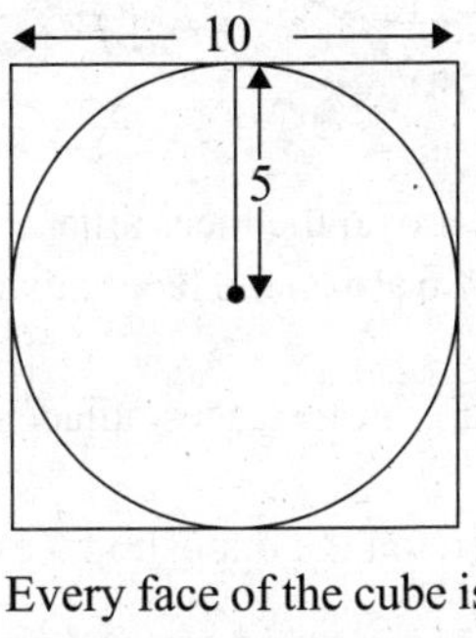

Every face of the cube is a square of side 10 cm. The radius of the largest circle that can fit into this square is 5 cm.

The area of the circle = $\pi \times 5^2 = 3.14 \times 25 =$ 78.5 cm^2.

The total area of this face = $10 \times 10 = 100$ cm^2.

Therefore, the unpainted area on this face = $100 - 78.50 = 21.50$.

As a cube has 6 faces, the total unpainted area on all its faces = $21.50 \times 6 = 129$ cm^2.

Hence, Option C.

26. Let the present ages of Sam and Amar be $5x$ and $4x$, respectively.

We have $\frac{5x + 3}{4x + 3} = \frac{8}{7}$

or, $35x + 21 = 32x + 24$

or, $3x = 3$

or, $x = 1$.

Therefore, the present age of Amar = $4x$ = 4 years.

Hence, Option B.

Shortcut: As the ages of Sam and Amar are in the ratio 5:4. Amar's age should be a multiple of 4. Only Option B gives us a multiple of 4.

28. Profit = 28.60 – 25.50 = 3.10.

Profit percentage $= \frac{3.10}{25.50} \times 100 = 12.15$ (approx.).

Hence, Option A.

Shortcut: $12.5\% = \frac{1}{8}$

and $3.1 < \frac{1}{8}$ of 25.5.

Therefore, the answer has to be less than 12.5%, and only Option A is less than 12.5%.

29. Let the total distance be $4d$.

Therefore, Ramesh travels d at 30 km/hr, another d at 20 km/hr and $2d$ at 60 km/hr.

Therefore, the total time taken by Ramesh

$$= \frac{d}{30} + \frac{d}{20} + \frac{2d}{60}$$

$$= \frac{d}{30} + \frac{d}{20} + \frac{d}{30} = \frac{2d}{30} + \frac{d}{20}$$

$$= \frac{d}{15} + \frac{d}{20} = \frac{4d + 3d}{60} = \frac{7d}{60}.$$

The average speed $= \frac{\text{total distance}}{\text{total time}} = \frac{4d}{\frac{7d}{60}}$

$$= \frac{4d \times 60}{7d} = \frac{240}{7} = 34.28 \text{ km/hr.}$$

Shortcut: As the involved speeds are 20 km/hr, 30 km/hr and 60 km/hr, let's assume the total distance to be 4 times the LCM of 20, 30 and 60. We can assume the distance to be anything, but we are carefully choosing a number for the ease of calculations.

Let the total distance be 240 km.

The total time $= \frac{60}{30} + \frac{60}{20} + \frac{120}{60} = 2 + 3 + 2$

= 7 hrs.

Therefore, the average speed $= \frac{240}{7} =$ 34.28 km/hr.

Hence, Option C.

30. The speed of the boat in still water
= 360 m in 120 seconds

$= \frac{360}{120}$ m/s = 3 m/s.

The speed of the stream = 2 m/s.

Therefore, the downstream speed of the boat = 3 + 2 = 5 m/s.

Therefore, the time taken by the boat to travel 360 m downstream $= \frac{360}{5}$

= 72 seconds.

Hence, Option D.

31. D E : 10 $\rightarrow$ $10 = \frac{4 \times 5}{2}$

4 5

H I : ? $\rightarrow$ $= \frac{8 \times 9}{2} = 36$

8 9

Hence, option C.

32.

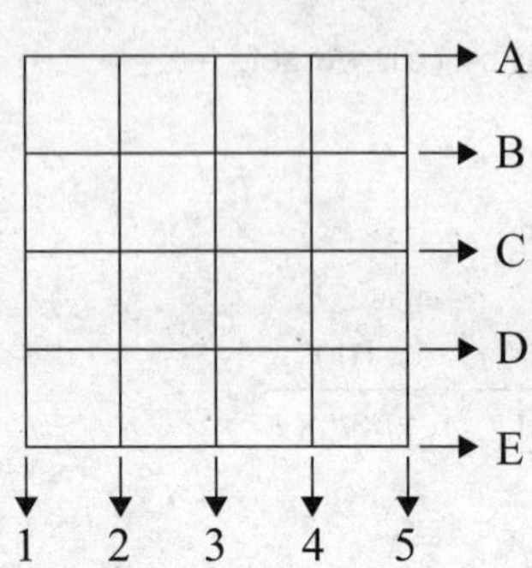

The figure above has 5 horizontal lines (A, B, C, D and E) and 5 vertical lines (1, 2, 3, 4 and 5).

We get a rectangle when we select any 2 out of the 5 vertical lines and any 2 out of the 5 horizontal lines.

Therefore, the number of rectangles $= {}^5C_2 \times {}^5C_2$

$$= \frac{5 \times 4}{2} \times \frac{5 \times 4}{2} = 10 \times 10 = 100.$$

Hence, Option D.

33. The actual time = 12:00 – the reflected time = 12:00 – 3:43 = 8:17.

Hence, Option C.

35.

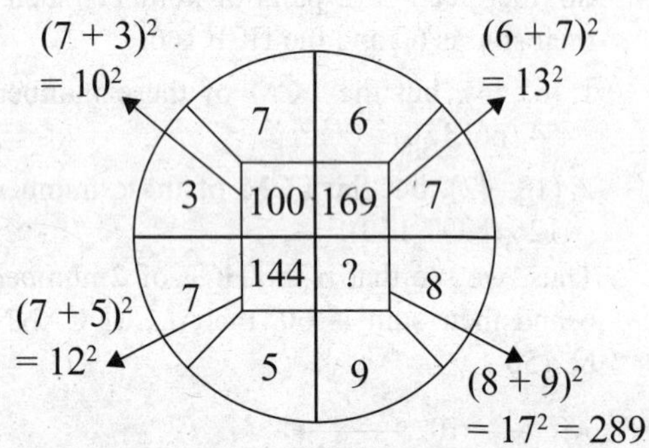

Hence, Option B.

38. In figure (i), 4 and 5 are on the faces adjacent to 3. In figure (ii), 2 and 6 are on the faces adjacent to 3.

Thus 2, 4, 5 and 6 are on the faces adjacent to the face having 3.

Therefore, 3 and 1 are on the opposite faces.

Hence, Option B.

40. 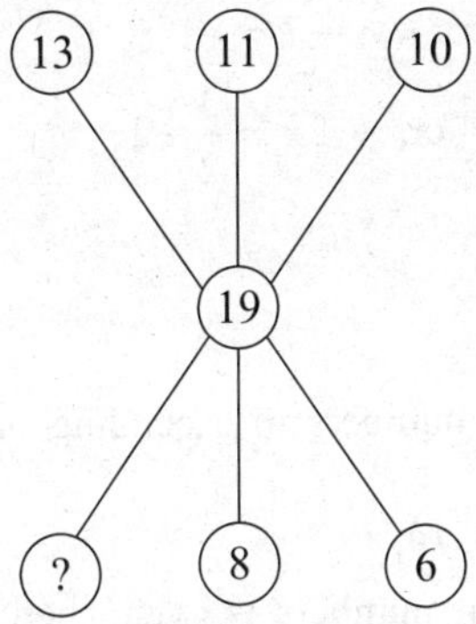

11 + 8 = 19 and 13 + 6 = 19.

Hence, 10 + 9 = 19.

⇒ ? = 9.

Hence, Option C.

Please refer to the table for explanations of questions 42–45:

Student	Type of Accommodation	Subject
A	**PG**	**Economics**
B	Home	**Zoology/ Accountancy**
C	**Home**	Philosophy
D	Hostel	Psychology
E	PG	Botany
F	Hostel	**Accountancy/ Zoology**

The information in **BOLD** is what you need to interpret. The rest is already given in the question.

42. Option D.

43. Option A (Economics-PG is the correct combination).

44. D stays in a hostel, and C stays at home.
Hence, Option B.

45. It is either Accountancy or Zoology.
Hence, Option C.

46. $256 = 4^4$

Hence, $? = 9^4 = 6561$.

Hence, Option B.

47. U Y : P T :: K O : (F) (J)

21 25 : 16 20 :: 11 15 : 6 10

(21 → 25: +4; 21 → 16: -5; 16 → 20: +4; 11 → 15: +4; 11 → 6: -5; 6 → 10: +4)

Hence, Option C.

52. 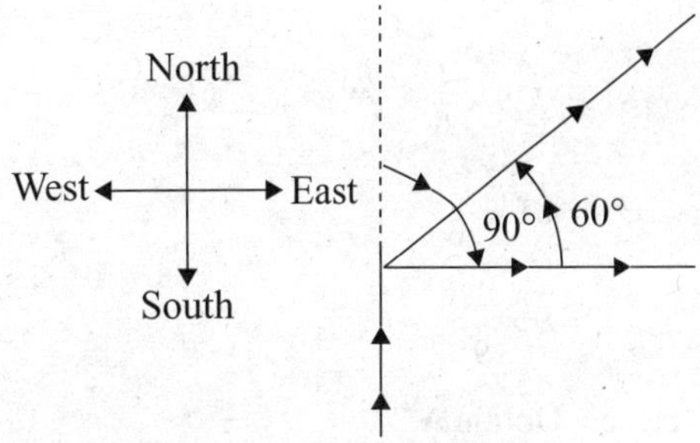

Hence, Option C.

53. Here,

69 = 67 + 2

73 = 71 + 2

75 = 73 + 2

81 = 79 + 2

85 = 83 + 2

So, each of the first five numbers is 2 more than a prime number. The prime numbers are 67, 71, 73, 79 and 83. The next prime number is 89, and hence, the next term of the series is 89 + 2 = 91.

Hence, Option C.

54. The number of days between the 31st and the 3rd of a month is 31 – 3 = 28
= 7 × 4 (zero odd days).

Therefore, the 3rd of the month will also be a Friday.

Hence, Option B.

55. 12, 20, 30, 42, 56, (72)

+8 +10 +12 +14 +16

Hence, Option A.

Alternative:

12 = 3 × 4

20 = 4 × 5

30 = 5 × 6

42 = 6 × 7

56 = 7 × 8

Hence, the next term is 8 × 9 = 72.

56. This is actually a GP with the common ratio $\frac{1}{9}$.

$$6561 = 59049 \times \frac{1}{9}$$

$$729 = 6561 \times \frac{1}{9}$$

$$81 = 729 \times \frac{1}{9}$$

$$9 = 81 \times \frac{1}{9}$$

$$1 = 9 \times \frac{1}{9}$$

Hence, Option A.

Note: It is always easier to deal with smaller numbers, and hence, looking at this series from the right to the left is advisable.

57.

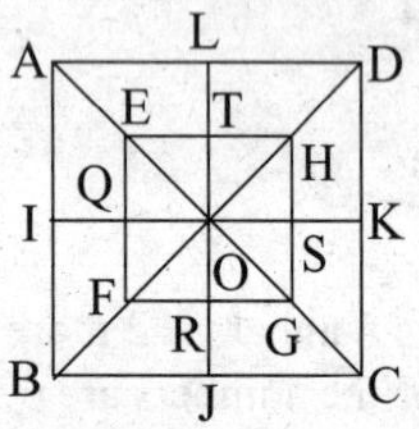

The squares are:

ABCD, AIOL, IBJO, OJCK, LOKD, EFGH, EQOT, QFRO, ORGS and TOSH.

Hence, Option B.

59.

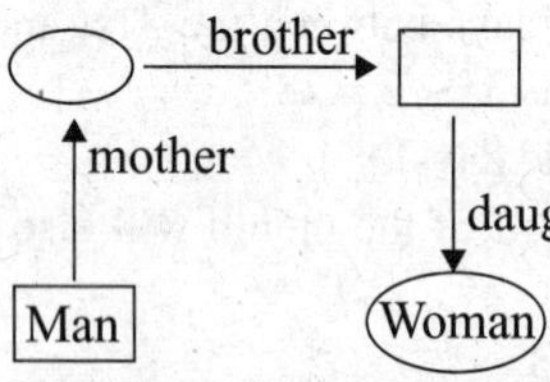

The woman is the daughter of the maternal uncle of the man, and thus, they are cousins.

Cousin is none of the options here.

It appears that the question intended to say, 'the daughter of the mother of his brother', but 'mother' and 'brother' got exchanged! This would have made the answer Option A (sister).

61. A. $5x + 2 = 0$ or, $x = -\frac{2}{5}$.

B. $-2x + \frac{5}{2} = 0$ or, $2x = \frac{5}{2}$, or, $x = \frac{5}{4}$.

C. $x + 7 = 6$ or, $x = 6 - 7 = -1$.

D. $-2x + \frac{3}{2} = 1$, or, $2x = \frac{3}{2} - 1 = \frac{1}{2}$, or, $x = \frac{1}{4}$.

Hence, Option A.

62. Arranging the 8 numbers in ascending order, we get,

3, 8, 9, 9, 11, 13, 14, 18.

As the number of numbers is even, there are two middle terms here: 9 and 11.

Therefore, the median $= \frac{9+11}{2} = \frac{20}{2} = 10$.

Hence, Option B.

63.

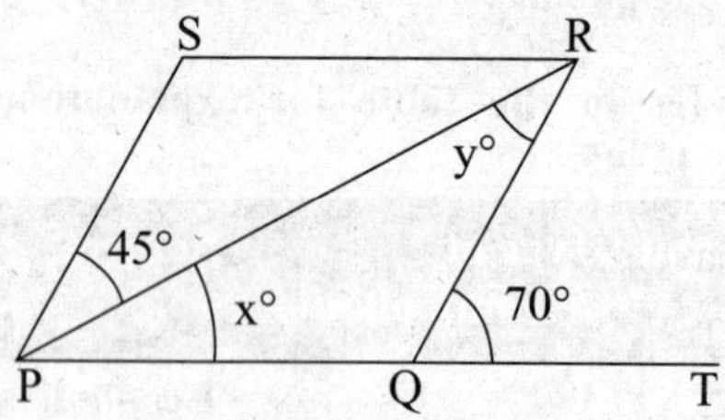

We have, $\angle RQT = \angle SPQ$ as $SP \| RQ$ (corresponding angles)

Therefore, $\angle SPQ = 70° = \angle SPR + \angle RPQ = 45° + x°$

Or, $x° = 70° - 45° = 25°$

Hence, Option D.

64. $8x + \frac{5}{7} = 12x - \frac{3}{5}$

or, $12x - 8x = \frac{3}{5} + \frac{5}{7} = \frac{21+25}{35}$

or, $4x = \frac{46}{35}$ or, $x = \frac{46}{35 \times 4} = \frac{23}{35 \times 2} = \frac{23}{70}$.

Hence, Option D.

65. $2x^2 + 3x + 1$

$= 2x^2 + 2x + x + 1$

$= 2x(x+1) + 1(x+1)$

$= (x+1)(2x+1)$.

Hence, Option B.

66. As $(2x - 7) \neq (2x + 7)$, they cannot be the opposite sides of a rectangle.

Therefore, they are adjacent sides.

The area of the rectangle = the product of its adjacent sides

$= (2x - 7)(2x + 7)$

$= (2x)^2 - 7^2 = (4x^2 - 49)$ square units.

Hence, Option D.

67. The speed of the train $= \dfrac{150 \text{ m}}{9 \text{ s}} = \dfrac{50}{3}$ m/s

$= \dfrac{50}{3} \times \dfrac{3600}{1000}$ km/hr = 60 km/hr.

Hence, Option B.

68.

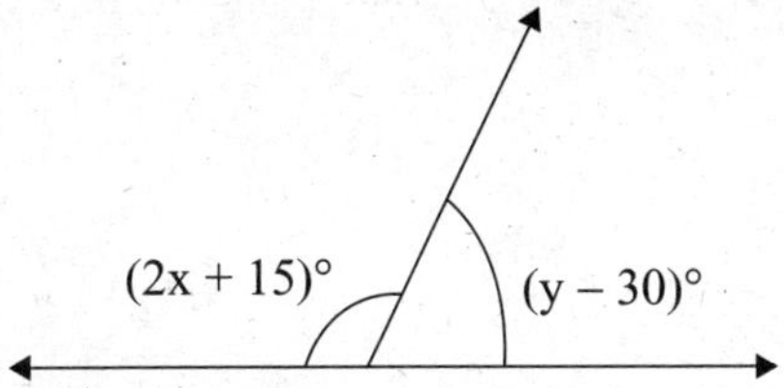

We have, $(2x + 15 + y - 30)° = 180°$

or, $(2x + y - 15)° = 180°$

or, $2x + y - 15 = 180$

or, $2x + y = 180 + 15 = 195.$

Hence, Option D.

69.

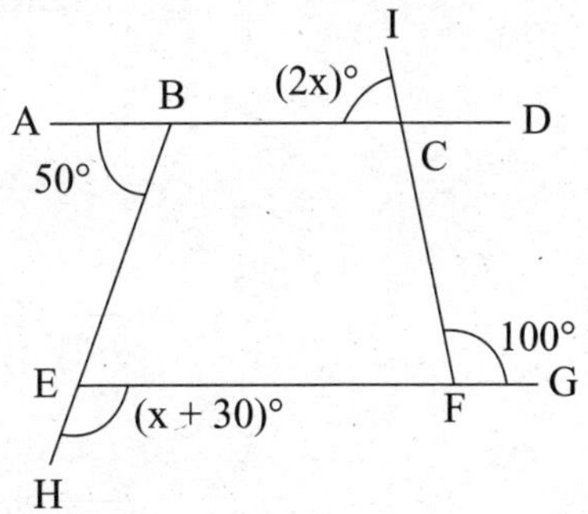

Here,

$\angle ABE + \angle CBE = 180°$

or, $50° + \angle CBE = 180°$

or, $\angle CBE = 180° - 50° = 130°.$

Again, $\angle CFG + \angle CFE = 180°$

or, $100° + \angle CFE = 180°$

or, $\angle CFE = 180° - 100° = 80°.$

Now, $\angle BEF + \angle FEH = 180°$

or, $\angle BEF + x° + 30° = 180°$

or, $\angle BEF = 180° - 30° - x°$

or, $\angle BEF = 150° - x°.$

Again, $\angle ICB + \angle BCF = 180°$

or, $(2x)° + \angle BCF = 180°$

or, $\angle BCF = 180° - (2x)°$

In the quadrilateral BEFC,

$\angle CBE + \angle BEF + \angle EFC + \angle FCB = 360°$

(the sum of all the angles of a quadrilateral is 360°)

or, $130° + 150° - x° + 80° + 180° - (2x)° = 360°$

or, $540° - (3x)° = 360°$

or, $(3x)° = 540° - 360° = 180°.$

or, $x = \dfrac{180}{3} = 60.$

Hence, Option B.

Note: You CANNOT assume that the opposite sides of the given quadrilateral are parallel.

Please refer to the following figure for explanations of questions 70–72.

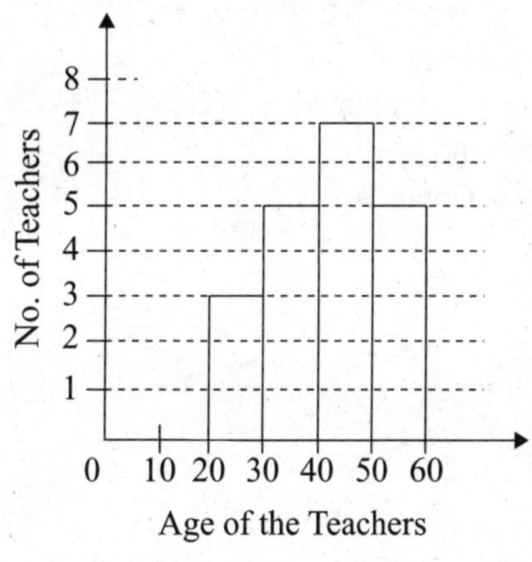

70. The number of teachers in the age group 20 to 40 is 3 + 5 = 8.

Hence, Option C.

71. The 'class' here refers to the class of the data.

Hence, Option D.

72. The number of teachers in the age group 40 – 50 = 7.

The number of teachers in the age group 20 – 30 = 3.

Hence, the difference = 7 – 3 = 4.

Hence, Option C.

Please refer to the following figure for the explanations of the questions 73–75.

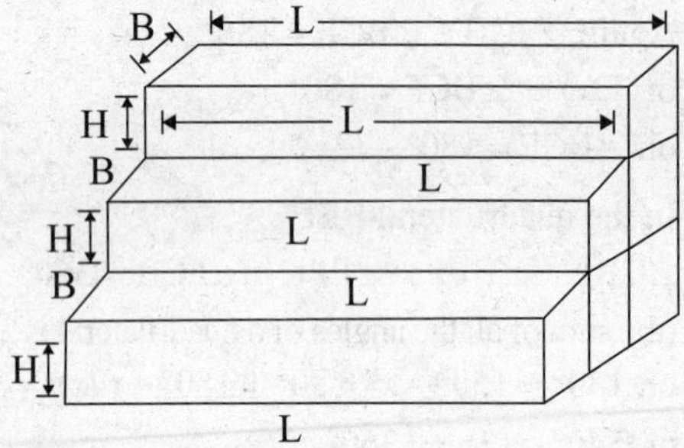

73. The side view:

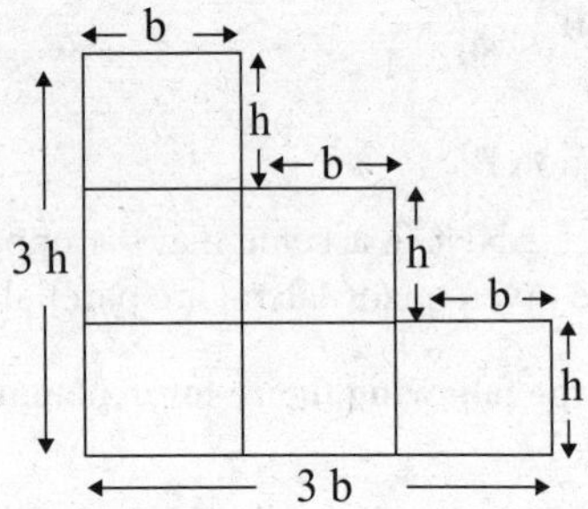

The perimeter

$= 6(b + h) = 6\ (45\text{ cm} + 30\text{ cm})$

$= 450$ cm.

Hence, Option A.

74. (Please refer to the figure given in the solution of question 73.)

The area of the side view $= 6 \times b \times h$

$= 6 \times 45 \times 30\text{ cm}^2$

$= 270 \times 30\text{ cm}^2$

$= 8100\text{ cm}^2$

Hence, Option C.

75. The perimeter of the bottom

$= 2\ (L + 3b) = 2(85 + 3 \times 45)$

$= 2(85 + 135) = 2(220) = 440$ cm

Hence, Option D.

CUET UG 2022 GENERAL TEST

August 20

INSTRUCTIONS:

1. You need to attempt any 60 out of the 75 questions in 60 minutes.
2. You get 5 marks for a correct response and –1 for an incorrect one. However, there is no reward or penalty for a question not attempted.

1. Arrange the IPL winner teams in a sequence of number of times they have won (from maximum to minimum or zero).

A. Kolkata Knight Riders
B. Mumbai Indians
C. Rajasthan Royals
D. Chennai Super Kings
E. Delhi Daredevils

Choose the correct answer from the options given below:

A. B, D, C, A, E B. B, D, A, C, E
C. E, B, C, D, A D. C, E, A, B, D

2. 'Address Book: A Publishing Memoir in the Time of COVID' is authored by:

A. Mahasweta Devi B. Arundhati Roy
C. Sudha Murty D. Ritu Menon

3. Match **List I** with **List II**.

List I (State)	List II (Governor)
A. Karnataka	I. Rajendra Vishwanath Arlekar
B. Madhya Pradesh	II. Mangubhai Chhaganbhai Patel
C. Mizoram	III. Thawar Chand Gehlot
D. Himachal Pradesh	IV. Dr. Hari Babu Kambhampati

Choose the correct answer from the options given below:

A. A-II, B-III, C-I, D-IV
B. A-I, B-II, C-III, D-IV
C. A-IV, B-III, C-I, D-II
D. A-III, B-II, C-IV, D-I

4. Which city has been named the world's most expensive city for foreign workers as per the 2021 cost-of-living survey by Mercer?

A. Tokyo B. London
C. New York D. Ashgabat

5. _________ satellite is used to telecast TV programs from one part of the world to another?

A. Geocentric
B. Geostationary
C. Polar
D. Natural

6. Match **List I** with **List II**.

List I	List II
A. < 20 Hz	I. Longitudinal waves
B. > 20000 Hz	II. Electromagnetic waves
C. X-rays	III. Infrasonic waves
D. Sound waves	IV. Ultrasonic waves

Choose the correct answer from the options given below:

A. A-I, B-IV, C-II, D-III
B. A-II B-III, C-I, D-IV
C. A-IV, B-II, C-I, D-III
D. A-III, B-IV, C-II, D-I

7. Which among the following are part of "The Eight-Fold-Path" suggested by Buddha?

A. Right Thought
B. Right Livelihood

C. Right Guru
D. Right Mindfulness
E. Right Blessing

Choose the correct answer from the options given below:

A. A, B and D Only
B. B, C and D Only
C. B, D and E Only
D. A, C and E Only

8. Match **List I** with **List II**.

List I (Mountain Peak)	List II (Country)
A. Cotopaxi	I. Tanzania
B. Tirich Mir	II. Ecuador
C. Mount Everest	III. Pakistan
D. Kilimanjaro	IV. Nepal

Choose the correct answer from the options given below:

A. A-III, B-I, C-IV, D-II
B. A-II, B-I, C-III, D-IV
C. A-IV, B-II, C-I, D-III
D. A-II, B-III, C-IV, D-I

9. "Writing with Fire" is a famous __________.

A. book
B. documentary
C. web series
D. movie

10. Match **List I** with **List II**.

List I	List II
A. World Mental Health Day	I. 11 October
B. International Day of the Girl Child	II. 24 October
C. World Students' Day	III. 10 October
D. World Polio Day	IV. 15 October

Choose the correct answer from the options given below:

A. A-II, B-III, C-IV, D-I
B. A-IV, B-I, C-III, D-II
C. A-III, B-I, C-IV, D-II
D. A-I, B-IV, C-II, D-III

11. A self-contained program that does not need to be a part of another program to propagate itself is called:

A. spyware
B. antivirus
C. worm
D. spam

12. Name of the first woman President of any country in the world.

A. Maria Estela Peron
B. Pratibha Patil
C. Sirimavo Bandaranaike
D. Golda Meir

13. Match **List I** with **List II**.

List I (Discovery)	List II (Discoverer)
A. America	I. Roald Amundsen
B. South Pole	II. Christopher Columbus
C. North Pole	III. Marco Polo
D. China	IV. Robert Peary

Choose the correct answer from the options given below:

A. A-II, B-IV, C-III, D-I
B. A-II, B-I, C-IV, D-III
C. A-IV, B-II, C-I, D-III
D. A-I, B-II, C-IV, D-III

14. __________ is the final value of the goods and services produced within the geographical boundaries of a country during a year.

A. Gross Domestic Product (GDP)
B. Net Domestic Product (NDP)
C. Gross National Product (GNP)
D. The Net National Product (NNP)

15. The articles of the Indian Constitution that correspond to the Rights to Equality are:

A. Article 11–13
B. Article 14–18
C. Article 19–22
D. Article 23–24

16. To find the profit % made on a transaction, which among the following is/are required?

A. Cost Price and Discount on the Marked Price
B. Marked Price and Discount %
C. Discount % of the Marked Price
D. Cost Price and Discount % on Marked Price

Choose the correct answer from the options given below:

A. only 'A' is required
B. only 'A' and 'B' are required

C. only A' and 'C' are required
D. only 'A' and 'D' are required

17. A seller earns a profit of 10% after selling an object at a 10% discount. What is the ratio of the cost price to the printed price of the object?
A. 7:11 B. 8:11
C. 9:11 D. 10:11

18. Find in whichever condition/conditions filling of the water tank is/are possible:
A. one tap filling the tank at 2 litres/minute
B. one tap filling the tank at 15 litre/minute and one tap emptying the tank with a speed of 1 litre/minute
C. two taps filling the tank with a uniform speed of 4 litre/minute and one tap emptying the tank with a speed of 500 ml/sec
D. one tap filling the tank in 2 litre/minute and one tap emptying the tank with a speed of 4 litre/minute

Choose the correct answer from the options given below:
A. filled in case 'A' only
B. filled in case 'A' and 'B' only
C. filled in case 'A' and 'C' only
D. filled in case 'A' and 'D' only

19. Viraj swims for $12\frac{1}{2}$ hours while going 24 km downstream and 36 km upstream. But he takes just 12 hours to swim 36 km downstream and 24 km upstream. At what rate is the river flowing?
A. 1.1 km/hr B. 2.1 km/hr
C. 3.1 km/hr D. 4.1 km/hr

20. The speed of a boat in still water is 20 km/hr, and the speed of the stream is 5 km/hr. Find the time taken to travel 50 km downstream and 30 km upstream by the boat.
A. 3.5 hours B. 4 hours
C. 3 hours D. 4.5 hours

21. A right-angled triangle is rotated along the base. If the perpendicular, hypotenuse and base of the triangle are 8 cm, 10 cm and 6 cm, respectively, then find the volume of the cone formed through the rotation. ($\pi = 3.14$)
A. 101.44 cm^3 B. 301.44 cm^3
C. 401.92 cm^3 D. 501.44 cm^3

22. The sum of two numbers is 44, and their difference is 16. The ratio of these numbers is:
A. 12:5 B. 15:7
C. 7:9 D. 11:13

23. The largest length of the scale that can measure exactly 20 cm, 90 cm, 1 m 25 cm and 1 m 30 cm length is:
A. 5 cm B. 15 cm
C. 20 cm D. 30 cm

24. A woman on vacation travels the first 150 km at 60 km/hr and the next 150 km at 25 km/hr. The average speed for the first 200 km of the tour is:
A. 44.44 km/hr
B. 66.66 km/hr
C. 33.33 km/hr
D. 55.55 km/hr

25. Two employees, X and Y, are paid a total of ₹4500 per week by their employer. If X is paid 125 per cent of the sum paid to Y, how much is Y paid per week?
A. ₹2500 B. ₹2000
C. ₹3000 D. ₹4000

26. The price of cooking gas has increased by 25%. By what per cent should a family reduce the use of cooking gas to not increase the expenditure on this account?
A. 10% B. 20%
C. 30% D. 25%

27. Two years ago, the ratio of the ages of Sita and Prakash was 5:8, respectively. After 4 years, this ratio would become 2:3. Find Sita's present age (in years).
A. 24 years B. 30 years
C. 32 years D. 35 years

28. Match **List I** with **List II**.

List I	List II
A. the sum of the first 5 primes	I. 15
B. the average of the first 5 primes	II. 28
C. the sum of the first 5 natural numbers	III. 3
D. the average of the first 5 natural numbers	IV. 5.6

Choose the correct answer from the options given below:

A. A-I, B-II, C-III, D-IV
B. A-II, B-I, C-III, D-IV
C. A-II, B-IV, C-I, D-III
D. A-III, B-I, C-II, D-IV

29. The ratio of the averages of the first five (05) odd and the first five (05) even natural numbers is

A. 3:2 B. 2:3
C. 6:5 D. 5:6

30. A bus travelled a 3 km distance in 5 seconds. What is the speed of the bus for this distance?

A. 2021 km/hr B. 2120 km/hr
C. 2160 km/hr D. 2130 km/hr

31. If × stands for –, ÷ stands for+, + stands for ÷ and – stands for ×, then 15 – 5 ÷ 5 × 20 + 10 is equal to

A. 12 B. 6
C. 72 D. 78

32. Pointing to a girl playing with her friends in a park, Rita said, "She is the daughter of the only daughter of my father." How is Rita related to that girl?

A. sister B. mother
C. grandmother D. sister-in-law

33. In this question, four words have been given, of which three are alike in some way, and one is different. Find the odd one out.

A. mango B. orange
C. watermelon D. sugarcane

34. Complete the series:
10.5, 7.5, __?__, 3.0, 1.5, 0.5

A. 6.5 B. 6.0
C. 5.5 D. 5.0

35. Complete the series:
20, 33, 48, 65, 84, ____

A. 95 B. 105
C. 115 D. 135

36. Today is Monday. After 75 days, what day will it be?

A. Wednesday B. Thursday
C. Friday D. Saturday

37. Complete the series:
7, 11, 13, 17, 19, _____

A. 20 B. 21
C. 23 D. 27

38. Rohan and Rita are standing in a park facing each other. When the sun rises, Rita's shadow falls on the right side of Rohan. Which direction is Rita facing?

A. East B. West
C. North D. South

39. If in a code language, LIFE is written as GOAL and SUN is written as CUT, what will be the code for FINE?

A. FUEL B. TOAL
C. AOTL D. ADET

40. Arrange the following words in a sequence in which they appear in a dictionary.

A. Combination
B. Coagulation
C. Companion
D. Cooperation
E. Corruption

Choose the correct answer from the options given below:

A. B, D, C, A, E
B. B, A, C, D, E
C. A, C, D, E, B
D. A, D, C, E, B

41. Goa : India : : Ontario: ?

A. Canada B. USA
C. England D. Africa

42. FHJL : IKMO : : ? : QSUW

A. NPRT B. MOPR
C. LNPQ D. NOQS

43. Ask : Inquire : : Beautiful : ?

A. Splendid B. Ugly
C. Terrible D. Unpleasant

44. Approached : Departed : : Admit : ?

A. Repudiate B. Fail
C. Accept D. Retreat

45. 5 : 3125 : : 7: ?

A. 343 B. 2401
C. 16807 D. 117649

46. The average of eight numbers is 6. If each number is multiplied by 5, then, the average of the new set of numbers is

A. 25 B. 30
C. 35 D. 40

47. A train running at a speed of 360 km/hr passes a platform with a length twice that of the train in 30 sec. Find the length of the platform.

A. 3 km B. 2 km
C. 4 km D. 1 km

48. The simple interest on an amount is $\frac{16}{25}$ of the principal. Find the rate % PA if the time and rate are numerically equal.

A. 8% B. 4%
C. 12% D. 16%

49. Consider the series:

2, 3, 5, 7, 11, 13, 17, 19, 21, 23, 29

Find the number which is different from the other numbers.

A. 29 B. 23
C. 19 D. 21

50. Find the value of $\left(\sqrt[3]{\frac{125}{27}} - \sqrt[3]{\frac{512}{729}}\right) \div \sqrt[3]{\frac{64}{5832}}$.

A. 2.5 B. 3.5
C. 4.5 D. 5.5

51. What is the smallest number of five digits formed using 2, 4, 0, 3 and 5?

A. 02345 B. 20345
C. 23450 D. 20354

52. Each side of a square is increased by 20%. Find the percentage increase in its area.

A. 20% B. 25%
C. 36% D. 44%

53. $296 \times 296 - 204 \times 204 = ?$

A. 29600 B. 46000
C. 20400 D. 36000

54. What was the day of the week on 16th June 1998?

A. Sunday B. Monday
C. Tuesday D. Friday

55. $-224 + (-314) \times 9 = ?$

A. 3050 B. –3050
C. –4842 D. 4842

56. $-\sqrt{8} + \sqrt{128} - \sqrt{32}$ is equal to

A. $-2\sqrt{2}$ B. $2\sqrt{2}$
C. $-3\sqrt{2}$ D. $3\sqrt{2}$

57. A clock seen through a mirror shows quarter to three. What is the correct time shown on the clock?

A. 8:15 B. 9:15
C. 8:45 D. 9:45

58. If P consumes 1500 ml of milk every day. How many litres of milk will be consumed in 4 weeks?

A. 42 B. 40
C. 44 D. 36

59. Find the smallest among the following.

$\sqrt[4]{6}$, $\sqrt{2}$, $\sqrt[3]{4}$ and $\sqrt{3}$

A. $\sqrt[4]{6}$ B. $\sqrt{2}$
C. $\sqrt[3]{4}$ D. $\sqrt{3}$

60. The angle of depression of a point situated at a distance of 500 m from the base of a tower is 45°. The height of the tower is ______.

A. $\frac{500}{3}\sqrt{3}$ B. $500(\sqrt{3} + 1)$ m
C. $500\sqrt{3}$ m D. 500 m

61. Arrange the following in a logical order:

A. Delhi
B. India
C. Parliament
D. Asia
E. World

Choose the correct answer from the options given below:

A. C, A, B, D, E B. A, B, C, D, E
C. C, A, D, B, E D. A, B, D, E, C

62. Which of the following collections of letters will look the same in the mirror?

A. XOTVA B. XOTPA
C. XOTOX D. XAOTS

63. A cylinder is painted in 6 colours - Green, Blue, Yellow, Violet, Red and Orange. Three positions are shown below:

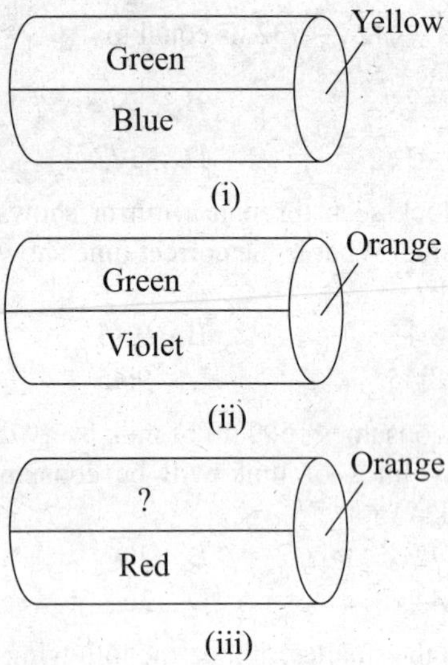

What is the missing colour?

A. Blue B. Green

C. Violet D. Yellow

64. Complete the pattern:

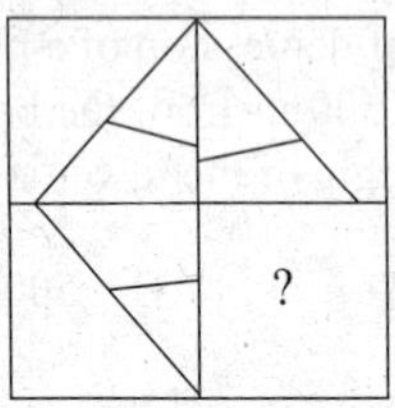

A. 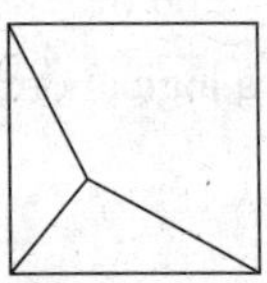 B. 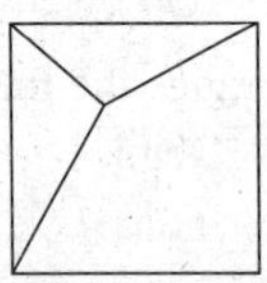

C. 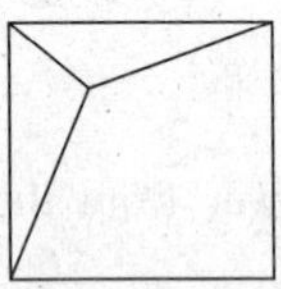 D. 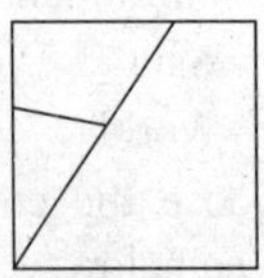

65. Find the area of the largest circle that can be drawn inside a rectangle with sides 8 m × 9 m.

A. 36 m^2 B. $50\frac{2}{7}$ m^2

C. $63\frac{9}{14}$ m^2 D. $201\frac{1}{7}$ m^2

66. Match **List I** with **List II**.

List I	List II
A. Car	I. Aviary
B. Aeroplane	II. Apiary
C. Bee	III. Garage
D. Birds	IV. Hangar

Choose the correct answer from the options given below:

A. A-III, B-IV, C-I, D-II

B. A-IV, B-III, C-II, D-I

C. A-III, B-IV, C-II, D-I

D. A-III, B-II, C-IV, D-I

67. Consider the figures:

A. 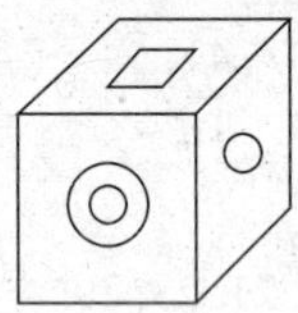 B. 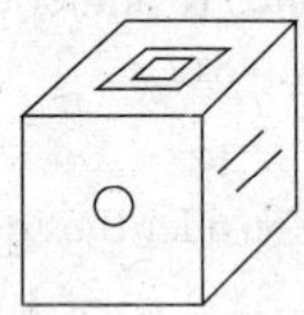

C. 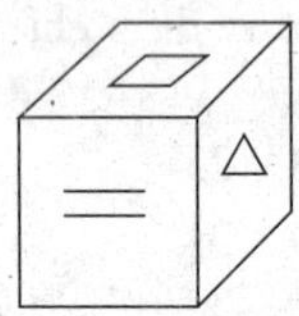 D. 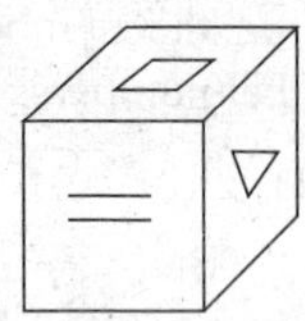

The symbol at the bottom of (D) is:

A.  B. 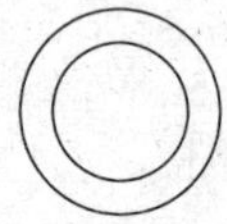

C. 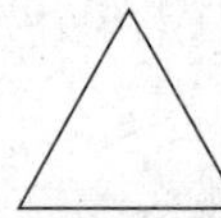 D. 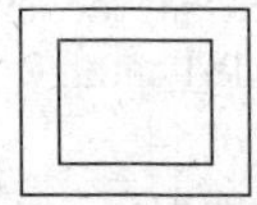

68. Choose the word least related to the word 'KNOWLEDGE':

A. teacher B. wisdom

C. learning D. power

69. Which Venn diagram correctly shows: Carrots, Food, Vegetables?

A. 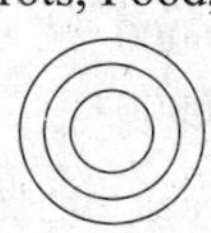 B. 

C. 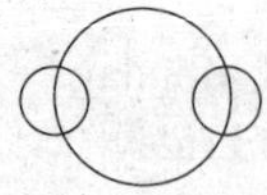 D. 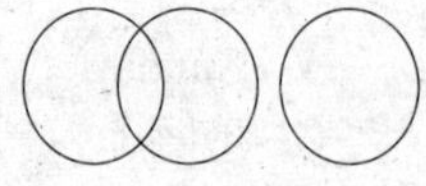

70. In the following question, arguments are followed by four diagrams.
Choose the correct diagram that shows/ represents the argument correctly.
All boys are houses.
No houses are huts.
No huts are boys.

A.
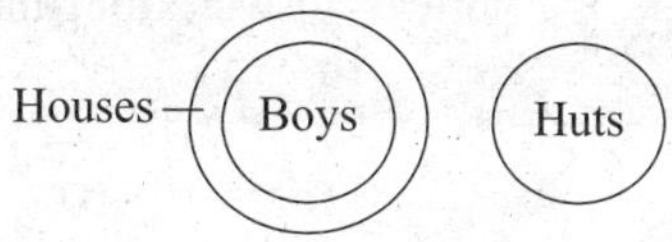

B.
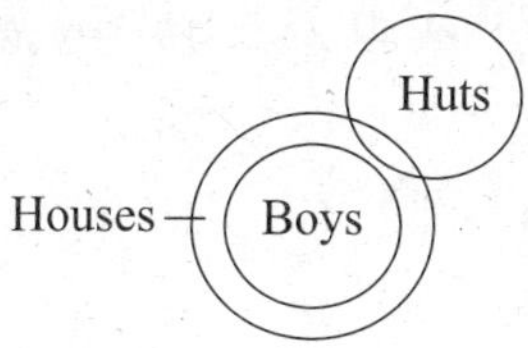

C.
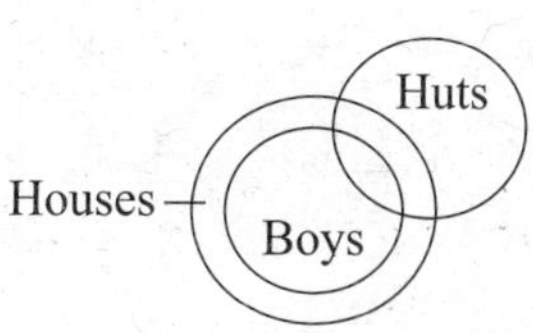

D.
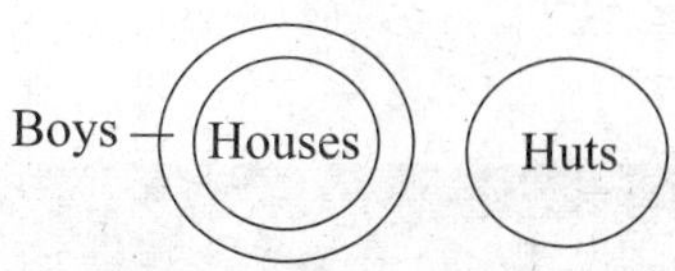

71. Choose the correct diagram which shows/ represents the arguments correctly.
No fishes are birds.
All pens are fish.
No pens are birds.

A.
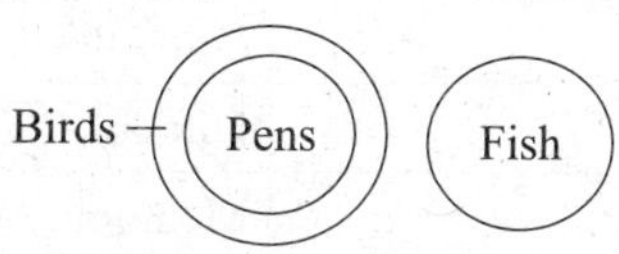

B.
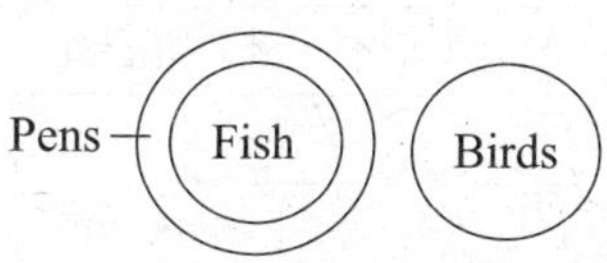

C.
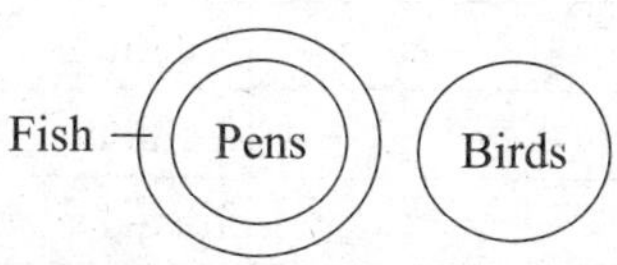

D.
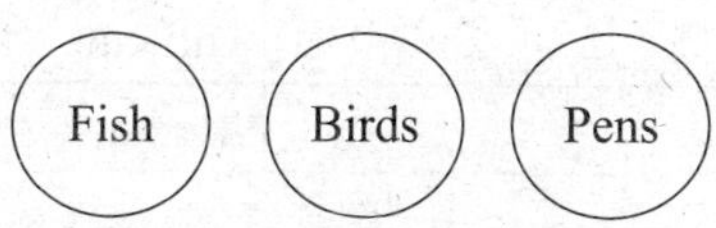

72. Choose the correct representation of the argument.
No students are illiterate.
All animals are illiterate.
No animals are students.

A.
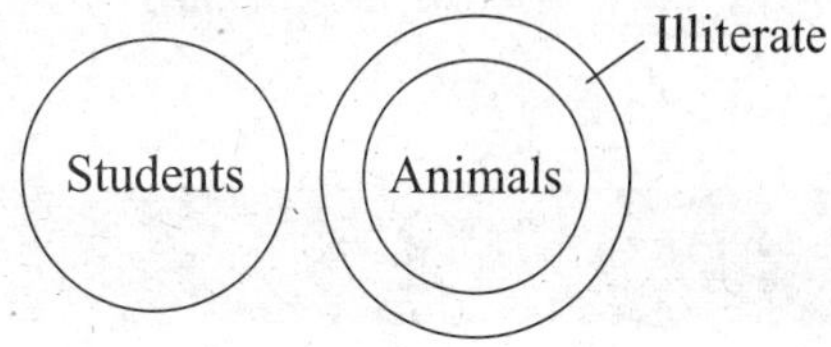

B.
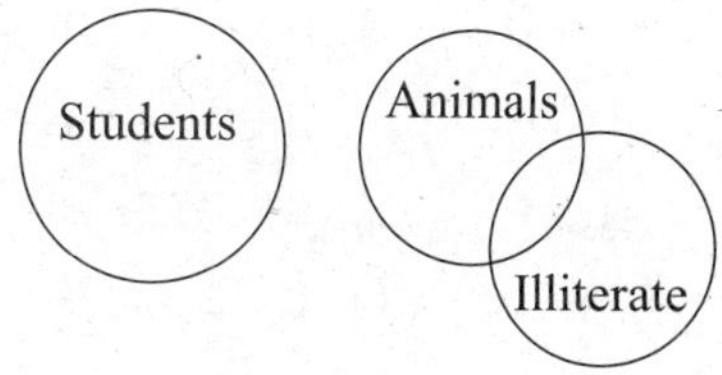

C.
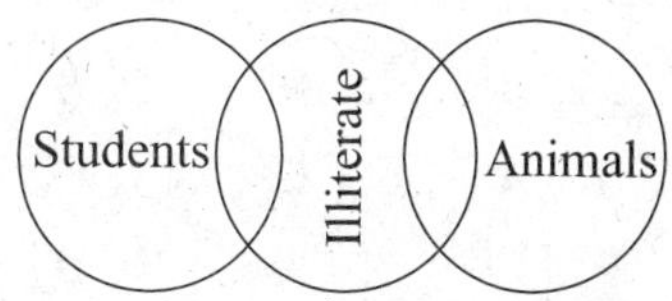

D.
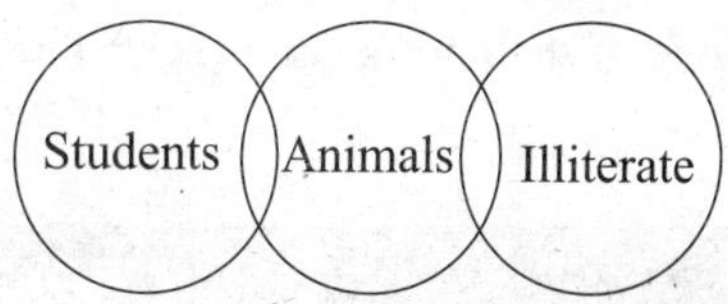

The following table shows the production of food grains (in million tonnes) in a state of India from 2001–2005. Analyse the table and answer questions 73–75.

Production (in Million Tonnes)

Years	Wheat	Rice	Maize	Grams	Total
2001	570	170	160	350	1250
2002	610	220	224	400	1454
2003	560	240	228	425	1453
2004	670	310	400	435	1815
2005	870	250	320	520	1960
Total	**3280**	**1190**	**1332**	**2130**	**7932**

73. During 2005, the percentage decrease in the production of Maize as against the previous year was
A. 25% B. 20%
C. 50% D. 40%

74. The increase in the production of Grams (over the previous years) was minimum during the year

A. 2002 B. 2003
C. 2004 D. 2005

75. During 2005, the percentage increase in production of Wheat over the previous year was

A. 26.47% B. 29.85%
C. 25.85% D. 22.98%

Answer Key

1. **B**	2. **D**	3. **D**	4. **D**	5. **B**	6. **D**	7. **A**	8. **D**	9. **B**	10. **C**
11. **C**	12. **A**	13. **B**	14. **A**	15. **B**	16. **B**	17. **C**	18. **B**	19.* None	
20. **B**	21. **C**	22. **B**	23. **A**	24. **A**	25. **B**	26. **B**	27. **C**	28. **C**	29. **D**
30. **C**	31. **D**	32. **B**	33. **D**	34. **D**	35. **B**	36. **D**	37. **C**	38. **C**	39. **C**
40. **B**	41. **A**	42. **A**	43. **A**	44. **A**	45. **C**	46. **B**	47. **B**	48. **A**	49. **D**
50. **B**	51. **B**	52. **D**	53. **B**	54. **C**	55. **B**	56. **B**	57. **B**	58. **A**	59. **B**
60. **D**	61. **A**	62. **C**	63. **C**	64. **D**	65. **B**	66. **C**	67. **D**	68. **A**	69. **A**
70. **A**	71. **C**	72. **A**	73. **B**	74. **C**	75. **B**				

***19. None of the options is correct. The correct answer is 50/99 kmph.**

Classification of Questions

Question No.	Subject	Topic	Level of Difficulty
1.	General Awareness	Sports	Easy
2.	General Awareness	Books & Authors	Difficult
3.	General Awareness	Polity	Difficult
4.	General Awareness	Current Affairs	Difficult
5.	General Awareness	Science & Technology	Medium
6.	General Awareness	Science (Physics)	Difficult
7.	General Awareness	History	Difficult
8.	General Awareness	Geography	Medium
9.	General Awareness	Current Affairs	Medium
10.	General Awareness	Miscellaneous	Difficult
11.	General Awareness	Computers	Easy
12.	General Awareness	Polity	Difficult
13.	General Awareness	Miscellaneous	Medium

Question No.	Subject	Topic	Level of Difficulty
14.	General Awareness	Economics	Easy
15.	General Awareness	Polity	Easy
16.	Quantitative Aptitude	Profit, Loss & Discount	Medium
17.	Quantitative Aptitude	Profit, Loss & Discount	Medium
18.	Quantitative Aptitude	Pipes & Cisterns	Easy
19.	Quantitative Aptitude	Boats & Streams	Medium
20.	Quantitative Aptitude	Boats & Streams	Easy
21.	Quantitative Aptitude	Mensuration	Difficult
22.	Quantitative Aptitude	Ratios	Easy
23.	Quantitative Aptitude	Numbers (HCF)	Easy
24.	Quantitative Aptitude	Time, Speed & Distance	Medium
25.	Quantitative Aptitude	Ratios	Easy
26.	Quantitative Aptitude	Percentages	Easy
27.	Quantitative Aptitude	Age-based problems	Easy
28.	Quantitative Aptitude	Averages	Easy
29.	Quantitative Aptitude	Averages	Easy
30.	Quantitative Aptitude	Time, Speed & Distance	Easy
31.	Reasoning	BODMAS	Easy
32.	Reasoning	Blood Relations	Easy
33.	Reasoning	Odd-one-out	Medium
34.	Reasoning	Number Series	Easy
35.	Reasoning	Number Series	Easy
36.	Quantitative Aptitude	Calendars	Easy
37.	Reasoning	Number Series	Easy
38.	Reasoning	Directions	Easy
39.	Reasoning	Coding	Easy
40.	Reasoning	Dictionary Order	Easy
41.	General Awareness	Analogy (Geography-based)	Easy
42.	Reasoning	Coding	Easy
43.	Reasoning	Analogy (word-based)	Easy
44.	Reasoning	Analogy (word-based)	Easy
45.	Reasoning	Analogy (number-based)	Easy
46.	Quantitative Aptitude	Averages	Easy

Question No.	Subject	Topic	Level of Difficulty
47.	Quantitative Aptitude	Time, Speed & Distance	Medium
48.	Quantitative Aptitude	Simple Interest	Medium
49.	Reasoning	Wrong Number Series	Easy
50.	Quantitative Aptitude	Simplification	Easy
51.	Quantitative Aptitude	Numbers	Easy
52.	Quantitative Aptitude	Percentages	Easy
53.	Quantitative Aptitude	Simplification	Easy
54.	Quantitative Aptitude	Calendars	Medium
55.	Quantitative Aptitude	Simplification	Easy
56.	Quantitative Aptitude	Simplification	Easy
57.	Reasoning	Mirror Image	Easy
58.	Quantitative Aptitude	Unitary Method	Easy
59.	Quantitative Aptitude	Irrational Numbers	Easy
60.	Quantitative Aptitude	Trigonometry (Heights & Distances)	Easy
61.	Reasoning	Words in a Logical Sequence	Easy
62.	Reasoning	Mirror Image	Easy
63.	Reasoning	Die-based problems	Medium
64.	Reasoning	Non-verbal	Easy
65.	Quantitative Aptitude	Mensuration	Medium
66.	Reasoning	Miscellaneous	Medium
67.	Reasoning	Die-based problem	Easy
68.	Reasoning	Miscellaneous	Easy
69.	Reasoning	Venn-diagram	Medium
70.	Reasoning	Syllogism	Easy
71.	Reasoning	Syllogism	Easy
72.	Reasoning	Syllogism	Easy
73.	Data Interpretation	Table-based	Easy
74.	Data Interpretation	Table-based	Easy
75.	Data Interpretation	Table-based	Easy

No. of questions on Quantitative Aptitude: 30

No. of questions on General Awareness: 16

No. of questions on Reasoning: 26

No. of questions on Data Interpretation: 3

Explanation to Select Questions

1. Update: When this exam was conducted, the Mumbai Indians had 5 titles and the Chennai Super Kings 4. Gujarat Titans won the title in 2022, and the Chennai Super Kings won their 5th title in 2023. Thus, at this stage, the Chennai Super Kings and the Mumbai Indians have 5 titles each. The answer is Option B (as per the status in 2022).

3. Update: The governor of Himachal Pradesh is Shiv Pratap Shukla now. Option D was the answer as per the status in July 2022.

4. As per the Mercer Cost of Living Rankings 2021, the world's most expensive city for foreign workers was Ashgabat, the capital of Turkmenistan.

Hence, Option D.

Update: As per these rankings of 2023, Hong Kong is the world's most expensive city for foreign workers.

8. Tirich Mir is the highest peak in the Hindu Kush Mountain system. Kilimanjaro is the highest mountain peak in Africa. The answer is Option D.

10. The World Students' Day is celebrated on 15 October every year as that is the birthday of Dr. A.P.J. Abdul Kalam. This day does not have much recognition outside India. The answer is Option C.

12. Maria Estela Peron became the first female president of any country in the world when she became the president of Argentina in 1974.

Sirimavo Bandaranaike became the first female prime minister of any country in the world when she became the prime minister of Sri Lanka (Ceylon then) in 1960.

In 1969, Golda Meir became the first female prime minister of Israel.

Hence, Option A.

Note: Option C is a trap.

13. In 1911, Roald Amundsen was the first to reach the South Pole. Christopher Columbus discovered America in 1492. Marco Polo reached China in 1271. In 1909, Robert Peary became the first person to reach the North Pole.

Hence, Option B.

17. Let the cost price of the article be 100.

Therefore, the selling price must be 110 (as there is a 10% profit).

Therefore, the printed price $= \dfrac{110 \times 100}{100 - 10}$ (as there was a 10% discount).

$= \dfrac{110 \times 100}{90} = \dfrac{1100}{9}$.

Therefore, the ratio of the printed price and the cost price $= \dfrac{1100}{9 \times 100} = \dfrac{11}{9} = 11{:}9$.

Hence, Option C.

Alternative: Check with the options.

Option A: The printed price of 11 and 10% discount $\Rightarrow$ selling price of $11 - 1.1 = 9.9$.

As the cost price is 7 here, a profit of $9.9 - 7 = 2.9$ on 7 is much more than 10%, and hence, it cannot be the answer.

Similarly, in Option B, there is a profit of 1.9 on 8 and this also is much more than 10%.

In Option C, there is a profit of 0.9 on 9, and that is 10%. Hence, this is the answer.

18. A. There is an inlet, but no outlet. Hence, filling is possible.

B. Here, the inlet fills at 15 litres/minute and the outlet 1 litre/minute. Therefore, it is a net inlet at $15 - 1 = 14$ litres/minute and hence, the tank will be filled.

C. Here the total inlet is $2 \times 4 = 8$ litres/minute and the outlet is 500 ml $\times$ 60 = 30 litres/minute.

Hence, overall, there is an outlet of $30 - 8 = 22$ litre/minute. and hence, the tank will not be filled

D. Here, there is an outlet of $4 - 2 = 2$ litre/minute, and hence, the tank will not be filled.

Hence, Option B.

19. Let the speed of Viraj in still water be x km/hr and the speed of the stream be y km/hr.

We have,

$$\frac{24}{x+y}+\frac{36}{x-y}=12\frac{1}{2}=\frac{25}{2}$$

$$\text{or, } 12\left(\frac{2}{x+y}+\frac{3}{x-y}\right)=\frac{25}{2}$$

$$\text{or, } \frac{2}{x+y}+\frac{3}{x-y}=\frac{25}{24} \qquad \text{(i)}$$

and

$$\frac{36}{x+y}+\frac{24}{x-y}=12$$

$$\text{or, } 12\left(\frac{3}{x+y}+\frac{2}{x-y}\right)=12$$

$$\text{or, } \frac{3}{x+y}+\frac{2}{x-y}=\frac{12}{12}=1 \qquad \text{(ii)}$$

multiplying equation (i) with 3 and equation (ii) with 2, we get:

$$\frac{6}{x+y}+\frac{9}{x-y}=\frac{25}{8} \qquad \text{(iii)}$$

$$\frac{6}{x+y}+\frac{4}{x-y}=2 \qquad \text{(iv)}$$

Subtracting (iv) from (iii), we get,

$$\frac{5}{x-y}=\frac{25}{8}-2=\frac{9}{8}$$

$$\text{or, } x-y=\frac{8\times 5}{9}=\frac{40}{9} \qquad \text{(v)}$$

Putting the value of $x-y$ in (ii), we get

$$\frac{3}{x+y}+\frac{2}{\frac{40}{9}}=1$$

$$\text{or, } \frac{3}{x+y}+\frac{9}{20}=1$$

$$\text{or, } \frac{3}{x+y}=1-\frac{9}{20}=\frac{11}{20}$$

$$\text{or, } x+y=\frac{20\times 3}{11}=\frac{60}{11} \qquad \text{(vi)}$$

Subtracting (v) from (vi), we get,

$$2y=\frac{60}{11}-\frac{40}{9}=\frac{540-440}{99}$$

$$\text{or, } 2y=\frac{100}{99}$$

$$\text{or, } y=\frac{50}{99} \text{ km/hr.}$$

None of the options is correct.

20. Here, the downstream speed = 20 + 5 = 25 km/hr. The upstream speed = 20 – 5 = 15 km/hr.

Therefore, the required time $=\frac{50}{25}+\frac{30}{15}=$ $2+2=4$ hours.

Hence, Option B.

21.

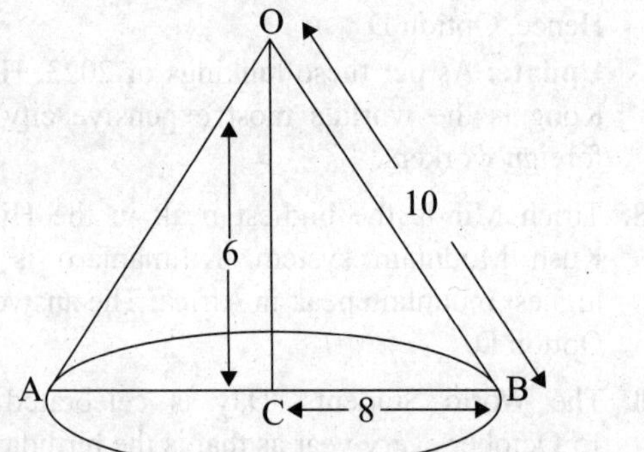

Let OCB be the right-angled triangle with base OC = 6, perpendicular CB = 8 and hypotenuse OB = 10.

When we rotate the triangle along the base, the height of the cone = 6 and the base radius of the cone = 8.

The volume of the cone $=\frac{1}{3}\pi 8^2\times 6$

$$=\frac{1}{3}\pi\times 64\times 6$$

$$=128\pi=128\times 3.14$$

$$=401.92 \text{ cm}^2.$$

Hence, Option C.

22. Let the numbers be x and y.

We have, $x+y=44$ (i)

and

$x - y = 16$ (ii)

Adding (i) & (ii), we get,

$2x = 60$ or, $x = 30$

Hence, $y = 44 - 30 = 14$.

Now, the ratio of the numbers $= \frac{30}{14}$

$= \frac{15}{7} = 15{:}7$.

Hence, Option B.

Shortcut: As the sum of the numbers is 44. The sum of the numerator and the denominator of their ratio (in the simplest form) should be a factor of 44, which is only in Option B $\left(15 + 7 = \frac{44}{2}\right)$.

23. 1 metre and 25 cm = 125 cm, and 1 metre and 30 cm = 130 cm.

We are looking for the HCF of 20, 90, 125 and 130.

$20 = 2^2 \times 5$,

$90 = 2 \times 3^2 \times 5$,

$125 = 5^3$ and

$130 = 2 \times 5 \times 13$.

So, their HCF is 5.

Hence, Option A.

24. Of the first 200 km of her journey, the woman travelled 150 km at a speed of 60 km/hr and 50 km at a speed of 25 km/hr.

The total time taken by the woman for the first 200 km $= \frac{150}{60} + \frac{50}{25} = \frac{5}{2} + 2 = 4.5$ hours.

Therefore, her average speed $= \frac{200}{4.5} =$ 44.44 km/hr.

Hence, Option A.

25. Let Y be paid $100a$ per week.

Therefore, X will be paid $125a$ per week.

Now, $100a + 125a = 225a = 4500$.

or, $a = \frac{4500}{225} = 20$.

Therefore, Y is paid $100a = 100 \times 20 = 2000$ per week.

Hence, Option B.

26. Let's assume that the price of the 100 units of cooking gas was ₹100 initially.

After the increase, 100 units cost ₹125.

But the family wants to spend only ₹100.

For ₹125, 100 units are available.

Therefore, for ₹100, $\frac{100}{125} \times 100 = 80$ units are available.

Hence the family needs to reduce its use of cooking gas by 20%.

Hence, Option B.

27. Let the ages of Sita and Prakash be $5x$ and $8x$, respectively 2 years ago.

Therefore, their present ages are $5x + 2$ and $8x + 2$

Their ages after 4 years will be $5x + 2 + 4 = 5x + 6$ and $8x + 2 + 4 = 8x + 6$.

We have, $\frac{5x + 6}{8x + 6} = \frac{2}{3}$ or, $15x + 18 = 16x + 12$.

or, $16x - 15x = 18 - 12$.

or, $x = 6$.

Therefore, the present age of Sita $= 5x + 2 = 5 \times 6 + 2 = 32$ years.

Hence, Option C.

Shortcut: As the ratio of the ages of Sita and Prakash was 5:8 two years ago, the present age of Sita should be 2 more than a multiple of 5 (of the form $5k + 2$, where k is a natural number), and only Option C ($32 = 5 \times 6 + 2$) is of that form.

28. The sum of the first 5 primes $= 2 + 3 + 5 + 7 + 11 = 28$.

The average of the first 5 primes $= \frac{28}{5} = 5.6$

The sum of the first 5 natural numbers $= 1 + 2 + 3 + 4 + 5 = 15$.

The average of the first 5 natural numbers $= \frac{15}{5} = 3$.

Hence, Option C.

Note: The sum of the first n natural numbers is $\frac{n(n+1)}{2}$,

The average of the first n natural numbers is $\frac{\frac{n(n+1)}{2}}{n} = \frac{n+1}{2}$.

Using these for the first 5 natural numbers:

their sum $= \frac{5 \times 6}{2} = 15$ and

their average $= \frac{5+1}{2} = 3$.

29. The sum of the first 5 odd numbers = $1 + 3 + 5 + 7 + 9 = 25$.

The average of the first 5 odd numbers $= \frac{25}{5} = 5$.

The sum of the first 5 even numbers = $2 + 4 + 6 + 8 + 10 = 30$.

The average of the first 5 even numbers $= \frac{30}{5} = 6$.

Therefore, the required ratio = 5 : 6.

Hence, Option D.

Note: Even if you take the ratio of the sum of the first 5 odd numbers, and the sum of the first 5 even numbers, the ratio will still be the same as the denominator is the same in both the cases when you calculate the averages.

Also, the sum of the first n odd numbers is n^2, and the sum of the first n even numbers is $n(n+1)$.

30. There are $60 \times 60 = 3600$ seconds in an hour.

Now, in 5 seconds, the bus travels 3 km.

Therefore, in 3600 seconds, it travels $\frac{3}{5} \times 3600 = 2160$ km.

Therefore, the speed of the bus = 2160 km/hr.

Hence, Option C.

31. $15 - 5 \div 5 \times 20 + 10$

$= 15 \times 5 + 5 - 20 \div 10$

$= 75 + 5 - 2$ (We have to follow the BODMAS rule.)

$= 80 - 2 = 78$.

Hence, Option D.

32.

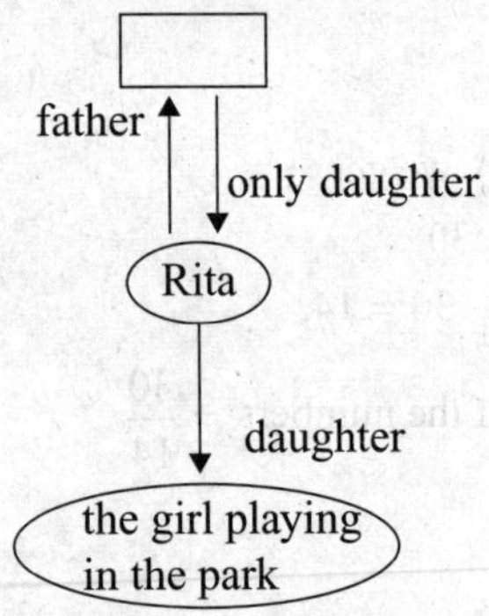

If Rita is a woman, she is the only daughter of her father and the girl in the park is her daughter.

Hence, Option B.

If Rita is a man, he is the maternal uncle of the girl playing in the park, but 'maternal uncle' is NOT among the options.

34. The terms from the right:

$1.5 = 0.5 + 1.0$

$3.0 = 1.5 + 1.5$

$5.0 = 3.0 + 2.0$

$7.5 = 5.0 + 2.5$

$10.5 = 7.5 + 3.0$

Hence, the difference between the consecutive terms increases by 0.5.

Hence, Option D.

35. 20, 33, 48, 65, 84, (105)

+13 +15 +17 +19 +21

Hence, Option B.

36. $75 = 7 \times 10 + 5$

Therefore, there are 5 odd days in 75.

Hence, after 75 days, it will be a day that falls 5 days after a Monday, a Saturday.

Hence, Option D.

37. 7, 11, 13, 17, 19, 23

These all are consecutive prime numbers.

Hence, Option C.

38.

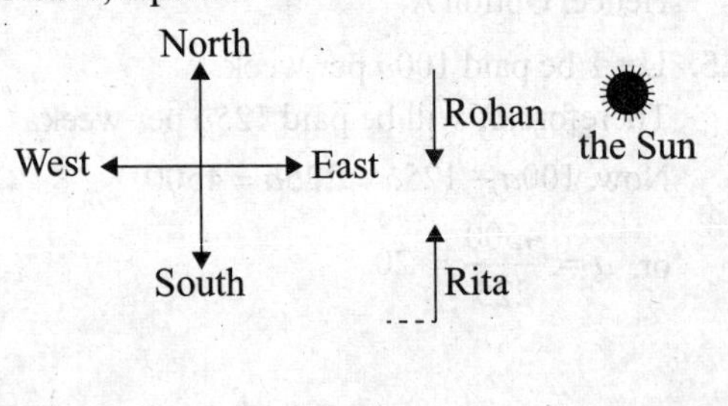

The sun rises in the east. Rita's shadow will be towards the west and it would be on the right side of Rohan only if Rohan is facing the south and thus Rita is facing the north.
Hence, Option C.

39. L I F E → G O A L; S U N → C U T

F I N E → A O T L

Hence, Option C.

41. Goa is a province in India, and Ontario is a province in Canada.
Hence, Option A.

42. F H J L: 6 8 10 12 (+2 +2 +2); I K M O: 9 11 13 15 (+2 +2 +2); +3

N P R T: 14 16 18 20 (+2 +2 +2); Q S U W: 17 19 21 23 (+2 +2 +2); +3

Hence, Option A.

43. 'Ask' and 'inquire' are similar. The word 'beautiful' has a positive connotation, as does 'splendid'. Option A is the best choice here, as the words in the remaining options have negative connotations.

44. 'Approached' and 'departed' are opposites, as are 'admit' and 'repudiate'.
Hence, Option A.
Repudiate means to refuse to accept (admit).

45. $3125 = 5^5$
$? = 7^5 = 16807$
Hence, Option C.

46. If each number gets multiplied by 5, the average will also get multiplied by 5.
Therefore, the new average $= 6 \times 5 = 30$.
Hence, Option B.

47. The speed of the train = 360 km/hr.
$= \dfrac{360 \times 1000}{3600} = 100$ m/sec.
The distance travelled by the train in 30 sec = $100 \times 30 = 3000$ m.
If the length of the train is x, then the length of the platform is $2x$.
$x + 2x = 3x = 3000$ m
$\Rightarrow 2x = 2000$ m = 2km.
Hence, Option B.

48. Let the principal be p, rate r and time t.
We have, $r = t$.

Also, the simple interest $= \dfrac{16p}{25}$.

The simple interest $= \dfrac{prt}{100}$

or, $\dfrac{16p}{25} = \dfrac{p \times r \times r}{100}$

or, $r^2 = \dfrac{16 \times 100}{25} = 64$.

or, $r = 8$.
Therefore, the rate of interest is 8% per annum.
Hence, Option A.

49. Only $21 = (3 \times 7)$ is a composite number in the series.
Hence, Option D.

50. $\left(\sqrt[3]{\dfrac{125}{27}} - \sqrt[3]{\dfrac{512}{729}}\right) \div \sqrt[3]{\dfrac{64}{5832}}$

$= \left(\sqrt[3]{\dfrac{5^3}{3^3}} - \sqrt[3]{\dfrac{8^3}{9^3}}\right) \div \sqrt[3]{\dfrac{4^3}{18^3}}$

$= \left(\dfrac{5}{3} - \dfrac{8}{9}\right) \div \dfrac{4}{18}$

$= \dfrac{15-8}{9} \div \dfrac{2}{9} = \dfrac{7}{2} = 3.5.$

Hence, Option B.

52. Let the side of the square be x initially.
$\Rightarrow$ its area $= x^2$.
After the increase of 20% in the length of the side, the new side $= 1.2x$

$\Rightarrow$ the new area = $(1.2x)^2$

$= 1.44\, x^2$

Percentage increase $= \dfrac{1.44x^2 - x^2}{x^2} \times 100$

$= \dfrac{0.44x^2 \times 100}{x^2} = 44.$

Hence, Option D.

Alternative: You can take two successive increases of 20% and 20% to get $20 + 20 + \dfrac{20 \times 20}{100} = 44\%$ as the answer.

53. $296 \times 296 - 204 \times 204$

$= 296^2 - 204^2 = (296 + 204)(296 - 204)$

$= 500 \times 92 = 46000.$

Hence, Option B.

54. The first of January of years 1, 401, 801, 1201, 1601 and 2001 were all Mondays.

The number of odd days between 1 January 1998 and 1 January 2001 = 4

(2 for the 2 non-leap years and 2 for the leap year 2000).

Therefore, 1 January 1998 must have been a day that falls 4 days before a Monday, a Thursday.

The number of odd days between 1 January 1998 and 16 June 1998 = 2 (in January) + 0 (in February) + 3 (in March) + 2 (in April) + 3 (in May) + 2 (June)

= 12, which is effectively 12 – 7 = 5.

Therefore, 16 June 1998 must be a day that falls 5 days after a Thursday, a Tuesday.

Hence, Option C.

55. $-224 + (-314) \times 9 = -224 - 2826 = -3050.$

Hence, Option B.

56. $-\sqrt{8} + \sqrt{128} - \sqrt{32}$

$= -\sqrt{4 \times 2} + \sqrt{64 \times 2} - \sqrt{16 \times 2}$

$= -2\sqrt{2} + 8\sqrt{2} - 4\sqrt{2} = 8\sqrt{2} - 6\sqrt{2} = 2\sqrt{2}.$

Hence, Option B.

57. The time shown in the mirror is a quarter to three (02:45).

The actual time = 12:00 – (02:45) = 9:15.

Hence, Option B.

58. The number of days in 4 weeks = $4 \times 7 = 28$.

The volume of milk consumed in a day = 1500 ml = 1.5 litre.

Therefore, the volume of milk consumed in 28 days = $28 \times 1.5 = 42$ litres.

Hence, Option A.

59.

$\sqrt[4]{6} = (6)^{\frac{1}{4}}$

$\sqrt{2} = (2)^{\frac{1}{2}}$

$\sqrt[3]{4} = (4)^{\frac{1}{3}}$

$\sqrt{3} = (3)^{\frac{1}{2}}$

Now, $\left(\sqrt[4]{6}\right)^{12} = \left(6^{\frac{1}{4}}\right)^{12} = 6^3 = 216.$

$\left(\sqrt{2}\right)^{12} = \left(2^{\frac{1}{2}}\right)^{12} = 2^6 = 64.$

$\left(\sqrt[3]{4}\right)^{12} = \left(4^{\frac{1}{3}}\right)^{12} = 4^4 = 256.$

$\left(\sqrt{3}\right)^{12} = \left(3^{\frac{1}{2}}\right)^{12} = 3^6 = 729.$

Therefore,

$\sqrt{3} > \sqrt[3]{4} > \sqrt[4]{6} > \sqrt{2}.$

Hence, Option B.

60.

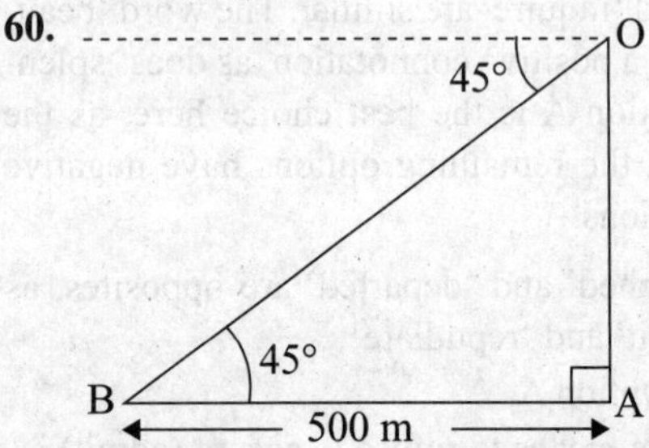

Let OA be the tower and B the point for which the angle of depression from the top of the tower is 45°.

In ΔOAB,

$\tan 45° = \dfrac{OA}{AB}$, or, $1 = \dfrac{OA}{500}$, or, OA = 500.

Hence, the height of the tower is 500 metres.

Hence, Option D.

63. Let's keep the Orange on the right-hand side in figures (i) and (ii).

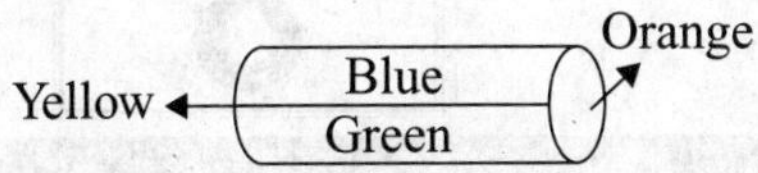

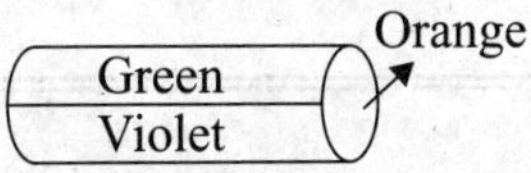

If we open the cylinder, keeping the Orange base on the right, it would appear like this:

Red
Blue
Green
Violet

Therefore, we have Violet in place of ?.

Note: Option A is a good trap.

Blue would be above red if we keep the yellow base on the right-hand side.

Hence, Option C.

65.

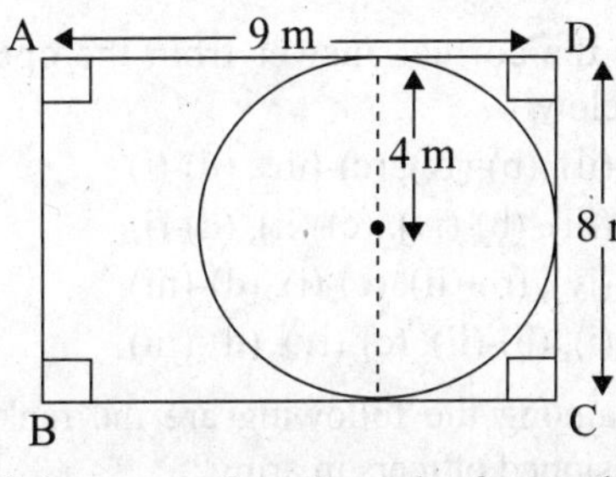

It becomes clear from the figure above that the radius of such a circle will be $= \frac{8}{2} = 4$ m.

Area of the circle $= \pi \times 4^2 = \frac{22}{7} \times 16 = \frac{352}{7}$

$= 50\frac{2}{7}$ m^2.

Hence, Option B.

Please refer to the table below for explanations of questions 73-75.

Production (in Million Tonnes)

Years	Wheat	Rice	Maize	Grams	Total
2001	570	170	160	350	1250
2002	610	220	224	400	1454
2003	560	240	228	425	1448
2004	670	310	400	435	1820
2005	870	250	320	520	1960
Total	3280	1190	1332	2130	7932

73. The production of maize in 2004 = 400.

The production of maize in 2005 = 320.

Therefore, the percentage reduction is $\frac{400 - 320}{400} \times 100 = 20$.

Hence, Option B.

74. The increase in the production of Grams in 2002 = 400 – 350 = 50.

The increase in the production of Grams in 2003 = 425 – 400 = 25.

The increase in the production of Grams in 2004 = 435 – 425 = 10.

The increase in the production of Grams in 2005 = 520 – 435 = 85.

Thus, we see that the increase in production of Grams over the previous year was the least in 2004.

Hence, Option C.

75. The production of wheat in 2004 = 670.

The production of wheat in 2005 = 870.

The percentage increase in 2005 over 2004

$= \frac{870 - 670}{670} \times 100 = \frac{200 \times 100}{670}$

= 29.85 (approx.)

Hence, Option B.

CUET UG 2022
General Test

August 8

Instructions:

1. You need to attempt any 60 out of the 75 questions in 60 minutes.
2. You get 5 marks for a correct response and –1 for an incorrect one. However, there is no reward or penalty for a question not attempted.

1. Which country is known as the "Land of the Rising Sun"?

A. Korea B. Japan
C. Finland D. China

2. Arrange the following days in the order of the date of observance in India.

(a) National Good Governance Day
(b) Armed Forces Flag Day
(c) Vijay Diwas
(d) Hindi Day
(e) Teachers' Day

Choose the correct answer from the options given below.

A. (c), (e), (b), (d), (a)
B. (e), (d), (b), (c), (a)
C. (e), (d), (c), (b), (a)
D. (d), (b), (e), (c), (a)

3. Which country successfully launched a new satellite named Shijian-21?

A. South Korea B. Pakistan
C. China D. UAE

4. The Reserve Bank of India has authorised ______ to collect direct taxes for the Central Board of Direct Taxes (CBDT).

A. Karur Vyasa Bank (KVB)
B. ICICI Bank
C. HDFC Bank
D. Axis Bank

5. Match the **List I** with **List II**.

List I (Country)	List II (Capital)
a. Belarus	i. Jerusalem
b. Angola	ii. Budapest
c. Hungary	iii. Minsk
d. Israel	iv. Luanda

Choose the correct answer from the options given below.

A. (a)-(ii), (b)-(iv), (c)-(iii), (d)-(i)
B. (a)-(iii), (b)-(iv), (c)-(ii), (d)-(i)
C. (a)-(iv), (b)-(ii), (c)-(i), (d)-(iii)
D. (a)-(i), (b)-(ii), (c)-(iv), (d)-(iii)

6. Which among the following are the ranks of commissioned officers in army?

(a) General
(b) Commodore
(c) Colonel
(d) Captain
(e) Group Captain

Choose the correct answer from the options given below.

A. (a), (c) and (d) only
B. (b), (c) and (e) only
C. (a), (b) and (d) only
D. (c), (d) and (e) only

7. Which among the following are the parts of the forebrain?

(a) Cerebrum
(b) Cerebellum
(c) Medulla Oblongata
(d) Hypothalamus
(e) Diencephalon

Choose the correct answer from the options given below.

A. (a), (d) and (e) only
B. (a), (c) and (e) only
C. (b), (c) and (d) only
D. (a), (b) and (d) only

8. Which among the following enzymes is required to digest protein?

A. Disaccharides B. Trypsin
C. Amylase D. Lipase

9. What is the name of the largest diamond in the world?

A. Cullinan B. Kohinoor
C. Sergio D. Woyie River

10. Which among the following countries have a lion on their national emblem?

(a) Spain
(b) Belgium
(c) Norway
(d) France
(e) Netherlands

Choose the correct answer from the options given below:

A. (a), (c) and (d) only
B. (a), (b), (c) and (e) only
C. (a), (b) and (d) only
D. (c), (b) and (e) only

11. The first Field Marshal of India was:

A. General KM Cariappa
B. General SHFJ Manekshaw
C. General V P Malik
D. General Bipin Rawat

12. Which team has won the men's cricket world cup the most number of times?

A. West Indies B. India
C. England D. Australia

13. Find the correct option.

$M \times N : 13 \times 14 :: F \times R : ?$

A. 7×19 B. 5×17
C. 14×15 D. 6×18

14. _________ transforms source code into the machine-readable code by converting into line by line.

A. Register B. Compiler
C. Cache Memory D. Interpreter

15. Match **List I** with **List II**.

List I	List II
a. Amartya Sen	i. Dreams from My Father
b. Amrita Pritam	ii. The Argumentative Indian
c. Aung San Suu Kyi	iii. Death of a City
d. Barack Obama	iv. Freedom from Fear

Choose the correct answer from the options given below:

A. a-ii, b-iii, c-iv, d-i
B. a-iii, b-iv, c-i, d-ii
C. a-iv, b-ii, c-i, d-iii
D. a-i, b-ii, c-iv, d-iii

16. The National Rail University has been established in India at

A. Gorakhpur B. Varanasi
C. Malda D. Vadodara

17. Find the number of rectangles in the figure below:

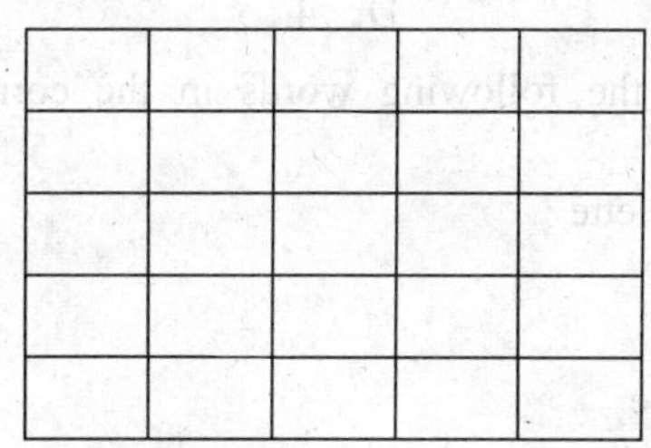

A. 25 B. 125
C. 225 D. 55

18. If the time appears in the mirror as 11:09, what time is it in the clock?

A. 1:51 B. 12:09
C. 12:51 D. 1:09

19. Identify the diagram that best represents the relationship among:
Men, Women, Human

A. 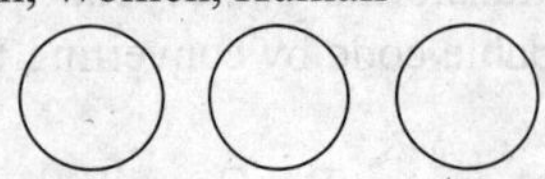

B. 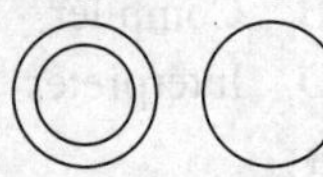

C. 

D. 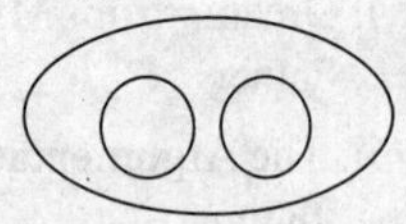

20. In the following diagram, the circle represents the police, the triangle represents the corrupt, the square represents the poet, and the rectangle represents the married.

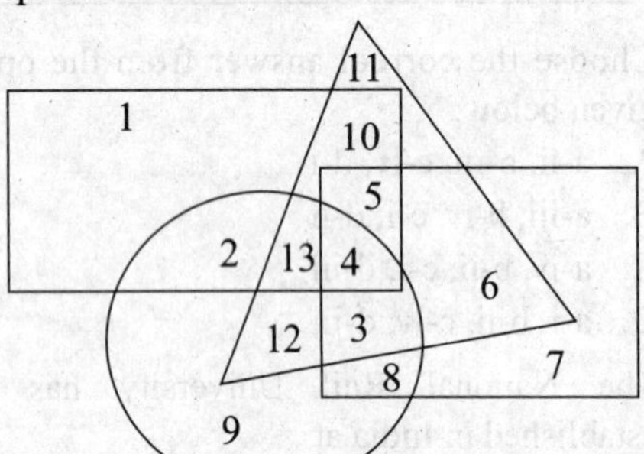

The number of unmarried police officers who are not corrupt but are poets is
A. 8 B. 9
C. 2 D. 4

21. Arrange the following words in the correct order:
(a) omelette
(b) hen
(c) roll
(d) serve
(e) egg
Choose the correct answer from the options given below:
A. b, e, a, d, c B. e, b, a, c, d
C. b, e, a, c, d D. b, a, e, c, d

22. Group the following figures into three classes based on identical proportions.

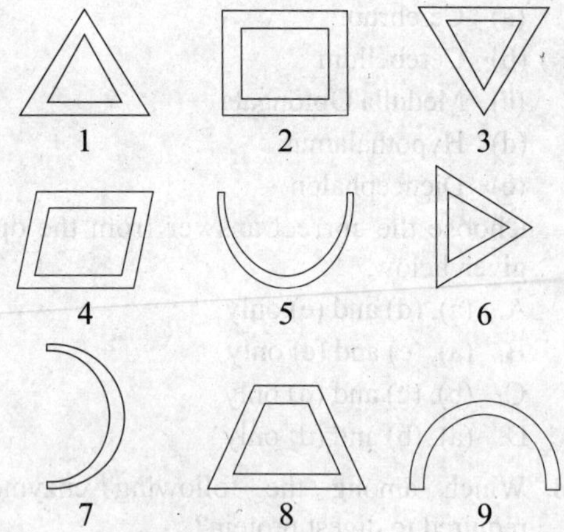

A. 1, 2, 3; 4, 5, 6; 7, 8, 9
B. 1, 3, 6; 2, 4, 8; 5, 7, 9
C. 2, 4, 5; 1, 3, 8; 7, 6, 9
D. 1, 4, 5; 2, 3, 8; 7, 6, 9

23. In a die, 1, 2, 3 and 4 are written on the adjacent faces in a clockwise order and 5 and 6 at the top and the bottom. When three is at the top, what will be at the bottom?

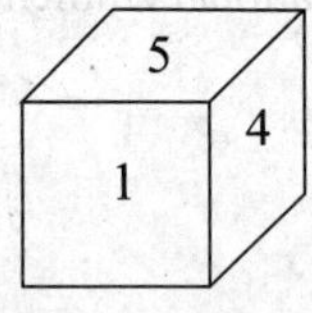

A. 1 B. 2
C. 3 D. 4

24. What is the mirror image of **SMILE**?
A. **ƧM⅃IEI** B. **ƧMIƎL**
C. **SM⅃ƎI** D. **Ǝ⅃IMƧ**

25. Find the missing number.

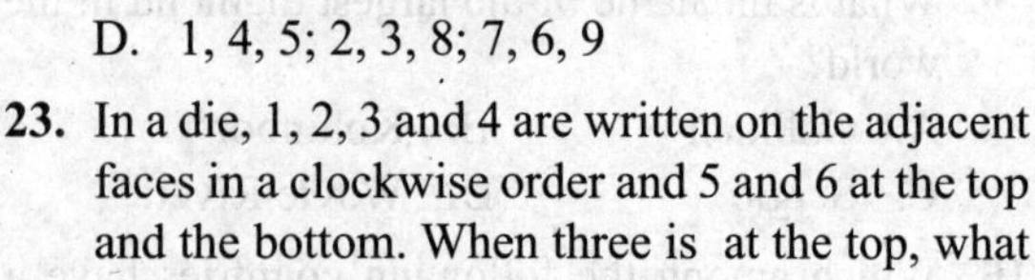

A. 64 B. 77
C. 48 D. 23

Read the passage to answer questions 26–29.

Five men, Ankur, Bharat, Chetan, Dev and Insan and their wives, Parveen, Qazi, Reshma, Sudha and

Tanu, join a dance party, but the order of husbands and wives doesn't need to be the same. This is also known that:

i. Husbands dance only with their wives.
ii. Chetan has a sister, Tanu, and only one brother, Ankur.
iii. If Dev has a dance with Tanu, that means he danced with another's wife.
iv. Bharat does not dance with Qazi, Tanu or Sudha.
v. Parveen is the wife of Ankur's brother.
vi. Qazi did not dance with Dev.

26. Who is Reshma's dance partner?
A. Insan B. Dev
C. Bharat D. Chetan

27. If Bharat and Chetan interchange their dance partners, who will dance with Bharat?
A. Reshma B. Parveen
C. Sudha D. Tanu

28. If Insan is Dev's son, how is Bharat related to Qazi?
A. Brother-in-law
B. Son
C. Sister-in-law
D. Cannot be determined

29. If such a dance programme is well organised, how many dances are possible, such that each woman dances with someone from the opposite sex?
A. 5 B. 4
C. 120 D. 25

30. Find the missing term:
31:961 : : ?:1369
A. 33 B. 37
C. 39 D. 43

31. ECA:QOM : : KIG:?
A. SUV B. WUS
C. TRP D. XVT

32. Acquire:Obtain : : Secure:?
A. Procure
B. Hover
C. Humorous
D. Amusing

33. Sweet:Sour : : Less:?
A. More B. High
C. Up D. Full

34. Fox:Vixen : : Drake:?
A. Bee B. Duck
C. Doe D. Drone

35. Arrange the following words in the sequence in which they appear in a dictionary:
A. Research
B. Resurgence
C. Respiration
D. Respective
E. Resources

Choose the correct answer from the options given below:
A. D, C, E, A, B
B. E, C, D, B, A
C. A, E, D, C, B
D. C, D, A, E, B

36. If in a certain language, D is coded as 2, I is coded as 1, N is coded as 7, M is coded as 5, A is coded as 0, O is coded as 8, then how is DIAMOND coded in that language?
A. 2105872 B. 2015782
C. 2108752 D. 2017582

37. Kiya drives her car 20 km west from her home, then turns left and goes 20 km more, then turns right and goes 10 km, and then turns right and goes 15 km. Finally, she goes 30 km further after turning right again. At what distance is she from the starting point?
A. 5 km B. 10 km
C. 15 km D. 25 km

38. Complete the series:
52, 58, 60, 66, 70, 76, ...
A. 80 B. 82
C. 86 D. 88

39. If the 9th day of a month is Sunday, what will be the last day of the month, on which a Sunday falls?
A. 28th B. 29th
C. 30th D. 31th

40. Complete the series:
7, 23, 95, 479, 2879, ….

A. 11519 B. 14399
C. 17279 D. 20159

41. Complete the series:
8192, 2048, … ? ..., 128, 32, 8

A. 256 B. 248
C. 1024 D. 512

42. How many squares are there in the given shape?

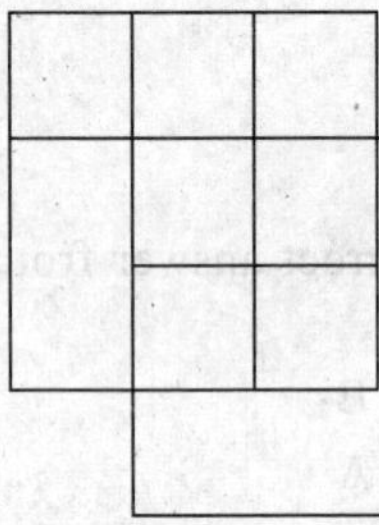

A. 11 B. 12
C. 13 D. 15

43. In this question, four words have been given, of which three are alike in some way, and one is different. Find the odd one out.

A. Rose B. Lotus
C. Jasmine D. Sunflower

44. Which image will appear if the following transparent sheet is folded?

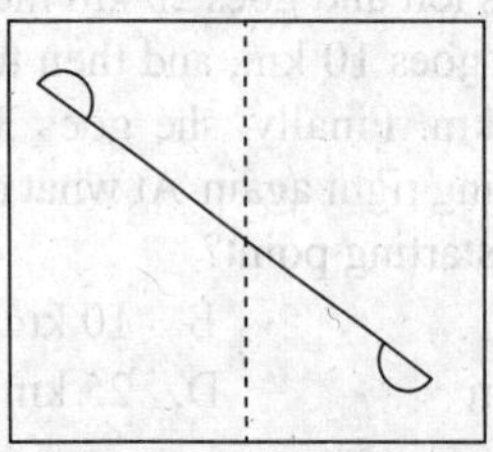

A. 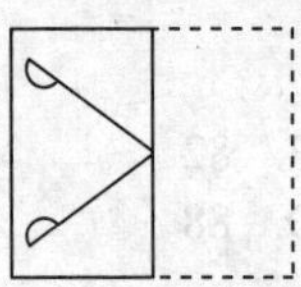 B. 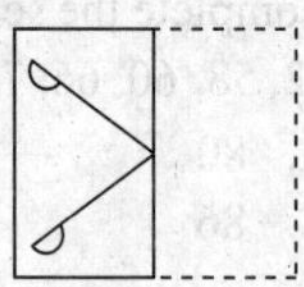

C. 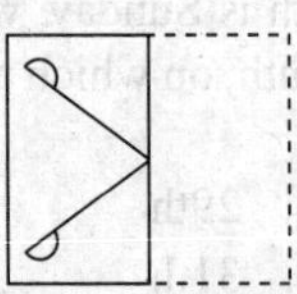 D. 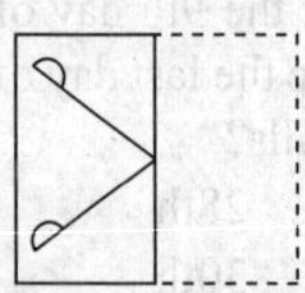

45. Pointing towards a person in the photograph, Mohit said, "He is the husband of the only daughter of the father of my sister's brother." How is that person related to Mohit?

A. uncle B. cousin
C. brother–in–law D. brother

46. What is the value of x if $4{:}x = x{:}16$ ______ ?

A. 16 B. 8
C. 9 D. 12

47. If P = ₹2000, R = 5% per annum, T = 5 years

A. total amount = ₹2200
B. SI = ₹200
C. SI = ₹500
D. total amount = ₹2500

Choose the correct answer from the options given below:

A. C and D only
B. A and C only
C. B and C only
D. A and D only

48. Find the LCM of $\frac{3}{5}, \frac{4}{9}$ and $\frac{5}{8}$.

A. 45 B. 55
C. 60 D. 65

49. In a swimming pool measuring 80 m × 60 m, 120 men take a dip. If the average displacement of water by a man is 6 m^3, then the rise in the water level is

A. 0.25 m B. 0.10 m
C. 0.15 m D. 0.35 m

50. The average age of a group of 5 friends is 32 years. The youngest friend amongst them is 4 years old. What was the group's average age at the time of birth of the youngest friend?

A. 36 years B. 35 years
C. 34 years D. 33 years

51. The volume of a wall is 128 cm^3. If the height of the wall is 6 times its breadth and the length is 9 times its breadth, then the breadth is

A. $\sqrt[3]{3.45}$ cm B. $\sqrt[3]{4.74}$ cm
C. $\sqrt[3]{2.37}$ cm D. $\sqrt[3]{2.38}$ cm

52. If P = x% of y and Q = y% of x, then which of the following is true?

A. P = Q
B. P > Q
C. P < Q
D. relationship between P and Q cannot be established

53. A man makes a profit of 20% after selling a product at a 28% discount on the printed price. Find the ratio of the printed price to the cost price.

A. 7:3 B. 5:3
C. 4:3 D. 8:3

54. Alice is faster than Bob. Each of Alice and Bob walks for 30 km. The sum of their speeds is 8 km/hr, and the sum of the time taken by them is 16 hours. Alice's speed (in km/hr) is equal to

A. 5 B. 4
C. 6 D. 8

55. A and B are two points in a river. Points X and Y divide the line AB into three equal parts. Let the flow of the river be from A to B. The ratio of the time taken to row from point A to Y and from B to Y is 3:4. Find the ratio of the boat's speeds upstream to the river's flow.

A. 5:6 B. 6:5
C. 4:5 D. 5:4

56. A and B can complete a work in 30 days, B and C in 10 days and C and A in 5 days. If all of them work together, the time taken to complete the work is

A. 4 Days B. 5 Days
C. 6 Days D. 7 Days

57. Suresh covers a distance by a cycle at 10 km/h. He returns to the starting point in a car at a speed of 50 km/h. Find the average speed for the entire journey.

A. 36.66 km/h B. 16.66 km/h
C. 26.66 km/h D. 30 km/h

58. A boy secures 70%, 40% and 60% marks on test papers with 100, 50 and 150, respectively, as maximum marks. The percentage of his aggregate is:

A. 55 B. 60
C. 56.66 D. 70

59. Radha sells her scooty for ₹50000 at a loss of 20%. At what price should she sell her scooty to make a profit of 10%?

A. ₹65750 B. ₹64750
C. ₹66750 D. ₹68750

60. The ratio between the ages of P and Q is 5:7. If 2 years ago, Q's age was 2 years more than the age of P after 4 years, then find the sum of their ages.

A. 30 years B. 35 years
C. 42 years D. 48 years

61. If $(a + b)^2 = 5 + 2\sqrt{6}$, then what can be a possible value of 'b' from the following?

A. $\sqrt{7}$ B. $\sqrt{3}$
C. $\sqrt{6}$ D. $\sqrt{5}$

62. If $x - \frac{1}{x} = 3$, then the value of $x^2 + \frac{1}{x^2}$ is

A. 9 B. 11
C. 7 D. 3

63. The distance from A to B is

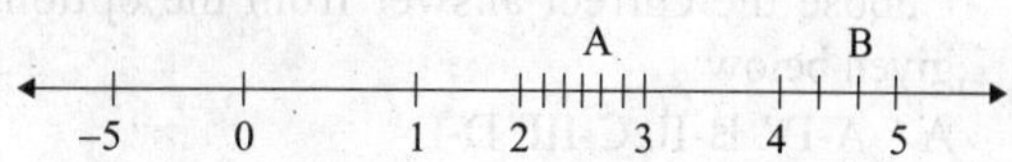

A. 1.8 units B. 1.9 units
C. 2 units D. 2.1 units

64. The ratio of the sides of the squares in the given figures is

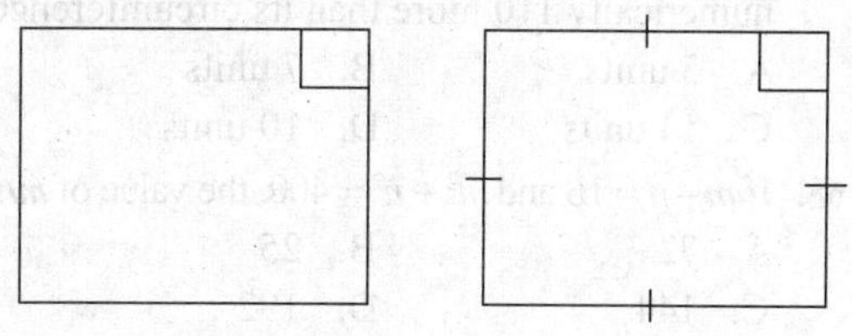

A. 13:4 B. 1:4
C. 4:3 D. 10:4

65. Find the mean of 12, 15, 7, 8 and 'x + 13', if x = 2.

A. 11.2 B. 9.5
C. 11.4 D. 12

66. Match **List I** with **List II**.

List I	List II
A. 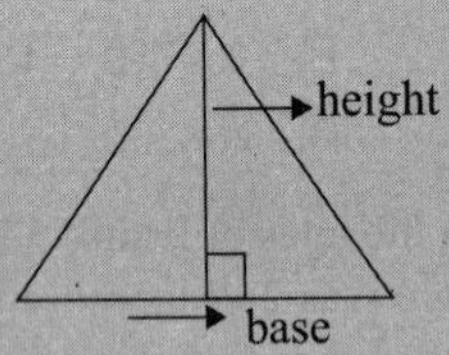	I. πr^2
B. 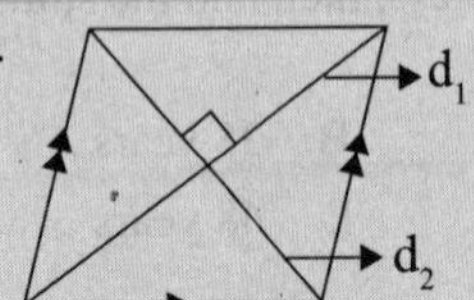	II. $\frac{1}{2} \times \text{base} \times \text{height}$
C. 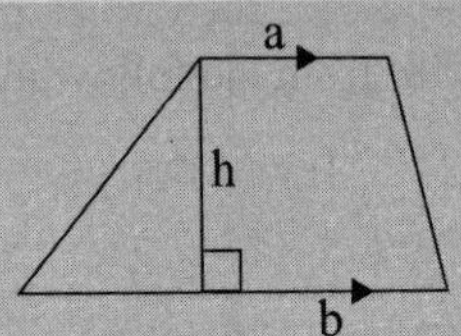	III. $\frac{1}{2} \times d_1 \times d_2$
D. 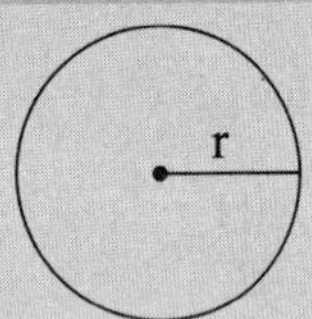	IV. $\frac{1}{2} \times (a+b) \times h$

Choose the correct answer from the options given below:

A. A-IV, B-II, C-III, D-I
B. A-III, B-IV, C-II, D-I
C. A-I, B-III, C-IV, D-II
D. A-II, B-III, C-IV, D-I

67. The diameter of a circle whose area is numerically 110 more than its circumference is

A. 5 units B. 7 units
C. 14 units D. 10 units

68. If $m - n = 16$ and $m^2 + n^2 = 400$, the value of mn is

A. 72 B. 25
C. 144 D. 192

69. The value of 'y' in the equation $2x + 3y - 7 = 0$, if $x = -\frac{3}{2}$, is

A. 10 B. $\frac{10}{3}$
C. $\frac{4}{3}$ D. $\frac{13}{3}$

Study the following histogram and answer questions 70–72.

A survey was done on the number of books owned by some people.

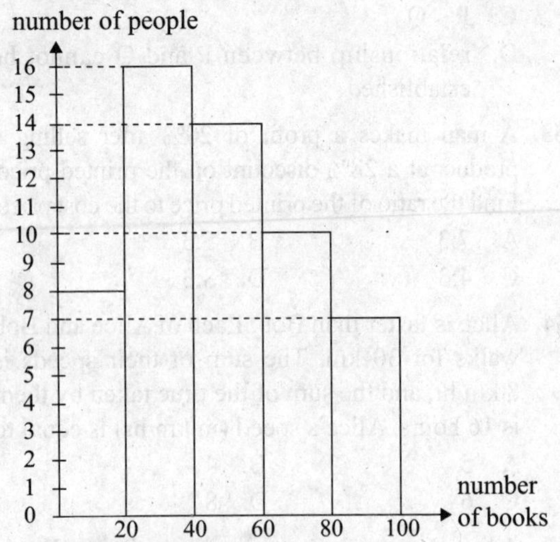

70. The total number of people owning more than '40' books is

A. 60 B. 31
C. 14 D. 30

71. The number of people owning more than 20 but less than 60 books is

A. 14 B. 16
C. 30 D. 40

72. The total number of people surveyed is

A. 16 B. 56
C. 54 D. 55

Study the following diagram and answer questions 73–75.

AC is 23 cm in the adjoining figure. Consider the figure and answer the questions.

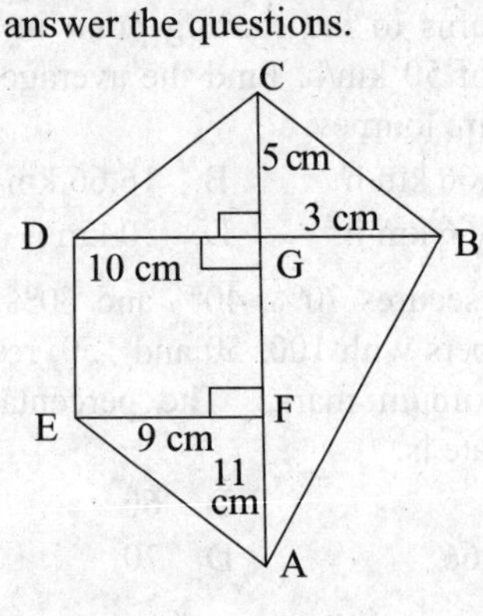

73. The area of the □DGFE is
A. 133 cm^2 B. 140 cm^2
C. 70 cm^2 D. 66.5 cm^2

74. The area of the ΔDBC, if DB is a straight line, is
A. 32.5 cm^2 B. 65 cm^2
C. 25 cm^2 D. 15 cm^2

75. The total area of the figure is
A. 184.5 cm^2
B. 205 cm^2
C. 175.5 cm^2
D. 153 cm^2

Answer Key

1. **B**	2. **B**	3. **C**	4. **A**	5. **B**	6. **A**	7. **A**	8. **B**	9. **A**	10. **B**
11. **B**	12. **D**	13. **D**	14. **D**	15. **A**	16. **D**	17. **C**	18. **C**	19. **D**	20. **A**
21. **C**	22. **B**	23. **A**	24. **D**	25. **B**	26. **C**	27. **B**	28. **D**	29. **D**	30. **B**
31. **B**	32. **A**	33. **A**	34. **B**	35. **C**	36. **A**	37. **A**	38. **B**	39. **C**	40. **D**
41. **D**	42. **B**	43. **B**	44. **C**	45. **C**	46. **B**	47. **A**	48. **C**	49. **C**	50. **B**
51. **C**	52. **A**	53. **B**	54. **A**	55. **B**	56. ***C**	57. **B**	58. **B**	59. **D**	60. **D**
61. **B**	62. **B**	63. **C**	64. **B**	65. **C**	66. **D**	67. **C**	68. **A**	69. **B**	70. **B**
71. **C**	72. **D**	73. **D**	74. **A**	75. **C**					

*In the question, the work done by B is negative!

Classification of Questions

Question No.	Subject	Topic	Level of Difficulty
1.	General Awareness	Geography	Easy
2.	General Awareness	Important Days	Medium
3.	General Awareness	Science & Technology	Medium
4.	General Awareness	Economics	Difficult
5.	General Awareness	Geography	Easy
6.	General Awareness	Miscellaneous	Easy
7.	General Awareness	Science (Biology)	Difficult
8.	General Awareness	Science (Biology)	Medium
9.	General Awareness	Miscellaneous	Medium
10.	General Awareness	Polity	Difficult
11.	General Awareness	Miscellaneous	Medium
12.	General Awareness	Sports	Easy

Question No.	Subject	Topic	Level of Difficulty
13.	Reasoning	Analogy (Letters-based)	Easy
14.	General Awareness	Computers	Medium
15.	General Awareness	Books & Authors	Easy
16.	General Awareness	Current Affairs	Easy
17.	Quantitative Aptitude	Permutations & Combinations	Medium
18.	Reasoning	Mirror Image	Easy
19.	Reasoning	Venn-diagram	Easy
20.	Reasoning	Venn-diagram	Easy
21.	Reasoning	Words in a Logical Sequence	Easy
22.	Reasoning	Non-verbal	Easy
23.	Reasoning	Die-based problem	Easy
24.	Reasoning	Mirror Image	Easy
25.	Reasoning	Missing Number	Medium
26.	Reasoning	Puzzle	Easy
27.	Reasoning	Puzzle	Easy
28.	Reasoning	Puzzle	Easy
29.	Reasoning	Puzzle	Easy
30.	Reasoning	Analogy (Numbers-based)	Easy
31.	Reasoning	Analogy (Letters-based)	Easy
32.	Reasoning	Analogy	Easy
33.	Reasoning	Analogy	Easy
34.	Reasoning	Analogy	Difficult
35.	Reasoning	Dictionary Order	Easy
36.	Reasoning	Coding	Easy
37.	Reasoning	Directions	Easy
38.	Reasoning	Number Series	Easy
39.	Quantitative Aptitude	Calendars	Easy
40.	Reasoning	Number Series	Medium
41.	Reasoning	Number Series	Easy
42.	Reasoning	Figure Counting	Medium
43.	Reasoning	Odd-one-out	Easy
44.	Reasoning	Non-verbal	Easy
45.	Reasoning	Blood Relations	Easy

Question No.	Subject	Topic	Level of Difficulty
46.	Quantitative Aptitude	Ratios	Easy
47.	Quantitative Aptitude	Simple Interest	Easy
48.	Quantitative Aptitude	Numbers (LCM of fractions)	Easy
49.	Quantitative Aptitude	Mensuration	Easy
50.	Quantitative Aptitude	Averages	Medium
51.	Quantitative Aptitude	Mensuration	Medium
52.	Quantitative Aptitude	Percentages	Easy
53.	Quantitative Aptitude	Profit, Loss & Discount	Medium
54.	Quantitative Aptitude	Time, Speed & Distance	Medium
55.	Quantitative Aptitude	Time, Speed & Distance	Difficult
56.	Quantitative Aptitude	Time & Work	Easy
57.	Quantitative Aptitude	Time, Speed & Distance	Easy
58.	Quantitative Aptitude	Percentages	Easy
59.	Quantitative Aptitude	Profit, Loss & Discount	Easy
60.	Quantitative Aptitude	Age-based Problems	Medium
61.	Quantitative Aptitude	Algebra (Equations)	Easy
62.	Quantitative Aptitude	Algebra (Equations)	Easy
63.	Quantitative Aptitude	Number Line	Easy
64.	Quantitative Aptitude	Mensuration	Easy
65.	Quantitative Aptitude	Averages	Easy
66.	Quantitative Aptitude	Mensuration	Easy
67.	Quantitative Aptitude	Mensuration	Easy
68.	Quantitative Aptitude	Algebra (Identities)	Easy
69.	Quantitative Aptitude	Algebra (Equations)	Easy
70.	Data Interpretation	Histogram	Easy
71.	Data Interpretation	Histogram	Easy
72.	Data Interpretation	Histogram	Easy
73.	Quantitative Aptitude	Mensuration	Easy
74.	Quantitative Aptitude	Mensuration	Easy
75.	Quantitative Aptitude	Mensuration	Easy

The no. of questions on General Awareness: 15
The no. of questions on Quantitative Aptitude: 29
The no. of questions on Reasoning: 28
The no. of questions on Data Interpretation: 3

Explanation to Select Questions

1. South Korea is called the 'Land of Morning Calm', and Japan is known as the 'Land of Rising Sun'.
Hence, Option B.

2.

Event	Date
Teachers' Day	5 September
Hindi Day	14 September
Armed Forces Flag Day	7 December
Vijay Diwas	16 December
National Good Governance Day	25 December

Hence, Option B.

Note: The Hindi Day is celebrated on 14 September, but the World Hindi Day is celebrated on 10 January.

Also, the National Good Governance Day is celebrated on 25 December as Atal Bihari Vajpayee was born on this date.

6. Commodore is a rank in the Indian Navy, and Group Captain is a rank in the Indian Air Force.
Hence, Option A.

9. Cullinan, the largest diamond in the world, was found in South Africa in 1905.
Hence, Option A.

11. General KM Cariappa became the first Indian Commander-in-Chief of the Indian Army in 1949. General SHFJ Manekshaw became India's first Field Marshal in 1973. General Bipin Rawat became India's first Chief of Defence Staff (CDS) in 2020.
Hence, Option B.

12.

Country	The Number of ICC Men's World Cup Titles	Year/years
Australia	6	1987, 1999, 2003, 2007, 2015 and 2023
India	2	1983 and 2011
West Indies	2	1975 and 1979
England	1	2019
Sri Lanka	1	1996
Pakistan	1	1992

This tournament has been held 13 times thus far.

Hence, Option D.

13. $M \times N : 13 \times 14$ as M and N are the 13th and the 14th letters of the alphabet. Similarly, F and R are the 6th and the 18th letters of the alphabet, and hence, it should be $F \times R : 6 \times 18$.
Hence, Option D.

17.

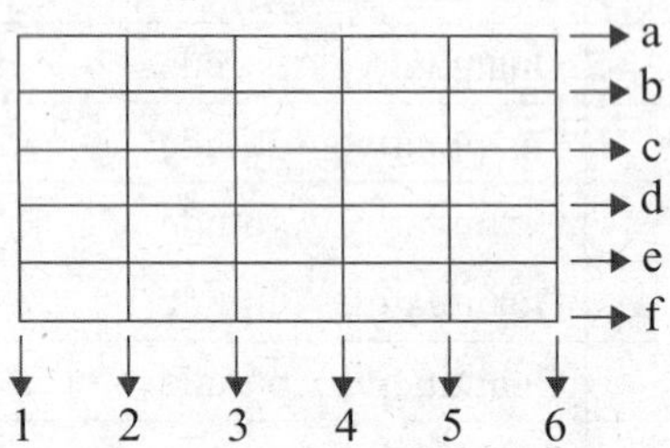

In this figure, there are 6 horizontal lines: a, b, c, d, e and f and 6 vertical lines: 1, 2, 3, 4 5, and 6.

To get a rectangle, we need any 2 of the 6 horizontal lines and any 2 of the 6 vertical lines.

It is possible in ${}^6C_2 \times {}^6C_2 = \frac{6\times5}{1\times2} \times \frac{6\times5}{1\times2} =$ $15 \times 15 = 225$ ways.

Hence, Option C.

18. The time in a clock = 12:00 – the image of its time = 12:00 – 11:09 = 00:51.
In any analogue watch, 00:51 is 12:51.
Hence, Option C.

21. Hens lay eggs with which we make omelettes, which are rolled and served.

Hence, Option C.

23.

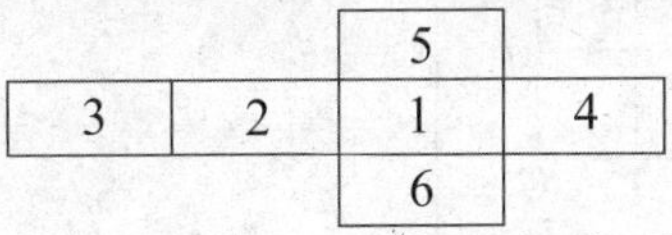

So, 3 and 1 are on the opposite faces.

Therefore, when 3 is at the top, 1 will be at the bottom.

Hence, Option A.

25.

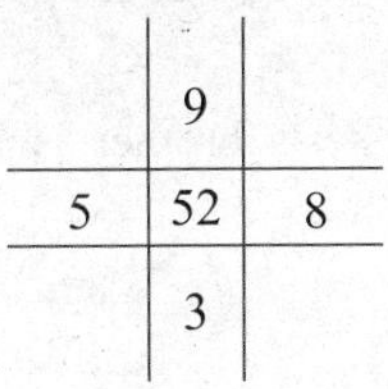

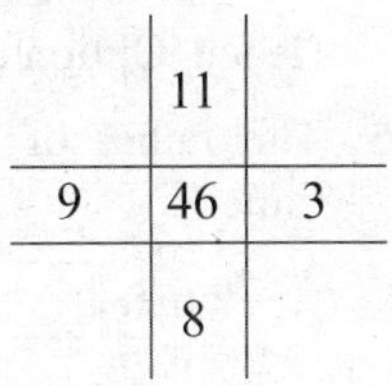

$52 = (5 \times 8) + (9 + 3)$ $46 = (9 \times 3) + (11 + 8)$

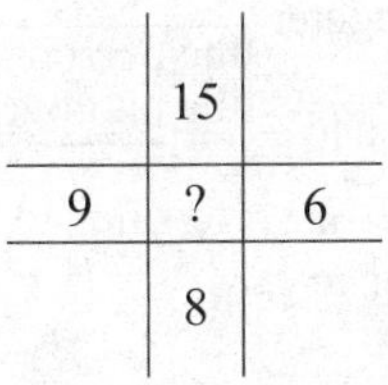

$? = (9 \times 6) + (15 + 8) = 54 + 23 = 77$

Hence, Option B.

Please follow this table for explanations of questions 26 to 29:

Man	His Wife	Important Information
Ankur	Qazi	Tanu is his sister and Chetan is his brother. Parveen is the wife of his brother.
Bharat	Reshma	He is not married to Qazi, Tanu or Sudha.
Chetan	Parveen	Tanu is his sister and Ankur is his brother.
Dev	Sudha	Tanu is NOT his wife.
Insan	Tanu	Qazi is NOT his wife.

The information in the 3rd column is given in the question.

26. As a man dances only with his wife, Reshma is Bharat's wife, and Bharat is her dance partner.

Hence, Option C.

27. Bharat is married to Reshma, and Chetan is married to Parveen. So, Reshma and Parveen are Bharat and Chetan's dance partners, respectively. Therefore, if Bharat and Chetan interchange their dance partners, Parveen will dance with Bharat.

Hence, Option B.

29. There are 5 women and 5 men. So, if each woman dances with someone from the opposite sex, the number of possible dances is $5 \times 5 = 25$.

Hence, Option D.

30. $961 = 31^2$ and $1369 = 37^2$.

Hence, Option B.

31.

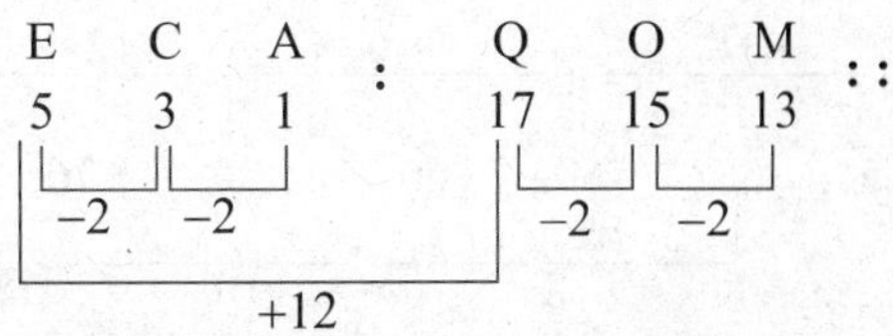

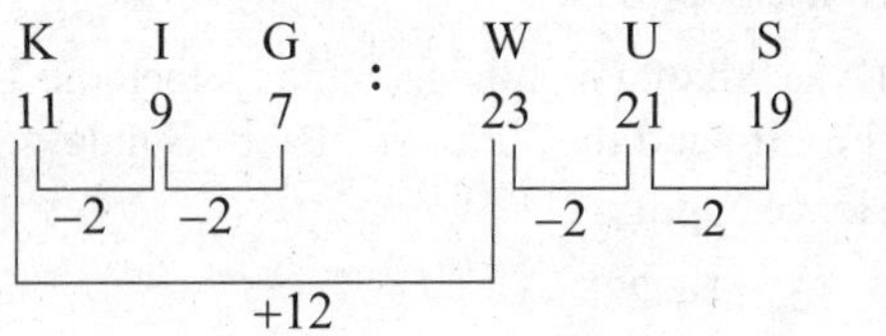

Hence, Option B.

32. 'Acquire' and 'obtain' are similar, as are 'secure' and 'procure'.

Hence, Option A.

33. 'Sweet' and 'sour' are opposites, as are 'less' and 'more'.

Hence, Option A.

34. A 'vixen' is a female fox, and a 'drake' is a male duck.

Hence, Option B.

A drone is a stingless male bee, and a doe is an adult female of deer, rabbit, or kangaroo.

37.

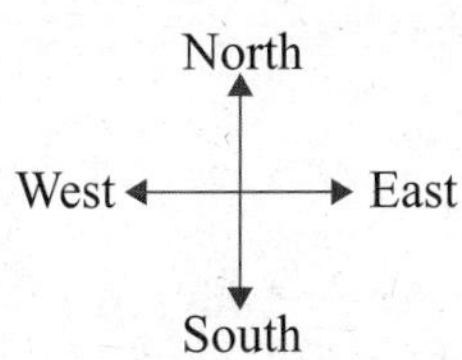

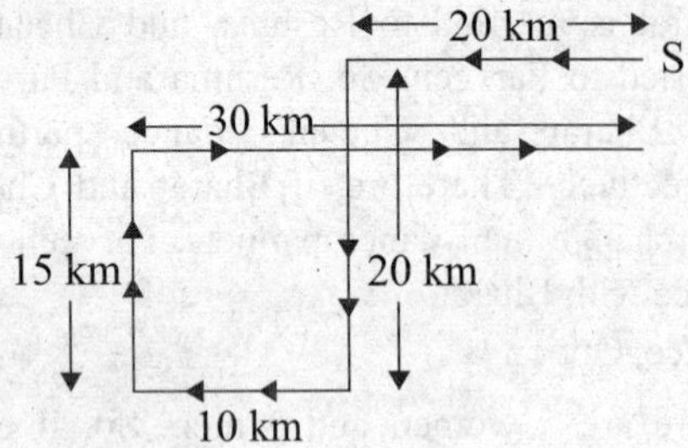

The total East-West displacement of Kiya = 20 (west) + 10 (west) – 30 (east) = 0.
The total North-South displacement of Kiya = 20 (south) – 15 (north) = 5 (south).
Hence, Kiya is at a distance of 5 km south from her starting point.
Hence, Option A.

38.

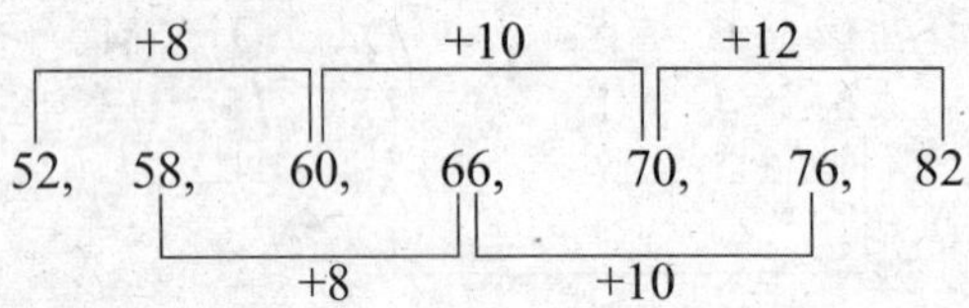

Hence, Option B.

39. If the 9th of a month is a Sunday, then the 16th, the 23rd and the 30th will also be Sundays.
Hence, Option C.

40. $7 \times 3 + 2 = 23$,
$23 \times 4 + 3 = 95$,
$95 \times 5 + 4 = 479$,
$479 \times 6 + 5 = 2879$ and
$2879 \times 7 + 6 = 20159$.
Hence, Option D.

41. $\frac{8192}{4} = 2048$,

$\frac{2048}{4} = 512$,

$\frac{512}{4} = 128$,

$\frac{128}{4} = 32$ and

$\frac{32}{4} = 8$.

Hence, Option D.

Note: It is easier to understand this series if you look at it from right to left.

42.

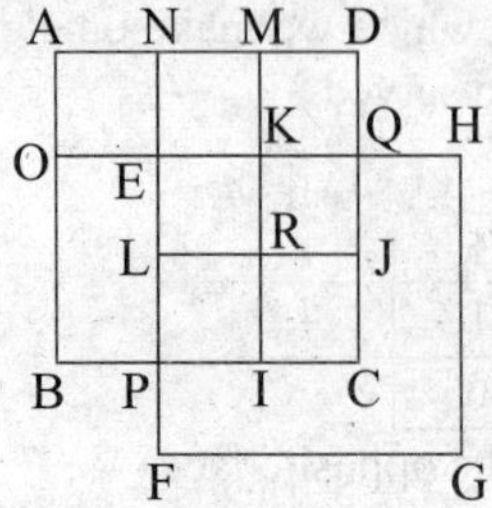

The squares are:
ABCD, EFGH, EPCQ, NLJD, OBIK, AOEN, NEKM, MKQD, ELRK, KRJQ, LPIR, RICJ.
Hence, Option B.

45. The father of one's sister's brother is one's father.

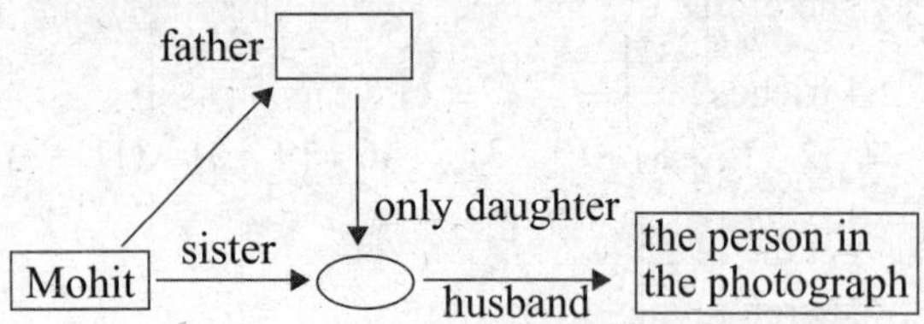

It is clear that Mohit is referring to the photograph of his brother-in-law.
Hence, Option C.

46. $\frac{4}{x} = \frac{x}{16}$ or, $4 \times 16 = x^2$

or, $x = \sqrt{64} = 8$.
Hence, Option B.

47. $SI = \frac{P \times R \times T}{100} = \frac{2000 \times 5 \times 5}{100} = 500$.

Total amount = Principal + Simple interest
= 2000 + 500 = 2500.
Hence, Option A.

48. The LCM of fractions = $\frac{\text{the LCM of the numerators}}{\text{the HCF of denominators}}$

The LCM of $\frac{3}{5}, \frac{4}{9}$ and $\frac{5}{8}$ = $\frac{\text{the LCM of 3, 4 and 5}}{\text{the HCF of 5, 9 and 8}}$

$= \frac{60}{1} = 60$.

Hence, Option C.

49. The rise in the water level

$$= \frac{\text{total volume of displaced water}}{(\text{length} \times \text{breadth}) \text{ of the pool}}$$

$$= \frac{6 \times 120}{80 \times 60} = \frac{3}{20} = 0.15 \text{ m.}$$

Hence, Option C.

50. The sum of the ages of the 5 friends = $32 \times 5 = 160$ years.

Therefore, the sum of the ages of these people 4 years back = $160 - 4 \times 5$ = 140 years.

But, 4 years back, the youngest friend was just about to be born, and there were only 4 people.

Therefore, the average age of the remaining 4 friends then $= \frac{140}{4} = 35$ years.

Hence, Option B.

51. Let the breadth of the wall be x cm.

Therefore, the height of the wall = $6x$ cm and the length of the wall = $9x$ cm

the volume of the wall = length × breadth × height

$= 9x \times x \times 6x$

$= 54x^3$

So, $54x^3 = 128$

or, $x^3 = \frac{128}{54} = \frac{64}{27} = 2.37$, or, $x = \sqrt[3]{2.37}$ cm

Hence, Option C.

52. $P = x\% \text{ of } y = y \times \frac{x}{100} = \frac{yx}{100}$

$Q = y\% \text{ of } x = x \times \frac{y}{100} = \frac{xy}{100} = \frac{yx}{100} = P$

Therefore, P = Q.

Hence, Option A.

53. Let the cost price be 100.

The selling price would be 120 as there is a profit of 20%.

The selling price is 120 after a discount of 28% on the printed price.

Therefore, the printed price $= \frac{120 \times 100}{100 - 28} = \frac{120 \times 100}{72} = \frac{500}{3}$.

Therefore, the ratio of the printed price to the cost price $= \frac{500}{3} : 100 = \frac{500}{3 \times 100}$

$= \frac{500}{300} = 5:3.$

Hence, Option B.

Alternative: Try the options.

Option A: If the printed price is 7, the selling is $7 - 7 \times \frac{28}{100} = 5.04$.

As the cost price (as per this option) is 3, a selling price of 5.04 is 68% profit. Hence, it cannot be the answer.

Option B: If the printed price is 5, the selling price is $5 - 5 \times \frac{28}{100} = 3.6$.

Now, 3.6 is 20% above 3, and hence, this is the answer.

54. Let's assume that Alice walks at a speed of x km/hour.

So, the speed of Bob is $8 - x$ km/hr.

As per the question:

$$\frac{30}{x} + \frac{30}{8 - x} = 16$$

$$\text{or, } 30\left(\frac{1}{x} + \frac{1}{8 - x}\right) = 16$$

$$\text{or, } \frac{8 - x + x}{x(8 - x)} = \frac{16}{30}$$

$$\text{or, } \frac{8}{x(8 - x)} = \frac{8}{15}$$

$$\text{or, } x(8 - x) = \frac{8 \times 15}{8} = 15$$

or, $8x - x^2 = 15$

or, $x^2 - 8x + 15 = 0$

or, $x^2 - 3x - 5x + 15 = 0$

or, $x(x - 3) - 5(x - 3) = 0$

or, $(x - 5)(x - 3) = 0$

or, $x = 3$ or, 5

But the speed of Alice is more than that of Bob. Hence, the speed of Alice is 5 kmph.

Shortcut:

Try with the Options.

Option A: Speed of Alice = 5 $\Rightarrow$ the speed of Bob = 8 – 5 = 3.

Now, $\frac{30}{5} + \frac{30}{3} = 6 + 10 = 16$.

As per the question also, the combined time taken by them is 16, and hence, Option A is the answer.

55. A · ← d → · ← d → · ← d → · B
X Y

Let the distance from A to B be 3d.

So, $AX = XY = YB = \frac{3d}{3} = d$.

Let the speed of the boat be p, and that of the stream be q.

As the flow of the stream is from A to B, the journey from A to Y is downstream and that from B to Y is upstream.

Time taken in travelling from A to Y = $\frac{d+d}{p+q} = \frac{2d}{p+q}$.

Time taken in travelling from B to Y = $\frac{d}{p-q}$

We have, $\frac{\frac{2d}{p+q}}{\frac{d}{p-q}} = \frac{3}{4}$

or, $\frac{2d}{p+q} \times \frac{p-q}{d} = \frac{3}{4}$

or, $\frac{p-q}{p+q} = \frac{3}{4 \times 2}$

or, $8p - 8q = 3p + 3q$

or, $8p - 3p = 8q + 3q$

or, $5p = 11q$

or, $\frac{p}{q} = \frac{11}{5}$.

Now, the required value = $\frac{p-q}{q} = \frac{p}{q} - \frac{q}{q} = \frac{p}{q} - 1 = \frac{11}{5} - 1 = \frac{11-5}{5} = \frac{6}{5}$.

Hence, Option B.

56. Let the work be of 30 units.

In 1 day, A and B do $\frac{30}{30} = 1$ unit.

In 1 day, B and C do $\frac{30}{10} = 3$ units.

In 1 day, C and A do $\frac{30}{5} = 6$ units.

So, in 1 day 2A, 2B and 2C do 1 + 3 + 6 = 10 units.

Therefore, in 1 day, A, B and C do $\frac{10}{2} = 5$ units.

Therefore, these 3 together can complete the work in $\frac{30 \text{ units}}{5 \text{ units}} = 6$ days.

Hence, Option C.

Caution: There is a catch in this question. In 1 day, A, B and C do 5 units, but A and C do 6 units. Therefore, B does – 1 unit every day! Option C was accepted by the CUET-UG.

57. Let the distance be d.

The total distance in going and coming back = $d + d = 2d$.

The total time taken in going and coming back $= \frac{d}{10} + \frac{d}{50}$.

The average speed = $\frac{\text{total distance}}{\text{total time taken}}$

$$= \frac{2d}{\frac{d}{10} + \frac{d}{50}} = \frac{2d}{d\left(\frac{1}{10} + \frac{1}{50}\right)}$$

$$= \frac{2 \times 10 \times 50}{10 + 50} = 16.67 \text{ km/h.}$$

Hence, Option B.

Shortcut: If you go to a place at a speed of x and come back at a speed of y, your average speed for the entire journey = $\frac{2xy}{x+y}$.

Applying it here,

the average speed $= \frac{2 \times 50 \times 10}{50 + 10} = \frac{1000}{60} = \frac{50}{3}$
$= 16.67$ km/h.

58. The maximum possible marks $= 100 + 50 + 150 = 300$.
The total marks obtained by the boy
$= 70\%$ of $100 + 40\%$ of $50 + 60\%$ of 150

$= 100 \times \frac{70}{100} + 50 \times \frac{40}{100} + 150 \times \frac{60}{100}$

$= 70 + 20 + 90 = 180.$

Therefore, the required percentage $= \frac{180}{300} \times 100 = 60$.
Hence, Option B.

59. A loss of 20% means that the selling price is 80% of the cost price and a profit of 10% means that the selling price is 110% of the cost price.
Now, 80% of the cost price = 50000.

Therefore, 110% of the cost price $= \frac{50000}{80} \times 110 = 68750$.

Hence, Option D.

60. Let the ages of P and Q be $5x$ and $7x$.
We have,
$(7x - 2) = 2 + (5x + 4)$
or, $7x - 2 = 5x + 6$
or, $7x - 5x = 2 + 6$
or, $2x = 8$
or, $x = \frac{8}{2} = 4$.

Therefore, the ages of P and Q are $5 \times 4 = 20$ and
$7 \times 4 = 28$ years, respectively. Also, the sum of their ages in $20 + 28 = 48$ years.
Hence, Option D.
Shortcut: As the ratio of the ages of P and Q is 5:7, the sum of their ages should be a multiple of $7 + 5 = 12$. Only Option 4 is a multiple of 12.

61. $(a + b)^2 = 5 + 2\sqrt{6} = \left(\sqrt{2} + \sqrt{3}\right)^2$.

Hence, b can be $\sqrt{2}$ as well as $\sqrt{3}$.
Hence, Option B.

62. $x - \frac{1}{x} = 3$

or, $\left(x - \frac{1}{x}\right)^2 = 3^2$

or, $x^2 + \frac{1}{x^2} - 2 \times x \times \frac{1}{x} = 9$

or, $x^2 + \frac{1}{x^2} - 2 = 9$

or, $x^2 + \frac{1}{x^2} = 9 + 2 = 11$.

Hence, Option B.

63. The required distance $= 4\frac{2}{3} - 2\frac{2}{3}$
$= 2$ units.
Hence, Option C.

64. The area of the square on the left = 1.69 cm².
Therefore, it's side $= \sqrt{1.69}$ cm = 1.3 cm.
The side of the square on the right = 5.2 cm.

The required ratio $= \frac{1.3}{5.2} = \frac{1}{4} = 1:4$.

Hence, Option B.

67. Let the radius of the circle be x.
We have,
$\pi r^2 - 2\pi r = 110$

or, $\frac{22}{7}r^2 - 2 \times \frac{22}{7}r = 110$

or, $\frac{r^2}{7} - \frac{2r}{7} = \frac{110}{22} = 5$

or, $r^2 - 2r = 5 \times 7 = 35$
or, $r^2 - 2r - 35 = 0$
or, $r^2 - 7r + 5r - 35 = 0$
or, $r(r - 7) + 5(r - 7) = 0$
or, $(r + 5)(r - 7) = 0$
or, $r = -5$ or, 7
But r cannot be negative.
So, $r = 7$.
Therefore, the diameter of the circle $= 2r = 2 \times 7 = 14$ units.
Hence, Option C.

Caution: The moment you get $r = 7$, you promptly feel like clicking this as your answer, but your answer is $2r$ and NOT r. *Beware of Option B.*

68. $m - n = 16$

or, $(m - n)^2 = 16^2$

or, $m^2 + n^2 - 2mn = 256$

or, $400 - 2mn = 256$

or, $2mn = 400 - 256$

or, $2mn = 144$

or, $mn = \frac{144}{2} = 72.$

Hence, Option A.

69. $2x + 3y - 7 = 0$

or, $2\left(-\frac{3}{2}\right) + 3y = 7$

or, $-3 + 3y = 7$

or, $3y = 7 + 3$

or, $y = \frac{10}{3}.$

Hence, Option B.

Refer to the following table for explanations of questions 70–72.

No. of Books	No. of People
less than 20 books	8
20 or more but less than 40 books	16
40 or more but less than 60 books	14
60 or more but less than 80 books	10
80 or more but less than 100 books	7

70. The total number of people owning more than 40 books = 14 + 10 + 7 = 31.

Hence, option B.

71. The number of people owning more than 20 but less than 60 books is 16 + 14 = 30.

Hence, Option C.

72. The total number of people surveyed is 8 + 16 + 14 + 10 + 7 = 55.

Hence, Option D.

Refer to the following figure for explanations of questions 73–75.

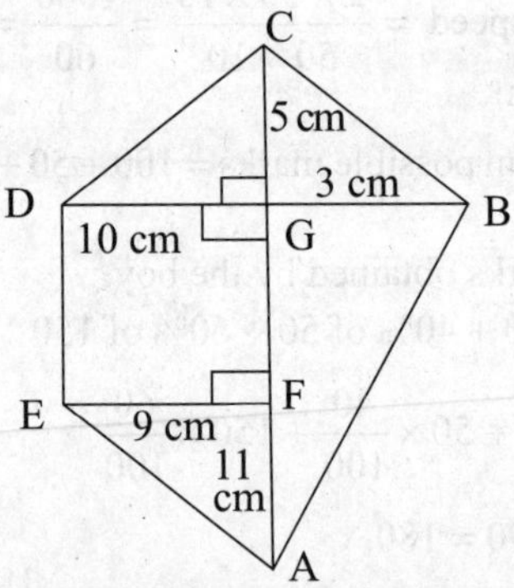

73. DGFE is a trapezium with DG||EF.

The area of a trapezium $= \frac{1}{2}$ (sum of the lengths of the parallel sides) × (the distance between the parallel sides).

$= \frac{1}{2} \times (10 + 9) \times 7 = \frac{133}{2}$ cm² = 66.5 cm².

Hence, Option D.

74. The area of the $\Delta DBC = \frac{1}{2} \times DB \times CG$ (as $CG \perp DB$)

$= \frac{1}{2}(DG + GB) \times CG$

$= \frac{1}{2}(10 + 3) \times 5 = \frac{65}{2} = 32.5$ cm².

Hence, Option A.

75. The total area of the figure = Area of the ΔDBC + Area of the trapezium DGFE + Area of the ΔEFA + Area of the ΔAGB.

$= 32.5 + 66.5 + \frac{1}{2} FE \times FA + \frac{1}{2} \times BG \times AG$

(as in ΔEFA, $EF \perp FA$, and in ΔAGB, $AG \perp GB$)

$= 99 + \frac{1}{2}(9 \times 11) + \frac{1}{2} \times 3(CA - CG)$

$= 99 + 49.5 + \frac{1}{2} \times 3(23 - 5)$

$= 148.5 + \frac{1}{2} \times 3 \times 18$

$= 148.5 + 27 = 175.5$ cm².

Hence, Option C.

CUET UG 2022 General Test

August 7

INSTRUCTIONS:

1. You need to attempt any 60 out of the 75 questions in 60 minutes.
2. You get 5 marks for a correct response and –1 for an incorrect one. However, there is no reward or penalty for a question not attempted.

1. 17:289 : : 23:?

A. 259 B. 952
C. 529 D. 959

2. Scatter:Collect : : Pliable:?

A. Slow B. Gentle
C. Pliant D. Rigid

3. DBF:JHL : : PNR:?

A. TVX B. VTX
C. XVT D. RTV

4. Odometer:Distance : : Anemometer:?

A. Air B. Pressure
C. Wind D. Temperature

5. Eager:Keen : : Fervent:?

A. Enthusiastic B. Contract
C. Delicious D. Indulge

6. Arrange the following words in the sequence in which they appear in a dictionary:

A. Experience
B. Exposure
C. Expression
D. Examination
E. Execution

Choose the correct answer from the options given below:

A. B, D, A, E, C
B. D, E, A, B, C
C. C, D, E, B, A
D. A, C, E, B, D

7. One morning, Rohita and Malvika were standing opposite each other. It was observed that Rohita's shadow fell to Malvika's left, then which direction was Rohita facing?

A. East B. West
C. North D. South

8. If in a code language, UGANDA is written as GUNAAD and AFRICA is written as FAIRAC, what will be the code of RUSSIA?

A. URSIAS B. URSAIS
C. URASSI D. URSSAI

9. Complete the series: 47, 59, 67, 73, 83, ?

A. 87 B. 89
C. 93 D. 97

10. Today is Wednesday. After 54 days, it will be:

A. Sunday B. Monday
C. Friday D. Saturday

11. Complete the series: 2, 6, 10, 14, 18, __

A. 20 B. 22
C. 26 D. 30

12. In this question, four words have been given, of which three are alike in some way, and one is different. Find the odd one out.

A. Platypus B. Kangaroos
C. Opossums D. Wombats

13. Complete the Series: 7560, 1080, ?, 36, 9, 3

A. 150 B. 180
C. 360 D. 540

14. Rashmi said to Anupam, "You are the daughter-in-law of the grandmother of my son." How is Rashmi related to Anupam?

A. Sister B. Mother
C. Grandmother D. Sister-in-law

15. How many squares are there in the given figure?

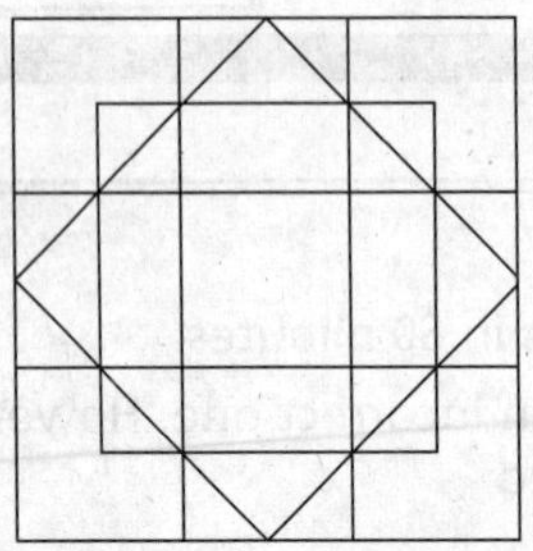

A. 16 B. 24
C. 25 D. 48

16. The average age of a family of 5 members was 15 years, five years ago. The birth of a new child kept the average age of the family at 17. How old is the child today?

A. 1 year B. 2 years
C. 3 years D. 4 years

17. In a library, 50% of books are in Hindi, and 30% of the remaining books are in English. If the number of books in English is 2400, find the number of books in Hindi.

A. 6000 B. 8000
C. 16000 D. 12000

18. A boat running downstream covers a distance of 8 km in 2 hours, while covering the same distance upstream it takes 4 hours. What time will it take to row 10 km downstream?

A. 3.5 hours B. 2.5 hours
C. 5.5 hours D. 4.5 hours

19. The ratio of the cost price to the selling price of an object is 5:4. Find the profit or loss %.

A. profit 10% B. loss 20%
C. profit 30% D. loss 10%

20. Suresh purchased a house at ₹100000 and gave the commission of ₹1200 to an agent. The painting cost on the house was ₹2000. Then he sold it with 40% profit. At what price did he sell it?

A. ₹1,35,520 B. ₹1,45,540
C. ₹1,44,480 D. ₹1,36,590

21. An auto going with $\frac{3}{4}$ of its standard rate covers 36 km in 1 hr, 30 min, 30 sec. What is the normal speed of the auto?

A. 29.15 kmph B. 31.82 kmph
C. 41.56 kmph D. 18.33 kmph

22. Four bells ring simultaneously at the starting and at intervals of 5 seconds, 10 seconds, 15 seconds, and 30 seconds, respectively. How many times do they ring together in 3 hours?

A. 361 times B. 436 times
C. 560 times D. 237 times

23. A, B and C can do a piece of work in 10 days. B and C can do it in 15 days and A and C can do it in 12 days. How long will B take to do it alone?

A. 45 days B. 50 days
C. 55 days D. 60 days

24. X is thrice as good as a worker as Y and, therefore, can finish a job in 40 days less than Y. Working together, they can do it in

A. 14 days B. 15 days
C. 12 days D. 13 days

25. If each side of a square is decreased by 10%, find the percentage decrease in its area.

A. 14% B. 17%
C. 19% D. 15%

26. A Pencil sharpened at two edges is an example of the combination of

A. one cylinder, two hemispheres
B. one cylinder, one cone
C. one cylinder, two cones
D. one cylinder, one hemisphere

27. The GCD of two numbers is 6 while their LCM is 120. Find the other number if one number is 12.

A. 40 B. 50
C. 60 D. 70

28. What is the simple interest of ₹125000 invested at the rate of interest of 6% per annum for a period from 5th April 2021 to August 28, 2021?

A. ₹2000 B. ₹3500
C. ₹4000 D. ₹3000

29. Find the value of x if $13:14 = x:8$.
A. 4.248 B. 7.666
C. 7.888 D. 7.428

30. A 450 m long train is running at a speed of 102 km/hr. In what time will it pass a man running at 16 km/hr in the same direction the train is going?
A. 17.05 sec B. 17.84 sec
C. 18.04 sec D. 18.84 sec

31. As per the Ease of Living Index 2020, The Most Livable Cities in India are given below. Arrange them in the ranking from the top to the bottom.
A. Chennai
B. Mumbai
C. Shimla
D. Bhubaneswar
E. Bengaluru
Choose the correct answer from the options given below:
A. EACDB B. CBEAD
C. ABCDE D. DCBEA

32. The economy of India is the ________ largest in the world by nominal GDP:
A. 5th B. 4th
C. 3rd D. 2nd

33. Atmospheric Pressure is measured by an instrument called
A. Vacuum gauges B. Barometer
C. Pressure gauge D. Pressure meters

34. The longest sea beach in India is
A. Ramayapatnam Beach
B. Kappil Beach
C. Junput Beach
D. Marina Beach

35. Which is the oldest Puranic text:
A. Skanda Purana B. Linga Purana
C. Matsya purana D. Brahma Purana

36. The intensity of the earthquake waves is recorded by:
A. Richter Scale B. Focus
C. Seismograph D. Mercalli Scale

37. Arrange the given names in the order given in Bloomberg Billionaires Index on May 21, 2021:
A. Bernard Arnault
B. Bill Gates
C. Elon Musk
D. Jeff Bezos
E. Mark Zuckerberg
Choose the correct answer from the options given below:
A. EACDB B. CBEAD
C. BDACE D. DCABE

38. "How the Earth Got Its Beauty" is authored by:
A. Sudha Murty B. Mulk Raj Anand
C. Jhumpa Lahiri D. Chetan Bhagat

39. Who won the gold medal in the 75kg Women's Middle category final at the Asian Boxing Championships 2021?
A. Mary Kom B. Pinki Rani
C. Pooja Rani D. Lovlina Borogohain

40. Which sports were inducted for the first time in the Tokyo Paralympics?
A. Badminton
B. Volleyball
C. Table Tennis
D. Taekwondo
Choose the correct answer from the options given below:
A. A and B only B. B and D only
C. A and D only D. C and D only

41. NITI Aayog has released the first-ever Multi-dimensional Poverty Index (MPI) to measure poverty at:
A. National level only
B. State level only
C. Union Territory level only
D. District level only
E. Block level only
Choose the correct answer from the options given below:
A. A, B and C only
B. A, B and D only
C. B, C, D and E only
D. A, B, C and D only

42. The Government of India has joined hands with the Government of ________ to create 150 'Villages of Excellence'.

A. USA B. Australia
C. Russia D. Israel

43. Who has won the title of Miss Universe 2021:

A. Nadia Ferreira B. Lalela Mswane
C. Harnaaz Sandhu D. Sushmita Sen

44. Women Equality Day is celebrated annually on:

A. 8 March B. 13 February
C. 26 August D. 10 December

45. Match **List I** with **List II**.

List I (Position)	List II (Individual)
A. Google CEO	I. C.P. Gurnani
B. Tech Mahindra CEO	II. Varun Sridhar
C. Apple Inc. CEO	III. Sundar Pichai
D. Paytm Money CEO	IV. Tim Cook

Choose the correct answer from the options given below:

A. A-I, B-III, C-IV, D-II
B. A-III, B-I, C-IV, D-II
C. A-II, B-IV, C-III, D-I
D. A-IV, B-III, C-I, D-II

46. The average of four consecutive odd numbers is 16. What is the sum of the first and the third numbers?

A. 28 B. 30
C. 32 D. 34

47. A simple interest of ₹22000 for 4 years at 5% PA is equal to the simple interest of ₹33000 at 10% PA for a fixed period. The fixed period is

A. $1\frac{1}{2}$ years B. $3\frac{1}{2}$ years
C. $1\frac{1}{3}$ years D. $2\frac{1}{2}$ years

48. Find out the wrong number in the sequence: 22, 33, 55, 66, 77, 121

A. 22 B. 55
C. 66 D. 77

49. $936 \times 296 - 936 \times 196$?

A. 93600 B. 936000
C. 29600 D. 296000

50. The area of a rectangular field is 108 m², and its diagonal is 15 m. Find the perimeter of the field.

A. 7.2 m B. 42 m
C. 42 m² D. 1620 m

51. What was the day of the week on 17th August 2010?

A. Tuesday B. Thursday
C. Friday D. Sunday

52. If $x = 5, y = 3$, and $z = 2$, then $\frac{x(y-z)}{y(x+y+z)} = ?$

A. $\frac{1}{3}$ B. $\frac{1}{6}$
C. $\frac{1}{9}$ D. 1

53. $\sqrt{x} + 24 = \sqrt{900}$, then the value of x is

A. 34 B. 36
C. 38 D. 32

54. How many rotations does the hour hand of a clock complete in 96 hours?

A. 4 B. 6
C. 8 D. 12

55. What least value must be assigned to x so that the number 19x25462 is divisible by 9?

A. 2 B. 4
C. 7 D. 9

56. The smallest positive integer P, for which 1125 × P is a perfect cube (cube of a natural number) is

A. 1 B. 2
C. 3 D. 5

57. Find the value of x.

$$(x)^{\frac{1}{4}} = \frac{56}{(x)^{\frac{3}{4}}}$$

A. $(56)^{\frac{3}{4}}$ B. 14
C. 56 D. $(56)^{\frac{1}{3}}$

58. 40.36 divided by 0.04 gives

A. 1096 B. 1093
C. 1090 D. 1009

59. An observer, 2 m tall, is $10\sqrt{3}$ m away from a tower. The elevation angle from his eye to the top of the tower is 60°. The height of the tower is:

A. 16 m B. 32 m

C. 30 m D. 28 m

60. The time taken by a 900m long train travelling at 42 km/hr to pass a women walking in the same direction at 6 km/hr will be ______

A. $1\frac{1}{2}$ minutes B. $1\frac{1}{3}$ minutes

C. $1\frac{1}{4}$ minutes D. $2\frac{1}{2}$ minutes

61. Arrange the following in a logical order:

A. Door

B. Seed

C. Plant

D. Wood

E. Tree

Choose the correct answer from the options given below:

A. AEDCB B. ACEDB

C. BCDEA D. BCEDA

62. By looking in a mirror, it appears 6:30 on the clock. What is the actual time?

A. 5:30 B. 8:30

C. 6:30 D. 9:30

63. Here are some words translated from an artificial language:Moolokarm means blue sky.

Wikospadi means bicycle race.

Moolowiko means blue bicycle.

Which word could mean 'race car"?

A. Wikozwet

B. Spadiwiko

C. Moolobreil

D. Spadivolo

64. Complete the following pattern.

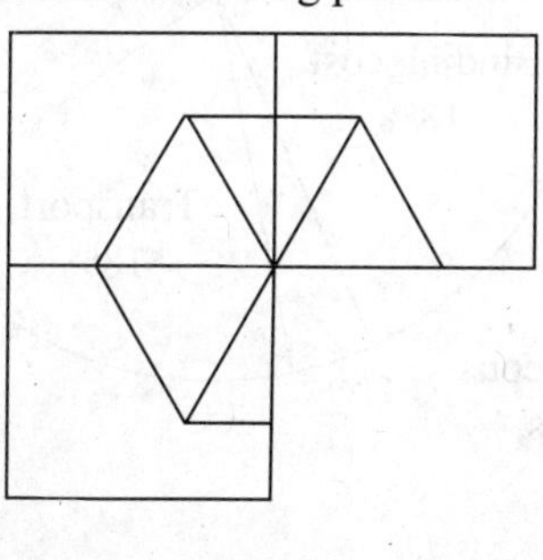

A. 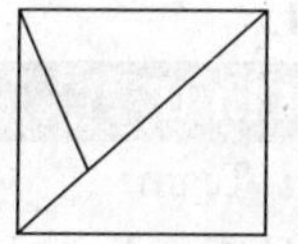 B. 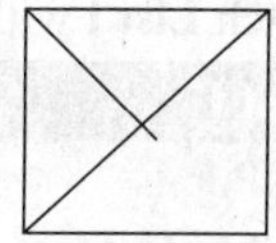

C. 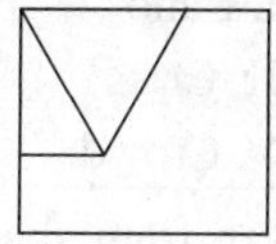 D. 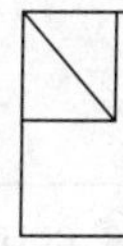

65. Match **List I** with **List II** based on the number of sides.

List I	List II
A. 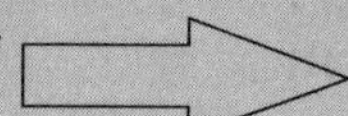	I. 18
B. 	II. 7
C. 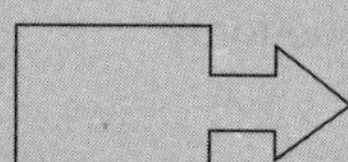	III. 5
D. 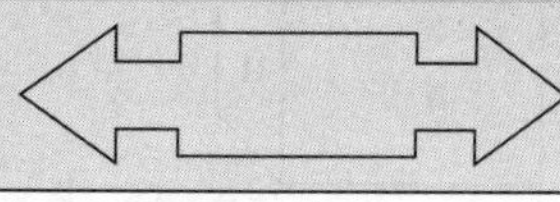	IV. 11

Choose the correct answer from the options given below:

A. A-II, B-III, C-IV, D-I

B. A-III, B-I, C-II, D-IV

C. A-II, B-IV, C-III, D-I

D. A-III, B-II, C-I, D-IV

66. Find out the symbol to make the given figure exactly.

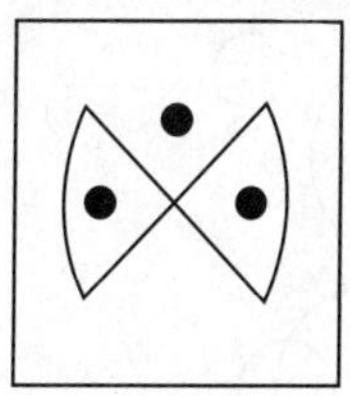

A. 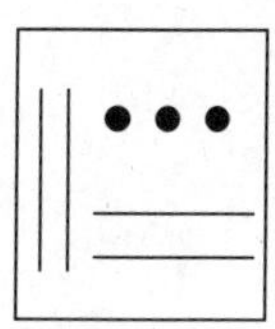 B. 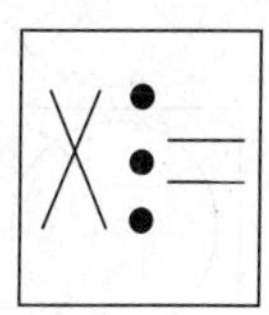

C. 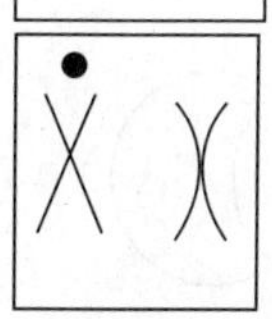 D. 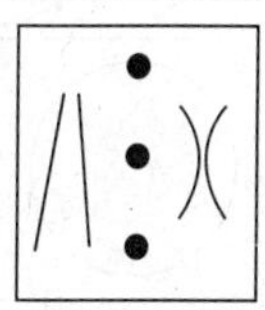

67. Match **List I** with **List II**.

List I	List II
A. Pupils	I. Team
B. Men	II. Band
C. Musicians	III. Class
D. Players	IV. Crowd

Choose the correct answer from the options given below:

A. A-VI, B-I, C-II, D-III
B. A-III, B-IV, C-II, D-I
C. A-III, B-II, C-IV, D-I
D. A-IV, B-II, C-I, D-III

68. In a die, 'a', 'b', 'c' and 'd' are written on the adjacent faces in a clockwise order and 'e' and 'f' at the top and the bottom. When 'c' is at the top, what will be at the bottom?

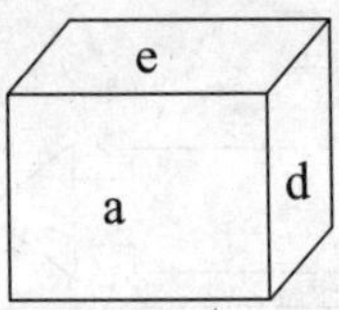

A. a B. b
C. e D. f

69. Choose the word that is necessary for the 'HARVESTING'.

A. AUTUMN B. STOCKPILE
C. PLOUGH D. CROP

70. Choose the correct representation of Primary: Secondary:School.

A.
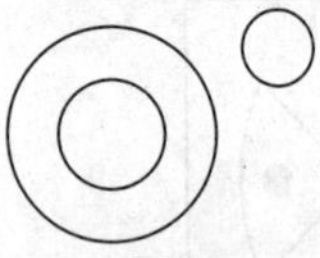

B.
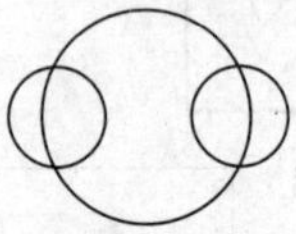

C.
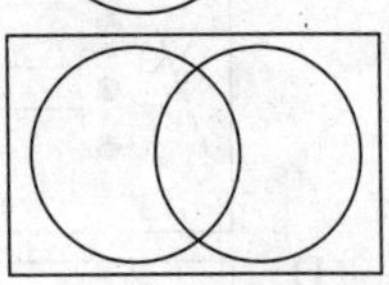

D.
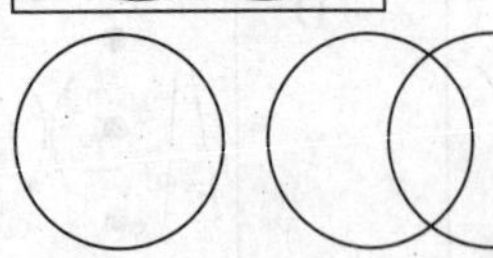

71. Study the diagram and find out the number that lies inside all the figures.

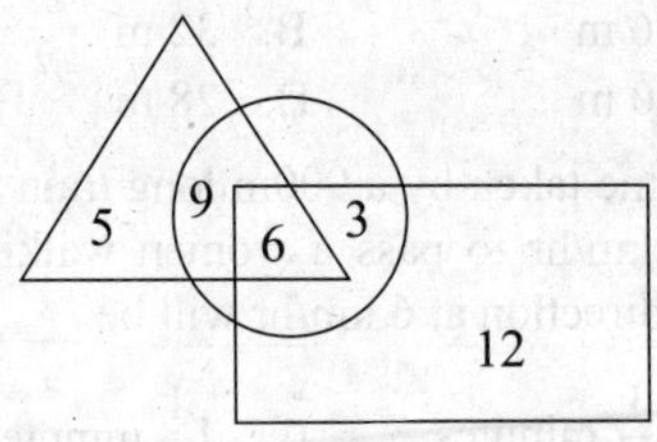

A. 3 B. 9
C. 6 D. 5

72. Find out the number that lies only in the circle.

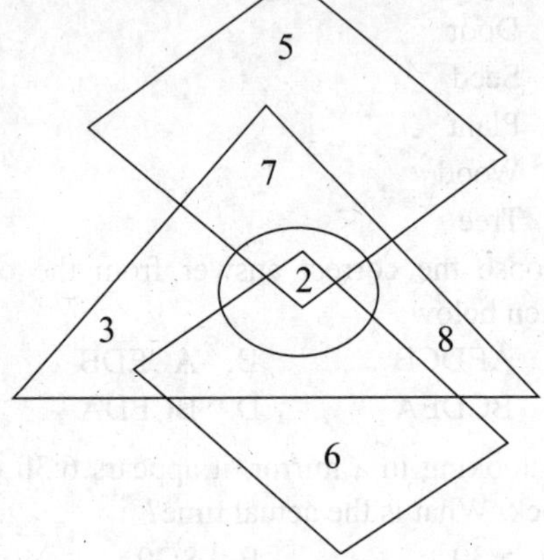

A. 3 B. 8
C. 7 D. 2

The pie chart gives the percentage of various items during the book production and sales. Answer questions 73–75 based on this pie chart.

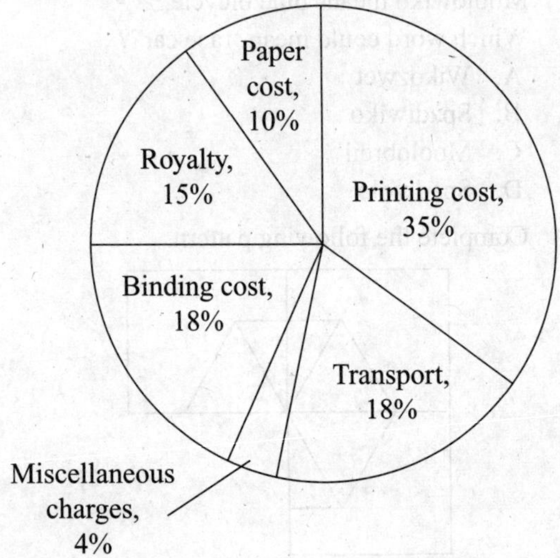

73. The cost of paper is approximately what per cent of the printing cost?

A. 20.3% B. 25.6%
C. 25.3% D. 28.6%

74. The central angle for the sector paper cost is:

A. $22\frac{1}{2}°$ B. 16°
C. 36° D. 10°

75. If the printing cost is ₹17500, then the royalty paid is:

A. ₹3150 B. ₹7500
C. ₹6300 D. ₹4550

Answer Key

1. **C**	2. **D**	3. **B**	4. **C**	5. **A**	6. **B**	7. **D**	8. **D**	9. **D**	10. **B**
11. **B**	12. **A**	13. **B**	14. **D**	15. **B**	16. **B**	17. **B**	18. **B**	19. **B**	20. **C**
21. **B**	22. **A**	23. **D**	24. **B**	25. **C**	26. **C**	*27. incorrect question			28. **D**
29. **D**	30. **D**	**31. **A**	32. **A**	33. **B**	34. **D**	35. **C**	36. **D**	37. **D**	38. **A**
39. **C**	40. **C**	41. **D**	42. **D**	43. **C**	44. **C**	45. **B**	46. **B**	47. **C**	48. **C**
49. **A**	50. **B**	51. **A**	52. **B**	53. **B**	54. **C**	55. **C**	56. **C**	57. **C**	58. **D**
59. **B**	60. **A**	61. **D**	62. **A**	63. **D**	64. **C**	65. **A**	66. **D**	67. **B**	68. **A**
69. **D**	70. **C**	71. **C**	***72. **D**	73. **D**	74. **C**	75. **B**			

*27. The question is wrong. The GCD of two numbers, 12 and 60, is 12 and NOT 6.
**31. This question was incorrect. There was NO consolidated list for the rankings of all the 5 cities in the question. There were 2 lists: Million Plus Population and Less than One Million Population. Also, there was NO entry called "Mumbai" (it had Greater Mumbai and Navi Mumbai).
***72. The question is incorrect. The answer given by the NTA was option D.

Classification of Questions

Question No.	Subject	Topic	Level of Difficulty
1.	Reasoning	Analogy (Number-based)	Easy
2.	Reasoning	Analogy	Easy
3.	Reasoning	Analogy (Letter-based)	Easy
4.	Reasoning	Analogy	Difficult
5.	Reasoning	Analogy	Easy
6.	Reasoning	Dictionary Order	Easy
7.	Reasoning	Directions	Easy
8.	Reasoning	Coding	Easy
9.	Reasoning	Number Series	Medium

Question No.	Subject	Topic	Level of Difficulty
10.	Quantitative Aptitude	Calendars	Easy
11.	Reasoning	Number Series	Easy
12.	Reasoning	Odd-one-out	Difficult
13.	Reasoning	Number Series	Easy
14.	Reasoning	Blood Relations	Easy
15.	Reasoning	Figure Counting	Medium
16.	Quantitative Aptitude	Averages	Medium
17.	Quantitative Aptitude	Percentages	Easy
18.	Quantitative Aptitude	Boats & Streams	Easy
19.	Quantitative Aptitude	Profit, Loss & Discount	Easy
20.	Quantitative Aptitude	Profit, Loss & Discount	Easy
21.	Quantitative Aptitude	Time, Speed & Distance	Medium
22.	Quantitative Aptitude	Numbers (LCM)	Medium
23.	Quantitative Aptitude	Time & Work	Medium
24.	Quantitative Aptitude	Time & Work	Medium
25.	Quantitative Aptitude	Percentages	Easy
26.	Quantitative Aptitude	Mensuration	Easy
27.	Quantitative Aptitude	Numbers (LCM & GCD)	Incorrect Question
28.	Quantitative Aptitude	Simple Interest	Medium
29.	Quantitative Aptitude	Ratios	Easy
30.	Quantitative Aptitude	Time, Speed & Distance	Medium
31.	General Awareness	Current Affairs	Medium
32.	General Awareness	Economics	Medium
33.	General Awareness	Science	Easy
34.	General Awareness	Geography	Medium
35.	General Awareness	History	Medium
36.	General Awareness	Science	Difficult
37.	General Awareness	Current Affairs	Difficult
38.	General Awareness	Books & Authors	Difficult
39.	General Awareness	Sports	Difficult
40.	General Awareness	Sports	Difficult
41.	General Awareness	Current Affairs	Difficult
42.	General Awareness	Current Affairs	Medium
43.	General Awareness	Current Affairs	Easy
44.	General Awareness	Important Days	Difficult

Question No.	Subject	Topic	Level of Difficulty
45.	General Awareness	Current Affairs	Easy
46.	Quantitative Aptitude	Averages	Easy
47.	Quantitative Aptitude	Simple Interest	Easy
48.	Reasoning	Number Series	Medium
49.	Quantitative Aptitude	Simplification	Easy
50.	Quantitative Aptitude	Mensuration	Easy
51.	Quantitative Aptitude	Calendars	Medium
52.	Quantitative Aptitude	Basic Arithmetic	Easy
53.	Quantitative Aptitude	Algebra (Equations)	Easy
54.	Quantitative Aptitude	Clocks	Easy
55.	Quantitative Aptitude	Numbers (Divisibility)	Easy
56.	Quantitative Aptitude	Numbers (Perfect Cubes)	Easy
57.	Quantitative Aptitude	Surds & Indices	Easy
58.	Quantitative Aptitude	Division	Easy
59.	Quantitative Aptitude	Trigonometry (Heights & Distances)	Easy
60.	Quantitative Aptitude	Time, Speed & Distance	Easy
61.	Reasoning	Words in a Logical Sequence	Easy
62.	Reasoning	Mirror Image	Easy
63.	Reasoning	Coding	Easy
64.	Reasoning	Non-verbal	Easy
65.	Quantitative Aptitude	Geometry	Easy
66.	Reasoning	Non-verbal	Easy
67.	Reasoning	Miscellaneous	Easy
68.	Reasoning	Die-based Problems	Easy
69.	Reasoning	Miscellaneous	Easy
70.	Reasoning	Venn-diagram	Easy
71.	Reasoning	Venn-diagram	Easy
72.	Reasoning	Venn-diagram	Question Incorrect
73.	Data Interpretation	Pie Chart	Easy
74.	Data Interpretation	Pie Chart	Easy
75.	Data Interpretation	Pie Chart	Easy

The no. of questions on Reasoning: 26
The no. of questions on General Awareness: 15
The no. of questions on Data Interpretation: 3
The no. of questions on Quantitative Aptitude: 31

Explanation to Select Questions

1. $289 = 17^2$
Therefore, the missing term is $23^2 = 529$.
Hence, Option C.

2. Scatter and collect are opposites, just as pliable and rigid are.
Hence, Option D.

3. 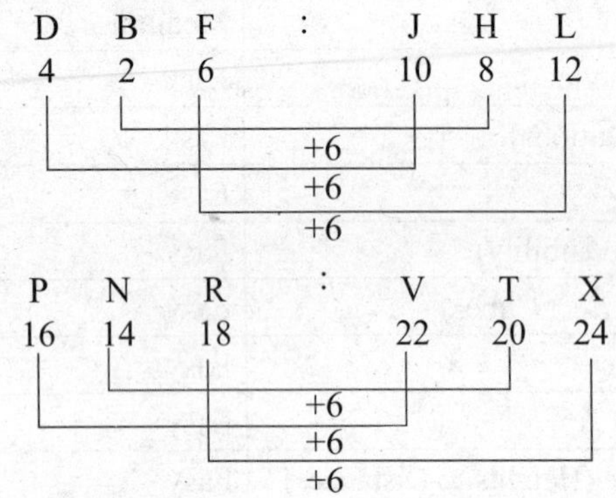

Hence, Option B.

5. Eager and keen are quite similar, and so are fervent and enthusiastic.
Hence, Option A.

7. 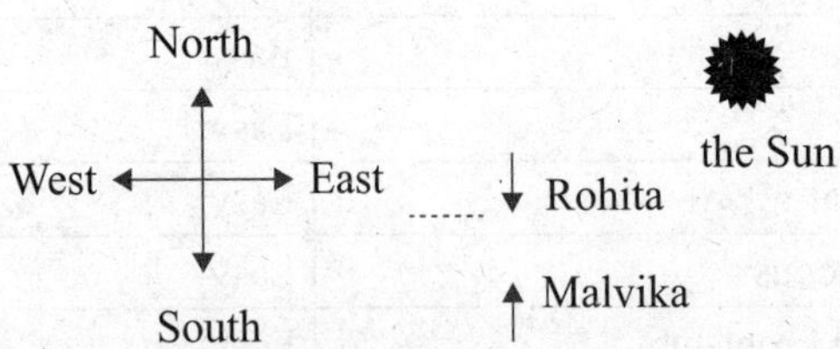

As it is morning, the Sun is in the East direction. For Rohita's shadow to be on Malvika's left, Malvika must be facing the North, and thus Rohita must be facing the South.
Hence, Option D.

8. 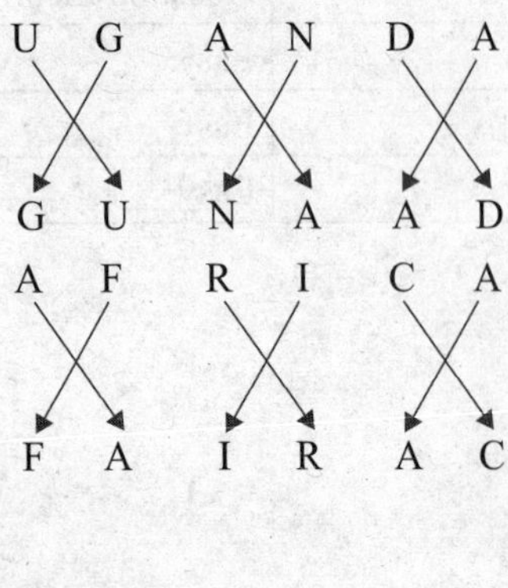

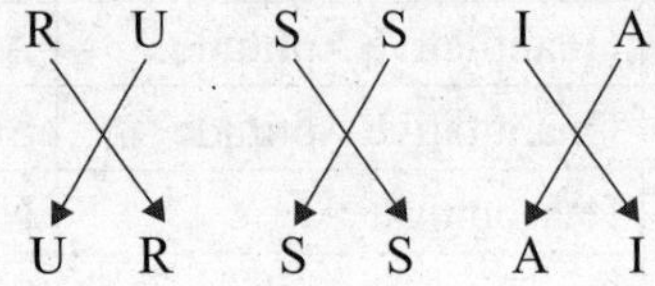

Hence, Option D.

9. All these five numbers are prime numbers. Actually, they are alternate prime numbers.

47, ~~53~~, 59, ~~61~~, 67, ~~71~~, 73, ~~79~~, 83, ~~89~~, 97.

So, starting with 47, every second prime number has been struck out.
Hence, Option D.

10. $54 = 7 \times 7 + 5$
Therefore, there are 5 odd-days in 54.
So, 54 days after a Wednesday, it would be a day that falls five days after a Wednesday, a Monday.
Hence, Option B.

11. The numbers in the given series are in an AP, and every term is 4 more than the previous term.
$6 = 2 + 4$, $10 = 6 + 4$, etc.
The next term of the series $= 18 + 4 = 22$.
Hence, Option B.

12. Kangaroos, opossums and wombats are marsupial mammals, but platypus is not.
Hence, Option A.

13. Starting from the right, the series is like:
$3 \times 3 = 9$
$9 \times 4 = 36$
$\mathbf{36 \times 5 = 180}$
$180 \times 6 = 1080$
$1080 \times 7 = 7560$
Hence, Option B.

14. 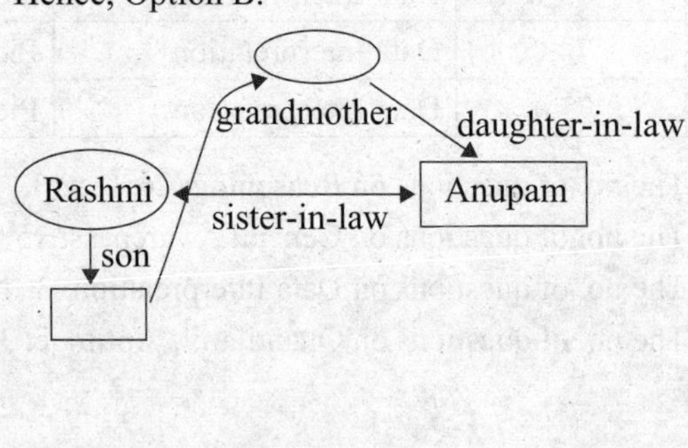

Thus, we see that Rashmi and Anupam are daughters-in-law of the same woman.

So, they must be sisters-in-law.

Hence, Option D.

15. 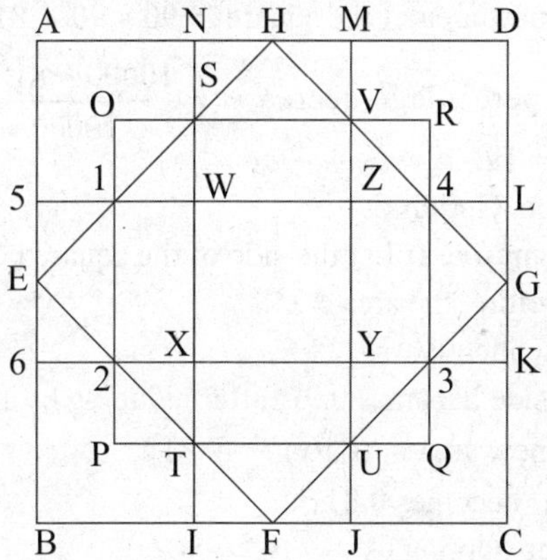

The squares are:

ABCD, A6YM, 5BJZ, WICL, NXKD, A5WN, 56XW, 6BIX, NWZM, WXYZ, XIJY, MZLD, ZYKL, YJCK, O1WS, 2PTX, YUQ3, VZ4R, O2YV, 1PUZ, WTQ4, SX3R, OPQR and EFGH.

Hence, Option B.

Note: Do NOT commit the blunder of counting WXYZ twice.

16. The total age of the 5 members, five years ago $= 15 \times 5 = 75$ years.

Each of these members is 5 years older now.

So, the total age of those 5 members now $= 75 + 5 \times 5 = 100$ years.

The total age of those 5 members and the child $= 17 \times 6 = 102$ years.

Therefore, the age of the child is $102 - 100 = 2$ years.

Hence, Option B.

17. Let the total numbers of books in the library be x.

The number of books in Hindi $= x \times \dfrac{50}{100} = \dfrac{x}{2}$.

The remaining books $= x - \dfrac{x}{2} = \dfrac{x}{2}$.

Now, 30% of these remaining books are in English.

So, $\dfrac{x}{2} \times \dfrac{30}{100} = 2400$

or, $x = \dfrac{2400 \times 2 \times 100}{30} = 16000$.

Therefore, the number of books in Hindi.

$= 16000 \times \dfrac{1}{2} = 8000$.

Hence, Option B.

Note: Option C is a trap.

Shortcut:

Books in Hindi = 50%

The remaining books = 50%

30% of 50% $= 50 \times \dfrac{30}{100} = 15\%$.

So, 15% of books are in English.

15% is equivalent to 2400 (books in English).

$\Rightarrow$ 50% (the number of books in Hindi)

$= \dfrac{2400}{15} \times 50 = 8000$.

18. The boat travels 8 km downstream in 2 hrs.

Therefore, it will travel 10 km downstream in $\dfrac{2}{8} \times 10 = 2.5$ hours.

Hence, Option B.

19. Let the cost price and the selling price be $5x$ and $4x$, respectively.

Therefore, the loss percentage $= \dfrac{5x - 4x}{5x} \times 100 = \dfrac{1}{5} \times 100 = 20$.

Hence, Option B.

20. The total cost $= 100000 + 1200 + 2000 = 103200$.

Profit $= 40\%$ of $103200 = \dfrac{103200 \times 40}{100} = 41280$.

Therefore, the selling price $= 103200 + 41280 = 144480$.

Hence, Option C.

21. 1 hour, 30 minutes and 30 seconds

$= 3600 + 1800 + 30 = 5430$ seconds.

In 5430 seconds, the auto travels 36 km at $\dfrac{3}{4}$ of its normal speed,

Therefore, In 3600 seconds, at its normal speed, the auto travels $36 \times \frac{3600}{5430} \times \frac{4}{3}$ = 31.82 km (approx.)

Hence, Option B.

22. The number of the seconds in 3 hours = 10800.
The LCM of 5, 10, 15 and 30 is 30.
So, all these bells ring every 30 seconds.

Therefore, they will ring $\frac{10800}{30} = 360$ times in 3 hours.

So, the number of times they ring together is 360 + 1 (for the beginning) = 361

Hence, Option A.

Note: They will ring simultaneously only 360 times in precisely 3 hours, but most of the exams follow this convention of adding 1.

23. Let the work be of 60 units.

So, A, B and C do $\frac{60}{10} = 6$ units in a day (i)

B and C do $\frac{60}{15} = 4$ units in a day (ii)

A and C do $\frac{60}{12} = 5$ units in a day (iii)

Comparing (i) and (iii),
B does 6 – 5 = 1 unit daily.
Therefore, B alone can complete the work in $\frac{60}{1} = 60$ days.

Hence, Option D.

24. Let X take n days to finish the job.
Y will take $3n$ days to finish this job as X is thrice as good a worker as Y.
We have, $3n - n = 40$ days.
or, $2n = 40$ days
or, $n = 20$ days.
So, X takes 20 days, and Y takes 60 days to finish this work.

Therefore, together they will take $\frac{1}{\frac{1}{20}+\frac{1}{60}} = \frac{1200}{80} = 15$ days.

Hence, Option B.

25. Let the side of the square be 100.
Its area = $100 \times 100 = 10000$.
The side of the square after a 10% decrease = 100 – 10 = 90.
The new area of the square = $90 \times 90 = 8100$.

The percentage decrease = $\frac{10000-8100}{10000} \times 100 = 19$.

Hence, Option C.

Alternative I: Let the side of the square be x.
Therefore, the area = x^2
Subsequently,
The side becomes $0.9x$ (after reducing by 10%)
The new area = $(0.9x)^2 = 0.81\,x^2$.
So, x^2 becomes $0.81x^2$.
Hence, Option C.

Alternative II: As the area of a square = side × side
The percentage decrease in the area after reducing the sides by 10% is a case of 2 successive reductions of 10%.

Net percentage change = $-10 - 10 + \frac{(-10)(-10)}{100} = -20 + 1 = -19\%$.

Hence, a 19% decrease.

Note: Two successive changes of x% and y% cause a net change of $\left(x + y + \frac{xy}{100}\right)$%.

27. Let the other number be x.
The product of two numbers = product of their LCM and HCF.
We have, $x \times 12 = 6 \times 120$

or, $x = \frac{6 \times 120}{12} = 60$.

Hence, the numbers 12 and 60.

Note: The CUET-UG marked Option C as the answer, **but the question is incorrect** as the HCF of 12 and 60 is 12 and NOT 6.

If the HCF and the LCM of two numbers are 6 and 120, respectively, none of the numbers can be 12.

In such a case (HCF = 6 and LCM = 120), there can be only two pairs of numbers: (6, 120) and (24, 30).

28. The number of days in the period 5th April 2021 to 28 August 2021 (including both the days) is 146.

Now, the principal = 125000

rate = 6% per annum

time = $\frac{146}{365}$ year

Therefore, the Simple interest

$$= \frac{125000 \times 6 \times \frac{146}{365}}{100} = 1250 \times 6 \times \frac{146}{365}$$

= ₹3000.

Hence, Option D.

29. $\frac{13}{14} = \frac{x}{8}$ or, $x = \frac{13 \times 8}{14} = 7.428$ (approx.).

Hence, Option D.

30. The relative speed of the train, with respect to the man = 102 – 16 = 86 km/hr

$= \frac{86 \times 1000}{3600}$ m/s.

$= \frac{215}{9}$ m/s

In order to pass the man, the train needs to pass its own length of 450 m.

Time taken $= \frac{450}{\frac{215}{9}} = \frac{450 \times 9}{215} = 18.84$ seconds (approx.).

Hence, Option D.

31. There is a problem with the way this question is structured. The Ease of Living Index comes with different categories of rankings for cities with a population above 1 million and cities with a population below 1 million. Option A was the best choice as, at that time, Bengaluru and Chennai were ranked 1 and 2, respectively, in India among million-plus cities.

36. Richter Scale and Seismograph measure the magnitude of an earthquake. Mercalli Scale records the intensity of the earthquake waves.

Hence, Option D.

37. The ranks were as per option D at the time when this test was conducted. The current ranks are:

1. Elon Musk
2. Jeff Bezos
3. Bernard Arnault
4. Bill Gates
5. Mark Zuckerberg

46. Let the numbers be $x, x + 2, x + 4$ and $x + 6$.

We have, $\frac{x + (x + 2) + (x + 4) + (x + 6)}{4} = 16$

or, $4x + 12 = 64$

or, $4x = 64 - 12 = 52$

or, $x = \frac{52}{4} = 13.$

So, the numbers are 13, 15, 17 and 19.

The sum of the first and the third numbers = 13 + 17 = 30.

Hence, Option B.

Alternative: As the four numbers are in AP, their mean (average) is equal to their median, and the median of the 4 numbers will be the average of the second and the third terms.

As 16 is the average of the second and the third terms, these two terms must be 15 and 17 (as they are two consecutive odd numbers).

Hence, the numbers are 13, 15, 17 and 19.

I expect you to do it mentally.

47. The simple interest on ₹22000 for 4 years at 5% per annum $= \frac{22000 \times 4 \times 5}{100} = 4400.$

The required time $= \frac{\text{simple interest} \times 100}{\text{principal} \times \text{rate}}$

$= \frac{4400 \times 100}{33000 \times 10} = \frac{4}{3} = 1\frac{1}{3}$ years.

Hence, Option C.

48. All numbers in the sequence are multiples of 11, but 66 is the only number that is a product of 3 prime numbers.

$22 = 11 \times 2$

$33 = 11 \times 3$

$55 = 11 \times 5$

$\boxed{66 = 11 \times 3 \times 2}$

$77 = 11 \times 7$

$121 = 11 \times 11$
Hence, Option C.

49. $936 \times 296 - 936 \times 196$
$= 936(296 - 196) = 936 \times 100 = 93600.$
Hence, Option A.

50. 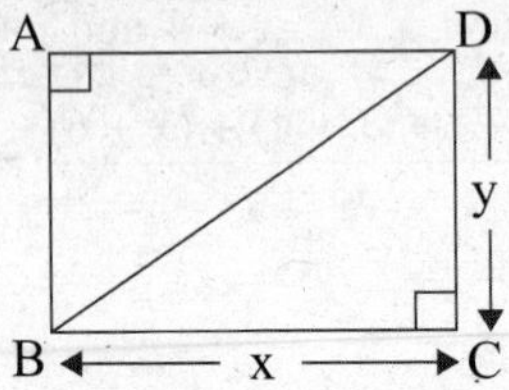

Let the length and the breath of the rectangle be x and y.
The area $= x \times y = 108$

The diagonal $= \sqrt{x^2 + y^2} = 15$

or, $x^2 + y^2 = 15^2 = 225$

$(x + y)^2 = x^2 + y^2 + 2xy = 225 + 2(108)$

$= 225 + 216 = 441 = 21^2$

So, $x + y = 21$.

The perimeter of the rectangle $= 2(x + y)$

$= 2 \times 21 = 42$ m.

Note: The perimeter is a length and NOT an area and hence, its unit cannot be m^2. So, option C should be discarded.
Hence, Option B.
Alternative: 9, 12 and 15 make a Pythagorean triple. We have, area = 12×9 and the diagonal $= \sqrt{12^2 + 9^2}$.
Hence, the perimeter = $2(9 + 12) = 42$ m.

51. 1.1.1 was a Monday and so, was 1.1.401, 1.1.801, 1.1.1201, 1.1.1601 and 1.1.2001.
The number of odd days between 1.1.2001 and 1.1.2010 = 11, which is effectively 11 – 7 = 4.
Therefore, 1.1.2010 fell on a day that comes 4 days after a Monday, a Friday.
The number of odd days between 1.1.2010 and 17.8.2010 is 2(January) + 0(February) + 3(March) + 2 (April) + 3(May) + 2(June) + 3(July) + 3(August) = 18, which is effectively 18 – 14 = 4 days.
Therefore, the day on 17th August 2010 was a day that falls 4 days after a Friday, a Tuesday.
Hence, Option A.
Note: The day does not change after a multiple of 7 days, and hence, anything in excess of a multiple of 7 is considered odd days.

52. $\dfrac{x(y - z)}{y(x + y + z)} = \dfrac{5(3 - 2)}{3(5 + 3 + 2)} = \dfrac{5}{3 \times 10} = \dfrac{1}{6}.$

Hence, Option B.

53. $\sqrt{x} + 24 = \sqrt{900} = 30.$

or, $\sqrt{x} = 30 - 24 = 6.$

or, $x = 36.$
Hence, Option B.

54. The hour hand of a clock completes one rotation in 12 hours.
Therefore, the number of rotations in 96 hours
$= \dfrac{96}{12} = 8.$
Hence, Option C.

55. A number is divisible by 9 if the sum of its digits is divisible by 9.
The sum of the digits of 19x 25462 is $1 + 9 + x + 2 + 5 + 4 + 6 + 2 = 29 + x$.
If we put $x = 7$, the sum becomes 36, divisible by 9.
Hence, Option C.

56. $1125 \times P = 3^2 \times 5^3 \times P$
If we put P = 3, the number becomes
$3 \times 3^2 \times 5^3 = 3^3 \times 5^3 = (3 \times 5)^3 = 15^3$.
Hence, Option C.

57. $x^{\frac{1}{4}} = \dfrac{56}{x^{\frac{3}{4}}}$ or, $x^{\frac{1}{4}} \times x^{\frac{3}{4}} = 56.$

or, $x^{\frac{1}{4}+\frac{3}{4}} = 56$

or, $x^1 = 56$

or, $x = 56.$

Hence, Option C.

58. $\dfrac{40.36}{0.04} = \dfrac{40.36 \times 100}{0.04 \times 100} = \dfrac{4036}{4} = 1009.$

Hence, Option D.

59.

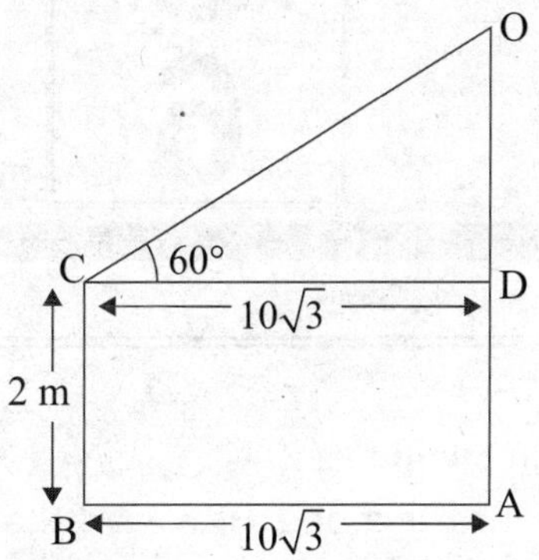

Let OA Be the tower and BC be the observer.

We have, BC = 2

$CD = BA = 10\sqrt{3}$

$DA = CB = 2$

$\angle OCD = 60°$.

In ΔOCD,

$$\tan 60° = \frac{OD}{DC} = \frac{OD}{10\sqrt{3}} \quad \text{or, } \sqrt{3} = \frac{OD}{10\sqrt{3}}$$

or, $OD = 10\sqrt{3} \times \sqrt{3} = 10 \times 3 = 30$.

The height of the tower OA = OD + DA = 30 + 2 = 32 m.

Hence, Option B.

60. The relative speed of the train with respect to the woman = 42 – 6 = 36 km/hr

$$= \frac{36 \times 1000}{3600} \text{ m/s} = 10 \text{ m/s}.$$

Now, in order to pass the woman, the train has to travel its own length, which is 900 m.

Therefore, the required time $= \frac{900}{10} =$ 90 seconds $= 1\frac{1}{2}$ minutes.

Hence, Option A.

61. A seed gives you a plant that matures into a tree and gives you wood with which you make a door.

Hence, Option D.

62. The actual time = 12:00 – the image of the time = 12:00 – 6:30 = 5:30

Hence, Option A.

63. Moolokarm:blue sky (i)

Wikospadi:bicycle race (ii)

Moolowiko:blue bicycle (iii)

On comparing (ii) and (iii), we get that 'wiko' is the code for bicycle and 'spadi' is the code for race. Hence, the code for 'race car' must have 'spadi', but not 'wiko. These conditions are met only in Option D.

68.

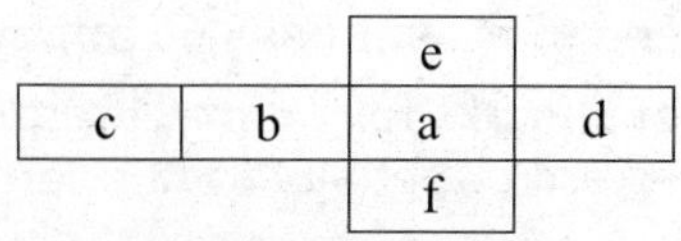

It is clear that the faces having c and a are opposite to each other.

Hence, Option A.

Please refer to the following figure for explanations of questions 73–75.

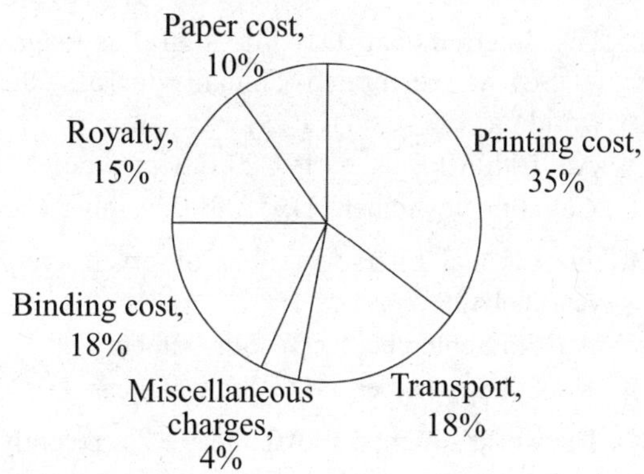

73. The cost of paper = 10%

The printing cost = 35%

Therefore, the required percentage $= \frac{10}{35} \times 100$

$$= \frac{2}{7} \times 100 = 28.6 \text{ (approx.)}$$

Hence, Option D.

74. The central angle for the paper cost = 10% of 360° = 36°.

Hence, Option C.

75. The printing cost = 35% = 17500

The royalty paid $= 15\% = \frac{17500}{35} \times 15 = 7500$.

Hence, Option B.

CUET UG 2022
General Test

August 6

Instructions:

1. You need to attempt any 60 out of the 75 questions in 60 minutes.
2. You get 5 marks for a correct response and –1 for an incorrect one. However, there is no reward or penalty for a question not attempted.

1. The Indian Army organised "Bijoya Sanskritik Mahotsav" from 26th to 29th September 2021 in

A. Pune B. Kolkata
C. Kanpur D. Prayagraj

2. The International Day of Sign Languages (IDSL) is celebrated annually across the world on

A. 10th April B. 23rd September
C. 20th November D. 10th December

3. International Literacy Day is observed every year globally on

A. 5th September B. 5th October
C. 8th September D. 8th October

4. The world's highest movie theatre has recently been inaugurated in

A. Ladakh
B. Himachal Pradesh
C. Jammu and Kashmir
D. Sikkim

5. Who created history as she became the first Indian woman finalist at the World Wrestling Championship 2021 and also the first female player from India to claim a silver medal?

A. Alka Tomar B. Vinesh Phogat
C. Anshu Malik D. Sakshi Malik

6. Three words are given here with something in common. Out of the four alternatives, choose the most appropriate description of these words.
Prakrit:Pali:Sanskrit

A. They are classical languages of Asia and Europe.
B. The Vedas are written in these languages.
C. They are ancient languages of India.
D. They are dead languages.

7. Select the combination of the correct pairs from the following.

(a) Netherlands:Euro
(b) UAE:Dinar
(c) Russia:Ruble
(d) Turkey:Lira
(e) Korea:Rial

Choose the correct answer from the options given below.

A. (b), (d), (c) B. (a), (c), (d)
C. (b), (e), (d) D. (c), (a), (b)

8. Arrange the given words in the sequence in which they occur in a dictionary.

(a) Bishop
(b) Bifocal
(c) Bicycle
(d) Bitter
(e) Brink

Choose the correct answer from the options given below.

A. (e), (b), (a), (d), (c)
B. (b), (c), (d), (a), (e)
C. (c), (b), (a), (d), (e)
D. (a), (c), (d), (e), (b)

9. Match **List I** with **List II**.

List I	List II
(A) Avesta	(I) Jew
(B) Torah	(II) Muslim
(C) Tripitaka	(III) Parsi
(D) Quran	(IV) Buddhist

Choose the correct answer from the options given below:

A. (A)-(II), (B)-(I), (C)-(III), (D)-(IV)
B. (A)-(III), (B)-(I), (C)-(IV), (D)-(II)
C. (A)-(IV), (B)-(II), (C)-(I), (D)-(III)
D. (A)-(I), (B)-(II), (C)-(IV), (D)-(III)

10. Match **List I** with **List II**.

List I	List II
(A) Botany	(I) Animals
(B) Zoology	(II) Blood
(C) Pathology	(III) Plants
(D) Haematology	(IV) Diseases

Choose the correct answer from the options given below:

A. (A)-(II), (B)-(III), (C)-(IV), (D)-(I)
B. (A)-(I), (B)-(II), (C)-(III), (D)-(IV)
C. (A)-(III), (B)-(I), (C)-(IV), (D)-(II)
D. (A)-(IV), (B)-(II), (C)-(III), (D)-(I)

11. Among the four options, three objects/things have the same properties. Find the odd one out.

A. Confluence B. Concourse
C. Concentration D. Radiation

12. Match **List I** with **List II**.

List I (Pass)	List II (State)
(A) Bomdila	(I) Jammu and Kashmir
(B) Banihal	(II) Sikkim
(C) Rohtang	(III) Arunachal Pradesh
(D) Nathu La	(IV) Himachal Pradesh

Choose the correct answer from the options given below:

A. (A)-(III), (B)-(I), (C)-(II), (D)-(IV)
B. (A)-(I), (B)-(III), (C)-(IV), (D)-(II)
C. (A)-(III), (B)-(I), (C)-(IV), (D)-(II)
D. (A)-(I), (B)-(III), (C)-(II), (D)-(IV)

13. Match **List I** with **List II**.

List I	List II
(A) High	(I) Peace
(B) Chaos	(II) Rejoice
(C) Mourn	(III) Deny
(D) Affirm	(IV) Low

Choose the correct answer from the options given below:

A. (A)-(III), (B)-(II), (C)-(I), (D)-(IV)
B. (A)-(I), (B)-(II), (C)-(IV), (D)-(III)
C. (A)-(IV), (B)-(I), (C)-(II), (D)-(III)
D. (A)-(II), (B)-(III), (C)-(IV), (D)-(I)

14. The following three words have something in common among themselves:

Ovary:Uterus:Cervix

Choose the most appropriate description of these three words from the four alternatives.

A. They are excretory organs.
B. They are reproductive organs.
C. They are endocrine glands.
D. They are organs for fertilisation in plants.

15. Arrange the given words in a sequence in which they occur in a dictionary.

(a) Leprosy
(b) Lessen
(c) Lesson
(d) Language
(e) Languid

Choose the correct answer from the options given below:

A. (a), (d), (e), (b), (c)
B. (d), (e), (a), (b), (c)
C. (a), (c), (d), (e), (b)
D. (a), (b), (c), (d), (e)

16. Match **List I** with **List II**.

List I	List II
(a) OZ	(i) 23
(b) KL	(ii) 27
(c) PK	(iii) 16
(d) DL	(iv) 41

Choose the correct answer from the options given below:

A. (a)-(IV), (b)-(II), (c)-(I), (d)-(III)
B. (a)-(III), (b)-(I), (c)-(II), (d)-(IV)
C. (a)-(IV), (b)-(I), (c)-(II), (d)-(III)
D. (a)-(I), (b)-(IV), (c)-(III), (d)-(II)

17. Who among the following were elected as the President as well as the Vice-president?

(a) Zakir Hussain
(b) Neelam Sanjeev Reddy
(c) Zail Singh
(d) K.R. Narayanan
(e) Shankar Dayal Sharma

Choose the correct answer from the options given below:

A. (a), (c) and (d) only
B. (b), (d) and (e) only
C. (b), (c) and (e) only
D. (a), (d) and (e) only

18. Which number will replace the question mark?

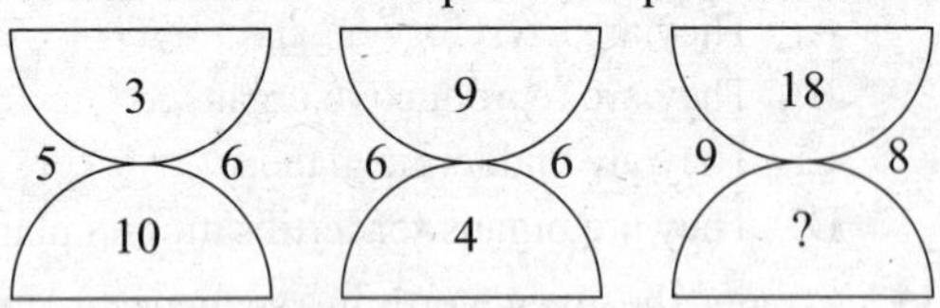

A. 9 B. 3
C. 8 D. 4

19. Bewilderment always comprises

A. Difficulty B. Anxiety
C. Helpless State D. Sharpness

20. The given set (2, 17, 31) is a set of

(a) Prime numbers
(b) Whole numbers
(c) Odd numbers
(d) Even numbers

Choose the correct answer from the options given below:

A. (a) only B. (a) and (b) only
C. (b) only D. (c) and (d) only

21. Find the next figure of the given series.

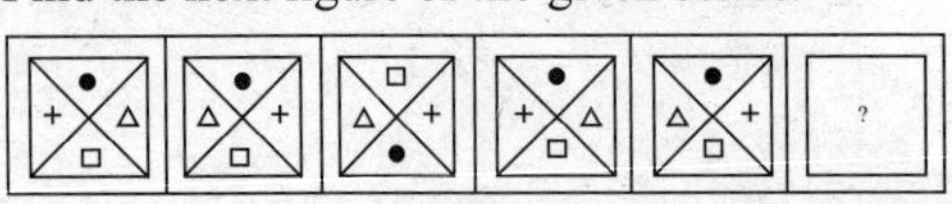

A.  B. 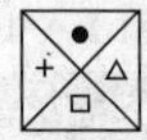
C.  D. 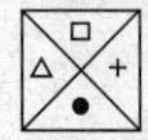

22. From the given options, which word can't be formed by using the letters of the word: "CATERING"

(a) CREATING
(b) REACTING
(c) RETIRING
(d) ARGENTIC

Choose the correct answer from the options given below:

A. (a) B. (b)
C. (c) D. (d)

23. The following three words have something in common among themselves:

Knight:Rook:Bishop

Choose the most appropriate description of these three words from the four given alternatives.

A. These are missionaries.
B. These are chessmen.
C. These are churchmen.
D. These are ranks of the military.

24. Arrange the given words in the sequence in which they occur in a dictionary.

(a) Amphibian
(b) Amorphous
(c) Ambidextrous
(d) Ambiguous
(e) Ambivalent

Choose the correct answer from the options given below:

A. (a), (c), (d), (e), (b)
B. (e), (b), (c), (d), (a)
C. (a), (c), (d), (b), (e)
D. (c), (d), (e), (b), (a)

25. Which among the following is a supercomputer of America?

A. Param
B. Mira
C. Anupam
D. SAGA-220

26. Eight friends A, B, C, D, E, F, G and H are placed in this manner:

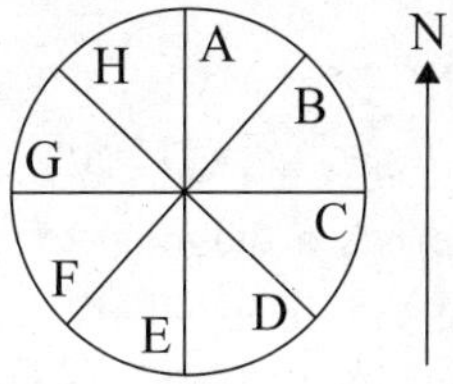

All are facing outward. If all of them move one position in the clockwise direction, then the direction E will be facing is:

A. Southwest B. Southeast
C. South D. West

27. Which among the following is a kharif crop?

A. Wheat B. Peas
C. Mustard D. Maize

28. Which was the first spacecraft to carry man to the Moon?

A. Sputnik-08 B. Sputnik-10
C. Apollo-11 D. Apollo-15

29. Which letters are midway between F and S in the English alphabet?

A. LM B. MN
C. KL D. JK

30. Consider a watch that gains 10 minutes daily. By what per cent does it become fast?

A. $\frac{5}{12}\%$ B. $\frac{1}{6}\%$
C. $\frac{25}{36}\%$ D. 2.5%

31. A 400 m long train passes a railway platform in 20 seconds at 90 km/hr speed. What is the length of the platform?

A. 105 m B. 102 m
C. 99 m D. 100 m

32. Match **List I** with **List II**.

List-I	List-II
(a) Cerebrum	(I) involuntary muscular coordination
(b) Diencephalon	(II) regulates heart rate
(c) Cerebellum	(III) intelligence
(d) Medulla oblongata	(IV) heat, cold and pain control

Choose the correct answer from the options given below:

A. (a)-(III), (b)-(IV), (c)-(I), (d)-(II)
B. (a)-(II), (b)-(III), (c)-(I), (d)-(IV)
C. (a)-(IV), (b)-(I), (c)-(II), (d)-(III)
D. (a)-(I), (b)-(III), (b)-(IV), (d)-(II)

33. An amount becomes its 3 times in 20 years. What is the rate of simple interest per annum?

A. 15% B. 10%
C. 6.67% D. 6%

34. Which of the following represents $x \cdot y = 64$?

A. $8{:}x = 8{:}y$ B. $x{:}8 = y{:}8$
C. $x{:}16 = y{:}4$ D. $32{:}x = y{:}2$

35. The ratio $5^{8\cdot14}{:}5^{5\cdot14}$ is equal to:

A. 1:5 B. 5:1
C. 25:1 D. 125:1

36. The sum of the ages of 5 children born at intervals of 3 years each is 50 years. What is the age of the youngest child?

A. 4 years B. 7 years
C. 9 years D. 10 years

37. The average of 3 consecutive even integers is 12. What is their product?

A. 1640 B. 1690
C. 1650 D. 1680

38. Find the average of the following numbers: 12, 15, 18, 14, 16, 13, 25, 28, 23, 27

A. 18.25 B. 12.5
C. 19.1 D. 16.1

39. Which among the following is a base?

A. NaCl B. NaOH
C. HCl D. $MgCl_2$

40. What per cent decrease in salaries would exactly cancel the 20 per cent increase?

A. $15\frac{1}{3}\%$ B. $14\frac{2}{3}\%$
C. $16\frac{2}{3}\%$ D. $33\frac{1}{3}\%$

41. The Escape Velocity at the Earth's surface is:

A. 11.2 km/sec B. 112 km/sec
C. 11.2 km/minute D. 112 km/hour

42. P, Q and R can complete a work in 12, 9 and 15 days, respectively.

Working together, they will complete the work in:

A. $3\frac{39}{47}$ days B. $5\frac{15}{42}$ days

C. $3\frac{38}{47}$ days D. $5\frac{39}{47}$ days

43. If 36 farmers can do a piece of work in 24 hours, in how many hours can 18 farmers do it?

A. 36 hours B. 42 hours

C. 48 hours D. 56 hours

44. The LCM and HCF of the two numbers are 35 and 15, respectively.
The product of these numbers is ________.

A. 625 B. 525

C. 425 D. 325

45. What will be the simple interest earned on an amount of ₹22000 in 8 months at $8\frac{1}{4}$ per annum?

A. ₹1013 B. ₹1012

C. ₹1210 D. ₹1215

46. The value of $3 - 3 \div 3$ is

A. 2 B. 4

C. 0 D. 1

47. If 20% of a number is 30, then the number is

A. 6 B. 150

C. 60 D. 15

48. Which city of the world is known as "the city of Golden Gate"?

A. Jaipur B. Amritsar

C. San Francisco D. Washington

49. The contribution of the agriculture sector to the GDP of India is around ________ at current prices.

A. 10% B. 12%

C. 20% D. 25%

50. The value of $x^{a-b} \times x^{b-c} \times x^{c-a}$ is

A. 1 B. 0

C. –1 D. x

51. If the adjacent angles of a parallelogram are $(2x + 30)°$ and $(3x - 15)°$, then the value of x is

A. 36 B. 39

C. 33 D. 35

52. If the lengths of two diagonals of a rectangle are $(2x - 3)$ cm and $(x + 2)$ cm, then the value of x is

A. 1 B. 5

C. 5/2 D. 5/3

53. If a square has a diagonal of length $6\sqrt{2}$ cm, then the area of the square is

A. 48 cm² B. 72 cm²

C. 16 cm² D. 36 cm²

54. The value of x in the equation $2x - 3 = 7 - 3x$ is

A. 10 B. 2

C. –2 D. 5

Direction: Read the following and answer questions 55–57.

In the given figure, ABCD is a square, and OE = 7 cm.

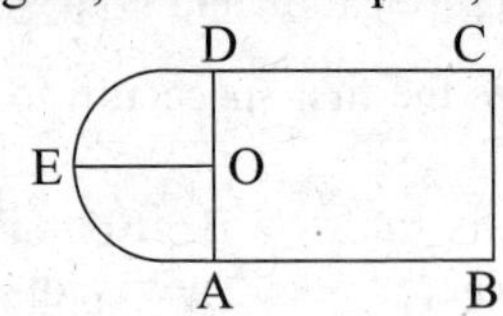

55. The perimeter of the figure is

A. 42 cm B. 44 cm

C. 64 cm D. 86 cm

56. The length of the diagonals of the square is

A. $14\sqrt{2}$ cm B. $7\sqrt{2}$ cm

C. 14 cm D. 7 cm

57. The area covered by the figure is

A. 350 cm² B. 273 cm²

C. 372 cm² D. 237 cm²

Direction: Please read the following carefully and answer questions 58–60.

The marks of 7 students in a unit test are given below:

9, 10, 7, 6, 9, 3, 5

58. The mode of the data is

A. 7 B. 9

C. 10 D. 6

59. The median of the data is

A. 6 B. 10

C. 9 D. 7

60. The mean of the data is

A. 9 B. 10

C. 7 D. 6

61. Five statements are given below, followed by options consisting of three statements put together in a specific order. Choose the option that indicates a conclusion drawn from the preceding two statements.

(A) All models are pretty.
(B) Some models are popular.
(C) Ruby is pretty.
(D) Ruby is a popular heroine.
(E) Some popular models are pretty.

Choose the correct answer from the options given below:

A. (A), (B), (E) B. (A), (C), (D)
C. (D), (C), (A) D. (E), (D), (C)

62. If A means addition, B means division, C means multiplication and D means subtraction, then find the value of 49B7D9A15C6.

A. –180 B. 180
C. 88 D. 38

63. In the given question, select the related word from the alternatives:

Man:Biography : : Nation:?

A. Population B. Autobiography
C. History D. People

64. Kalam says, "Ravi's mother is the only daughter of my mother." How is Kalam related to Ravi?

A. Father B. Brother
C. Maternal Uncle D. Uncle

65. If * stands for addition,
⊗ stands for subtraction,
⇔ stands for division,
↕ stands for multiplication,
≠ stands for equal to,
then which of the following alternatives is correct?

A. 2 ↕ 5 ⊗ 6 * 2 ≠ 6
B. 5 * 7 ⊗ 4 ⇔ 2 ≠ 4
C. 3 ↕ 6 ⇔ 2 * 3 ⊗ 6 ≠ 5
D. 4 ⇔ 7 * 4 ≠ 2 ↕ 3 ⊗ 1

66. Introducing a man *X*, *Y* said, "His wife is the only daughter of my father." How is *X* related to *Y*?

A. Brother B. Uncle
C. Husband D. Father-in-law

67. Find the missing number.

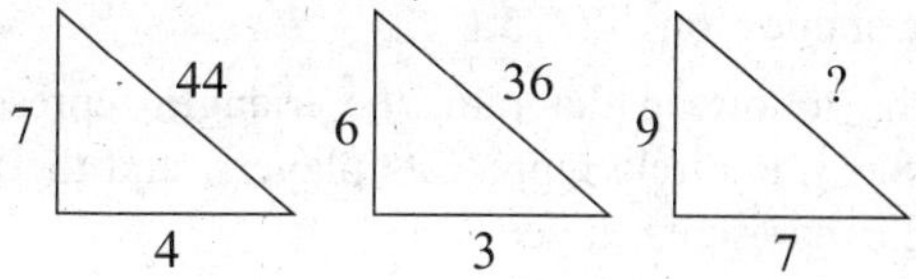

A. 64 B. 63
C. 16 D. 66

68. Match **List I** with **List II**.

List I	List II
(A) Raj Ghat	(I) Dr. Rajendra Prasad
(B) Vijay Ghat	(II) Morarji Desai
(C) Abhay Ghat	(III) Mahatma Gandhi
(D) Mahaprayan Ghat	(IV) Lal Bahadur Shastri

Choose the correct answer from the options given below:

A. (A)-(IV), (B)-(I), (C)-(II), (D)-(III)
B. (A)-(III), (B)-(IV), (C)-(II), (D)-(I)
C. (A)-(II), (B)-(III), (C)-(I), (D)-(IV)
D. (A)-(II), (B)-(III), (C)-(IV), (D)-(I)

69. In the given question, select the related letters/words/numbers from the given alternatives:

Mirage:Desert : :

A. Rain:Rainbow
B. Rainbow:Sky
C. Image:Water
D. Sky:Illusion

70. Find the missing number.

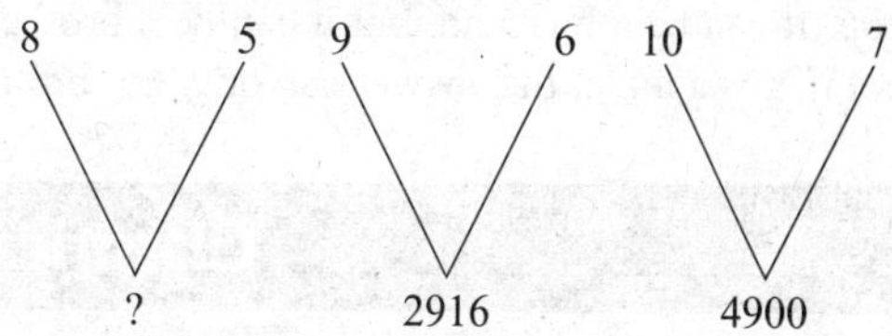

A. 400 B. 169
C. 1600 D. 80

71. Among the four options below, three have similarities. Find the odd one out.

A. Sepals
B. Petals
C. Petiole
D. Stamen

Direction: Please read the details carefully and answer questions 72–75.

In the following diagram, the triangle represents doctors, the circle represents players, and the rectangle represents singers.

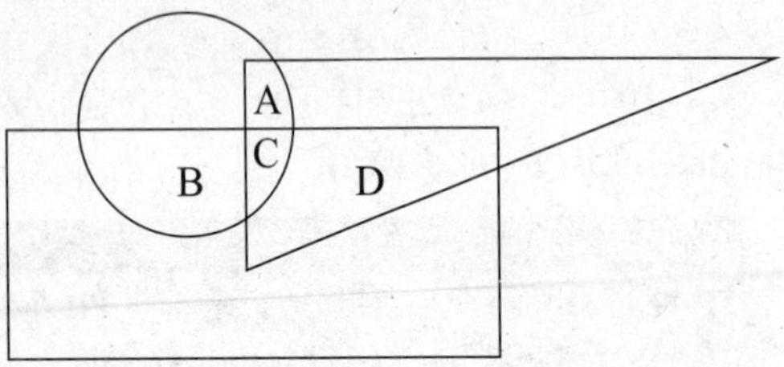

72. Which region represents the doctors who are singers but not players?

A. A B. B
C. C D. D

73. Which region represents the doctors who are players but not singers?

A. A B. B
C. C D. D

74. Which region represents the doctors who are players as well as singers?

A. A B. B
C. C D. D

75. Which region represents the individuals who are players as well as singers but not doctors?

A. A B. B
C. C D. D

Answer Key

1. **B**	2. **B**	3. **C**	4. **A**	5. **C**	6. **C**	7. **B**	8. **C**	9. **B**	10. **C**
11. **D**	12. **C**	13. **C**	14. **B**	15. **B**	16. **C**	17. **D**	18. **D**	19. **B**	20. **B**
21. **D**	22. **C**	23. **B**	24. **D**	25. **B**	26. **A**	27. **D**	28. **C**	29. **A**	30. **C**
31. **D**	32. **A**	33. **B**	34. **D**	35. **D**	36. **A**	37. **D**	38. **C**	39. **B**	40. **C**
41. **A**	42. **A**	43. **C**	44. incorrect question			45. **C**	46. **A**	47. **B**	48. **C**
49. **C**	50. **A**	51. **C**	52. **B**	53. **D**	54. **B**	55. **C**	56. **A**	57. **B**	58. **B**
59. **D**	60. **C**	61. **A**	62. **C**	63. **C**	64. **C**	65. **A**	*66. **C**	67. **A**	68. **B**
69. **B**	70. **C**	71. **C**	72. **D**	73. **A**	74. **C**	75. **B**			

*66. It can be a husband, but it can be a brother-in-law as well. If Y is a female, the answer is 'husband', but if Y is a male, the answer can only be 'brother-in-law'.

Classification of Questions

Question No.	Subject	Topic	Level of Difficulty
1.	General Awareness	Current Affairs	Easy
2.	General Awareness	Important Days	Difficult
3.	General Awareness	Important Days	Difficult
4.	General Awareness	Current Affairs	Medium
5.	General Awareness	Current Affairs	Difficult
6.	General Awareness	History	Easy

Question No.	Subject	Topic	Level of Difficulty
7.	General Awareness	Country and Currency	Medium
8.	Reasoning	Dictionary Order	Easy
9.	General Awareness	Major Religions	Easy
10.	General Awareness	Different Studies	Easy
11.	Reasoning	Odd-one-out	Easy
12.	General Awareness	Geography	Medium
13.	Reasoning	Miscellaneous	Easy
14.	General Awareness	Science (Biology)	Easy
15.	Reasoning	Dictionary Order	Easy
16.	Reasoning	Coding	Easy
17.	General Awareness	Polity	Medium
18.	Reasoning	Missing Number	Easy
19.	Reasoning	Miscellaneous	Medium
20.	Quantitative Aptitude	Types of Numbers	Easy
21.	Reasoning	Non-verbal	Easy
22.	Reasoning	Miscellaneous	Easy
23.	Reasoning	Miscellaneous	Easy
24.	Reasoning	Dictionary Order	Easy
25.	General Awareness	Science & Tech	Difficult
26.	Reasoning	Directions	Easy
27.	General Awareness	Geography	Medium
28.	General Awareness	Science & Technology	Medium
29.	Reasoning	Orders & Rankings	Easy
30.	Quantitative Aptitude	Percentages	Easy
31.	Quantitative Aptitude	Time, Speed & Distance	Easy
32.	General Awareness	Science (Biology)	Medium
33.	Quantitative Aptitude	Simple Interest	Easy
34.	Quantitative Aptitude	Ratios	Easy
35.	Quantitative Aptitude	Ratios	Easy
36.	Quantitative Aptitude	Algebra (AP)	Easy
37.	Quantitative Aptitude	Averages	Easy
38.	Quantitative Aptitude	Averages	Easy
39.	General Awareness	Science (Chemistry)	Easy
40.	Quantitative Aptitude	Percentages	Easy
41.	General Awareness	Science (Physics)	Medium
42.	Quantitative Aptitude	Time & Work	Easy
43.	Quantitative Aptitude	Time & Work	Easy

Question No.	Subject	Topic	Level of Difficulty
44.	Quantitative Aptitude	Numbers (LCM & HCF)	Incorrect Question
45.	Quantitative Aptitude	Simple Interest	Easy
46.	Quantitative Aptitude	Arithmetic (BODMAS)	Easy
47.	Quantitative Aptitude	Percentages	Easy
48.	General Awareness	Geography	Medium
49.	General Awareness	Economics	Easy
50.	Quantitative Aptitude	Surds & Indices	Easy
51.	Quantitative Aptitude	Geometry	Easy
52.	Quantitative Aptitude	Geometry	Easy
53.	Quantitative Aptitude	Mensuration	Easy
54.	Quantitative Aptitude	Algebra (Linear Equations)	Easy
55.	Quantitative Aptitude	Geometry	Easy
56.	Quantitative Aptitude	Geometry	Easy
57.	Quantitative Aptitude	Geometry	Easy
58.	Quantitative Aptitude	Statistics (Mean, Median & Mode)	Easy
59.	Quantitative Aptitude	Statistics (Mean, Median & Mode)	Easy
60.	Quantitative Aptitude	Statistics (Mean, Median & Mode)	Easy
61.	Reasoning	Syllogism	Medium
62.	Reasoning	Miscellaneous	Easy
63.	Reasoning	Analogy	Easy
64.	Reasoning	Blood Relations	Easy
65.	Reasoning	Miscellaneous	Easy
66.	Reasoning	Blood Relations	Medium
67.	Reasoning	Missing Number	Medium
68.	General Awareness	Miscellaneous	Easy
69.	Reasoning	Analogy	Easy
70.	Reasoning	Missing Number	Easy
71.	General Awareness	Science (Biology)	Difficult
72.	Reasoning	Venn-diagram	Easy
73.	Reasoning	Venn-diagram	Easy
74.	Reasoning	Venn-diagram	Easy
75.	Reasoning	Venn-diagram	Easy

The no. of questions on Quantitative Aptitude: 27
The no. of questions on Reasoning: 26
The no. of questions on General Awareness: 22

Explanation to Select Questions

5. Anshu Malik (57-kg category) won a silver medal in the World Wrestling Championship 2021 held in Oslo, Norway.

Hence, Option C.

Alka Tomar (59-kg category) was the first Indian woman to win a medal (bronze) in the World Wrestling Championship, in 2006 held at Guangzhou, China.

Udey Chand (67-kg, Men's freestyle) was the first Indian to win a medal (bronze) in the World Wrestling Championship, in 1961 at Yokohama, Japan.

Update: Antim Panghal (Women, 53-kg category) won a bronze medal at the World Wrestling Championship 2023 held at Belgrade, Serbia.

7. The currency of the UAE is the Dirham (NOT Dinar). The currency of Korea (the North as well as the South) is the Won (NOT the Rial). The Rial is the official currency of Iran.

So, statements (b) and (e) are incorrect.

Hence, Option B.

9. Torah is the compilation of the first 5 books of the Hebrew Bible. We all know that the Quran is the holy book for Muslims, and the combination (D)-(II) is there only in Option B.

Hence, Option B.

16.

O	Z	K	L	P	K	D	L
15	26	11	12	16	11	4	12
$15 + 26 = 41$		$11 + 12 = 23$		$16 + 11 = 27$		$4 + 12 = 16$	

Hence, Option C.

18.

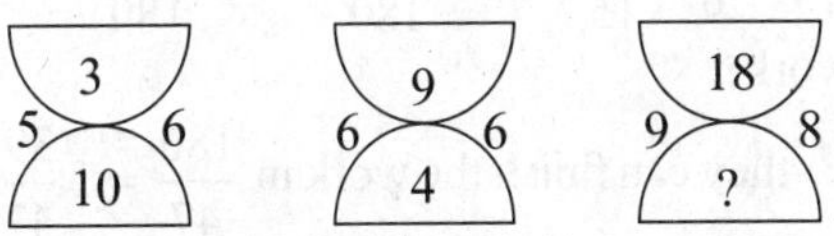

$3 \times 10 = 5 \times 6$ $9 \times 4 = 6 \times 6$ $18 \times ? = 9 \times 8$

or, $? = \dfrac{9 \times 8}{18} = 4$

Hence, option D.

25. Mira was developed by the USA. Param was developed by the Centre for Development of Advanced Computing (C-DAC), India. Anupam was developed by the Bhabha Atomic Research Centre (BARC), India. SAGA-220 was developed by the ISRO.

Hence, Option B.

27. Wheat, Peas and Mustard are all Rabi crops. Maize is a Kharif crop.

Hence, Option D.

30. The number of minutes in a day $= 24 \times 60 = 1440$.

The percentage gain of 10 over 1440

$= \dfrac{10}{1440} \times 100 = \dfrac{25}{36}$.

Hence, Option C.

31. The speed of the train = 90 km/hr.

$= \dfrac{90 \times 1000}{3600} = 25$ m/s.

Distance travelled by the train in 20 seconds $20 \times 25 = 500$ metres.

The total distance travelled by a train in passing a platform = length of the platform + length of the train

or, 500 = length of the platform + 400

or, length of the platform = 500 – 400 = 100 m.

Hence, Option D.

33. Let the initial amount be ₹100.

100 becomes 300 in 20 years,

So, an interest of 300 – 100 = 200 is generated in 20 years.

⇒ The amount of interest generated in 1 year

$= \dfrac{200}{20} = 10$.

Therefore, the rate per annum is 10%.

Hence, Option B.

34. Option A. $\dfrac{8}{x} = \dfrac{8}{y} \Rightarrow x = y$

Option B. $\frac{x}{8} = \frac{y}{8} \Rightarrow x = y$

Option C. $\frac{x}{16} = \frac{y}{4}$ or, $4x = 16y$ or, $x = \frac{16y}{4}$ or, $x = 4y$

Option D. $\frac{32}{x} = \frac{y}{2}$ or, $xy = 32 \times 2$ or, $xy = 64$.

Hence, Option D.

35. $5^{8.14}:5^{5.14} = \frac{5^{8.14}}{5^{5.14}} = \frac{5^{8.14-5.14}}{1} = \frac{5^3}{1} = 125:1$

Hence, Option D.

36. Let the age of the youngest child be x years. Therefore, the ages of the 4 other children will be $x + 3$, $x + 6$, $x + 9$ and $x + 12$ years.

We have,

$x + (x + 3) + (x + 6) + (x + 9) + (x + 12) = 50$

or, $5x + 30 = 50$, or, $5x = 50 - 30 = 20$, or, $x = \frac{20}{5} = 4$

Hence, Option A.

37. Let the three consecutive integers be x, $x + 2$ and $x + 4$.

The average of these three integers $= \frac{x + x + 2 + x + 4}{3}$

$= \frac{3x + 6}{3} = x + 2.$

As per the question, $x + 2 = 12 \Rightarrow x = 10$.

Therefore, the numbers are 10, 12 and 14.

Therefore, their product is $10 \times 12 \times 14 = 1680$.

Shortcut: As three consecutive numbers are in an AP, their average (mean) is equal to their median (the middle number). So, 12 is the middle number.

Therefore, the numbers are 10, 12, and 14 and their product is $10 \times 12 \times 14 = 1680$.

Hence, Option D.

38. The sum of these 10 numbers = 12 + 15 + 18 + 14 + 16 + 13 + 25 + 28 + 23 + 27 = 191

Therefore, their average $= \frac{191}{10} = 19.1$

Hence, Option C.

39. NaCl is a salt; HCl is hydrochloric acid; $MgCl_2$ (magnesium chloride) is also a mild acid. NaOH (sodium hydroxide or Caustic Soda) is a base.

Hence, Option B.

40. Let the initial salary be 100.

The salary after a 20% increase = 120.

Now, in order to get back to the old salary, 20 out of 120 needs to be decreased.

Therefore, the percentage decrease

$= \frac{20}{120} \times 100 = 16\frac{2}{3}\%$

Hence, Option C.

42. P, Q and R can complete a work in 12, 9 and 15 days.

Therefore, in 1 day, they can do $\frac{1}{12}, \frac{1}{9}$ and $\frac{1}{15}$ of the work, respectively.

So, working together they can do

$\frac{1}{12} + \frac{1}{9} + \frac{1}{15} = \frac{15 + 20 + 12}{180} = \frac{47}{180}$ of the work.

$\Rightarrow$ they can finish the work in $\frac{180}{47} = 3\frac{39}{47}$ days.

Hence, Option A.

43. Since 36 farmers can do the work in 24 hours, 1 farmer can do the work in 24×36 hours and 18 farmers can do it in $\frac{24 \times 36}{18} = 48$ hours.

Alternative: If we halve the number of workers, the time taken will be twice.

Hence, $24 \times 2 = 48$ hours.

Hence, Option C.

44. The product of two numbers = the product of their LCM and HCF.

Therefore, the product of these numbers = $35 \times 15 = 525$.

This is what most of the people do and think that Option B is the answer. Please bear in mind that the LCM of a group of numbers is always a multiple of their HCF. If the HCF of two numbers is 15, their LCM CANNOT be 35. Hence, this question is incorrect.

45. Principal = ₹22000, Rate = $8\frac{1}{4}\% = \frac{33}{4}\%$

Time = 8 months $= \frac{8}{12}$ year $= \frac{2}{3}$ year.

$$\text{Simple interest} = \frac{\text{Principal} \times \text{Rate} \times \text{Time}}{100}$$

$$= \frac{22000 \times \frac{33}{4} \times \frac{2}{3}}{100} = 220 \times \frac{33}{4} \times \frac{2}{3} = ₹1210.$$

Hence, Option C.

46. $3 - 3 \div 3 = 3 - (3 \div 3) = 3 - 1 = 2.$

We need to follow the BODMAS rule here, and hence, the division must be done before the subtraction.

Hence, Option A.

47. Let the number be x.

As per the question,

$$x \times \frac{20}{100} = 30,$$

$$\text{or, } x = \frac{30 \times 100}{20} = 150.$$

Hence, Option B.

50. $x^{a-b} \times x^{b-c} \times x^{c-a} = x^{a-b+b-c+c-a} = x^0 = 1.$

Hence, Option A.

51.

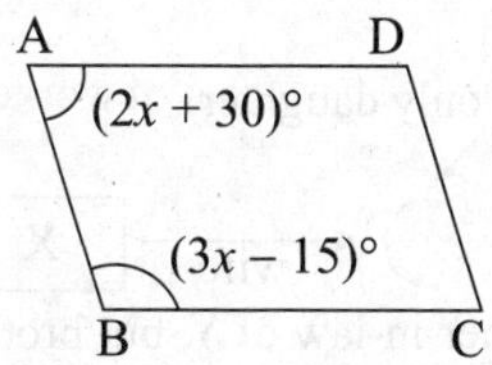

The sum of the adjacent angles of a parallelogram is 180°.

So, $(2x + 30)° + (3x - 15)° = 180°$

or, $5x + 15 = 180,$

or, $5x = 165,$

$$\text{or, } x = \frac{165}{5} = 33.$$

Hence, Option C.

52.

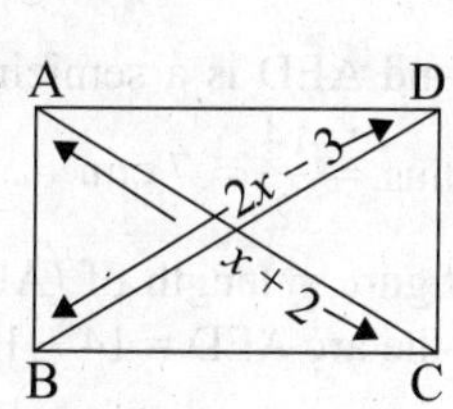

The lengths of both the diagonals of a rectangle are the same.

Therefore, $2x - 3 = x + 2.$

or, $2x - x = 3 + 2$ or, $x = 5.$

Hence, Option B.

53.

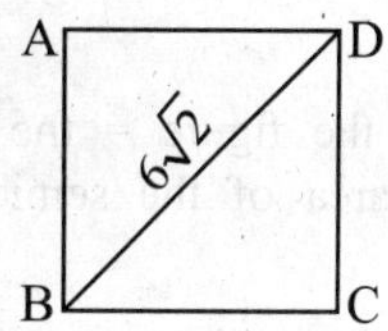

The length of the diagonal of the square $= 6\sqrt{2}$

Therefore, the length of a side of the square

$$= \frac{6\sqrt{2}}{\sqrt{2}} = 6.$$

So, the area of the square $= 6 \times 6 = 36\ \text{cm}^2$.

Alternative: A square is a rhombus and the area of a rhombus $= \frac{1}{2} \times$ product of the diagonals.

In a square, both the diagonals are of the same length.

Therefore, the required area

$$= \frac{1}{2} \times 6\sqrt{2} \times 6\sqrt{2} = 36\ \text{cm}^2.$$

Hence, Option D.

54. $2x - 3 = 7 - 3x,$ or, $2x + 3x = 3 + 7,$

or, $5x = 10,$ or, $x = 2.$

Hence, Option B.

Refer to the following figure for the explanations of the questions 55–57:

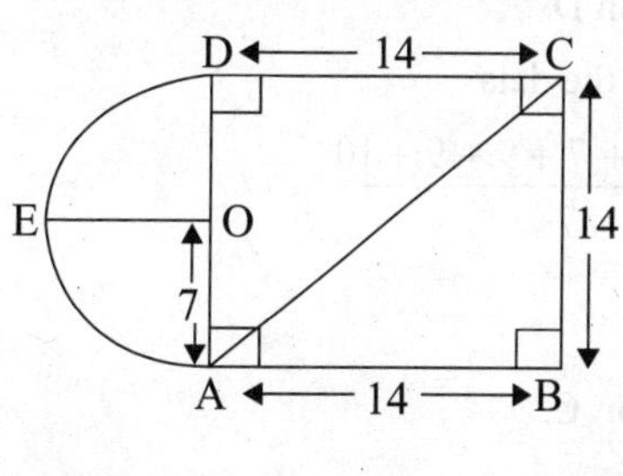

Here, ABCD is a square, and AED is a semicircle with its centre at O and radius $= \frac{14}{2} = 7$ cm.

55. The perimeter of the figure = length of (AB + BC + CD) + length of the arc AED = 14 + 14 + 14 + $\pi \times 7$

$= 42 + \frac{22}{7} \times 7 = 42 + 22 = 64$ cm.

Hence, Option C.

56. The length of the diagonal of the square $= \sqrt{2} \times 14 = 14\sqrt{2}$ cm.

Hence, Option A.

57. The area covered by the figure = the area of the square + the area of the semicircle

$= 14 \times 14 + \frac{1}{2}\pi 7^2$

$= 196 + \frac{1}{2} \times \frac{22}{7} \times 7^2$

$= 196 + 77 = 273$ cm^2.

Hence, Option B.

Refer to the following data for explanations of questions 58–60.

The marks of the 7 students: 9, 10, 7, 6, 9, 3, 5

The marks in ascending order: 3, 5, 6, [7], 9, 9, 10

58. The mode of the data is the most frequent number.

In the given 7 numbers, only 9 gets repeated, and hence, 9 is the mode.

Hence, Option B.

59. The median of the data is the middle number after arranging the numbers in ascending/descending order.

Of these 7 numbers, the 4th one is 7, and hence, it is the median.

Hence, Option D.

60. The mean of the data

$= \frac{3+5+6+7+9+9+10}{7}$

$= \frac{49}{7} = 7.$

Hence, Option C.

62. 49B7D9A15C6

$= 49 \div 7 - 9 + 15 \times 6$ (We need to follow the BODMAS rule.)

$= (49 \div 7) - 9 + (15 \times 6)$

$= 7 - 9 + 90 = 88.$

Hence, Option C.

64.

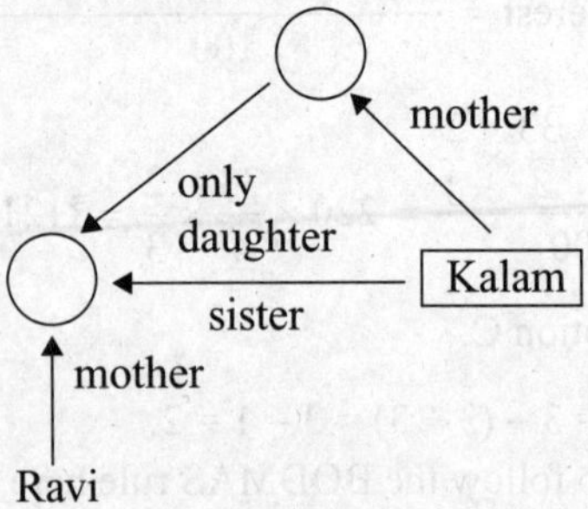

It is obvious that Ravi is a child of Kalam's sister.

Hence, Kalam is Ravi's maternal uncle.

Hence, Option C.

It is assumed in the question that Kalam is a male. If Kalam is a female, the answer would be 'mother', but that is NOT among the options.

65. Option A

$2 \updownarrow 5 \otimes 6 * 2 \neq 6$

or, $2 \times 5 - 6 + 2 = 6$ (BODMAS)

or, $10 - 6 + 2 = 6$

or, $6 = 6$

Hence, Option A.

66. There are two cases possible here:

(I) If Y is a male:

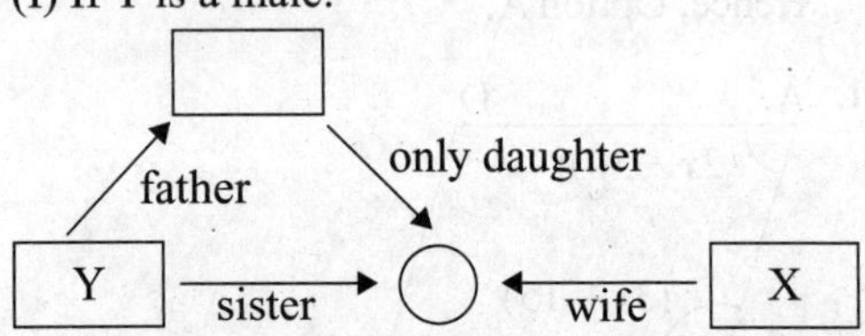

Here, X is the brother-in-law of Y, but brother-in-law is not among the options.

(II) If Y is a female:

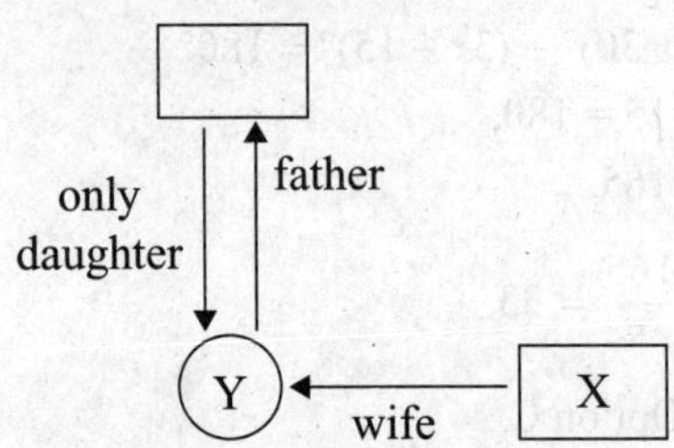

In this case, Y is the only daughter of her father and the wife of X.

Therefore, X is the husband of Y.

Hence, Option C.

67.

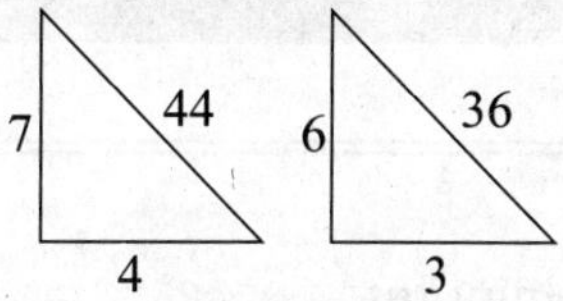

$44 = 4(7+4)$ $36 = 4(6+3)$

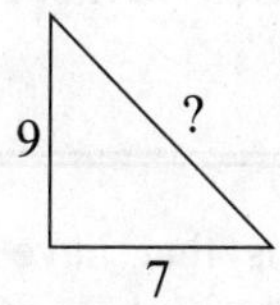

$? = 4(9+7) = 4 \times 16 = 64$

Hence, Option A.

70.

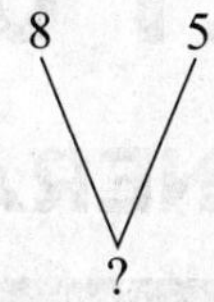

$? = (8 \times 5)^2 = 40^2 = 1600$

$2916 = (9 \times 6)^2 = 54^2$ $4900 = (10 \times 7)^2 = 70^2$

Hence, Option C.

71. Sepals, Petals and Stamen are all parts of the flower, but a Petiole joins a leaf to its stem.

Hence, Option C.

CUET UG 2022
General Test

July
15

Instructions:

1. You need to attempt any 60 out of the 75 questions in 60 minutes.
2. You get 5 marks for a correct response and –1 for an incorrect one. However, there is no reward or penalty for a question not attempted.

1. Constitution Day or Samvidhan Divas is observed every year in India on:
A. 26 January B. 26 November
C. 25 January D. 14 April

2. Who is nicknamed the "Milkman of India":
A. Verghese Kurien
B. M.S. Swaminathan
C. Sam Pitroda
D. Vishal Tewari

3. Which state has been adjudged as the state with the highest level of multidimensional poverty in 2019–21?
A. Bihar
B. Madhya Pradesh
C. Rajasthan
D. Odisha

4. Who has been appointed as the new CEO of Twitter?
A. Mark Zuckerberg
B. Parag Agrawal
C. Jack Dorsey
D. Azim Premji

5. The world's largest national flag, made up of Khadi cloth, has been installed in _______ on the occasion of the 152nd birth anniversary of Mahatma Gandhi on October 02, 2021.
A. Bhopal, Madhya Pradesh
B. Shimla, Himachal Pradesh
C. Lucknow, Uttar Pradesh
D. Leh, Ladakh

6. These are three words that have something in common among themselves. Out of the four alternatives, choose the most appropriate description of these three words:
Paper : Pen : Colours
A. These are drawing items.
B. These are stationery items.
C. These are study materials.
D. These are official items.

7. From the following pairs, select the combination of the correct pairs from the given options:
(A) Angle : Radians
(B) Pressure : Volt
(C) Luminous Intensity : Candela
(D) Work : Joule
(E) Power : Current
Choose the correct answer from the options given below:
A. (A), (C) and (B) only
B. (C), (B) and (D) only
C. (A), (C) and (D) only
D. (E), (B) and (A) only

8. Arrange the given words in the sequence in which they occur in the dictionary:
(A) Miniscule
(B) Minimalist
(C) Minority
(D) Miniature
(E) Ministerial

Choose the **correct** answer from the options given below:

A. (A), (C), (D), (E), (B)
B. (D), (B), (A), (E), (C)
C. (B), (C), (A), (D), (E)
D. (E), (B), (A), (D), (C)

9. Match **List I** with **List II**.

List I	List II
(A) Ram Nath Kovind	(I) United States of America
(B) Joe Biden	(II) India
(C) Gotabaya Rajapaksa	(III) Russia
(D) Vladimir Putin	(IV) Sri Lanka

Choose the **correct** answer from the options given below:

A. (A) - (II), (B) - (III), (C) - (IV), (D) - (I)
B. (A) - (II), (B) - (I), (C) - (IV), (D) - (III)
C. (A) - (II), (B) - (III), (C) - (I), (D) - (IV)
D. (A) - (I), (B) - (II), (C) - (IV), (D) - (III)

10. Match **List I** with **List II**.

List I (Dance)	List II (State)
(A) Bharatanatyam	(I) Andhra Pradesh
(B) Kuchipudi	(II) Tamil Nadu
(C) Kathak	(III) Kerala
(D) Kathakali	(IV) Uttar Pradesh

Choose the **correct** answer from the options given below:

A. (A) - (III), (B) - (I), (C) - (IV), (D) - (II)
B. (A) - (II), (B) - (IV), (C) - (I), (D) - (III)
C. (A) - (III), (B) - (II), (C) - (IV), (D) - (I)
D. (A) - (II), (B) - (I), (C) - (IV), (D) - (III)

11. Among the four options given below, three have similarities. Find the odd one out.

A. Mayonnaise
B. Cumin
C. Berry leaf
D. Turmeric

12. Match **List I** with **List II**.

List I (Chief Minister)	List II (State)
(A) Shivraj Singh Chouhan	(I) Rajasthan
(B) Yogi Aditya Nath	(II) Bihar
(C) Ashok Gehlot	(III) Madhya Pradesh
(D) Nitish Kumar	(IV) Uttar Pradesh

Choose the **correct** answer from the options given below:

A. (A) - (III), (B) - (IV), (C) - (II), (D) - (I)
B. (A) - (II), (B) - (IV), (C) - (III), (D) - (I)
C. (A) - (IV), (B) - (II), (C) - (III), (D) - (I)
D. (A) - (III), (B) - (IV), (C) - (I), (D) - (II)

13. Direction: Among the four options given below, three have similarities. Find the odd one out:

A. Kolkata B. Gangtok
C. Indore D. Gandhinagar

14. Arrange the following words in a logical sequence:

(A) Thousand
(B) Hundred
(C) Trillion
(D) Million
(E) Billion

Choose the **correct** answer from the options given below:

A. (B), (A), (D), (C), (E)
B. (B), (D), (A), (E), (C)
C. (B), (A), (D), (E), (C)
D. (B), (D), (A), (C), (E)

15. Which one of the following would be a meaningful order of the following?

(A) Preface
(B) Introduction
(C) Table of contents
(D) Bibliography
(E) Chapter

Choose the **correct** answer from the options given below:

A. (C), (B), (A), (E), (D)
B. (A), (C), (B), (E), (D)
C. (B), (C), (A), (E), (D)
D. (D), (A), (C), (B), (E)

16. Among the four options given below, three have similar properties.
Find the word that does not match with others:
A. Aryabhata
B. Sridhara
C. Ramanujan
D. Chanakya

17. Find the related option.
Sports : Logo : : Nation?
A. Anthem B. Sobriquet
C. Emblem D. Ruler

18. Among the four options given below, three have similarities. Find the word that does not match with others.
A. Retina B. Cornea
C. Pupil D. Eyebrow

19. After walking 6 km, Sonu turned right and covered a distance of 2 km, then turned left and covered a distance of 10 km. In the end, he was moving towards the North. From which directions did he start his journey?
A. East B. West
C. South D. North

20. Neha is facing east. She turns 100° in the clockwise direction and then 145° in the anticlockwise direction. Which direction is she facing now?
A. North-East
B. South-West
C. North
D. East

21. Arrange the words given below in a meaningful sequence:
(A) Population
(B) Disease
(C) Unemployment
(D) Poverty
(E) Death
Choose the **correct** answer from the options given below:
A. (A), (C), (D), (B), (E)
B. (C), (D), (A), (B), (E)
C. (D), (C), (A), (B), (E)
D. (D), (C), (B), (E), (A)

22. Match **List I** with **List II**.

List I	List II
(A) Pen	(I) Page
(B) Clock	(II) Blade
(C) Fan	(III) Nib
(D) Book	(IV) Needle

Choose the **correct** answer from the options given below:
A. (A) - (III), (B) - (II), (C) - (IV), (D) - (I)
B. (A) - (II), (B) - (III), (C) - (I), (D) - (IV)
C. (A) - (III), (B) - (IV), (C) - (II), (D) - (I)
D. (A) - (II), (B) - (I), (C) - (III), (D) - (IV)

23. Arrange the following words in a meaningful order:
(A) Sea
(B) Ocean
(C) River
(D) Glacier
(E) Rivulet
Choose the correct answer from the options given below:
A. (E), (D), (C), (A), (B)
B. (E), (D), (A), (C), (B)
C. (D), (E), (C), (A), (B)
D. (D), (E), (A), (C), (B)

24. A box consists of 28 mangoes and 46 Bananas. How many bananas must be removed from the box so that 70% of the pieces of fruit in the box are mangoes?
A. 12 B. 24
C. 34 D. 48

25. If 'Good' can be coded as 14, 30, 30, 8, then 'BAD' will be coded as:
A. 2, 4, 8
B. 8, 2, 4
C. 4, 2, 8
D. 8, 4, 2

26. If 'GREEN' can be coded as 21, 54, 15, 15, 42, then 'YELLOW' will be coded as:
A. 75, 36, 15, 15, 45, 69
B. 75, 15, 36, 36, 45, 69
C. 75, 45, 36, 36, 15, 69
D. 75, 36, 45, 45, 15, 69

27. Introducing a boy, a girl said, "His wife is the only daughter of my mother." How is that boy related to the girl?

A. Husband B. Brother-in-law
C. Son D. Father-in-law

28. Which of the following diagrams represents schools, classrooms and blackboards?

A.
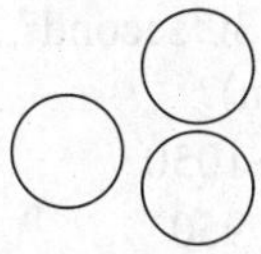
B.

C.

D.
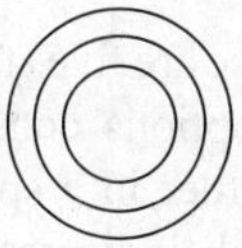

29. Arrange the words given below in a meaningful sequence:

(A) Door
(B) Key
(C) Lock
(D) Room
(E) Switch on

Choose the **correct** answer from the options given below:

A. (A), (C), (B), (D), (E)
B. (C), (B), (A), (D), (E)
C. (B), (C), (A), (D), (E)
D. (D), (A), (C), (B), (E)

30. Match **List I** with **List II**.

List I	List II
(A) Ram	(I) Mahabharata
(B) Arjun	(II) Mantra
(C) Krishna	(III) Ramcharitmanas
(D) Gayatri	(IV) Geeta

Choose the **correct** answer from the options given below:

A. (A) - (II), (B) - (III), (C) - (IV), (D) - (I)
B. (A) - (I), (B) - (II), (C) - (III), (D) - (IV)
C. (A) - (III), (B) - (I), (C) - (IV), (D) - (II)
D. (A) - (II), (B) - (III), (C) - (I), (D) - (IV)

31. Arrange the following waves in the increasing order of their wavelength?

(A) X-ray
(B) Gamma ray
(C) Infrared
(D) Ultraviolet
(E) Microwaves

Choose the **correct** answer from the options given below:

A. (A), (C), (E), (B), (D)
B. (B), (A), (D), (C), (E)
C. (E), (A), (D), (B), (C)
D. (D), (E), (B), (A), (C)

32. If the edge of a cube is 22 cm, then its volume is:

A. 10848 cm^3
B. 10648 cm^3
C. 10548 cm^3
D. 10748 cm^3

33. Which among the following is a fat-soluble vitamin?

A. Vitamin A B. Vitamin B_2
C. Vitamin B_{12} D. Vitamin C

34. If 45% of P = $\frac{3}{4}$ of Q, then P:Q is:

A. 5:4 B. 5:3
C. 4:5 D. 3:5

35. ________ is a major highway, economic corridor and expressway development scheme of the government in India; launched in 2015, it is the biggest road construction plan in the country.

A. Bharatmala
B. Golden Triangle
C. Golden Quadrilateral
D. Belt and Road Initiative

36. Sanchi's age after 15 years will be 4 times her age 6 years back. What is the present age of Sanchi?

A. 15 years B. 12 years
C. 13 years D. 8 years

37. The sum of the ages of A, B and C is 93 years. Ten years ago, the ratio of their ages was 2:3:4. What is the present age of B?

A. 21 years B. 28 years
C. 31 years D. 38 years

38. The name of the first woman to climb Mount Everest is:

A. Bachendri Pal B. Arunima Sinha
C. Santosh Yadav D. Junko Tabei

39. Find the average of the first ten multiples of 7.

A. 48.5 B. 28.5
C. 39.5 D. 38.5

40. Match **List I** with **List II**.

List I	List II
(A) x% of 25 = 2.125	(I) 70
(B) 9% of x = 6.3	(II)16
(C) x% of 45 = 22.5	(III) 8.5
(D) 0.25% of x = 0.04	(IV) 50

Choose the **correct** answer from the options given below:

A. (A) - (I), (B) - (III), (C) - (II), (D) - (IV)
B. (A) - (III), (B) - (I), (C) - (IV), (D) - (II)
C. (A) - (II), (B) - (III), (C) - (IV), (D) - (I)
D. (A) - (III), (B) - (IV), (C) - (I), (D) - (II)

41. What percent of 3 metric tonnes is 90 quintals?

A. 30% B. 270%
C. 300% D. 330%

42. In the formula "Work = Fs cosθ", if the angle between the force and displacement (θ) is less than 90°, the net work done will be:

A. Infinity B. Positive
C. Negative D. Zero

43. Forty-eight persons can complete a part of a work in 35 hours. In how many hours will 20 people do it?

A. 48 hours B. 56 hours
C. 74 hours D. 84 hours

44. Match **List I** with **List II**.

List I	List II
(A) Land of Maple	(I) Norway
(B) Land of Morning Calm	(II) Canada
(C) Land of the Midnight Sun	(III) Japan
(D) Land of the Rising Sun	(IV) South Korea

Choose the **correct** answer from the options given below:

A. (A) - (II), (B) - (III), (C) - (IV), (D) - (I)
B. (A) - (III), (B) - (IV), (C) - (I), (D) - (II)
C. (A) - (II), (B) - (IV), (C) - (I), (D) - (III)
D. (A) - (I), (B) - (III), (C) - (IV), (D) - (II)

45. A train running at a speed of 150 km/hr crosses a 300 m-long platform in 30 seconds. What is the length of the train (in m)?

A. 1000 B. 1050
C. 900 D. 950

46. These are five statements given below, followed by options consisting of three statements put together in a specific order, choose the option which indicates a conclusion drawn from the preceding two statements.

(A) Teachers are in great demand.
(B) Shashi and Manshi are in great demand.
(C) Shashi is in great demand.
(D) Manshi is in great demand.
(E) Shashi and Manshi are Teachers.

Choose the **correct** answer from the options given below:

A. (A), (B), (E)
B. (A), (E), (B)
C. (E), (B), (A)
D. (E), (C), (D)

47. If P means plus, M means minus, N means multiply, and S means divide, then find the value of 18M6N24S8P17

A. 71 B. 53
C. 35 D. 17

48. Pointing towards Peeyush, Saksham Said, "I am the only son of her mother's son." How is Peeyush related to Saksham?

A. Mother B. Niece
C. Aunt D. Cousin

49. Arrange these historical milestones of the Indian Economy (from older to recent):

(A) Sarvodaya Plan
(B) Planned Economy for India
(C) People's Plan
(D) National Planning Committee
(E) Bombay Plan

Choose the **correct** answer from the options given below:

A. (B), (D), (E), (C), (A)
B. (D), (A), (E), (B), (C)
C. (C), (A), (D), (E), (B)
D. (B), (E), (C), (A), (D)

50. If $A + D = B + C$, $A + E = C + D$, $2C < A + E$ and $2A > B + D$, then:

A. $A > B > C > D > E$
B. $B > A > D > C > E$
C. $B > C > D > E > A$
D. $D > B > C > A > E$

51. Find the missing number from the following given options:

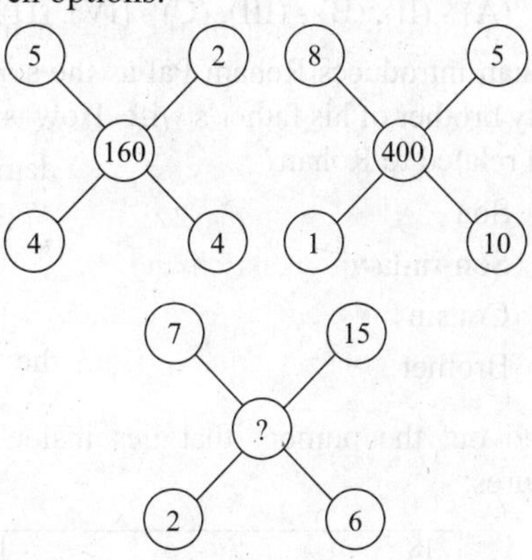

A. 225 B. 1260
C. 800 D. 30

52. Among the given options, find the odd one out:

A. ulna B. malleus
C. incus D. stapes

53. Find the missing number from the following given options:

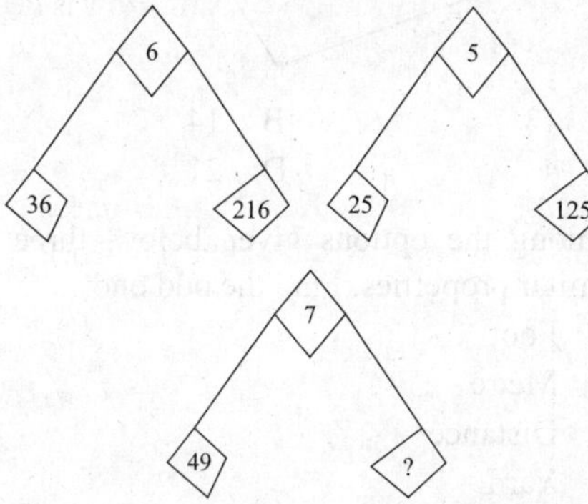

A. 98 B. 343
C. 56 D. 27

54. In the following question, select a figure from the four given alternatives that would complete the pattern when placed in the blank space (?) of the problem figure.

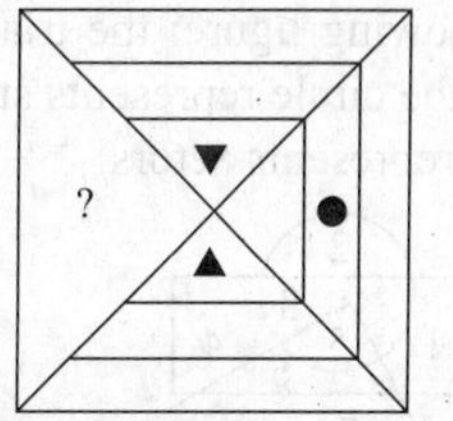

A.
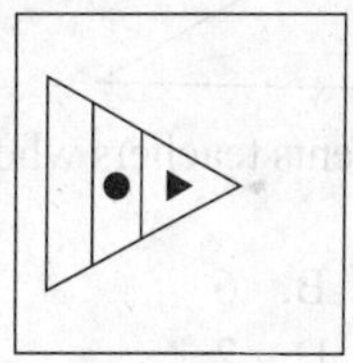
B.
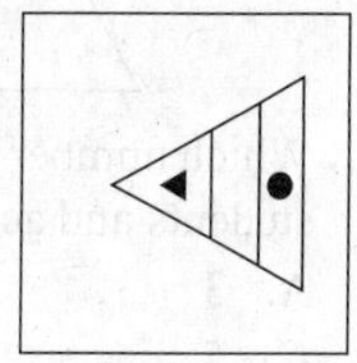
C.
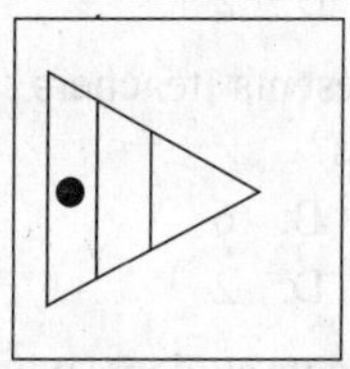
D.
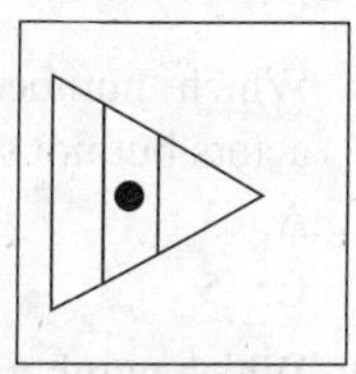

55. In the following question, select a figure from the given four alternatives that would complete the pattern when placed in the blank space (?) of the problem figure.

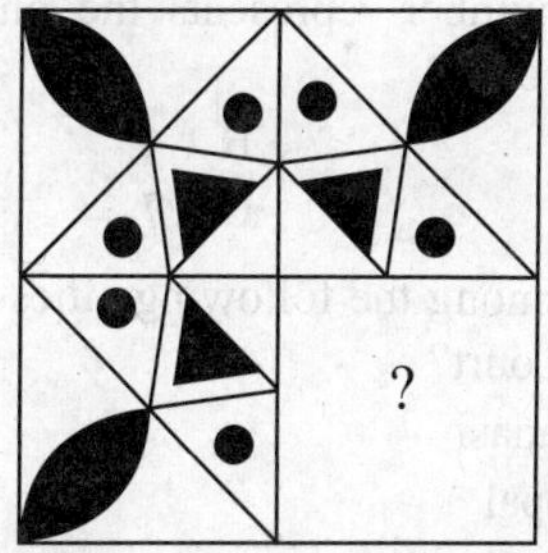

A.

B.
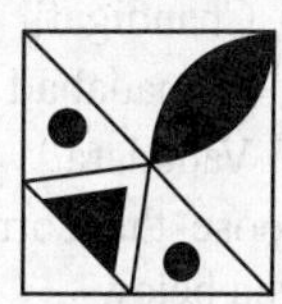
C.

D.

56. The network in the graphical area spread over 1 km to 10 km or within the same building is known as:

A. LAN B. VAN
C. MAN D. WAN

Read the details carefully for questions 57–60 in the following figure: the triangle represents teachers, the circle represents students, and the rectangle represents actors.

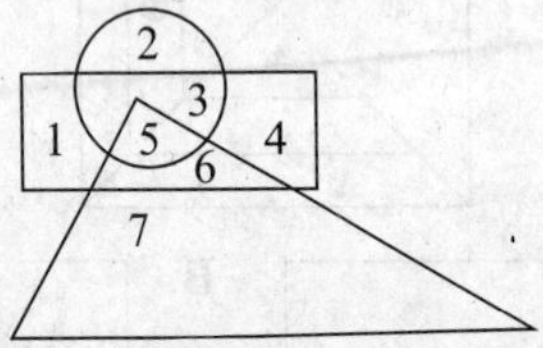

57. Which number represents teachers who are also students and actors?

A. 3 B. 6
C. 5 D. 2

58. Which number represents teachers who are actors but not students?

A. 3 B. 6
C. 5 D. 2

59. Which number represents students who are also actors but not teachers?

A. 2 B. 3
C. 4 D. 7

60. Which number represents the ones who are teachers only?

A. 1 B. 4
C. 2 D. 7

61. Which among the following cities do not have a High Court?

(A) Varanasi
(B) Bhopal
(C) Chandigarh
(D) Ahmadabad
(E) Vadodara

Choose the correct answer from the options given below

A. (B), (C) and (E) only
B. (A), (C) and (D) only
C. (A), (B) and (E) only
D. (A), (D) and (E) only

62. Match **List I** with **List II**.

List I	List II
(A) Nyaya	(I) Patanjali
(B) Vaisheshika	(II) Gautam
(C) Sankhya	(III) Kanad
(D) Yoga	(IV) Kapil

Choose the **correct** answer from the options given below:

A. (A) - (III), (B) - (II), (C) - (I), (D) - (IV)
B. (A) - (IV), (B) - (I), (C) - (II), (D) - (III)
C. (A) - (I), (B) - (IV), (C) - (III), (D) - (II)
D. (A) - (II), (B) - (III), (C) - (IV), (D) - (I)

63. Rohan introduces Reham Pal as the son of the only brother of his father's wife. How is Reham Pal related to Rohan?

A. Son
B. Son-in-law
C. Cousin
D. Brother

64. Find out the number that lies inside all the figures:

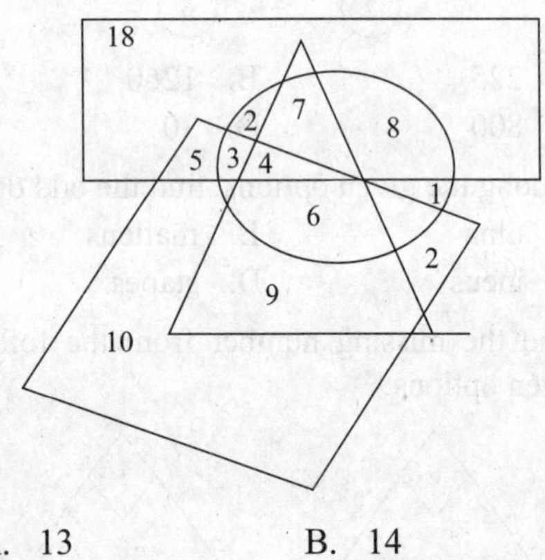

A. 13 B. 14
C. 4 D. 21

65. Among the options given below, three have similar properties. Find the odd one:

A. Foot
B. Metre
C. Distance
D. Yard

66. Which number is in all the geometrical figures?

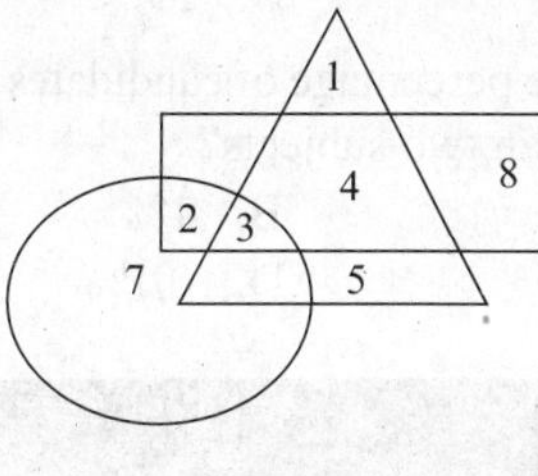

A. 4 B. 3
C. 2 D. 8

67. Match **List I** with **List II**.

List I	List II
(A) Rice	(I) Beverages
(B) Tea	(II) Pulses
(C) Beans	(III) Juice
(D) Fruit	(IV) Cereals

Choose the **correct** answer from the options given below:

A. (A) - (IV), (B) - (I), (C) - (II), (D) - (III)
B. (A) - (I), (B) - (II), (C) - (III), (D) - (IV)
C. (A) - (IV), (B) - (II), (C) - (I), (D) - (III)
D. (A) - (I), (B) - (III), (C) - (II), (D) - (IV)

68. If the ratio of the selling price and cost price of an apple is 11:10, the percentage of profit is:

A. 8% B. 10%
C. 12% D. 18%

69. The **correct** sequence from the given words will be:

(A) School
(B) Child
(C) Job
(D) Playschool
(E) College

Choose the **correct** answer from the options given below:

A. (B), (D), (A), (E) (C)
B. (A), (B), (E), (D), (C)
C. (B), (D), (E), (A), (C)
D. (B), (A), (D), (E), (C)

70. The given figure after rotation is:

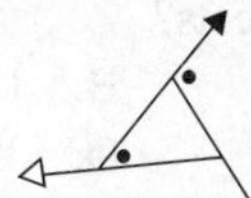

A.

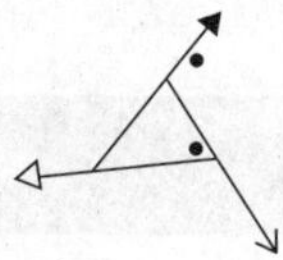

B.

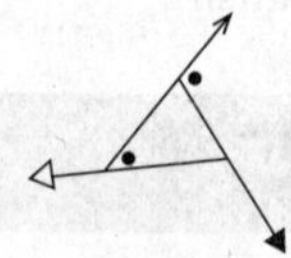

C.

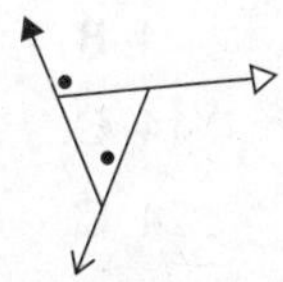

D.

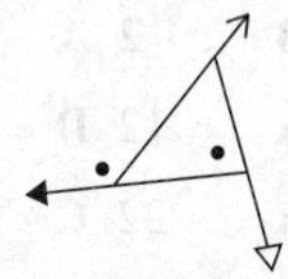

71. The rate at which the RBI lends short-term money to the banks against securities is called:

A. Repo Rate B. Reverse Repo Rate
C. Bank Rate D. Cash Reserve Ratio

72. Find the missing number from the following options:

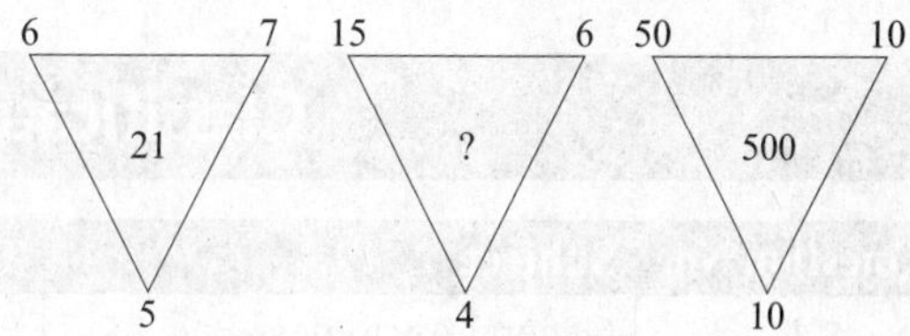

A. 94 B. 22.5
C. 25 D. 36

Observe the following diagram carefully and answer questions 73–75.

In an examination, 500 candidates appear for English, Hindi and Mathematics tests. The diagram presents the number of candidates who failed in different tests.

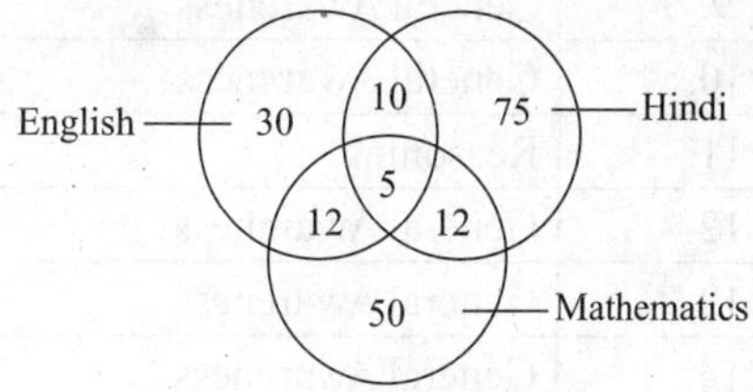

73. What is the number of candidates who failed in at least two subjects?

A. 5 B. 12
C. 17 D. 39

74. What is the number of candidates who failed in English?

A. 75 B. 30
C. 57 D. 39

75. What is the percentage of candidates who failed in more than two subjects?

A. 1.8% B. 1%
C. 1.2% D. 0.1%

Answer Key

1 **B**	2 **A**	3 **A**	4 **B**	5 **D**	6 **B**	7 **C**	8 **B**	9 **B**	10 **D**
11 **A**	12 **D**	13 **C**	14 **C**	15 **B**	16 **D**	17 **C**	18 **D**	19 **C**	20 **A**
21 **A**	22 **C**	23 **C**	24 **C**	25 **C**	26 **B**	27 **A**	28 **D**	29 **C**	30 **C**
31 **B**	32 **B**	33 **A**	34 **B**	35 **A**	36 **C**	37 **C**	38 **D**	39 **D**	40 **B**
41 **C**	42 **B**	43 **D**	44 **C**	45 **D**	46 **B**	47 **D**	48 **C**	49 **A**	50 **B**
51 **B**	52 **A**	53 **B**	54 **D**	55 **A**	56 **A**	57 **C**	58 **B**	59 **B**	60 **D**
61 **C**	62 **D**	63 **C**	64 **C**	65 **C**	66 **B**	67 **A**	68 **B**	69 **A**	70 **D**
71 **A**	72 **D**	73 **D**	74 **C**	75 **B**					

Classification of Questions

Question No.	Subject	Topic	Level of Difficulty
1.	General Awareness	Polity	Easy
2.	General Awareness	Economics	Easy
3.	General Awareness	Current Affairs	Medium
4.	General Awareness	Current Affairs	Easy
5.	General Awareness	Current Affairs	Easy
6.	Reasoning	Miscellaneous	Easy
7.	General Awareness	Science (Physics)	Medium
8.	Reasoning	Dictionary Order	Easy
9.	General Awareness	Polity	Easy
10.	General Awareness	Art & Culture	Easy
11.	Reasoning	Odd-one-out	Easy
12.	General Awareness	Polity	Easy
13.	General Awareness	Polity	Easy
14.	General Awareness	Miscellaneous	Easy
15.	General Awareness	Miscellaneous	Difficult
16.	General Awareness	Miscellaneous	Easy

Question No.	Subject	Topic	Level of Difficulty
17.	Reasoning	Analogy	Easy
18.	Reasoning	Odd-one-out	Easy
19.	Reasoning	Directions	Easy
20.	Reasoning	Directions	Easy
21.	Reasoning	Logical Sequence of Words	Easy
22.	Reasoning	Miscellaneous	Easy
23.	Reasoning	Logical Sequence of Words	Easy
24.	Quantitative Aptitude	Percentages	Easy
25.	Reasoning	Coding	Easy
26.	Reasoning	Coding	Easy
27.	Reasoning	Blood Relations	Easy
28.	Reasoning	Venn-diagram	Easy
29.	Reasoning	Logical Sequence of Words	Easy
30.	General Awareness	Hindu Mythology	Easy
31.	General Awareness	Science (Physics)	Difficult
32.	Quantitative Aptitude	Mensuration	Easy
33.	General Awareness	Science (Biology)	Medium
34.	Quantitative Aptitude	Ratios	Easy
35.	General Awareness	Geography	Medium
36.	Quantitative Aptitude	Age-based problems	Easy
37.	Quantitative Aptitude	Ratios	Easy
38.	General Awareness	Sports	Medium
39.	Quantitative Aptitude	Averages	Easy
40.	Quantitative Aptitude	Percentages	Easy
41.	Quantitative Aptitude	Percentages	Easy
42.	Quantitative Aptitude	Miscellaneous	Easy
43.	Quantitative Aptitude	Time & Work	Easy
44.	General Awareness	Geography	Easy
45.	Quantitative Aptitude	Time, Speed & Distance	Easy
46.	Reasoning	Syllogism	Easy
47.	Quantitative Aptitude	BODMAS	Easy
48.	Reasoning	Blood Relations	Easy
49.	General Awareness	Economics	Difficult
50.	Quantitative Aptitude	Inequalities	Difficult
51.	Reasoning	Missing Number	Easy
52.	General Awareness	Science (Biology)	Difficult

Question No.	Subject	Topic	Level of Difficulty
53.	Reasoning	Missing Number	Easy
54.	Reasoning	Non-verbal	Easy
55.	Reasoning	Non-verbal	Easy
56.	General Awareness	Computers	Medium
57.	Reasoning	Venn-diagram	Easy
58.	Reasoning	Venn-diagram	Easy
59.	Reasoning	Venn-diagram	Easy
60.	Reasoning	Venn-diagram	Easy
61.	General Awareness	Polity	Medium
62.	General Awareness	History	Easy
63.	Reasoning	Blood Relations	Easy
64.	Reasoning	Venn-diagram	Easy
65.	General Awareness	Science	Easy
66.	Reasoning	Venn-diagram	Easy
67.	General Awareness	Geography	Easy
68.	Quantitative Aptitude	Profit, Loss & Discount	Easy
69.	Reasoning	Words in a Logical Sequence	Easy
70.	Reasoning	Non-verbal	Medium
71.	General Awareness	Economics	Easy
72.	Reasoning	Missing Number	Easy
73.	Quantitative Aptitude	Set Theory	Easy
74.	Quantitative Aptitude	Set Theory	Easy
75.	Quantitative Aptitude	Set Theory	Easy

No. of questions on Reasoning: 31

No. of questions on Quantitative Aptitude: 17

No. of questions on General Awareness: 27

Explanation to Select Questions

1. The Constitution Day is observed every year on 26 November as the Constitution of India was adopted on this day in 1949. It is also celebrated as the National Law Day.
Hence, Option B.

4. Parag Agrawal was the CEO of Twitter till 27 October 2022.
Hence, when this exam was held, the answer was Option B.

Update: Twitter is now called X, and Linda Yaccarino is its current CEO.

7. (B) and (E) are incorrect. The unit of pressure is Pascal (Pa) - NOT Volt- and the unit of power is Watt (W) - NOT current.
Hence, Option C.

9. UPDATE: Droupadi Murmu is the current president of India. Ranil Wickremesinghe is the current president of Sri Lanka.

11. Mayonnaise is a man-made sauce, whereas the remaining three options are natural.
Hence, Option A.

12. **UPDATE:** The current chief minister of Rajasthan is Bhajan Lal Sharma, and the current chief minister of Madhya Pradesh is Mohan Yadav.

13. Kolkata, Gangtok and Gandhinagar are capital cities, but Indore is not.
Hence, Option C.

14. Hundred (100) < Thousand (1000) < Million (1000000) < Billion (1000000000) < Trillion (1000000000000)
Hence, Option C.

16. Chanakya was a politician, but the remaining 3 options were Mathematicians.
Hence, Option D.

18. The retina, cornea and pupil create vision, but the eyebrows just protect the eyes from sweat and other such debris.
Hence, Option D.

19.

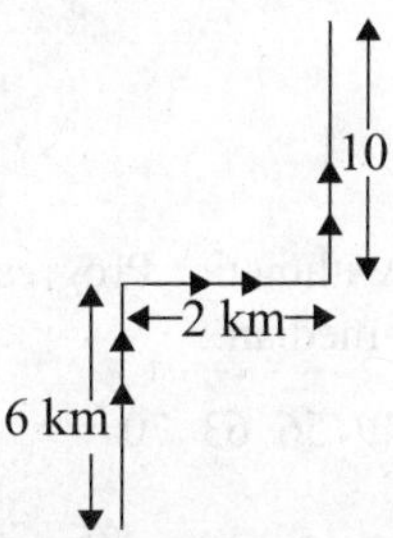

The question does NOT ask which direction Sonu was travelling in initially; it asks from which direction Sonu started his journey. It is clear that Sonu started from the South (relatively).
Hence, Option C.

20.

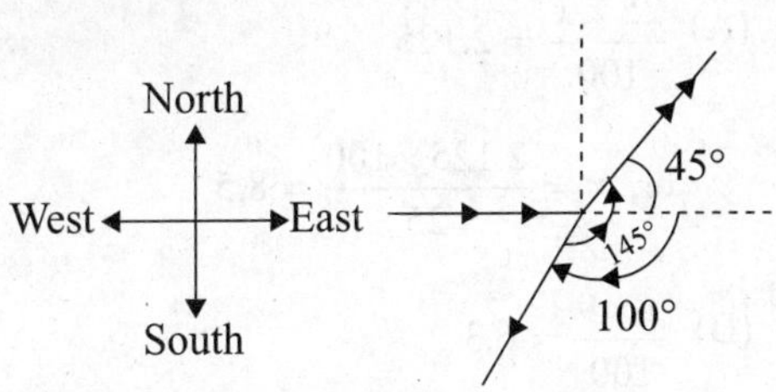

If one turns 100° in the clockwise direction and then 145° in the anticlockwise direction, she effectively turns 145° – 100° = 45° in the anticlockwise direction.
Hence, Option A.

24. The number of mangoes in the box = 28.
We want 28 to be 70% of all the fruits in the box, so we should have $28 \times \frac{100}{70} = 40$ fruits in the box.
Therefore, other than the 28 mangoes, we should have 12 fruits in the box.
But there are 46 bananas in the box.
So, we need to take out 46 – 12 = 34 bananas.
Hence, Option C.

25.

G	O	O	D
7	15	15	4
×2	×2	×2	×2
14	30	30	8

B	A	D
2	1	4
×2	×2	×2
4	2	8

Hence, Option C.

26.

G	R	E	E	N
7	18	5	5	14
×3	×3	×3	×3	×3
21	54	15	15	42

Y	E	L	L	O	W
25	5	12	12	15	23
×3	×3	×3	×3	×3	×3
75	15	36	36	36	69

Hence, Option B.
Shortcut: E is the 2nd letter in YELLOW, and the code for E is 15, which is only in Option B.

27.

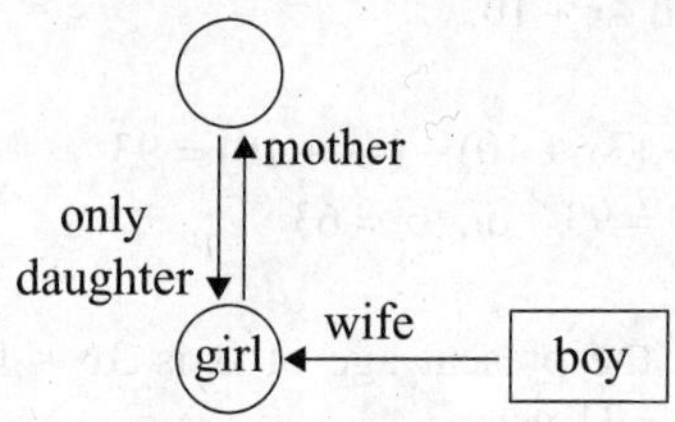

31. The important waves in increasing order of their wavelengths:
Gamma Ray < X-ray < Ultraviolet Rays < Optical Waves < Infrared Rays < Microwave < Radio Waves
Hence, Option B.

32. The volume of a cube is equal to the cube of its edge.
Therefore, the required volume = 22^3 = 10648 cm^3.
Hence, Option B.

33. There are 8 varieties of Vitamin B, and all of them are water-soluble. Vitamin C is also water-soluble. Vitamins A, D, E and K are fat-soluble.
Hence, Option A.

34. 45% of $P = \frac{3}{4}$ of Q

$$\text{or, } \frac{45}{100} \times P = \frac{3}{4} \times Q$$

$$\text{or, } \frac{9}{20} \times P = \frac{3}{4} \times Q$$

$$\text{or, } \frac{P}{Q} = \frac{3 \times 20}{4 \times 9} = \frac{5}{3}.$$

Hence, Option B.

36. Let Sachin's present age be x years.
We have,
$(x + 15) = 4(x - 6)$,
or, $x + 15 = 4x - 24$
or, $4x - x = 24 + 15$
or, $3x = 39$ or, $x = 13$.
Hence, Option C.
Shortcut: There is only one option- C- that will be a multiple of 4 after 15 years!

37. Let's assume that 10 years ago the ages of A, B and C were $2x$, $3x$ and $4x$ years, respectively. Therefore, their present ages are $2x + 10$, $3x + 10$ and $4x + 10$.
We have,
$(2x + 10) + (3x + 10) + (4x + 10) = 93$
or, $9x + 30 = 93$ or, $9x = 63$
or, $x = 7$.
Therefore, the present age of B is $3x + 10 = 3 \times 7 + 10 = 31$ years.
Hence, Option C.
Shortcut: Ten years ago, the age of B was the mean of the ages of A, B and C as the ratio of their ages was 2:3:4 and $3 = \frac{2+3+4}{3}$.
So, even the present age of B must be the mean of the present ages of A, B and C.

$\Rightarrow$ B's present age $= \frac{93}{3} = 31$ years.

38. Bachendri Pal was the first Indian woman to scale Mount Everest. This option is a good trap! The first woman in the world to do so was Junko Tabei from Japan.
Hence, Option D.

39. The required average

$$= \frac{7 + 14 + 21 + 28 + 35 + 42 + 49 + 56 + 63 + 70}{10}$$

$$= \frac{7(1 + 2 + 3 + \cdots + 10)}{10}$$

$$= \frac{7\left(\frac{10 \times 11}{2}\right)}{10} = \frac{7 \times 5 \times 11}{10} = 38.5.$$

Note: The sum of the first n natural numbers $= \frac{n(n+1)}{2}$.

Shortcut:
For numbers in an Arithmetic Progression (AP), their mean = their median.

7 14 21 28 | 35 42 | 49 56 63 70

The median of the numbers above $= \frac{35 + 42}{2} = 38.5$
Therefore, their mean = 38.5
Hence, Option D.

40. (A) $\frac{25 \times x}{100} = 2.125$

$$\text{or, } x = \frac{2.125 \times 100}{25} = 8.5$$

(B) $\frac{x \times 9}{100} = 6.3$

$$\text{or, } x = \frac{6.3 \times 100}{9} = 70.$$

(C) $\frac{45 \times x}{100} = 22.5$

or, $x = \frac{(22.5) \times 100}{45} = 50.$

(D) $\frac{x \times 0.25}{100} = 0.04$

or, $x = \frac{(0.04) \times 100}{0.25} = 16.$

Hence, Option B.

41. 1 metric ton = 1000 kg.
1 quintal = 100 kg.

The required value $= \frac{90 \times 100}{3 \times 1000} \times 100 = 300.$

Hence, Option C.

42. For $\theta < 90°$, Cos θ is positive and hence FsCos θ will also be positive.
Hence, Option B.

43. $\because$ 48 people can do the work in 35 hours.
$\therefore$ 1 person can do the work in 35 × 48 hours.
$\therefore$ 20 people can do the work in $\frac{35 \times 48}{20}$ = 84 hours.
Hence, Option D.

45. The speed of the train = 150 km/hr.

$= \frac{150 \times 1000}{3600}$ m/s

$= \frac{125}{3}$ m/s.

The distance travelled by the train in 30 seconds

$= \frac{125}{3} \times 30 = 1250$ metres.

In order to cross a platform, a train has to travel the sum of the lengths of the platform and itself.
Therefore, 300 + the length of the train = 1250.
$\Rightarrow$ the length of the train = 1250 – 300 = 950.
Hence, Option D.

47. 18M6N24S8P17
$18 - 6 \times 24 \div 8 + 17 = 18 - 6 \times 3 + 17 = 18 - 18 + 17 = 17$
Hence, Option D.
Note: We need to follow the BODMAS rule.

48.

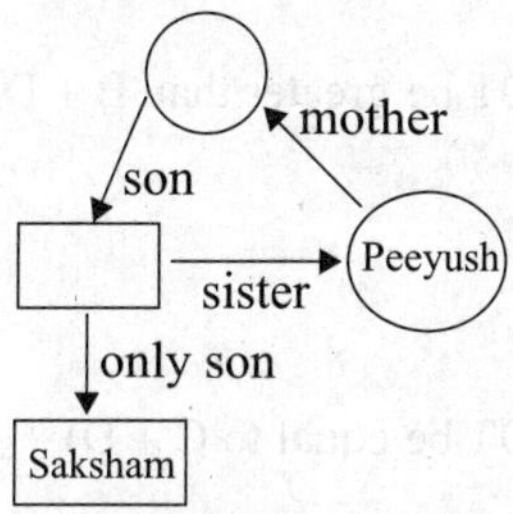

Please notice that Peeyush is a woman here as the possessive pronoun used for her is 'her'.
It becomes clear from the graph above that Peeyush is a sister of Saksham's father.
Therefore, she is his aunt.
Hence, Option C.

49.

Plan	Year	Planner
Planned Economy of India	1934	M. Visvesvaraya
National Planning Committee	1938	S.C. Bose
Bombay Plan	1944	Major industrialists of the country
People's Plan	1945	M.N. Roy
Sarvodaya Plan	1950	Jayaprakash Narayan

Hence, Option A.

50. We have,
A + E = C + D (i)
and
2C < A + E (ii)
Combining (i) and (ii), we get
2C < A + E = C + D
or, 2C < C + D
or, C < D (iii)
We also have,
A + D = B + C
but, D > C (from iii)
Therefore, B > A (iv)
(else A + D will become greater than B + C)
We also have,
2A > B + D
or, A + A > B + D
as A < B (from iv)

A > D (v)

(else A + A will NOT be greater than B + D)

Again,

A + E = C + D

As A > D (from v)

C > E (vi)

(else A + E will NOT be equal to C + D)

So, we have,

C < D, B > A, A > D, and C > E.

Combining all these, we get,

B > A > D > C > E.

Hence, Option B.

51. 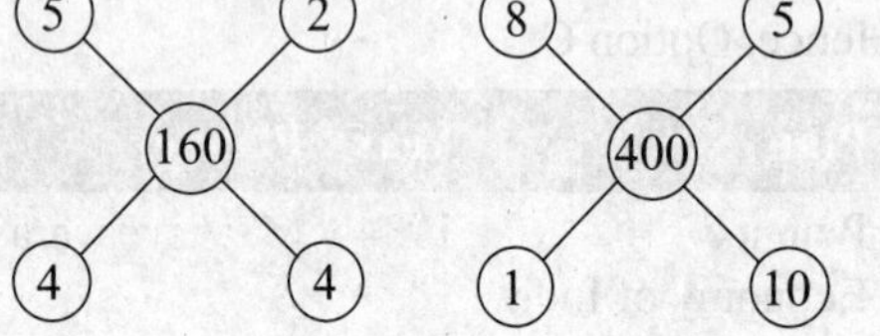

160 = 5 × 2 × 4 × 4 400 = 8 × 5 × 10 × 1

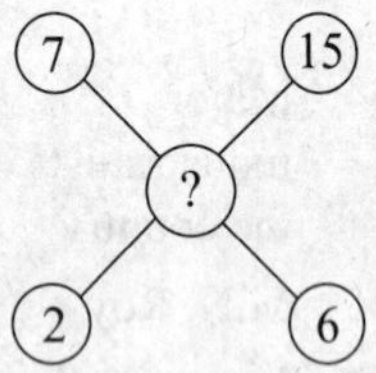

? = 7 × 15 × 6 × 2 = 1260

Hence, Option B.

52. The malleus, incus and stapes are the bones of the middle ear, but the ulna is the bone of the forearm.

Hence, Option A.

The stapes is the smallest bone in the human body.

53. 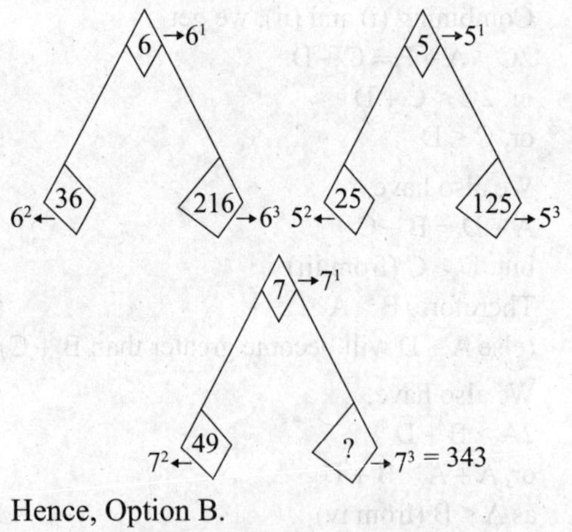

Hence, Option B.

56.

Network	Full form	Geographical Area Spread
LAN	Local Area Network	1 km to 10 km
MAN	Metropolitan Area Network	5 km to 50 km
WAN	Wide Area Network	above 50 km

Hence, Option A.

VAN stands for Value Added Network.

63. 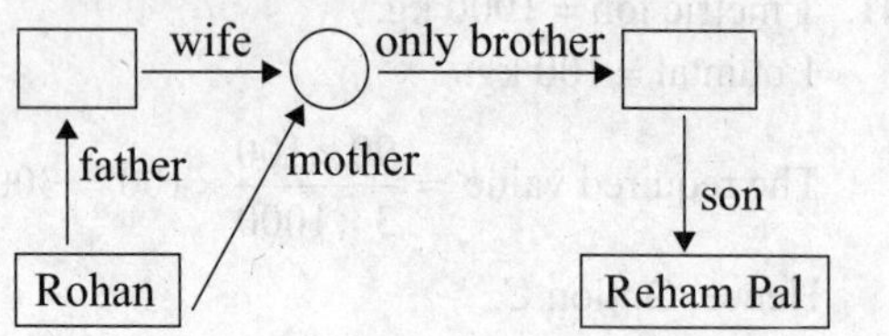

Thus, Reham Pal is the son of Rohan's maternal uncle.

⇒ Rohan and Reham Pal are cousins.

Hence, Option C.

68. Let the selling price be $11x$ and the cost price be $10x$.

Profit = $11x - 10x = x$.

Percentage of profit $= \frac{x}{10x} \times 100 = 10$.

Hence, Option B.

72. 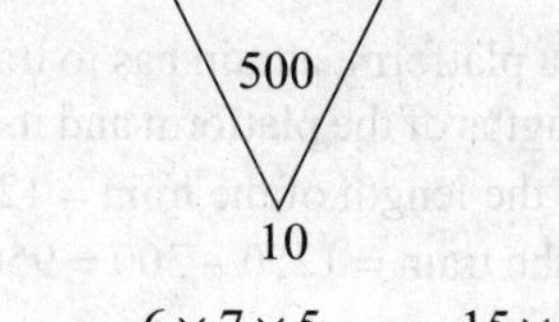

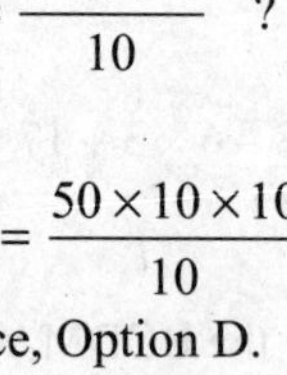

$21 = \frac{6 \times 7 \times 5}{10}$ $? = \frac{15 \times 6 \times 4}{10}$

$= 36$

$500 = \frac{50 \times 10 \times 10}{10}$

Hence, Option D.

Please refer to the following figure for the explanations of the questions 73–75:

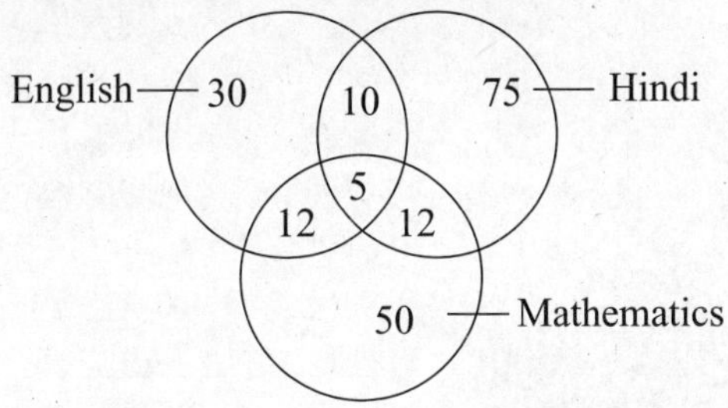

73. The number of candidates who failed in at least two subjects = 12 + 12 + 10 + 5 = 39.

Hence, Option D.

74. The number of candidates who failed in English = 30 + 12 + 5 + 10 = 57.

Hence, Option C.

75. The total number of candidates = 500.

The number of candidates who failed in more than 2 subjects = the number of candidates who failed in all three subjects = 5.

Therefore, the percentage of such candidates

$= \frac{5}{500} \times 100 = 1.$

Hence, Option B.